THE LAWYER'S GUIDE TO
Fact Finding
ON THE
Internet

Carole A. Levitt

Mark E. Rosch

(First Edition entitled **The Internet Fact Finder for Lawyers:
How to Find Anything on the Net**
by Joshua D. Blackman and David Jank)

ABA **LawPracticeManagementSection**
MARKETING • MANAGEMENT • TECHNOLOGY • FINANCE

PJC WARRINGTON CAMPUS LRC

Commitment to Quality: The Law Practice Management Section is committed to quality in our publications. Our authors are experienced practitioners in their fields. Prior to publication, the contents of all our books are rigorously reviewed by experts to ensure the highest quality product and presentation. Because we are committed to serving our readers' needs, we welcome your feedback on how we can improve future editions of this book.

Screen shots reprinted with permission from their respective owners. All rights reserved.

Cover design by Jim Colao.

Nothing contained in this book is to be considered as the rendering of legal advice for specific cases, and readers are responsible for obtaining such advice from their own legal counsel. This book and any forms and agreements herein are intended for educational and informational purposes only.

The products and services mentioned in this publication are under or may be under trademark or service mark protection. Product and service names and terms are used throughout only in an editorial fashion, to the benefit of the product manufacturer or service provider, with no intention of infringement. Use of a product or service name or term in this publication should not be regarded as affecting the validity of any trademark or service mark.

The Law Practice Management Section, American Bar Association, offers an educational program for lawyers in practice. Books and other materials are published in furtherance of that program. Authors and editors of publications may express their own legal interpretations and opinions, which are not necessarily those of either the American Bar Association or the Law Practice Management Section unless adopted pursuant to the bylaws of the Association. The opinions expressed do not reflect in any way a position of the Section or the American Bar Association.

Printed in the United States of America.

10 09 08 07 06   5 4 3 2 1

Library of Congress Cataloging-in-Publication Data

Levitt, Carole A.
   The lawyer's guide to fact finding on the Internet / by Carole A.
 Levitt, Mark E. Rosch. -- 3rd ed.
      p. cm.
   Includes index.
   ISBN 1-59031-671-1
   1. Legal research—United States—Computer network resources. 2. Legal research—Computer network resources. 3. Internet research. I. Rosch, Mark E. II. Title.

   KF242.A1L48 2006
   025.06′34—dc22

                                                                2006036532

Discounts are available for books ordered in bulk. Special consideration is given to state bars, CLE programs, and other bar-related organizations. Inquire at Book Publishing, American Bar Association, 321 N. Clark Street, Chicago, Illinois 60610.

Contents at a Glance

Contents

About the Authors

Carole A. Levitt

Carole Levitt is a nationally recognized author and speaker on Internet legal research. She has over twenty years of extensive experience in the legal field as a law librarian, legal research and writing professor (Pepperdine University School of Law), California lawyer, and Internet trainer. She is a skilled online searcher, focusing on legal, public record, investigative, and business research. She is also the coauthor of *The Cybersleuth's Guide to the Internet* (IFL Press, 2006).

As president and founder of Internet For Lawyers (**www.netforlawyers .com**), she provides customized Internet research training to legal professionals (with continuing legal education credit). Ms. Levitt has made Internet research presentations at the ABA TECHSHOW®; the LegalWorks and LegalTech technology conferences; the annual meetings of the American Bar Association, the National Association of Bar Executives, the Association of Continuing Legal Education (ACLEA), the California State Bar Association, the worldwide Gibson, Dunn & Crutcher corporate lawyer retreat, and at many law firms, bar associations, and library associations throughout the United States.

Ms. Levitt serves on the executive council of the American Bar Association's Law Practice Management Section, as well as the section's publishing board. Previously, she was chair of the California State Bar's Law Practice Management and Technology Section and now serves as a special advisor to that group. She also served on the executive board of the Los Angeles County Bar Law Practice Management Section, and is a past chair of the Southern California Association of Law Libraries.

She is a regular contributor to *Los Angeles Lawyer* magazine's "Computer Counselor" column (reaching 25,000 lawyers throughout California), and has also written for the following magazines and newsletters: *Internet Lawyer, Computer and Internet Lawyer, Research Advisor,* and *Nashville Lawyer,* as well as the Web sites FindLaw, CEB Case N Point, and LLRX.

Ms. Levitt received her Juris Doctor from the John Marshall Law School, where she graduated with distinction and was a member of the school's law review. She earned her bachelor's degree in political science and her master's degree in library science at the University of Illinois. Ms. Levitt can be contacted at **clevitt@netforlawyers.com**.

Mark E. Rosch

As vice president of Internet For Lawyers (IFL), Mr. Rosch is the developer and manager of the Internet For Lawyers Web site (**www.netforlawyers.com**). He is editor of IFL's newsletter, and he writes and speaks about how to use the Internet for research and marketing, and also on technology implementation for the legal community.

Mr. Rosch is coauthor of *The Cybersleuth's Guide to the Internet* (IFL Press, 2006). Mr. Rosch has presented at the ABA TECHSHOW®; the Legal-Works and LegalTech technology conferences; the annual meetings of the American Bar Association, the National Association of Bar Executives, the Association of Continuing Legal Education (ACLEA), the California State Bar Association, and at numerous law firms, bar associations, and library associations throughout the United States.

During his nearly twenty years of marketing experience, Mr. Rosch has developed, implemented, and supervised the publicity, promotions, and marketing campaigns for numerous and varied clients, from prestigious legal portals to new media developers. He also provides electronic-marketing consulting services to law practices of all sizes that seek to improve online marketing campaigns, increase the effectiveness of their current efforts, or optimize their Web sites to improve their search-engine rankings. He has also provided Web management consulting to the State Bar of California Law Practice Management and Technology Section's Web site, in addition to various law firms and solo practitioners. He has written on the subject of building and managing effective Web sites for the Legal Marketing Association, and *GP Solo* and *Los Angeles Lawyer* magazines. Mr. Rosch has also written about the application of computer technology to the law office for *Law Office Computing, Los Angeles Lawyer,* and the *Los Angeles Daily Journal,* among other publications.

Mr. Rosch is a member of the ABA and the ACLEA, serving as chair of ACLEA's marketing section. He has also served as a member of the Academy of Television Arts & Sciences' public relations steering committee, the Television Publicity Executives Committee, and the American Film Institute.

He graduated from Tulane University in New Orleans with a bachelor's degree in sociology. Mr. Rosch can be reached at **mrosch@netforlawyers .com**.

Introduction

In 1999, we combined Carole's dual background as a lawyer and law librarian with Mark's background in marketing and his penchant for technology to create Internet For Lawyers and teach lawyers how to use the Web effectively and efficiently. To create our first seminars and training materials, we reviewed a lot of Internet research books to find the most useful sites for lawyers that were available for free on the Internet. In all of the books we used, we never found an Internet research book that was everything we thought such a book should be.

When the ABA asked us to write a new edition of Joshua Blackman's *The Internet Fact Finder for Lawyers*, which was re-titled *The Lawyer's Guide to Fact Finding on the Internet*, Second Edition, our goal was to write a book that would save researchers time and money and help them avoid frustration. We looked at it as our chance to write the book we had been searching for, but never found—and our chance to correct all the pet peeves we found in other books. We wanted to share what we learned about the best of the hundreds of Web sites we've used while conducting real-world research or while testing for evaluation purposes.

What's New in the Third Edition?

As we re-entered the Internet superhighway to revise this book, we began by testing and reevaluating each site discussed in the second edition. From there, we updated our discussion about each site by pointing out any new (or deleted) features and new URLs (if they changed). We also refreshed almost every single screen shot.

We then added hundreds of pages of new information to the third edition, including detailed discussions of new Web sites, a new chapter on blogs and podcasts, a glossary of Internet technology terms, and information about new laws and cases affecting Internet research such as: (1) access to public records and non-public records on the Internet; (2) Internet privacy issues; and (3) security breaches of commercial databases; and much more.

We were pleased to learn from our readers that the second edition of the book met our goal—to help them save time and money with their Internet research and to avoid frustration!

Our goal with this new edition remains the same.

This Book Differs From Other Internet Books— It Will Empower You!

The following was a rundown of the pet peeves we had with other Internet research books, and an explanation of how we hoped the second edition (and now the third edition) would this book overcome those shortcomings in order to empower you to become a more efficient and effective researcher.

But, Is It Free?

The authors of the other Internet research books rarely warned us if the Web site they were describing was a pay site. There's nothing more bothersome than going to a site expecting to find information for free, and instead being greeted by a registration and payment screen asking for your credit card. On the other hand, these other authors usually also failed to bother to clue us in when a site was free.

We know, as it is with most anything, that price is a major consideration when deciding between alternative research resources—and we all agree that free is better (all other things being equal!). Our first goal, then, was to label the Web sites we included in the book to show whether they are free (or free but requiring registration) or pay. Some sites have different levels of access. For example, a Web site might offer some limited information for free and then charge for more extensive information (such as those sites that are free to search but require a paid subscription to view the full text of search results). Some sites are completely free, while others, though costing no money, require registration to access all or part of the sites.

However a Web site is arranged, it's good to know before you get there. We label the sites with the icons shown below to indicate what kind of access is offered. If we use more than one icon, it means the site offers varying levels of access.

$** Pay   **($) Free   Registration Required

We also tell you when free is not better—that is, when you're not going to find it for free or when free won't be the most efficient route. In such instances, we recommend a pay site. We want to save you time and money by clueing you in—in advance.

So, What's the Purpose of this Site and What Content Does It Offer?

Some of the authors of other books we reviewed simply pointed to a laundry list of Web sites but failed to describe their content or failed to indicate the purpose of the site. Our second goal was to provide an overview of each site's content and to suggest in what situations the Web site should be used. When applicable, we also suggest alternative sites. We want to save you the frustration of visiting Web sites that don't have the content you need or don't allow you to search in the manner you want. For example, if you need to know the owner of a certain piece of real estate in Los Angeles, we recommend a pay site to find that information, and explain that while the Los Angeles County assessor's office offers a free, searchable Web site, it doesn't allow you to search by owner's name, only by the property address. Even then, the free site does not provide the owner's name—only the assessed value.

What's with This Alphabetical List of Titles?

Some Internet research books we looked at listed Web sites in alphabetical order by the name of the site. A research book is not useful if it's simply an alphabetical list. Even one of the authors of this book, who is a librarian by training and who lives and dies by alphabetical order, doesn't find it useful when organizing a research book— in fact, she abhors it! And this is from someone who organizes her spice rack (and even the credit cards in her wallet) alphabetically.

We want to save you time and money by thinking the way you do. So, our third goal was to organize by subject. Researchers don't think in alphabetical title order—they think in subject order. To make this book more useful, we have chosen to organize it in subject order.

But, Which Sites Are We Recommending, and Where Should You Start?

Even those few authors who did organize their books by subject couldn't stay completely away from alphabetical order. They always seemed to revert to an alphabetical list of Web sites within each subject when it would have been more meaningful to organize in a way that showed the reader in which order they should use the sites, starting with the most useful. The reader seeks and depends on the judgment of the author, who is the expert searcher. The author is there to guide searchers down the superhighway—to draw the road map, showing the searcher which sites to stop and visit in order to gather the most useful information.

Our fourth goal was to list the Web sites in a meaningful order within each topic. Thus, our list of sites begins with what we judge to be the best starting-point sites. We want to save you time and money by listing sites in a way that quickly displays our judgment of each site—by showing you which ones to begin with, and then which sites to visit next. We only show you the best sites.

Are There any Tips or Tricks to Using This Site?

Most other Internet research books failed to provide practical tips and tricks about the Web sites listed in the book. Our book is designed to save searchers from the wrong turns, dead-ends, and even wrong destinations that we encountered along the way while evaluating the sites. To do this, we include tips about the best aspect of each site (content and functionality) and a how-to for those sites that have great content but are not intuitive to use. For example, some Web sites bury the search function, or their most useful information. Some sites use cryptic labels for parts of the site, such as **More** or **Download**. We tell you what you'll find if you click on the **More** or **Downloads** link and very often, that's where the most useful information is found!

Our goal is to uncover that information and those features for you—to translate those sites for you. We want to save you time and money by detailing the information we learned by visiting and testing out the hundreds of sites included in this book.

Show Me the Site

Finally, most authors failed to display the Web sites that they described! The Internet is a graphic-intensive medium, chock-full of icons and links—not just text. When getting driving directions, most people find it useful to look at a map while the instructions are being given. It's the same with the Internet. So, rather than just describe Web sites, we also provide screen shots of the more important sites, or the ones that have some hidden trick.

This book is written in a style that mixes narrative with a standardized template presentation. First, we give you an introduction to the topic in a narrative fashion, and then we highlight the best sites in a template format so you can quickly learn about each individual Web site. The template, as shown below, displays the site name, whether it's free or not, its URL, its purpose, its content, our view of the site, and our tip or tips for using the site.

Internet For Lawyers

Articles, tips, and links: Online CLE: **$**

http://www.netforlawyers.com

Purpose: To provide information to the legal professional about how to use the Internet for legal, business, and investigative research.

Content: The site offers articles about Internet research and also has online CLE courses to help you hone your Internet research skills by having you test out the sites discussed in the CLE articles in order to answer the quiz questions. Some of the articles explain how to find free case law on

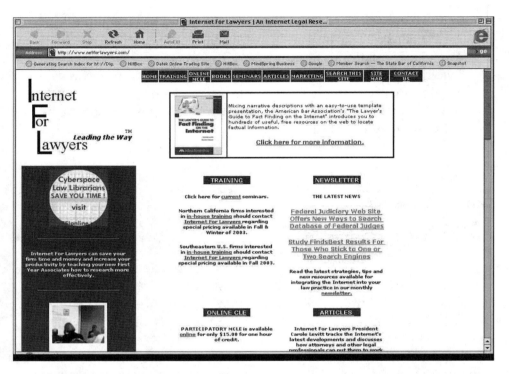

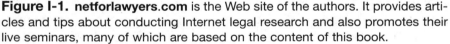

Figure I-1. netforlawyers.com is the Web site of the authors. It provides articles and tips about conducting Internet legal research and also promotes their live seminars, many of which are based on the content of this book.

the Internet, how to find information about companies, and how to find free public records.

Our View: It's our site, so we're probably a bit biased, but here goes! You'll like the clickable links included in the articles—it makes it easy for you to visit the sites for your own research. The online CLE quizzes are probably the least expensive you'll find on the Internet at $15 per credit hour.

Tip: Use the blue tabs at the top to navigate the site, or click on **SEARCH THIS SITE** to search with keywords. The **TRAINING** tab informs you about in-house courses and the **SEMINARS** tab tells you in which city (from Alaska to Atlanta) you can attend an Internet For Lawyers bar-association-sponsored seminar.

How to Use the CD

To make it easier to locate and access the sites you want to use in the book, we have included a CD-ROM that features links to all of the sites discussed in the book. The sites are all indexed, by name and by topic so you can easily navigate to them without typing URLs into your browser! The index is included as a PDF file and requires the free Adobe Acrobat Reader to view. See Chapter 2 for more information on using Acrobat effectively to get the most out of this index.

Also provided are some of the helpful checklists featured in the book, including a Source Credibility Checklist, a handy Methodology Checklist, and more. These are included as Microsoft Word files so that you can copy them to your hard drive, print them out and make notations for your own Web searches.

Keeping Up to Date

We have been teaching legal professionals where to find the information they need on the Internet at seminars for more than seven years, so nobody knows more than we do that useful new sites appear on the Internet daily. That's why we are working with the ABA to keep you up-to-date on these developments by including, free, a bi-monthly, companion update service for this book to inform you of the newest sites and any useful new developments at old favorites. This update will be delivered to your e-mail inbox every other month, so you can print out the pages and keep them with your copy of the book, or near your computer for easy access. More information about subscribing to this service is available online at **http://www.lawpractice.org/factfinder**, and a Subscription Request Card can be found on the last page of this book.

*CHAPTER***ONE**

Using the Internet for Factual Research

War Stories from Internet Fact Finders

In legal practice, research involves *much* more than the case law, statutes, and regulations explained in law school. For example, medical malpractice lawyers need to know about anatomy, and how to find medical experts. Product liability lawyers need to know how to find corporate family trees to deduce parent-subsidiary relationships, and to trace the path of a product—from manufacturing to distributorship to sales—in order to ascertain liability. The Internet is extremely well-suited to such fact finding. This book is aimed at factual research only. While we may discuss some legal research and government sites, it is because those sites can be used for digging up *factual* information.

For example, in Chapter 9, "Finding and Backgrounding Expert Witnesses," we talk about court opinions, but only in the context of using court-opinion databases to find experts who are referenced in cases that have similar facts to your case and for which you are seeking an expert. When we talk about bills and legislative histories in that chapter, once again it is not in the legal context, but in the context of finding experts who have testified about a certain matter in a pending bill, or been referred to in a legislative report about a similar issue you are involved with. In the discussion of dockets in Chapter 8, "Accessing Public Records," we talk about how to use dockets for client development, recruiting, and learning about the opposition lawyer or even the judge you're going before. Once again, we are not discussing dockets from a legal-research perspective.

If you're not yet convinced that you should bother with the Internet, or if you're uncertain whether anything of practical value is available on the Internet, read the examples below from practicing lawyers describing how they've used the Internet to find factual information to solve problems. In most of the war stories, we note the lawyer's name. But if a matter is still ongoing, to protect the confidentiality of the parties (and in one case an innocent dog) we need to shield the lawyer's name.

War Story: Drunk Driving

Wes Pittman of Pittman & Perry, P.A., in Panama City, Florida (wes@pittmanfirm.com), describes how he finished a trial for which he used the Internet to generate some ideas for opening statements and summations. He said that it worked "marvelously well."

"I represented a plaintiff in a personal injury case. The defendant was a drunk driver who crossed the center line of a highway one dark rainy night and struck her car head-on. I had a claim not only for compensatory but also for punitive damages. Under Florida law, we are permitted to argue that punitives are to deter flagrant conduct by the defendant and by others, and we are able to argue that the conduct is pervasive, etc., much like in other jurisdictions. I needed to use only one search phrase, 'drunk driving,' to generate forty-nine-thousand-plus hits and to find, within the first twenty-five, two great ideas to use. Both ideas related to the widespread practice of drinking while driving and how it has become a joking matter. I took it one step further, of course, to say in closing that the only way to keep people like the defendant from continuing to make drunk driving a joke is to send a message by a punitive award.

"The two hits which were so useful were about a card game called 'Drunk Driver, Drunk Driver' in which successive cards are dealt, each accompanied by the consumption of an entire drink, until the driver 'safely makes it off the road' (all the cards are dealt). [The second useful site included] an article that at first sounded serious enough in its title to divert me to it. [I thought I might] want to print it for use in future product liability cases. Its title was something like 'The Steering Propensities of Pickup Trucks at Highway Speeds.' As I read the article, I quickly learned that the author had written the three-page paper as a (poor) joke to describe how a pickup has become 'the only beer-guided vehicle in the country,' how pickups stall in front of bars, how to balance a beer to keep it from spilling in the crotch, etc."

Pittman's use of the Internet to easily find examples of how our culture perceives drunk driving, and then his using that information to demonstrate to the court the strength of his arguments, perfectly demonstrates the Internet's great strength. Because the Internet enables virtually anyone to publish material for the world to see, it makes a remarkably rich repository.

While professional researchers can take the time to search the database sites Dialog or LexisNexis to find pertinent articles, most people have neither the expertise to search those databases (especially Dialog), nor wish to pay for access. Online databases generally are collections of commercial publications, professional journals that are peer reviewed, and newsletters. While there is undeniable value in such collections, they also necessarily omit vast bodies of data and knowledge that, before the Internet, had little to no distribution. In addition, such databases do *not* include articles written "as a joke," the very articles that proved most useful to Pittman to make his point that drunk driving is considered a joke when, in fact, it's a deadly serious problem.

Before the Internet, Pittman may have been able to search Dialog or LexisNexis for published articles on the subject, or he may have sought to collect anecdotal information on the subject, but it's unlikely he could have done either from the comfort of his office on the weekend, within a short period of time, for virtually no cost. The informal information he personally collected from the Internet, which proved useful for defending his client, was only available from the unique "library" we know as the Internet. And, to share with the jury that he received forty-nine-thousand-plus hits by searching for the phrase "drunk driving" is more impressive than saying, "I spoke to a few people about 'drunk driving' and they said. . . ."

The fact is that the Internet is rich with free, valuable information that legal professionals and anyone else can conveniently access day or night. It's simply become an easy way to get smart fast about topics we may otherwise know nothing about. It's one thing to know the law on a given subject; it's another to be armed with the factual information required to make a winning argument. Besides getting ideas for an opening or closing as Pittman did, the Internet is just the place to find a useful statistic or the perfect quote to use in that opening or closing.

War Story: Case Research and Lawyer Referral

Several lawyers volunteered anecdotes describing how the Internet is being used in law offices across the country to solve research problems.

Bruce L. Dorner (callmylawyer@choiceonemail.com), who practices law in Londonderry, New Hampshire, relates these incidents:

"I had a client who was seriously injured in a propane explosion. I searched the Internet for references to propane. Once I filtered down to the better items, I found a link to the home page for the American Gas Association (**http://www.aga.com**). They had all the standards of the industry posted, including comments about the particular appliance implicated in my case. Best of all, there was a phone number and an Internet mail address for further information. I got some good materials for the case."

Disappearing Sites

An attempt to recreate Dorner's search several years later found that the Aga.com site was no longer the site of the American Gas Association, but now belonged to a private international gas company, Linde Gas. That site, obviously, would be of no help to Dorner if he needed the same information today. What happened to the American Gas Association site? On February 15, 1999, the American Gas Association changed its URL to **http://www.aga.org** (they changed ".com" to ".org"). Their old URL was purchased by Linde Gas, but used only as a "redirect" to Linde's corporate site at **http://www.lindegas.com**. This type of information can be discovered by tracking the original URL through Archive.org (**http://www.archive.org**), an amazing site that you can read more about in the "Finding Extinct Pages" section of Chapter 4, "Search Tools."

Dorner has another story. "Another client wanted to adopt a child. A third party told him about a prospective birth mother in Tennessee, and my client thought this might be worth pursuing. My client needed the name of a lawyer in Tennessee who handled interstate adoptions. A quick trip to the West Legal Directory (**http://www.wld.com**) and a search using the phrase 'interstate adoption' produced the information in just a few minutes."

Lawyer Searches

Recreating this adoption search also revealed that the original URL used was no longer valid. The old URL redirected to another site—FindLaw's lawyer directory (**http://lawyers.findlaw.com**) that contained the same information as the old West Legal Directory site. (Since its purchase of FindLaw in 2001, West now posts its directory there).

Now, searching for the phrase "interstate adoption" was no longer possible. Instead, only a preselected set of practice areas was available for use as search terms (and interstate adoption was not one of them). Also, the site now requires you to select not only the practice area from the list, but also to indicate the state and city.

Lawyer searches can also be conducted at an online version of the printed Martindale-Hubbell directory (**http://www.martindale.com**). Searching at the Martindale site is more flexible, because you are not limited to preselected practice areas. (Click the **Location/Area of Practice** tab on the site's home page). You can also search nationally, internationally, or statewide. Searching for the two words "interstate adoption" for Tennessee returned no results. It was necessary to insert the Boolean connector AND between the words "interstate" and "adoption" to find lawyers who listed interstate adoption as their area of practice. While none were currently listed as practicing in Tennessee, the search returned numerous names of lawyers in other states.

War Story: Immigration Cases

Greg Siskind, of Siskind, Susser, Bland in Tennessee (gsiskind@visalaw.com), explains how his firm uses the Internet for various nonlegal questions relating to their immigration cases:

"[We have used the Internet for] finding documentation to support human rights violation claims in connection with an asylum case (we actually found specific references in an obscure UN document to the torture of our client by the government of Equatorial Guinea).

"We have located expert witnesses for our cases; we have gotten procedures sent to us by e-mail from officials at various U.S. consulates around the world; [and] we frequently submit National Interest Waiver green-card applications that require a demonstration that the applicant's work will provide a substantial, prospective benefit to the U.S. The key to winning these cases is documentation, and we often find articles and other support material on the Internet."

War Story: Weather Evidence

Michael C. Zusman (mikez@evanszusman.com), who practices commercial litigation with emphasis on securities, real property, and creditor's rights, describes how one of his partners "was preparing to try a case involving an allegedly defective concrete floor laid by our client. One of the issues was whether the concrete was poured on a day where our client knew or should have known that the weather was too warm for the concrete to set properly. I hopped on my PC and, after linking around for a while, located a Web site for the Oregon Climate Service (**http://www .ocs.orst.edu**) and obtained the name and e-mail address for our state climatologist, George Taylor. He responded, and I was able to obtain hour-by-hour temperatures for the relevant locality on the day in question which, as I recall, my partner was able to introduce into evidence."

War Story: A Law Librarian's Unusual Search

When a lawyer needed to discover the manufacturer of an item responsible for burning down a client's farm, he turned to the ultimate Internet fact finder—his law librarian. The item that was responsible for burning down the farm was a white heated pet bowl, which, unfortunately, had met the same demise as the house, making the research a tad tricky. Despite that, the law librarian took up the challenge. (Because this matter is an ongoing case, and to protect the innocent dog, we have changed the color of the bowl and are not using any of the names of the cities, manufacturers, hardware stores, the lawyer, the law librarian—or the dog).

The librarian first began his search by using a general search at Yahoo! with the phrase "heated dog bowls." He began looking at some of the search results. The first one he found that sold heated dog bowls was **http://www.petco.com**. It had a picture of a blue heated dog bowl, but not a white one. The librarian then turned to his law-librarian mailing list for some suggestions. Here is his story:

"Four days ago I asked for help [from a law-librarian list] to find a specific model of a white heated dog bowl (which burned down the farm). I received over twenty-five replies from the list . . . providing . . . sites with heated dog bowls—undoubtedly, pet lovers were attracted to the search by the pictures of cute dogs and cats. Indirectly, they were all helpful. Yesterday, I purchased two of the correct models (one for testing by an expert, the other for demonstrative evidence).

"The key to the find was to distinguish the marketing chain: (1) *manufacturing* from (2) *wholesale distribution* from (3) *retailing*.

"Most of the leads [from the list] were to retailers on the Internet. By themselves, the Internet retailers did not solve the problem. Most pictures on the Internet were of bright blue bowls (a visual expert ruled out color blindness by our client). EBay had started a cut-and-paste service of all products by type, but it looked like that Internet service had just started building its database [so it wasn't useful]. Then we analyzed all the retailers and narrowed the search down to three manufacturers (X, Y, and Z). Then we obtained written lists of all products made by each manufacturer and compared them with their Web sites and some of the more comprehensive sites of the retailers.

"We discovered one product on manufacturer Z's product list that was *not* shown on Z's Web site or any retailer Web site. We called the manufacturer (posing as a pet groomer) and asked for the product—of course, they had none in stock, but did provide us with a list of wholesale distributors in our area. None of the distributors, however, were in the [current] phone directories. One, however, was listed in an old city directory. The distributor had a small downtown office just two blocks from our office. With the specific model number, the distributor confirmed that he had fifty-two of the bowls in a nearby warehouse. The warehouse supplied the part number and local hardware stores to whom it distributed [the bowls]. We called several of the retail hardware stores. Of course, none stocked heated pet bowls in the heat of August. So we ordered two bowls from one hardware store. Eureka!!! They are the model that burned down the farm."

Jumpstarting a Search on the Internet

This is a great example of how the power of the Internet and a searcher's good use of various search strategies coalesced to successfully use the Internet to hunt down what seemed like an impossibility. Fact finders should take note of these search strategies: (1) because he had no idea of where to begin, and knew he would need to cast a wide net, he chose a general search engine; (2) he entered very specific keywords into the general search engine so he could zero in on the specific item; and (3) he took advantage of an Internet mailing list he had joined earlier (for law librarians from around the world). From the search-engine search he was able to start identifying manufacturers and retailers of the item. From the mailing list, he received numerous suggestions of more names of retailers who sold this type of product. He was then able to immediately turn to the retailers' product catalogs by finding their Web sites. From their sites, he was able to search for pictures of a white heated pet bowl and compile a list of retailers' phone numbers to start making phone calls to learn about the distribution chain. This is a also a great example of using information found via the Internet to jump-start what otherwise would have been a tedious manual search through product directories at a library, in the hopes that they would even have pictures of the product—and in color.

Yet, it's important also to realize the role that old-fashioned research played here—from obtaining print copies of the product lists in case the lists on the Internet weren't complete (which, as it turned out, they weren't), to thinking about who else to ask for assistance (in this case, fellow librarians) to making dozens of phone calls to manufacturers, retailers, and distributors—mostly from phone numbers found on the Internet, but also from printed directories.

War Story: The Internet Advantage

What is the advantage of using the Internet? Why not go the route before there was the Internet—the library? Why use the Internet at all? Lawyer Ted Claypoole (**http://www.wcsr.com/default.asp?id=86& objId=75**), who is the senior member of the Intellectual Property practice group at Womble Carlyle (a firm with over 500 members and offices throughout the Southeast and mid-Atlantic), answers these questions this way:

"[I use the Internet for] convenience and a broad general search to find what is out there. If I want to get a feel for what is going on in the area, I can sit down in the comfort of my own home and take an hour or two in the evening with the radio or TV on and do a general search and get some very good ideas of where I might want to go. I usually do not consider that a serious search. I still think it has advantages though. I think it will continue to have advantages to that and as you move forward, if you look at it as not a serious search you will find the sites that have what you want. In other words, if I am on it even once a week, and looking at legal topics, I will eventually know that Emory University (an example used before) has Sixth Circuit opinions—I bookmark that, and the next time I want Sixth Circuit opinions and I am home and I want to word-search them, I can go to that site. It just takes far more time than it is worth to actually say that 'I am going to do all this research on the Web.' You would spend way more time than you would need to. If you know where you are going already, then it is a very good tool. If you do not know at all what is out there and you want to get an idea, it is a very good tool."

All of these Internet research war stories have common threads: in each one, the researcher really had no idea of where to begin his search and simply threw some key words out to a general search engine. In each case, one Internet link led to another, until each person found their answer, whether directly from the Internet or indirectly. For those who got their answers indirectly from the Internet, the Internet quickly pointed them to the persons who held the answers.

We hope that this book can help you figure out where to begin your search. As you read through Chapter 3, "Search Strategies," and Chapter 4, "Search Tools," you'll get a sense for how to use general search engines effectively. Then, as you read through the subject-oriented chapters, you'll learn about specific sites that may hold the answer to your question. We'll also attempt to tell you how to use those sites, and not simply point you to them to find your own way.

Distinguishing Legal Research from Factual Research

This is a book about Internet fact finding for the legal researcher. Among the first steps in learning how to conduct factual research on the Internet is distinguishing between factual and legal research, and learning where to find the factual sources. Legal research on the Internet seems to be more organized than factual research on the Internet. So, the online-legal-researcher-turned-Internet-factual-researcher may find that conducting factual research on the Internet is more of a challenge.

Utilizing the Internet effectively is a challenge for any type of researcher. Unlike a traditional library, with catalog access to every book and every book shelved in order, the Internet is more like a vast highway where someone tossed billions of books out the car window in no particular order, and where catalog records are kept of some, but not of others. From this smorgasbord of sources strewn about the information superhighway, we are continually challenged to bob, weave, and select carefully, knowing that some of the information cannot even be accessed because it's not cataloged (indexed) by a search engine.

Differences in Research Terms

Legal researchers and factual researchers use similar terms in describing their sources. While both speak in terms of *primary, secondary*, and *tertiary* sources, these terms have very different meanings to each group.

Primary, Secondary, and Tertiary Research Sources Compared

	Factual Reasearch	**Legal Research**
Primary	• Obtained by either conducting in-person interviews with experts, listening to taped recordings of speeches or commentaries, or requestng permission to view some piece of original documentation not available from another source. • Consulting with primary sources can sometimes be referred to as "going to the source" or "getting it from the horse's mouth."	• Sources of law—compilations of legislation, regulations, and court opinions. • Includes state and federal statutory codes, municipal ordinances, constitutions, the Code of Federal Regulations, case law (court opinions), etc., whether found in books or databases.
Secondary	• Data that is compiled, organized, and distributed publicly for mass consumption. • Includes books, newspapers, magazines, journals, published papers, public speeches, directories, reference guides, and almanacs (to name just a few); electronic formats of these materials are also secondary sources.	• Materials that discuss, illuminate or otherwise provide reference to primary materials. • Includes law journals and legislative committee hearing transcripts, which provide commentary, explanation and guidance to the law, but not necessarily access to the full-text of statutes or case law and treatises (that may provide narrative overviews of an area of law, or references to case law and statutes).
Tertiary	• Materials or sources referred to by other primary or secondary sources. • Includes sources referred to by footnotes, bibliographies, quotations, or other mentions in primary or secondary sources.	• Materials that direct the researcher to other primary or secondary sources; also known as "finding tools." • Includes case digests and statutory indexes (to direct researchers to primary source materials) and legal periodical indexes (to direct researchers to secondary source materials such as law reviews or legal newspapers.

How a Factual Researcher Uses Sources

When you don't know much about a topic, secondary factual sources are generally good places to *start* conducting research because they lead to primary sources that, in addition, lead to other sources, which the factual researcher refers to as tertiary sources. Secondary legal sources can also be a good place to start legal research for the same reasons—because they lead the legal researcher to primary sources (cases, statutes, and regulations) for citing to a judge, and also lead to other secondary legal sources.

Let's say a factual researcher is researching e-mail spam. He starts by conducting a quick search of the Electronic Privacy Information Center (EPIC) Web site, (**http://www.epic.org**) and finds an article, "SPAM: Unsolicited Commercial E-Mail," that's full of good information. This article is a *secondary* source.

The article refers to Timothy Muris, then-chairman of the Federal Trade Commission (FTC), who released a new privacy agenda for the agency. The article also refers to an article by David Sorkin, *Technical and Legal Approaches to Unsolicited Electronic Mail*. The references to the agency's new privacy agenda and to Sorkin's book are both *tertiary* sources, because they were referenced in a secondary source. (A legal researcher would label these sources secondary.)

If the factual researcher phones Muris and Sorkin and interviews them, they become *primary* sources. If the legal researcher phones them, they remain secondary sources. If either of these people refers the legal researcher to a statute, regulation, or case about the topic, these become primary sources when the legal researcher locates them.

Judging Sources for Worth and Credibility

To determine which sources are worthy of use for a research project, the expert researcher needs not only to judge their worth by assessing their relevance and quality, but to judge also their credibility. Distinguishing the relevant and credible sources from the irrelevant and suspect sources is a critical research skill, especially so when using the Internet—where anyone can (and anyone does) publish. See the section "Internet Source Credibility" later in this chapter to learn how to apply the credibility test to material found on the Internet.

> The most valuable skill an Internet researcher can have is to know when *not* to use the Internet.

When to Use the Internet

Prior to jumping onto the Internet, knowing how accessible a resource is in a nonelectronic format can save lots of time. If you are about to invest time in accessing, searching, and sifting through Internet sources, it ought to be worth the trip. There is no better testament to the need to choose the right resource than watching a colleague pull a copy of the *World Almanac* right off the shelf sitting next to you while you are hyperlinking through home pages, and seeing him flip to the page with the data you are looking for in less than half the time it takes you to find it online.

However, if an Internet surfer can verify the toxicity of an accidental overdose of an over-the-counter drug by accessing a pharmaceutical encyclopedia online that is not located on the shelf right next to you, then the Internet has more than proved its worth as a research tool.

> On the other hand, it can also be said: always use the Internet—everyone else is.

In fact, lawyers may run the risk of competency claims if they do not have access to and make use of the Internet. At least one federal court has held that in order to avoid negligence, and to satisfy due diligence considerations, lawyers should be plugged into the Internet. Seventh Circuit Judge Kanne wrote that in the context of a Securities Exchange Act Rule 10b-5 securities fraud action, "nondisclosure of enacted or pending legislation and industry-wide trends is not a basis for a securities fraud claim" because the information was in the public domain and accessible to the plaintiff. "In today's society, with the advent of the information superhighway, federal and state legislation and regulations, as well as information regarding industry trends, are easily accessed. A reasonable investor is presumed to have information available in the public domain, and therefore Whirlpool is imputed with constructive knowledge of this information." (*Whirlpool Financial Corporation v. GN Holdings, Inc.*, 67 F.3d 605 (7th Cir. 1995) *available at* **http://www.law.emory.edu/7circuit/sept95/ 95-1292.html**.) Reading this decision might make you think that this chapter might be more aptly titled "Always Use the Internet—Everyone Else Is." Almost ten years later, the Third Circuit agreed with *Whirlpool* in *In re: Adams Golf Securities Litigation*, 381 F.3d 267 (3rd Cir. 2004) *available at* **http://vls.law.villanova.edu/locator/3d/August2004/033945p.pdf**. Not only is there a duty to use the Internet, but there is a duty to "google" a missing party. In a recent decision, *Munster vs. Groce*, 829 N.E.2d 52 at n. 3 (Ind. App. 2005), the court was incredulous that plaintiff failed to "google" the missing defendant as part of his due diligence process and upheld the defendant's claim of insufficient service of process. The Court stated:

> We do note that there is no evidence in this case of a public records or Internet search for Groce or the use of a skip-trace service to find him. In fact, we discovered, upon entering "Joe Groce Indiana" into the Google™ search engine, an address for Groce that differed from either address used in this case, as well as an apparent obituary for Groce's mother that listed numerous surviving relatives who might have known his whereabouts. We note that . . . advances in modern technology and the widespread use of the Internet have sent the investigative technique of a call to directory assistance the way of the horse and buggy and the eight track stereo.

In contrast, only six years prior to *Munster*, a district court cautioned against relying on "voodoo information" from the Internet. *St. Clair v. Johnny's Oyster & Shrimp, Inc.*, 76 F. Supp. 2d 773, 775 (S.D. Tex. 1999). The court wrote:

> While some look to the Internet as an innovative vehicle for communication, the Court continues to warily and wearily view it largely as one large catalyst for rumor, innuendo, and misinformation. . . . Anyone can put anything on the Internet. No Web site is monitored for accuracy and nothing contained therein is under oath or even subject to independent verification absent underlying documentation. Moreover, the Court holds no illusions that hackers can adulterate the content on any Web site from any location at any time. For these reasons, any evidence procured off the Internet is adequate for almost nothing. . . .

Lawyers have an obligation to clients (and to themselves, in order to remain competitive) to have access to the most comprehensive, cost-effective research resources. The Internet provides an unparalleled opportunity to find the facts relevant to legal issues.

Maintaining an Edge over Research

The researcher's judgment must remain sharp when determining whether to use the Internet for fact finding (or for legal research). Maintaining an edge over research is a process of continually asking yourself what types of sources you need and where you might find them.

Internet Methodology Checklist

1. What type of information do I need?
2. What sources do I need in order to locate the information?
3. What is the likelihood of finding these sources on the Internet?
4. How immediately can these sources be accessed elsewhere, if at all?
5. What will the research cost, in time and money?

This thought process may appear to be painstaking at the outset, but it is crucial to the researcher, especially if there are limitations on time and expense. When well integrated into the research mix, this Internet Methodology Checklist becomes second nature to the researcher, and often can be processed in no time. It is, in fact, not very different from the step-by-step approach employed for many years by researchers using printed materials. It is at the heart of truly effective Internet use, and is mastered not simply by learning how to surf the Internet like a pro, but by remembering to think like a researcher. The checklist can be applied to both legal research and fact-finding research.

We'll use the following fact pattern to illustrate how to use the Internet Methodology Checklist for legal research and fact finding research: Let's say you are working on a case that involves a school bus accident. A child was injured in the accident. It appears that her injuries were caused from the seat belt that she was wearing on the school bus. The child and her parent want to know who's liable.

❑ *Checklist Item 1: What Type of Information Do I Need?*

To put this question into law school exam lingo, "What is the call of the question?" To start assessing liability, the legal researcher in you decides that the first bit of information you need is to figure out *why* there were seat belts on this school bus to begin with. When you rode a school bus, there were no seat belts. You're going to need legal data and information to answer the following question:

- Did the school bus company install seat belts because a new law was passed mandating their installation in school buses, or did they install them on their own, without any mandate?

The factual researcher in you has other questions. You're going to need factual data and information to answer the following questions:

- What type of seat belt was it (lap or shoulder)?
- Who manufactured it? Who installed it?
- Was it manufactured or installed defectively?
- Were other children injured on the bus?
- Were they wearing seat belts?
- Have there been similar accidents?
- Were children in those other accidents injured by the seat belts?

❏ *Checklist Item 2: What Sources Do I Need in Order to Locate the Information?*

The following legal sources are needed to locate information about whether a law was passed recently that mandated seat belts on school buses:

- Codes (probably state, but possibly local or federal)
- Bills (if it's a new statute, it might not be in the code yet, so you'll need to search current bills)
- Legislative history (to find the intent behind the law and to learn if there was any conflicting data as to whether it is safe to place seat belts on school buses)
- Newspaper articles (there were probably articles written about this new law)

The following factual sources are needed to locate the answers to all the other questions relating to the manufacture and installation of the seat belts, and statistics about other similar accidents:

- Product directory (to help identify the seat belt manufacturer and other manufacturers of similar products)
- Company Web site (to see if the manufacturing specs are on any of the manufacturers' sites, and to learn about this specific company structure so you know who to name)
- Government statistics (about school bus and seat belt accidents)

- Articles from newspapers or journals about safety issues concerning placing seat belts on school buses and about similar accidents (and cases) elsewhere
- Newsgroups or Internet mailing lists (to find unofficial or informal reports about school bus and seat belt accidents)

❑ *Checklist Item 3: What Is the Likelihood of Finding these Sources on the Internet?*

The likelihood is high that you'll find many of these legal and factual research sources on the Internet, but you'll need to verify that they are current and credible sources. It won't do any good to rely on an old code, for instance, especially if you suspect that this is a new law.

The following federal legal sources are on the Internet, and they are free:

- U.S. Code
- Bills
- Legislative history

The following state legal sources are likely to be on the Internet, and free (this varies from jurisdiction to jurisdiction):

- Codes
- Bills
- Legislative history
- Local codes and ordinances

The likelihood is high that the following factual resources will be on the Internet for free:

- Bus accident and injury statistics—probably in some government agency Web site related to transportation (see Chapter 6, "Government Resources Online," Chapter 17, "Statistical Research," and Chapter 18, "Transportation Research")
- Articles about school bus and seat belt safety issues and other accidents and cases (see Chapter 9, "Finding and Backgrounding Expert Witnesses," to learn how to find experts' articles)
- Company Web sites (see Chapter 10, "Company Research")
- Product directories (see Chapter 10, "Company Research")
- Newsgroup (such as Google Groups) and Internet e-mail lists. The Internet is the only likely place where you might get information directly from the source by searching newsgroups and e-mail lists (see Chapter 3, "Search Strategies," and Chapter 10, "Company Research")

❏ *Checklist Item 4: How Immediately Can These Sources Be Accessed Elsewhere, If at All?*

Codes: If you have ready access to any of the codes in print, start there. Otherwise, start searching the Internet. Most (if not all) free sites with codes lack case annotations. Even though you can immediately access both the code and the case annotations at a pay site, we wouldn't advise starting with a pay site. Instead, use the free Web sites to find the statute's citation. In case it takes a while to find the citation, you can do it without worrying about the cost of being on a pay site. However, once you find the citation, then turn to a pay database and enter the citation to find annotations.

Local codes: Most people don't have ready access to local (county or city) codes and it's hardly worth a commercial publisher's effort to try to place every municipality's code online—the money is just not there. It's more likely that the local codes, if online at all, can be found on a free site on the Internet.

Statistics and company Web sites: It's unlikely that you have immediate access to injury statistics or information about seat belt manufacturers at your fingertips, and there's no saying that you can find these resources more quickly on a pay site than on the free Internet. Obviously, a company's Web site won't be immediately accessible anywhere but on the free Internet.

Articles: Magazine articles are unlikely to be immediately accessible in print. You might try a free site on the Internet first (such as FindArticles.com), but you may want to turn to a pay database of articles, where more articles and more years' worth of articles are indexed. For newspaper articles, try a few free sites first, but you'll need to search each newspaper's site one by one (unless you know how to access a free newspaper index that searches many simultaneously—see the section "Free Internet Access to Library Databases and Catalogs" in Chapter 5, "General Factual Research"). For newspaper articles, we also recommend using a pay site where you can search hundreds of newspapers in one simultaneous search.

❏ *Checklist Item 5: What Will the Research Cost, in Time and Money?*

It will cost you less money to use the free Internet to find the statute's citation, and because it's usually less expensive to do a citation search than a keyword search in a pay database, you will spend less money if you first find the statute's citation, then use a pay database to find case annotations.

It should cost you little time and no money to search for the company Web site on the Internet. However, if you need very detailed information about the corporate structure, in order to know who to name in the suit, a pay database may be the quicker way to go. We recommend the Directory of Corporate Affiliations database for an instant answer (found on Lexis or Westlaw). Granted, you could piece the information together through various sources on the free Internet (see Chapter 10, "Company Research," and Chapter 11, "Competitive Intelligence Research"), but it may take too long and end up costing you in billable hours.

Finding statistics will probably be less costly on free sites than in a pay database, but in both cases it might be time-consuming, so this might be the perfect research project for a "virtual law librarian" (see the section "Getting Help: Expert Research Support" in Chapter 3, "Search Strategies").

Finding Something Responsive to Your Research

As you can see from the sample search above, you may be able to retrieve most of the information for free from the Internet. This is because the Internet's breadth has continued to widen, and it is becoming a first stop for research of all sorts (including traditional legal research) and particularly for factual research. The openness of the Internet, which enables virtually anyone to publish, has resulted in a continually expanding collection that covers the scope of human knowledge. This is not to say that you can find *everything* on the Internet, but that it's likely you'll find something responsive to your research—something that will point you in a productive direction, even if it does not actually answer your precise question.

Lack of Documentation on the Free Internet

With the openness of the Internet, however, comes the caveat that not everything on the Internet is current or credible (see the section on "Internet Source Credibility" in this chapter). This is where the pay databases sometimes have an advantage over the free Internet sites—you can pretty much assume the pay sites' data are credible and current without doing the extra checking you might need to do when using a free source. Documentation is still somewhat lacking at the free sites on the Web. If you need documentation regarding the credibility or currency of the data found in pay databases, there's 24-7 customer service to provide the answers. (Fee-based Internet customer service is just evolving for the legal professional—see the section on "Getting Help: Expert Research Support" in Chapter 3, "Search Strategies.")

Internet Source Credibility

A good researcher needs to be a sleuth, someone who specializes in finding facts, in understanding why some facts can't be found, and in figuring out whether any of the found facts are credible. Surrounded by today's ocean of information on the Internet, a lawyer now needs to be a "cybersleuth." Lawyers need to be able to look through endless buckets of data to find the relevant drops. We are faced with so many data sources that simply keeping track of them, let alone vouching for their credibility, can be overwhelming. Just because a search engine brings you back Web site results doesn't mean the information at the sites comes from credible sources or is necessarily quality information. Anyone can put up a Web site (or a Web log), post to a newsgroup or an advice site, or join an Internet mailing list, and say anything he wants.

One of the tenets of sound research technique is that a healthy ounce of skepticism is worth a pound of information. There is an adage in accounting that states, "Figures don't lie, but liars figure." The computer-expert version is "Garbage in, garbage out." For most researchers, the adage can be stated even more simply: "Just because it's published doesn't mean it's true." Regular users of the Internet recognize that sentiment. The Internet puts a means of instantaneous worldwide publication at everyone's fingertips, from established commercial publishers to schoolchildren.

Case in point: In a two-week period, "Lawguy1975" dispensed 939 legal answers to 943 questions posed on Askme.com (which was an advice site at the time). By mid-July, Lawguy1975 was the number-three-rated expert in criminal law on AskMe.com. Beneath him in the rankings were 125 licensed lawyers and a wild assortment of ex-cops and ex-cons. When asked why he hadn't answered the other four questions out of the 943 posed, "Traffic law," he said. "I'm sorry, I don't know traffic law." Lawguy1975 finally came clean and admitted on Askme.com that he wasn't a lawyer, just Markus Arnold, a 15-year-old kid with an obvious penchant for Court TV. He didn't know about traffic law because, at age 15, he hadn't learned how to drive . . . yet. (Arnold's exploits were included in the book *Next: The Future Just Happened*, by Michael Lewis.)

So, your job is to evaluate a site's credibility before relying upon the information. How do you do this? The easiest way is to use this book for suggested Web sites. The authors of this book have tested the sites and evaluated them—not only for content, but also for credibility—before recommending them.

There are also a number of Web sites that offer advice on determining the credibility of other sites you find on your own. Consumer Union's

Consumer WebWatch site offers a set of recommended guidelines for Web sites to follow (**http://www.consumerwebwatch.org/bestpractices/index.html**). The site also offers a report on its 2002 research survey, "A Matter of Trust: What Users Want From Web Sites" (**http://www.con sumerwebwatch.org/news/1_abstract.htm**). Other sources for guidelines for testing Web site credibility include **http://www.webcredibility.org/guidelines**, and LLRX's article "Getting It Right: Verifying Sources on the Net" (**http://www.llrx.com/features/verifying.htm**).

For other Web sites that you encounter, try running them through the following checklist to see how they stand up.

Internet Source Credibility Checklist

1. Can you tell the site's owner, editor, or authors when you visit the site?
2. Run the domain name through a registry database to discover the owner.
3. Verify credentials by doing an independent search, not just by relying upon what is given on the site.
4. Discover who else relies on a particular site by conducting a link search.
5. How fresh is the content?
6. What is the quality of the content?
7. Is the site missing any content? Is it as complete as its print version (if there is one)?
8. Verify all information by trying to find the same data at another site.
9. Ascertain the top-level domain (TLD) to help decide credibility.
10. Document your search.

❑ Checklist Item 1: Can You Tell Who the Site Owner Is When You Visit the Site?

Look for a publication statement on the site to ascertain the owner, editor, and authors. Be suspicious if you don't find it easily. A credible site owner should post his name and contact information in a readily visible place on the site in case you want to verify the owner's identity or contact him via e-mail or phone. We've contacted site owners countless times to ask about their credentials or the currency of their data, or even to let them know that links weren't working.

When we went to the Jurist.law site (**http://jurist.law.pitt.edu/about.htm#Masthead**), for example, it was easy to find out that it was hosted by the University of Pittsburgh and that the site editors and founder were a group of law professors (although when we noticed one of their names was "Lawless" we were momentarily concerned about creditability!).

❏ *Checklist Item 2: Run the Domain Name Through a Registry Database to Discover the Owner*

To *try* to discover who is behind a Web site, type the URL into a registry such as DomainTools (**http://domaintools.com**), Better-Whois (**http://www.betterwhois.com**) or Allwhois (**http://www.allwhois.com**). Allwhois also provides links to other countries' registries. The reason why we emphasized "try" in the first sentence of this paragraph is because no registry, for a variety of reasons, seems to be "completely complete." A registry may claim to be the "most complete 'whois' service on the Internet," but this doesn't mean complete as in "comprehensive"—just the most complete that it can be, given all the obstacles. It's difficult to create a comprehensive registry because registries may receive less-than-complete records when a domain is registered, and most registries only cover the most popular TLD types such as .com, .net, or .org, thus leaving out many records from the less popular TLD's such as .biz or .museum.

Even if you do find the registration statement, it's hard to say whether you have found the site owner because anyone can list themselves as the contact person on the registration statement—the site owner, the IT manager, or the Web site's outside designer.

DomainTools (formerly Whois Source)

http://www.domaintools.com

Purpose:	To find out who is behind a Web site, and to learn whether a URL is available, on hold, or deleted, and more.
Content:	There are many sites that help you learn who is behind a Web site and they all allow you to search by the site's URL, but DomainTools offers more search parameters and more features than the others.
	As to extra features, DomainTools provides a site registrant's name and contact information just as the other sites do, but only DomainTools provides a thumbnail (image) of the site's home page, information about the site's purpose, its IP address, and also a list of its meta tags (and other information).

As to search parameters, while DomainSurfer.com and DomainTools both offer partial site name searching and allow you to anchor the search to the beginning of the name, DomainTools goes a step further by allowing you to search by several other options if you click on the **Domain Search Advanced** tab: (1) for partial names, you can also anchor the search to the end of the name (right anchor) besides the beginning (left anchor); (2) search only hyphenated names, or block them, or search both; or (3) search active names, or deleted names, or both.

Our View: Although you need to register to access some extra information, the registration process is quick and easy—enter only your e-mail address and your password. We like the flexibility in searching offered at this site. We also find it convenient to view the home page thumbnail and read about the site's purpose information—that way we can avoid linking to the site if it's apparent that it's not what we're looking for. A timesaving feature is **Bulk Check** where you can check the availability of multiple domain names simultaneously.

Tip: The following are the additional services and features you'll receive by registering (free) or subscribing to the pay portion (silver membership) of the site. Click on the **Members Area** tab to subscribe.

- **Mark Alert**: Monitor a specific word to find out when it is used in a new URL and to find out when your monitored word is found in a URL that is about to expire.
  - Silver Member: 10 Alerts
  - Registered Member Limit: 1 demo alert
- **Reverse IP**: Search by IP address such as "66.863.22.111" (.COM, .NET, .ORG, .INFO, .BIZ, and .US domains only).
  - Silver Limit: 2000 URLs
  - Registered Member Limit: 3 URL views
- **Domain History**: Only Silver Members can view the complete history of a domain's Domain Record (back to 2001).

❏ *Checklist Item 3: Verify the Owner or Author's Credentials by Doing an Independent Search*

Don't just rely on the information that is given on the site. If the site owner says he's a lawyer in California, run his name through the California bar association's member records to verify his license and review his discipline record. If the site owner claims to be an author, run his name through the Library of Congress online catalog (**http://catalog.loc.gov**) and its copyright database (**http://www.loc.gov/copyright/search**).

❏ *Checklist Item 4: Discover Who Else Relies on the Site*

Sometimes the best way to verify credibility is to see who thinks highly enough of the site to link to it from another site. For example, to

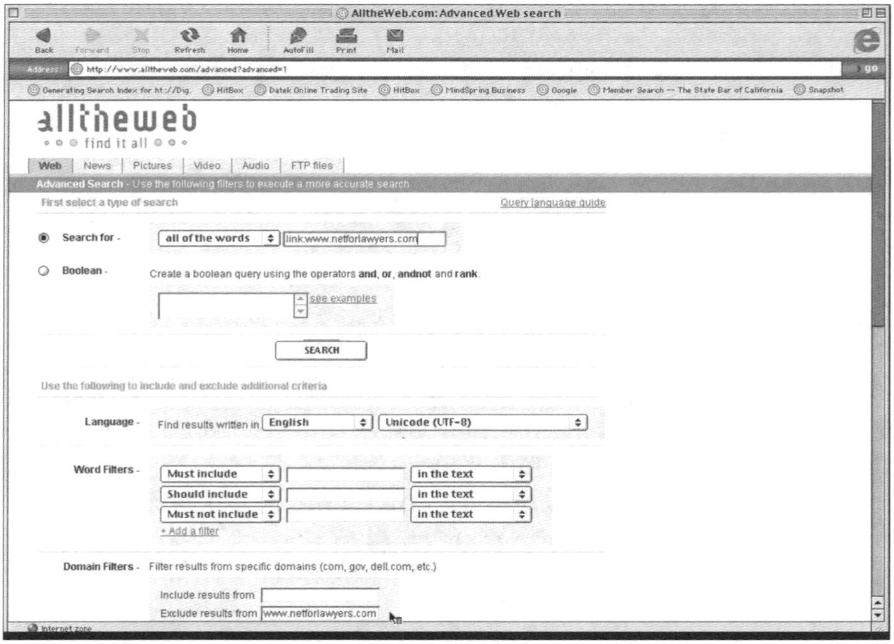

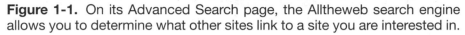

Figure 1-1. On its Advanced Search page, the Alltheweb search engine allows you to determine what other sites link to a site you are interested in.

see if others rely upon a site called www.sitename.com, conduct a link search using the Alltheweb search engine. Using Alltheweb's Advanced Search page, enter "link:www.sitename.com" in the **all of the words** query box and also enter the same URL (**www.sitename.com**) in the **Domain Filter-Exclude Results From** query box.

❏ *Checklist Item 5: How Fresh Is the Content?*

Look for a statement saying when the site as a whole was last updated. Also look for publication dates for the articles or other material posted on the site. For example, on November 7, 2005, we visited the Jurist.law site (**http://jurist.law.pitt.edu/**) and found a 2005 copyright statement at the bottom of the home page. We then looked for a publication date for any of the material posted on the site and found exact dates that indicated when each piece of information had been added right at the top of each article. Other headlines on the home page listed the dates on which they were posted. When stories were posted on the same day as we visited the site, those headlines carried the time at which the stories were posted. All this indicated that the site was being kept fresh.

❑ *Checklist Item 6: What Is the Quality of the Content?*

Is the content one-sided or objective? One-sided information might be acceptable if it's being used to persuade. For example, the Electronic Privacy Information Center (EPIC) states that it is "a public interest research center . . . established . . . to focus public attention on emerging civil liberties issues and to protect privacy, the First Amendment, and constitutional values." Is this site biased? You bet. But, as noted above, it clearly states its bias on its home page by way of its purpose message. Is the information of high quality? Yes—it's just presented from a privacy advcate's viewpoint.

❑ *Checklist Item 7: Is the Site Missing Any Content? Is It as Complete as Its Print Version (if There Is One)?*

Ever since the *Tasini* decision, many publications have had to remove individual author's articles from their Web sites (*New York Times Co. v. Tasini*, 533 U.S. 483 [2001]). Thus, many Web sites are no longer as complete as their corresponding print versions. Sometimes the opposite occurs—a Web site may contain more content than the print publication. This is the case with sites that continually update throughout the day.

❑ *Checklist Item 8: Verify All Information by Trying to Find the Same Information at Another Site*

Just by reviewing your results, you can often tell that the information is being published at many sites. Does this make it any more credible? Not necessarily, but you can click on a few of the sites and apply the credibility test. We typically don't verify information if we've already run the site through a credibility test, or if someone else whose judgment we trust has done so. Whom do we trust? People who test out sites before writing about them. These are some of the sites where we know the authors test sites before recommending them: Virtual Chase, SearchEngineWatch,

Search Engine Showdown, LLRX, and Netforlawyers (just add a .com to each to visit the sites) and the ABA's Site-tation (**http://meetings.abanet .org/ltrc/index.cfm**).

❑ *Checklist Item 9: Ascertain the TLD to Help Decide Credibility*

Does the TLD indicate it's a government (.gov), educational (.edu), or commercial (.com) site?

Can you trust a site with a .gov TLD? The U.S. General Services Administration Federal Technology Service (GSA FTS) validates each .gov top-level domain name before registering it. It's likely then that a site with the .gov TLD is actually sponsored by the government. We say "likely" because on Jan. 24, 2003, the GSA was faced with the first "hijacking" of a .gov TLD, and pulled the domain of AONN.gov after CNET site (**http://news.com**) questioned the site's governmental status.

Even when you're sure a .gov site is authentic, there are other aspects of credibility that must be considered, such as whether the information on the site is current. For example, the U.S. Code is published by two governmental entities—the House of Representatives and the Government Printing Office (GPO)—but the House site is the more current (**http://uscode.house.gov/lawrevisioncounsel.shtml**). On October 20, 2005, for example, Title 1, section 1 on the GPO site (**http://gpoaccess .gov/uscode/index.html**) was current only up to laws that took effect on January 7, 2003, while the House site showed dates of January 1, 2004.

Another credibility issue is whether the information on a government site is the "official" record? For example, many court sites warn that their site is for informational purposes only and that the information is *not* the official record. This is especially true for courts that publish their slip opinions because the court can later modify the opinion.

Can you trust the .edu TLD? Just because an academic institution sponsors a site doesn't mean an academician is writing the content. Case in point: we did a search using the words "lemon" and "law" and came up with a .edu site with a page written by an elementary school child, who liked lemonade and root beer and wanted to be a law professor when he grew up! Needless to say, this site didn't help us with our lemon-law questions. Not all such instances will be as obvious, unfortunately.

Therefore, as with all information sources, data retrieved from the Internet must be viewed with skepticism until its credibility has been verified. Any cybersleuth can access data sources. But if you are after genuine knowledge, only a *good* cybersleuth knows to judge credibility before relying on the data.

Can you trust well-known pay resources? Even pay resources can contain errors. While you don't have to go through the same credibility checklist to identify owners and sponsors of pay resources (such as Lexis-Nexis or Westlaw), you still need to verify the veracity and currency of the information you find there.

❑ **Checklist Item 10: Document Your Search**

Print out a paper copy of the pages you will be relying upon so you can prove credibility to others.

Free Versus Pay Resources

Although Lexis, Westlaw, and other legal research, fee-based databases originally provided access only to the law, they have added reams of factual information to their databases. Though you can now turn to them for factual research, the best researchers know that there are often many ways to access the same information for free on the Internet. Sometimes the information you seek will only be found in a free Internet source (such as a small-town newspaper that a pay database wouldn't bother to index). On the flip side, the best researchers also know that sometimes it's worth the money to use pay databases (even if you think the information can be found for free on the Internet).

The Myth of the "All-Comprehensive" Database

Although a savvy searcher knows how to evaluate which method (free or pay) is the best route to take, the *really* savvy searcher knows that there is no such thing, even in a pay environment, as a definitive and comprehensive database (in scope and content) for any area of knowledge. For example, there is no pay database that will search every type of public record that was ever filed, in every government agency, and in every jurisdiction.

The savvy searcher also knows that whether using free or pay databases, the type and amount of information available varies greatly from jurisdiction to jurisdiction. Some states, such as Florida, have a wide variety of public records available for free on the Internet (such as Uniform Commercial Code filings (UCC), trademark owner names, corporate records, and annual reports), and they also provide a large amount of information in each record by placing the image of the original public record online (**http://ccfcorp.dos.state.fl.us**). Other states may not provide access to the same data Florida does, or may provide some of it free and require payment for some.

And finally, the savvy searcher knows that to conduct what comes closest to a comprehensive search sometimes involves all, or a combination of, the following:

- Pay database searching
- Free Internet searching
- Print resource searching
- Hiring expert researchers
- Contacting the source, such as a government agency or an individual, via:

  - In-person visit
  - Phone call
  - E-mail message
  - Letter

When to Use Pay Databases

We recommend using pay databases in the following instances:

- **If it's going to be quicker than surfing the Internet.** You might know exactly where to find the information in a pay database because you've been there before, or perhaps you need to document that the data are credible and current, and you don't have time to evaluate a free Internet source (documentation is usually better on the pay sources).

- **If you need older data.** Pay databases often offer earlier date coverage. The free Internet is fairly new compared to pay databases, many of which have been around for at least twenty-five years. Thus, the pay databases are more comprehensive in scope because they have been building their archives longer than the free sites have.

- **If you need to perform a somewhat complex search.** Pay sites often have better search functions—allowing for easier access to data (and sometimes the only, or the only reasonable, access), such as:

  - Performing national or multistate searches
  - Searching a broad swath of unrelated material (for example, searching through thousands of articles in hundreds of individually owned newspapers or magazines)
  - Field searching (by name, date, and so on)

- **If the information is only available at a pay source**.
  - A pay database may have purchased a certain category of public records from a government entity and created an online product where one did not exist before
  - A pay database may have purchased publicly available information to fill in any information gaps in public records
  - A pay database is commonly known as the only source—such as a D & B company or a credit report for a private company

Examples of Pay Database Searches

Below are some examples of the types of searches best suited to pay sites.

National and Multistate Searching

If a searcher wants to search a corporation in every state in which it is registered (and therefore needs to find the registered agent in each state), a multijurisdictional secretary of state search using the corporation's name is in order. If the searcher needs to discover in which state a company is incorporated or licensed to do business, again, a multijurisdictional secretary of state search by the corporation's name is in order. Neither of these types of simultaneous multistate searches can be done for free on the Internet. Conceivably, you could search the free Internet, state by state, but in a time and cost analysis, it would not be worth your while. Thus, a pay site is the best (and only reasonable) option. Also, not every state has posted its corporate records for free on the Internet, but the records are likely to be available in a pay database.

Field Searching

Field searching allows you to search with almost any nugget of information, or with a combination of nuggets. For example:

- If you *only* know someone's Social Security number and need to find his or her name, address, and phone number, you can perform a reverse search on a fee-based database that provides a Social Security number search field.
- When searching using a name is getting you nowhere and you suspect the spelling provided to you was wrong, if you have any other nugget of information (such as a Social Security number, a phone number, or an address), entering that information into the appropriate field to conduct a reverse search can get you the correct spelling.

- If you need to know if a specific person is a registered agent in a state, this typically requires a pay search, because most free sites don't provide multiple-field searching options where you can search by either a corporation's name or a registered agent's name. Most free sites only allow you to perform a one-field search, and that is typically a corporation name search. Most pay sites also allow you to also conduct a registered agent name field search. (However, in Florida, you *can* search by a registered agent's name for free at Florida's Secretary of State site. Thus, it never hurts to first visit a state's free site to review the search functions.)

Advanced Searches

Pay sites allow sophisticated and flexible types of searches, such as the following searches of public records:

- In a single search, being able to search one public-record category for one or more states (for example, searching using an individual's name through all online real estate records nationwide to marshal his or her assets)
- In a single search, being able to search through multiple public-record categories in unrelated agencies in one or more states (for example, searching on an individual's name to find all of his or her property records, bankruptcies, liens, and judgments)

Publicly Available Information at Pay Sites

The content found in a fee-based database is usually more comprehensive than that of a free public-record database, because pay sites add data from publicly available information that was voluntarily provided to nongovernmental entities. This information is extracted from sources such as a product warranty cards, where purchasers divulge income, gender, and age; phone directories; utility customer lists; and so on.

Examples of Major Pay Databases

Throughout the book, we refer to pay databases, such as Lexis, LexisONE, Westlaw, Choicepoint, Accurint, Merlin, and KnowX. We discuss specific aspects of the data available on these pay sites when it relates to the chapter's subject, and we indicate when it's best (or necessary) to use the pay sources. For example, in the section on real estate records in Chapter 8, "Accessing Public Records," we discuss free real estate assessor sources first. But if a jurisdiction doesn't have this data online for free, or if the pay database has a better search feature, we discuss the pay database too. In some of the chapters, we introduce pay databases in addition to the major ones noted above.

When to Use Free Internet Sources

Below are just some of the myriad situations when it's best to use the free Internet. Throughout this book, we give examples of each type of situation listed below, and suggest specific free Web sites to use to find the factual answers. Use a free site in these circumstances:

- If you don't need a comprehensive search, only a targeted one
- If the free site provides more information than the pay site
- If you have a lot of clues about a person or if he has a unique name
- If you want both official and unofficial information—such as rumors or opinions about a company, a product, an event, or a person, or to see what nuggets of information "pop up"—use the following free Internet sources:

  - Search engine
  - Newsgroup
  - Your subject's Web site
  - Your subject's Web log (also known as a "blog")
  - Internet mailing list
  - Archive of magazine or newspaper articles
  - Conference papers

- If you're looking for very local or regional information
- If you're looking for up-to-the-minute (literally) news—some search engines and some sites add news continually throughout the day (see the section on news in Chapter 5, "General Factual Research")
- If you're looking for other types of up-to-the-minute information such as:

  - Stock quotes
  - Time
  - Weather
  - Sports scores

- If you're looking for anything that might have been created in the following file formats:

- Microsoft Word
- Microsoft Excel (spreadsheets)
- Microsoft PowerPoint (presentations)
- Adobe Portable Document Format (PDF)

- If you're looking for government information, such as:

  - Public records
  - Statistics
  - Reports

- If you're looking for forms

- If you're looking for something created privately and later posted to the Internet, such as:

  - Brochures
  - Newsletters
  - Family trees
  - Conference papers

Examples of Searches on Free Sites

Targeted Search

If a searcher needs to locate a company's corporate record, and only needs to search one specific state, the free route usually is satisfactory if that state's secretary of state database is free on the Web. In this case, it doesn't pay to search virtually the same database at a pay site. To easily link to all states that do provide free corporate record databases over the Web, use the National Association of Secretaries of States metasite (**http://www.nass.org/sos/sos.html**) or Residentagentinfo.com (**http://www.residentagentinfo.com**). For more details on these two databases, see Chapter 10, "Company Research."

Free Site with More Information

In state trial-court docket databases, some of the pay sites may only contain the party name and the docket number, while the free government sites may also contain the lawyers' names and the case disposition (and sometimes even more).

However, even though the free site may have more information, you still might first need to use a pay site to get to the free information because the pay site offers better searching! For example, if you only have the party's name, and the free docket site doesn't allow for party name field searching (it only allows docket number field searching), a pay site comes in handy because it typically allows for party name field searching. By doing a party name field search at the pay site, you can discover the docket number. Then to find more information, such as the attorneys of record or the disposition, you can visit the free site and search by the newly found docket number. It's a roundabout method, but one we've had to use.

If the first key to successful, efficient research is to first know where to start—in a pay database or free on the Internet—the next step to success is deciding which specific sources to use. For instance, if using the free Internet, in which Web site or search engine should you start your research? See Chapter 3, "Search Strategies," and Chapter 4, "Search Tools," for tips on how to begin to identify specific sources.

Citing Internet Resources

For insight into how to cite to a Web site, *The Bluebook: A Uniform System of Citation, Eighteenth Edition,* finally provides some detailed solutions beyond the *Bluebook's* previous edition's cursory examples. The *Bluebook* still discourages citing to Web sites unless the materials are unavailable in printed form because sites are so transient and can disappear from the Internet. If no one is able to find and verify your citation to a Web site, you will not be able to rely upon it any longer for your argument. However, the rules about citing the Internet (Rules 18.2 through 18.2.4), have been revised and expanded to acknowledge the increasing reliance people have placed upon information found on the Internet. Examples of the expanded rules vary from how to cite to blogs to an instruction to cite to a PDF rather than an HTML document, if the document is available in both formats.

Although the full text of the official *Bluebook* is not online, the official Bluebook Web site has a list of changes to the new Eighteenth edition at **http://legalbluebook.com/changes.shtml**. Also available online is a basic guide to the *Bluebook* entitled *Introduction to Basic Legal Citation,* by Peter Martin, with examples on how to cite Internet sources. It can be found at Cornell University's Web site, **http://www.law.cornell.edu/citation**. It was first written in 1993, but was most recently updated in January of 2006. To find examples, click on **How to Cite** (in the left column) and then click on **Electronic Sources**.

Martin also refers to an alternative citation manual for examples on citing electronic sources, the *ALWD Citation Manual: A Professional System of Citation* (2003), written by the Association of Legal Writing Directors.

An Internet citation is required if the source is only found on the Internet. However, it may be added as a parallel citation to a print version's citation if providing it makes the source more accessible. The Internet citation should consist of all the elements required by the *Bluebook* for any of the basic document types found in print. If the Internet citation is added as a parallel citation to the print source, indicate this by adding the explanatory phrase *available at* prior to the Internet citation. For example, you would cite to a print version of U.S. Supreme Court case that is also found on the Internet at the Cornell site in this manner:

Hill v. Colorado, 200 U.S. 404 (2000), *available at*
http://supct.law.cornell.edu/supct/html/98-1856.ZS.html.

According to Rule 18.2.3, if the electronic source is the only known source, or is not widely available in a commercial database (such as an e-mail or unpublished dissertation), no explanatory phrase is used.

If a journal appears only on the Internet, in addition to including the author's name, include (1) the volume number; (2) the title of the journal; (3) the sequential article number; (4) the paragraph number (if doing pinpoint citing); (5) the publication date if available (or the most recent modification date of the site or the date you visited the site); and (6) the URL without the *available at* explanatory phrase. For example:

Levitt, *How to Use the Internet for Legal Research*, 3 Net for Lawyers L.J. 1, par.8 (July 20, 1999), **http://www.netforlawyers.com/levitt.html**.

A word about using angle brackets to set off URLs: opinion on this is divided into two camps. The first camp believes in following *The Chicago Style of Manual,* which does not favor using angle brackets because they can cause confusion (Web site designers also use angle brackets as part of Web page mark-up languages, such as HTML or XML). The other camp thinks angle brackets are useful to show where a URL begins and ends. To avoid the mark-up language confusion and to indicate where the URL begins and ends, in this book we often place URLs in parentheses. The eighteenth edition of the *Bluebook* no longer appears to use the angle brackets.

In 1996, the American Bar Association (ABA) approved a resolution recommending that courts adopt a uniform public domain citation system "equally effective for printed case reports and for case reports electronically published on computer disks or network services." About twelve states and the Sixth Circuit Court have adopted the ABA's resolution for uniform citation. For a full copy of this report, go to **http://www.abanet.org/tech/ltrc/research/citation/report.html**. (The American Association of Law Libraries published the *Universal Citation Guide* to implement the ABA's resolution. To order this book, see **http://www.aallnet.org/products/pub_universal.asp**.)

The following example is offered by the ABA for citation to a federal court of appeals decision found on a Web site:

> *Smith v. Jones*, 1996 5Cir 15, ¶ 18, 22 F.3d 955

The ABA instructs that if a case is only available on the Internet, print it out for opposing counsel and the court.

Finally, if you don't find a specific rule or example in any of these sources, provide as much information as you can and print out a copy of the material (as the ABA instructs you to do for cases on the Internet) or use citation examples from either of the two nationally recognized general citation style manuals, *The Chicago Manual of Style* or the *American Psychological Association* (APA) *Publication Manual*. The *APA Publication Manual* has a Web page about electronic references at **http://www.apastyle.org/elecref.html.** The *Chicago Manual* is not online, but an updated frequently-asked questions (FAQs) page (**www.press.uchicago.edu/Misc/Chicago/cmosfaq/cmosfaq.html**) offers helpful Internet citation tips, and the editors welcome your questions. (A revision date is now posted on the FAQ page to let visitors know the last time information was added to the page.) The editors' replies may come as individual responses or may appear on the FAQ page. Here is an example of a *Chicago Manual* citation for a private e-mail message:

> Ford, Cory <cford@soil.com>, "Soil Ecology Discussion," private e-mail message to author. 7 March 1998.

Internet Copyright Issues

All we can definitively say about copyright and the Internet is that as courts try to superimpose traditional copyright rules (Title 17 of the U.S. Code) onto the digital world, the two concepts will continue to clash, and the rules will be constantly shifting. When copyright laws were written, no one dreamed that books, articles, and other text, and even music, images, and videos would be posted in cyberspace on this thing we call the Internet.

Ask a typical Internet user about copyright and the Internet and you'll probably get the reply that if it's on the Internet for free, then it's free to copy! This, of course, is patently wrong if the material is copyrighted (unless it fits within fair use), but it's the common belief (or hope) of most Internet users.

When digital data appears on a computer screen, is it considered to be
- A copy?
- Distribution?
- Publication?
- Public display?
- Fair use?

Or, do these questions only arise when the digital material is actually printed out as a hard copy?

Ownership of Digital Rights to Freelance Work: The Tasini Decision

Digital rights are now typically a standard part of a freelancer's contract, but when contracts were signed over a decade ago, they were not. In *New York Times Company v. Tasini*, 533 U.S. 483 (2001), the U.S. Supreme Court ruled that print publishers must seek copyright permission from freelancers before placing their work into an electronic database. This decision has affected many Web site archives that contained freelancers' articles from over a decade ago because many works have now been taken off line. While this decision was a victory for freelancers, it was a loss for researchers who can no longer rely on digital archives necessarily being complete.

Ownership of Digital Rights to an Author's Works

The case of Rosetta Books also dealt with the question of digital rights. Rosetta Books paid various authors for the electronic publishing rights to their books. Random House then filed suit, claiming those rights were already theirs by virtue of agreements from twenty to forty years before, when each author granted to Random House the exclusive right to "print, publish and sell in book form." Random House asserted that those agreements should be interpreted as including the right to publish those books in an e-book format. Random House's appeal, from the denial of a preliminary injunction that sought to enjoin Rosetta Books from selling the e-books that it claimed it had exclusive rights over, was affirmed by the Second Circuit in *Random House v. Rosetta Books*, 283 F.3d 490 (2002) available at **http://laws.lp.findlaw.com/2nd/017912.html**. Eventually, the pending litigation was settled, with no financial payment made by either party. Instead, they agreed to partner in developing the e-book market.

The question of who owns digital rights to an author's work if digital technology was not even imagined when the contracts were signed remains unanswered.

In-line Linking and Framing

Is it fair use for sites to use in-line linking or frames to display content that actually resides on a third party's server? Not according to the Ninth Circuit and its decision in *Kelly v. Arriba Soft Corporation*, 280 F.3d 934, (9th Cir. 2002). In *Kelly*, the Arriba (now Ditto.com) search engine located and reproduced Kelly's images as thumbnails on the Arriba Web site, and also displayed Kelly's full-sized images on the site using in-line linking and framing. This means, basically, that Arriba linked to the image on Kelly's server, but placed an Arriba frame around the image so it looked as though it was posted on Arriba's site. Although Arriba did not *copy* Kelly's Internet images onto its site (and thus did not violate Kelly's right of reproduction under fair use), the Court held that Arriba did infringe on Kelly's copyright because it unlawfully *distributed* and publicly *displayed* Kelly's images. The Copyright Act protects against unlawful distribution and public display of copyrighted material. However, one year later, the Court replaced its *Kelly vs. Arriba Soft Corporation* opinion. See 336 F.3d 811 (9th Cir. 2003) *available at* **http://images.chillingeffects.org/cases/ Kelly_v_Arriba.html**. While it affirmed that the thumbnails were fair use, it stated that (for procedural reasons) the district Court should not have reached whether Arriba's display of Kelly's full-sized images was fair use. The Court reversed its holding that the display of the full-sized images was not fair use and remanded to the district court.

Screen Shots

Does using a screen shot of a Web site for illustrative purposes (as we do in this book) invoke copyright issues? The Ninth Circuit faced a somewhat similar issue in a "comparison advertisement" case. In *Sony Computer Entertainment America v. Bleem*, 214 F.3d 1022 (9th Cir. 2000), the court had to decide "whether the unauthorized use of a 'screen shot'—a frozen image from a personal video game [in this case]—falls within the fair use exception to the law of copyright." The court stated, basically, that there was no market in screen shots and held that use of the screen shot was fair use, explaining that:

1. Although Bleem is . . . copying Sony's copyrighted material for the commercial purposes of increasing its own sales . . . there is very little corresponding loss to the integrity of Sony's copyrighted material.
2. A screen shot is merely an inanimate sliver of the game.
3. A screen shot is such an insignificant portion of the complex copyrighted work as a whole.
4. Bleem's use of a handful of screen shots in its advertising will have no noticeable effect on Sony's ability to do with its screen shots what it chooses.

What if those screen shots are of government Web sites? Does the concept that the government cannot copyright its data because it is in the public domain change in cyberspace? When we wrote for copyright permission to show a screen shot of the government's FedStats Web site (**http://www.fedstats.gov**), the reply was, "Fedstats is in the Public Domain, therefore no special permission is needed to link to our site or place a screen shot on your site or in your publication." Just as we thought. But there are some other intellectual property issues to consider when taking screen shots of government Web sites, such as trademark issues, as pointed out by the reply from the U.S. Security and Exchange Commission (SEC) **EDGAR** site (**http://www.sec.gov/edgar.shtml**) when we sought copyright permission to publish a screen shot of **EDGAR**. "While the Commission has no copyright interest in the web page, it does own a trademark in the **EDGAR** name and logo . . ." However, the commission went on to say that "a display of the name or logo incidental to publication of an image of the web page in a book about Web sites is unlikely to cause public confusion. . . ."

The Internet and the Entertainment Industry

When the ruling in *Napster* was made in favor of the entertainment industry, it was hoped by the industry that the issue of illegally downloading copyrighted music had finally been put to rest (*A&M Records, Inc. v. Napster* 284 F.3d 109 9th Cir. 2002). But, in April 2003, a new case posed another threat to the entertainment industry's music and movie copyrights. In *MGM Studios, Inc. v. Grokster Ltd.*, 269 F. Supp. 2nd 1213 (C.D. Cal, 2003) *aff'd* 380 F.3d 1154 (9th Cir. 2004), District Court Judge Wilson ruled that Grokster is not liable for copyright infringement merely because buyers of its software can copy copyrighted music and movies (thus infringing on copyrights) because the Grokster networks do not monitor or control what people do with the software (unlike Napster, which did). Judge Wilson stated that Grokster is no more liable for copyright infringement than Sony was for distributing the Betamax VCR.

Then, in 2005, the U.S. Supreme Court disagreed with the District Court and the 9th Circuit's holdings and held that:

> The question is under what circumstances the distributor of a product capable of both lawful and unlawful use is liable for acts of copyright infringement by third parties using the product. We hold that one who distributes a device with the object of promoting its use to infringe copyright, as shown by clear expression or other affirmative steps taken to foster infringement, is liable for the resulting acts of infringement by third parties. 125 S. Ct. 2764 (U.S. 2005) *available at* **http://caselaw.lp.findlaw.com/scripts/getcase.pl?court=us&vol=000&invol=04-480**

The Court vacated the judgment of the Court of Appeals and remanded it for further proceedings consistent with its opinion.

On November 7, 2005, the Recording Industry Association of America (RIAA) announced a settlement under which Grokster would cease operation immediately.

The RIAA statement read in part, "the settlement includes a permanent injunction prohibiting infringement—directly or indirectly—of any of the plaintiffs' copyrighted works. This includes ceasing immediately distribution of the Grokster client application and ceasing to operate the Grokster system and software."

Grokster ceased operation that same day, posting the following notice on its own Web site:

> The United States Supreme Court unanimously confirmed that using this service to trade copyrighted material is illegal. Copying copyrighted motion picture and music files using unauthorized peer-to-peer services is illegal and is prosecuted by copyright owners. There are legal services for downloading music and movies. This service is not one of them.

The notice went on to indicate, however, that, "Grokster hopes to have a safe and legal service available soon" at **www.grokster3g.com**.

Copyright Clearance Center

Using the Copyright Clearance Center (CCC), you can request permission to reproduce copyrighted material (**https://www.copyright.com**).

From articles and book chapters, to Web sites, e-mails, and more, CCC manages the rights to over 1.75 million works of more than 9,600 publishers and hundreds of thousands of authors. Over 10,000 corporations and thousands of government agencies, law firms, document suppliers, libraries, educational institutions, photocopy shops, and bookstores use CCC to clear rights. You can search CCC's online catalog to discover if a work is registered: if it is, you can find out what it would cost to reproduce the work and then instantly have CCC clear the rights you need. The cost depends on how many copies are to be reproduced and for what purpose (to use in a newsletter, for a brochure, and so on).

Other Copyright Issues

These are only a few of the issues confronting lawyers involved in copyright and the Internet. For a look at myriad issues in this area, see the Electronic Frontier Foundation site (**http://www.eff.org**).

*CHAPTER***TWO**

Internet Tools and Protocol

Browsers and Favorites

Web Browsers: A Quick View

- A browser is a program that allows you to view pages on the Internet.
- Browsers (such as Microsoft Internet Explorer or Netscape Communicator) often come pre-installed when you purchase a new computer.
- The different browsers have many similar characteristics . . . and some subtle differences.
- You can cut and paste material from visited sites.
- You can use the Find function to locate text in a long Web page.
- You can bookmark sites you find especially useful to make them easy to return to.

Pick the Browser That Best Suits Your Needs

Aside from the software that connects you to your Internet Service Provide (ISP), the single most important piece of software required for surfing the Internet is the Web browser, also referred to as simply the browser.

The browser is the computer program that allows users to reach out onto the Internet, locate innumerable Web pages on any number of topics, and translate these computer documents from their HTML programming language into the graphical Web sites we are now all used to seeing.

While all Web browsers perform basically the same functions, they each have their own characteristics. Netscape was first-to-market with a commercial version of a graphical Internet browser with the introduction of its Navigator browser in 1994. Realizing the importance of the Internet as an information platform, Microsoft introduced its Internet Explorer browser the following year. Exhibiting some of the marketing savvy (and muscle) that has made it the largest software publisher in the world, Microsoft went on to capture the lion's share of the browser market. In December 2002, OneStat, a provider of Internet usage statistics, reported that "Microsoft's Internet Explorer has a total global usage share of 95%," while "the global usage share of Netscape is 3.0%" (**http://www.onestat .com/html/aboutus_pressbox15.html**). Less than four years later however, Internet Explorer had lost significant market share to the open source browser upstart Mozilla. In July 2006, OneStat reported that "Mozilla's browsers have a total global usage share of 12.93 percent," while Internet Explorer had slipped to 83.05 percent. At the same time, OneStat reported that Netscape had dropped to just 1.16 percent of browser usage, behind Opera and Apple's Safari browser. (**http://www.onestat.com/html/about us_pressbox44-mozilla-firefox-has-slightly-increased.html**) This ongoing competition between browser developers for browser market share has resulted in an incredibly rapid evolutionary pace. For a while, new versions of major browsers were being released every six months or so. After a lull in development in the early 2000s, developers are again introducing new browser versions with more and more features. It is pointless to discuss all of these features here in any depth, since any information may soon be irrelevant.

Practical Point

Let's say you're conducting research designed to challenge your opponent's expert witness. If the expert is a physician, you might click over to the American Medical Association site (**http://www.ama-assn.org**) to get the expert's basic background. Once you find her address, school attended, and other basics, you might highlight the data with your mouse, copy it using the Ctrl+C sequence (hold down the Ctrl key, and hit C), open your word processor (either a new or existing document), and paste the information (using Ctrl+V) onto the dossier page you're building.

Practical Point

Suppose you're interested in adding to your law firm's corporate clients. As part of the preparation for your marketing effort, you'd like to look into a particular target company's recent legal matters. Assuming your target is a public company, you might start by looking at the relevant portion of the SEC 10-K filing, (Part 1., Item C. Legal Proceedings). So, you could click over to the SEC's EDGAR site (**http://www.sec.gov/cgi-bin/srch-edgar**), and pull up the 10-K. Then, if you're using Navigator or Explorer, you could hit Ctrl+F (hold down the Ctrl key, and hit F) to invoke the Find tool. Note that this tool searches only the document that appears in the browser window. It does not search the entire Internet the way search engines like AltaVista and Google do. When the Find search window pops up, type "legal proceedings" (upper or lower case—it doesn't matter), hit the Enter key, and you should be taken to the Legal Proceedings section of the 10-K.

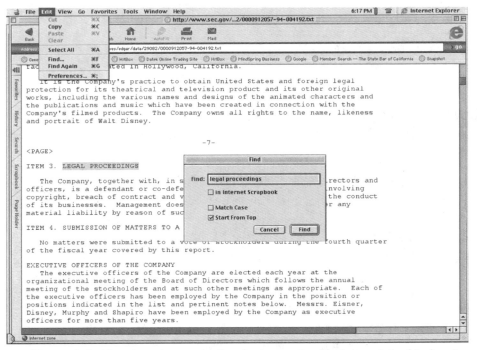

Figure 2-1. Here is a demonstration that uses the Find search tool to locate the Legal Proceedings section of a Walt Disney Company 10-K from the SEC's EDGAR site.

It is worth noting, however, the essential browser features that a researcher ought to be familiar with:

- Browsers provide the ability to bookmark favorite Internet sites and easily access those bookmarks.
- Arrows in the upper left-hand corner of the browser window allow you to move back and forward between Web pages you have viewed.
- Like many other programs, browsers offer you the ability to copy text from sites you visit and paste it into your own word processing documents (such as Microsoft Word or Corel WordPerfect). This can be a very handy feature when compiling a dossier on an individual, a company, or when you're getting up to speed on a new subject.
- Another excellent browser feature is the ability to conduct a text search on any Web page viewable in your browser, using the Find function.

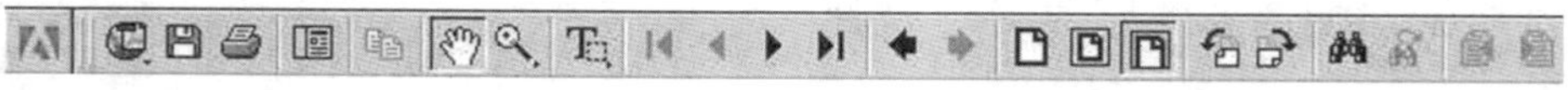

Figure 2-2. To do a similar search when viewing a PDF document on the Internet, click the Binocular icon on the special Adobe® Acrobat Reader® toolbar that opens near the top of your Web browser window whenever you're reading a PDF document. Adobe product screen shot reprinted with permission from Adobe Systems Incorporated.

Practical Point

Many government documents are posted on the Internet in the Adobe Portable Document Format (PDF). While these documents can be viewed in your browser (if you have installed the Acrobat Viewer plug-in), they are searched differently than described above. An additional toolbar is seen (see Figure 2-2) when the browser displays a PDF document. On this toolbar is a Binocular icon that is used to search the PDF. Clicking that icon brings up the search box into which you type your search term. Clicking Ctrl+F will bring up the browser's Find box, but it will not actually find your search term even if it is in the PDF document. (To make matters even more confusing, not all PDF documents are searchable—even when clicking the Binocular icon and entering search terms. This is dependent on how a document was originally created.)

Choosing a Web browser boils down to personal preferences, especially when you consider the Microsoft versus Mozilla versus Netscape battle for desktop supremacy, that has made the leading browsers' (functionally) nearly identical. You may have a preference, however, for the way Netscape handles bookmarks, or for the screen layout employed by Internet Explorer or the tabbed searching and browsing in Mozilla's Firefox. To each his own.

Those without the luxury of an in-house computer support staff must decide for themselves whether to follow the software developers and regularly update their chosen browser by downloading each new version as soon as it becomes available. Often, the newest version of any program can be plagued by small problems known as bugs. As these bugs are discovered and repaired, the browser's creators periodically issue "patches" that must be downloaded and installed on your computer to fix the known bugs. Putting off the updating for a while and waiting for the bugs to be fixed in subsequent versions can cut down on headaches for experienced and novice computer users alike.

Internet Explorer

http://www.microsoft.com/windows/ie

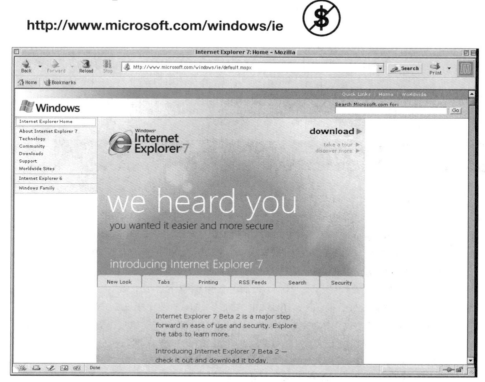

Figure 2-3. Despite losing some market share, Microsoft's Internet Explorer is still the most-used Web browser in the world.

Purpose: Software necessary to access Web sites.

Content: Most computers sold commercially come pre-installed with a Microsoft operating system (such as Windows XP), and the latest version of the Internet Explorer (IE) browser. Recent additions to Internet Explorer include Auto Address Completion (which presents a list of possible matches for a URL you are typing from previous URLs you have visited) and improved handling of Internet programming standards to insure that pages are displayed as their designers intended.

Our View: According to some statistics, there's a better than 83 percent chance that this is the browser you're currently using. By virtue of Microsoft's dominance in the software publishing industry, Internet Explorer is the de facto Web browser standard. A new version currently in development (Version 7), promised to address some of the security issues that have plagued many browsers (especially Internet Explorer) in recent years.

Tip: The browser is available as a free download for Windows and select handheld operating systems. In June 2003, Microsoft announced that it would no longer be developing new versions of its Internet browser for Apple operating systems.

Internet Explorer Version 7 (beta)

As of this writing, Microsoft has not yet released the final incarnation of its flagship Web browser's newest version. It has made a public *beta* version (the final stage of software development before a product is released) available for users to download. It is only available for users of the newest Windows Operating Systems (XP Pro & Home—Service Pack 2 only and Server 2003—Service Pack 1). This new version adopts many of the features and functions first seen in the Mozilla and Firefox browsers. Note that features of the beta version mentioned here may change (or disappear) from the final version.

Version 7 introduces a new, sleeker, user interface that eliminates the familiar "Tool Bar" and "Menu Bar" of previous editions, replacing them with a streamlined button bar where users can view their "Favorites," check or clear their "History" and access other browser tasks and tools.

Version 7's "Tabbed Browsing" allows Internet Explorer users to more easily navigate between multiple open Web pages. Rather than opening a separate browser "window" for each site, multiple "Tabs" can be visible along the top of a single browser "window" with the title of each site clearly visible. A single click on one of the tabs brings that tab's page to the forefront while moving the previously viewed page to a "background" tab. Users can also group and save tabs for later access to those pages. A single click can open a group of tabs containing multiple pages.

A search box is integrated into the upper right-hand corner of the interface allowing users to conduct Internet searches without having to leave the Web site they're viewing, or open a new tab. Similar functions are available to users of older versions of Explorer via the Google and Yahoo! Tool Bars. The default search engine in version 7 is Microsoft's own MSN Search. Users can select other search engines from a pull-down menu, or add their own choices if they are not already on the list.

An RSS icon on the new button bar automatically illuminates when it detects RSS feeds on sites the user is visiting. A single click on the icon presents a preview and gives users the option of subscribing to the site's RSS feed. The browser also recognizes the XML language used to create the feeds, so users can read RSS feeds directly in the browser, and then scan for important stories, or use the browser's "Find" function to locate particular stories of interest.

One particularly useful new feature is the "Advanced Printing" option that automatically formats pages so that if they are wider than the printer's settings, the text will not "run off" the printed page, truncating words or sentences.

Much has been made over the past few years about the security vulnerability of the Internet Explorer browser. It has been a favorite target of malicious coders, primarily because it is employed by so many computer users. Version 7 addresses many of these security concerns by including filters and barriers to thwart some of the most common malicious "phishing" or "pharming" (*see Glossary*) practices used to trick computer users into revealing personal/financial information. The new "Security Status Bar" promises "awareness of website security and privacy settings by displaying color-coded notifications next to the Address Bar." In the forthcoming Windows Vista Operating System, Version 7 will run "in isolation from other applications in the operating system. Exploits and malicious software are restricted from writing to any location beyond Temporary Internet Files without explicit user consent," offering even more security from malicious programs.

As of this writing, no firm date has been announced for the final release version of version 7.

Netscape Communicator

http://wp.netscape.com/computing/download

Purpose:	Software necessary to access Web sites.
Content:	With each new version released, the perceptible differences between Internet Explorer and Netscape Communicator become fewer and fewer. In 1998, Netscape was purchased by America Online (AOL).
Our View:	Versions of the browser since 1998 have shown more and more integration with AOL services like e-mail and Instant Messenger. Other recent additions include Web page saving, group bookmarks, full-screen mode (which devotes more screen space to Web page content) and pop-up blocking. Some people prefer to use it, and its accompanying e-mail application (Netscape Messenger), because it is not as often the victim of malicious viruses as is Internet Explorer.

Figure 2-4. Netscape introduced the first commercial (graphical) Web browser in 1994. This is version 8.

Tip: The browser is available as a free download for Windows operating systems only. Version 7.2 was the last available for Apple or Linux operating systems.

Firefox (aka Mozilla)

http://www.mozilla.org

Purpose: Software necessary to access Web sites.

Content: Mozilla was the original code name for the browser that became Netscape Navigator and Communicator. In January 1998, Netscape Corporation announced that it would make the source code for the Netscape browser freely available. Since then, volunteer software developers around the world have revised and refined that original code to create a new browser also known as Mozilla. (This is what is known as an "open source" project.) Until November 2004, Mozilla was a suite of software that included a browser and an e-mail handling program. On November 9, 2004, Mozilla split into the separate Firefox browser and Thunderbird e-mail program.

Our View: Firefox includes many of the most up-to-date features of the more well-known browsers, as well as variations on those features. Users familiar with either Internet Explorer or Netscape Communicator will be very comfortable with Firefox.

Tip: The browser is available as a free download for Windows, Apple, and Linux operating systems. In July 2005, *PC World* magazine voted Firefox its "Product of the Year." For more information on how Firefox differs from Internet Explorer and Netscape Communicator, see *PC World's* review of Firefox that accompanied the announcement of the award (**http://www.pcworld .com/reviews/article/0,aid,118959,00.asp**).

Opera

http://www.opera.com/download   **$**

Purpose: Software necessary to access Web sites.

Content: The Opera browser has long been popular with "power" Internet users. They praise the program's small size and the speed with which it opens Web pages. Opera is available for most major operating systems, including Windows, Apple, Linux, OS/2, and select handheld computers. After many years of offering a free version (that included banner ads) and a paid version (that did not), in September 2005, Opera removed the advertising banners from the free version.

Our View: Opera is a full-featured, easy-to-use browser for locating information on the Internet. It includes many of the same advanced features found in better-known browsers, such as tabbed browsing, RSS support, and integrated searching. Also, pages load very quickly when using this browser to surf the Web.

Tip: While there are numerous free troubleshooting resources on the Opera site, if you need additional support installing or using the Opera browser, you can buy a subscription to their "Premium Support" (e-mail) for $29. A version of the Opera browser is also available for selected web-enabled cell phones for $29. For a more in-depth discussion of the benefits of the newest version of the Opera browser, see the e-Week article "Opera Raises Curtain on New Browser Version" at **http://www.eweek.com/article2/0,1759, 1788085,00.asp.**

Safari

http://www.apple.com/safari

Purpose:	Software necessary to access Web sites from a computer.
Content:	This is Apple's Mac OS-X-only Web browser.
Our View:	The Apple engineers have added a number of refinements to the basic browser functions. These include a "naming sheet" that allows bookmarks to be easily and immediately named and put into folders for easy access, and a "snapback" feature. If you've linked from one site to another, to another, and so on, snapback takes you back to the last page where you typed a URL into the address bar at the top of the browser. Some of the functions added to the new Version 2 include easy archiving of Web pages on your own hard drive, and the ability to keyword search through your bookmarks.
Tip:	The browser is available as a free download from Apple.

---

iCab

http://www.icab.de/dl.php

Purpose:	Software necessary to access Web sites.
Content:	ICab is another Apple-only browser from Germany. The newest version is available for operating systems from 8.5 through the current OS X. (older versions, compatible back to Mac OS 7.1, were once again available as of this writing.)
Our View:	Devotees appreciate iCab's small size, fast page loading, and its search tool that users can configure to use their search engine of choice.
Tip:	A free copy of (public beta) version 3 is available for download. A Pro version with added features is available for $29.

Bookmark Your Favorite Sites

All Web browsers allow you to create your own list of Web sites that you find particularly useful. Internet Explorer calls these "Favorites." Netscape Communicator and Mozilla Firefox call them "Bookmarks." Selecting a Web site from your **Bookmarks** or **Favorites** on subsequent Internet sessions takes you directly back to the bookmarked site. Because Internet Explorer is the most widely used browser, we will outline the process of adding "Favorites" when using that browser. The process is similar in other browsers.

To create a Favorite in Internet Explorer, select **Favorites** at the top of the screen, and then **Add to Favorites**. Internet Explorer then displays the name of the site in a name dialog box. You can change the name (if you would rather call it something else) by clicking into the Name box and typing in your new name. Click **OK**, and the site will be added to your Favorites list.

As you add Favorites, your list can grow quite long. Just as you do with other documents on your computer, you can arrange your Favorites into folders (and subfolders) to help you easily locate the one you're looking for.

Using the **Organize** Favorites dialog box, you can move a Favorite into an existing folder or move it into a newly created folder, rename a Favorite, rename a folder, delete a folder, or delete a Favorite. You can organize your folders by jurisdiction (International and Foreign), by subject (Corporate), by types of materials (Public Records or Forms), or by a combination (by jurisdiction and subject, such as California Statistics), or by any other system that is useful to you.

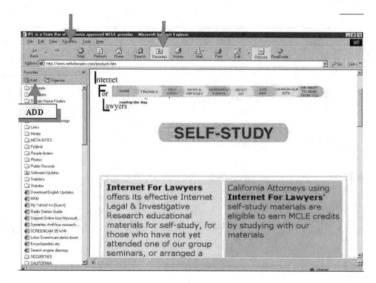

Figure 2-5.
To create a Favorite in Internet Explorer, select Favorites at the top of the screen, and then **Add** to Favorites.

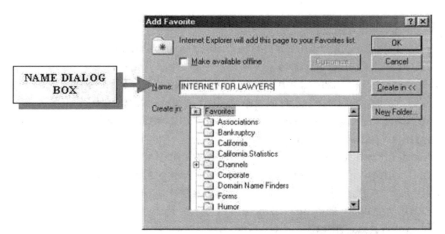

Figure 2-6. Internet Explorer's Favorites **Add Favorite—Name** dialog box.

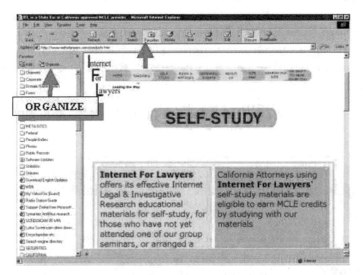

Figure 2-7. Select **Favorites** and then **Organize Favorites** to create folders to classify your Favorites to find them more easily.

Netiquette and Internet Ethics

Netiquette

Most lawyers are familiar with the term "netiquette," which is the code of proper behavior online. Generally, the rules of netiquette date back to the earliest days of the Internet. Those rules, which came together in the days when Usenet newsgroups were the "killer app" that drew people online, have evolved and expanded to cover all electronic communication, including e-mail sent directly to others and to Web sites, in addition to behavior on Internet mailing lists and discussion groups.

Generally, these rules include the following:

- The use of capital letters is the online equivalent of SHOUTING. DON'T DO IT!
- Don't send messages with a vague subject line (or no subject at all).
- Keep messages concise. (For discussion groups, you should also append "Long Response" to the subject for those who might not want to read a long response.)
- A brief "signature" (four or five lines) identifying yourself and including your contact information is acceptable (and not viewed as advertising) and has come to be expected.
- Don't regularly forward jokes (particularly long or risqué jokes) to people who have not asked you to send them.
- If you don't have anything nice to say, don't say anything at all. (Negative messages, particularly in newsgroups or discussion groups, are referred to as "flames." They're considered a no-no and can elicit more flames in return, touching off a "flame war.")
- Be aware whether you're clicking the **Reply** or the **Reply All** button!

While this list is not comprehensive, it's a good place for any "netizen" to start.

The Invention of Spam

No discussion of netiquette would be complete without mention of "spam"—that bane of nearly everybody with an e-mail address. For those who may not be familiar with the term, spam refers, essentially, to electronic junk mail—unsolicited e-mail messages that are trying to sell you something you probably don't want.

There is no agreed upon origin of the spam label. According to the Internet dictionary Webopedia (**http://www.webopedia.com**):

... the generally accepted version is that it comes from the Monty Python song, 'Spam spam spam spam, spam spam spam spam, lovely spam, wonderful spam . . . ' Like the song, spam is an endless repetition of worthless text. Another school of thought maintains that it comes from the computer group lab at the University of Southern California who gave it the name because it has many of the same characteristics as the lunchmeat Spam:

- Nobody wants it or ever asks for it.
- No one ever eats it; it is the first item to be pushed to the side when eating the entree.
- Sometimes it is actually tasty, like 1% of junk mail that is really useful to some people.

There is, however, a point in Internet history that is generally accepted to be the birth date of spam. It's ironic, however, and particularly appropriate for this book, that the invention of this form of unsolicited mass e-mail is traced to two Arizona lawyers in 1994.

Internet lore has it that on April 12, 1994, a husband-and-wife pair of immigration lawyers sent a solicitation regarding the INS "green-card lottery" to thousands of Usenet newsgroups. One of the lawyers, Laurence Canter, created a small computer program that automatically sent their message with the subject line "Green Card Lottery—Final One?" to as many of the groups as the program could find. The posting was indiscriminate—targeted groups included rec.music.makers.bass, comp.programming.literate, and sci.physics.electromag, among hundreds of others.

Response from the Internet community to this blatant advertisement—a breach of their unwritten code of netiquette—was swift. Thousands of people angrily called for retribution in their own subsequent posts. One poster to sci.physics.electromag offered this advice in his April 14, 1994 post:

"Here's a suggestion. Everyone send these lawyers a note telling them what you think of their ads . . . which have appeared on *every* newsgroup. Include 10-15 copies of their original posting, just for fun . . . "

Many people had the same idea, and soon Canter and his then-wife and law partner, Martha Siegel, were indeed bombarded with angry responses.

The barrage of e-mail caused one ISP after another to drop Canter and Siegel's account. While the lawyers capitalized (quickly) on the firestorm they'd created by publishing *How to Make a Fortune on the Internet Superhighway* in 1994, by 1995 they had stopped practicing law. In 1996, the couple divorced. In 1997, Canter was disbarred by the Tennessee Supreme Court. This e-mail campaign was cited as one of the reasons for that action. (Canter is now a software developer in San Francisco. Siegel died in 2000.)

> ***TIP:*** You can use the information in this story to locate the actual e-mail Canter and Siegel sent by conducting a search of the Google Group archives (**http://groups.google.com**). On the Advanced Groups Search page, enter "canter" in the Author box, "green card lottery" in the Subject box, and in Message Dates set the date range from April 12, 1994 to April 14, 1994. (For more information on conducting searches of Google Groups, see the "Search Engines" section of Chapter 4, "Search Tools.")

Federal Legislation of Internet Ethics: CAN-SPAM

In an effort to control Spam, the federal legislature, in 2003, passed the "Can-Spam" Act, 15 U.S.C.A. 7701–7713 *available at* **http://www4.law .cornell.edu/uscode/html/uscode15/usc_sec_15_00007701----000-notes .html** (click "next" or "previous" at the bottom of the screen to move between sections of the act). See also the FTC's site regarding Can-Spam, **http://www.ftc.gov/bcp/conline/pubs/buspubs/canspam.htm**.

"Can-Spam" stands for: Controlling the Assault of Non-Solicited Pornography and Marketing." To understand the Can-Spam act, let's first look at what type of e-mail it does *not* apply to: "e-mail that facilitates an agreed-upon transaction or updates a customer in an existing business relationship" or e-mail sent to someone who gave "affirmative consent" to be contacted by e-mail. Thus, you probably can send e-mail to both current and past clients without worrying about violating Can-Spam.

The Can-Spam Act, however, does apply to e-mails sent to prospective clients because such e-mails are considered non-solicited (or "commercial") e-mails under the act.

To comply with Can-Spam, commercial e-mails must include:

- An "Advertisement" or "Solicitation" identifier somewhere in the body of the e-mail. (Like the ABA rule it does NOT have to be in the subject line of the e-mail, but see below for further ABA rules.)
- A physical address. (The law is silent as to whether a post office box or mail-drop address can be considered "physical.")
- An opt-out procedure that is clear and conspicuous.
- A "Reply to" return address for the opt-out (The "Reply to" address must be valid for at least thirty days from the date of the e-mail transmission. Senders have ten calendar days to remove someone from their mailing list.

Further, the Act prohibits any false or misleading transmission of information, such as a false header (e.g., the "to" and the "from" information) and also prohibits a deceptive subject line. A penalty up to $250 per e-mail address can be imposed for a violation of Can-Spam.

In addition to complying with the Can-Spam law, lawyers must also comply with the ABA ethics rules (or their state's rules) when sending an e-mail to a prospective client because ABA Ethics Rule 7.3 (b) considers an e-mail (referred to as "electronic communication" in the rules) as a solicitation. As such, the e-mail should be labeled "Advertising Material" at the beginning and ending (but not in subject line) of the e-mail.

Rule 7.3 (b) states:

> A lawyer shall not solicit professional employment from a prospective client by written, recorded or <u>electronic communication</u> (*emphasis added*) or by in-person, telephone or real-time electronic contact even when not otherwise prohibited by paragraph (a), if:
>
> > (1) the prospective client has made known to the lawyer a desire not to be solicited by the lawyer; or
> > (2) the solicitation involves coercion, duress or harassment.

Bar Associations Create Internet Ethics Rules

Basic netiquette applies as much to the legal professional as it does to a lay person. The ABA's 2004–2005 Legal Technology Survey found that a large majority of respondents use e-mail at least once a day for work-related tasks (84%), with 97 percent of them "using e-mail most to send routine correspondence." This growing reliance on online communications between lawyers and clients has moved bar associations to create more specific rules to guide the online behavior of lawyers.

As early as 1996, many state bar associations began issuing opinions on Internet ethics, often focusing on law firm Web sites. The formalization of the rules of netiquette to address lawyers' behavior online varies from state to state, but most of the rules and opinions relating to online communications apply the state's existing rules for print advertising.

The State Bar of California, for example, did not issue an opinion on Web site ethics until 2001. (Formal Opinion No. 2001-155 of the State Bar of California Standing Committee on Professional Responsibility and Conduct at **http://www.calbar.org/2pub/3eth/ca2001-155.htm**). The 2001 opinion deals specifically with the ethical issues lawyers must address when creating and displaying Web sites relating to their law practices.

The specific question that the bar addressed was "What aspects of professional responsibility and conduct must a lawyer consider when providing an Internet Web site containing information for the public about her availability for professional employment?" In a nutshell, the opinion views Web sites as a "communication" under the Bar rules (1-400(A) of the California Rules of Professional Conduct) and an "advertisement" under the state's Business and Professions Code (Sections 6157 to 6158.3), applying those existing criteria to lawyer Web sites in the state. The principles behind the opinion, however, may be applied to all forms of online communication, including e-mail, domain names, e-mail addresses, online articles, discussion groups, and chat rooms, in addition to Web sites.

It was four more years until California issued another Internet ethics opinion(**http://calbar.ca.gov/calbar/pdfs/ethics/2005-168.pdf**). California is not alone in applying existing principles of attorney-client communication to new forms of electronic correspondence.

In Arizona, State Bar Opinion 2001-05 holds that while a firm's domain name does not have to be identical to the firm's actual name, the domain name must not be false or misleading. Furthermore, a law firm's domain name cannot state or imply any special competence or unique affiliations unless the claim is factually true (**http://www.myazbar.org/Ethics/opinionview.cfm?id=273**). The opinion also indicates that a for-profit law firm domain name should not use the .org suffix or use a domain name that implies that the law firm is affiliated with a particular nonprofit or governmental entity. Thus, a private firm's request to call itself "arizonalawyer.org" was rejected.

The registration of descriptive domain names, rather than domain names that reflect the actual name of your law firm, should therefore be examined carefully. For example, registering a law firm Web site with the URL "bestresults.com" or "bestattorney.com" would almost certainly violate the Arizona and California rules. It is possible that a naive consumer may assume that a lawyer with these domain names is promising to be the best or is guaranteeing the best results. The ABA's 2004–2005 Legal Technology Survey found that nearly all (95 percent) of the survey's respondents indicated that their law firm Web sites utilized the name of the firm or some variation for their domain name.

Descriptive domain names might also violate ABA Model Rule 7.1, which prohibits using superlatives to distinguish one law firm from another without factual proof. A bankruptcy lawyer who uses the domain name dontpaythosebills.com might, likewise, expect to face ethical problems if, for example, the domain name misleads a client who is reorganizing rather than declaring outright bankruptcy.

ABA Model Rule 7.1 also prohibits communications that contain "guarantees, warranties, or predictions regarding the result of the representation." Thus, advertising past client successes on a lawyer's Web site or in e-mail messages could also be deemed unethical because it could indicate to a potential client that he or she can expect similar results. Personal injury lawyers who use their sites to detail past successes or advertise damage awards may therefore want to reconsider, or if in New York, clearly display an appropriate disclaimer as suggested in New York Ethics Opinion 771. Internet ethics issues are now arising with blogs. For example, the Kentucky Attorney's Advertising Commission is considering exerting jurisdiction over law related blogs and assessing a $50 Filing Fee each time a blog is modified.

Lawyers should also consider the ethics of their e-mail signature line or tag line (a signature block that includes "King of Torts," for example, might not be a good idea). A lawyer's e-mail signature should not include anything that could be interpreted as false, deceptive, or tending to confuse or mislead the public.

Another ethics issue for lawyers online is giving legal advice or soliciting clients in chat rooms or discussion groups. The Florida Bar Standing Committee on Advertising held in Opinion A-00-1 (see **http://www.flabar.org**—click on Ethics Opinions) that "[a]n attorney may not solicit prospective clients through Internet chat rooms, defined as real time communications between computer users." On the other hand, chatting in a chat room to prospective clients is not prohibited in California because chatting in a chat room is NOT considered as a "solicitation." (State Bar of California Formal Ethics Opinion No. 2004-166.) Instead, chatting is considered as a communication (and thus ethical) unless the lawyer's conduct in a chat room involves coercion, duress or harassment, at which time it becomes a prohibited communication and, thus, an ethical violation.

Thankfully for lawyers who write for magazines, articles that are published online—with or without the author's knowledge—are probably protected by the First Amendment. If someone in or out of state reads the article and relies upon the information to his or her detriment, the lawyer-author may not be liable for either the unauthorized practice of law or malpractice. This ethical area becomes more problematic, however, when lawyers begin expressing their opinions in chat rooms or discussion groups that feature, as most do, two-way communication.

The ethical principles that apply to lawyer advertising and communications in traditional media may serve as a guide for lawyers seeking to avoid ethics difficulties online. Therefore, lawyers and firms should review their state's advertising and communication rules and determine if their Web sites meet those existing criteria. Finally, it pays to observe common netiquette. Lawyer Laurence Canter, for example, violated netiquette rules by spamming (see "The Invention of Spam" sidebar in this chapter), thus drawing complaints from offended computer users. Your online manners can matter just as much as your in-person manners.

*CHAPTER***THREE**

Search Strategies

Finding It Online

It is no longer sufficient only to understand how to use traditional print sources for secondary research. There are numerous sources that exist only on the Internet and have no counterpart in the print world. While simply knowing what types of traditional print sources contain the information that you need is a start, it's no longer enough.

There are two reasons for this: first, more and more material is being posted directly (and only) to the Internet, so there is no traditional print correlation. Examples range from electronic-only journals and newsletters, to postings made on Internet discussion groups, to the creation of personal Web logs (also known as "blogs"). To find information these days, you need to look to new developments and sources placed only on the Internet instead of just looking back to Internet versions of traditional print sources.

Second, you must truly understand the basic workings of the Internet in order to find information on it. This entails understanding the distinction between the "visible" and "invisible" Web and knowing how to find information in each. Thus, understanding the nuances of search engines that search both parts of the Web is imperative.

The Invisible Web

The information which is not readily indexed by most search engines is said to reside in the Invisible Web. (For a more detailed discussion of the Invisible Web, see the section "Search Engines" in Chapter 4, "Search Tools.")

Of the vast amount of information posted on the Internet, only a small portion is actually indexed by search engines or directories. Although Internet search engines do an amazing job of collecting and keyword searching millions of Web sites and billions of pages, some of the most valuable data is not indexed by search engines because:

- The data is in a format that the search engines do not recognize.
- The data is contained in a database that must be queried before the data can be retrieved.
- The search engine does not know that the Web site containing the data exists because the site has not been submitted to the search engine for indexing.
- The search engine has chosen (or been instructed by a site's owner) not to index a particular site.

That said, there is a small group of search engines that *do* index many of the Web sites that are invisible to numerous other search engines. Currently, the most useful are Google, Yahoo!, Alltheweb, AltaVista and First Gov.gov (for government documents only). There are a few other ways to locate information on the Invisible Web, as noted below.

Finding Invisible Databases

To penetrate the Invisible Web for the valuable data that often lurks deep within a Web site's database, you have to know where to go by having the URL, or using some of the methods we discuss in this chapter and in Chapter 4, "Search Tools." For example, if you want to find out what a specific stock was worth on July 22, 1970, just typing that date and the stock name or ticker symbol into a search engine will *not* find the answer. The answer is on the Internet, in a database of historical stock quotes maintained by Yahoo!. The specific answer is not findable by a search engine because a search engine cannot index databases. But even though the database is invisible to a search engine, the information is still findable—but only if you know where to go.

So, using one of our invisible Web strategies for finding databases, we use a search engine, such as Google, Yahoo!, Alltheweb, or AltaVista and type the keyword "database" plus any keywords, such as "historical stock quotes," that describe the type of database you are seeking into the search box. If you use the home-page search box of any of the aforementioned databases, you can type the words in without any Boolean connectors since they default to the AND Boolean connector. (For a discussion of Boolean connectors, see the Search Strategy Checklist on pages 64–66.) The keywords "historical stock database" will lead you to a discussion of where to find this sort of information, and then provide a link to the relevant database for you to query.

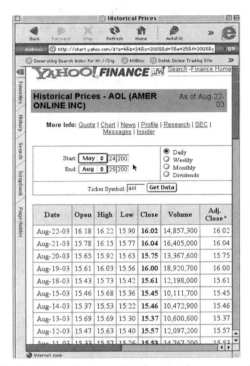

Figure 3-1. This illustrates the results of a database search of Yahoo!'s historical stock database. Enter your ticker symbol and your ending and starting dates into the blanks and then choose a daily, weekly, or monthly report (or dividends). Reproduced with permission of Yahoo! Inc. © 2003 by Yahoo! Inc. YAHOO! and the YAHOO! logo are trademarks of Yahoo! Inc.

Search Engines: Last Resort or First Resort?

While search engines have their place in the fact finders' search toolbox, their results can sometimes be too broad to be immediately useful. Using a book like this one can be a shortcut to finding relevant sites or specific search engines that might return more relevant results. For instance, if you know you are after a government document, first look at Chapter 6, "Government Resources Online," where you'll be advised to use FirstGov.gov over Google. For those times when you simply have no clue as to where to find the data, turning to a search engine—as long as you choose the right one—is your best option. (See also the section "Getting Help: Expert Research Support" later in this chapter to learn where to find an experienced law librarian who—for a fee—will cobrowse the Internet with you.)

These search tools take time and experience to master—but you've already got a head start by using this book. Refer to Chapter 4, "Search Tools," where the nuances of Google and a few other search engines are highlighted, and use some of the search tips found in the section "Cost-Effective and Time-Saving Search Tips" later in this chapter. You'll improve your search strategies tenfold and become a search-engine guru in no time. Don't try to overwhelm yourself, though; learning the nuances of two or three search engines should do it—we recommend Google, Yahoo!, Alltheweb, and AltaVista (and for government documents, First Gov.gov).

Search Strategy Checklist

1. Peruse this book to locate a likely Web site to begin your search.
2. Review your own bookmarks (hopefully, you will add the metasites discussed later in this chapter to your bookmarks).
3. Go to Google and type your search terms into the search box and then click on **I'm Feeling Lucky**. This will bring you to the one site that Google deems the most relevant to your search terms. Very often, the site selected by Google will contain enough information to answer your question. If it does, you've just saved yourself the time you might have spent slogging through dozens of results (or even slogging through hundreds if you are one of the truly compulsive) and then deciding that the first one would have done it after all. Occasionally, the site returned by an **I'm Feeling Lucky** search may only be the most popular and not necessarily the most relevant.
4. If you don't have luck, then use your back arrow, and click on the **Google Search** button next to the **I'm Feeling Lucky** button. This will automatically run the same search through Google's entire index, and display all of the results.
5. Too many results? Add more search words to focus in on the topic. Connect the search words with Boolean connectors (AND, OR, NOT). If you need a refresher on Boolean logic and Boolean connectors, see **http://www.google.com/help/refinesearch.html**. Google supports the Boolean concepts of the connectors AND, OR, and NOT. When you are entering your search words into the search box on the Google home page, there is no need to use the AND

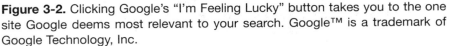

Figure 3-2. Clicking Google's "I'm Feeling Lucky" button takes you to the one site Google deems most relevant to your search. Google™ is a trademark of Google Technology, Inc.

Boolean connector at all—Google automatically defaults to it whenever there is a space between words. Use the minus (-) symbol for NOT (such as "cat -kitten" to represent "cat NOT kitten"). To search with an OR connector, you must type "OR" in uppercase (cat OR kitten). Enclose phrases in quotation marks ("contributory negligence"). For more information on how different search engines handle Boolean connectors, see the "Search Engines" section in Chapter 4, "Search Tools."

6. Not enough results? Check your spelling—is it correct? Are there multiple ways to spell the word or name? If yes, add them to your search (smith OR smyth). If there are synonyms for your original search word, you can also try adding them to the search. For example, to add the following synonyms (connected with the OR Boolean connector) to your original search for the word "car," enter "car OR auto OR automobile OR vehicle."

7. If you don't want to think too much about Boolean connectors and symbols, then select Google's Advanced Search option (see Figure 3-3), where Boolean logic search boxes are already set up for you (such as **Find results with the exact phrase**). Type your keywords or phrases into the appropriate Boolean search boxes. The box labeled **Find results with all of the words** is the same as using the Boolean AND connector. The box labeled **Find results**

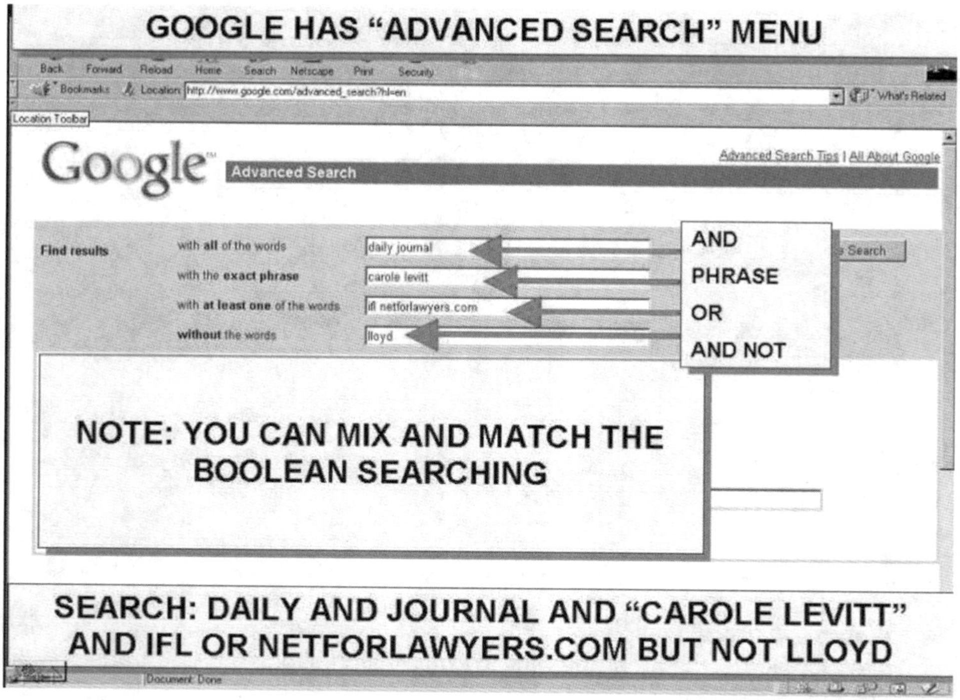

Figure 3-3. Google's Advanced Search page makes it easier to construct sophisticated searches using Boolean logic such as AND, OR and AND NOT. Google™ is a trademark of Google Technology Inc.

with at least one of the words is the same as using the OR connector. The box labeled **Find results without the words** is the same as using the minus (-) sign (equivalent to the Boolean NOT connector). Typing the three words "robert bob bobby" into the **Find results with at least one of the words** box is automatically interpreted by the search engine to mean "robert OR bob OR bobby" without you having to type in the ORs. It is important to note, however, that Google has a limit of ten terms per search.

8. Use the other features on the Advanced Search page to create even more complex or targeted searches, such as a file format search (see Figure 3-4), which allows you to search for specific types of data commonly found on the invisible Web (Microsoft PowerPoint presentations, PDFs, and so on).

File Format Searching

Selected search engines allow you to limit results to a specific type of file format, such as a PowerPoint presentation, Word document, Excel

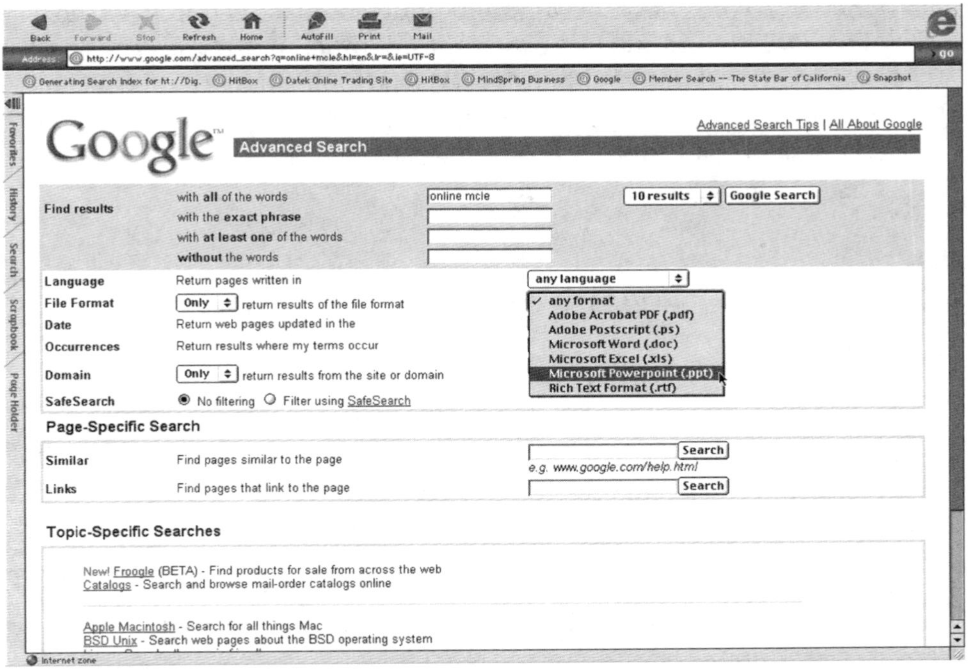

Figure 3-4. The Advanced Search page of the Google search engine allows you to select a specific file format, such as Microsoft PowerPoint (.ppt), among others. Google™ is a trademark of Google Technology Inc.

spreadsheet, or a PDF file. Until recently, search engines did *not* index *any* of these file formats—they were simply invisible. But Google, Yahoo!, Alltheweb, AltaVista, and FirstGov.gov index all of them (although First-Gov.gov is limited to government documents while the others are not). To conduct file format searches, you'll need to visit the Advanced Search pages of the respective search engines.

PowerPoint Presentation

Use Google to restrict your search to a PowerPoint presentation if you are looking for:

- Your expert witness's (or the opposition's) presentation at a conference—to see if there are any public inconsistencies in an opinion he'll be giving at your upcoming trial. Many presentations are created in PowerPoint and many people post them on the Web, so you might be in luck.
- A "hot" topic that no one has had time to write about yet. It's possible that someone may have given a recent presentation on the topic and posted the PowerPoint slides. For example, this was the case

when everyone was scrambling to understand and comply with the new 2005 Bankruptcy Act. There wasn't much written on the topic that you could put your hands on quickly, but there were scores of PowerPoint presentations created and posted on the Web that you could download, created by lawyers, accountants, law school professors, and government agencies.

PDF File

Restrict your search to PDFs if you are looking for:

- Forms
- Newsletters
- Charts
- Graphs
- Government Documents
- Brochures

A number of the major search engines index PDF files posted on the Internet. Currently, these include Alltheweb, AltaVista, FirstGov.gov, Google, and Yahoo!.

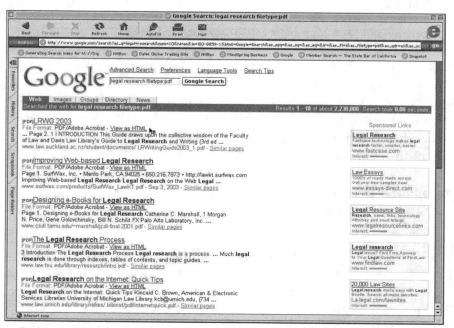

Figure 3-5. Google usually offers an alternative to viewing files with the Acrobat Reader software when PDF files are included in a list of search results. Clicking on the **View as HTML** link opens a stripped-down, text-only version of the document. Google™ is a trademark of Google Technology Inc.

PDF Search Tip

When Google returns a document in PDF in its search results list, it usually also includes an identical document in the plain text (HTML) format. (Only Google and Yahoo! offer this option.) You'll want to click on **View as HTML** for the text version if you want to easily copy and paste any of the text into your own document. We once ran across a Federal Aviation Administration (FAA) document posted in PDF format that must have been corrupted; every time we tried to either print or download it from the FAA Web site, it crashed the computer on which we were conducting our search. Instead of giving up and calling the FAA for a print version, as someone suggested, a simple click on the **View as HTML** link displayed the document on the computer screen and we were able to print it without crashing the computer. Granted, the text document lacked the attractive formatting and graphics of the PDF document—but the all-important content was intact.

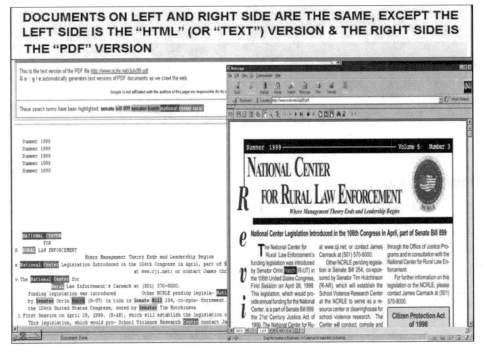

Figure 3-6. These two images illustrate the differences in the coding (the document's instructions to the computer detailing the content, layout, and so on) between a PDF and an HTML version of the same document.

Excel Spreadsheet

Restrict your search to Excel documents if you are looking for:

- Financials
- Charts
- Graphs

Word Document

Restrict your search to Word documents if you are looking for:

- Someone's resume
- A conference paper
- An agenda for a meeting
- A chart created by a committee

Word Search Tip

In a search for information on the Sarbanes-Oxley Act, we searched using the keywords "Sarbanes Oxley" and limited the search to Word file format only. We found a detailed comparison chart prepared by KPMG International for a meeting of an audit committee. The search also netted an agenda for a meeting on the same topic, held by the Nashville Audit Committee Institute Roundtable. It listed the place and the time of the meeting, and the speakers.

Domain Searching

Many search engines such as Alltheweb, AltaVista, FirstGov.gov, Google, and Yahoo! allow you to limit a search to a specific domain. Alltheweb, Firstgov.gov, and Google also allow you to exclude a specific domain from your search. These functions are available on the Advanced Search page of each of these respective search engines. This type of search can be extremely helpful when you can't find something that you *know* is on a specific site. Sometimes the site has poor navigation, lacks a good internal search engine (or doesn't have one at all), or doesn't have a site map.

By conducting a domain search, you are more or less superimposing the search engine's capabilities onto a specific site. It is important to remember, though, that not every search engine has indexed every page of every Web site. Therefore, it may be necessary to run this type of domain search with more than one search engine to find the data you are looking for.

Domain Search Tip

We found a domain search useful in pinpointing the Minimum Continuing Legal Education (MCLE) rules for providers on a state bar Web site when it was not clear on the site where the information was located. We knew they had to be there—they were the bar's rules, after all. Google helped us locate the rules within seconds when we restricted our search to the bar's domain and used the search phrase "mcle rules" and the additional search term "provider."

If you still aren't finding what you need on the Internet, see the section "Free versus Pay Resources" in Chapter 1, "Using the Internet for Factual Research," for some pay database suggestions, and see the section "Getting Help: Expert Research Support" in this chapter.

Cost-Effective and Time-Saving Search Tips

"Time is money." "Every minute counts." Everyone in the legal profession, especially those in the billable-hour world, knows these mantras. Here are some time-saving search tips that will save you time *and* money, since time is money and every minute counts.

Look for the Free Sites! ($)

If there is more than one site on the Internet to answer your question, use this book to identify the free site and use that first. But, read "Our View" and the "Tip" to be certain that the free site is going to meet your needs.

Save Time with an Auto-fill-in Program

With so many free sites now requiring registration, a time-saving search tip from Catherine Sanders Reach, Director of the ABA's Legal Technology Resource Center, is to use an auto-fill-in program. She suggests Roboform (**http://www.roboform.com**). Reach says, "It's an automated form filler and password keeper. It automatically fills in forms with amazing accuracy and remembers all my passwords (so I can dump my cookies without having to go through them). It is free [30-day free trial], but you can get a 'professional' edition [for $29.95] and a networked edition. It saves all the information on your hard drive (passwords, etc.) so someone would have to have access to it or hack it."

Bookmark Metasites

Bookmark subject-specific metasites (such as ResidentAgentInfo noted in Figure 3-7) instead of hundreds of individual sites for the types of sites you only use occasionally. Metasites are created to assist you in linking to hundreds or thousands of other sites. Metasites are either set up like a directory (think Yahoo!, FindLaw, or the Google directory), a simple laundry list, a site with an internal search engine, or a combination of any of these features.

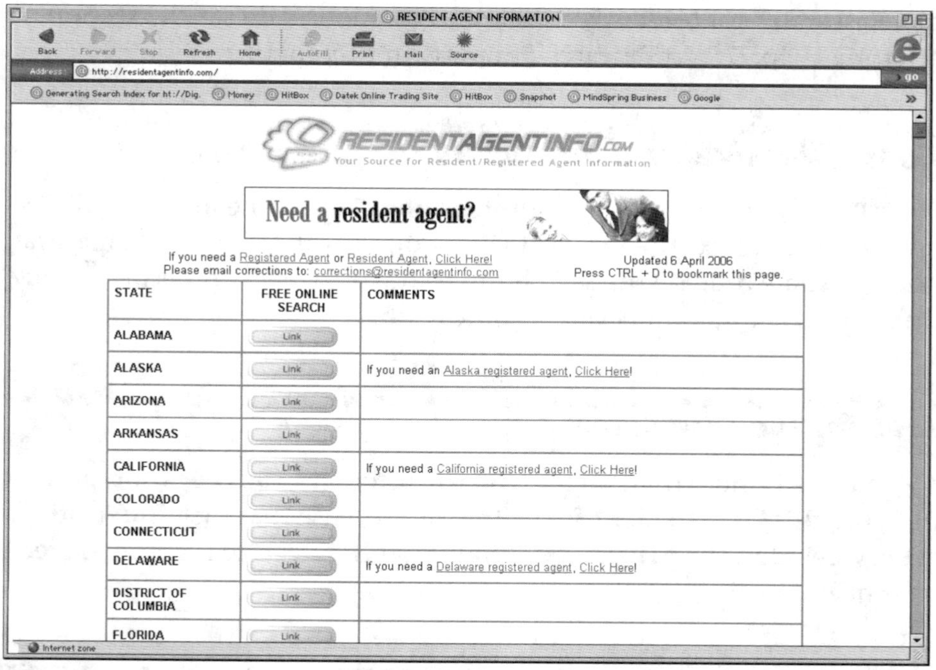

Figure 3-7. ResidentAgentInfo (**http://www.residentagentinfo.com**) is a free metasite maintained by Maryland lawyer Terry A. Berger. The site offers a state-by-state breakdown of information regarding sources for locating information on registered agents for service of process. Information is also included on selected foreign countries, such as Canada and the United Kingdom.

For example, if you only occasionally need to search for public records, use SearchSystems.net or Pretrieve.com as your jumping-off points for locating and searching public records in various jurisdictions. Search Systems is a good example of a metasite that has a directory and an internal search engine, while Pretrieve is a "metasearch" site that acts as a "front-end" to submit users' searches to multiple public records resources. However, if you regularly search your state's secretary of state Web site, then by all means, bookmark it individually. In each of our factual research chapters, we endeavor to list the metasites for that topic—and usually it's the first site we list.

First, You Google . . . Yahoo!

Throughout this book we discuss the many useful functions of the Google search engine. It was the first major search engine to offer many of the robust advanced search functions we discussed above. Until recently, it was the undisputed leader in terms of the number of documents its searches encompassed and the relevancy of the results it returned. In February 2004, Yahoo! introduced a new search index and search methods that rivalled Google with the relevancy of its results. Then in August 2005, Yahoo! announced that the size of its index encompassed over 20 billion "Web objects" (nearly twice the size of Google's.) Since Yahoo! made its claim, much has been written about the accuracy of both Yahoo! and Google's self-reported index sizes. Despite that controversy, we find that Google and Yahoo! both return extremely relevant results. Many of the advanced search functions that will help you locate the information you are looking for are similar at both Google and Yahoo!. Throughout this book, we will use Google to illustrate many of those functions, noting where Yahoo! functions in the same way. Even with all its strengths, Google is not perfect. There has been much debate in the online research community regarding Google's limit on the number of terms you can use per search. The limit had been ten, but sometime in early 2005, the limit was quietly raised to thirty-two search terms. To test the search terms limit, we entered 74 search terms into the Google search box. It was a string of text contained on a page of our own Web site (**http://www.netforlawyers.com/online_mcle.htm**) that we knew had been indexed by Google. The search returned the Web page on which the text is contained, along with the notation by Google near the top of the results page that "'MCLE' (and any subsequent words) was ignored because we limit queries to 32 words."

Google has also been criticized for limiting the amount of information it indexes in a long document. Generally, Google has only indexed the first 101 kilobytes of information in a document. (If any of your search terms do not appear until after the first 101 kilobytes of HTML in a long document, that document would not be returned in a Google search.) In the first half of 2005, search engine enthusiasts found repeated evidence that Google occasionally indexed further than this 101K and believed that Google was poised to officially increase that limit. In February 2005, when Search Engine Watch Webmaster Danny Sullivan questioned Google about the limit, he received a very non-committal "isn't it interesting what you can spot" response from Google (**http://blog.search enginewatch.com/blog/050202-111155**). To test this limit, we searched for a 10-K for the "Walt Disney Company." One result was for a recent filing by Disney. The amount of data included in the Google cache for that page was listed as "262k." Comparing the cached version to the live version (as displayed at the Web site where Google found the information) revealed that Google had stored the entire contents of the page in its cache. Another result on the list was for a Disney 10-K with the cache size listed as "513k." Comparing that result revealed that the cached version covered only the first 48 and a half pages of the 107 pages found in the live version of the same document. While this would seem to indicate that the new cache limit is 513k, we have occasionally found other documents whose cache sizes were as large as 906k, and were complete versions of the live document to which they referred. Google's limit is larger for other file types (e.g., one Gigabyte for PDF documents). Yahoo! has similar limits (thought to be larger than Google's), but not as much research is available on that subject.

So, if you don't find what you're looking for using Google, try Yahoo!, Alltheweb, and AltaVista. If you're looking for a government document, skip over Google and the rest of the engines and go directly to FirstGov.gov.

See Chapter 4, "Search Tools" and the earlier part of this chapter for more on "Googling" and other tips.

Try the Google Toolbar

A free tech tool, the Google Toolbar (**http://toolbar.google.com**), is favored by Ben M. Schorr, Director of Information Services at the law firm Damon Key in Honolulu, Hawaii (**http://www.hawaiilawyer.com**). "For folks who use Google frequently, it's a fantastic add-on. It sits quietly on your toolbar, lets you quickly search Google from anywhere, gives you quick ways to search within the page or within the site, search Google

Groups and its dictionary, and just about anything else you'd want to search. It'll highlight the search terms you used . . . and you can even have it take you to the next hit or prior site in your results list." Some of the lawyers at the twenty-five-member firm probably do not even realize they are using this tool because Schorr installs it by default on all new firm machines. Schorr notes, "About two-thirds of them have it and quite a few are actually using it regularly. They rave about it, generally." Yahoo! and Microsoft's MSN Search (**http://search.msn.com**) also offer feature-packed search toolbars.

Yahoo! and Google Search Shortcuts

What's a shortcut? It's a way to tell the search engine what TYPE of information you want—such as a definition or a synonym, by typing the word "define" or the word "synonym" before the word for which you want a definition or a synonym. A search for *define "sprinkling trust"* displayed 22 results—all of which defined a sprinkling trust. A search for *"sprinkling trust"* (without the word "define" preceding the phrase) displayed 285 results. Although many of the 285 results were definitions, some were not. For instance, one of the results, instead of defining "sprinkling trusts," was a quiz that asked that very question, "What is a sprinkling trust?"

> *Tip:*   The shortcut links at the top of the Yahoo! Shortcuts Cheat Sheet page work best in the Internet Explorer Web browser. For a list of these search shortcuts, see the Shortcuts Cheat Sheet at Yahoo! (**http://help.yahoo.com/help/ us/ysearch/tips/tips-01.html**).

> *Tip:*   Google's version of shortcuts can be found at **http:// www.google.com/help/features.html**.

Use a Metasearch Site

Metasearch sites such as DogPile (**http://www.dogpile.com**), Teoma (**http://www.teoma.com**), and Vivisimo (**http://www.vivisimo.com**) query several different search engines at once and display the results from each on a single page (or in a series of pages or folders). Metasearch sites can be time savers, and anything that saves you time saves you money. However, most metasearch sites impose a time limit for each of the various search engines to respond. If a particular search engine takes longer to respond, the metasearch site will display zero results from that search engine—

when, in fact, that particular search engine might have returned relevant results if given a few more seconds to respond. Therefore, it can sometimes be better to take your search to a search engine individually if a metasearch site shows zero results since you might find more data that way. Additionally, most of the individual search engines offer Advanced Search functions that the metasearch sites may not have access to.

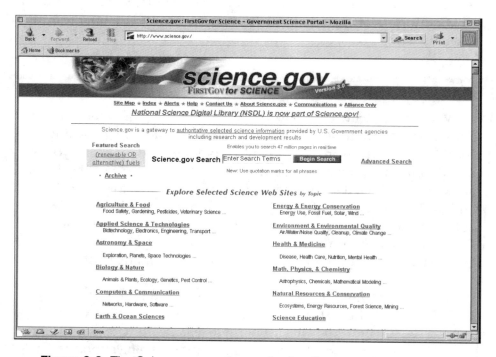

Figure 3-8. The Science.gov metasearch site allows you to query over 1,700 Web sites and databases from 16 scientific and technical organizations maintained by 12 federal agencies (such as EPA, Agricola, PubMed, MedLine, and many more). Each of the individual participating agencies has selected the resources, including research and development results, from within their agency for inclusion. New resources are added to the Science.gov website every six weeks, presenting a large cross-section of federal science resources. Results are listed in order of relevance (based on a four-star system). The site also allows you to set up alerts to keep up to date as new information is added.

Use High-Speed Internet Access on the Road

Sometimes a cost-effective tip is one that will cost you some money, but will save you time and, in the end, save you more money.

When traveling on business, obtain a local dial-up number to your Internet Service Provider (ISP) to avoid long-distance charges when dialing into the Internet. However, in some states (such as Florida), hotels meter even local phone calls to the extent that local access to the Internet can quickly become more expensive than the room. Therefore, it may be a good idea to stay at a hotel with high-speed Internet access (for between $10 and $20 per day extra), because high-speed access will save you time while you are on the Internet and may save you money, in the long run, on your hotel phone bill. Check the following sites for information regarding hotels that offer high-speed Internet access: **http://www.wayport.net/ locations** and **http://www.stsn.com**.

Some hotels also offer wireless access to the Internet for guests who have the necessary wireless access hardware on their laptop computers or cell phones. While wireless connectivity can be convenient, it is significantly less secure than a hard-wired connection to the Internet.

Use Small Tools for Big Savings

Expensive technology, with all its bells and whistles, sometimes promises to save us time and money, increase our efficiency, and at least double our productivity.

But sometimes it's the smaller tech tools or even the free tech tools that help us save time and money and increase our efficiency and productivity. Two very small tech tools—one software and one hardware—that provide very big solutions are TinyURL and a thumb drive.

TinyURL

Anyone who has clicked on a link from an e-mail message or a posting where the URL is longer than one line soon learns that the link will not work because browsers only recognize the first line of a URL. TinyURL can solve this problem. Next time you need to post or e-mail a long URL, you can save the recipient the trouble of copying and pasting the long URL into a browser by transforming it into a much shorter (yes, tiny) URL. Visit **http://www.tinyurl.com**, and type the long URL into the **Make TinyURL** box. Voila! It is transformed into a much shorter URL for you to e-mail or post. Die-hard TinyURL users can add it to their browser toolbar to automatically create a TinyURL for any page they are viewing by using a single click on their toolbar. Best of all, TinyURL is free.

Thumb Drive

The second small tool that packs a large punch is a mini USB drive, also known as a thumb drive. When asked for her favorite tech tool, Cindy Chick, manager of Latham & Watkins' Information Services Department, literally whipped out her thumb drive. The drives, used for document storage, are actually about the size of a thumb (with a capacity of up to 2 Gigabytes). For lawyers who transport documents between office and home PCs, these USB drives offer extreme portability. For those who travel with a laptop and worry about having it stolen before arrival, loading documents onto the thumb drive adds security since it can be placed in a pocket or hung around the neck with a lanyard (usually included with the drive). To use a thumb drive, simply plug it into the USB port of almost any computer (newer operating systems do not require a driver). The thumb drive is a good alternative to storing files on either Zip disks or CDs. Prices vary (a 256-megabyte thumb drive was recently advertised for $15.99 after rebates).

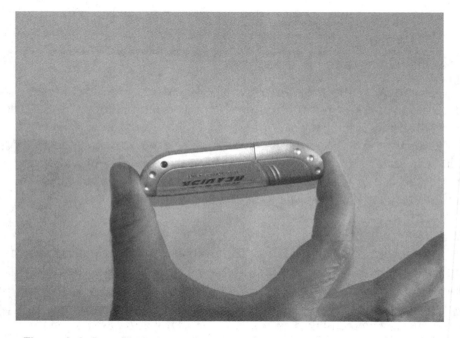

Figure 3-9. Despite their small size, thumb drives can store up to 2 Gigabytes of data. Their size makes them extremely portable.

Switch Browsers If You Need To

If you're having trouble using a site (perhaps parts of it are obscured, you click and nothing happens, or a site won't even open), chances are you're using Netscape Navigator. Some sites tell you up front that they only work (or work better) with Internet Explorer. However, some don't mention it at all, leaving you to figure it out. The solution? Use IE for those sites. You can install both browsers for free on your desktop for easy access to either one. You don't have to use the browser that was the default when you purchased your PC.

To install IE, go to **http://www.microsoft.com/windows/ie/default .mspx**. To install Netscape, go to **http://browser.netscape.com/ns8/**. To install Firefox, go to **http://www.mozilla.com/firefox**. For more details on Web browser choices and features, see "Browser & Favorites" in Chapter 2.

Tracking Changes Automatically and Setting Up Alerts

Are you spending money for a pay database to track or set up alerts about a specific company, individual, case, event, or product? Since there may be information unique to the Web (such as blogs, forums, mailing lists, and auctions), you might also want to track the same data on free sites that you're currently tracking on a pay site. Or you may be able to discontinue the pay alert altogether if you can locate the same service on the Web for free. For example, some legislatures and some courts allow you to sign up for an e-mail alert every time there is any action affecting a pending bill or taken in a case. Just visit the site and see if they offer the service, then specify what to track (such as *senate bill 213* or *docket number 2002-98*). If you're paying for an alert like this, consider canceling it. Or, you might want to track a specific page on a Web site, such as a client's company site or the opposition's company site. You decide how often you want to be alerted to changes. You also decide whether you want an e-mail alert or whether you want to visit the tracking service and check for changes at your convenience. The best known free alert service is Google Alerts. Additionally, Chris Sherman of SearchEngineWatch (**http://www.searchenginewatch.com**) recommends the following alert services:

- WebSite-Watcher (**http://www.aignes.com**): It's powerful and highlights all changes, but is desktop-based. A free 30-day trial is offered. Thereafter, the cost is $38.25 for personal use and $126.42 for corporate use.
- WatchThatPage (**http://www.watchthatpage.com**): It's Web-based, so you can access it from anywhere and it's free to individuals. (It requires registration.)
- InfoMinder (**http://www.infominder.com**): It highlights changes, is Web-based, and offers a variety of page mining options at a variety of prices. The "Pro" version of the service tracks the pages you indicate once per day and offers five volumes of service, tracking from 20 pages ($9/year) to 1000 pages ($179/year). The "Premium" version tracks up to four times per day tracking from 100 pages ($65/year) to 1000 pages ($499/year). An in-house, server edition is also available that can monitor higher volumes of web pages as often as once per hour.

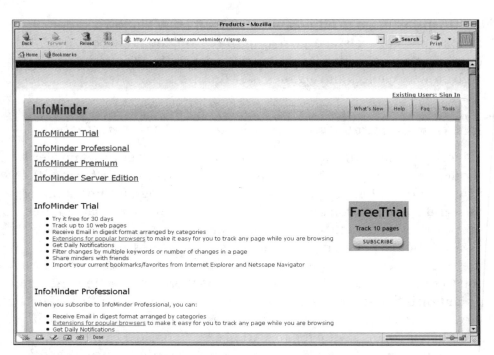

Figure 3-10. Infominder allows subscribers to track changes made on up to 5,000 Web pages at a time.

Setting Up Alerts

GoogleAlerts.com

http://www.google.com/alerts

Purpose: Google Alerts sends you up to the minute e-mail Alerts so you can monitor the Web via Google's search engine or via Google's current news database (or both), or via its Groups database based on your keyword search.

Content: To create a *Google Alert* you need to enter your keywords into the first box and then answer three simple questions: (1) the type of alert you would like (*Web, News,* or *News & Web* or *Groups;* (2) how often you would like the alerts e-mailed (daily, weekly, or as they occur); and (3) your e-mail address.

On the bottom left of this same page, Google asks if you would like to manage your Alerts. If you click on this link, Google will then require you to sign up and register with an e-mail address and password. The benefit of this process is that every time you log on to Google Alerts you can view your list of Alerts that you have created, as well as edit or delete them easily. For example, we originally created a Web Alert for the topic Iraq that we wanted sent to us daily. Later, it was simple to revise the Alert to add *News* to have the Alert also monitor Google's *News* database in addition to the Web. We also revised the Alert to request the Alert be sent as it happens, instead of just daily.

If you decide to forgo this option, you will not be able to edit your search queries at all. You will have to delete the Alert entirely (by clicking on a link at the bottom of an Alert e-mail) and then create a brand new Alert to your new specifications.

Our View: Google has created a simple way to keep you in touch with the information you need, when you need it. When we signed up for the Iraq *News* Alert, our first e-mail arrived within two hours. Granted the topic is pretty newsworthy, but Google Alerts still deserves kudos for their speedy entry of our information and queries.

Although the Alerts home page technically says it is still in its Beta stage, that doesn't mean it hasn't been around for a while. Google seems to keep their services in Beta mode longer than most other companies, apparently so they can continue to add and "play" with their products. We found this to be a really good service, and one of the few free ones on the Internet.

Tip: For those who can't wait to receive their automatic alerts, another neat option of the **Manage** page allows you to click on your Alert to run your search on the spot.

WatchThatPage

http://www.watchthatpage.com/

Purpose: To track any changes on a Web site, even U.S. Supreme Court dockets.

Content: To register (free) for WatchThatPage, click on the **Register** tab on the site's home page. You will be asked to create a profile page where you must enter your e-mail address, name, and country, and create a password. You then scroll down the page to set up your delivery options. You can choose to receive an e-alert:

- on a daily or weekly basis
- at a specific time of day
- with only the URL of the pages that have changed listed or with the text of what has changed on the monitored page displayed (this is the more useful choice)

WatchThatPage also allows you to restrict the monitoring to specific keywords on your watched pages instead of monitoring all changes on a page. After you are a registered user, you can log in on the home page and add URLs to be monitored, such as a URL for a specific U.S. Supreme Court docket.

Our View: While some courts do offer a monitoring/e-alert service for dockets, the U.S. Supreme Court does not; therefore, as noted by Paul Bush of Legal Dockets Online, using WatchThatPage is a perfect substitute to monitor new activity on a case.

To obtain the URL for a specific U.S. Supreme Court docket of a case that you want to monitor, visit the U.S. Supreme Court's Web site (**http://www.supremecourtus.gov**) and click on the **Docket** tab. Enter a docket number (if you know it), a party name, or even a keyword into the **Search For** box to find the case in question (e.g., enter "IBP" to find the *IBP* vs. *Alvarez* case). Select the link to the case, and notice in the address bar that there is a unique URL address for the case's docket (**http://www.supremecourtus.gov/docket/03-1238.htm**). Highlight and copy this URL. Then visit **www.watchthat page.com**, click on **Your Pages** and copy this URL into the **Add Page** box. WatchThatPage will now monitor the docket sheet for you and alert you to any new actions. There are several choices on **Your Pages**, such as **Add new channel**. If you click on **Add new channel** you can request that:

- All new content on all of your watched pages be collated into one e-mail
- New content on your various watched pages be sent in separate emails
- Different watched pages get different update rates
- Different keywords be used for your various watched pages

Tip: (1) The help screens are very useful if you want to learn how to add new channels. (2) You can also use WatchThatPage to let your visitors know they can get notified when the pages on your site change (for details, see **http://watchthatpage.com/webMasterInfo.jsp**). (3) Although the service is free, WatchThatPage is requesting donations of $20 or more for one year of priority service (your changes are processed before anybody else's and you will receive changes at the time you have specified in your profile). (4) For those who do not want to receive an e-alert, a personal Web page, which you would visit to view changes, can be set up.

IRS GuideWire

http://www.irs.gov/newsroom/page/0,,id=123315,00.html

Purpose: To provide people (primarily tax professionals) with advance notice of any tax-related information before it is to be published in the *Internal Revenue Bulletin*.

Content:	Subscribers will receive free e-mail notification of IRS Revenue Procedures, Revenue Rulings, Notices, and Announcements. The e-mail will also include links to PDFs of the documents. Subscribers will *not* receive *all* IRS guidance, but only "advance" guidance.
Our View:	It's easy to set up the alert and also easy to "unsubscribe" by using the above URL.
Tip:	Visit **http://www.irs.gov/newsroom/content/0,,id= 103381,00.html** to set up one or more of the twelve other alerts that the IRS offers for free.

Find, Find, Find!

This tip can't be emphasized enough: Use your browser's "Find" function or the PDF binocular icon to quickly scan through long documents. For more detailed information on this helpful hint, see the "Browsers and Favorites" section in Chapter 2, "Internet Tools and Protocol."

Keeping Informed About Internet Research Resources

The best way to begin educating yourself about the vast resources available on the Internet is to purchase a comprehensive research reference book like this one. This book is designed to give you a definitive overview of research resources available across a broad collection of factual research categories—and some guidance in using those sites.

As with any reference book, this one offers a snapshot of the available resources as they appeared at the time of publication. Because new sites are added to the Internet with startling regularity, and existing sites can add or delete features just as quickly, it is also important to keep up to date with the sites with which you are already familiar. To help keep you informed, the authors and the ABA offer a bi-monthly e-mail companion newsletter to this book that highlights the changes that can impact your research needs. More information on the newsletter is available at **www.lawpractice.org/factfinder** and on the last page of this book.

There are also a variety of Web sites and Web-based Internet newsletters, magazines, and e-mail alerts to update you about the Internet and technology in general, Internet legal research, and Internet legal issues.

Pay Resources

The Internet Lawyer

http://www.mddailyrecord.com/newsletters/internetlawyer/pub   **$**

Purpose: To keep up to date with research resources.

Content: This print newsletter reviews free law-related Web sites, books, and paid (online) research services.

Our View: Internet resources are only a small part of what this newsletter covers. Its content is well written and insightful. Subscriptions are $149 for twelve print issues.

Tip: The site includes a search engine for the newsletter's archives. Returned results include the title, publication date, and abstract of the article. Online access to the full text of the newsletter's articles is available only to print subscribers.

Legal Information Alert

http://alertpub.com/contents_lia.html   **$**

Purpose: To keep up to date with research resources.

Content: This print newsletter reviews law-related Web sites, books, and paid (online) research services.

Our View: Internet resources are only a small part of what this newsletter covers. While targeted primarily at librarians, this newsletter is valuable to lawyers who conduct research on a regular basis. Subscriptions are $149 for twelve print issues.

Tip: The site offers free online access to its article index only. No online access is available to the full text of the newsletter's articles.

Internet Connection

http://www.glwinternetconnection.com 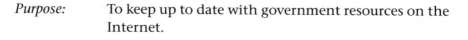 **$**

Purpose:	To keep up to date with government resources on the Internet.
Content:	The articles in this print newsletter review the contents of government Web sites at the federal and state level. It also includes discussions of the policy and legal issues surrounding government information on the Internet.
Our View:	If you use a lot of government resources on the Internet, this newsletter can help you stay on top of new developments. Subscriptions are $114 for ten print issues.
Tip:	Subscribers can also access online versions of the newsletter's articles.

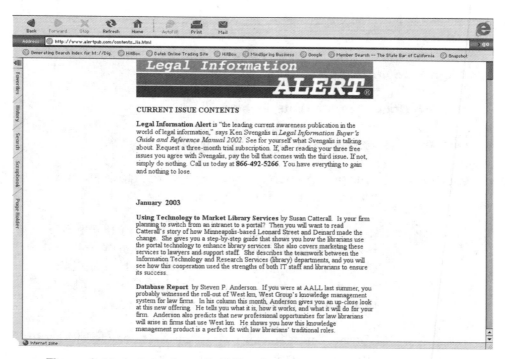

Figure 3-11. Legal Information Alert is a newsletter that reviews law-related Web sites, books, and paid (online) research services.

Internet Law Researcher

http://www.internetlawresearcher.com   **$**

Purpose: To keep up to date with research resources on the Intenet.

Content: This print newsletter discusses the content of law-related Web sites, and important Internet-related court decisions. Additionally, it covers technical issues important to the lawyer computer user.

Our View: The newsletter covers Internet resources for a wide variety of legal areas, including bankruptcy, legislative research, litigation, and intellectual property, among others. Subscriptions are $200 for eleven print issues.

Tip: Subscribers can also access online versions of the newsletter's articles.

Free Resources

Below, we have listed a number of "traditional" Web sites where you can get up-to-date information about online research resources. Personal Weblogs (or "blogs") can also be excellent resources for current information on this topic. See Chapter 20, "Weblogs, RSS Feeds, and Podcasts" for details on specific sites. Additionally, you can consult a directory of law-related blogs such as the annotated Blogs of Law (**http://www.theblogsoflaw.com**).

The Virtual Chase (TVC)

http://www.virtualchase.com

Purpose: To keep up to date regarding online research sites and resources.

Content: The Virtual Chase (TVC) offers articles about the most useful Internet research sites. It covers various areas of factual and legal research, as well as offering articles about Internet law and technology.

Our View: This site is sponsored by a Philadelphia law firm and run, full time, by the firm's former librarian. News and articles are added to the site daily. The content is presented in a very useful and practical manner.

Tip: Sign up for the editor's free daily e-mail alert with headlines of the day's Internet-related new stories.

LLRX (Law Library Resource Xchange)

http://www.llrx.com

Purpose: To keep up to date regarding online research sites and resources.

Content: LLRX provides up-to-date information on a wide range of Internet research and technology-related issues, applications, resources, and tools.

Our View: Since its inception in 1996, LLRX has consistently provided some of the most useful, in-depth coverage on the subjects of conducting legal and law-related research online.

Tip: Sign up for the site's free e-mail alert with headlines of the newest articles added to the site. For daily updates covering copyright, privacy, censorship, the Patriot Act, identity theft, and freedom of information issues, also check out the editor's Web log (**http://www.bespacific .com**).

SearchDay

http://www.searchenginewatch.com/searchday/index.php

Purpose: To keep up to date regarding search engine features and functions.

Content: SearchDay is the daily publication of SearchEngine Watch.com. The site provides tips and information about using search engines effectively, and analysis of the search engine industry.

Our View: An excellent resource for anyone conducting research on the Internet. While extremely informative, the daily e-mail update might be overwhelming to all but the most devoted Web researchers (**http://e-newsletters .internet.com/searchday.html**).

Tip: If the daily update is too much for you, sign up for the editor's free monthly newsletter Search Engine Report **(http://e-newsletters.internet.com/searchengine.html**). Also, this site can be very useful if you are trying to learn how to improve your own Web site's placement in search engines.

Search Engine Showdown

http://www.searchengineshowdown.com

Purpose: To keep up to date with search engine nuances.

Content: Search Engine Showdown contains in-depth examinations of the search functions of various search engines. The site owner, Greg Notess, has also compiled detailed comparisons of popular search engine features and functions, including sizes of results lists, freshness of data, and database overlap.

Our View: The site's easy-to-read search-engine news feature is updated regularly, with the most recent entries at the top of the list.

Tip: Check out the search engine comparison chart at **http://www.searchengineshowdown.com/ features.** (A screen shot is included in Chapter 4, "Search Engines.")

Site-tation

http://meetings.abanet.org/ltrc/index.cfm

Purpose: To keep up to date regarding Internet resources.

Content: The site covers all angles of law office technology, not just research resources. This includes practice-related software, search-engine optimization, and computer security. Each issue includes brief descriptions of useful online resources for lawyers, and even includes a few entries on subjects like travel and gardening.

Our View: "Site-tation" is just one resource of the ABA's Legal Technology Resource Center (LTRC). By their own description, "The ABA's Legal Technology Resource Center is the starting point for lawyers seeking information about implementing and understanding technology."

Tip: Sign up for the LTRC's free monthly e-mail newsletter by clicking the link on the Site-tation (**http://meetings .abanet.org/ltrc/index.cfm**) home page. Check out the LTRC's other online technology features at **http://meet ings.abanet.org/ltrc/index.cfm**.

Law Technology News

http://www.lawtechnologynews.com

Purpose: To keep up to date regarding Internet resources.

Content: This monthly magazine covers a wide range of technology subjects applicable to lawyers in any size practice.

Our View: The Web Watch column specifically devoted to Internet research and practice-related resources is particularly useful for keeping up with Internet resources.

Tip: You can either register for a free print subscription or access the columns and news online (it requires registration).

———————————

There are a number of other free newsletters and discussion lists that also include information on Internet research resources in the course of their discussions of practice-related technology, including TechnoLawyer Community (**http://www.technolawyer.com**), ABA's Solosez list (**http://www.abanet.org/solosez.net**), and ABA's LawTech (**http://mail.abanet.org/archives/lawtech.html**). TechnoLawyer also offers e-newsletters and an archive of both its discussion postings and e-newsletters. The archive provides an advanced search menu that is searchable by date, keyword, topic, and content type (e.g., a posting or a feature article and so on). Searching the archive is free but to read the full-text, registration is required.

Getting Help: Expert Research Support

At the end of an Internet research seminar, we often hear the following comment: "That was a great seminar. I really understand the Web now and everything I can find on it. *But*, where do I go now to find someone to do it for me?" The goal of our seminars is twofold: (1) to teach lawyers how they can use the Web for research on their own, and (2) for those lawyers who don't have the time (or inclination) to use the Web on their own, to inform them of what's available on the Web so they know what to ask for when handing a research assignment over to an associate, librarian, or paralegal. However, for many of you in a small or solo practice, there is no one else to take over the research task! Maybe you have an assistant, but in certain instances the subject matter is beyond that person's knowledge base. In either case, this is the time to seek expert research support.

There are a number of options for those of you who prefer to have someone else conduct your online research. There are a variety of independent librarians, information brokers, and other researchers who can help you find the information you need on a per-project basis. Some of the areas they in which they can find information include:

- People Finding (e.g., missing witnesses, missing heirs)
- Competitive Intelligence (e.g., profiling an opposing counsel, expert, prospective client, etc.)

- Asset Searching
- Company Background
- Criminal Records (note: availability of information varies widely from jurisdiction to jurisdiction)
- Legal Research

Depending on your needs, you might want to seek ones who are degreed law librarians or lawyers. Most of these researchers have access to a variety of pay databases from which to draw information not available for free on the Internet, and the experience to locate it quickly. While no electronic search is absolutely complete, an experienced researcher will be able to cross-match and combine their results from their various sources to deliver a dossier of information that can help make or break your case.

When There's No One to Help You, Think Virtual

If you need expert help, but you also want to be more involved in the research process, consider working with a virtual law librarian.

You can also interact with a virtual law librarian to assist you the minute you're in crisis mode—whether you need help finding an answer from a free Web site, from a pay database, or even from a print resource. Legal Reference Service Inc. (LRSI) (**http://www.lrsionline.net**). See Figure 3-12) allows you to interact with a law librarian as if you were on the

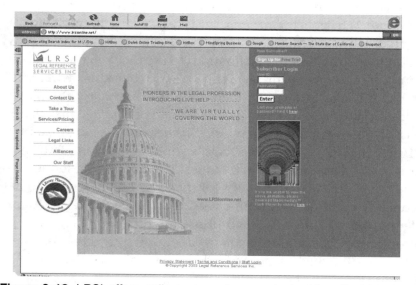

Figure 3-12. LRSI offers online access to experienced law librarians who can assist you with your research.

phone or face to face. This virtual librarian can even "walk through" the research project with you over the Internet in a secure, cobrowsing mode.

Let a Librarian Take Control of Your Browser

In cobrowsing, the librarian takes control of your browser and brings you to the same free Web sites or pay databases she is using to research your query. All along, you are viewing the results live and chatting over the Internet as the search session is in progress. You can make comments or suggestions or ask questions while the search is going on. This gives you not only an element of control over the research, but can also serve as a training tool so you can do the same type of search on your own, if you choose, the next time. This service is available from LRSI (**http://www.lrsionline.net**) from 2:00PM–5:00PM ET.

After each interactive session is completed, a transcript containing links to the sites visited during the cobrowsing session is immediately produced and e-mailed to both the lawyer and the virtual librarian for follow-up on either side (see Figure 3-13).

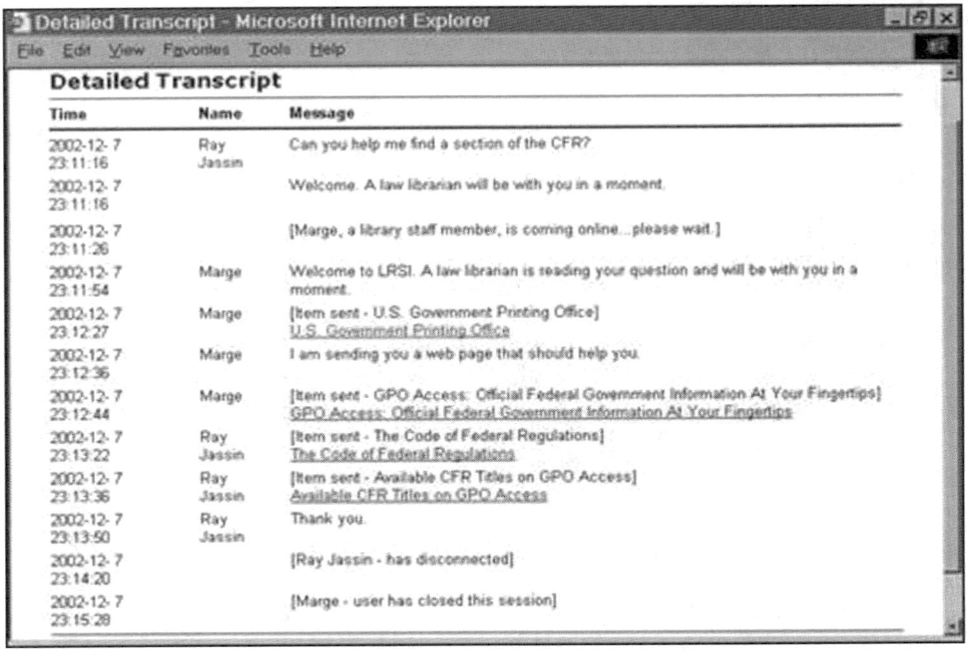
Detailed Transcript - Microsoft Internet Explorer

File Edit View Favorites Tools Help

Detailed Transcript

Time	Name	Message
2002-12- 7 23:11:16	Ray Jassin	Can you help me find a section of the CFR?
2002-12- 7 23:11:16		Welcome. A law librarian will be with you in a moment.
2002-12- 7 23:11:26		[Marge, a library staff member, is coming online...please wait.]
2002-12- 7 23:11:54	Marge	Welcome to LRSI. A law librarian is reading your question and will be with you in a moment.
2002-12- 7 23:12:27	Marge	[Item sent - U.S. Government Printing Office] U.S. Government Printing Office
2002-12- 7 23:12:36	Marge	I am sending you a web page that should help you.
2002-12- 7 23:12:44	Marge	[Item sent - GPO Access: Official Federal Government Information At Your Fingertips] GPO Access: Official Federal Government Information At Your Fingertips
2002-12- 7 23:13:22	Ray Jassin	[Item sent - The Code of Federal Regulations] The Code of Federal Regulations
2002-12- 7 23:13:36	Ray Jassin	[Item sent - Available CFR Titles on GPO Access] Available CFR Titles on GPO Access
2002-12- 7 23:13:50	Ray Jassin	Thank you.
2002-12- 7 23:14:20		[Ray Jassin - has disconnected]
2002-12- 7 23:15:28		[Marge - user has closed this session]

Figure 3-13. At the end of an online reference session with one of LRSI's online librarians, users receive a transcript of the entire session, including clickable links to any Web sites visited as part of the session.

The service is available as a subscription service (ten hours minimum), based on a fee of $50 per hour. LRSI will also handle e-mailed reference requests where a librarian works on a project on her own and e-mails back the results.

If you need public record retrieval, LRSI may be able to handle this too. But another option is to visit the BRB Public Record Retriever Network site (see Figure 3-14) and contact one of their recommended retrievers (**http://brbpub.com/PRRN**).

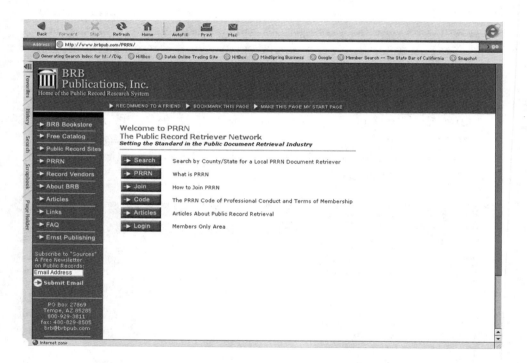

Figure 3-14. Research book publisher BRB Publications maintains a searchable database of members of the Public Record Retrieval Network (PRRN), a trade organization for contractors who retrieve documents from local government agencies in over 2,000 counties in all 50 states.

Free Local Library Virtual Reference Services

Many local libraries offer free virtual (chat) reference services (but not to the extent of a commercial service like LRSI). For example, the New York Public Library hosts a chat at **http://ask.nypl.org**. At Asknow.org (**http:// www.asknow.org**), public-library patrons can chat 24/7 with a librarian. A patron can also choose to chat with a Spanish-speaking librarian, a law librarian, or a medical librarian. Locate your local public library's Web site at the LibWeb site to find out if they offer a similar service (**http://sunsite.berkeley.edu/Libweb**). Use the LiveRef directory to link to various types of libraries (government, university, or special libraries) that offer free chat reference services (**http://www.public.iastate .edu/~CYBERSTACKS/ LiveRef.htm**). An example of a special library offering this service is the Illinois CPA Society (**http://www.icpas.org/ icpas/library/library.asp**).

Pay Library Virtual (Chat) Reference Services

Many libraries also offer pay reference services in a virtual (chat) mode. With the advent of the Web, you don't even need to be restricted to your *local* library, but can make use of any library's services remotely. For example, the New York Public Library's pay reference service can assist you in "locating a discrete fact to compiling a report." See NYPL Express at **http://www.nypl.org/express/fees.html**. Fees range from $75 to $125 per hour, depending on the turnaround time requested. The Los Angeles County Library hosts FYI Research Services (**http://www.colapublib.org/ fyi.html**). They are strong in business references (among other subjects). These pay services use both electronic and print resources to answer your questions. Academic libraries and county law libraries also may offer pay reference services.

Other Reference Assistance

The Association of Independent Information Professionals offers a free referral service at their site to obtain contact information for fee-based reference assistance (**http://www.aiip.org/AboutAIIP/referral.html**). Finally, take a look at Chapter 9, "Finding and Backgrounding Expert Witnesses," for ideas on where else to find subject specialists. Often, a professional or trade association has a staff person (or even a library) where you can make inquiries about research assistance.

*CHAPTER***FOUR**

Search Tools

Search Engines

Search Engines: A Quick View

- Not all information is available on the Internet.
- Not all the information on the Internet is findable via a search engine.
- No search engine can actually search the entire Web, no matter what the propaganda says. Among the places no public search engine can search are sites requiring passwords, and the content of sites that can only be viewed by searching a database contained at the site.
- Google and Yahoo! are two of the best search-engine starting points. (Combined, those two search engines search a little over 12 percent of the total number of documents that the Bright Planet report (see page 99) predicts should currently be on the Internet.)
- Take advantage of advanced-search options. Very often, you'll get different results over using the "plain vanilla" search offered on the opening page.
- Use more than one search engine per search.
- Metasearch sites use multiple engines for each search.
- If you plan to rerun a search at a later date, consider bookmarking the search results page.

- If you want to refer to a search throughout your browsing session, you can leave the search open in its own browser window, and open subsequent Web pages in new browser windows.
- If you are using a newer version of the Internet Explorer, Netscape Navigator, or Firefox browser, you can open subsequent sites in their own tabs—allowing you to move back and forth between the sites.

The majority of this book is designed to steer the researcher toward specific resources that contain information directly related to their search topic, thereby skipping an initial visit to a search engine to (hopefully) locate those resources. Because of the volume of results returned by search engines, and the invariable questions of the relevance and credibility of those results, it is preferable to use a resource that has already been tested and evaluated by a reputable reviewer. Search engines, however, can be useful for general Internet searching, particularly if you are not familiar with the subject area in which you're searching. Some of the most well-known of these include Google, AltaVista, and Yahoo!.

One of the frequent complaints concerning search engines is that they return too much irrelevant information in response to search requests. Admittedly, at times when the researcher has no clue what he is really looking for, and needs the search software to make suggestions in the form of a variety of Internet destinations, this search engine flaw is a good thing. But the more common and disappointing experience is to receive 2 million responses to a simple request, which then need to be reviewed, page by page, until the most worthwhile and informative sites are found. Even though the experienced researcher can sense right away whether the responses are relevant and likely to lead to an appropriate site, it would, obviously, be a poor use of time to scroll through those 2 million responses. Additionally, the highest-rated results are most likely to be the most relevant to the search request. Ordinarily, the relevance of the search results (as determined by the engine's search algorithms) diminishes the further down the list you look. If the first few hits are irrelevant, the best thing to do is to review the original search and construct a new search to produce more-pointed results.

Search Engines' Limitations

That part of the Web that is not indexed by search engines is referred to as the "Invisible Web." (Other terms used to describe this segment of the Internet include Hidden Web, Deep Web, and Dark Web.) These pages might be invisible for any number of reasons. They may be protected by a firewall or password, be contained in a database, be in a format other than HyperText Markup Language (HTML), such as Macromedia's Flash (.swf) or be information maintained in a searchable database (such as membership records).

The first thing to remember about search engines is that no single search engine has indexed the contents of every Web site on the Internet. In a widely cited March 2000 report, Web search technology developer Bright Planet (**http://www.brightplanet.com/technology/deepweb.asp**) concluded that:

- One billion documents were findable via a search engine on the "surface" [visible] web.
- There was 400 to 550 times that amount of information that search engines could access and index, if the search engines knew where to look. The report referred to this as the "deep Web."

The report estimated that the Web was growing at a rate of 7.5 million documents per day. If that is correct, then there are approximately 133.8 trillion documents on the Internet as of late 2005, with 243 billion of those supposedly being visible to search engines. The last publicly professed index sizes show Yahoo! at 21 billion and Google at 8.2 billion.

Despite the superior size of Yahoo!'s index (as reported by Yahoo! itself) there is still a great deal of overlap in the top-ranked results when running similar searches at both Google and Yahoo!. A number of search industry watchers think that Yahoo!'s 21 billion Web object claim may be overstated, as searches at Yahoo! do not return significantly larger numbers of results when compared to the same searches run at Google. In fact, shortly after Yahoo!'s claim of 21 billion became public, in the summer of 2005, Google removed the reference to the nearly 11.3 billion Web objects (8.2 billion Web pages, 2 billion images, and 1 billion Usenet postings) in its database that had been displayed on the bottom of its homepage. (It should be noted, however that the "8.2 billion" number had not been increased/updated since Google had placed it on the homepage more than a year earlier.)

To their credit, despite this large quantity of un-indexed material, the major search engines generally do a fairly good job of returning something useful in the first few hits. You will often retrieve different results even if you conduct the same search using different search engines. For example, if a search engine is designed to only look for your search terms in the document's title, but the terms for which you're searching are only in the document's abstract, the search engine will not return results. However, engines that search through abstracts or, better yet, do full-text searches of pages, tend to find more documents.

Because no search engine has catalogued the entire contents of the Internet, for more in-depth results it is advisable to conduct the same search on two or three of the most comprehensive search engines in order to retrieve the highest volume of useful information.

The quality of search results is dependent on choosing the right search engine and creating the best search. A lousy search strategy will be unsuccessful no matter what search engine is used, and a precise search string will generate better results, even with the weakest search tool. But the optimal situation is for the researcher to understand the nuances of each engine, and to submit focused search requests that take advantage of such nuances. This takes practice, but is possible. It also requires keeping on top of the all-too-frequent enhancements made to search engines' functionality. This book's companion e-letter is a valuable resource for the researcher who wishes to keep up with these enhancements. The newsletter is published electronically every other month and delivered via e-mail to all purchasers of this edition who return the subscription card enclosed with this book. On the Web, Search Engine Report (**http://www.searchenginewatch.com/sereport**), SearchEngineWatch (**http://www.searchenginewatch.com**), and Search Engine Showdown (**http://www.searchengineshowdown.com**) are good sources for new developments regarding search engines.

All search engines provide some limited Boolean logic capabilities (meaning the ability to use logical operators to connect words and phrases, such as AND, OR, NOT, and so on). Most free Internet search engines do not reach the level of Boolean search sophistication that online researchers have come to expect from pay services like Lexis and Westlaw. Most free search engines also lack the proximity connectors (such as "within two words") that lawyers use in pay databases. With enough practice and training, you could one day be certain that you could extract any piece of information contained in these pay services' databases. Unfortunately, there are no such certainties on the free Internet.

That's where this book comes in. It is designed to be a researcher's user manual for the Internet, a tool that has not existed before.

Learning How to Search

The best way to learn how each search engine works is to read the instructions and tips found in the **Help** or **Tips** pages offered by each of the respective search engines. Such instructions demonstrate how the designers recommend using the engine. What the Help pages don't usually tell you is exactly how the engine was built, or how the search algorithms weight the search-string elements you submit. These are the main criteria that determine how the engines work, why they return some pages instead of others, and why they rank certain pages higher than others. Search engines usually do not divulge this information in an effort to keep unscrupulous Web developers from exploiting their index and ranking systems.

After reading the **Help** pages, the next best way to learn how to use search engines effectively is simply to use them. Familiarity leads to expertise. By trying out various engines, and using them frequently, you'll get a sense of the strengths and weaknesses of each. We recommend Google, Yahoo!, AltaVista, and Alltheweb, for reasons we explain below.

If you take the time to read the instructions and suggestions at each of the individual search engines, your searches will be more accurate. One thing you'll find, however, if you study the various engines, is that each search engine indexes the Internet differently, and that each offers different search functions. What works well on Google may not work at all on Yahoo!. Some vary slightly from one to the next, and some vary a lot. With so many available search engine options, remembering what search strategies to use at which site can be a challenge. Therefore, it might be more realistic to become familiar with two or three of the most comprehensive search engines—and stick with them. Searchengine Showdown provides a useful chart of search engine features.

When switching between search engines, it's important to remember that different search engines recognize different proximity connectors. For example, Google allows you to use an asterisk as a wildcard to replace a word (or more than one word) in a search string, while Yahoo! does not allow any wildcards. So, a Google search for:

John * Jones

could retrieve John Paul Jones, John Howard Jones, John William Henry Jones, John asked Mr. Jones, etc.

By representing one word or a series of words, the asterisk serves a sort of imprecise "near" connector. The problem is, however, that we're not sure how "near" this "near" places our search terms. In test searches, we have seen our search terms separated by as many as twenty-eight other terms, even though we've used only one asterisk. Aside from using the wild card to replace a word or series of words as we did above, another handy option on Google is to use the wild card to replace **one number or a series of numbers**. You might use this type of wild card search in the following scenarios:

1. You need to find someone's full phone number and you only know part of their name and part of their phone number. Try

Search Engine Showdown
The Users' Guide
to Web Searching

Home Chart Reviews Statistics Learn Directories Search

Search Engine Features Chart

* See also Search Engines by Search Features.

* Search engines grouped by size; all words link to more detailed reviews.

Last updated Apr. 25, 2005.
by Greg R. Notess.

Search Engines	Boolean	Default	Proximity	Truncation	Case	Fields	Limits	Stop	Sorting
Google Review	-, OR	and	Phrase, GAPS	No, but stemming, word in phrase	No	intitle, inurl link, site, more	Language, filetype, date, domain	Varies, + searches	Relevance, site
Yahoo! Review	AND, OR, NOT, ( ), -	and	Phrase	No	No	intitle, url site, inurl, link, more	Language, file type, date, domain	Very few	Relevance, site
Ask Jeeves/Teoma Review	-, OR	and	Phrase	No	No	intitle, inurl	Language, site, date	Yes, + searches	Relevance, metasites
MSN Search Review	AND, OR, NOT, ( ), -	and	Phrase	No	No	link, site, loc, url	Language, site	Varies, + searches	Relevance, site, sliders
WiseNut Review	- only	and	Phrase	No	No	No	Language	Yes, + searches	Relevance, site
Gigablast Review	AND, OR, AND NOT, ( ), +, -	and	Phrase	No	No	title, site, ip, more	Domain, type	Varies, + searches	Relevance
Exalead Review	AND, OR, NOT, ( ),-	and	Phrase, NEAR	Yes	No	title	Language, file type, date, domain	Varies, + searches	Relevance, date

A Notess.com Web Site
©1999-2006 by Greg R. Notess, all rights reserved

Search Engine Showdown
Greg's Writings
Greg's Presentations

Figure 4-1. It is important to know what Boolean connectors are recognized by the search engine you are using. It is equally important to know what the search engine you're using automatically adds as a default Boolean connector. Search Engine Showdown offers a comprehensive chart of the features of numerous search engines (arranged by search engine) at **http://www.searchengine showdown.com/features.** © 1999-2006 by Greg R. Notess. All rights reserved. Reprinted with permission.

searching the partial name (e.g., "Wilson") and as much of the phone number as you know (e.g., you might know that the area code is "310" and the last four digits are "6789"). Using the Google wild card, your search would look like this:
Wilson 310 * 6789

This search could retrieve Wilson and 310-555-6789, Wilson and 310-777-6789, etc.

2. You want to run your own Social Security number or credit card number through Google to assure yourself that none of those numbers are on the Internet. However, for various security reasons, you don't want to type the full number into the Google

search box. Using the Google wild card, a search for your Social Security number would look like this:

010 * 1098 (you could also add your first or last name)

Google API Proximity Search (GAPS)

http://www.staggernation.com/cgi-bin/gaps.cgi

Purpose: To superimpose a proximity connector search function on the Google search engine.

Content: Using Google's Application Program Interface (API), Web developer Kevin Shay created a more precise proximity search, giving us a way to search the Google index for keywords within one, two, or three words of each other. Returned results include a notation of how many words separate your search terms.

Our View: GAPS offers the flexibility of searching individual keywords, or multiword phrases in close proximity to one another. A pull-down menu between two search boxes allows you to choose whether you want your terms to be within one, two, or three words of each other. A separate pull-down menu lets you choose in which order the words should appear in the web page. A third search box allows you to add more terms to the search.

Tip: Proximity searching can be useful when searching for information about a person—if the person uses one (or more) middle initials or a middle name. Therefore, a search for "Lee" within two words of "Oswald" should return more relevant information than a phrase search for "Lee Oswald."

Common words (also called "noise" or "stop words"), such as "of," "the," "an," or numbers are ignored by most search engines. Some search engines, such as Google, can be forced to include these terms if it is important to your search. For example, to force Google to search for the phrase "to be or not to be," put the phrase in quotation marks. To search for "Star Wars Episode I," place a plus sign (+) before the word you want to force it to search for (Star Wars Episode +I). Each of these strategies returns different results. It might be useful to try both for a tricky set of search terms.

Figure 4-2. Search Engine Showdown also provides an excellent comparison review of the major engines' features (arranged by feature) at **http://www .searchengineshowdown.com/features/byfeature.shtml**. (At the time of this writing, the site was being reconstructed, so you will need to visit the site to learn if an update of this chart has been posted.) © 1999-2006 by Greg R. Notess. All rights reserved. Reprinted with permission.

Who Owns What?

In recent years, the search engine industry has undergone a major ownership shuffle, leading to greater ownership consolidation among major search engines. The chart below offers a snapshot of some of the biggest deals. With Yahoo!'s 2003 purchase of Overture, Yahoo! now owns Inktomi, Overture, AltaVista, and Alltheweb.

	Ask Jeeves	Yahoo!	Overture	Overture	Yahoo!	InterActive Corporation
Date of Purchase	October 2001	December 2002	February 2003	February 2003	July 2003	March 2005
What It Purchased	Teoma	Inktomi	AltaVista	Alltheweb	Overture	Ask Jeeves
Reported Purchase Price	$4 million	$235 million	$140 million	$100 million	$1.6 billion	$1.85 billion

Sponsored Links

Most search engines place links labeled "Sponsored" or "Partner" above the results generated from their own index. These types of links are advertisements generated to correspond to your search terms. These sites may or may not be the most relevant to your search, but they have paid to appear at the top of the list for certain search terms. There is no harm in clicking to see if those sites are useful to you. Very often, though, the best results are found below in the regular Web search results.

One of the originators of paid placement search results is Overture (**http://www.overture.com**). Overture, owned by Yahoo!, supplies its paid placement search to numerous other search engines, including Yahoo!, MSN, and CNN.

Google has taken a different direction with its Adsense advertising service (**https://www.google.com/adsense/**). Adsense supplies ads to any Web site publisher that creates an account to receive those ads. Ads are sent to those sites based on keywords detected by Google on the sites' pages. Advertisers pay only when Web surfers click on one of their ads.

For more information about effective searching than the search engine **Help** screens offer, try the detailed search engine reviews published by SearchEngineShowdown.com (**http://searchengineshowdown.com/reviews/**).

How Search Engines Work

No search engine is comprehensive in scope or time. When you enter your search terms into the search box of any search engine, you are not searching the entire Internet. You are only searching those pages that a particular search engine has previously found ("visited") and added to its index. Additionally, depending on the frequency with which the search engine revisits pages, search result lists might be based on Web page content that is one week to many months old.

Search engines are essentially large, automatic classifiers. To gather information about the content of various Web pages, the search engines send out robots (also known as spiders) that automatically add information from Web pages to the search engine's index. This process is known as indexing or spidering. It is from this index that the search engine returns its list of results when you enter your search terms into the search box.

After completing the search, the search engine displays a list of links to sites that include your search terms. This is your list of results or hits. Sometimes the results will be right on target and other times completely irrelevant, even though they contain your search terms. Ordinarily, the results that the search engine deems to be the most relevant to your search terms will be at the top of the list.

Advanced Searches

Most search engines offer an advanced search capability. *Find it and use it!* The advanced search gives you significantly more options for conducting your search. These might include sophisticated Boolean-connector searching or limiting the search to a certain Internet domain or specific file format (such as PDF) that is not available to you if you use the "plain vanilla" search box offered on the search engine's home page. A link to the advanced search functions is often on the right-hand side of a search engine's opening screen.

Figure 4-3. Clicking on the **Advanced Search** link opens the Advanced Search page. Google™ is a trademark of Google Technology Inc.

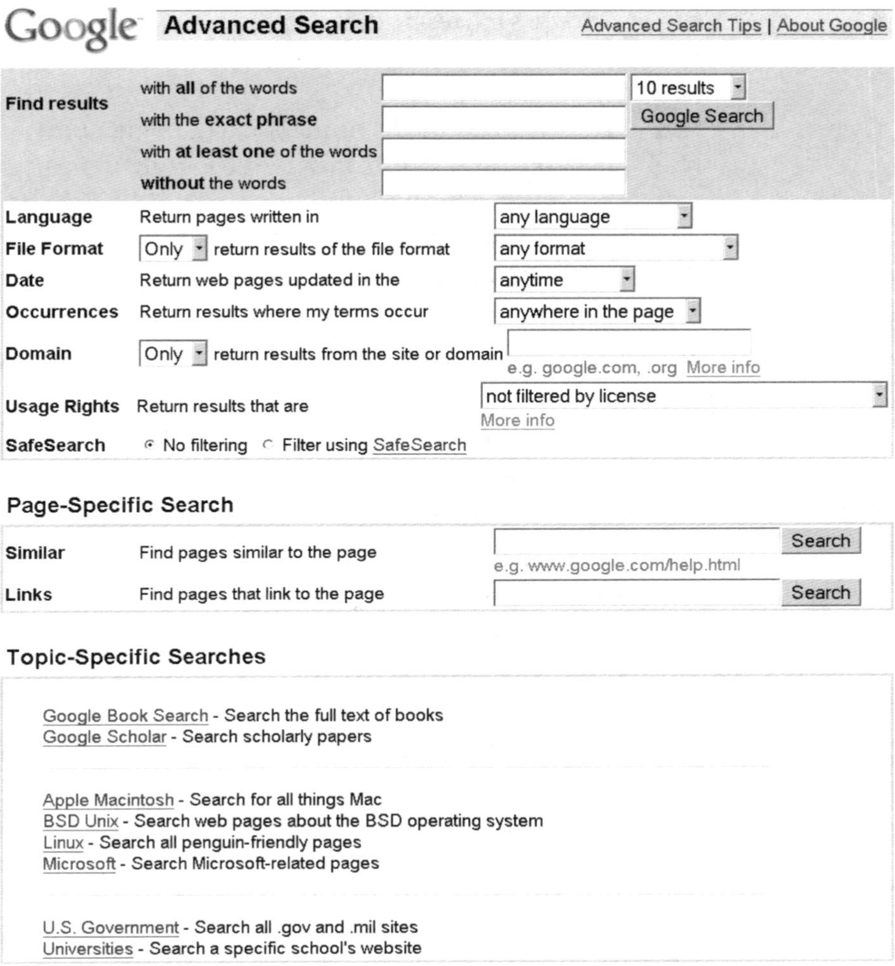

Google **Advanced Search**   Advanced Search Tips | About Google

Find results	with **all** of the words		10 results ▾
	with the **exact phrase**		Google Search
	with **at least one** of the words		
	without the words		

Language	Return pages written in	any language ▾
File Format	Only ▾ return results of the file format	any format ▾
Date	Return web pages updated in the	anytime ▾
Occurrences	Return results where my terms occur	anywhere in the page ▾
Domain	Only ▾ return results from the site or domain	e.g. google.com, .org More info
Usage Rights	Return results that are	not filtered by license ▾
		More info
SafeSearch	⦿ No filtering ○ Filter using SafeSearch	

Page-Specific Search

Similar	Find pages similar to the page		Search
		e.g. www.google.com/help.html	
Links	Find pages that link to the page		Search

Topic-Specific Searches

Google Book Search - Search the full text of books
Google Scholar - Search scholarly papers

Apple Macintosh - Search for all things Mac
BSD Unix - Search web pages about the BSD operating system
Linux - Search all penguin-friendly pages
Microsoft - Search Microsoft-related pages

U.S. Government - Search all .gov and .mil sites
Universities - Search a specific school's website

©2006 Google

Figure 4-4. Google's Advanced Search page offers greater search strategy options. Google™ is a trademark of Google Technology Inc.

Use Automatic Alerts to Stay on Top of Important Searches

GoogleAlerts.com

http://www.google.com/alerts

Purpose: Google Alerts sends you up-to-the-minute e-mail Alerts
              so you can monitor the Web via Google's search engine

or via Google's current news database (or both), or Google Groups, based on your keyword search.

Content: After arriving at Google's home page (Google.com), click on **More**, which is located on the right-hand side of the page. This will lead you to Google Services, which offers several options, with **Alerts** being one of them. Clicking on the **Alerts** icon will bring you to their welcome page.

To create a *Google Alert* you need to enter your keywords into the first box and then answer three simple questions: (1) the type of alert you would like (*Web, News,* or *News & Web together, or Groups*); (2) how often you would like the alerts e-mailed (daily, weekly, or as they occur); and (3) your e-mail address.

On the bottom left of this same page, Google asks if you would like to manage your Alerts. If you click on this

Figure 4-5. Create a Google Alert to receive e-mails about any topic, person, or company you need to closely monitor. Besides monitoring the Web and News, Google Alerts now offers Alert users the option of also monitoring Google Groups. Google™ is a trademark of Google Technology Inc.

link, Google will then require you to sign up and register with an e-mail address and password. The benefit of this process is that every time you log on to Google Alerts you can view your list of Alerts that you have created, as well as edit or delete them easily. For example, we originally created a Web Alert for the topic "Iraq" that we wanted sent to us daily. Later, it was simple to revise the Alert to add *News* to have the Alert also monitor Google's *News* database in addition to the Web. We also revised the Alert to request the Alert be sent as it happens, instead of just daily.

If you decide to forgo this option, you will not be able to edit your search queries at all. You will have to delete the Alert entirely (by clicking on a link at the bottom of an Alert e-mail) and then create a brand new Alert to your new specifications.

Our View: As previously stated, Google has created a simple way to keep you in touch with the information you need, when you need it. When we signed up for the Iraq *News* Alert, our first e-mail arrived within two hours. Granted the topic is pretty newsworthy, but Google Alerts still deserves kudos for their speedy entry of our information and queries.

Although the Alerts home page technically says it is still in its Beta stage, that doesn't always mean it hasn't been around for a while. Google seems to keep their services in Beta mode longer than most other companies, apparently so they can continue to add and "play" with their products. We found this to be a really good service, and one of the few free Alert Services on the Internet.

Tip: For those who can't wait to receive their automatic alerts, another neat option of the **Manage** page allows you to click on your Alert to run your search on the spot.

Indices and Directories Versus Search Engines

While search engines operate off a large index of automatically spidered pages, directories and indices contain fewer links that have been

Figure 4-6. In addition to its search engine, Google also offers a directory of topics that include Internet resources reviewed and selected by human editors. Google™ is a trademark of Google Technology Inc.

hand-selected by humans who are (usually) subject specialists. These directories divide sites into increasingly more-narrow subjects based on their content (such as Government > Law > Legal Research > Libraries). Yahoo! started out life as the personal directory site of two Stanford grad students before growing into the media titan it is today. Google, the search engine that started out as a project of two other Stanford grad students, later added a directory (see Figure 4-6).

Some directories only allow users to click through the categories until they come to the level that holds the information they're looking for. This practice is often referred to as drilling down. Others add the ability to search through the index with an internal search engine that points the user to the category where he'll find the information he needs.

Our Favorite Search Engines

The following is a list that includes some of the most comprehensive search engines and directories (beginning with our most favorite to least favorite). Google is our top pick; of law-related sites, our favorite is Lawcrawler.com.

- **Google at** http://www.google.com. Many believe that Google delivers the most relevant results of any major search engine. Google was the first major search engine to search many types of files that until then had been relegated to the Invisible Web. For a long time, it had very little competition in these areas, but recently Yahoo! and MSN Search have made impressive progress. Beginning in mid-2004, Google claimed to index nearly 8.2 billion pages of the Internet (although it is important to note that there is no way to independently confirm this self-reported number). In late 2005, after attempting to refute Yahoo!'s claim of indexing more than 20 billion items (see below), Google removed the reference to the size of its index from their home page. (Google had not updated or increased the number since first claiming 8.2 billion pages in 2004.) Google utilizes a proprietary "PageRank" technology to determine a Web page's relevance and importance based on each page's content, the number and types of other Web pages that link to it, and other criteria. Google updates the entirety of its index (on average) every 28 days, although some Web sites are spidered more often.

- **Yahoo! at** http://search.yahoo.com. In February 2004, Yahoo! implemented a new search index of its own (reportedly based on an index and spidering technology created by Inktomi, which Yahoo! acquired in 2002). This new index quickly distinguished itself by returning high-quality, relevant results. In fact, many of their results are very similar to Google results for the same search, in size and order of the search results. In an August 2005 posting to the Yahoo! Search Blog, Yahoo! claimed that its search index had grown "to over 20 billion items . . . this update includes just over 19.2 billion Web documents, 1.6 billion images, and over 50 million audio and video files" (**http://www.ysearchblog.com/archives/000172.html**). Some veteran search engine watchers didn't embrace that claim, but no definitive evidence is available one way or another (**http:// battellemedia.com/archives/001790.php** and **http://vburton.ncsa .uiuc.edu/indexsize.html**). Previously, Yahoo! had relied on Google to return its Web search results.

- **MSN Search at** http://search.msn.com. In November 2004, MSN Search implemented a new search index based on technology it developed in-house. Like Yahoo!, MSN Search has made great strides in terms of the relevance of its search results, and its ability to search non-HTML documents that had previously been relegated to the Invisible Web. MSN last reported its index size as 5 billion documents, in mid-2003. Previously, MSN Search had also relied on Google to return its Web search results.

- **AltaVista at http://www.altavista.com.** Despite being owned by Yahoo!, AltaVista generally returns different Web search results than its corporate parent's search engine. However, AltaVista's image and current news searches often return results similar to the results for the same searches conducted at Yahoo!
- **LawCrawler at http://lawcrawler.lp.findlaw.com.** Law Crawler searches the World Wide Web, but only sites that contain law-related information by limiting its search to (primarily) government and educational sites. You can limit LawCrawler to a specific state, to federal legal sites, or to international legal sites. Because this search engine is powered by Google, it returns very relevant results.

Our Favorite Search Engine Functions

There are a number of advanced search functions that make Google and Yahoo! our first choices. For a long time these were solely the dominion of Google, but Yahoo! has made significant strides to improve and extend its search functions:

- Large indices of Internet pages
- Search file types on the Internet that some other search engines do not
- Robust Advanced Search page
- Return relevant results
- Can conduct an image and news searches
- Can perform a newsgroup search (of Google Groups)
- Also include a browsable directory

Additional File Formats

For more-sophisticated search options, click on **Advanced Search** to search a variety of non-HTML file formats that Google and Yahoo! include in their indices. The most useful of these may be the Microsoft Office files, including Word, Excel, and PowerPoint, as well as Adobe PDF. For example, a regular Google search for "accounting expense report forms" returns results that include Word, Excel, and PDF files, with each file type clearly labeled, as noted below. Clicking on the document's title downloads the file to your computer and automatically opens it in the corresponding software.

Both Google and Yahoo! have limitations on how much information in a document they index. Yahoo! apparently searches the first 500 kilo-

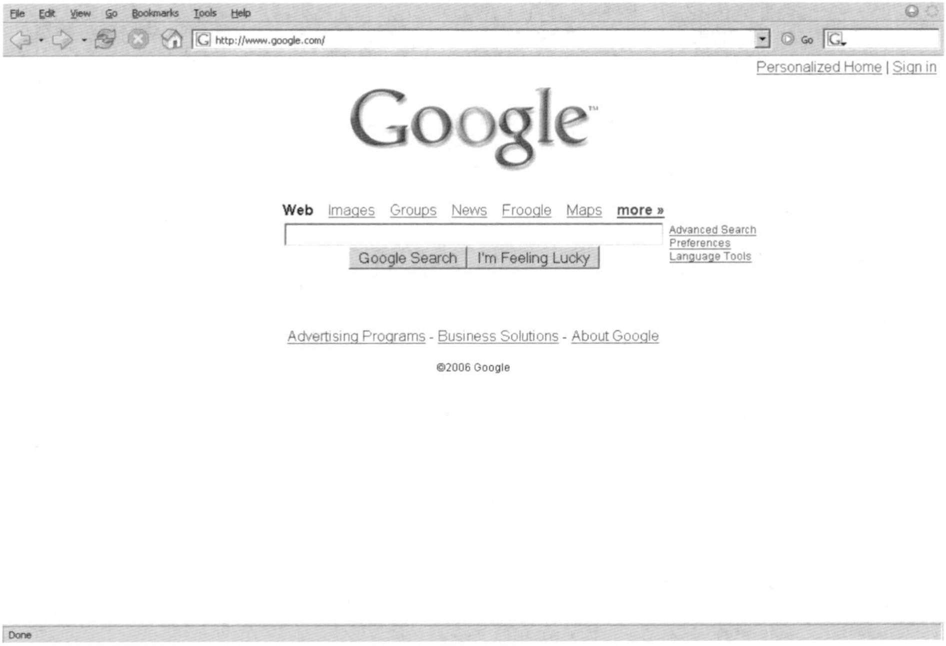

Figure 4-7. Beneath its minimalist home page, Google hides a powerful search engine. Google™ is a trademark of Google Technology Inc.

bytes of a document. In contrast, Google seems to index varying amounts of different documents it finds on the Web. We encountered this varying limitation in a recent search for a 10-K for the "Walt Disney Company." In that search, we received results that had been indexed to 262k, 513k, and 906k. Even at these higher indexing thresholds, the larger limits did not necessarily mean that Google had indexed the entire document. (For more details regarding this test search and its results, see page 74 in Chapter 3.) This is an improvement over Google's previous limit of 101 kilobytes.

To reduce download time, and to lessen the possibility of download-ing a virus or worm along with the file, you should take advantage of the **View as HTML** link both search engines provide. Clicking this link dis-plays a stripped-down version of the file (in plain text) in the Web browser rather than downloading it to your hard drive. You can save the lengthier process of downloading (and scanning for viruses) for only the most important or relevant files.

Google was the first major search engine to move beyond indexing just the traditional HTML format by indexing documents in Adobe's popu-lar PDF format, adding them to its search results in 2001. This marked a

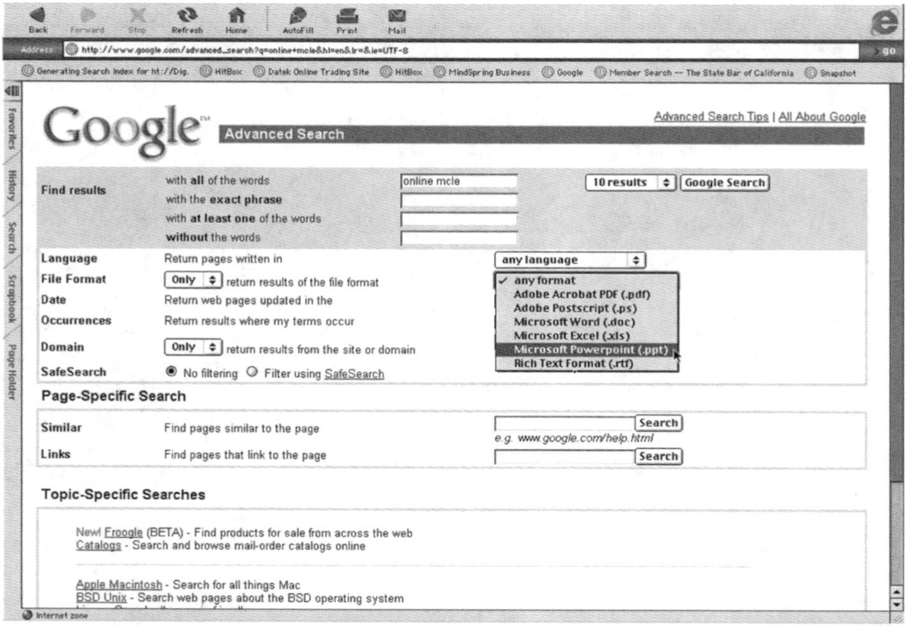

Figure 4-8. Because Google is able to index many files types, such as Microsoft Word, Microsoft Excel, Microsoft PowerPoint, and Adobe Acrobat, a search for "accounting expense report forms" returns results in all of those file formats. Google™ is a trademark of Google Technology Inc.

significant advance in searching the "Invisible Web." Other search engines followed suit, adding PDF files to their search results including Alltheweb, AltaVista, Adobe's specialty PDF search at **http://searchpdf.adobe.com**, and FirstGov.gov (for government documents). When Yahoo! began to re-invigorate its own search technology in 2004, they also expanded to more non-HTML Web documents, including PDFs. Since many researchers and universities use the PDF format for their papers, theses, and other research results, the availability of PDF files in search engine indices is a boon to all researchers. Many government documents are also created in the PDF format, especially forms.

Because the PDF format requires users to download the Adobe Acrobat Reader software before viewing, search engines clearly high-light any PDF document returned in a search with a **[PDF]** designation next to the returned item. For those who do not have the Acrobat Reader software, you can also use the **View as HTML** option to view a text version of the document (with the formatting and special fonts removed).

Google and Yahoo!'s Advanced Search pages can also limit your results to one of the specific popular Microsoft Office file formats these search engines index. The file format is noted by an abbreviation (the same as the file extension the programs use when saving a file on a user's hard drive) in brackets (Google) or parentheses (Yahoo!) to the left of the document's title. They are

- [DOC] for Word files
- [XLS] for Excel files
- [PPT] for PowerPoint files
- [RTF] for Rich Text Format files
- [PS] for PostScript files

The ability to search various formats is very useful in locating memos, tables, or other documents published on the Internet that might not be easily accessible or indexed by most search engines.

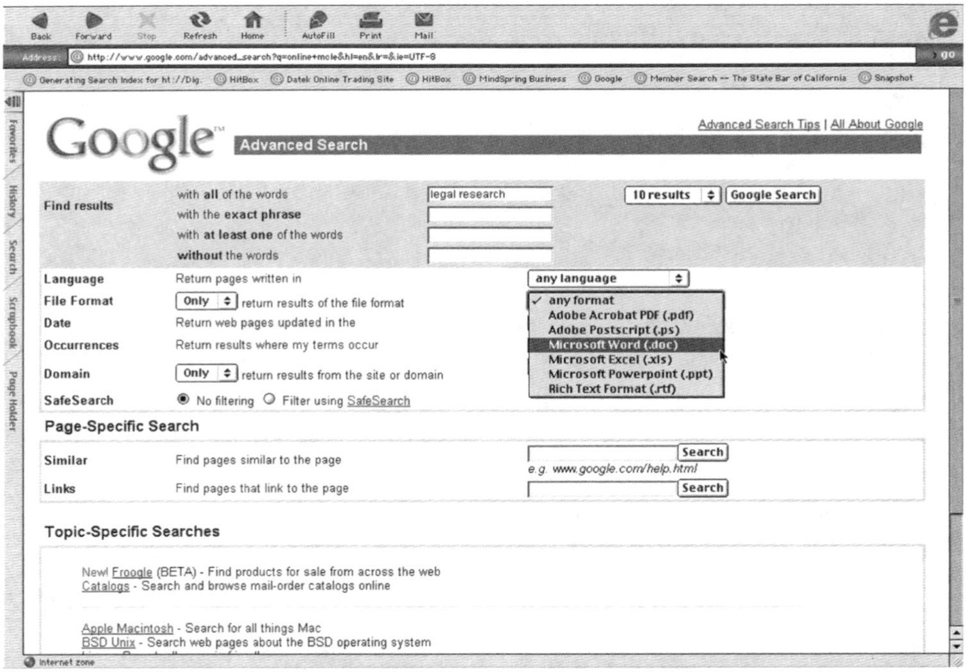

Figure 4-9. You can also use Google's Advanced Search page to limit your search to specific file formats. For example, entering the search terms **legal research** and selecting **File Format: Only return results of the file format Microsoft Word (.doc)** returns only Word documents containing the keywords "legal" and "research." Google™ is a trademark of Google Technology Inc.

Cache Is King

As stated earlier, no search engine offers a complete picture of all the content that is on the Web. Depending on how often a Web site is updated, or how often a search engine revisits the sites in its index, the information on which a search engine bases its results may be many weeks or months old.

For example, if a client wanted to sue for libel, based on a libelous statement posted on a Web site, the site owner could remove the libelous statement by the time a lawyer visited the site to view the statement. Clicking on Google or Yahoo!'s **Cached** link, you can access a version of the page as it appeared the last time the search engine's "robot" visited the site, that visit may have occurred before it was altered—and you can view the version that contained the allegedly libelous statement in question (as saved on the search engine's own server). There is a chance, however, that the cached page may still be displaying "live" information from a Web site. For more information on locating archival information on Internet sites, see the section on "Finding Extinct Pages and Archived Material" later in this chapter.

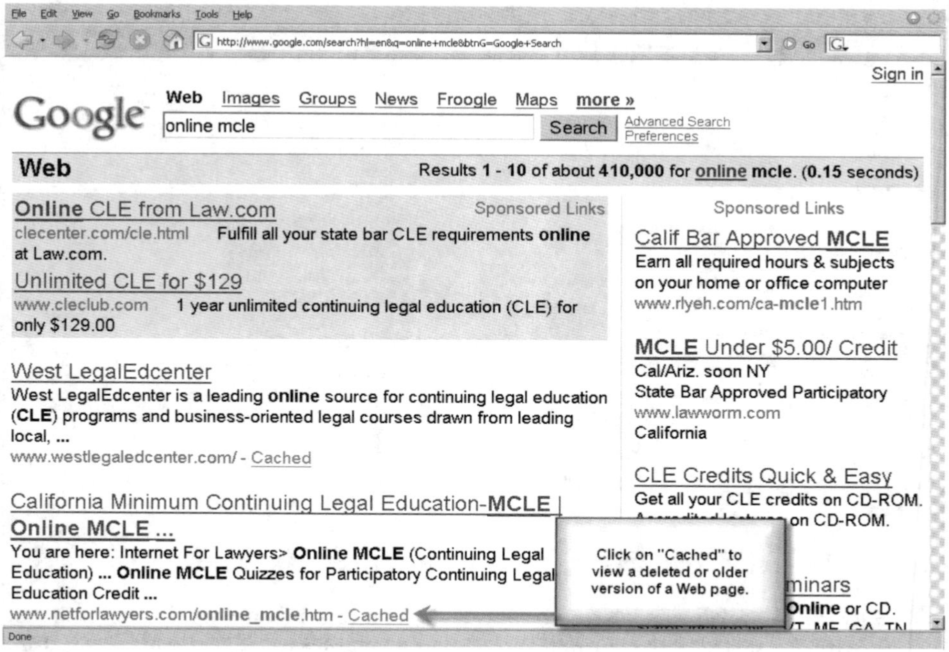

Figure 4-10. Google offers a **Cached** link accompanying nearly all of its returned results. **Cached** links to a saved version of the returned Web site as it appeared on the day that the Google search engine last visited the site. Google™ is a trademark of Google Technology Inc.

News Search

Yahoo! News and Google News searches collect recent news stories from sources around the world, updating them continuously throughout the day.

Google (**http://news.google.com**) searches over 4,500 news sources on a continual basis. Yahoo! News compiles its news from 7,000 news sources in 35 languages, continuously updating them. Both retain news stories in their index for approximately 30 days.

A recent Google News search for "iraqi oil" returned over 6,000 results. The first result included a story from the BBC that carried the qualifier "less than 11 hours ago." (You can sort your results list by **Date** or by **Relevance**.) Other stories listed the time they were collected as "less than 30 minutes ago," indicating the up-to-date nature of the search results. Under the first result were related news stories from other publications around the world. A sampling of some of the sources from which Google indexes news stories include

- Islamic Republic (of Iran) News Agency
- *Washington Post*
- News24 (South Africa)
- *Melbourne Herald Sun* (Australia)
- *Taipei Times*
- MSNBC
- Al-Jazeera (Qatar)
- *San Jose Mercury News*
- *Christian Science Monitor*

You can also browse the latest news headlines at both sites. The Google News home page lists news in a variety of categories (including **Top Stories, World, U.S., Business, Science/Technology, Entertainment,** and so on) in a directory style. Within those categories, stories are grouped together by subject, with stories from multiple sources that cover the same news subject arranged in subgroups. Google has recently added a prominent **Customize this Page** option in the upper right-hand corner of its News home page that allows you to arrange the categories in whatever order you prefer, or to add your own custom news category that includes results of a news search you define. Yahoo! News offers similar news content, organized into categories such as: **Top Stories, World, U.S. National, Politics, Business, Science, Technology, Entertainment, Sports, Odd News,** and **Opinion**. On its Advanced Search page, Google also added the ability to limit news searches by country or state, or to a specific publication.

For more information on locating news resources on the Internet, see Chapter 5, "General Factual Research."

Image Search

To build its index of images, Google looks at the text on the Web page surrounding an image, the accompanying caption, and other elements to determine the content and context of the 2.2 billion images (as of September 2005) in its searchable database at **http://images.google.com**. Yahoo! Images (**http://search.yahoo.com/images**) contains 1.6 billion images (as of September 2005). Both search engines display image results similarly, as thumbnail images, up to 20 per page. Each thumbnail lists the size (in bytes and pixels), file type, and URL of the image. Clicking on the thumbnail displays two frames. The top frame displays a larger view of the image. The lower frame shows the picture in context on the Web page where it resides. The images can also be viewed alone.

The image searches can be very effective. A Yahoo! Image search for "Carole Levitt" resulted in five hits, four of which were (different) photos of this book's coauthor. The fifth was a picture of the second edition of this book. Despite claims in the Google Image Search Frequently Asked Questions that "Google also uses sophisticated algorithms to remove duplicates," when we ran our "Carole Levitt image search at Google, we received twenty-two results, many of which were duplicates of the same image. Another strike against Google here is that eight of the images were not of (or related to Carole), and Yahoo! turned up two images that Google did not.

For more information on locating images on the Internet, see the section "Finding Video, Audio, and Images" later in this chapter.

Why Google is Still Our Favorite Search Engine

There are still a few functions/features found only at Google that make it stand out from the other search engines.

The opening screen features four tabs, two buttons, and a search box for entering search terms. There are no flashy ad banners. In fact, there's no advertising at all on the home page. The gaudiest thing on the page is the site's multicolored logo. The site's clean, uncluttered opening screen indicates that Google is ready to get down to the business of searching. (Yahoo! users can bypass that site's cluttered home page by going directly to **http://search.yahoo.com**).

As an antidote to the multitude of results returned for a search, more adventurous researchers can try Google's **I'm Feeling Lucky** button. This search returns just one site—and the searcher is taken directly to it. No list of results is presented. That site is the one deemed most relevant by Google's search algorithm and relevance weighting system.

As part of its quest to deliver relevant search results, Google employs a proprietary "PageRank" system to determine a Web site's value in relation to other pages. Similar to a lawyer using *Shepard's* or *Key Cite* to determine which other cases have relied on a case they are reading, the Page-Rank system weighs the number and quality of other Web sites that link to the site being ranked. As explained on its Web site, "Google interprets a link from page A to page B as a vote, by page A, for page B. But, Google looks at more than the sheer volume of votes, or links a page receives; it also analyzes the page that casts the vote. Votes cast by pages that are themselves 'important' weigh more heavily and help to make other pages 'important.'" To return the most useful and relevant search results, Google considers this PageRank as it matches the keywords of a search query with the text contained in Web pages its spiders have added to its index.

Search Within Results

Like the "Focus" feature on the pay version of LexisNexis and the "Locate" feature of Westlaw, Google also allows users to narrow down their list of results. By selecting the **Search within results** link at the bottom of each page of results, Google searchers can add additional key-

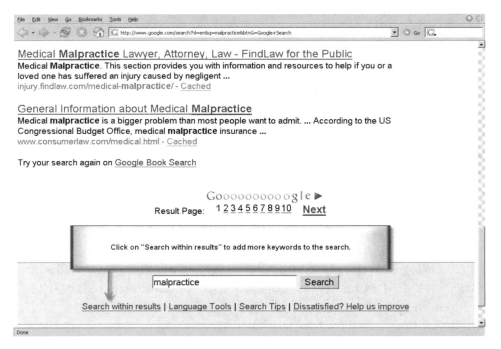

Figure 4-11. Google allows you to narrow your search by adding additional search terms and clicking the **Search within results** link on the bottom of the first page of your results. Google™ is a trademark of Google Technology Inc.

words to their search, instructing the search engine to search for those keywords only within the list of sites included in the results list currently being displayed.

Google People Finder

Google offers an easy way to retrieve phone numbers and addresses from its database.

The search engine has added street address and phone number information for residences and businesses to the results returned by a standard Google search. Results are limited to published, United States phone listings. To find listings for a business, you only need to type the business name, city, and state into the Google search box. The business's ZIP code can be substituted for the city and state if you know it. Conversely, you can conduct a reverse search to retrieve a complete listing for a business by entering only the area code and phone number.

To retrieve residential listings, users can type any of the following combinations into the Google search box:

- First name (or first initial), last name, city (state is optional)
- First name (or first initial), last name, state
- First name (or first initial), last name, area code
- First name (or first initial), last name, ZIP code
- Phone number, including area code
- Last name, city, state
- Last name, ZIP code

Phone number and address results are displayed at the top of results pages. Residential results have a phone icon to the left, while business results feature a compass icon to their left. (The compass icon identifies this as a "Google Local" result which includes address and phone number, and distance from the center point of the city indicated in the search. Clicking on the result link brings up additional information about the business, as well a map. (Yahoo! offers a similar "Local" search for business-related information. See page 143 for more information.)

In addition to the phone number results, if any, these searches will retrieve HTML documents on the Internet that contain the keywords included in the query.

Individuals can have their contact information removed from the Google database by filling in the form found at **http://www.google.com/help/pbremoval.html**.

Google Uses Wildcards for Proximity Searching

Google allows you to use a wild card (represented by an asterisk*) to take the place of one or more words. See pages 100-102 for a more-detailed description on conducting searches using Google.

Usenet Postings

Google offers a searchable archive of over 1 billion messages posted to public Usenet news groups back to 1981 at **http://groups.google.com**. Using the Advanced Groups Search, you can perform full-text searches or narrow the results down to a specific newsgroup or author. Locating postings by a specific author assumes that the author used their real name, or that the researcher knows the e-mail address or online alias of the individual for whose messages they are searching.

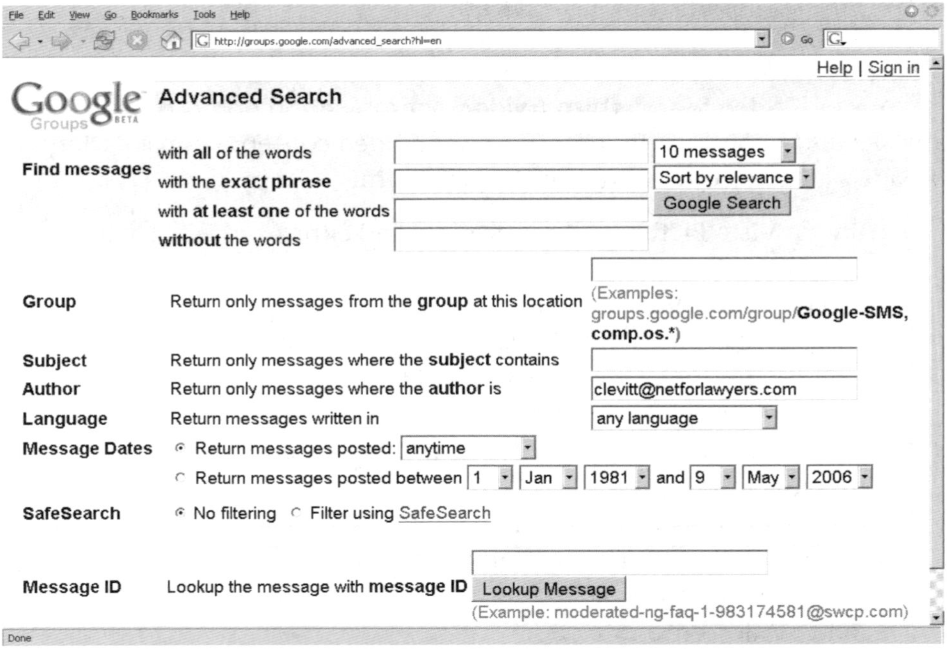

Figure 4-12. Google Groups Advanced Groups Search allows you to search for Usenet postings by a specific author using the person's name or e-mail address. Google™ is a trademark of Google Technology Inc.

Other Reasons Yahoo! Has Become a Strong Second

There are also some very useful features offered by Yahoo! that Google does not offer:

Subscription Search

On its Advanced Search page, Yahoo! allows you to search multiple, selected subscription sites—even if you don't have a subscription. You can search subscription content from a range of publications, including *Consumer Reports*, Factiva, Forrester Research, FT.com, IEEE, Lexis-Nexis (via its *Ala Carte* offering to solos and small firms), the *New England Journal of Medicine*, TheStreet.com and the *Wall Street Journal*. Check boxes allow you to pick which resources you want to search through. Subscriptions results are listed at the top of the results list. Next to the title of the result is the source from which the result comes. Clicking on any "Subscriptions" result brings up an abstract of the full item. The full article related to each result is available for sale by the site where the result resides. Prior subscriptions are not necessary, as the sites offer individual articles for sale on an ad-hoc basis. If you already have a subscription to the source, you can enter your username and password to access the item.

Video Search

Yahoo! Video Search (**http://video.search.yahoo.com/**) offers searchable access to commercial/entertainment video content from a variety of broadcast, cable, and online sources, including

- Buena Vista Pictures: Movie trailers and clips
- CBS News: News clips
- CMT: Video entertainment
- Discovery Communications: Video clips from Animal Planet, Discovery Channel, Discovery Health, Discovery Home, FitTV, TLC, Travel Channel, and Science Channel.
- IFILM: Movie clips and trailers, shorts/independent movies, viral movies, and music videos
- Internet Archive: Open Source movies, Prelinger Archives, Brick Films, Election 2004, PBS Computer Chronicles, and more
- Internet Broadcasting Systems: Local news clips
- MTV: Video entertainment
- Reuters: News clips
- Scripps Network: Home & Garden Television video clips, The Food Network video clips
- Stupid Videos: Fun and independent videos across a variety of genres
- The One Network: Movie trailers, celebrity interviews, music videos
- TVEyes: Bloomberg news clips including Morning Markets, World Financial Report, Marketline, Bloomberg on the Markets,

Bloomberg Now, Morning Call, In Focus, European Market Report, and Money & Politics
- VH1: Video entertainment

On the Advanced Search page, you can indicate specific file types for which you want to search:

- AVI
- MPEG
- Quicktime
- Windows Media
- Real
- Flash

You can also limit results by size or duration, as well as limit your search to specific Top Level Domains (TLDs—.com, .org, .edu, or .gov) or limit your search to a single URL.

A recent search for *Hurricane Katrina* returned over 7,700 results from CBS, CNN, Reuters, Bloomberg, and other local TV stations, among other sources.

FactBites.com

http://www.factbites.com/

Purpose: A topic-based search engine that offers users meaningful and more-detailed abstracts for every site in their search results.

Content: FactBites.com dares you to compare it to Google's search engine abilities, especially when it comes to presenting encyclopedia-style content. It is a beta version and its Web site is clean and simple. Similar to the Google interface, you enter your search request into a box under the FactBites logo and click the "Find" button. Underneath the search box, you can click on **More** or **Info**.

When you enter your request, the results page will list a three-sentence abstract of each listing. FactBites offers a topic-based search refinement that allows a more relevant search on your topic. For example, we asked for information on former President Bill Clinton and received many results from encyclopedia Web sites. On the top of the results page we could click on the following to further refine our search: **People, United States,** and **Government and Politics**. On the right-hand side of the results page another search opportunity appears: **Related Topics**.

Our View: FactBites is an interesting and useful, if limited, search engine. Many of the topics that would be of interest to lawyers (e.g., "online mcle" or "malpractice insurance") yield less-than-useful results; however, a search for "insurance fraud" did yield worthwhile resources. Fact-Bites is somewhat limited in scope, but if used with that in mind, you could discover quite a bit of useful information from using this site.

Metasearch Sites

Another variety of Internet search engine is the metasearch site, which enables simultaneous searching using several individual search engines—a search engine of search engines. Metasearch sites are good for searching for very obscure subjects or for searching the most Internet space possible. The downside of these tools is that they are generally less precise and accurate than an individual search using each search engine. They also do not include results from the most comprehensive search engines (including Google) or those that (usually) return the most relevant results. Some of the more popular metasearch sites are

- Clusty at **http://www.clusty.com**
- Teoma at **http://www.teoma.com**
- Dogpile at **http://www.dogpile.com**
- HotBot at **http://www.hotbot.com**
- Ixquick at **http://www.ixquick.com**
- Metacrawler at **http://www.metacrawler.com/**
- Surfwax at **http://www.surfwax.com**
- Webcrawler at **http://www.webcrawler.com/**

Twingine

http://www.twingine.com

Purpose: To search Yahoo! and Google simultaneously

Content: Twingine is a metasearch site that simultaneously submits your search to Yahoo! and Google. All you do is enter your search terms into the search box and click the **Search** button. Twingine displays results from Yahoo! and Google in side-by-side windows.

In the Twingine frame that remains above the results, the **Maximize** link above the Yahoo! results window opens the Yahoo! results window full screen. Clicking your browser's **Back** button returns you to Twingine's side-by-side display. (There is also a **Maximize** link that does the same for the Google results.) Clicking the **Next** link will display the next page of results from both search engines.

Our View: You may have read about this site when it was originally launched in the spring of 2005 with the name YaGoohoo!gle.com. It started out as an April Fool's posting on the Slashdot "News for Nerds" site (**http:// slashdot.org/article.pl?sid=05/03/31/2117206**), by 31-year-old Norwegian technology architect Asgeir Nilsen. In that post, Nilsen claimed to have knowledge that Yahoo! and Google were planning to announce a merger and that the new company would be called YaGoohoo!gle. Soon however, Nilsen found that thousands of people were seeking out the fictitious company via search engine searches or by visiting the YaGoohoo!gle.com Web address that Nilsen had registered just days before. So, Nilsen created a site at the YaGoohoogle.com domain that displayed Yahoo! and Google results next to one another.

Yahoo! and Google apparently didn't appreciate the April Fool's joke—particularly the YaGoohoo!gle logo, which was comprised of the Yahoo! and Google logos cut and pasted back together to form the new name. Within a month of launching YaGoohoo!gle, Nilsen wrote on his blog, "Both Yahoo! and Google have issued notices of trademark infringements. Instead of contacting me directly, they sent intimidating e-mails to my DNS provider. I have tried to argue with them, but have not had any success with that (yet)."

The issue seems to be resolved with the re-launch of the simultaneous search under the Twingine banner. A search of the Betterwhois domain registration database shows that the YaGoohoo!gle domain is now owned by Yahoo!.

Tip: While you can view Yahoo! and Google results side-by-side using Dogpile, Twingine's display is less cluttered and makes the "Sponsored Links" stand out more than they do in Dogpile's display.

For more information on using metasearch sites in your searching, see the "Cost-Effective and Time-Saving Search Tips" section in Chapter 3, "Search Strategies."

Finding Video, Audio, and Images

More and more each day, the Internet-age axiom "you can find anything online" becomes truer. It is especially true of multimedia content. Whether you're looking for audio clips from famous films (at **http://www.moderntimes.com/palace/audio.htm** or h**ttp://www.moviesounds.com**), from the Kennedy White House (**www.gwu.edu/~nsarchiv/nsa/cuba_mis_cri/audio.htm**), of aviator Charles Lindbergh (**www.charleslindbergh.com/audio/index.asp**), or of the U.S. Supreme Court's "Greatest Hits" (oral arguments at **http://www.oyez.org/oyez/frontpage**), it's all available online for free.

When preparing client presentations, or multimedia arguments for arbitration or mediation, the addition of video news coverage, stock photos, sound effects, and clip art can make your compelling argument even more memorable. Additionally, photos, diagrams, or videos of a product from a manufacturer's Web site might be useful in a product liability case.

Finding the video, audio, or image files is just half the battle. If you want to use them you have to download them to your own computer; and they can be *very large*. If you do not have a high-speed connection to the Internet, it can take a very long time for the files to download to your computer. If you are using a dial-up connection to the Internet, there is also the possibility that you could get disconnected before the file has downloaded completely.

Once you have the files on your own computer, you'll find that the audio and video files come in a variety of file formats. The different formats are distinguishable by the three-letter extension that follows the file-name (such as .wav, .ram, .asf, .mov, .mp3, and so on). To see and/or hear these clips, it is necessary to have the appropriate media player software installed on your computer. The three major media player programs are available as free downloads. Versions are available for Windows and Mac operating systems. (Paid versions with more features are also available.)

The major media players are

- Quicktime, at **http://www.apple.com/quicktime/download**
- RealOne Player, at **http://www.real.com**
- Windows Media Player, at **http://www.windowsmedia.com/download**

Not all media players play all types of files. Therefore it is advisable to have more than one player installed.

With any online audio or video resource, be sure to check the source Web site for any usage requirements or restrictions, or copyright information. When necessary, be certain to obtain permission to use the audio or video element in your own work.

Finding Video

For news coverage, check out the Yahoo! Video search mentioned earlier in this chapter or your local TV stations' sites for footage of local events. Internet For Lawyers maintains a page linking to major market and network news gathering organizations at **http://www.netforlawyers .com/TVlinks.htm**. Also see Chapter 5, "General Factual Research," for more information on locating news sources online.

AltaVista

http://www.altavista.com/video

Purpose:	To locate video clips on the Internet for download.
Content:	AltaVista offers the ability to limit your search results to video files. The results are returned with small still images from the videos (called thumbnails), as well as links to the full video on the Internet.
Our View:	By using the drop-down menu and check boxes under the search box, you can specify file types (AVI, MPEG,

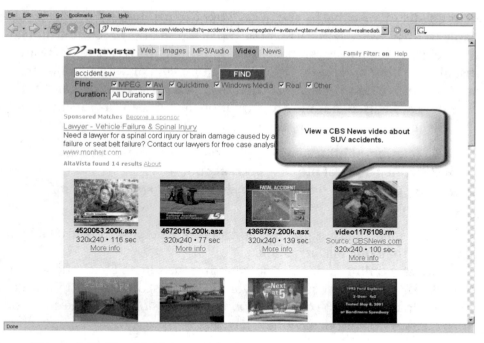

Figure 4-13. The AltaVista search engine is an excellent resource to search for multimedia content. In early 2003, the company expanded its index of multimedia files to encompass over 240 million unique media files, including images, video clips, MP3s, and other audio files. Reproduced with permission of AltaVista Company. All rights reserved.

Quicktime, Windows Media, Real, and Other), as well as selecting the duration of the audio clips returned. Additionally, you can choose to limit your search to include content from AltaVista partner sites, which include MSNBC and RollingStone.com. (Content from the partner sites is copyrighted material.)

Tip: The Advanced Search also allows you to filter out so-called "noise" images such as buttons and banners that might be included on a Web site.

Alltheweb

http://www.alltheweb.com

Purpose: To locate streaming video and video clips on the Internet for download.

Content: Alltheweb claims to have "hundreds of millions" of multimedia files in its index. To search for video, click the **Video** tab at the top of the home page.

Our View: To conduct the most targeted search, click the **advanced search** option next to the search box. This allows you to specify file types (such as AVI, MPEG, Real, Quicktime, and so on), as well as giving you the option to view results from static downloadable files, or from streaming video sources.

Tip: For the greatest number of results, select **All** formats and **Both** streams or downloads.

Prelinger Video Archive at Archive.org

http://www.archive.org/details/prelinger

Content: The archive contains links to more than 4,000 films digitized by the Prelinger Archive. The collection consists primarily of instructional, educational, advertising, and documentary films (in a mixture of AVI and MPG file formats), as well as home movies dating from 1903 through the 1980s. Most films can be viewed as streaming media or downloaded. All material is in the public domain. In 2002, the Library of Congress acquired the Prelinger Archive of over 48,000 titles. (See **http://www.oc.gov/rr/mopic**.) The 4,000 titles currently at this site were collected by Rick Prelinger subsequent to the Library of Congress acquisition.

Our View: This offbeat collection of films includes cigarette commercials from the 1950s, Civil Defense films regarding preparation for a nuclear attack, and other items that might prove worthwhile in certain class action suits.

Tip: The Prelinger Archive is just one of many video collections accessible from the Archive.org site.

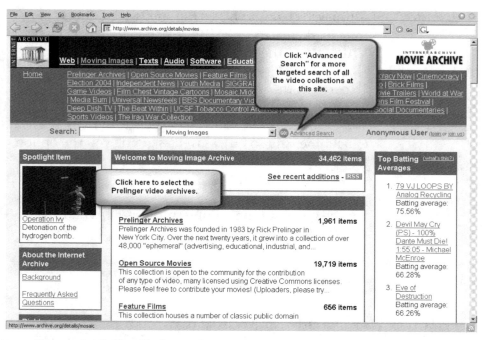

Figure 4-14. The Prelinger Archive presents a searchable database of over 48,000 advertising, educational, industrial, and amateur films dating back to 1903. The Advanced Search allows you to create a very targeted search of all the video collections on the Archive.org Moving Image site. Search by creator, title, date, description, etc.

Finding Audio

Podcasts, a recent phenomenon in Web audio, allows anyone with a Web connection and a Web site to post their own (sort of) taped radio shows, on any topic, to the Web for others to download. Though not initiated or endorsed by Apple Computers, the name comes from the company's popular iPod portable digital audio player. You can use a specialized directory such as **iPodder.org** to locate podcasts on numerous general topics. To locate law-related podcasts, click the "podcast" category of the law-related directory, The Blogs of Law (**http://www.theblogsoflaw .com**). For more information on podcasts, see Chapter 20, "Weblogs, RSS Feeds, and Podcasts."

FindSounds.com

http://www.findsounds.com

Purpose: To locate various sounds on the Internet for download.

Content: FindSounds doesn't have content of its own, *per se*. It is an Internet search engine, like Google and AltaVista, that searches only for sound effects and musical instrument samples on the Internet. Clicking on any of the results usually opens or plays the sound automatically. You can usually save the sound to your computer to use in your own work.

Our View: You can choose three types of sound files (WAV, AIFF, and AU) for which to search. You can also dictate the quality of the sound returned by selecting the minimum resolution (8-bit or 16-bit) and minimum sample rates (8,000 to 44,100 Hertz).

If you are making a presentation to a claims adjuster about your client's accident, the addition of screeching tires, crashing glass, or an ambulance siren coupled with pictures from the accident scene or of the client's injuries could help punctuate the seriousness of the accident.

Tip: To return the largest number of sound results, select all three sound file types, 8-bit minimum resolution, and 8,000 Hertz as the minimum sample rate. Also, the site claims to filter out audio files containing obscenities, claiming " . . . this site is safe for children."

AltaVista

http://www.altavista.com/audio

Purpose: To locate various sounds on the Internet for download.

Content: AltaVista is a general-purpose search engine that offers you the ability to limit your search results to just audio files. Clicking on any of the results takes you to the Web page where the sound file can be accessed.

Our View: You can specify file types (WAV, MP3, Windows Media, Real), as well as selecting the duration of the audio clips returned.

Tip: AltaVista includes copyright information in its results. You should note, however, that lack of information in the copyright field does not mean it is in the public domain.

Alltheweb

http://www.alltheweb.com

Purpose: To locate various types of audio clips and sound on the Internet for download.

Content: Alltheweb boasts "hundreds of millions" of multimedia files in its index. To search for audio, click the **Audio** tab at the top of the home page.

Our View: Alltheweb's audio search is the weakest of its multimedia search functions. It currently offers no Advanced Search options. While the search results include only MP3 files (primarily songs), Alltheweb offers a unique **see other files in this folder** link under each of the results. Clicking it returns a new page of results that lists other audio files stored in the same location on the Internet.

Finding Images

Google

http://www.images.google.com

Purpose: To locate various types of images on the Internet for download.

Content: In September 2005, Google boasted that it had indexed nearly 2.2 billion images, up from nearly a half million in 2003.

Our View: To return the images most relevant to your search terms, Google looks at the text on the Web page around the image and the accompanying caption, among other elements, to help determine an image's content. The Advanced Search page offers sophisticated search combinations, including:

- Boolean logic
- Phrase searching
- File type limitation
- File size limitation
- Color or black and white

Results are displayed as thumbnail images, up to twenty per page. Below each thumbnail is the file name showing the file type (such as JPG or GIF), image resolution (in pixels), file size (in bytes), and the URL of the image. Clicking on a thumbnail brings a larger view of the image in the upper frame of the page, and a view of the picture in context on the Web page where it resides in the lower frame. The images can also be viewed alone.

Tip: Use the Advanced Image Search page. There, you can also limit your search to a single domain (such as www.netforlawyers.com). This can be extremely useful if you are looking for photos of executives or products from a particular company. Using the **Return images from the site or domain** option, you can search only that company's Web site.

Yahoo Image Search

http://search.yahoo.com/images

Purpose: To locate various types of images on the Internet for download.

Content: As of September 2005, Yahoo! Images boasted 1.6 billion images.

Similar to Google's Image Search, Yahoo! Image Search's Advanced Search page offers sophisticated search combinations, including:

- Boolean logic
- Phrase searching
- File size limitation
- Color or black and white

Also similar to Google, Yahoo! Image Search results are displayed as thumbnail images, up to twenty per page. Below each thumbnail is the file name showing the file type (such as .JPG or .GIF), image resolution (in pixels), file size (in bytes), and the URL of the Web page where the image was found.

Clicking on a thumbnail brings a larger view of the image in the upper frame of the page, and a view of the picture in context on the Web page where it resides in the lower frame. The images can also be viewed alone.

Tip: Use the Advanced Image Search page. There, you can also limit your search to selected Top Level Domains (e.g., only ".com" or ".gov" sites) or a single domain (such as **www.netforlawyers.com**). This can be extremely useful if you are looking for photos of executives or products from a particular company. Using the "Only search in this domain/site" option, you can search only that company's Web site.

AltaVista

http://www.altavista.com/image

Purpose: To locate various types of images on the Internet for download.

Content: AltaVista also offers the ability to limit your search results to image files. Like AltaVista's video search, results are returned with thumbnails, as well as a link to the original image on the Internet.

Our View: You can choose to search for either photos or graphics (or both), as well as designating color or black and white (or both). Additionally, you can choose to search the Web only, or also include content from AltaVista partner sites that include Corbis.com and Rolling-Stone.com. (Content from the partner sites is copyrighted material.)

Tip: You can filter out "noise" images such as buttons and banners by not selecting the **Buttons/Banners** check box.

Alltheweb

http://www.alltheweb.com

Purpose: To locate various types of images on the Internet for download.

Content: Alltheweb boasts "hundreds of millions" of multimedia files in its index. To search for images, click the **Pictures** tab at the top of the home page.

Our View: To conduct the most targeted search, click the **advanced search** option next to the search box. This allows you to use check boxes to specify file types (.JPEG, .GIF, .BMP), color (color, grayscale [black and white and shades of gray], line art (black and white only), and background transparency (transparent, nontransparent)

Tip: For the greatest number of results, select these check boxes: for files types, **All formats;** for color, **All types;** and for background, **Both types.**

Corbis Archive

To search: To license: **$** [Registration Form]

http://www.corbis.com

Purpose: To locate professional and news photos.

Content: Founded in 1989 by Microsoft's Bill Gates, the Corbis collection is made up of more than 65 million images, 2.1 million of which are online. The collection includes the holdings of the former Bettman and United Press International photo archives and contains images that date back (at least) to the Civil War.

Search the database by entering keywords or phrases into the image search box on the home page. Thumbnail versions of corresponding images are returned in the results list. Clicking on a thumbnail opens a larger version of the image (with a Corbis "watermark"). Click the **Information** tab above the image for more information on the photo and its permitted uses. Usage restrictions and licensing fees vary from image to image.

Our View: The famous images and news photographs available from the Corbis Archive can be very persuasive to mediators, arbitrators, and jurors, or in business presentations. Images include asbestos cleanups, lung cancer effects, car crashes, cigarette ads with celebrities, among many other subjects.

Tip: Be certain the image you select is available for the use for which you want it. Also see Corbis's business presentation site at **http://bizpresenter.corbis.com** to license business-themed photos, cartoons, and illustrations for inclusion in presentations.

Finding Extinct Pages and Archived Material
Isn't the Most Current Information Better?

You might wonder why you'd want to find old information that has been altered or removed from the Internet completely. After all, aren't we supposed to be looking for the most current information?

- What if your client claims to have been libeled on a competitor's Web site? Your client swears the offending comments were posted, but when you visit the site, the offending statements are nowhere to be found.
- What if your client is being sued for theft of trade secrets by a competitor? Your client swears he got the information off their Web site, but when you visit the site, the information is nowhere to be found.
- What if you'd read an article on opposing counsel's Web site that ends up contradicting a point they made later in arbitration, but the other firm has taken it down from the site when you go back to look for it?

There may still be a way to find the information you need!

War Story: Using the Wayback Machine

Marcia Burris, library manager at Ogletree, Deakins, Nash, Smoak & Stewart, P.C., in Greenville, South Carolina, tells this story:

"I needed to confirm the contents of a two-year-old news article that appeared on the Internet. The story was about a mugging and was needed to verify an individual's date of injury in a litigation matter our firm was involved in. The story had appeared in the *Daily Star,* 'The First Bangladeshi Daily Newspaper on the Internet,' but the archives from that year were no longer online.

"My e-mail to the editor may have gone through, but I got no response. My e-mail to the Webmaster bounced back.

"I also tried looking in other sources on Westlaw and Lexis for coverage of the same story, but found nothing.

"After posing the question on a research LISTERV, a number of people suggested the Wayback Machine. I was able to find the archived version of the online paper for the date I was looking for and printed out the article I needed."

As we have mentioned many times in this book, material on the Internet changes constantly. This can be a boon or bane to a lawyer searching for information. While Web page changes usually result in more information being available, the opposite can also be true.

For a variety of reasons, a Web site owner might remove information from a Web site. Just because information has been removed from a site does not (necessarily) mean that it is gone forever. Here are two ways you might be able to retrieve that information after it has been deleted from the site owner's Web server.

Internet Archive (the Wayback Machine)

http://www.archive.org

Purpose: To retrieve older versions of Web pages.

Content: In 1996, the Internet Archive set about building a permanent historical record of that ephemeral new

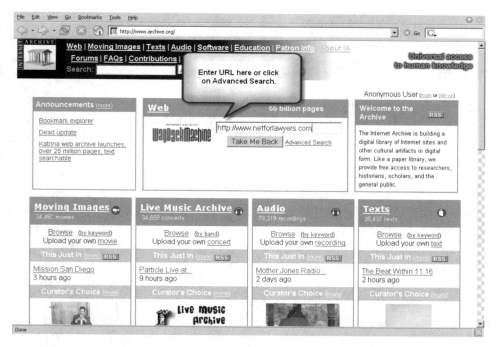

Figure 4-15. The Wayback Machine at Archive.org has archived versions of many Web sites dating back to 1996. Its Advanced Search allows you to see side-by-side comparisons of current and archived versions of a particular Web site.

medium, the World Wide Web. Since then, the Internet Archive has been collaborating with the Library of Congress, the Smithsonian Institution, and others to store and record Web pages. The Internet Archive made its collection available to the public via its Wayback Machine Web site in October 2001. In August 2006, the site boasted more than 55 billion Web pages in its archive, up from 10 billion only three years earlier.

Our View: While the Wayback Machine's archive is not complete, it does offer a rare opportunity to view Web site content that has been changed or removed from the Internet. Type the URL of any site you are interested in viewing into the search box on the Archive.org home page to comb the archive's hundreds of terabytes of data. Results are returned in a table listing the target site's stored pages by the date they were modified and added to the archive. Clicking on any of the returned links brings up the stored version of that page as it appeared on the date indicated.

Clicking on the **Advanced Search** option underneath the **Take Me Back** button on the site's home page gives you additional options for homing in on the pages you want from the target Web site. You can request results be returned only within a specific date range. (If you don't select a date range, the results will include links to all of the versions of your target site in the Wayback Machine's archive.) You can also request that the results show check boxes to allow comparison of two versions of a page.

Tip: • The archive has seemingly stored complete versions of the Web sites for that particular date. For example, if you were to view the Internet For Lawyers Web site as it appeared in May of 2000, you would be able to click through all the various pages then available.
  • If available, a side-by-side comparison of the opposition's Web site, showing changes detrimental to your client, can be very persuasive in an arbitration, mediation, or trial.

- Selecting a date range in the Advanced Search results in the first instance of an archived page for the target site within the specified range. Not specifying a range and using the comparison feature will give you a better sense of the changes made to the site over time.

Google

http://www.google.com

Purpose: To retrieve older versions of Web pages.

Content: When Google adds most pages to its index, it also takes a snapshot of the page, adding it to Google's cache of stored Web pages. This allows Google to show you where your keywords appear in the returned page, or to display the page in the event that it later becomes unavailable. It also creates a viewable record of the page before it changed or became unavailable. The date on which Google captured its "cached" version of the page is displayed at the very top of the page.

Our View: If a page is changed (or removed from the Internet) after it was added to the Google index and before your search, you may still be able to access an earlier version by clicking on the **Cached** link, if one accompanies your search result (see Figure 4-16 on the next page). When the cached page is displayed, your search terms are highlighted on the page.

Tip:
- We can't really be certain how long an archived version of a Web page will remain in the Google cache. On average, Google revisits Web pages once a month (though some are visited on a significantly more frequent basis). The older cached version is replaced by a newer cached version after Google revisits the page.
- Additionally, the **Cached** link is not available for all results. Web site owners can request that Google not cache their pages.

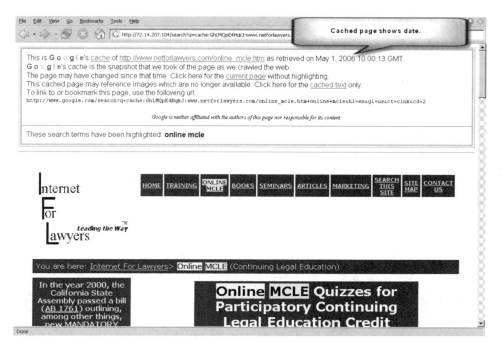

Figure 4-16. Clicking on the **Cached** page link returns a snapshot of the text of the target Web page on the day that Google's robots last visited it (including the date of the visit, which is displayed at the top). Nontext elements such as images or movies seen in a cached page are not actually cached on the Google servers, but are fed live from the target Web page's server if still loaded there.

The Google cache stores only the HTML content of a Web page on Google's servers (the actual HTML code that makes up the page, including any text visible on the page). One major drawback of the Google cache is that it *does not* store non-HTML information such as images (photos, buttons, banners, and so on), video, audio, or multimedia files (such as Macromedia Flash files). When displaying the cached page, Google's server retrieves this non-HTML content from its original location on the Web server where the cached page was originally stored. Therefore you might find large empty spaces with little red X's in place of the non-HMTL content if those files have been removed from their original locations; or you might be viewing more current, live graphics or video content from the current version of a page along with the archived text content stored in the Google cache.

Yahoo now also offers cached versions of many of the sites in their index. Yahoo! presents its cached material in much the same way as Google. Yahoo! does not include the date on which the cached version was captured, but it does include a link directly to the Archive.org collection of old versions of the same page.

Like Google and Yahoo!, Archive.org also stores primarily the HTML content of the pages it archives, but in many instances, it does also store non-HTML content associated with the pages stored in its archive, but not all of the images, and not for all of the pages. Therefore, you may or may not get to see the full view of the old version of the Web page when viewing these old versions of pages stored in the Google or Yahoo! cache or at Archive.org.

Fagan Finder URLinfo

http://www.faganfinder.com/urlinfo/

Purpose: Provides comprehensive information about URLs.

Content: URLinfo presents a number of tools for finding information about a URL or Web site all in one place. To begin, you would enter a URL in the box at the top of the screen. Clicking the **View Page** button opens that URL in a frame under a series of tabs at the top of the page. There are tabs labeled **General Information** (Alexa stats, Google PageRank, page count, text analyzer, etc.); **Cache** (from different sources including Google, Gigablast, and the Internet Archive); **Develop**; and **Blogs/Feeds**. You can get all of this detailed URL information from this one page. Another nifty time-saving device that can be found on the site is the ability to create bookmarklets (see Glossary).

Our View: Fagan Finder's URLinfo makes gathering large amounts of information about a Web site, from a variety of sources, quick and simple. An easy layout allows for anyone to discover the necessary information.

Tip: URLinfo can be a good source to access cached versions of pages that are no longer available on the Internet from many sources, including the *Internet Archive*.

Local Searching

If you are traveling to meet with a prospective client or to take (or defend) a deposition in an unfamiliar city, it can be very useful to get information on the neighborhood where you'll be visiting in order to plan your time there. In the past, this would usually require buying a tourist guide or some similar book. These books were usually limited to major metropolitan areas. Even the tourbooks offered by the AAA might not cover the precise neighborhood you needed.

Now, Google and Yahoo! have created "local" searches that allow us to locate businesses by name or type within geographical boundaries we determine.

Google Local Search (New Feature)

http://local.google.com

Purpose:	To locate businesses in a particular region.
Content:	From its database of billions of Web pages and other sources. Google Local Search delivers information regarding local (U.S.) businesses in a particular area, based on the search parameters you enter. The company also plans to include local information for international markets in the future.
	Returned results include: a phone number, street address, a list of Web sites of related business in the locality in which you're searching, store reviews, and other related information where available. Clicking on a business name delivers a new page featuring a map and directions to the selected business, and more related Web pages.
Our View:	Using the local search function is as easy as typing in a keyword that describes a business (e.g., photocopying) and a ZIP code, or the name of a city or town. Google combines this information with comprehensive local business, map, and service information drawn from a wide variety of U.S. databases, such as the yellow pages and other sources.

Figure 4-17. Searching the keywords *bar association Chicago* in the Google Local Search brings back results showing the address, phone number, and map of various bar associations in Chicago. Google™ is a trademark of Google Technology Inc.

Tip: If needed, users can limit or expand their results to include listings within a 1-mile, 5-mile, 15-mile, or 45-mile radius of a specific location by using the links in the upper right-hand corner of the results pages.

Yahoo! Local Beta

http://local.yahoo.com

Purpose: To locate businesses and services within a local area.

Content: Yahoo! has also developed a local search option. It combines Yahoo Yellow Pages, Yahoo Maps, and Yahoo Search to deliver its results. This easy-to-read home page asks you to enter the type of business or service you are looking for and a location (by street, city, state, or ZIP code).

Search results are displayed 10 to a page, similar to regular Yahoo! search results, sorted by relevance to your search terms. You may also choose to sort the results alphabetically, by rating (stars given by personal reviews), by price, or by distance (or other criteria depending on the type of business or service you're looking for) by selecting those options on the left-hand side of the results list. Another interesting option is the ability to view the 10 listed results on a map together. This can be done by clicking on **View Results on Map** using the map icon in the upper right-hand corner. It is also possible to view your result on a map as a single entity.

Each result offers address, phone, and Yellow Pages category information. Some may also have Web sites listed.

Our View: Despite all of these useful features, the database needs some refinement. Initial searches for "restaurants" within 50 miles of "Los Angeles, CA" and "Chicago, IL" returned zero results, while a similar search for "New York, NY" retrieved over 24,000 listings. (More recent searches have returned similar results for Los Angeles and Chicago.) This will be a handy search source once these bugs are worked out. It's an easy-to-use tool that combines many of Yahoo!'s features and performs well when it returns results. This site would be especially helpful for travelers, or those looking to plan lunch or dinner meetings near their clients' (or potential clients') offices, as well as those traveling out of town for depositions, etc.

Tip: The **Find Nearby** option that's available when you click on a results map link is very useful. This allows you to locate ATMs, hotels, parking, transportation, and restaurants that are in the area of your search result. Once you click on one of those options, a map will pop up indicating the locations of nearby amenities, with numbers that correspond to names listed on the right side of the page. From here you can conduct another **Map Nearby** search to look for anything else you might need.

Organizing & Retrieving the Information You Find

Once you have found all of this information on the Internet and made note of the most useful, one of the most daunting tasks is finding that information again, when you need it at some point in the future. Thankfully, there are some useful, free tools that can help you organize, locate, and retrieve the information when you need to refer to it later.

Google Desktop Search

http://desktop.google.com/

Purpose:	How many times have you searched for a document in your Word files only to learn hours later it was actually in an e-mail message? The Google Desktop Search application solves this problem by full-text searching through everything on your hard drive simultaneously—from Word documents to e-mail to Web history and chats to Web pages you've visited previously (even when you're not online)—and even to documents you've deleted (documents that are still in the Recycle Bin or Trash). The Google Desktop Search, like the Google search engine, creates an index of documents on your hard drive and maintains cached versions of the documents as you make changes.
Content:	To download the desktop, visit **http://desktop.google.com/**. It's free and takes only seconds if you have a high-speed connection. Your computer must have Windows® XP or Windows® 2000 Service Pack 3+ and you must be using Microsoft Internet Explorer version 5 or newer, Netscape 7.1 or newer, Mozilla 1.4 or newer, or Firefox. Once the download is complete, you'll have an

icon on your desktop labeled, aptly enough, "Desktop Setup.exe." Double click on this to begin the installation process. During the installation process you are given the opportunity to opt out of providing Google with non-identifying search usage information. After the installation process is complete, double click the Google Desktop Search icon that appears on your desktop. The Google Desktop Search page appears. Enter your keywords into the search box and select **Search Desktop**. (You can also select **Search the Web** from here).

In a sample search, we entered the words *Google Deskbar* into the Google search box and "8 results stored in your computer" appeared at the top of the results list. We clicked on this link and found a link to a current document titled "To Do" and a link to eight previously cached versions of the same document maintained by the Google Desktop Search. Although the search terms did not appear in the current document, it did appear in some of the cached versions.

Our View: The Desktop Search is useful, but still has a number of quirks to be worked out. For example, when we first searched the words *Google Deskbar* no results appeared, but when we ran the same search later, results appeared. Another quirk seems to be that the Desktop Search includes documents in the results list that may not include your search term. However, the term is usually found in one or more of the cached versions of the document that the Google Desktop Search has created as part of its index. When viewing a current document from the Desktop Search result list, search terms are not highlighted, but if you view a cached version, they are. We'd prefer to see the words highlighted in the current version.

Tip: Even if you are not using the Google Desktop Search, but simply conducting a traditional Google search of the Web, the results listed at the top will show what's available on your hard drive and then the Web results follow. By clicking on **Desktop Preferences**, you can turn the integration of desktop results into Google Web searches on or off. There are also a variety of other customization options available on the **Desktop Preferences** page.

Google Desktop's Sidebar

http://desktop.google.com/features.html#sidebar

Purpose: Sidebar is an application that, as the name implies, sits on the side of your computer's desktop. It automatically gathers personalized weather, stock updates, e-mail, RSS/Atom feeds, news, and other information that you can define.

Content: Sidebar is a feature that works only if you have first installed the Google Desktop. Once installed, Sidebar is automatically personalized to the user—no manual configuration is required—although it is possible to make your own customizations. The following functions (called "plug-ins") are included in Sidebar:

- **Weather**: A 4-day forecast, a multiple-location weather locator, and the ability to click on weather locations to see more details are just some of the features provided in this pane.
- **Stocks**: When available, prices are shown in real time. Click on the ticker symbol to get all the relevant information (point change, current price, percent change, daily graph, news, etc.). Individual stock tickers are added or deleted in the **Options** menu.
- **E-mail**: You can read your e-mail as soon as it arrives. The **Options** menu allows you to add filters, based on what you want to receive or do not want to receive.
- **Web Clips & Photos**: You can read RSS and Atom feeds that are retrieved and updated every 30 minutes from the Web. Feeds are automati-

cally added based on the Web pages you visit, but it is also possible to manually add a feed by entering its URL into Sidebar's **Options** menu. Photos found in frequently visited RSS/Atom feed Web pages will also be automatically added to the **Photos** panel (a manual option is available as well). These photos can be viewed in a slide show format.

- **News**: The latest news headlines are automatically displayed in the **News** pane. Sidebar "learns" what news is interesting to you by tracking which stories you read, and Sidebar also allows you to mark items as "uninteresting" by clicking the **Don't show me items like this** button.

- **Scratch Pad**: The **Scratch Pad** offers a space to type and save notes. Each keystroke that you make in the Scratch Pad is automatically saved to the Scratch Pad, so there is little chance of losing data. It also includes an option that saves the entire Scratch Pad anywhere on your hard drive that you specify, which clears the pad entirely, letting you begin again with a clean slate.

- **Quick View**: **Quick View** is a handy list of frequently used Web pages, files, and applications. Double-click any entry to open it. You can even "star" items to move them to the top of the list.

Our View: With Sidebar, Google moves one step closer to usurping Microsoft's control of the computer desktop. It is hard to say if the clutter would increase or decrease. Certainly the intention is to simplify. We like the idea that it keeps track of the frequently visited Web sites and automatically adds that information into the various plug-in areas (such as News, Stocks, or RSS/Atom feeds). If you are already a user of Google Desktop, the Sidebar is a useful addition.

Tip: If you don't want Sidebar to automatically add information from the various Web sites you visit, you can go to **Options** to uncheck the box for that particular plug-in.

For example, if you only want to add stocks manually, click on **Options** and choose to uncheck the **Automatically add stocks** check box. Additional plug-ins are available to extend the features of sidebar at **http://desktop.google.com/plugins/**. Sidebar works only with Windows XP and 2000 (Service Pack 3) Operating Systems. Also, be sure you have plenty of memory before installing Sidebar.

MyStuff (from Ask.com) [formerly MyJeeves]

http://mystuff.ask.com/

Purpose:	To save/organize searches and results to build your own personal Web "database."
Content:	MyStuff can be accessed by clicking on the **MyStuff** link on the **search tools** menu on the left hand side of the Ask Jeeves homepage, or going directly to **http://mystuff.ask.com**. Registration is requested, but is not required. Benefits of registration include expanded storage space (you have a limit of 1,000 saved items without registration), access to your information from any Internet-connected computer, and privacy protection.

On the left side of your personal MyStuff page, under the heading **Saved Results,** are links to your saved **Web Pages, Images,** and **Search History**. Below that is the **My Folders** heading that will remain empty until you create a folder by clicking on **New**. You may also click on **Edit** to rename a previous folder or delete it.

Search terms are entered into the box at the top of the page. You can choose to conduct either an Ask Web Search, or search just the personal MyStuff database you have constructed. To build that personal database, you save results by clicking the **Save** link to the right of any Web search result that you want to save. The saved results are combined into one long list of results viewable at your MyStuff home page. Also at your MyStuff home page, you can organize these saved pages by putting them in folders you define.

Once placed in folders, you can choose to look at results saved in each individual folder separately, or all of your saved results as one long list. You may also add personal notes to your saved searches by clicking on the **Add Note** link that appears at the far right of each saved result. Saved results can be sorted in several ways, including chronologically (by date/time saved); or alphabetically by title, folder name, or the first word contained in the accompanying notes by clicking on the column header above the list of saved results.

Our View: Taking the browser's idea of Favorites to a more extreme degree, MyStuff does a good job allowing you to organize your search results. Adding notes is a nice bonus to personally annotate your results and offering a multitude of sorting techniques helps sort through all the possible chaos. MyStuff is off to a good start in customizing search results.

Tip: (1) MyStuff requires Firefox version 1.0 or Internet Explorer 5.5 Web browser or later for Windows. The service did not work properly with any browser we tested under Mac OS 9.1 and some links did not appear when the site was viewed in Netscape Communicator 7.1 for windows.

(2) In the lower left-hand corner of your account page is **Today's Tip**, a short, helpful idea for those using MyStuff.com. While I was using the database, the **Tip** changed several times, so keep on the lookout for some useful communication, such as the best way to organize your result pages.

(3) The sorting functions of MyStuff still have some bugs to work out. For example, if you sort alphabetically by the **Notes** field, saved results to which you have not added notes (blank notes) appear before those saved results with notes added. One way

around this problem is to click on the **Notes** column header a second time to resort the notes in descending alphabetical order.

(4) A binocular icon appears to the left of the URL of selected search results. Hovering over the binoculars pops up a preview image of the Web site associated with the URL—allowing you to see what it looks like (in miniature) before clicking on the link to actually visit the site.

Yahoo! My Web

http://myweb2.search.yahoo.com/

Purpose: To save and categorize Web sites you find while searching.

Content: Yahoo!'s **My Web** service allows you to track the pages you click on in your Yahoo! searches, save specific pages (or links to those pages), and assign your own keywords ("tags") to those pages so you can group like pages together. It also allows you to share your list of saved pages and tags with a group of other **My Web** users you define or all other users. The service is free, but does require setting up a Yahoo! account. (If you currently have a "yahoo.com" e-mail address, then you already have a Yahoo! account.

From the first **My Web** screen (after log-in), adding a Web page to your list is as easy as clicking the **Add** link near the top of the page. You can then enter the URL for the site, your own title, and description, and also assign category tags. These tags can be whatever you want them to be. Doing all of this would save a link to the page, along with your tags. You can also opt to save a copy of the page as it appears today (for future reference).

For example, if you are searching for information about the opposition's expert, you may find their biography on their Web site. You can add that page to your **My Web** collection by clicking the **Add** link. You would enter the URL for the biography page, assign it a title (e.g., "Their Expert's Bio") and description (e.g., "Their expert Joe Smith has an MBA, PhD, and 35 years of experience. He'll sound credible to a jury."). You can then add tags that will be meaningful to you in the future (e.g., the case name, opposition expert, expert bio, area of expertise, etc.). Finally, you can determine who can have access to the information you've saved for this site (i.e., **Me**—only you; **My Community**—additional **My Web** users you invite into your community; or **Everyone**—anyone who has signed up for **My Web**). Completing this process adds the site to your list of saved sites.

Accessing your list of sites is as easy as clicking the **My Pages** or **My Tags** links on the left-hand side of the **My Web** page. Selecting **My Pages** brings up the list of all the pages you saved (which can be sorted by date saved, the title you've assigned, or URL). You can review all of the information you've saved or assigned for a site. You can click on the link to visit the site, or if you checked the **Store a copy of this page** box when you initially added the site to your list, you can view the cached version of the page, as it appeared on the day you added it to your list. Selecting **My Tags** brings up an alphabetical list of all of the tags you have created/assigned. They are displayed as a continual list in the center of the page. The more often you have assigned a specific tag to different Web pages, the larger and bolder the tag will appear on the list. Clicking on any tag will display a list of sites on your list to which you have assigned that tag.

Our View: Though still in beta, this is a worthwhile tool for saving and categorizing useful sites you have found in your search results. It can even help you better organize and share your existing Bookmarks/Favorites. The first time you launch **My Web** it gives you the option of importing your Bookmarks/Favorites. **My Web** also allows you to omit a site from your Yahoo! search results, if you find sites appearing that are not useful to you.

Tip:

(1) The way the tags are displayed can take a bit of getting used to. It almost resembles a ransom note with its different size type for each tag. You can also access your list of tags on the left-hand side of the **My Pages** page.

(2) If you also download the Yahoo! toolbar, you'll have more flexibility in saving pages to your **My Web**.

CHAPTER FIVE

General Factual Research

Standard Reference Resources

From elementary school through college, we've been trained that the solutions to all of our research questions can be found by going to the library. While this is still true, the Internet now brings much of the library to us, allowing us to access a great amount of information from the comfort and convenience of our home or office.

Many tried-and-true resources that we are used to using in print form, such as the *Merriam-Webster Collegiate Dictionary* and the *Encyclopedia Britannica*, are now available online, along with a host of other resources.

Another quick way to find a definition is via Google. It's **define** command retrieves definitions from within the billions of Web pages in the Google index. To retrieve definitions with Google, type **define:** in the search box on the Google home page, followed by the term you are interested in defining and then clicking **Google Search**. For example, entering "define: broadband" returned 27 definitions of the term from a variety of Web sites including telecom giant Sprint and the University of New Orleans.

Don't Count Out the Library Yet!

In addition to the sites included here, many public libraries offer their patrons access to some of the online pay databases used by the libraries' reference staffs. Ordinarily, all you need to access these normally expensive resources on your home computer is a library card and an Internet connection. Some of these include

- Selected news, periodical indices, and full-text articles
- Gale's Biography Resource Center
- Oxford English Dictionary
- Physician's Desk Reference (PDR)
- Reference USA
- Standard & Poor's

Starting-Point Web Sites for General Research

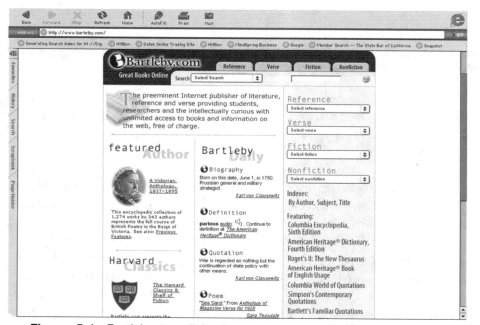

Figure 5-1. Bartleby.com links to numerous general reference resources, including dictionaries, encyclopedias, and thesauri of all types.

Bartleby.com

http://www.bartleby.com

Purpose: To locate general information from various references.

Content: Bartleby.com offers a wide range of reference resources searchable online, including the dictionaries, encyclopedias, Gray's *Anatomy of the Human Body,* the *King James Bible,* and various thesauri.

Our View: Bartleby is a good place to start when looking for various types of general information. The site allows you to keyword search through all of the site's five dozen reference works (a sampling of which are noted above) all at once or individually.

Selecting the **Reference** drop-down menu on the right-hand side of the home page displays a list of suggested resources in which to search for information on your keyword, including dictionaries, thesauri, encyclopedias, quotations, and nine other subcategories, rather than returning the actual definition or synonyms. To retrieve definitions or synonyms, select **Dictionary** or one of the thesauri names from the list and search those resources directly.

Tip: The site also features a searchable and browsable version of Strunk's English language usage guide, *The Elements of Style.*

Refdesk.com

http://www.refdesk.com

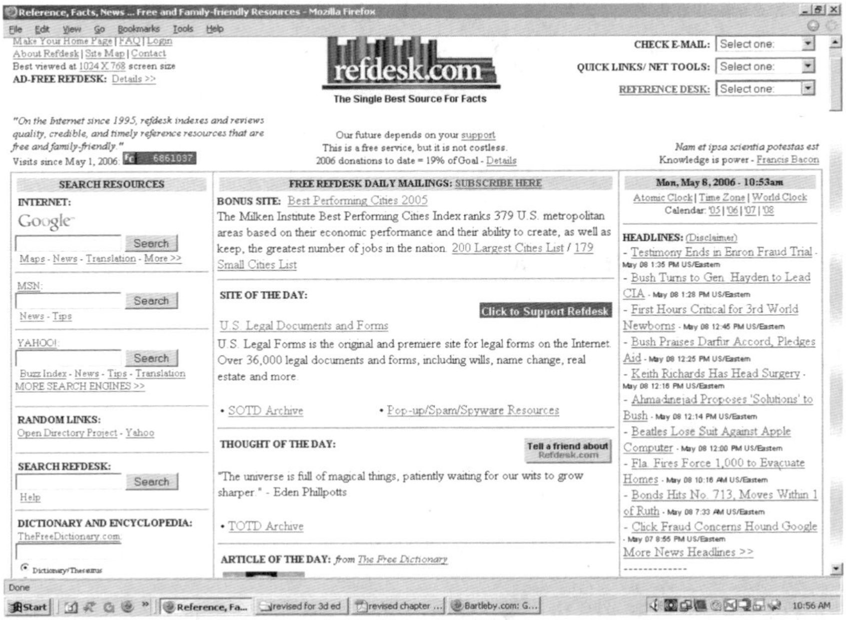

Figure 5-2. Access to the Refdesk site is like having your own virtual reference collection right at your fingertips.

Purpose: To locate general information and reference material on various subjects.

Content: The site links to more than 20,000 other resources in numerous categories, including news, weather, sports, reference, dictionaries, encyclopedias, and search engines, among others. Among its many **Refdesk Subject Categories Tools** (scroll down the center of the home page to locate this list) are **Dictionaries** and **Encyclopedias** categories that include links to nearly 100 different sites. The home page also includes news headlines from sources such as ABC News, CNN, and Reuters.

Our View: A good site to bookmark for links to all sorts of useful general information. Making all of this information accessible from the home page gives it a cluttered look, but it's well worth scrolling through the page for pointers to resources on the subject you need.

Tip: Cut your book budget by asking every lawyer and staff person in the office to bookmark this site. That way you won't have to buy each person their own standard dictionary and legal dictionary!

Interesting side note: the Refdesk creator and Webmaster, Robert Drudge, is the father of Internet muckraker Matt Drudge, the creator and "citizen reporter" behind the *Drudge Report* Web site.

Dictionaries and Thesauri

Merriam Webster

http://www.m-w.com

Purpose: To locate definitions and synonyms for common (and not-so-common) words.

Content: The site offers a searchable version of *Merriam-Webster's Collegiate Dictionary, Tenth Edition.* Access to a larger, unabridged Webster's dictionary is available for $29.95 annually, or $4.95 per month. (A fourteen-day free trial is available for the unabridged version subscription. Currently, there is a **Free Premium Access** offer giving one-day's access to users in return for viewing an ad.)

Dictionary and thesaurus search boxes are available at the top of the home page. If you're not certain of the spelling of the word you're looking up, you can use wild card characters. A question mark (?) can be used to take the place of one letter and an asterisk (*) can be used to take the place of more than one letter. For example, a search for "m?n" will find "man" and "men," as well as the abbreviations "min," "mon," "mtn," and "mun." A search for "m*n" will find those entries, as well as entries for "macaroon," "magnification," "maiden," "maintain," and many other words that begin with "m" and end with "n."

Our View: The site is fairly straightforward and easy to use. The wild card capabilities of its searches are especially helpful. The results can be inconsistent, though. For example, the synonyms returned as part of a dictionary search may not correlate to the results of a thesaurus search for the same word. A sample dictionary search for the word "scion" included two synonyms along with the definition. Clicking the **Thesaurus** tab revealed that the site had no thesaurus entries for the word scion, but on the list of similar words were entries like "chain" and "gum." Apparently including consonants and vowels is enough to be considered similar! Therefore, if you do not find a thesaurus listing for the word you're seeking, try clicking the **Dictionary** tab to see if there are any synonyms listed along with the definition.

Tip: • Definitions also include audio pronunciations of the word. Clicking on the Speaker icon next to the main entry plays a recording of the proper pronunciation of the word you've looked up.
• Based on sample searches, such as this "scion" search, this thesaurus is not as comprehensive as the *Roget's Thesaurus* discussed below.

The American Heritage Dictionary

http://www.bartleby.com/61

Purpose: To search for definitions and meanings.

Content: Based on the *American Heritage Dictionary of the English Language,* Fourth Edition, this site offers 90,000 entries and audio pronunciations for 70,000 words. This dictionary does not offer a direct link to a thesaurus entry, although many entries do include synonyms.

Our View: The site's search options can be a bit confusing. To locate the definition of a word, you must select **Entry Word** from the pull-down menu located next to the search box. Selecting **Definition** from the pull-down menu instructs the dictionary to look for the word you input in the definitions of other words. For example, an **Entry Word** search for "scan" returns one result—the definition of that word. A **Definition** search for the word "scan" returns twenty results, nineteen of which are for the definitions of other words where the word "scan" appears in the definition.

Tip: Included with the dictionary definitions are notes regarding the word's history and information regarding the etymological origins of the word.

OneLook Dictionary Search

http://www.onelook.com

Purpose: To search for definitions and translations of words and phrases.

Content: With a single search, the OneLook dictionary search engine can return the definition of one of more than

7 million words from its database of nearly 1,000 dictionaries, broken down into a dozen categories.

Our View: The site can be particularly helpful if you are not sure of the correct spelling. OneLook offers the asterisk (*) and question mark (?) wild card search options to fill in the blanks when you're not sure how the word you're looking for is spelled. (See the entry above on the **Merriam-Webster** dictionary for more information on searching with these wild cards.)

To help narrow down your search, click the **Browse Dictionaries** link on the upper right-hand side of the home page to see the list of available dictionaries by category. For example, clicking **Browse Dictionaries** and then selecting **Science** brings up a list of over 100 dictionaries on scientific topics, from a dictionary of scientific units to an online browsable version of the periodic table of the elements. From these pages, you can also see the date when each particular dictionary was indexed by the OneLook directory.

Tip: You can also use wild cards to search for words (if you aren't sure how to spell them) in a particular category. For example, searching for "f*:construction" will return all words that start with the letter F that are related to the topic of construction. This can be especially helpful in deciphering terms of art from other industries heard in meetings or in conversation.

OneLook Reverse Dictionary

http://www.onelook.com/reverse-dictionary.shtml

Purpose: Locate words by their meaning.

Content: OneLook's reverse dictionary lets you enter a definition or describe a concept to retrieve a list of words and phrases related to that concept. Your description can be a few words, a sentence, a question, or even just a single word. Type your query into the **Describe Concept Here** box and hit the **Find words** button. In most cases you'll get back a list of related terms with the best matches shown first.

Our View: This reverse dictionary can be helpful when you're searching for "just the right word," however, double-check the dictionary definitions of any words returned for your query. For example, a search for words related to the concept "being tried twice for the same crime," listed "double jeopardy" as the first result. Further down the list, however, entries included "accusatorial," "call," and "old."

Tip: Shorter queries yield the best results.

LookWAYup

http://lookwayup.com/free/default.htm Free Trial: $\cancel{\$}$ Purchase: **$**

Purpose: To find definitions, meanings of words, phrases, and acronyms.

Content: LookWAYup is a downloadable addition to your Web browser. Clicking the **LookWAYup** button that it adds to your browser pops up a search box that allows you to search for the definition of a word without leaving the Web site you're viewing. A 31-day free trial is available. After that LookWayUp can be purchased for $15.

Our View: This can be a handy tool if you often have to define words or technical terms in Web pages, but don't want to leave that site to find a dictionary. LookWAYup is available in English, German, French, Dutch, Spanish, and Portuguese. Small Web sites may also install a server-based free version, as long as the site receives no more than 1,000 visits per day (for nonprofit volunteer organizations, the limit is 25,000 visits).

Tip: LookWAYup works with version 4 and above of the Netscape, Internet Explorer, and Opera browsers, on Windows, Unix, and Mac operating systems.

Roget's Thesaurus

http://www.bartleby.com/thesauri

Purpose: To find synonyms of words.

Purpose: To find definitions, meanings of words, phrases, and acronyms.

Content: Two editions of *Roget's Thesaurus* are available to search online (via Bartleby.com): *Roget's International Thesaurus of English Words and Phrases* (1922), and *Roget's II: The New Thesaurus, Third Edition* (1995).

Our View: Searching is straightforward. Returned results also include thesaurus entries for synonyms of the word you've looked up. For example, a search for "scion" returned that word's entry, as well as entries for "progeny," "offspring," "descendant," and so on.

Tip: Based on sample searches, such as this "scion" search, these thesauri are more comprehensive than the thesaurus offered at the Merriam-Webster site noted above.

Legal Dictionaries

FindLaw's Legal Dictionary

http://dictionary.lp.findlaw.com

Purpose: To find definitions of legal words and phrases.

Content: The dictionary at FindLaw is licensed from *Merriam-Webster's Dictionary of Law* (1996). It is keyword searchable by words or partial words.

Our View: We prefer this to any of the other legal dictionaries because it not only provides very complete definitions, it also includes pronunciations, hyperlinks to related words or comparative words, and in some instances, citations for cases where the word has been used. (It would be even better if it then hyperlinked to those cases.)

Everybody's Legal Dictionary (NOLO's Shark Talk dictionary)

http://www.nolo.com/lawcenter/dictionary/wordindex.cfm

Purpose: We'll let NOLO tell you the purpose: it's "your life-raft in the sea of legal jargon."

Content: It has plain-English definitions for over 1,000 legal terms.

Our View: We like that you can either browse alphabetically by clicking on any letter in the alphabet, or you can type a word (or partial word) into a search engine. The definitions are very thorough.

Tip: If you don't find the word you want, check back—it's being built word-by-word.

Duhaime's Law Dictionary

http://www.duhaime.org/dictionary/diction.htm

Purpose: To find legal concepts defined in plain language, created as a public service by the Canadian law firm Duhaime Law.

Content: An alphabetical list of definitions of legal concepts.

Our View: It's an easy-to-use site, with easy-to-understand definitions. We'd prefer a search engine, too.

Tip: There may be one or more hyperlinks within each definition. When you click on one, it takes you to the definition of the word used in the entry you've just looked up.

Morse Code Applet (Morse Code translator)

http://www.babbage.demon.co.uk/morse.html

Purpose: To translate messages into Morse code.

Content: The site is powered by a Java applet that turns the text you type in the message box into a Morse code message that you can hear. As the audio Morse Code message is being played, the individual letters are displayed in a separate text box so you can identify the specific sound patterns associated with each letter. A translation table, listing the dot and dash patterns of each letter of the Morse Code alphabet, is also included at the site.

Our View: Morse Code decoding is one of those things that falls into the "you never know what you're going to need" category. It's included here for that reason. The applet is compatible with most current Web browsers. See the site for a current list of incompatibilities.

Acronym Finder

http://www.acronymfinder.com

Purpose: To decode acronyms and abbreviations.

Content: Acronymfinder.com offers a searchable database of over 480,000 acronyms and abbreviations. The database is limited to acronyms of up to 24 characters, and definitions are limited to a maximum length of 255 characters.

Our View: Acronym Finder has undergone a number of changes, not all for the better. The **Option** drop-down menu is now relegated to the **Search Tips** or **Help** page and only offers two options:

- Acronym
- Word in meaning (reverse keyword lookup)

The first method is self-explanatory. Entering letters into the search box and clicking **Find** returns a list of definitions for the acronym entered. For example, a search for "FBI" returns not only Federal Bureau of Investigation, but also Faith Based Initiatives and Farm Bureau Insurance, among other results.

Selecting **Word in Meaning** from the **Option** menu allows a reverse lookup to determine any acronyms related to a specific subject by allowing users to search by keywords. For example, a search for the keywords "oil" and "drilling" returned 26 oil-industry-related hits, including PHPA (Partial Hydrolytic Polyacrylamide) and ERD (Extended Reach Drilling), among other results.

Tip:
- The site will not return more than 300 results for a search. If a search returns more than 500 definitions, no results are returned and an error message is displayed.
- Look below your search results to see if there are any additional definitions found in the *Acronym Attic*—the site's collection of 3 million acronyms/definitions that have not been verified or reviewed.

Abbreviations and Acronyms of the U.S. Government

http://www.ulib.iupui.edu/subjectareas/gov/docs_abbrev.html

Purpose: For specialized acronym decoding.

Content: The Indiana University-Purdue University Indianapolis Library offers a browsable list of nearly 800 U.S. government acronyms and their definitions.

Our View: The list is included on one long page, with the ability to jump to any particular letter in the alphabet from a row of alphabetical links at the top of the page. A search function would be helpful.

Tip: Use your browser's Find function to search for an acronym quickly, rather than scrolling through the list.

Military Acronyms and Glossaries

http://www.ulib.iupui.edu/subjectareas/gov/military.html

Purpose: For specialized military acronym and term decoding.

Content: The Indiana University-Purdue University Indianapolis Library also offers a metasite listing nearly twenty on-line resources for decoding military terms.

Our View: The majority of the sites are maintained by the military (.mil domain names), so you can be sure you're going right to the source.

Jane's Defence Glossary

http://www.janes.com/defenceglossary/

Purpose: Define military/defense-related terminology.

Content: Jane's Defence Glossary contains a searchable database of over 20,000 defense-related acronyms and abbreviations from around the world. Acronyms and abbreviations are entered in the **Acronym** search box, and words or phrases are entered in the **Term** search box. Clicking the **View the glossary alphabetically** link offers drill down, browseable access to the collection of definitions.

Our View: Jane's Information Group is one of the world's leading providers of military and defense-related information and analysis from around the world. The glossary is easy to use and its searches are clearly labeled.

Tip: The glossary automatically "stems" an acronym search—creating a search for the precise acronym you've entered, or any acronym starting with those letters. For example, a search for the acronym "RAF" returns the expected meaning of "Royal Air Force (UK), but it also returns "RAFO" (Royal Air Force Oman) and "RAFTS" (Reconnaissance Attack Fighter Training System-US) among the 19 results for the search.

Searching for a term looks for that word anywhere in the definition of an acronym. For example, a search for the term "engagement" returns the definitions for "ATESS" (Advanced Tactics & Engagement Simulation System) and "BATES" (Battlefield Artillery Target Engagement System-UK) among the 38 results.

SEARCH Publications Criminal Justice Acronyms

http://www.search.org/conferences/2006symposium/
registration/packet/acronymsv020806.pdf

Purpose: To decode law-enforcement-related acronyms.

Content: This document provides a list of nearly 150 selected criminal justice acronyms, their definitions, and relevant links. (For example, one entry is "NIJ, National Institute of Justice, U.S. DOJ http://www.ojp.usdoj.gov/nij.")

Our View: The list is all contained on one long page. The list is short enough that it's not a great chore to scroll through it to find the acronym you might be looking for, although a search function would still be helpful.

Tip: Use the PDF **Find** function to search for an acronym quickly, rather than scrolling through the list.

Encyclopedias

Zimmerman's Research Guide

http://www.lexisnexis.com/infopro/zimmerman/

Purpose: To point legal researchers who need advice on where to begin their research in the right direction.

Content: The Guide is a database of resources (print, online, free, pay, etc.) that can be searched by keyword or browsed by topic. For example, say you are trying to find a resource for historical stock quotes. Browsing to **stock prices** links to a lengthy entry about stock prices and a paragraph on "Historical Quotes." The "Historical Quotes" entry provides links to (and explanations of) a variety of sources that can be used to find historical quotes. The sources include URLs for free sites and pay sites; phone and fax numbers of companies that will research the stock's history (for a fee); and print sources such as books, periodicals, and newspapers. You could also have found the appropriate entry by typing "historical stock quotes" into the site's internal search engine.

Our View: Besides finding this a useful source, we enjoyed learning about the author of Zimmerman's Research Guide. Andrew Zimmerman is a law librarian who began this project one afternoon as a way to start "my own black book" after seeing another librarian's "black book." He explains, "Mostly I just took notes on anything I learned in the library. At first I kept my notes to myself, but soon I started printing out copies for other librarians. . . ." The Guide could, however, use a few Help screens to let the visitor know whether phrases should be placed in quotation marks (they should) and whether the site supports Boolean connectors (it does not—the default connector is AND; other connectors are ignored).

Tip: Your search can be narrowed by limiting your keywords or phrases to the **heading** or to the **text of entry** or broadened by selecting **All Fields**. The author encourages collaboration, so if you want to contribute any information to the site, click on **email the author** at the bottom of the page.

The Columbia Encyclopedia, Sixth Edition (2002)

http://www.bartleby.com/65

Purpose: To search for information on a topic, person or place.

Content: The online edition of this encyclopedia includes nearly 51,000 entries. Entries can be searched full-text, or just by the entry titles. You can also browse the entries from an alphabetical table of contents.

Additionally, there is a separate index covering the encyclopedia's more than 17,000 biographical entries. They are classified into 140 subject categories.

Our View: Just like a print encyclopedia, this site offers informative entries on myriad topics. One advantage of the online format is the more than 80,000 hypertext cross-references sprinkled throughout the individual entries. For example, within the entry for Albert Einstein there are links to related topics discussed, including his special theory of relativity, the photoelectric effect, and Brownian movement, among other topics.

Calculators and Converters

Martindale's Calculators OnLine Center

http://www.martindalecenter.com/Calculators.html

Purpose: For help on calculations and conversions of various types.

Content: This site has an impressive collection of over 21,000 specialized online calculators from over 3,000 sources. The calculators are created and maintained by a variety of public and private sources around the world. They are broken down into two main categories: **Agriculture, Science and Math Calculators**, and **General**. There are several subcategories for science and math, such as **statistics** and **chemistry**, and the general calculators are arranged alphabetically.

Our View: Whether you need to convert ounces to milligrams, barrels of oil to U.S. and Imperial gallons, or calculate the field of view for a particular type of camera, you're bound to find the source for your solution here.

CalendarHome.com

http://calendarhome.com/date.shtml

Purpose: To calculate the number of days between two dates.

Content: The basic **enter two dates** calculator allows you to calculate the number of days, months, years, hours, etc., between two specific dates in time.

Our View: This site is easy to use with a very simple interface. It's a quick and painless way to calculate how many days a lawyer needs to prepare for a case or to calculate the due date of a filing. It does not calculate court/business days, only calendar days.

Tip: Explore the rest of CalendarHome.com for useful tools when scheduling events, trials, and clients. For example, if you have a client in Israel who is using the Hebrew calendar, you can quickly translate any dates your client gives you to our calendar system (the Gregorian calendar system).

Maps

MapQuest

http://www.mapquest.com

Purpose: To retrieve maps of various locations, as well as driving directions and other helpful information.

Content: The site is probably most often used for its Driving Directions feature. It also provides maps of the U.S. and of foreign countries, as well as aerial photographs of selected locations.

Our View: MapQuest is an easy-to-use tool for creating maps and getting driving directions. You can get (usually) clear driving directions and maps simply by putting your starting address and destination address into the appropriate boxes on the Driving Directions page.

Clicking on the **Maps** icon on the home page allows you to enter a place name, address or intersection to retrieve a map from in the U.S. or Canada.

Tip: • MapQuest can also be a handy way to calculate mileage between two points for expense or tax purposes.
• Additionally, you might want to include a link to a MapQuest map of your office on your Web site.

TerraFly

To search: (**$**) To purchase photos (and conduct advanced searching): **$**

http://www.terrafly.fiu.edu

Purpose: To view satellite images of neighborhoods.

Content: This site allows you to search for aerial photos by
                address. The returned maps include labels for streets,
                parks, schools, restaurants, hotels, and homes listed for
                sale (including price), among other information. Click-
                ing on the map takes you to a page where you can access
                more information, such as demographic data, median
                household income, and population, as well as local
                businesses and hospitals, among other categories. Using
                the control panel on the left-hand side of the screen you
                can "fly" over the area. (Click the direction you want to
                fly on the red directional crosshairs to select a direction.
                Click in the center of the crosshairs to stop.) You can
                also select from several major cities (click the **Browse**
                button on the home page to see a list of states and
                cities). After selecting a city from the list, click on **Fly
                over aerial imagery starting at [name of city you
                selected]**.

                Subscriptions to see non-waterworked images and addi-
                tional demographic data begin at $10 for a 24-hour
                period to $25,000/year depending on the size of the
                subscribing organization.

Our View: This is the most flexible of the free sources for aerial
                photos, but also the slowest loading. The maps and Java
                control panel took nearly a minute to load over a stan-
                dard DSL connection. Once they do load, these maps
                offer the most information. Clicking the **Layers** button
                and then checking the zip box changes the view to show
                ZIP codes. Click the **Mark** button to draw a box around
                the specific area for which you would like to order a cus-
                tom map, then the **Dispense** button to order. Prices
                vary. This site is run by the High Performance Database
                Research Center (HPDRC), which is associated with the

School of Computer Science at Florida International University.

Unfortunately, a number of useful features are no longer available without paid registration.

Tip: Currently, the closest resolution is one mile. The site promises to add one-foot resolution for the entire country in the future. (Fort Lauderdale is the first city available for viewing at one-foot resolution.)

Terraserver

To search: Ⓢ To purchase images (and conduct advanced searching): **$**

http://www.terraserver.com

Purpose: To retrieve aerial photos of selected locations.

Content: Terraserver provides satellite and aerial photographic images of selected cities around the world. The majority of coverage is in North America and Europe, with some coverage of Australia, Asia, and the Middle East.

Our View: Terraserver started as a joint research project among Terraserver.com, Microsoft, the U.S. Geological Survey (USGS), and Compaq.

You can view all imagery for free down to 8 meters of detail. As a Terraserver subscriber you can view high-resolution images of 1 or 2 meters of detail and then purchase the images immediately. Subscription fees range from $9.95 (for 7 days) to $119.95 (for one year). Free searches can be conducted by:

   • City
   • ZIP code
   • USGS

- Address (U.S. Only)
- County
- Coordinates

Tip: This site can be useful for lawyers who need demonstrative evidence (such as for a car accident). More detailed images require a paid subscription. Microsoft also maintains a separate free service where you can access more-detailed photos at **http://terraserver-usa.com**. Searches for U.S. addresses can be conducted for free at this site using the search boxes on the home page. **Terraserver-usa.com** does not have photos from as many sources as **Terraserver.com**.

Unlike the aerial photos available at MapQuest, those available at the Microsoft site include the date the photo was taken.

Geographic Names Information System

http://geonames.usgs.gov/#db

Purpose: To locate places throughout the U.S.

Content: The U.S. Geological Service maintains this database of "almost 2 million physical and cultural geographic features in the United States" (states, territories, and protectorates). These include airports, beaches, cemeteries, dams, lakes, military installations (historical only), parks, populated places (cities, towns, and so on), schools, and more. Click on **Domestic Names** and then **Search GNIS** to begin searching.

Our View: This database can be extremely useful if you're trying to pinpoint a geographic landmark or location in an area you are unfamiliar with. You can enter as much or as little information as you know about a place to conduct a search. Search fields include feature name, state or territory, and feature type. Returned results include the state and county where the feature is located, the type of feature, its latitude and longitude, and the name of the USGS map where it can be found. Clicking on the feature's name in the search results brings additional information, as well as links for maps, aerial photos (if available), and other information.

Tip: Foreign place names are searchable at the National Geospatial-Intelligence Agency's GeoNet Name Server Site (**http://gnswww.nga-mil/geonames/GNS/index.jsp**).

Maporama

http://www.maporama.com/

Purpose: To easily convert any address into longitude and latitude and retrieve maps of various locations and driving directions.

Content: Like many other map sites on the Web, Maporama provides driving directions and points of interest relative to an address you specify. One unique function is the site's ability to generate latitude and longitude coordinates from the address quickly.

To generate these coordinates (as well as a standard map with the address highlighted and various "points of interest" noted), select the country where the address is located from the "Country" drop-down menu, then enter the address, city, state, and ZIP code into the appropriate boxes, and then click the "Go" button. The latitude and longitude information is displayed on the left-hand side of the screen.

You can also **Personalise Your Map** using the size, color/style, and miles/kilometers drop-down menus or you can **Export the Map** to your printer, e-mail or PDA. Both functions are located to the left of the map. **Quick Links**, just to the right of the home page's center, offers maps of popular cities such as New York or Chicago with one click.

Our View: Latitude and longitude data can be useful when researching precise historical weather data or verifying/comparing data recovered from a Global Positioning System (GPS) device. Maporama makes it easy to convert any street address into latitude and longitude. A function to convert latitude and longitude into a street address would also be helpful (but is not offered).

Tip: The **Airport** drop-down menu provides maps of European airports and the **Real-time traffic info** drop-down menu offers traffic maps for various French cities only.

U.S. Postal Service Official Abbreviations

http://www.usps.com/ncsc/lookups/abbreviations.html

Purpose: To verify postal abbreviations.

Content: The U.S. Postal Service offers a list of its official abbreviations for U.S. states, possessions, military "states," street suffixes (e.g., street, alley), and secondary unit designators (e.g., apartment, basement). Links at the top of the page jump directly to each of the three categories of abbreviations.

All of the categories are presented on one very long page.

Our View: While most of us are familiar with common abbreviations such as "St" for "street" and "Apt" for "apartment," the preferred postal abbreviations for "shoal" and "hangar" are probably not as well known—but they're all here.

Tip: The list of street suffixes is very long, so be sure to use the alphabetical links at the top of the list to jump to the letter your suffix begins with.

ZIP Info

http://www.zipinfo.com/search/zipcode.htm

Purpose: To locate the ZIP code (or all ZIP codes) for a particular city

Content: Offered by CD Light, the publishers of numerous ZIP code (and related) databases on CD-ROM, this site gives you the ability to enter a city and state and retrieve all of the ZIP codes for that city. Checkboxes let you also retrieve additional information with your results, including

- County name & FIPS (Federal Information Processing Standard) code
- Area code
- Time zone
- Latitude & longitude
- MSA (Metropolitan Statistical Area)/PMSA (Primary Metropolitan Statistical Area)

The U.S. 50

http://www.theus50.com

Purpose: Locate information about the individual states

Content: The us50.com includes general information about all 50 U.S. states. Selecting a state from the **Visit** pull-down menu on the left-hand side of the home page delivers a **General State History**, as well as information on **Historic Figures** from, or connected to, that particular state. (Note that these **Historic Figures** can range from John Sutter and Leland Stanford in California to Hank Aaron and Rosa Parks in Alabama.

Additional information is provided in the following categories:

- Geography (location and state map)
- Outdoors (state parks, camping, hunting, fishing, hiking, and other outdoor activities)
- Tourism (historic sites and tourist attractions)
- Information (general state information such as (capital, agriculture, industry, flag, flower, bird, etc.)
- State links (official state homepages and state related links)
- State quiz

Our View: The site is a good source for general information regarding a particular state.

Phone Books

Area Decoder

http://www.areadecoder.com

Purpose: Determine area code or dialing codes for specific localities; or the city in which a phone number is located.

Content: The site is best known for its database of area codes retrievable by city and state, and international dialing codes retrievable by country name. You can also perform reverse lookups by entering domestic or international calling codes. It includes information on more than a quarter million cities around the world.

Area Decoder has recently added the ability to return information about specific exchanges within a domestic area code. To search for a specific exchange, enter the area code in parentheses, followed by a minus sign and then the exchange, e.g., (xxx)-yyy. For example, a search for the "559" exchange in the "310" area code would be written as (310)-559. Information returned for this search would include the state and top 10 major cities (by population) covered by the area code, the date the area code was established, the city where the exchange is located and the owner of the exchange/telephone office. The results also include a link to an area code map of the state (or region).

Our View: The Area Decoder is easy to use and can help you quickly determine the city in which an area code is located (by entering the area code), or all of the area codes for a particular city (by entering the city and state). The site does not provide any information regarding specific phone numbers.

Tip: To determine the country for a specific foreign country dial code, put a plus sign (+) before the country code and a dash before the city code—without spaces. For example, a search for +49 will display "Germany" while a search for +49-30 will display "Berlin, Germany." You may also need to drop leading zeros on country codes.

See Chapter 7, "Finding and Backgrounding People," for an in-depth discussion of phone directories available online.

Quotations

Bartleby.com

http://www.bartleby.com/quotations

Purpose: To locate famous quotes (mostly) from well-known authors.

Content:	Bartleby.com offers a searchable index of over 87,000 quotations from four primary sources: Bartlett's *Familiar Quotations* (10th ed., 1919), *The Columbia World of Quotations* (1996), *Simpson's Contemporary Quotations* (1988), and *Respectfully Quoted: A Dictionary of Quotations* (1989).
Our View:	Searching is fairly logical. You can either perform a keyword search, or you can select any of the three sources and browse their subject categories to find the quote that best suits your need.
Tip:	A good, famous quote (when it's on point, of course) can be a good addition to a brief, opening statement, or closing argument.

Quoteland

http://www.quoteland.com

Purpose:	To locate famous quotes (mostly) from well-known authors.
Content:	Quoteland also offers a database of quotations searchable by keyword, or browsable by topic.
Our View:	One advantage to this site is that its search engine allows for use of the percent sign (%) as a wild card to represent one or more characters. This can be extremely helpful if you know the name of an author, but are unsure of the correct spelling. (For example, keyword searches for "Clark%" return results from Chris Clark and Arthur C. Clarke.)
Tip:	This site offers the added ability to purchase your favorite quote on a T-shirt, coffee mug, and more.

The Quotations Page

http://www.quotationspage.com

Purpose: To locate famous quotes (mostly) from well-known authors.

Content: This site offers quotations from more than 2,000 authors in categories ranging from **Ability** to **Youth**.

Our View: This site is also easy to use. The database is full-text searchable, or you can browse through an alphabetical list of categories or authors. Individual quotation entries include cross-references to other quotations by the same author, other quotations in the same category, and biographical information (on selected authors).

Tip: If you don't find a category in the list that matches your needs, try doing a keyword search. If those quotes don't fit the bill, use the cross-reference links to locate other related quotes that might work.

Online Translators

AltaVista's Babel Fish Translation

http://world.altavista.com

Purpose: To translate words, phrases, or Web pages.

Content: Babel Fish was one of the first online translation sites. It offers three dozen possible translation possibilities among one dozen different languages, including:

- English to Chinese
- English to French
- English to German
- English to Italian
- English to Japanese

- Chinese to English
- French to English
- French to German
- German to English
- German to French

- English to Korean
- English to Portuguese
- English to Spanish

- Italian to English
- Japanese to English
- Korean to English
- Portuguese to English
- Russian to English
- Spanish to English

Our View: Babel Fish allows you to enter up to 150 words at a time for translation. Once your translated phrase is returned, you are offered the option of searching the Web with that translation as your keyword phrase.

The site also allows you to type in a URL to have that Web site translated into your choice of language.

Tip:
- For a "quick-and-dirty" translation of a document, you can "cut and paste" or type the text into Babel Fish (150 words at a time).
- Despite the stated 150-word limit per translation, we were able to translate a document that was 2,344 words in length without the site cutting off any words.

Online Translators

While useful, online translators are no substitute for a human translator. The online translations can sometimes be a bit too literal or stilted to make sense. For example, translating the sentence "Where are you going?" from English to Spanish (using both the Babel Fish and Google translation sites noted above and below) produces the following Spanish translation: "¿Adónde usted va?" Translating that exact phrase from Spanish back into English produced the following result: "Where you go?" While understandable, it is not exactly a proper translation. The bottom line is that online translation sites can be useful in a pinch to translate a document or Web site on the spot or to make yourself understood to a client. But for important case-related issues, use a qualified live interpreter or translator to ensure a proper result.

Google Translate

http://translate.google.com/translate_t

Purpose: To translate words, phrases, or Web pages.

Content: Google also offers a translation site covering 20 translation combinations of 10 languages, including:

- English to French
- English to German
- English to Italian
- English to Portuguese
- English to Spanish

- French to English
- French to German
- German to English
- German to French
- Italian to English
- Portuguese to English
- Spanish to English

Our View: Google offers the same features and functions as Babel Fish, albeit with a shorter list of languages and combinations. Google, however, seems to have no limit on the size of document you can translate. We were able to translate a document of over 12,000 words with no signs of rejection. Longer documents take significantly longer to translate than shorter ones.

ZIP Codes

ZIP Code Lookup

http://www.usps.com/zip4

Purpose: To search for ZIP code and related information.

Content: This page is part of the U.S. Postal Service's Web site. Here you can search various ZIP code information by selecting one of the following tabs:

- Search By Address
- Search By City
- Find all Cities in a ZIP code
- Search By Company

Free Internet Access to Library Databases and Catalogs

Since the first edition of this book was written we've come a long way in terms of access to library resources over the Internet. In the first edition the chapter was simply called "Library Catalogs Online" and the authors lamented, "At present, however, only Gale's *Encyclopedia of Associations* is available in full text on the Internet, and, as with all of the Net-converted Gale sources, pre-payment is required."

Oh, how far we've come; libraries are now providing library patrons with *free* remote access over the Internet to selected pay databases that contain a wealth of factual information, even to the above-mentioned *Encyclopedia of Associations*. Who would have foreseen that you'd be able to have remote access for free into expensive databases such as Gale's *Encyclopedia of Associations*? Consequently, we've added "databases" to the front of this section's title and relegated "catalogs" to the end of the title. To say that the addition of free remote access to pay databases is a valuable resource is an understatement! In fact, it's invaluable. It not only saves you a commute to the library, it opens up amazing amounts of expensive and useful information to you, free—saving you from investing in database subscriptions that you might need only occasionally.

Whether a library offers remote access at all varies widely from library to library. To find out if your local public library does, visit their Web site. Don't know your public library's URL? You can locate it at the LibWeb site (**http://sunsite.berkeley.edu/Libweb**). If your library does have remote access, you'll need to have a library card. Some libraries allow you to apply online and then pick the card up in person. Once you have your card, you'll need to enter your library card number into the library's remote access database Web page. You may have to also enter a password or your ZIP code. For those libraries that offer remote access to databases, the number and type of databases vary widely. Here are links to three library remote access databases: Chicago Public Library (CPL) at **http://piscator2.chipublib.org/ChicagoAuth.asp**, Los Angeles Public Library (LAPL) at **http://databases.lapl.org**, and New York Public Library (NYPL) at **http://www.nypl.org/databases/**.

The following are examples of the types of databases that can be accessed at NYPL. Many of these can also be accessed at LAPL and CPL, among other libraries:

- Academic Search Premier: 3,288 scholarly publications (full text) covering social sciences, humanities, education, computer sciences, engineering, medical sciences, and more

- Biography Resource Center: information on over 335,000 people
- Business and Company Resource Center (Gale): subjects include finance, acquisitions & mergers, international trade, money management, new technologies & products, local & regional business trends, investments, and banking
- Business Source Premier: 2,470 scholarly business journals (full text) covering management, economics, finance, accounting, international business, and more
- Clinical Pharmacology
- *Encyclopedia Americana*
- Funk & Wagnalls New World Encyclopedia
- Health Source, Consumer Edition: access to nearly 300 full-text consumer health periodicals, 1,200 health-related pamphlets, and 20 health reference books
- Health Source, Nursing/Academic Edition
- *New York Times* and *New York Post* Full-text (Gale): full-text newspaper articles from 2000 to the present
- Newspaper Source: full text of more than 200 regional U.S. newspapers, 18 international newspapers, 6 newswires, the *Christian Science Monitor,* the *Los Angeles Times,* and more
- Psychology and Behavioral Sciences Collection: the database has nearly 480 full-text titles

You will find that some of the databases that are available at one library on a remote basis may be completely unavailable at another library (remotely or in-person). Other times, you will find that one library's remote database is another library's in-person database only. There's no rhyme or reason. For example, at LAPL, Reference USA and the Oxford Dictionary are remote access databases, but not so at NYPL. They can be accessed only by an in-person visit to NYPL. All of the libraries in this discussion offer remote database titles that the others do not. For example, CPL has remote access to ABI Inform while the other two libraries don't carry this database at all. And the *Encyclopedia of Associations*, coveted by the prior authors, is available remotely (free) only at LAPL. This title is extremely useful for locating experts—especially those in unusual fields. See Chapter 9, "Finding and Backgrounding Expert Witnesses," for our quest for a chewing gum expert.

As you peruse the NYPL list of remote databases, you should have one foot out the door—heading over to visit your local library to pick up your library card. These databases have truly remarkable information. We'll give some detailed examples throughout this book describing situations when lawyers (or when we) made use of remote databases. They are especially useful for company research and competitive intelligence. Remote databases, particularly the full-text articles from newspapers, journals, or books, are also useful for any type of subject-specific research or for finding experts.

The convenience of being able to search remotely (and for free) through the full text of so many databases for information, and to read and print the full text of the materials from your office or home computer, surpasses anything we imagined just a few years ago. The usefulness of browsing through a library's online catalog to locate books or journals probably now pales in comparison to what you've just learned you can find in the remote databases.

Free Internet Access to Library Databases and Catalogs
Inspire

http://www.inspire.net/otherstates.html

Purpose: Although the primary purpose of this site is to provide all Indiana residents remote access to pay databases, free of charge, it is useful to non-Indiana residents because it has a list of all states that have a program similar to Indiana's.

Content: The following states are listed as having free remote access to databases on a statewide level. The list is currently being updated, and Oregon is expected to soon be added to the list.

Alabama	Maryland
Alaska	Massachusetts
Colorado	Michigan
Delaware	Minnesota
Florida	Nebraska
Georgia	Nevada
Idaho	New Hampshire
Illinois	New Jersey
Indiana	New Mexico
Kansas	New York
Kentucky	North Carolina
Louisiana	North Dakota
Maine	Ohio

Oklahoma	Texas
Pennsylvania	Utah
Rhode Island	Virginia
South Carolina	West Virginia
South Dakota	Wisconsin
Tennessee	Wyoming

Our View: This is a really useful list if only it were easier to find. Although we had read about this list, we were unable to find a link to it on the site's home page. The method we used to find the list illustrates that using a site's internal search engine can work well at times. In this case, we knew Alaska had a statewide program like Indiana's, so we assumed that if there were indeed a list on the site, "Alaska" would be on it. With that idea, we simply typed the word "Alaska" into the site's search engine and voila . . . the list appeared. You don't have to bother looking for it that way—just use the direct URL noted above.

Tip: If your state is not listed here, that only means there is no statewide program. Check your local library's site to see if there is a similar program on a local level.

News, Periodicals, and Broadcast Media

News coverage can be a valuable source of factual information on hot topics, or background information on high-profile individuals or select businesses. News sites on the Internet provide you with the unique ability to choose the topics you want to see when you want to see them. In addition, many sites provide archives that can be searched as needed.

Because news is constantly changing, it used to be useless to search for the latest news with *most* search engines. There are three search engines that do a good job of keeping up with changing news (Google, Yahoo!, and AltaVista); otherwise it's best to go directly to the source.

There are many news sources on the Internet. Some are Internet versions of respected media sources such as CNN, *USA Today*, the *Wall Street Journal*, and so on. Often, content from newspapers and magazines that is available for a fee from a commercial database (such as LexisNexis or Dialog Service) might be available for free on the Internet or via a public library's remote database.

However, that doesn't necessarily imply that the content on the Internet duplicates what is found on the commercial sources, or what was originally disseminated by the media source. Some material, such as audio, is not yet compiled into searchable databases by commercial database sites. However, broadcasters such as National Public Radio (NPR) at **http://www.npr.org** offer the ability to conduct keyword searches to retrieve audio (free) of past NPR news and feature coverage, back to 1996. (Some searches may return abstracts of stories from before 1996. No audio is available for those stories, although transcripts of some are offered for purchase.)

In some instances there are differences between the Internet version of a story and what's been published by the same media source elsewhere. For example, there may be a limit to the number of articles displayed on the Internet from each edition of a periodical, or only headlines may be provided, or the news may be summarized. Additionally, news stories on the Internet are occasionally updated throughout the day—long after the print version of a story has been finalized.

Some news sources are exclusive to the Internet. Whenever a big news story happens, whether it's floods in the Midwest or a war in a third-world country, Web sites are set up just to give people a way to exchange information and find ways to help victims. This seems to happen spontaneously. Such is the nature of the global publishing forum available to everyone, and known as the Internet.

Everyone has their favorite local or national newspaper or magazines that they turn to for their news fix. For news of local interest, the Web sites for local newspapers, radio, and TV stations may be your best source for information. Regionally, news outlets in large, nearby cities may also yield useful information on a particular topic. When conducting research, it can be necessary to look beyond those usual sources for regional or specialty news topics.

PBS's "The NewsHour with Jim Lehrer"

http://www.pbs.org/newshour/video/

Purpose: To locate video of select stories that appeared on PBS's "The NewsHour with Jim Lehrer."

Content: PBS has created a searchable database of select news stories that have aired on the "The NewsHour with Jim Lehrer" going back to February 7, 2000. To locate video on specific topics, enter a keyword or topic in the search box, or select a topic from the drop-down list beneath the search box. You can also use the drop-down list in combination with keywords, to further target your search.

The default Boolean connector for the search is "AND." You can also enclose a phrase in quotations marks to conduct an exact phrase search, or to exclude a word from your search, include a space, then a "minus sign" before the word (e.g., Zimbabwe—travel).

Results are seemingly located through a search of the video clip's transcript. The results are displayed in chronological order. Each returned result also includes a helpful **E-mail this!** link that allows you to send the video clip to a client, colleague, or yourself, and a cumbersome drop-down menu with a transcript of the entire clip.

Our View: "The NewsHour with Jim Lehrer" offers insightful and in-depth coverage on a wide range of topics. This search of video files from the program can be a good source of current awareness information about specific companies, business and economic trends, medical research, or even legal issues. We like the inclusion of the videos' transcript, but, as noted above, putting the entire transcript in a drop-down menu makes it less useful.

Tip: Be careful when you're typing your search terms. The search engine is case sensitive IF YOU USE CAPITALIZATION. Therefore, if you capitalize any letters, your search will look for results that contain the same use of capital letters. However, if you enter search terms in all lowercase letters, the search will return results without case sensitivity.

It is also important to note that this database does not include all stories that aired on "The NewsHour" since February 17, 2000, but "only segments that the NewsHour has the legal right to stream over the Internet."

Burrelle's Transcripts

http://tapesandtranscripts.burrellesluce.com/

To search: Ⓢ⃠   To purchase: **$**

Purpose: To purchase transcripts from 11 national channels/net-works, other syndicated programs and the Council on Foreign Relations.

Content: From Burrelle's home page, you can click the network logos along the top of the page, or click the **All Programs** tab near the middle of the page to access the full list of the following channels:

- CBS News
- NBC News
- CNBC
- C-SPAN
- Christian Broadcasting Network
- The Discovery Channel
- Fox News
- MSNBC
- MTV
- PBS
- WNBC-TV
- Syndicated programs
- Council on Foreign Relations

You will then see which programs each entity makes available for purchase (e.g., CBS News offers *48 Hours, 60 Minutes,* etc.). After selecting a program, a list of years is displayed. Some programs only offer the most recent years, while others go back as far as 1968 (*60 Minutes*). You may also order by phone or by mail. Most transcripts cost $6 to $16 per show.

Our View: If you need a transcript, this is the site to use because the fee is so minimal. Unfortunately, information on specific show air dates and ordering information for specific dates was no longer available on our most recent visit. (It was only available for *Oprah* and *Dr. Phil*.) A keyword search engine would make the site more useful. There didn't seem to be any rhyme or reason as to what was offered. Some of the abstracts (when available) were quite long, allowing you to glean enough information without having to even order the transcript if all you needed to know was who appeared on the show or what the topic involved.

Tip: Besides transcripts of programs, Burrelle's also offers videotapes for a number of programs. The company indicates whether or not they are available next to your selection of shows.

British Broadcasting Corporation

http://www.bbc.co.uk/

Purpose: To research programs and links for general news and other information.

Content: Throughout its long lifespan, the BBC has presented extensive programs on virtually all major political, economic, and entertainment news events. Unlike most American broadcasting systems' Web sites, the BBC treats their Web site as a separate entity, covering specific issues in more depth than on television and radio. The Web site combines television, radio, and local and national news, accompanied by online blogs and QuickTime video streams, to transmit their information in a terse yet well-developed fashion. All radio programs, as well as transcripts of many programs, are available on the Web site only weeks after broadcast.

Our View: Although you won't find much about American pop culture, a foreign point of view can often be very helpful. BBC's easy-to-use navigation system, where you can browse by topic, search its index, or keyword search its search engine, creates a viable source for old and new issues alike, expanding its role as an information leader. The **A to Z index** at the bottom of the left-hand column is where you will find virtually everything that was in the news recently and also many articles that date back several years. Index entries include names of topics, programs, or individuals.

Tip: If you're a "mobile lawyer" you can access the BBC on your cell phone or PDA by visiting **www.bbc.co.uk/ mobile**.

Also, click the **Podcasting Trial** buttom at the bottom of the home page to access downloadable audio versions of select BBC radio programs.

Links to many major market newspapers, television networks, and national news magazines can also be found at the Internet For Lawyers Web site (**http://www.netforlawyers.com/news.htm**).

News Directory

http://www.newsdirectory.com

Purpose: To locate and link to newspapers, magazines, and television stations from around the world.

Content: The news directory offers more than 20,000 links to more than 3,600 newspapers and nearly 5,000 magazines and other media resources around the world.

You can browse links to the world's newspapers by country (drilling down to the state or city in which you're interested) or browse magazines by subject or region. You can also search for newspapers and magazines by title, or locate U.S. and Canadian resources geographically by searching for publications using the telephone area code for the locality in which you're interested.

Our View: The site is mostly well organized and easy to use. The browse options are clearly labeled and accessible. The site's extensive collection of media links can help you easily locate news sources in regions with which you are not familiar. While clearly marked, the site's search functions leave something to be desired. Therefore, we suggest relying more on the site's "browse" capabilities more than its "search" capabilities.

No database, especially one this size, is infallible. An area code search for links to media sources in the 310 area code returned nine results for newspapers whose offices are located in that area code, but did not include a link to the dominant newspaper serving that area code (the *Los Angeles Times*). In fact, an area code search for the four most common area codes in the greater Los Angeles area failed to return a link to the *Los Angeles Times*, including the 213 area code where the *Times* headquarters is located. A **title** search for *"Los Angeles Times"* did return two links to the *Times'* primary Web site. A link to the *Times'* site could also be found by browsing to the United States> California> page of the site's directory.

Tip:
When using any of the site's search functions, you MUST click the **Go** button next to the search box and not press the <**Enter**> key on your keyboard to initiate the search. Even though pressing the <**Enter**> key successfully initiates searches on most other sites, any search initiated with the <**Enter**> key at the News Directory site returns no results. We conducted a number of searches (pressing the <**Enter**> key after typing our search term in the search box) and all returned no results. When we re-ran those searches and clicked the **Go** button, a number of those same searches returned links to the media we were looking for.

The site's area code search function also does not return links to local TV stations. To find these, click on the **Broadcast TV Stations** link on the home page.

Try a name search in conjunction with an area code search. Better yet, browse the links by region or subject to find the links to the media that will help you most.

Don't Forget Your Local Library for Remote Access to Newspapers, Too!

Many libraries offer patrons remote access to local newspapers and other papers from major cities around the country. For example, the Beverly Hills (California) public library offers its patrons remote access to Newsbank with its full-text content of the *Los Angeles Times, Christian Science Monitor, USA Today, Orange County Register, Riverside Press-Enterprise, San Diego Union-Tribune,* and *San Francisco Chronicle.* All a patron needs is a library card. The National Newspaper Index, offered remotely by some libraries, provides access to an index of the *New York Times,* the *Wall Street Journal,* the *Christian Science Monitor,* as well as to news stories written by the staff writers of the *Los Angeles Times* and the *Washington Post.* Local libraries may also other local and regional databases that offer full-text searchable archives of various papers.

See the discussion of free remote database access offered by libraries beginning on page 185 for information on more resources that may be available.

Search Engines for News

Google News

http://news.google.com

Purpose:	Search engine for news.
Content:	This site uses Google's search and page-ranking technologies to gather stories from over 4,500 news sources around the world, ranging from the BBC, CNN, and the Boston Globe to press releases from selected companies. News stories displayed on the Google News home page or in News search results are updated continuously throughout the day. (On a recent visit to the site, the "freshest" story was only five minutes old.) Headlines and abstracts are prominently displayed on the main page under Top Stories. Users can also perform keyword searches for links to news stories on particular subjects. Returned results can include stories up to (approximately) thirty days old.
Our View:	The search results page lists news in a variety of categories (including **Top Stories, World, U.S., Business, Entertainment,** and more) in a directory style. Within those categories, stories are grouped together by subject,

Figure 5-3. Google News home page. Google™ is a trademark of Google Technology Inc.

with stories from multiple sources—covering the same news subject—in subgroups.

A recent search for "Fidel Castro" returned over 1,900 results. In Google's ordering of the stories by relevance, the first result linked to a story from Moscow's *Pravda* that was two weeks old, while the second result from the *Washington Post* was from "19 hours ago," indicating the up-to-date nature of the search results. Under the third result were related news stories from other publications around the world.

A sampling of other sources included

- The BBC
- *Christian Science Monitor*
- CNN
- *Hindustan Times*
- *Miami Herald*

- *Jordan Times*
- *San Jose Mercury News*
- WPTV (Florida)

The oldest story in the results list was nine days old.

It is important to take note of a story's source, since Google may also include company press releases in its news search results.

Tip: Use the site's **Sort by date** function (on the right-hand side of the results page) to put the most current results at the top of the list.

AltaVista News

http://www.altavista.com/news/default

Purpose: Search engine for news.

Content: The AltaVista News search includes over 4 million articles from 3,000 sources, worldwide. It is powered by the stand-alone news search engine Moreover.

Our View: In addition to conducting standard keyword and phrase searches, you can use the AltaVista News index to search only for articles that contain images (with a check box) or to limit your search with user-definable parameters in drop-down menus. You can select

- Date range
- Topic category
- Geographical region
- News source

Tip: While there is no Advanced Search option in the AltaVista News search, it supports all search commands also used on its Web search. If you enter multiple words, AltaVista returns only articles that have all of the words.

- To exclude words, put a minus sign (-) in front of them
- Use quotation marks for phrase searches
- Use Boolean commands including AND, OR, AND NOT, NEAR
- To return results from a specific source, use the "host:" command to indicate its Web site. For example "host:latimes.com presidential election" (no quotation marks required) will return results containing the words "presidential" and "election" found at the *Los Angeles Times* Web site.

News Metasites

There are several metasites that link to general newspapers and magazines, business newspapers and magazines, and wire services.

Drudge Report

http://www.drudgereport.com

Purpose: To search for news and information through various links to news organizations.

Content: The Drudge Report site offers a comprehensive set of links to major news organizations around the world. The site also includes a list of American columnists (listed alphabetically), Chinese, Japanese, and English language wire services, and even the *National Enquirer*.

Our View: While best known for the "shoot-from-the-hip" muckraking style of his own reporting, Webmaster Matt Drudge provides a good list of links to more-established news organizations on this site. Along with the links comes Drudge's own (conservative) opinions on the news stories he chooses to highlight.

Tip: For links to many of the same news resources, and thousands of other resources in dozens of other categories, see the Refdesk.com site (discussed in the "Standard Reference Resources" section of this chapter) maintained by Matt Drudge's father, Robert Drudge.

BuzzFlash

http://www.buzzflash.com

Purpose: To search for news and information through various links to news organizations

Content: BuzzFlash offers a comprehensive set of links to major news organizations around the world. The list includes links to wire services and major market newspapers in the United States, as well as selected international news resources.

Our View: Many of the links to news sources at BuzzFlash are also available at other sites mentioned in this section. The site offers a decidedly more liberal view of current news than the Drudge Report. The top 80 percent of the Web site's home page contains links to current news stories, opinion, commentary, and satire from a liberal perspective.

Tip: There are media links buried near the bottom of the page.

Today's Front Pages

http://www.newseum.org/todaysfrontpages/

Purpose: To view and link to the current front page of newspapers from around the world.

Content: Maintained by the non-profit Newseum, "Today's Front Pages" is an online version of popular live exhibit of the same name. Every morning, more than 507 newspapers from 46 countries submit their front pages to the Newseum via the Internet. Thumbnail images of all of these front pages are then posted on the Newseum's Web site by 9:30 A.M. each day. Each image includes a clickable link to the corresponding newspaper's Web site.

Our View: Not only does this site offer a view of numerous newspaper front pages from around the world, but it also serves as a good collection of links to those papers.

Thumbnail images of the newspaper's front pages are arranged in alphabetical order by country, with U.S. papers listed first (and then alphabetically by state). The front page images are arranged in alphabetical order by country, with only 48 front pages displayed per page. To view additional front pages, you must click the **View More Pages** link at the bottom of the page you're viewing.

Navigating to specific newspapers is easier now that the Newseum has added links to two browsing options near the top of the home page. The **Map View** option displays a world map containing pinpoints representing each newspaper available via the Newseum. Hovering over any pinpoint pops up an image of that newspaper's front page. Clicking the pinpoint opens a larger image of the front page in a window that contains links to the newspaper's Web site and a downloadable PDF version of the front page. The **List by Region** option offers you broad regional categories from which to select (e.g., **USA, Asia, North America, South America,** etc.). Within those regions, you can choose the **List by Name** or **List by State** buttons (in the lower left-hand corner) to further organize the list. Hovering over a publication name pops up an image of its front page on the right-hand side of the screen. Clicking on the **Load** link next to the paper's name causes the image of that paper's front page to remain on the right-hand side of the screen. (Only one paper's front page can be "loaded" into the right-hand portion of that screen.)

| *Tip:* | If you're in Washington, D.C., be sure to catch the live exhibit of "Today's Front Pages"—updated daily. Sixty-eight of the submitted front pages are selected for an exhibition at the future site of the Newseum located at Pennsylvania Avenue and Sixth Street in downtown Washington. Front pages are chosen to represent each of the fifty states as well as a selection of international newspapers. The display is updated by 8:30 A.M., seven days a week. |

Online Newspapers

http://www.onlinenewspapers.com/

Purpose:	To search for news and newspapers from specific countries.
Content:	Developed and maintained by the Australian search engine Web Wombat, Online Newspapers contains links to over thousands of newspapers around the world. (The site lists more than 100 newspapers for Japan alone.) Links to individual counties' newspapers can be accessed through the series of regional pull-down menus on the site's home page (e.g., "Central America," "Africa," West Indies," etc.), or from the alphabetical list of all countries for which links are included.
Our View:	This is another good place to start a search for news sources in specific foreign countries.

Bizjournals

http://www.bizjournals.com

| *Purpose:* | To locate business news from forty-one cities around the U.S. |

Content:	Bizjournals is from American City Business Journals, which publishes local business newspapers in forty-one cities across the country. Some of their major markets include Atlanta, Austin, Baltimore, Boston, Dallas, Nashville, San Francisco, and Tampa, among others. Clicking the **Search Archive** link (next to the search box on the home page) gives you the option to search any of their publications (or all of them at once) back to 1996. All articles on the site can be read full-text.
Tip:	RSS Feeds are available covering specific industries and cities.

NewsLink

http://newslink.org

Purpose:	To locate links to various news organizations.
Content:	The site offers links to television and radio stations across the country, as well as to newspapers and magazines in the U.S. and around the world.
	You can view lists of these sources broken down by:

- Geographical area (state for the U.S., country for foreign media)
- Daily or nondaily newspapers
- Network affiliation (TV)
- Subject matter (such as alternative, business, and so on)

Our View:	NewsLink is run by University of Illinois journalism professor Eric Meyer. He is also a research scientist at the school's National Center for Supercomputing Applications (the birthplace of the Mosaic browser that became Netscape Navigator). While it would be difficult for any worldwide database of media sources to be complete, with his credentials, it would seem that if anyone could create a comprehensive list, Meyer could.

CEOExpress

http://www.ceoexpress.com

Purpose: For information and news on business.

Content: CEOExpress contains links to hundreds of business-oriented newspaper and magazine sources arranged by subject. These include:

- Daily news
- Business news
- International news
- News feeds
- Tech news
- Lifestyle publications

Our View: The site's layout can be a bit hard on the eyes, but the volume and quality of the links make it worth visiting.

Current News

The Web sites of the 24-hour cable television news networks are all good sources for news on the Internet. Because they are constantly updating and rewriting stories to appear on TV, the news on their sites is generally very up to date. The most popular all-news network Web sites are

- CNN at **http://www.cnn.com**
- Fox News at **http://www.foxnews.com**
- MSNBC at **http://www.msnbc.com**

Current news is also available from newspapers and magazines (see above) and wire services (see below).

Wire Services

Wire services are collectives, or membership organizations, that gather and report news, distributing the resulting stories to their members. With the recent trend toward shrinking news-gathering budgets, the international wire services have become more and more important to news coverage around the world.

Tip: Use the Drudge Report for News Archives. The most convenient way to search the archives of the major news services is via the news metasite the Drudge Report (**http://www.drudgereport.com**). You can search the AP and Reuters archives back fourteen days via search boxes offered on the Drudge site. (See the "News Metasites" section earlier in this chapter for more information on this site.)

The major wire services listed below (in alphabetical order) offer headlines and links to their most recent stories, as noted.

AFP (Agence France Presse)

To read current news: ($)   To read or download archive stories: **$**

http://www.afp.com/english/home

Purpose: For current and archived news stories from around the world.

Content: AFP is the successor of the world's first international press agency, founded in 1835. Its site offers headlines and links to select current articles.

Our View: The site is a good source to browse breaking news, and has added a search engine to retrieve archival news stories. The cost to read or download archived stories is $2–$5 per story.

Tip: Searches for current news stories from AFP can be conducted via the Yahoo! News page (**http://news.yahoo .com**).

Associated Press (AP)

http://customwire.ap.org

Purpose: To locate current and archived news stories from around the world.

Content: AP is the oldest American wire service. Its site offers access to its headlines through the Web sites of its member newspapers. From this page, you can select your local paper, or any member paper whose Web site you wish to visit. These pages usually offer headlines and abstracts of the latest stories, with links to the full articles.

Our View: The Associated Press is probably the best known wire service in the United States. Its vast resources, coupled with the resources of its member newspapers, make this wire service an excellent source of breaking news. Having to select a member paper and click through to that paper's AP search page can be cumbersome. That's why we recommend using the AP search box provided at the Drudge Report Web site (**http://www.drudgereport.com**). Drudge has tapped directly into the AP search page of the *Washington Post* to provide this service.

Bloomberg.com

http://www.bloomberg.com

Purpose: To locate news stories from around the world.

Content: Bloomberg.com presents news coverage with a heavy focus on business news coverage. Its site offers headlines and links to selected, current news stories.

Our View: Founded in 1990, Bloomberg is the newest of the wire services discussed here. Even though no archive search is available, the site is still a good source for breaking news—particularly for business and financial subjects.

Reuters

http://www.reuters.com

Purpose: To locate current and archived news stories from around the world.

Content: The site offers headlines and links to current news stories and stories from the recent past. It presents browsable headlines in over a dozen categories, ranging from **Technology** to **Oddly Enough** (strange stories), as well as a search engine to retrieve recent stories by keyword.

Our View: The easy-to-use keyword search function makes the Reuters site simple to use. The results can go back as far as one month, but are limited to the 20 newest stories. Therefore, if there are 300 stories on a particular subject over the course of a week, a keyword search for that subject will only show the headlines and links for the most recent 20, regardless of what day they appeared (even if all appeared today). You cannot see or access stories number 21 through 300.

With optional free registration, you can access raw news video and receive news alerts via e-mail, among other features.

United Press International (UPI)

http://www.upi.com

Purpose: To read selected current news stories.

Content: UPI offers links to current news stories on its home page, and has added a robust search function to access the archive. Most articles are viewable for free, with "UPI International Analysis" stories requiring a free registration to access.

Our View: Previously, the UPI site functioned as little more than a sales tool for UPI's packaged news products—offering little access to current or archived news. Now it offers one of the most robust search engines for accessing archived news stories. The search also features results "clustered" by Clusty. (See page 124 for information on Clusty.com).

Company Press Releases

In addition to the traditional news wires mentioned above, there are services that distribute news releases (for a fee) for the companies that issue them.

While press releases often put the most positive spin on a story, it can be extremely interesting and important to see what a company said about itself or a given situation in retrospect—especially in intellectual property, business transactional, and family law cases, and in stockholder lawsuits.

Below are the two largest such distribution services. While there may be some overlap in the companies that use these two services, it's a good idea to check both when you're looking for company news. You can also locate some company press releases by using the Google News search engine (discussed earlier in this chapter).

You should also keep in mind that not all companies utilize these types of services. An excellent source of company press releases is often the Web site of the company itself.

Business Wire

http://www.businesswire.com To search: To read releases:

Purpose: To locate business news and press releases.

Content: The site offers a full-text, searchable database of all company press releases issued through Business Wire over the past 30 days.

You can search or browse the latest headlines by:

- Industry (from Accounting to Universities)
- Subject (from Bond/Stock Ratings to Webcasts)
- Language

Our View: If you're looking for news from a particular company or industry, the press releases they issue can be an excellent source of information. For older news, click on **Company News Centers** for an alphabetical list of companies distributing news through Business Wire and links to each of their news releases. Some companies also proffer an online media kit. Additional information can also be obtained by clicking on **Company Profiles.**

Once Registered, you can also create a "watch list" of companies you're interested in receiving updates about by clicking on **My Companies** on the right-hand side of the home page.

PR Newswire

For Current Press Releases: (🚫$)   For Archived Press Releases: **$**

http://www.prnewswire.com/news

Purpose: To locate business news and press releases.

Content: Like Business Wire, PR Newswire offers headlines and browsable lists of the most recent news releases by subject or industry. Use the **Company or Organization** search box to find news released by a particular company. There you have the option of searching (by company name) for all releases sent by a company, or include its name, during the past thirty days. Additionally, you can click the **Company News** link on the right-hand side of the home page to browse an alphabetical listing of PR Newswire member companies to view all of the press releases sent by a particular company back to 1996. The **Archive Search** link allows you to search from any date between May 30, 1992 through thirty days ago. Abstracts of archived press releases can be accessed for free, but full-text versions must be bought—$9.95 for 3 (minimum even if you only want to read one) to $279.95 for 500.

Our View: The availability of an archive of press releases from a particular company can be a valuable tool in charting that company's history.

Locating Books and Videos

While the Internet offers ready access to millions of information sources, there are still many instances when only a hard copy of a book or video will do. For example, when you are locating or researching an expert, you may want to find a book the expert has written that relates to the testimony you need. The book can help establish expertise, and also give you an idea of the expert's perspective on the issue. (For more information on researching experts, see Chapter 9, "Finding and Backgrounding Expert Witnesses.") The Internet may come in handy in tracking down materials from experts. Here are some resources that can help.

Books

It's hard to imagine anyone with an Internet connection who has not heard of the Internet's premiere bookseller, Amazon.com (**http://www .amazon .com**). Launched in July 1995, Amazon offers what it describes as "Earth's Biggest Selection" of books (and other consumer goods). While there are any number of other traditional book retailers that have entered the online book sales fray, none has approached the notoriety of Amazon. Even book retailing giant Borders Group (owner of the Borders, Waldenbooks, and Brentano's chains) has teamed up with Amazon.com to provide online sales. Barnes & Noble online bookstore can be located at **http://www.barnesnoble.com**. Amazon and Barnes & Noble's sites both also offer videos of current and recent film releases.

Likewise, major retail video outlets have staked their claim on the Internet. New and recent releases can be purchased from Blockbuster Video (**http://www.blockbuster.com**). Other online retailers include

Buy.com (**http://www.buy.com**) and Reel.com (**http://www.reel.com**), which has teamed up with Amazon to handle its sales.

It should also be noted that Amazon maintains an auction service where users can offer personal copies of books or videos for bid. (Select **Auctions** from the list of **Product Categories** at the top of the Amazon opening screen.) Also on the auction front, you shouldn't discount the possibility that the book or video you're looking for might be available on eBay (**http://www.ebay.com**).

Hard-to-Find and Out-of-Print Books and Periodicals

Powell's Books

To search:    To purchase: **$**

http://www.powells.com

Purpose: To locate new and used technical, hard-to-find, and rare books.

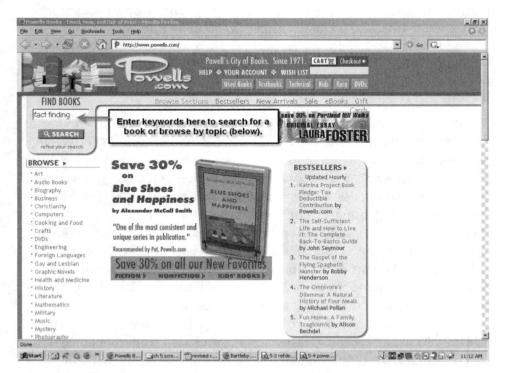

Figure 5-4. Powell's Books offers thousands of new and used books for sale in (nearly) every imaginable category.

Content: Powell's has divided its collection into more than 200 browsable categories and offers a sophisticated search engine. You can keyword search by author or title, among other criteria.

Our View: The site's clean design and clear navigation make it easy to go directly to the genre, author, or title you're looking for. The site also includes an incredible breadth of titles, from the latest Harry Potter release ($29.99, hardcover) to an 1853 first-edition French translation of selected works of Edgar Allan Poe ($1,550.00, paperback). Additionally, Powell's has an extensive selection of technical books and text books if you are searching for or conducting background research on an expert.

Tip: Click on **refine your search** to create the most targeted searches.

Abebooks

To search: To purchase: **$**

http://www.abebooks.com

Purpose: To locate new and used technical, hard-to-find, and rare books.

Content: Abebooks (from Advanced Book Exchange) has created a searchable database of the combined inventory of a network of more than 13,000 independent booksellers. All told, these booksellers hold more than 40 million books. This inventory is a mix of popular, mass-market titles; scientific and technical books; and rare, out-of-print, limited, or first-edition printings.

Our View: Returned results feature full information for the books including binding, cover type, ISBN, price, and location of the bookseller who owns each particular copy that's available.

Tip: You can search by author, title, or keywords to find the title you need. Additionally, an asterisk (*) can be used as a trailing wild card to truncate search terms ("Ste*" would stand in for "Stephen" or "Steven").

Alibris

To search: To purchase: **$**

http://www.alibris.com

Purpose: To locate new, used, hard-to-find, and rare books.

Content: Like Abebooks, Alibris connects thousands of independent booksellers and their 60 million new, used, and hard-to-find titles with the people who are looking for them. You can browse through the more than 29 categories (and innumerable subcategories) or use the site's comprehensive search engine.

Our View: You can search by author, title, or keywords to find the title you need. Returned results indicate a book's availability and pricing (new and used). Clicking on a book's title displays details for each copy of the book selected, including condition, cover type, number of pages, price, ISBN, and name of the bookseller that has the book for sale.

Tip: Alibris also utilizes the asterisk (*) as a wild card at the end of a search term.

Keep Media

http://www.keepmedia.com

Purpose: To access back issues of periodicals

Content: Founded by Borders bookstore co-founder, Louis Borders, this site offers unlimited access to more than two-dozen consumer and over 100 trade publications ranging from *Business Week* and *Esquire* to *National Hog Farmer.* The site also includes content from a number of major-market newspapers, including the *Miami Herald, San Jose Mercury News, St. Paul Pioneer Press,* and the *Philadelphia Inquirer.* Some articles are available free of charge.

Our View: At $4.95 per month for unlimited access to all of the periodicals in the Keep Media database, the charge is less than some magazines charge for a single article, not to mention services like Nexis. Articles from the current issues of publications may also be displayed. These articles can be purchased individually (recent articles included in a test search were priced at only $1) or you can wait until the articles are added to the archive that is available as part of the paid subscription.

The default display mode for returned search results is by perceived relevance. Clicking the **Date Published** link at the top of the results list reorders the list in reverse chronological order—with the most recent results listed first. Results can be further refined by publication title or by date (range).

Trussel.com

www.trussel.com/books/magdeal.htm

Purpose: To find providers of back issues of magazines and newspapers.

Content: This site provides an alphabetical list of 94 magazine and newspaper back-issue providers, including contact name, address, and phone number for each. Some listings also include an e-mail address and URL. Some of the links provide more in-depth information about the provider.

Our View: This is a great way to find that particular back issue, especially if you need publications of a specialized variety, because many of the providers list their specialties (from the esoteric to the more mainstream). For example, Al's Cine Collectibles offers "AL'S SPANISH magazines and books on all subjects, antique and modern. What is not in stock, Al, Your Man in Spain, will find for you," and Magazine Memories, Inc., offering *Life* magazine (1936 to the present, 2,000 different ones); *Time*, *Newsweek* (1920 to 1979) . . ." and more.

Tip: There is also a state and country index. We first thought that the index would be to providers who carried periodicals about that specific state or country or published in that state or country, but when we clicked on "California," for example, we found a list of providers simply located in California. Also, ordering processes vary from provider to provider. Most, however, do not offer the option to order and pay for publications over the Internet.

Million Magazines

http://www.millionmagazines.com/

Purpose: Acquire back issues of select periodicals.

Content: The Million Magazines site claims to possess more than 1 million foreign and domestic magazines dating back to 1843. Titles include:

- *Time* (1923-present)
- *Newsweek* (1933-present)
- *Life* (1883–2000)
- *Fortune* (1930–1981)
- *TV Guide* (1956–2001)

Prices range from $29.95 for the most recent issues to $79.95 for the oldest magazines listed on the site.

Our View: This is not the prettiest or most intuitive site you'll find on the Internet. In fact, the online ordering process is quite quirky; it's included here mostly as a way to access this vendor's offline contact information to help you locate the magazines you might need. While not comprehensive in title or date coverage, this service can be a good place to locate hard-to-find issues of specific magazines.

Tip: For those who do want to make their purchases online from this site, only issues of a half-dozen select magazines from 1936 to the present are available for purchase on the site. For older issues, you have to e-mail or call the site owners.

Videos

The TV MegaSite

To search: (no $) To purchase: $

http://www.tvmegasite.net/prime/store/videostobuy.shtml

Purpose: To locate obscure or hard-to-find videos.

Content: This site's Videos to Buy page maintains a list of nearly thirty sources for all types of videotapes.

Our View: The list runs the gamut from commercial video clubs (CBS Video Club) offering new and recent releases, to small specialty retailers around the country. Not all of the sources listed have Web sites or e-mail addresses, so you'll have to contact those by phone or snail mail.

Tip: See the Video Trading Post at **http://tvmegasite.net/ trading** for a list of links to other trading lists and resources where specific programs might be obtained.

The Video Den Collection

To search: **($)**   To purchase: **$**

http://www.rarevideo.com

Purpose: To locate obscure or hard-to-find videos.

Content: The Video Den Collection maintains a database of "tens-of thousands" of hard-to-find titles in a fully searchable database. You can search by:

- Film title
- Director's name
- Stars' names

Our View: The site contains a wide range of titles and genres, from special collector's editions of *E.T. The Extraterrestrial* to both versions of *Jacob Two Two Meets the Hooded Fang* (1979, starring Alex Karras; and 1999, starring Gary Busey). You can also browse the titles alphabetically. Prices vary (wildly).

Tip: If the Video Den does not have the title you're looking for in its collection, they can help you locate it on a "'collector-to-collector' basis with no rights given or implied." Click the **Inquiry** tab to submit information on the title you need.

Traditions Military Videos

To search: **($)**   To purchase: **$**

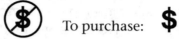

http://www.militaryvideo.com

Purpose: To locate military-themed and military-produced videos.

Content: The site maintains a growing catalog of over 600 training films and documentaries produced by the U.S. military dating from the 1930s through the 1980s.

Our View: You can browse the entire catalog by title, by service branch (Navy, Army, and so on), by theaters (such as Vietnam, Korea, World War I), or perform a keyword or title search. Prices vary from title to title.

Tip: If you are looking for a particular title or subject, on return visits to the site you can use its **New Videos** option to see new titles added in the previous two weeks or previous month.

The Video Beat

To search: To purchase: **$**

http://www.thevideobeat.com

Purpose: To locate hard-to-find genre videos.

Content: The Video Beat specializes in video copies of fifties and sixties movies. Their genre list includes Rock 'n' Roll Movies; Teen, Beach & Hippie Movies; Rock 'n' Roll TV Shows; and more. From the 1956 "seedy art house film" *Dance Hall Racket* starring Lenny Bruce to a collection of Elvis-Presley-insider Joe Esposito's rare 8mm home movies of Presley, this site is filled with esoteric and difficult-to-locate items.

Click the **Go Shopping** icon to access the site's search engine.

All tapes cost $25 and run two hours in length. Shorter programs are filled out with filler material of the same genre.

Our View: While the focus of the Video Beat collection is narrow, you never know what you'll need some day.

Tip: It should be noted that the site carries the following dis-
              claimer: "All videos are VHS NTSC and for home use
              only. All titles are sold on a 'collector-to-collector' basis
              with no rights given or implied. All titles have been
              researched and found to be in the public domain."

A Million and One World-Wide Videos

To search: 🚫$ To purchase: **$**

http://www.wwvideos.com

Purpose: To locate obscure or hard to find videos.

Content: While they do not maintain a list of available titles, this
              site claims to have "video detectives" who locate "out-
              of-print videos, rare movies, and lost films." They adver-
              tise in numerous consumer and video specialty publica-
              tions to locate the videos their clients are looking for.
              Once you have asked them to locate a video, "Your only
              obligation is to guarantee with your credit card, that
              you'll pay for it when we mail it to you," according to
              the site. If they do not find your video there is no charge
              to you.

Our View: While offering a valuable service, this Web site is diffi-
              cult to navigate. To inquire about locating and purchas-
              ing a title, click on the **Get Free Information Now**
              link at the bottom of the home page (not the **Search**
              link). That takes you to a form to fill in the title and star
              or director, along with your name and e-mail address.
              The site promises an answer to queries "within minutes."

Tip: Be certain your video is really hard to find before con-
              tacting A Million and One World-Wide Videos.

   For more information on locating video on the Internet, see Chapter
4, "Search Tools."

Locating Print Advertisements

adflip

http://www.adflip.com/ 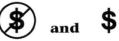 and **$**

Purpose:	To locate print advertisements back to the 1950s.
Content:	The site provides access to six decades of classic print advertising in a searchable database on a member basis (and limited access to nonmembers). Adflip's home page is a jumble of Search options. Some are available to non-members, but only a member can perform the more useful searches (such as a search by keywords, a search of a specific publication, a company name search, or to view a "Top 100" list). Membership options include a one-week, one-month, or one-year access fee. Nonmembers can only search by category, by decade, or by year and, even then, the number of results is limited. Adflip lets you know just how many more ads you could view if you were a member.
Our View:	Lawyers could either use this database in a proactive mode—to regularly search for unauthorized uses of a client's image in an advertisement, or in a reactive mode—to find an advertisement once they are made aware of the unauthorized use. Depending on what you are looking for, it is possible to search this database as a nonmember and receive enough information to be successful. However, the one-week and one-month access fees ($14 and $34, respectively) are not terribly expensive and might be worth the cost to be able to perform the more useful searches.
Tip:	When searching for older print advertising, we suggest Ad*Access, **http://scriptorium.lib.duke.edu/adaccess/**, which presents over 7,000 images appearing in U.S. and Canadian newspapers and magazines from 1911 to 1955. Ads can be searched in five main subject areas: **Radio, Television, Transportation, Beauty and Hygiene,** and **World War II**.

CHAPTER **SIX**

Government Resources Online

Generally, government Web sites end with the .gov (federal) or .us (state or local) domain. Military sites usually end with the .mil domain. In many instances, the government had the foresight and ability to also register .com and .org domain names for its sites; in other instances it did not. For example, **http://www.usps.com**, **http://www.senate.com**, and **http://www.culvercity.org** will take you to the Web sites of the U.S. Postal Service, the U.S. Senate, and the city of Culver City (California) respectively. But **http://www .whitehouse.com**, **http://www.house.com**, and **http://www .culvercity.com** will take you to a public record referral site, a real estate site, and a personal Web site, respectively—rather than to the White House site (**http://www.whitehouse.gov**), the U.S. House of Representatives site (**http://www.house.gov**), and the site for the city of Culver City. Similarly, **http://www.co.bexar.tx.us** and **http://www.bexar.org** both lead to the official Web site of Bexar County, Texas, while **http://www.bexar.com** is the personal site of a former San Antonio resident.

A domain ending in .gov or .mil can almost certainly be counted on to be authentic government sites, as there is no mechanism to register those domains outside of the federal government. Many domain registrars do offer .us domains to the general public, so it's worth a second look to be certain you are visiting the "Real McCoy."

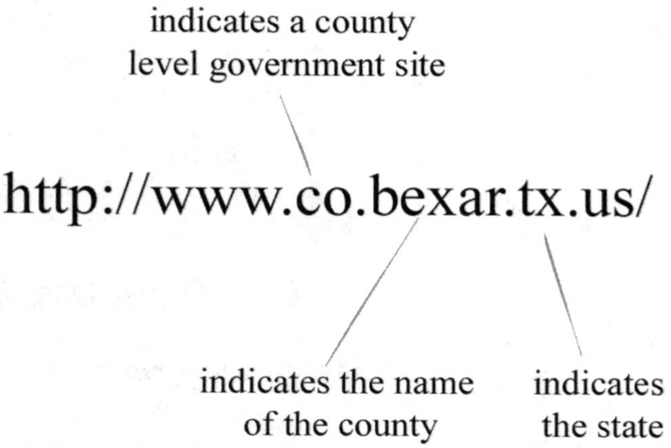

indicates a county
level government site

http://www.co.bexar.tx.us/

indicates the name   indicates
of the county   the state

Figure 6-1. In official local government sites, .us is usually preceded by a two-letter designator for a city or county (.ci and .co respectively), the name of the city or county, and a two-letter abbreviation for the state.

Federal, state, and local governments regulate, license, and collect data on a broad cross section of our professional and personal lives. More and more, government Web sites are making this information available online, but the amount and type of information varies from site to site. The George W. Bush White House has developed an action plan to create a government-wide, citizen-centered e-government program. The U.S. Office of Management and Budget regularly reports on the progress of these initiatives (**http://www.whitehouse.gov/results/agenda/egov.html**), even issuing a quarterly scorecard on the performance of particular agencies (**http://www.whitehouse.gov/results/agenda/scorecard.html**). Additionally, almost every jurisdiction (from the state down to the city level) is implementing or planning some type of online access to its services and information.

Currently, some government sites provide only utilitarian information, such as directories of agency staff, regulations, and reports. Other sites offer juicier information like administrative decisions, background information about the industries (or individuals) they regulate, the companies within those industries, and in some instances, any action taken against those companies.

For more topic-specific government Web sites, see the following chapters in this book: Chapter 8, "Accessing Public Records;" Chapter 7, "Finding and Backgrounding People;" Chapter 10, "Company Research;" Chapter 12, "Medical Research;" Chapter 14, "Environmental Research;" Chapter 17, "Statistical Research;" and Chapter 18, "Transportation Research."

Government Metasites

There are a number of metasites that can help you locate the federal, state, and local government resources you need.

FirstGov.gov

http://www.firstgov.gov

Purpose: To locate government documents and Web sites at all levels.

Figure 6.2. FirstGov.gov is the government portal. The site is a public-private partnership through which you can search millions of federal, state, District of Columbia, and U.S. territory government Web pages and the documents they contain.

Content: FirstGov provides a comprehensive search engine and a drill-down index covering millions of government Web pages at the federal and state level, including the District of Columbia and U.S. territories. Using the drop-down menu in the Search box, you can select **Federal Only, Federal & All States, All States, One State,** or **Federal & One State**. You can choose topics and subtopics (such as **Environment, Energy and Agriculture** or **Science and Technology**) by clicking on **Information by Topic**. The returned results include direct links to Web pages and other documents from the resources you have selected to search. This includes PDF, Power-Point, Word, and Excel documents, in addition to HTML Web pages.

The **News and Features** section in the lower right-hand corner of the home page includes links to press releases and free e-mail newsletters from numerous federal agencies.

For an alphabetical list of federal agencies, click the **A-Z Agency Index** link (under the **Agencies** heading) in the upper left-hand corner of the home page. This list also includes links to state agencies. (Entries for the states are in alphabetical order by the name of the state.)

Our View: This site is a good first stop when you're looking for government information on the Web. It can be especially useful if you're unsure what federal agency might oversee a particular issue, or when more than one agency might have jurisdiction. For example, a search of **Federal & All State** sites for "toxic waste" returned results from the U.S. Department of Agriculture, the Army Corps of Engineers, the Texas attorney general, and the King County (Washington) government site.

To narrow down your search results, click on **Advanced** in the upper-right corner of the home page to go to the Advanced Search page, which offers additional criteria with which you can focus your query.

In mid-2005, FirstGov made a number of changes to its Advanced Search—some for the better and some not. You can use the Advanced Search to:

1. Restrict keywords to a specific part of the web page (e.g., title, URL, or text), or to a specific domain (e.g., doe.gov).
2. Search file formats other than just HTML (e.g., Word and PowerPoint).
3. Restrict search results to a specific jurisdiction.
4. Restrict search results to a specific language.

Unfortunately, one of the less-than-useful changes is that FirstGov no longer supports the "OR" Boolean connector.

Because so many government documents and forms are created for distribution in print and posted on the Web in non-HTML formats (such as PDF), it's best to start with a broad search that includes all of the file formats searchable by FirstGov.

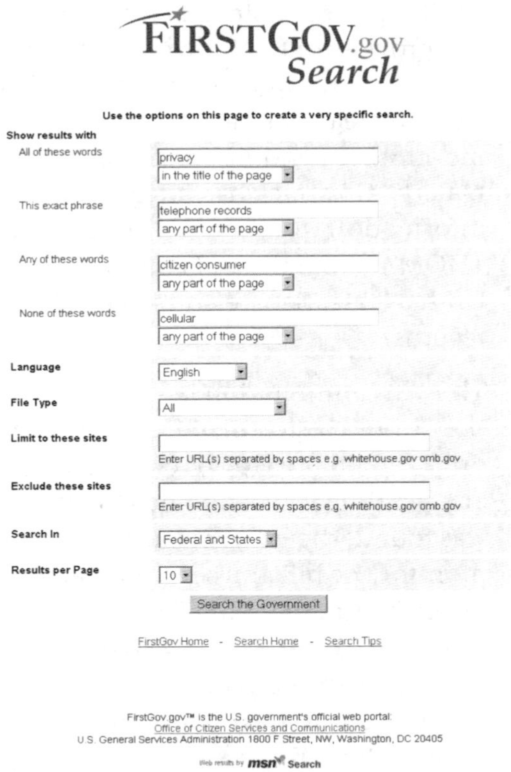

Figure 6-3. You can use FirstGov's Advanced Search to do more sophisticated and targeted searching. For instance, you can target only PDF or PowerPoint results by selecting one of them from the **File Type** drop-down menu. You could also request results only from a specific site (or sites) by entering its URL into the **Limit to these sites** search box or you can exclude results from one or more sites by entering its URL into the **Exclude these sites** search box.

Tip: • For links to Native American tribal government sites, and federal government agencies dealing with the tribes, use the **Tribal** link, listed under **By Organization**, on the left-hand side of the home page.

GovTrack

http://www.govtrack.us/

Purpose: An E-monitoring and E-alert service that assists you in monitoring any pending legislation in Congress.

Content: While the official federal legislative site, THOMAS, does not provide an E-monitoring or E-alert feature, a University of Pennsylvania Department of Linguistics graduate student created a site that does: GovTrack. For ease of monitoring pending legislation and sending users E-alerts, GovTrack has integrated, into one database, information from a variety of official sources, including THOMAS (for bills and committee reports), and the United States Senate and House Web sites (for voting records).

Thus, an immigration lawyer who has clients claiming they would be tortured if returned to their country of origin could use GovTrack to research whether there was any pending legislation on this topic. If a relevant bill was found, the lawyer would request that GovTrack monitor the bill and send an E-alert when action is taken. To find pending legislation on the topic "torture," click on the **Legislation** tab at GovTrack and select **Search Legislation**, enter the word "torture" in the search box and choose the current congress or one back to 1999. **Browse Bills by Subject or Committee**, another search method is to click on the **What Interests You** tab, select "T" from the alphabetical list, and then click on "torture." Using both methods during a recent test search, fifteen bills appeared. If you are only interested in one bill, such as Senate Bill 654, click on it and a screen will be displayed that shows the origin of the information (THOMAS), the status of the bill, and links to the full text of the bill. There is also a tab labeled **Monitor** (to the right of the status information) that can be selected to monitor Senate Bill 654. The **Monitoring** feature requires you to register at login to the site to visit your **customized tracked events** page. (To end the monitoring, simply click **Stop Monitoring**.) To monitor all bills under the topic "torture," select the topic from the **What Interests You** list.

To instead receive an E-alert from GovTrack about Senate Bill 654, the immigration lawyer at this point would click on **Sign Up for free e-mail updates**. The lawyer would then enter his or her e-mail address and select a password. From here, the lawyer would be able to select from the drop-down menu **Don't Send Me Updates, Send Me Daily Updates**, or **Send Me Weekly Updates**, and then click on **Update Settings**.

Our View: The site is easy to search, and setting up the E-Monitoring and E-Alert features was also fairly easy. Often times, multiple bills are introduced regarding the same topic and this is why we like the **What Interests You** feature, which allows you to set up E-Monitoring and E-Alerts for a topic, rather than a specific bill. This way, you won't miss information about a newly introduced bill on your topic. We also like how the Tracked Events and E-Alert features are two separate services, allowing those who don't want to receive an E-alert to still go back to the site and review any action on their selected bills or topics by logging in and clicking on **Your Tracked Events**.

Tip: After logging in and selecting **Your Monitors**, do *not* choose, under **Miscellaneous Monitors**, any of the following: **Activity on all Legislation, Upcoming Committee Hearings,** or **All Roll Call Votes,** unless you really want E-alerts about *all* pending congressional bills, hearings, or roll call votes.

For those who would rather set up the alert as an RSS feed instead of an e-mail, this option is also available.

University of Maryland Thurgood Marshall Law Library

http://www.law.umaryland.edu/marshall/crsreports/index.asp $\textcircled{\$}$

Purpose: The University of Maryland Thurgood Marshall Law Library maintains an online archive of Congressional Research Service (CRS) reports to make them accessible to the public.

Content: CRS is an arm of the Library of Congress and is charged with providing Congress with nonpartisan, in-depth reports about various topics. Over 3,000 reports are issued yearly, none of which are publicly released. The archive of reports is browseable alphabetically by report title or by general topics. The full text of each report is available free—in PDF format. The archive also references other free subject collections.

Our View: This is a great resource. Not only does Thurgood Marshall Law Library link to CRS reports that they happen to find on the Internet, they also purchase reports that they don't readily find and then archive them at this site. We tested this out by trying to see if we could readily find a CRS report on FirstGov that we had already found at the Thurgood Marshall site. Sure enough, we got no results at FirstGov. Some sort of keyword search feature would be helpful, however.

Tip: The list of Reports can be sorted by date, by order code, or by title. Sorting by date shows you the most recent reports first. By using the **Sort By Date** feature, we learned that a report entitled "The Department of State's Patterns of Global Terrorism Report: Trends, State Sponsors, and Related Issues" had been issued only one month ago.

Pennyhill.com (to search) (to obtain CRS Reports)

http://pennyhill.com/ $\textcircled{\$}$ (to search)   **$**   (to obtain CRS Reports)

Purpose: To supply Congressional Research Service (CRS) publications to the public.

Content: Any CRS document issued since 1995 (and selected documents from 1993-94, and some prior to 1993) is available for purchase at Penny Hill Press, the only private supplier of all CRS publications. However, the documents can only be searched by topic. The documents can be purchased on an ad-hoc basis or by subscription. The collection is updated at least weekly and sometimes more frequently.

Our View: This is a useful resource that could be more useful if it was keyword searchable. It's reasonably priced at $7.95 per report (subscribers), $29.95 per report (nonsubscribers) or $19.95 per report (students), plus postage. Each additional same-day order by non-subscribers is offered at 50 percent off.

Tip: If you cannot find a CRS report, Pennyhill suggests that site visitors call them at 301-330-9224 or e-mail them at congress@pennyhill.com. They will attempt to obtain the report within one week of the request.

If you prefer to keyword search to find your CRS report (an option that Pennyhill does not offer), go to Zfacts (**http://zfacts.com/p/576.html**). There, you will be able to keyword search for CRS reports. You will be presented with a list of results, one of which will most likely be Pennyhill. Before linking to it, however, link first to the other results in case one is a site where your report is available at no charge. Otherwise, click on the Pennyhill.com result and order the report.

Three of the most oft-requested government sites are for the White House (**http://www.whitehouse.gov**), the U.S. Senate (**http://www.senate.gov**) and the U.S. House of Representatives (**http://www.house.gov**). For links to other government sites at the federal, state, and local level, there are four metasites in particular that have each compiled hundreds of useful links to government resources at every level. While no list is complete, a combination of these four should point you to the information you're looking for:

- GovSpot at **http://www.govspot.com**
- FindLaw
  - Federal Resources at **http://www.findlaw.com/10fedgov**
  - State Resources at **http://www.findlaw.com/11stategov**
- University of Michigan Library's Government Resources on the Web at **http://www.lib.umich.edu/govdocs/govweb.html**
- LexisONE
  - Federal Resources at **http://www.lexisone.com/legalresearch/ legalguide/federal_resources/federal_resource_center_ index.htm**
  - State Resources at **http://www.lexisone.com/legalresearch/ legalguide/states/states_resources_index.htm**

These metasites offer drill-down directories to select the particular information you need. Each site organizes and presents its information differently. Your preference of one over another will depend on how you like to retrieve and review information.

GovSpot offers links to executive, legislative, and judicial resources at the federal level, as well as links to individual state and local government resources. For example, click the **Executive Branch** link on the left-hand side of the GovSpot home page to access links to cabinet-level agencies such as the Departments of State, Commerce, and so on. (Don't miss the site's list of toll-free phone numbers for a variety of federal agencies at **http://www.govspot.com/lists/800numbers.htm**.)

Similarly, clicking the **Executive Branch** link on FindLaw's federal government resource page (**http://www.findlaw.com/10fedgov**) and then clicking **Executive Agencies** returns a list of links to the same cabinet-level agencies. Also included are links to the Web sites of other government entities they supervise. For example, beneath FindLaw's link to the Department of Justice Web site are links to the Drug Enforcement Administration, the Federal Bureau of Investigation, and the Office of the Solicitor General. (FindLaw also offers links to state government information, as noted above.)

At the University of Michigan Library page, clicking the **Federal** link on the left-hand side, and then clicking **Executive Branch** returns a long list of links to other sites where you can find information and links to federal agencies, but not direct links to the agencies themselves. (This site also provides links to state and local government resources by clicking the **State** or **Local** links, respectively, on the left-hand side of the page.)

LexisONE's federal and state government resource pages are also organized similarly to GovSpot's. Clicking on the **Federal Executive Departments** link returns an annotated list of links to cabinet level agencies. Links to independent agencies such as the Central Intelligence Agency are found by clicking the page's **Federal Independent Agencies** link.

For links to historical data and documents, visit the U.S. National Archives and Records Administration site at **http://www.archives.gov**.

TRACfed

http://tracfed.syr.edu

Purpose:	To locate government regulatory data; civil, criminal, and enforcement data; judicial data; and track trends in those areas.
Content:	Syracuse University's Transactional Records Access Clearinghouse (TRAC) has compiled a massive database of information detailing how the federal government "enforces the law, where it assigns employees, and how it spends our money." TRAC has developed a set of forms-driven pages to help you extract the data you need. Individual subscriptions of $50 per month allow twenty queries per month. TRACfed offers pricing for organizational subscriptions and site licenses.

To access search forms for specific types of data, select a topic from the brightly colored buttons on the home page (e.g., Criminal, Civil, etc.).

Each topic offers a variety of options for manipulating data, including: **Express, Going Deeper,** and **Analyzer.** Within these options are more detailed perspectives of the data.

The **Express** view might contain a broad **Overall** view of the topic, data related to actions brought by specific

Agencies or present the data organized by cause of action (labeled **Causes**). Researchers can select any of these views by clicking the **Express** link and then the **Overall, Agencies,** or **Causes** links on the left-hand side of the screen. Each of these is then broken down into more specific examinations, including comparisons between agencies or causes of action, and trends from year to year in a given information category.

The **Going Deeper** link on the left-hand side of the screen allows users to set specific search parameters (e.g., "Fiscal Year," "Outcome in Court [raw numbers for/against the U.S.]," or "Court Outcome" [percentage of cases found for/against the U.S.]) more narrowly define the results. Criteria are added using a series of check boxes.

The **Analyzer** option offers a more powerful data mining tool to retrieve very specific information based on criteria you define in the **Analyzer's** fill-in forms. It is offered on the left-hand side of the page in the "Criminal," "Civil," and "Staffing" categories only.

Our View: The "drill-down" structure, pull-down menu and fill-in-the-blank forms used to generate these reports are very easy to use. The available data can be worthwhile as you formulate your strategy for a particular case. For example, you can discover the percentage of convictions in cases brought by federal enforcement agencies in a specific district (or the entire country). A search of this data, in the Central District of California, revealed that 42.6 percent of cases filed by the Bureau of Alcohol, Tobacco and Firearms, in the most recent year for which data were available, ended in conviction of the defendant. The data also showed that the percentage had dropped steadily each year over the five years for which data were presented.

TRACfed does not require an annual subscription, so you can subscribe for just one month if you do not need continued access to this kind of information.

Registered users can also save selected results to their **Web Locker** (information is saved on the TRACfed servers for later recall). The Web Locker can hold up to 20,000 records.

Tip: When using the **Analyzer** function, it is necessary to click the **Select** link next to a drop-down form field to select the criteria to be included in that field.

See Chapter 17, "Statistical Research," to locate resources on the Internet that offer free access to some of this type of information.

LSU Libraries Federal Agency List

http://www.lib.lsu.edu/gov/fedgov.html

Purpose: To locate links to hundreds of federal government agencies, boards, commissions, committees, and so on.

Content: This site from Louisiana State University links to hundreds of federal agency, commission, board, and committee Web sites. The links are accessible either as an alphabetical list or as a hierarchical list arranged by level (such as **Boards, Commissions and Committees, Independent,** and **Quasi-Official**)

Our View: LSU's list is best suited for use when you know the name of the agency you're looking for, but don't know the URL of its Web site. It can also be useful when you have only the partial name of an agency. Unlike FirstGov, which searches the content of millions of government Web sites, this site's search box only searches within its own database of agency Web site names. For example, a search for "toxic waste" returned no results, since there is no agency with those words in its name, while a search for "energy" returned links to Web sites that con-

tain that word in their title (such as Department of
Energy and Federal Energy Regulatory Commission).

Government Publication Sites

GPO Access

http://www.gpoaccess.gov

Purpose: To locate government publications on the Web, or for
purchase in print.

Content: GPO Access is an online service of the U.S. Government
Printing Office (GPO) providing free electronic access to
the official, published versions of information products
produced by the federal government. Available information ranges from the federal budget and the Code of Federal Regulations to topic-specific books published by the
GPO. The publications are also offered for sale through
their online bookstore.

Our View: Use the **Federal Resources by Topic** link near the
bottom of the home page to access the **GPO Access
Resources Organized by Topic** drop-down menu to
select the topic in which you're interested. Many topics
include links to Congressional committees related to the
topic, as well as links to regulations and pending legislation.

The GPO Access internal search engine uses the FirstGov
search index. Therefore, any search results returned via
GPO Access can also be located through a search at First-
Gov. However, you can use the GPO Access Advanced
Search options check boxes to further narrow your
results to **All of GPO, Only GPO Access,** or **Only the
U.S. Government Online Bookstore,** among other
options.

Our most recent tests, however, return no results when
searching from the GPO Access site. Regular and

Advanced searches bring up the FirstGov search page . . .
no results, just the FirstGov search page. You can still
run your searches there, however.

Tip: Also see the site's **Finding Aids** page at
             http://www.access.gpo.gov/su_docs/tools.html for
             links to available materials.

Uncle Sam Migrating Government Publications

**http://exlibris.memphis.edu/resource/unclesam/
migrating/mig.htm**

Purpose: To locate U.S. government publications on the Internet.

Content: The University of Memphis Library maintains this index
             of U.S. government publications available on the Inter-
             net. The site includes links to documents that have been
             converted from print to the online format, as well as to
             some that are only available on the Internet. The docu-
             ments come from a wide variety of entities, from the
             Department of Agriculture to the (House) Committee
             on Ways and Means. The "Migrating" in the site's title
             originally referred to those documents that were being
             converted ("migrating") from print to electronic for-
             mats.

Our View: To locate the document you're looking for, you must
             know its title or its SuDoc number (similar to a library's
             call number). There is no keyword searching. One main
             advantage to the site is that it links directly to these doc-
             uments, and not just to the Web sites of the agencies
             that authored them. While the site is extremely useful,
             the ability to locate documents through a topical search
             engine would make it more useful.

U.S. Government Manual

http://www.gpoaccess.gov/gmanual/browse-gm-05.html

Purpose:　To access the official handbook of the federal government.

Content:　The United States Government Manual provides comprehensive information on the agencies of the legislative, judicial, and executive branches. Each section (such as Office of National Drug Policy or Department of Commerce) is presented as a separate PDF or text document that can be read online or downloaded to your computer. From this page, you can access the current or past editions of the manual.

　　To browse, go to **http://www.gpoaccess.gov/gmanual/browse.html**, and click on an edition (back to 1997). Each section of the Manual is presented as a separate PDF or text document. To access the search engine, go to **http://www.gpoaccess.gov/gmanual/search.html**, select an edition of the manual (back to 1995) and type a keyword, phrase, or name into the search box. Searches can include Boolean operators (AND, OR, NOT, ADJ). For phrase searching, place quotation marks around the phrases. Truncation is an option (use the asterisk wildcard) to find variations of a word. For example: agen* will retrieve agency, agencies, agent, agents, etc.

Our View:　The Government Manual includes useful background information, such as lists of staff and office locations. The table of contents, with its descriptive chapter titles, is easy to browse. The inclusion of page number references to the print version of the manual is helpful if you need to later refer to or cite the print version. The text version of the manual includes the URLs of agencies discussed, but does not include clickable links to those sites. Clickable links are accessible in the PDF version (if you're using version 7 of the Acrobat Reader.)

Tip:　To search multiple editions of the Manual in consecutive order (e.g., 2003-2004 and 2002-2003) or to search a range of editions (e.g., 2003-2004 through 1999-2000), go to **http://www.gpoaccess.gov/gmanual/search.html**, highlight the first edition, and then hold down the <SHIFT> key and highlight the last item. All items within this range will be selected. To search non-contiguous editions of the Manual (e.g., 2002-2003 and 1999-2000), hold down the <CTRL> key and use the mouse (left click) to highlight each individual edition of the Manual.

Other Useful Government Sites

Google's Uncle Sam Search

http://www.google.com/unclesam

Purpose:	To search only military and government Web sites.
Content:	Google has created a specialty search engine that returns results only from the .gov and .mil domains reserved for government and military Web sites, respectively.
Our View:	As we've mentioned a number of times throughout this book, Google is our preferred search engine. The fact that you can utilize the Advanced Search features, just as you would in a regular Google search, while limiting the search to .gov and .mil sites makes it that much easier to narrow your search for the precise government-related information you need.
	When we compared this search engine to its mainstream counterpart (Google) and to the Firstgov.gov Web site, using the phrase "class action," Google's Uncle Sam returned more than 3 million results, starting with a link to FindLaw's Class Action and Mass Tort Center— clearly not a government site. The rest of the first page of results did include government sites though, from bills and lawsuits to settlements about "class actions." Google's main search engine returned over 4 million results, starting with links to News and Books about class actions. The **News** link allows you to view the day's top stories in regard to your topic and the **Book** link

shows you if there are any class action books available on the Internet. The first result after the News and Books sections was a link to Stanford University Law School's Class Action Clearinghouse. A link to FindLaw's Class Action and Mass Tort Center was also returned on the first page, but no government related links—only commercial links—many to law firm sites.

We searched "class action" in Firstgov.gov and opted to search "Federal and All States" (use the drop-down menu on the top right of the home page to make a jurisdictional selection). More than 7,000 results were returned, mostly having to do with settlements, lawsuits, and bills about "class action."

Of the three sites mentioned here, our preference was Google's main search engine—for when you are interested in news and books about the topic and not just information from government sites. However, for hardcore government information on the topic, our preference was FirstGov or Google's Uncle Sam—especially if you do not want to see any law firm sites displayed. We were surprised that FirstGov had fewer results than Google's Uncle Sam.

Tip: See Chapter 4, "Search Tools," for more information on conducting effective Google searches.

CyberCemetery

http://govinfo.library.unt.edu

Purpose: To locate Web sites of defunct federal government entities.

Content: Maintained by the University of North Texas Libraries (in partnership with the GPO), this site offers archived versions of nearly four dozen Web sites of now-defunct federal government agencies and commissions dating back to 1995. The Web sites are stored with all of the pages that were available at the time the Web site was closed down.

Our View: While the sites was easy enough to browse when it was only an alphabetical list of archived sites (now you can-click the **Browse the Cybercemetery** link on the left-hand side of the screen to access the list), the addition of a search engine for the expired site is very helpful. Click **Search the Cybercemetery** link to access the search.

Tip: Also see Chapter 4, "Search Tools," for more information regarding locating archived material no longer available in its original location on the Internet.

The Educator's Reference Desk

http://www.eduref.org/

Purpose: To locate education-related research and information.

Content: ERIC is the Educational Resources Information Center from the U.S. Department of Education. This site offers a collection of over 3,000 educational resources organized into a Yahoo!-style directory. Within the directory's twelve primary topics are hundreds of subtopics covering many aspects of educational theory and practice. Each subtopic includes links to Internet sites, answers to related questions, and links to related lesson plans.

The site also offers a keyword or phrase search engine that searches all of the topics simultaneously, as well as an archive of questions posed to the site's experts by previous visitors.

Our View: You can access the high volume of information in whatever manner suits you best: by drilling down through

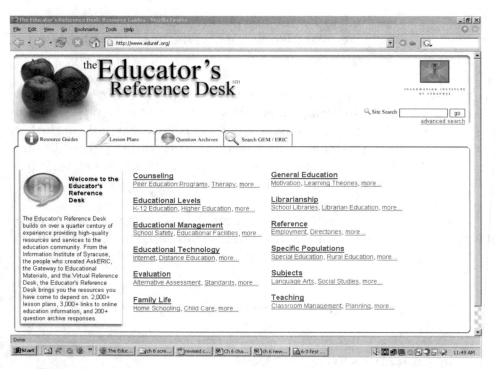

Figure 6-4. If you can't find the education-related information you need in one of ERIC's nearly four hundred subtopics, you can pose a question directly to one of ERIC's education experts.

the directory, by selecting the subtopic that looks most relevant (click on the **Topics A-Z** link at the bottom of the home page), or by conducting a keyword or phrase search.

You can also use the **Advanced Search** page to construct more sophisticated phrase searching or to limit your search to a particular grade level.

The Downside

Despite the explosion of the Internet in the 1990s as an information distribution platform, not all government agencies provide as much information as some of the sites discussed here. For example, it wasn't until 2002 that the U.S. Immigration and Naturalization Service (now the Bureau of Citizenship and Immigration Services) created an online database to check the status of applications made to the agency (**https://egov.immigration.gov/cris/jsps/index.jsp**).

Also, easy access to all these government computers and information via the Web isn't always a good thing. In 2001, U.S. District Court Judge Royce Lamberth ordered the U.S. Department of Interior to take down all of its Web sites. The order was part of a long-running case in which the Department was charged with mismanaging billions of dollars held in trust since the late nineteenth century for millions of Native Americans. As part of the underlying class-action suit filed in 1996, the judge hired a security expert who was able to access sensitive information regarding the Indian trust funds by entering the Department of Interior computer network through its Web site. This security breach brought about the judge's order to essentially quarantine the Department's network from any outside contact until the data in question were secured. This led to the Department closing all of its Web services, including e-mail. Though the services eventually returned to the Web, some of the agency's sites were off line well into 2002.

After the September 11, 2001 terrorist attacks on the United States, many government agencies removed some of the more sensitive information publicly available on their Web sites. For example, the U.S. National Imagery and Mapping Agency (NIMA) suspended online and off-line sales of maps of military installations; the U.S. Office of Pipeline Safety (OPS) restricted access to its Internet mapping application, pipeline data, and drinking water data; and visitors to the Nuclear Regulatory Commission (NRC) Web site were greeted with the following disclaimer: "In support of our mission to protect public health and safety, the NRC is performing a review of all material on our site. In the interim, only select content will be available. We appreciate your patience and understanding during these difficult times."

*CHAPTER***SEVEN**

Finding and Backgrounding People

Finding Versus Backgrounding

Lawyers frequently have to find people, from a missing heir to an expert witness. Other times lawyers need to "background" a person. Backgrounding can be defined simply as finding information about people and about their background. It's a term commonly used by private investigators. There are two major ways to find and background people: by searching through public records and by sifting through bits and pieces of publicly available information. While public records are filed with government agencies, publicly available information is not. Publicly available information is that information that you voluntarily provide to a private entity or publish in a public place (such as the Internet). For example, you provide your phone number and address to a private entity—the telephone company. You publish information on the Internet—from postings to an online community, to the content on your own Web site, to the information you provide to Classmates.com. That information is now publicly available and may be found by anyone surfing the Internet. It may also be sold to marketing companies or public record database companies. In a recent study, 70 percent of the respondents gave personal information to a commercial Web site to get a product or service (but only 29 percent did so to a government Web site). The fact is that information about each of us is scattered among countless computer files held by the government, by private entities, and now by the public entity known as the Internet.

This chapter focuses on using the publicly available information found on the Internet to find and background people. We'll discuss both traditional resources found on the Internet—such as phone directories, and nontraditional resources—ones that you'll need to "think outside the box" to find, such as online communities. Some of this publicly available information contained within nontraditional resources would never be found on a pay database, yet could provide you with the "smoking gun."

The next chapter, "Accessing Public Records," focuses on using public records to find and background people.

Try the Internet First

There's nothing as convenient or as cheap as using the Internet to search for people via public records or publicly available information. This is not to say that the Internet provides access to all records. For example, there is no comprehensive site on the Internet to search for all reported state or federal court decisions going back to the time when each court first began publishing its decisions. If you want to search for something like that, you'd be better off using a pay database such as Lexis or Westlaw. However, the convenience of the Internet's perpetual availability from almost any computer (or hand-held device) with an Internet connection, and the negligible cost of using the Internet, makes it a logical first choice for finding and backgrounding people, even if you end up accessing a fee-based database later.

Backgrounding People

Although we noted that the term backgrounding is one used by private investigators, which conjures up images of cloak and dagger surveillance, it actually refers to investigating a person via research instead of by surveillance. Backgrounding can be as straightforward as finding someone's biography in a *Who's Who* directory or as offbeat as finding out something mentioned about them in a posting in an online community or in an eBay feedback profile. (The eBay feedback profile includes a rating number for the bidder and the seller, as well as written comments about either. Because not everyone uses their real name in these types of communications, you might not have any luck finding information about your subject, but it's worth a try.)

eBay Feedback Profiles

A California judge cleared eBay in a libel suit brought by one of its users who asked eBay to remove a seller's negative comments about him in the feedback profile (see **http://www. law.com/jsp/article.jsp?id=1090180161293**).

Backgrounding can include the following information about a person:

- Address
- Phone number
- Social Security number
- Date of birth (or death)
- Marriages and divorces
- Education
- Occupation
- Professional or occupational license
- Place of employment
- Publications by or about the subject found in books, articles, e-newsletters, blogs, and Web sites (such as an employer's site)
- Biography or profile
- Image
- Hobbies
- Interests
- Assets (assessment value of the subject's home, and whether he or she owns a plane, boat, trademarks, copyrights, patents, stocks, businesses, and so on)
- Liens, judgments, and bankruptcies
- Lawsuits
- Political party membership
- Campaign contributions
- Civic and volunteer work
- A PowerPoint presentation, Excel spreadsheet, or Word document created and posted on the Internet by the subject or about the subject
- Postings to, from, or about the subject (found in the ongoing discussions or archives of online communities)

Other Backgrounding

Much of the same data can be gathered for background information about companies, their executives, products, and experts as well. See Chapter 10, "Company Research;" Chapter 11, "Competitive Intelligence Research;" and Chapter 9, "Finding and Backgrounding Expert Witnesses."

Finding People

War Story: Finding Someone Without Having a Name

Sometimes lawyers have the name of the person they are trying to find and sometimes they don't. Even when you don't know the name of the person you seek, the Internet can be the answer to your problem. Lawyer and law librarian Cathy Pennington Paunov tells this story:

"One of my favorite examples is the case where someone in Ohio was working on a salmonella ice cream case. She was desperate. She needed additional information. We only wanted to get hold of practitioners that had worked on cases like this. So I went to AltaVista, which is my favorite search engine on the Internet, and searched the Internet for the following three words: "salmonella" and "ice cream." I got something like three hundred hits. One of them, and it was in the first batch—the nice thing about AltaVista is it ranks the stuff in order of probable relevance—the third or fourth hit down, was some law firm in Chicago. Their Web site said that one of their senior litigation partners had handled the largest salmonella ice cream case in the country. I actually picked up the phone because I knew how desperate this poor lawyer was. I picked up the phone and called the lawyer in Ohio and said, 'Listen, here's someone in Chicago.' I also called the Chicago lawyer and warned him I was doing this—and he said, 'Fine, I'd be happy to help her out.'

"I don't think I would have found the salmonella ice cream guy but for the Internet. There's no way I could have found him anywhere else. That was the most incredible story. I've got one very happy small-town lawyer and she's got the name of the top legal expert in the field."

Free Is Sometimes Best

If Paunov had tried searching for this information before we were using the Internet for research, she might have racked up a huge bill by running a nationwide search looking for court opinions in a commercial database about salmonella ice cream cases. And to boot, she may have come up empty-handed if there were only state trial-level opinions on the topic, since trial-level cases are not usually published. The beauty of the Internet is you might find a story about an unreported trial-level case right on point on some firm's Web site as Paunov did, or in a posting in an online community—information resources that the commercial databases don't index (yet).

Search for the Expertise

When you don't have the name of an expert, you often need to search by the expertise to discover names of potential experts. See Chapter 9, "Finding and Backgrounding Expert Witnesses," for various places to find and background experts.

The Internet is an excellent source for finding people if you know something about the individual. For example, if you're looking for a lawyer, there are two comprehensive lawyer directories available free on the Internet: the West Legal Directory found on their FindLaw site (visit **http://lawyers.findlaw.com/lawyer/lawyer_dir/search/jsp/adv_search.jsp** to search by practice area, and visit **http://lawyers.findlaw.com/lawyer/lawyer_dir/search/jsp/name_search.jsp** to search by lawyer or firm name) and Martindale Hubbell (**http://www.martindale.com**) for searching by practice area, name, language spoken, and more. In addition, private companies, universities, government agencies, and other entities provide staff directories online, so if you know that the person you seek is on the faculty at Rutgers University, you can use the Internet to find a way to contact that person even when it's after normal business hours and nobody's answering the telephone at the university's main number. If you're looking for an American physician, the American Medical Association (**http://webapps.ama-assn.org/doctorfinder/home.html**) pro-vides a database that can locate over 690,000 doctors by name, specialty, and location who are licensed to practice in the U.S.

Reverse Searching

If you don't have the name of the person you are trying to locate (or if you are unsure of the spelling or there has been a name change), but you do have other clues about the person, reverse searching is a possible option. The following clues about a person can be turned into a reverse search and lead you to that person (sometimes a combination of these clues needs to be employed):

- Social Security number
- An alias
- Phone number or address (current or past)
- Date of birth
- Age range
- Occupation

Problems with Name Searching

Even if a lawyer has the name of the person he is trying to find or background, the search can prove difficult if any of the following events have occurred:

- Address or phone number change
- Name change due to marriage or divorce
- A misspelled name
- Death

Another problem with name searching is you can't always be sure that you have the right person since many people share the same name. Also, because many people refer to themselves in various ways, it's hard to be certain that you've done a thorough search. Name searching requires finding all the various names (and variations) that the subject uses and then searching using all of them. You need to discover what name your subject uses:

- First and last name only?
- First and last name, with a middle name or middle initial?
- Nickname?
- Aliases?

- Married name?
- Maiden name?

Tips for Name Searching

If you think the person uses only a first and last name, enter the name into a search engine as a phrase by surrounding it with quotation marks ("carole levitt"). This will help narrow your search.

If it's possible that the subject uses a middle name or initial (either regularly or sporadically) or if you don't know the middle name, use a Boolean connector between the first and last name (carole AND levitt) to find any document with the name "carole" and the name "levitt"—and anything in between those two names. This can give you many irrelevant results, though—you might find a Carole Brown and a Robert Levitt in the same document, which is technically a correct result but not the one you're looking for.

Or, better yet, enter your name search into Staggernation (**http://staggernation.com/cgi-bin/gaps.cgi**), a proximity search function created to work with Google. It allows one to search Google's index with a keyword, such as a first name, within one, two, or three words of another keyword, such as a last name. The search can be limited to the exact order in which the words are entered (e.g., *john* within one word of *brown*) or in either order (e.g., *john* within one word of *brown* or *brown* within one word of *john*).

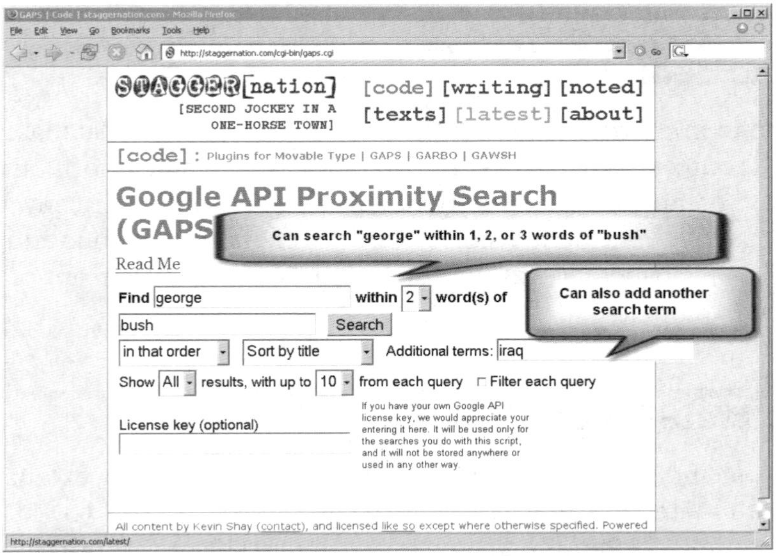

Figure 7-1. Use the drop-down menu at the Staggernation site to choose whether to search a keyword within one, two, or three words of another keyword.

If a name is commonly misspelled (or has an alternative spelling), search for the subject by the misspelled (or alternatively spelled) name, too. A Lexis search for Carole Levitt's property records found she owned nothing, until we entered "Leavitt," which is the common misspelling of her last name.

Use the OR Boolean connector for names that have various spellings (Smith OR Smyth) or have nicknames (Andy OR Andrew).

Privacy Issues

Computers are incredibly useful tools if you're looking for someone or backgrounding them, and slightly scary if you're concerned about personal privacy (especially your own). After we've already disclosed personal data, it is difficult to recall it. Some sites do offer you the chance to remove your data, however. For instance, if you find your contact information available at Swithchboard.com (**http://www.switchboard.com/**) and you want to remove it, simply click on the **Update/Remove This Listing** link that is positioned to the right of your entry. In order to protect our personal privacy, the most useful thing we can do is to be aware of the power of digital communications, and be cautious about what personal data we release. But if you're looking for someone, maybe because they owe you money, or because an estate you're administering owes them money, or just simply to invite them to a reunion, computers make the process easy, and even fun.

Off-line Searching

Keep in mind that although the free Internet and pay databases can be useful sources for public record and publicly available information research, a comprehensive search may also involve physically traveling to court houses, government agencies, and other archives (public and private) to review paper records. It's estimated that only 20 percent of public records are online.

Using Web-Based Traditional Resources

To find and background people, researchers used to rely extensively upon print materials (such as directories and phone books), CD-ROMs, microfilm, microfiche, and proprietary databases. These resources would often be inaccessible to many researchers because they were expensive, cumbersome to use, cumbersome to store, or geographically inaccessible.

But as more and more of these traditional research resources have been converted to Web-based resources, they have become much more accessible in every way and thus much more useful for finding people. Take print phone directories that are now Web-based, for example: since many are free, the expense of buying and storing them is no longer an issue; since they are searchable in a digital format, there is no longer a need to manually search through multiple directories so they are no longer cumbersome to use; since they are stored on the Internet, they are no longer cumbersome to store; and since they can be accessed by anyone with a computer and an Internet connection, there is no longer an issue of geographical inaccessibility.

Phone Directories on the Web

The most common (though often overlooked) way to find people is to use the most common reference book there is—the telephone book, now found free in Web-based phone book directories. The thousands of U.S. regional phone directories are perfectly suited to the quick lookup speed of computer databases. Results usually include street address, telephone number, and sometimes an e-mail address, a map to the address, and more. At present, there is no comprehensive directory for cellular phones. Later in this chapter, we'll provide some limited assistance for finding cellular phone numbers and even records of calls made from both cellular and land-line numbers—for a fee. While some years ago a number of CD-ROM publishers seized the opportunity to issue national phone directories on disk, Internet-based phone books are a step ahead of CD-ROM phone books in some ways. The Internet makes databases easier to update and distribute, so they can be more current than a CD-ROM, although it's hard to tell how often the Web-based directories are actually updated. Using the Internet avoids the need to change disks. Internet phone books are accessible from anywhere (assuming you have an Internet connection, of course) and Internet phone books are free.

On the flip side, if you want to print large phone lists, CD-ROM is superior because Internet-based directories generally allow you to display only a few names and phone listings at a time. Karen Olson, an independent information specialist (**kolsoninfopro@adelphia.net**), still finds that phone directories on CD have several advantages over the Web directories. Olson explains, "The CD has an auto-type-ahead feature, which the Web lacks. This makes it possible to see the list of query results fill in as you type the search terms. Often with both individual and business names, the searcher is trying to find a name and is handicapped with an incorrect spelling. The auto-type-ahead feature lets you see the possible answer set at each character stroke. Secondly, although it is true that the CD is not up to the minute in currency, the product at least lets the user know what release date they are working with whereas the Web directories don't provide any date information at all. Finally, the CD directories search faster. Not only does the CD have a faster search response time, but it saves you the time from going from one phone Web directory to the next since the CD is more comprehensive than any one Web directory site."

Unpublished and Unlisted Phone Numbers

Many of the Web phone directories draw data from the same sources—published White Pages directories and other publicly available sources. If a phone number is unpublished or unlisted, you most likely won't find it in one of these Web phone directories. (There is some debate about whether there is any difference between an unpublished and an unlisted number. Some say "no" while a law librarian/former telephone company employee says there are some similarities and some differences. For example, both unlisted and unpublished numbers are similar to each other because neither appears in the phone book and neither is sold to other companies. However, an unpublished number is different from an unlisted number because it is also not included in the directory assistance database while an unlisted number is (and may be given out when one phones directory assistance.) But sometimes people with unpublished or unlisted phone numbers do provide their phone numbers to sources other than the phone company. You might be able to find the number in those sources, especially if it's in a public record or private database. Also, if the person has a Web site, you might find the number listed on the site or in an Internet Domain Registry application (using one of the Whois registries noted in Chapter 10, "Company Research"). Unpublished and unlisted phone numbers may also be found by name searching at Accurint. If you need to find out the owner of an unpublished or unlisted phone, reverse phone searching of these numbers is possible using Merlin. (See Chapter 8's pay database section for more information about Merlin and Accurint.)

More Information?

Nearly all of the phone book sites are advertiser-supported, with enticements labeled **More Info** or **Public Record Click Here**. For example, after finding Carole Levitt's name, address, and all three phone numbers in a free Yahoo! People Search (**http://people.yahoo.com**), we were offered a **Sponsor Results by Intelius** link. Upon clicking the link, we were brought to Intelius' Web site, which is a pay site that you will see over and over again—at various telephone directory sites and other people finding sites. We were informed that for $49.95, Intelius could find "Criminal Report, Lawsuits, Judgments, Liens, Bankruptcies, Property Ownership, 30 Year Address History, Relatives & Associates, Neighbors, Licenses, Marriage records, and more." At that price, we weren't willing to bite. If you need past addresses and phone numbers or possible aliases, you would be better off with a subscription to Accurint.com or Merlindata.com, where some of this information could cost as low as $1 and up with an average cost of about $8.50.

Traditional Directory Searching and Reverse Searching

For finding phone numbers, addresses, neighbors, maps, e-mail addresses, and so on, we prefer Infospace out of all the Web phone directories because it has so many ways to locate people and businesses through both traditional searching and reverse searching.

Reverse phone number or address searching is the perfect tool when you are uncertain of someone's name (or the spelling), but you know that person's phone number or address. With a reverse phone search (or address search) the person's name (and correct spelling) should be retrieved. Reverse phone or address searching is also the perfect tool for business searching when you don't know the company name (or its correct spelling), but do have its address or phone number. Address searching is also useful when you want to be certain you are naming all relevant parties and you suspect that multiple businesses owned by the same person are operating out of one address. The reverse address search results may show you all the company names related to that one address. If Infospace doesn't bring any results, try using a phone directory metasite, such as theultimates.com (see below), to identify other phone directory sites, and if the free sites there fail, then see the information on pay sites below.

Phone Directory Metasite

The Ultimates

http://www.theultimates.com/

| *Purpose:* | To locate various types of people-finding and business-finding directories. |

Content: The Ultimates.com allows one to search a variety of White Page, Yellow Pages, and e-mail directories free from its site instead of visiting each site one by one. After filling information into a template for the first displayed directory (e.g., Infospace.com), all information is automatically copied to the other directories' templates. Click the **Search** button on the first directory's template. A new browser window opens with your search results displayed. One can switch back to the original window and click the **Search** button connected to the next directory's template, and so on. There is also a pay version ($12 annually) called Ultimates Plus that has some added features, such as storing your previous search (using a cookie) up to a month and displaying results in the same window instead of having you switch back and forth.

Our View: We use this when we can't find the person we're looking for and want to view a variety of other phone directories. It would be useful if the Ultimates allowed one to search the various databases simultaneously.

Figure 7-2. After selecting the **White Pages** link, enter your information into the first set of White Pages directory templates (Infospace.com) and the other White Pages directory templates will automatically be filled in with the same information **(http://www.theultimates.com/white).**

Tip: Craig Ball's Phone Finder (**http://www.craigball.com/ phonefind.html**) also does not offer simultaneous searching, but it too automatically fills in the other templates once you fill in the first one.

Infospace

http://www.infospace.com $\oslash$ (to search and view contact information) **$** (to obtain public records)

Purpose: To find people and businesses (phones numbers, addresses, and e-mail addresses) and maps to homes and businesses. Also, see the Tip below for how to find neighbors.

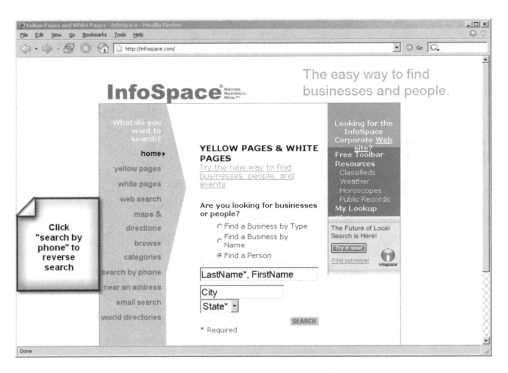

Figure 7-3. Infospace offers numerous resources to search for telephone number information, including White Pages, Yellow Pages, and a Reverse Lookup to help locate a name when you only have a phone number or address. © 2006 InfoSpace, Inc. All rights reserved. Reprinted with permission of InfoSpace, Inc.

Content: Infospace has separate White Pages and Yellow Pages searches and reverse search options.

White Pages:

- Search by last name and first name (or initial), city, and state. Only the last name is a required field, but the more fields you fill in, the more you are assured of finding the correct party.
- When you click on a specfic result from the list of results for a personal listing, you will see the following information, links and features:

  —An address and phone number

  —A map to the address

  —Links to: **Find Neighbors** (use this feature to automatically display names and contact information of neighbors), **Directions, Find Businesses Near This Location** (use this feature to link to specific types of businesses, such as hotels, restaurants, etc. that are near the "found" address), **Add to Outlook** (use this feature to add the "found" contact information to your Outlook address book), **Update/Remove** (use this feature to: (1) update your own InfoSpace listing; (2) add an e-mail address if one does not already appear, or (3) remove your name and all contact information entirely from the InfoSpace database) and **Send Listing to Friend** (use this feature to forward the "found" information via e-mail)

  —Almost any other link will be to a pay background research service, Intelius (See Chapter 8 for other less expensive options to Intelius such as Accurint or Merlin).

Reverse lookup (**http://www.infospace.com/home/ white-pages/reverse-phone**):

- To reverse search by phone number, address, email, area code, ZIP code or international dialing code, first click **Search by phone.**

  —To reverse phone search, click the **business** or **residential** button to find a name and address (U.S. only). Use this to identify who called you when they failed to leave their name, but left a phone number on your voicemail (or on your caller ID).

—Click on **Area Code Lookup** to search by area code to find a city (this can help trigger your memory if you're not sure how you know the person who left a voicemail message with an out-of-town phone number).

—Click on **Area Code Lookup** to search by city and state to find an area code.

—Click **Address Lookup** to search by address to find name and phone number: (To search by address, enter one or more of the following: the house number, street name, city, or state (required).

—To find an international dialing code, click **International Dialing Codes look up**

Yellow Pages: There are two types of searching: by **Name** or **Type**.

- **Name search**: Enter a business name and choose a state—this is required on the main Yellow Pages search screen at **http://www.infospace.com/home/yellow-pages**; however, a **Nationwide search** by business name is an option on the Advanced search page at **http://www.infospace.com/home/yellow-pages/advanced-search**. Limiting the search to a specific city is optional. To find a specific business by its name, search by its exact name. However, if you are uncertain of the exact name, enter the letters you think the name begins with or if the name has multiple words, enter any one of the words in its business name. The displayed results will show an address and also links to a: **map, business profile,** and **phone**. Some results will also show a link to their web site, general information such as business hours, and type of business.

- **Type search**: To identify names of businesses in a state that fall within a certain category, search by a business type and state. You can also limit the **Type** search further to one or more of the following: an address (street number, street name, or both), a city, or a ZIP code (the "Type" search box must be filled in with a business type before adding these restrictions to the search).

> • **E-mail search**: search by last name, first name, city, state, and country to find e-mail addresses of people worldwide (the full e-mail address is no longer displayed--only the domain is displayed and you will have to send the e-mail via Infospace).

Our View: The **Near An Address** search (**http://www.infospace .com/home/yellow-pages/near-address**) is also useful. Use this option when you want to find out what businesses are near a specific home or office address (from one to one hundred miles). For example, if you are meeting a client at his home or office and you will need a notary, type "notary" into the **Business Type** field and type the client's address into the **Address** field.

Tip: If you are searching for someone who has moved or is being evasive, the automatic **Find Neighbors** feature is especially useful. By clicking on the **Find Neighbors** feature, you will be armed with the names and contact information of their neighbors. You might then be able to track the missing/evasive person through a neighbor.

If you want people to be able to find your e-mail address readily, then update your listing and add the e-mail address.

There are dozens of phone directory sites that have features similar to Infospace (such as Bigfoot.com, Whitepages.com, and Switchboard.com), or are powered by other phone directory sites. For example, Bigfoot's White Pages search is powered by Whitepages.com. Each one includes traditional and reverse White Pages and Yellow Pages for phone, address, area code, and city searching. They also include maps, international calling code lookup by country, and e-mail listings (but they only found Carole Levitt's former e-mail address, which is defunct).

Other Phone Directories' Features

While Anywho.com's free site includes many of the same search features as Infospace described above, you can also type in a company name to discover its toll-free number (**http://anywho.com/tf.html**).

Don't believe Anywho.com's claim for a free preview of "More Information" when you bring up search results from a person name search. All you get is an advertisement to conduct a pay background database search at US Search for $39.95 and up. Our usual admonition: Read about less expensive sites in Chapter 8, such as Accurint and Merlin, etc.

International Phone Directory

Infobel (formerly teldir)

http://www.infobel.com/teldir/default.asp

Purpose: To link to the White Pages, Yellow Pages, business directories, and other people-finding directories in more than 216 countries.

Content: There are two ways to search for available telephone directories. While the first way allows you to select from the drop-down menu any country from the alphabetical list, we prefer the second way, which is to click on the icon of one of the continents or countries listed to the right of the continent icon. The second way is preferable because it offers an annotation about the types of phone directories available and whether any are in English.

Our View: We found this site to be a wealth of information and easy to use. For example, when we searched for a listing in Denmark and couldn't recall the exact spelling of the city we wanted, all we had to do was click on **City list** and type in part of the name ("Hel"). This brought us to a city list showing three cities beginning with "Hel" (ours was Helsingor).

Tip: Because each country's telephone directory is hosted by a separate site, search functions will vary at each of the country directory sites. The Denmark phone directory, for example, allows you to click on **Extended Search** to add in first names and postal codes to refine the search, and you can also click on **Reverse search**.

Pay Database Phone Directory

MasterFiles

http://www.masterfiles.com/index.html **$**

Purpose: Its Reach411 product provides real-time access to over 130 million listings.

Content: Listings of U.S. residences, businesses, and government agencies for all fifty states (since the last edition of this book, Hawaii and Alaska have been added). Data is from Ameritech, Bell South, Cincinnati Bell, PacBell, QWEST, Southern New England Telephone, Southwestern Bell, and Verizon.

Our View: Considering you can search by name, phone, or address for 20¢ to 45¢ (based on search type and volume), and that the content is refreshed continually, this may be useful to find someone who has recently moved or who is continually on the move. There is a $60 start-up fee to fund your debit account.

Tip: Make sure the coverage fits your needs. If you're searching for international listings, this won't do much good.

Pay Site Directory Searching

Most of the pay public record databases we discuss in Chapter 8, "Accessing Public Records," have all sorts of traditional or reverse phone and address searching functions. Most noteworthy is that they allow you to search by an old address or phone number and get an updated result. You won't find this option at the phone directory sites noted in this chapter.

Cellular Phones

As mentioned earlier, there is no comprehensive cellular phone directory. The following section offers some assistance for first determining (for free) whether a phone number is a wireless phone number (see FoneFinder), to a free self-reporting directory that allows one to search by name (see MobilephoneNo.com), to a pay site for conducting a reverse wireless phone number search to discover who owns the specific cellular number (see Cell-Phone-Numbers.com). Accurint (see Chapter 8) allows for name searching to find cellular numbers and may be less expensive than the pay sites discussed below.

Cell Phone (Wireless) Searching

FoneFinder

http://www.fonefinder.net/

Purpose: This site can be used free to discover if a specific phone number is for a land line or a wireless phone. It also links to phone number searching sites that require payment.

Content: Search by the area code, prefix, and the first number following the prefix of a phone number. The results do not show the name of the person who owns the phone number but shows the type and name of the phone company that "owns" the prefix (a wireless company or a regional Bell operating company, like Pacific Bell or Bell Atlantic). It also displays the city and state connected to the prefix. This site can be used for U.S., Canada, and international phone *number* searching. Reverse searching by city or ZIP code will bring back prefix results for that city or ZIP code. This site also allows one to search by name of country to find the country's phone code.

Our View: This can be very useful when you're having trouble tracing a phone number, because you are tipped off right away whether it's a wireless number. And, if it's wireless, you won't be able to use the same avenues to find out who owns it as you would for a land line.

Tip: Once you've identified the number as wireless, see the two listings below for further tips on how to identify who owns the wireless number.

MobilephoneNo.com

http://www.mobilephoneno.com

Purpose: To discover who owns a wireless number.

Content: This site offers free listings to people who choose to register their wireless number here. Searching (by name) is also free.

Our View: Though it's nifty to be able to find the name and address of a wireless owner, the content is very limited—to those who have chosen to self-register.

Tip: If you want others to be able to locate you by your wireless number, you might want to register it here. A cell number is kept online for one year only, so you need to remember to renew your registration (for free). If you provided this site with your e-mail address when you initially listed your cell number, they will notify you two weeks prior to your listing expiration. Just as with the initial listing, there is no cost to re-list.

Figure 7-4. The content at Mobilephoneno.com is accessible to only those who have chosen to self-register at the site.

Cell-Phone-Numbers.com

http://www.cell-phone-numbers.com

Purpose: To discover who owns a wireless number

Content: For $79 you can request a reverse wireless number search to discover the name and address of the person who owns the number.

Our View: We haven't used this service, but there was an interesting story in the *Chicago Tribune* about Eric Smith, a 21-year-old student at the University of New Orleans, who used it when he needed to find the name and address of someone who had defrauded him of $3,000 on eBay. It worked!

Tip: You wouldn't use this service until after discovering that the number is wireless and after being unable to locate it at MobilephoneNo.com. Bestpeoplesearch (**http://www.bestpeoplesearch.com**), among others, also offers this service. Bestpeoplesearch states, at its site, that if "You supply: Name, Address (if available), City & State" they will, "conduct a search from all cell providers offering cell service to the City and State where you think your subject resides. . . . If a cell account is located, your investigator will provide the primary cell phone number on the account along with the billing address."

How to Obtain Records of Phone Calls

Whether a call has been made from a land-line, cell phone, or voice over IP, it is possible to obtain records listing all phone calls made from that number. The record shows the phone number of the recipient of the phone call and the day, time, and duration of the call. Phone records can be useful to divorcing spouses, identity thieves, criminal lawyers looking for ties between people to show evidence of a conspiracy, or a myriad of other people in a myriad of other scenarios. But, is any of this legal?

Until it was shut down by the Missouri Attorney General in January of 2006, Locatecell.com provided a list for $110, of the outgoing calls from your subject's phone, up to 100 calls of the last billing cycle. All that was required was your subject's name, address, and phone number. One could place an online order and get results within hours. How did Locatecell.com obtain these records? Law enforcement surmises that either telephone company employees are violating their companies' rules and simply selling customers' phone call records to independent information brokers and investigators, or that information brokers and investigators are using age-old pretexting (pretending to be the customer) to obtain records from the phone companies. Both Verizon and Cingular Wireless have sued companies who have sold their customers' cell phone records to third parties.

As discussed later in this chapter, pretexting financial institutions is illegal, but it's a gray area as to whether it's illegal to pretext non-financial entities, although Joel Winston (Associate Director of the Federal Trade Commission's Financial Practices Division), was quoted in a July 8, 2005 *Washington Post* article (**http://www.washingtonpost.com/wp-dyn/ content/article/2005/07/07/AR2005070701862_pf.html**) as saying, "The FTC views pretexting as a deceptive practice even without a specific ban on its use for telephone records."

The Electronic Privacy Information Center filed a complaint (*available at* **http://www.epic.org/privacy/iei/ftccomplaint.html**) on July 7, 2005 with the Federal Trade Commission against a data broker, Intelligent e-Commerce Inc., of Encinitas, California, which hosts the Web site **http://www.bestpeoplesearch.com**. This site advertises the sale of cell phone records, among other personal information. When we visited the site on January 20, 2006 (*available at* **https://secure.bestpeoplesearch .com/c-CBO,Service.aspx**), we learned through their January 18, 2006 press release that, "Due to controversy surrounding the availability of phone records via the internet we have decided to discontinue offering these searches. We apologize to anyone with a legitimate need for these searches." However, see above, for information about what the site still offers to do.

In a January 17, 2006 press release (*available at* **http://hraunfoss.fcc .gov/edocs_public/attachmatch/DOC-263216A1.pdf**), FCC Commissioner Jonathan S. Adelstein stated that he was, "[a]larmed by reports that data brokers are obtaining and selling customers' personal telephone records without the customers' consent or knowledge." Further, he stated, that "[a] petition for rulemaking on enhanced consumer data protection standards filed by the Electronic Privacy Information Center (EPIC) in August 2005 could be an appropriate vehicle for tightening our rules."

Using Mark Rosch's cell number, in November 2005, we tested out whether a third party would be able to obtain Mark's most recent cell phone bill. Within hours we received a fax of Mark's bill with a record of his calls. The fax also had a cover page showing Mark's home and office land-line numbers and a statement that his land-line numbers were listed as belonging to Carole Levitt.

On the first day of the 2006 legislative session, two bills were introduced to combat the pretexting employed to obtain a third party's phone records without the person's permission or accessing the information from their online account. The bills are the Consumer Telephone Records Protection Act of 2006, S. 2178, 109th Congress (*available at* **http://frweb gate.access.gpo.gov/cgi-bin/getdoc.cgi?dbname=109cong_bills& docid=f:s2178is.txt.pdf**), and the Phone Records Protection Act of 2006, S. 2177, 109th Congress (*available at* **http://frwebgate.access.gpo.gov/ cgi-bin/getdoc.cgi?dbname=109cong_bills&docid=f:s2177is.txt.pdf**), S. 2178 is meant to, "[m]ake the stealing and selling of telephone records a criminal offense" and applies to cell phone, land-line, and voice over IP records. S. 2177 is meant to, "[make] the sale or fraudulent transfer of telephone records a criminal offense."

Fax Number Searching

Finding fax numbers is not as straightforward as finding phone numbers (or even e-mail addresses). To find a fax number for a person at his place of employment, try locating the company Web site to see if it is listed there.

Thinking Outside the Box to Find and Background People

Aside from the traditional resources now available over the Internet for finding and backgrounding people, there are numerous other nontraditional avenues to take. Most of these resources would never be found in any of the traditional places noted earlier in this chapter, nor in public records or pay databases. We'll call our searching of these nontraditional avenues "thinking outside the box."

Thinking outside the box, however, does not entail doing anything illegal, such as obtaining a credit report without a permissible business reason or "pretexting" (see below). Let's take a look at those two issues and see why those aren't part of our thinking-outside-the box search strategy.

Consumer Credit Reports

For anyone who wants to use a consumer credit report to simply locate a person or to obtain general and financial information about a subject, beware of the Fair Credit Reporting Act (FCRA), 15 U.S.C. §§ 1681b-1681u (2000). Section 1681b prohibits the disclosure of consumer credit reports by consumer credit reporting agencies, except in response to the following kinds of requests:

(a) In general

Subject to subsection (c) of this section, any consumer reporting agency may furnish a consumer report under the following circumstances and no other:

(1) In response to the order of a court having jurisdiction to issue such an order, or a subpoena issued in connection with proceedings before a Federal grand jury.

(2) In accordance with the written instructions of the consumer to whom it relates.

(3) To a person which it has reason to believe—

(A) intends to use the information in connection with a credit transaction involving the consumer on whom the information is to be furnished and involving the extension of credit to, or review or collection of an account of, the consumer; or

(B) intends to use the information for employment purposes; or

(C) intends to use the information in connection with the underwriting of insurance involving the consumer; or

(D) intends to use the information in connection with a determination of the consumer's eligibility for a license or other benefit granted by a governmental instrumentality required by law to consider an applicant's financial responsibility or status; or

(E) intends to use the information, as a potential investor or servicer, or current insurer, in connection with a valuation of, or an assessment of the credit or prepayment risks associated with, an existing credit obligation; or

(F) otherwise has a legitimate business need for the information—

(i) in connection with a business transaction that is initiated by the consumer; or

(ii) to review an account to determine whether the consumer continues to meet the terms of the account.

(4) In response to a request by the head of a State or local child support enforcement agency (or a State or local government official authorized by the head of such an agency).

(Note: There are other conditions one must comply with in relation to using consumer reports for employment purposes—see 1681b(b))

A consumer credit report is different from "credit headers" which are discussed in Chapter 8. Credit headers refer only to that portion of the consumer report (the "header") that credit bureaus sell to third parties such as investigative database vendors and marketing companies. Credit headers include personal identifier information, such as the creditor's name, address, phone number, date of birth, and Social Security number and not the financial information in the report (which was never divulged to third parties such as investigative database vendors and marketing companies).

In the case of *Phillips v. Grendahl*, 312 F.3d 357 (8th Cir. 2002), *available at* **http://caselaw.lp.findlaw.com/data2/circs/8th/012616p.pdf**, a "concerned" Minnesota mother, Mary Grendahl, hired a private investigator from McDowell Investigations. She asked him to check out her daughter's fiancé, Lavon Phillips. The PI retrieved Phillips's Social Security number from a database and then contacted Econ, a company in the business of furnishing consumer reports, finder's reports, and credit scoring to creditors and PIs. Econ provided a finder's report, showing the fiancé's credit card accounts and child support obligations.

The Eighth Circuit Court held that the finder's report was actually a consumer report under FCRA and that none of the actors in this escapade had a permissible business reason under § 1681b(a)(3) for the information. The court remanded the case for trial, ruling that it was an error to grant summary judgment to the defendants (Grendahl, McDowell Investigations, and Econ) regarding Phillips's claim for wrongful disclosure of a consumer report. While the act allows access to consumer reports for decisions bearing on extending credit to, insuring, or employing someone, it does not allow access for decisions about marriage, noted the court. However, the court held that Phillips's invasion of privacy claim relating to disclosure of his child support order (noted in the finder's report) couldn't support this claim. Even though the information was sensitive, it was not considered a publication of a matter that would be "highly offensive to a reasonable person" because it already was of public record. (The daughter ended up not marrying her fiancé, by the way.)

The Fair and Accurate Credit Transaction Act of 2003 (FACTA)

FACTA, Pub. L. 108-159, 111 Stat. 1952 (2003), amended FCRA by adding new sections to FCRA. Its stated purpose was "to prevent identity theft, improve resolution of consumer disputes, improve the accuracy of consumer records, make improvements in the use of, and consumer access to, credit information. . . ."

While FACTA took effect in 2004, the Federal Trade Commission, among other agencies, was responsible for drafting regulations to implement the Act. The adopted regulations can be found at the FTC's site at **http://www.ftc.gov/os/statutes/fcrajump.htm.**

The FTC Penalizes ChoicePoint for Providing Credit Information to Illegal Subscribers

In the continuing saga of identity theft and privacy violations involving the FCRA and consumer reports, in January of 2006, the FTC alleged that consumer data broker ChoicePoint violated the FCRA by turning over consumers' sensitive personal information to subscribers who did not have a permissible purpose for the information and whose applications raised obvious "red flags." While it is absolutely correct that sensitive information about approximately 163,000 Americans was obtained by criminals with the intent of perpetrating credit card fraud and identity theft on those individuals, these criminals DID NOT electronically "break into" the ChoicePoint database despite early reporting about hacking! The criminals acquired the information the same way you or I would— they applied for an account with ChoicePoint and purchased the records from ChoicePoint. The criminals used stolen identities and credit card information to apply for a ChoicePoint account with assumed business names that passed ChoicePoint's account vetting process.

ChoicePoint, Inc. will pay $10 million in civil penalties and $5 million in consumer redress to settle Federal Trade Commission charges that its security and record-handling procedures violated consumers' privacy rights and federal laws. The FTC alleges that ChoicePoint did not have reasonable procedures to screen prospective subscribers, and turned over consumers' sensitive personal information to subscribers whose applications raised obvious "red flags." Indeed, the FTC alleges that ChoicePoint approved as customers individuals who lied about their credentials and used commercial mail drops as business addresses. In addition, ChoicePoint applicants reportedly used fax machines at public commercial locations to send multiple applications for purportedly separate companies. According to the FTC, ChoicePoint failed to tighten its application approval procedures or monitor subscribers even after receiving subpoenas from law enforcement authorities alerting it to fraudulent activity going back to 2001.

The FTC charged that ChoicePoint violated the Fair Credit Reporting Act (FCRA) by furnishing consumer reports—credit histories—to subscribers who did not have a permissible purpose to obtain them, and by failing to maintain reasonable procedures to verify both their identities and how they intended to use the information. The agency also charged that ChoicePoint violated the FTC Act by making false and misleading statements about its privacy policies. ChoicePoint had publicized privacy principles that addressed the confidentiality and security of personal information it collects and maintains with statements such as:

ChoicePoint allows access to your consumer reports only by those authorized under the FCRA. . . "Every ChoicePoint customer must successfully complete a rigorous credentialing process. ChoicePoint does not distribute information to the general public and monitors the use of its public record information to ensure appropriate use.

The stipulated final judgment and order requires ChoicePoint to pay $10 million in civil penalties—the largest civil penalty in FTC history—and to provide $5 million for consumer redress. It bars the company from furnishing consumer reports to people who do not have a permissible purpose to receive them and requires the company to establish and maintain reasonable procedures to ensure that consumer reports are provided only to those with a permissible purpose. ChoicePoint is required to verify the identity of businesses that apply to receive consumer reports, including making site visits to certain business premises and auditing subscribers' use of consumer reports. The order requires ChoicePoint to establish, implement, and maintain a comprehensive information security program designed to protect the security, confidentiality, and integrity of the personal information it collects from or about consumers. It also requires ChoicePoint to obtain, every two years for the next 20 years, an audit from a qualified, independent, third-party professional to ensure that its security program meets the standards of the order. Choice-Point will be subject to standard record-keeping and reporting provisions to allow the FTC to monitor compliance. Finally, the settlement bars future violations of the FCRA and the FTC Act.

"The message to ChoicePoint and others should be clear: Consumers' private data must be protected from thieves," said Deborah Platt Majoras, Chairman of the FTC. "Data security is critical to consumers, and protecting it is a priority for the FTC, as it should be to every business in America."

ChoicePoint, however, does not admit any wrongdoing. In an interview with the Associated Press, ChoicePoint Chief Executive Derek Smith has been quoted as reacting to the situation with what could be described as the understatement of the decade: "Looking back, I certainly wish the situation hadn't occurred."

ChoicePoint will continue to offer products and services that contain sensitive personal information. In order to access this information, users will need to meet one of three tests:

- Support consumer-driven transactions where the data is needed to complete or maintain relationships, such as insurance, employment, and tenant screening, or to provide access to their own data;

- Provide authentication or fraud prevention tools to large, accredited corporate customers where consumers have existing relationships. For example, information tools for identity verification, customer enrollment, and insurance claims; or
- Assist federal, state, and local government and criminal justice agencies in their important missions.

For a copy of the FTC complaint against ChoicePoint, see **http://www.ftc.gov/os/caselist/choicepoint/0523069complaint.pdf**, and for a copy of the Stipulated Final Judgment and Order for Civil Penalties, Permanent Injunction, and Other Equitable Relief, see **http://www.ftc.gov/os/caselist/choicepoint/0523069stip.pdf**.

Pretexting with Financial Institutions

We've often been asked to get information about a person's bank account balance. There is no database for this information and if anyone has obtained this information for you in the past, then it was done by "pretexting," which is illegal. Pretexting, the practice of obtaining consumers' private financial information under false pretenses, was specifically outlawed in 1999 by the Gramm-Leach-Bliley Act (GLB), 15 U.S.C. 6821 and 6822(a). Under GLB, it is also illegal to solicit others to obtain financial information via pretext.

In April 2001, the Federal Trade Commission (FTC) filed suit in three U. S. district courts to halt the operations of three information brokers, all of whom allegedly used false pretenses, fraudulent statements, or impersonation to illegally obtain consumers' confidential financial information—such as bank balances—and sell it. The brokers were asked to find out how much money a woman's fiancé had in his bank account. The woman (actually an FTC investigator involved in Operation Detect Pretext) supplied the brokers with her fiancé's name and the name of his bank and other "limited information," (though not stated, it was probably his Social Security number and his mother's maiden name). In each case, the broker used pretexting by posing as the fiancé to obtain the information (**http://www.ftc.gov/opa/2002/03/pretextingsettlements.htm**).

The FTC and the brokers ended up in settlement. The brokers had to forfeit any money they made while using pretexting to obtain information. Also, they were prohibited from engaging in any activity in connection with the obtaining, offering for sale, or selling of customer information of a financial institution, obtained by:

- Misrepresenting their identities or their right to receive customer information
- Using others who will obtain information using deception
- Selling or disclosing customer information obtained from a financial institution
- Making false and misleading statements

Paying for Pretexting

Since pretexting is illegal, it would be an ethical violation for a lawyer to use pretexting. It would also be an ethical violation for a lawyer to hire someone (such as a private investigator or information broker) to do the same. According to the ABA Model Rules of Professional Conduct, Rule 5.3, Responsibilities Regarding Nonlawyer Assistants, a lawyer is responsible for the conduct of nonlawyers hired to do something that would be a violation of the Rules of Professional Conduct if engaged in by the lawyer himself and if "the lawyer orders or, with the knowledge of the specific conduct, ratifies the conduct involved."

Pretexting with Other Institutions

Until recently, we've always said the jury is out on whether it's illegal to use pretexting to obtain nonfinancial information. The jury may not be out any longer on this question. In *Remsburg v. Docusearch*, 816 A.2d 1001 (N.H. 2003), Liam Youens wanted to find out Amy Boyer's work address. He paid an Internet research company, Docusearch, to find her home address, phone number, and Social Security number, but Docusearch was unable to find her work address.

Docusearch then hired an information broker who placed a pretext call to Boyer at her home. The broker lied about her identity and the purpose of her call. She convinced Boyer to reveal her work address. On October 15, 1999, Youens drove to Boyer's workplace and fatally shot her as she left work. Youens then shot and killed himself. A subsequent police investigation revealed that Youens maintained a Web site containing references to stalking and killing Boyer. The court said, "We conclude that an investigator who obtains a person's work address by means of pretextual phone calling, and then sells the information, may be liable for damages under [New Hampshire] RSA Chapter 358-A to the person deceived."

Maiden Names

As illustrated above, it wasn't too hard to find Boyer's Social Security number, so you can see how the information brokers in Operation Detect Pretext (above) could have gotten the fiancé's Social Security number if the FTC investigator hadn't provided it.

Finding someone's mother's maiden name, which the information broker in Operation Detect Pretext probably had to do to convince the bank he was the FTC investigator's fiancé, on the other hand, is tougher. We'd try various pay public record databases that link people to their relatives and associates (such as Accurint at **http://www.accurint.com**), and we'd also try a free family tree search at RootsWeb.com at **http://www.rootsweb.com** (as discussed later in this chapter).

Summarization Search Engines

While we frequently search someone's name or company name through a search engine (e.g., Google or Yahoo!), we find that we often get overwhelmed by the number of results. Instead, you might consider trying a summarization search engine that creates a summary sheet about a person or company from information gathered from various sources of the Web.

ZoomInfo.com

http://www.zoominfo.com/

Purpose:	ZoomInfo describes itself as a summarization search engine. It locates, collects, and categorizes information on people and their business, personal, and university affiliations, and allows users access to their own biographical data, which they can update, correct, or supplement.
Content:	Formerly known as Eliyon.com (before a name change in March 2005), ZoomInfo creates a summary information sheet for about 27 million people and more than 2 million companies gleaned from a variety of outlets,

such as electronic news services, SEC filings, press releases, corporate Web sites, and other online sources.

The ZoomInfo Web site offers both free and subscription-only options.

To conduct a people search, you can enter an individual's name into the box and click find, or you can click on the advanced search option. This will allow you to enter either a company or a university along with the person's name. Your search results will be listed ten to a page, ranked by Web popularity. Clicking on any of the results brings up the summary sheet. For instance, a search for Mark Rosch offered five results. By clicking on the first result, a summary sheet with information populated by 18 Web sources provided a summary of Mark, from his title, to board memberships, education and work history (past two companies only) and full biographies about Mark Rosch (taken from various conferences where he has spoken, in addition to his company Web site).

Users may also access their own Web information by clicking on *My Web Summary*, but it is necessary to register first. Once registration is completed, ZoomInfo creates an online location for you to store your information. They will continue to add to this page as they find information about you on the Web.

ZoomInfo also has a tiered subscription-based service that allows you to search by 20 fields:

- <u>On Demand</u>—$99 for 30 searches ($3.30 for each search thereafter)
- <u>Professional</u>—$12,000 for an annual membership
- <u>Enterprise</u>—custom packages available; prices vary

Our View: ZoomInfo's data can be useful in recruiting, client development, backgrounding individuals, competitive intelligence, and other general business. Valuable intelligence can be gained gathering background information on businesspeople and companies, to prepare for a meeting, or perhaps just for a better business relationship. Because ZoomInfo collects and compiles all of this data automatically, it is not always completely accurate, but it can be a good point to begin or continue one's research.

Tip: Subscribers can export ZoomInfo's information results to a spreadsheet, address book, or save them to an online folder.

A Narrower Summarization Search Engine

Zabasearch.com

http://www.zabasearch.com/

Purpose: A narrower summarization search engine for finding people's addresses, phone numbers, and birth month and birth year free, with links to fee-based people backgrounding sites.

Content: ZABA, a derivative from the Greek word "tzaba" which means "free," searches available public records and publicly available information, including, but not limited to: court records, phone listings, subscriptions, and real property records. However, they are not all free! The search box asks for a name and the pull-down menu lists the states. We typed in the name of our research assistant, Kristine K. Pike, and then chose California with the pull-down menu—an "all-states" option is available, too, and were shown two exact matches in the first result group, three matches for a K.K. Pike, and seven matches for a Kristine Pike.

After clicking **Search**, "Premium" results are listed on top—linking you to a pay background-check database, Intelius (you will also link to Intelius if you click on the link "**More information on. . . .**"). Scroll down past the premium results to view your subject's address, phone number, and birth month and year. If you click on the person's name, another window opens with choices to run the person's name in a variety of search engines, such as Yahoo!, Yahoo! Image, Highbeam, Dogpile, Lycos, A9, AltaVista, or AltaVista Image. This new window also allows you to link to Google Maps and Mapquest.com for maps and/or directions.

Our View: What makes ZabaSearch different from some of the other free people-search engines on the Web is that it offers month and year of birth for free. If you were looking to discover that bit of information, this would be the engine to use. Otherwise, ZabaSearch's free results are not too helpful.

Using a Search Engine

To locate a person and to find information about him, first enter the name into a search engine (such as Google). You never know what you're going to find on the free Internet and sometimes it's more than you would find using a pay database. The second step is to run their name through a newsgroup site (like Google Groups at **http://groups.google.com**).

War Story: A Search Engine Finds Fraud Convictions

"Not using the Internet [to find people or find out about them] is malpractice," asserts Steve Whiteside, J.D., from Sheppard, Mullin in San Diego, California. "I'm a law firm librarian . . . and an incident the other day pointed out the importance of Internet research. I was asked to find information on a person believed to be involved in tax fraud schemes. I happened to be on Westlaw at the time, so I searched their news database. Only one hit came up on the name and that was some insignificant committee the person was on. Without the Internet, the guy checked out OK. I then ran the name on the Internet and received dozens of hits on his multiple convictions for tax fraud and various news items on schemes he was involved with. The main difference was the PDF files that I could access through Google from the Treasury Department and attorneys general sites."

PDFs

Lucky that Whiteside knew to choose Google as his search engine, which at the time was one of the few general-purpose search engines (aside from AltaVista) that indexed PDF files. If he hadn't, he would have missed these documents. He also may have had luck at FirstGov.gov, a government site that indexes PDFs, considering that some of the PDF documents Google found were from government sites (see Chapter 6, "Government Resources online," for more on FirstGov.gov). Yahoo! now also indexes PDFs.

Standard of Care

Diane Karpman, a California ethics expert, asks the question, "Will the use of technology change the standard of care?" In a scenario where the average lawyer uses online resources to find the most current information, while another lawyer fails to, then "the failure to do so is below average and therefore below the ordinary standard in the community. Falling below the average, typical, ordinary standard in the community opens the door to charges of professional negligence. In this case liability would not be for failing to use technology, but for failing to find the information that other lawyers could find and use for their clients' benefit." ("Keep Up or Face Peril," 20 GPSOLO, Number 4 [June 2003]) available at **http://www.abanet.org/genpractice/magazine/june2003/keepup.html.**)

War Story: A Search Engine Leads to a Settlement

Charlie Cochran, a lawyer in Northern California, relates this story of how thinking outside the box allowed him to settle a case the day before the trial, for a fraction of the original settlement demand: "Anyhow, after attending your seminar I tried to implement some of your research tools to a trial I had scheduled in March 2003. The Plaintiff was a well-known musician and producer who claimed he had brain injury from an auto accident and could no longer play the piano. My search began with a Google 'I'm feeling lucky' which sent me to the Plaintiff's home page. On the home page he was selling an album that he had recorded after our auto accident. The Google search naturally hit many online sites where his albums were being sold. One of the Google hits had him giving an online interview with an entertainment reporter where he discussed his auto accident, that he could not play piano for a few months but after that he was back to playing and writing with a new spirit and inspiration. Google image hits are amazing. It's fascinating what people post on the Internet. One image of the Plaintiff was a concert he did about a year after the accident where he was shown playing piano in front of a class of graduate level pianists. The look on their faces showed that they were really impressed with his abilities. We ended up issuing a trial subpoena to the woman that held the concert and interviewed the Plaintiff for the online interview. The case settled the day before the trial for a fraction of the original settlement demand because, in my opinion, we were going to confront the Plaintiff with the photo of him playing the piano, the words from his online interview, and albums that he was selling over the Internet."

I'm Feeling Lucky

The **I'm Feeling Lucky** search button returns one Web site only and, as illustrated here, often it's the most relevant. Using Google's **I'm Feeling Lucky** search button quickly led lawyer Cochran directly to the plaintiff's own Web site. To obtain more results, Cochran returned to his original search page and merely clicked on the **Google Search** button. This search led him to an online interview of the musician and to sites selling his recent albums, information that he probably would not have found without the Internet. Finally, using Google's Images feature, Cochran proved that a picture is indeed worth a thousand words.

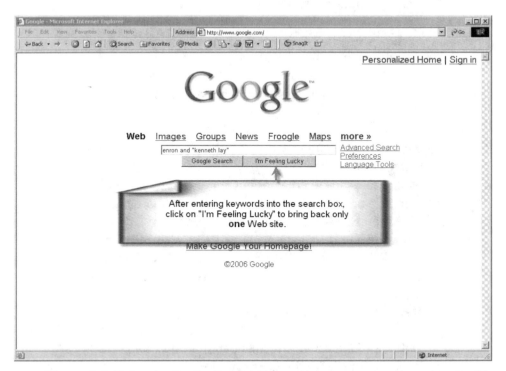

Figure 7-5. Using the I'm Feeling Lucky search button returns just one site; it's often the most relevant, especially when searching by a person or company's name. Google™ is a trademark of Google Technology Inc.

Definitions of Online Communities

- Usenet (also called newsgroups): a global online electronic bulletin board of Usenet newsgroups, covering thousands of topics. They are different from mailing lists because they do not communicate through passive e-mail. Instead, messages reside on central newsgroup servers where they can be read and commented upon like a community bulletin board.
- Mailing lists (also called LISTSERVs or discussion groups): a group discussion via e-mail. To actively participate, members first must e-mail a subscribe request to the list manager. Then, the subscriber can both post and receive messages. All messages are e-mailed to a central server where they are then distributed to each subscriber's e-mail in-box. Some lists distribute messages automatically while others are moderated. If the list is moderated, then the e-mails are reviewed by an actual person—the moderator—to be sure the discussion stays on topic, and so on, before being distributed. Some people mistakenly use LISTSERV as a generic term for all mailing lists. It's not. LISTSERV is a type of mailing list software.
- Message (or bulletin) boards: messages are posted to a Web-based bulletin board where visitors can read, comment upon, or leave new messages (or files). Requires users to visit the site.
- Forums: Same as message (or bulletin) board
- Blogs (Web logs): a Web site "light." Blogs have been compared to an online diary. They are easy to create and to update. They can be educational, entertaining, or frivolous, depending on the person who set up the blog. Blogs are indexed and searchable at such sites as Daypop.com (**http://www.day pop.com**) and Blogstreet.com (**http://www.blogstreet.com**). Google's Web search engine and Yahoo!'s will both return results that include some blogs. To display blog-only results from Google, use its Blog Search at **http://blogsearch.google.com/**. While Yahoo! (**http://www.yahoo.com**) does not have a blog-only search, it segregates its blog results (in a column on the right-side of the news results page) when one performs a "news" search. The initial list of blog results found on the News search results page will include four to five blog results. Click on the **More Blog Results** link to display blog-only results.

- Blawgs: same as a blogs, but topics are law related only. (See Theblogsoflaw at **http://www.theblogsoflaw.com** for an annotated list of law-related blogs and podcasts.) There are numerous sites offering tools to create blogs, such as Blog-ger.com (**http://www.blogger.com**). See Chapter 20 for more information about blogs and blawgs.

Searching Online Communities

The ease of communicating over the Internet has fostered the creation of a countless number of online communities (which focus on countless topics) used for the public exchange of ideas. There are various types of (and labels for) online communities, such as LISTSERV lists, mailing lists, discussion groups, Usenet newsgroups, forums, message (or bulletin) boards, and blogs, and there are various ways that people join and participate in a community on the Internet. Despite the variances, we'll discuss them generically and focus only on those that are public, have been archived, and are searchable by anyone.

There are various ways to participate in an online community:

- You can initiate the discussion.
- You can respond to someone else's discussion.
- You can "lurk," which means you simply read the discussions posted by others and do not join in the discussion.
- You can visit the group's archives (if the group has one and it's public) and search the archived postings by keyword (or by a person's name or e-mail address) to see what has been discussed in the past (and by whom).

Some groups have strict membership rules for joining (for example, to join the Los Angeles County Bar Association's Family Law Section group you first would need to join and pay your dues to the association and the section). Some types of groups require registration before you can join (but place no restrictions on who can join), while others may not require registration at all. Some groups require you to visit the group each time you want to participate (or even to lurk) while others "visit" you via e-mail. For instance, each time you want to participate in a message board, you need to visit that board by typing its URL into your browser's address box and then either read messages, answer a message, or post your own message. On the other hand, to participate in a mailing list, you only need visit once—to subscribe. Once you've done that, you'll automatically begin receiving e-mails from other participants. You can then respond to the entire list (or just to the individual sender) if you want to join the discussion and you can also initiate a discussion by sending an e-mail to the list. Once again, for convenience's sake, we'll label any online community communication a "posting."

Why do we care about online communities? Because, from the ongoing discussions in the online community to the postings that are archived, online communities can contain a treasure trove of information. Reading a posting might help you to find someone or to find out about someone. From a person's hobbies, to opinions, to concerns, it's all available to any Internet researcher who knows where to look. Many people use their actual names and e-mail addresses when posting to an online community, failing to realize that their postings are being archived and can be searched. This is a boon to the researcher (assuming the postings have relevant information). A further boon to a researcher is when a subject has configured his e-mail with an automatic signature block (with all his contact information) that attaches to any e-mail sent.

On the other hand, online communities can be a complete black hole. For instance, in your quest to find someone (or find out about him) you may come up empty-handed if that person has joined a community using an alias or using an anonymous e-mail address. There is always the chance that even if the subject has joined an online community, he joined one that has restricted membership or one that lacks a searchable archive.

Google Groups

Google Groups (**http://groups.google.com**) is one of the best-known online communities. (Google Groups is a feature separate from Google's general-purpose search engine, Google.com.) Using Google Groups, one can anonymously search through over 850 million postings. There is no need to subscribe to a Google Group to be able to search and lurk. The postings are from the archives of thousands of Usenet newsgroups, dating back to 1981, that Google purchased from Deja.com. While the Google Groups' archive is full-text keyword searchable, there is an even more useful feature available on the advanced search page for finding information about a specific individual: the ability to search for a specific person's message by their name or their e-mail address. (See section later in this chapter titled, "Google Groups People Finding Search Strategy "Tips.")

War Story: Online Community Search Finds Hobbies

If you know something about the person, add a descriptive keyword (such as the name of his city, his company, or his profession) to the name search when searching through an online community's archives (or search engine). For example, one of this book's authors, Carole Levitt, was looking for background information about the president of Elite.com because she had to introduce him at a conference. She decided to search Google Groups and because he had a very common name, she searched using his name in conjunction with the name of his company and came up with some interesting information, including his hobby—he's a Trekkie.

When else might these types of tidbits come in handy? Sometimes it's useful to find out a potential client's hobby before your first meeting. Or, according to Texas lawyer Craig Ball, he uses these tidbits of information at deposition to show the deponent that Craig Ball knows all! Ball swears deponents are more forthright when they think he already knows everything—even information about their hobbies. He also uses information found on the Internet about a deponent to "bond" with the deponent and help them feel more comfortable.

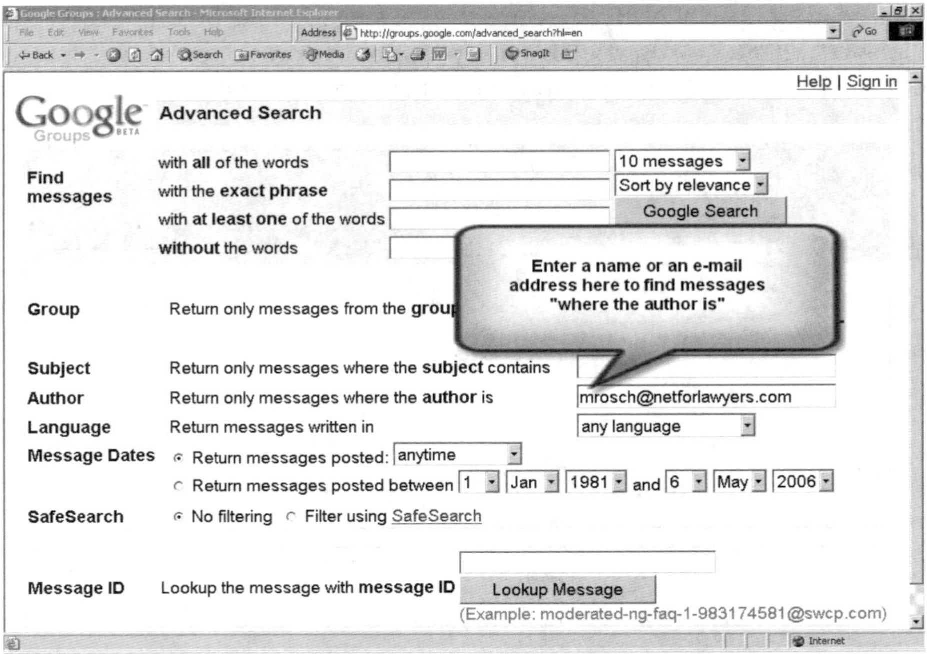

Figure 7-6. The Google Groups Advanced Groups Search allows you to search for group postings by the name or e-mail address of the person who posted the message. Google™ is a trademark of Google Technology Inc.

Google Groups People Finding Search Strategy Tips

To find a specific person's messages, users should conduct a few different types of searches on Google Group's Advanced Groups Search page (**http://groups.google.com/advanced_group_search**).

First, search the name in the **Return only messages where the author is** field. However, keep in mind that some people surf anonymously by using pseudonyms, so you may find nothing.

Second, search the specific person's e-mail address in the **Return only messages where the author is** field. After all, besides a Social Security number, what other identifier is more unique than an e-mail address? Since many people share the same name, searching by a unique e-mail address will help you verify that you've found the correct person. Because some people have more than one e-mail address, try to discover all of them to conduct a complete search of their postings. There are various ways to discover someone's e-mail address, from simply asking them (whether informally or through discovery) to "Googling" their name through Google and Google Groups. After performing a search through Google Groups and displaying results, the author's e-mail address used to be displayed, but Google is now masking the author's e-mail address. Although there is a work-around for unmasking the address once someone's posting is displayed, there are several steps to take before it can be displayed: First, click on the **Show Options** link on the posting. A partial address will be displayed. It will have ellipses inserted between the first

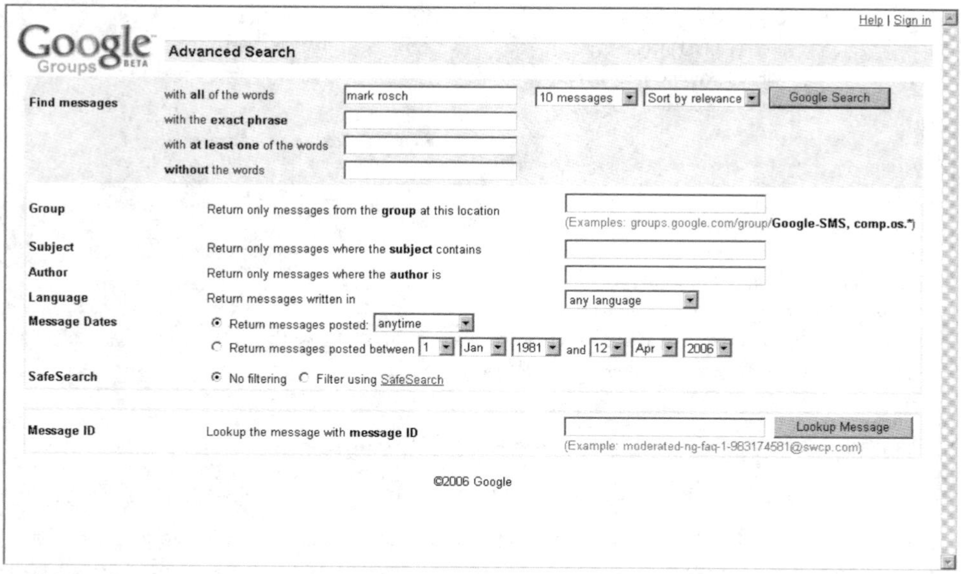

Figure 7-7. Is someone else discussing the person you're interested in finding out about? You can also use Google Group's Advanced Groups Search page to search using your target's name as a keyword (phrase). Google™ is a trademark of Google Technology Inc.

part of the e-mail address and the domain ("m ...@aol.com"). Click on the ellipses. Then, enter the characters in the picture to "unlock" the full e-mail address. The posting is shown again but the e-mail address is still masked. Click **Show Options** once more and it will be unmasked.

The third search method is to search for the specific person's name in one of the keyword fields of the Advanced Groups Search page (either in the **with all of the words** field or the **with the exact phrase** field). This may disclose other people's messages that contain your subject's name. You might learn about someone's opinion of your subject or the message may disclose some contact information about your subject. You can also attempt to e-mail the author of the message to learn more.

Finding Other Online Communities

To find other online communities to join or to search through, aside from Google Groups, visit CataList (**http://www.lsoft.com/lists/listref .html**), a directory and search engine of 55,295 public LISTSERV lists that can be searched by keywords found in the list name, list title, or host name or browsed by host countries, country, or by number of subscribers. Topica (**http://lists.topica.com/**), a newsgroup directory and search engine that you can either keyword search or browse by categories and subcategories to find the right group, is another site for finding online communities.

CataList

http://www.lsoft.com/lists/listref.html

Purpose:	To find a LISTSERV list that will meet your purposes.
Content:	CataList is the official catalog of LISTSERV mailing lists, covering 55,295 public lists out of 397,588 LISTSERV lists. There are several ways to use this catalog of lists: view lists by host country; view lists by number of subscribers; search the list by keyword, with the option of limiting your keyword search to list name, host name, or list title; and search lists that only have a Web archive interface.
Our View:	A search for "research" returned over 1,200 mailing lists. Results included the name of the list, a one-line description, and the number of subscribers. Clicking on the

title provided additional information, including host name and some features of the lists. The amount of information in the annotation for each list varied considerably. While it was useful that some of the lists had an Eye icon indicating access to archives, some of those archive links worked and some of them didn't.

Tip: If you don't find what you need at CataList, use a search engine and type in keywords that describe the type of list you are seeking and the word "listserv" (or "list") or try searching a newsgroup directory and search engine such as Topica (**http://lists.topica.com/**). At Topica, you can either search by keywords or browse categories and subcategories to find the right group.

A Private Investigator's "Thinking Outside the Box" Metasite

Black Book Online and

http://www.crimetime.com/online.htm

Purpose: Lists a wide spectrum of links useful for investigative research.

Content: The site is sponsored by Crime Time Publishing, a publisher of books geared toward private investigators. While it has links to some typical people-finding sites, such as contractor's licensing boards and phone directories, it also links to sites that fall more in the realm of "thinking outside the box." Some of the "thinking outside the box" sites are listed under "Unique Searches," such as the "Former Employee Index." We've always said there's no database of where people work (or worked), but this site lists 20,162,268 former employees (search by company name). The data is derived from profiles found on corporate and personal Web sites, government filings, press releases, etc. We searched the names of companies where we were former employees, but didn't find our names. We did, however, find names of people we recognize as former employees from our former companies (but also recognized some names that are current). Some other "thinking outside the box" sites include reverse directories for pay phones and for mail drops.

Our View: We like this site because it doesn't just link to the sites, but also annotates many of them, telling you in advance what you'll find at the site and offers tips as to why you might want to use them. See below for an example of a tip for finding bank accounts.

Tip: Although the left side of the site has a column labeled "Free Searches," not all the searches listed there are free. For example, click on "Bank Accounts" and you will find links to free sites that help you identify bank routing numbers, but you'll also see an ad for a report that you can purchase for $9.95 that purports to give you nine lawful tips for finding bank accounts. (One tip is offered free—"a standard DMV check may identify a lien holder for the vehicle—a financial institution where the subject of the investigation may also have a banking relationship.")

Locating a Picture of a Person

See the section "Finding Video, Audio, and Images" in Chapter 4, "Search Tools," to learn how to search the Web for someone's picture. If a person's picture is on a Web site or in a faculty directory, for instance, it can be found. We use this whenever we are meeting a new client at a public place and want to be able to readily spot the person.

Locating the Dead

People often ask us how to locate where a particular relative has been buried. This is after they have been unable to verify the death through the Social Security Death Index (SSDI). For information on where (and how) to search the SSDI, see the "RootsWeb SSDI Search" entry in Chapter 8. People who ask this question are always certain that the relative died, and that the relative left them a fortune, even though they'd been out of touch with the decedent for a good long time. There are some other options besides the SSDI for the hopeful heir trying to verify a death. For instance, locating the gravesite or an obituary can help establish the place of death. From there you can narrow down the search to a specific jurisdiction and begin your phone and letter inquiries.

Cemeteries and Graves

Find A Grave

http://www.findagrave.com

Purpose: To locate gravesite locations of 9.7 million people.

Content: The site contains information on gravesites of both the celebrity and the mere mortal. Search by name, (**http://www.findagrave.com/cgi-bin/fg.cgi**) or date, or browse by location. Name searching can be further limited by date of birth or death or by the state in which the person is buried. It even includes noncemetery burial sites, such as cremation "sites." A link to the SSDI's advanced search page is also offered.

Our View: While over 200,000 contributors to this site have more free time than most of us, we're happy to take advantage of their work. Although 5.5 million more people have been added to the site between 2003-2006, we still did not find a name we searched for back in 2003 when we tried again in 2006.

Tip: Another site to check is Interment.net (**http://www .interment.net**), which has fewer records than Find A Grave: 3,897,472 cemetery records across 8,375 cemeteries from around the world. You can search by last name and first name and, if known, add in the location. Connect search terms with either the AND Boolean connector or the "near" proximity connector. You can also add quotation marks when a surname is two words, and you can use a wild card for prefix searching (for example, john* will find Johnson, Johnston, and so on)

If you don't find your decedent at one of these cemetery sites, try one of the obituary sites noted below.

Obituaries

Obituary Daily Times

http://obits.rootsweb.com/cgi-bin/obit.cgi

Purpose: To discover in which newspaper an obituary is published when you don't know where to begin your search.

Content: The site is an index of published obituaries. While the actual obituary is not online, the index tells you in which newspaper it was published. To learn which newspapers participate in this index, see **http://www.rootsweb.com/~obituary/publications.htm**. To receive an e-mail alert (often twice a day) of new obituaries or to volunteer, see the instructions at **http://www.rootsweb.com/~obituary**.

Our View: This free index of published obituaries, which adds over 2,500 entries a day, is a good place to start a search if you don't know where someone died. With so many newspapers online, it should not be too difficult to obtain an obituary from a specific newspaper. Volunteers are responsible for monitoring each newspaper's obituaries and then adding them to the index, but not all newspapers have been adopted by a volunteer.

Tip: Another obituary index is the National Obituary Archive (NOA), with almost 58 million obituaries (**http://www.arrangeonline.com**). By clicking on the **Search** button (toward the top and center of the home page), an advanced search menu will pop up. Fill in the last name of the decedent and any (or all) of the following criteria: first name, city, state/province, country, or approximate date of death. If unsure of the spelling of a name, a "wild-card" search can be performed. The percent sign is used as the wild card. For instance, a search for bosl* will find bosley, boslin, and so on. With funeral directors across North America serving as contributing members to this site, it contains very recent data. On April 28, 2003, a search for Chester Wazny at the SSDI came up empty, but his April 26, 2003 death was listed at NOA.

If you know where someone died, check the Web to see if the local library or historical society has a site because they often have local obituaries online. To find library Web sites, see Libweb (**http://lists.webjunction.org/lib-web/**), which offers keyword searching by location, library type, and name, or browsing by library type or by region for foreign countries' libraries. To find links to many local historical societies, see RootsWeb.com (**http://www.rootsweb.com**).

Searching with a Mother's Maiden Name

We know your mother's maiden name. What else can we do with this information besides something illegal, like using it for pretexting? Let's say you're searching for a missing person. If anyone knows where that person is, it would be his or her mother. You can use this information to contact her and try to find the missing person that way—but don't pretext. See the section below, Family Trees, for information on how to find someone's mother's maiden name. Also, read Chapter 8, where you can learn about various background/investigative databases (such as Accurint and Merlin) which may provide leads to a mother's maiden name.

Family Trees

RootsWeb

http://worldconnect.rootsweb.com

Purpose:	Primarily for genealogy research, but the family trees may be useful for finding relatives of missing witnesses, missing heirs, mother's maiden names, and so on, who may be willing to assist you in finding the missing person.
Content:	There are over 239 million names on file in the Family Tree database.
Our View:	You'll learn more than you can imagine. Some family trees include, along with family members' names, dates of births, deaths, marriages, links to the family's home

page, (with pictures), e-mail address contact information—and we even found pictures of ancestor's head-
stones and someone's will (search for Jordan Sanders).

Tip: Check for your own family tree in case your third cousin
         twice removed put one up—it has more information
         than you want publicized.

Genealogy Library and Online Databases

Godfrey Memorial Library

http://www.godfrey.org/

Purpose: Godfrey Memorial Library is located in Middleton, Con-
             necticut, and specializes in genealogical materials. Its
             Godfrey.org Web site offers users remote access to its
             online databases 24/7.

Content: The library's mission has been to collect genealogical
             materials, with the majority of its information from pre-
             1875. Its list of titles includes a number of reference
             books, genealogies, and indexes, including the 226-vol-
             ume *American Genealogical-Biographical Index (AGBI)*—
             the largest reference set ever published.

             There are two ways to access Godfrey's databases. The
             free option allows guests to search resources that include
             newspaper, military, and Vital Records indexes. You can
             conduct this search by scrolling down Godfrey.org's
             home page and clicking on the **Library Online Cata-
             logue** link. If you are in need of a more in-depth search,
             the Godfrey Scholar library card is your other option.
             Clicking the **Sign Up Online** link will lead the user to a
             registration page. The cost is $35 a year for access to all
             of Godfrey's thousands of digital records. Once you have
             been given a library card number, you can click on the
             Online Resources Portal link to search the complete
             database.

Our View: Godfrey.org is a very specific library database, and the fact that we can now access it online is pretty phenomenal. In an earlier chapter, we wrote about how far libraries have progressed by now offering remote access to some of their databases, and Godfrey.org fits in with that model. However, this may be one of the first libraries to offer Internet access to such specific content (genealogical resources), and a good portion of it is available for free. The pages are perhaps not as sophisticated as some of the other larger libraries, but they are manageable and there is a help section if you get into trouble.

Tip: Whenever she needs to work on a quiet title action, Tamara Thompson, a private investigator from Oakland, California, makes use of Godfrey.org by using its older genealogical and census records.

State Genealogy Records Metasite

USGenWeb Project

http://www.usgenweb.com/

Purpose: USGenWeb.com is a genealogical Web site that provides links to all the state Web sites, which then can direct the user to the individual counties in each state. This site could be useful to lawyers who are searching for a missing person, verifying a death, or researching offspring in a quiet title action.

Content: USGenWeb.com is completely volunteer-driven, and it is the responsibility of the individual volunteer to maintain each site. Thus, each state and county Web site varies to a certain degree. Many states also have different ongoing projects as diverse as reuniting families with lost photos, or transcribing Civil War regiments. All of the counties provide links to access the archives, the state's home page, and to post queries.

On the left-hand side of the home page, there is a list of the fifty states. Clicking on California to start a search, we found ourselves on the CAGenWeb home page. Scrolling down to the bottom of the page we found the following nine options: **Counties Table; Counties Map; Archives; Mailing List; California Research Help; CAGenWeb Supporters; About CAGenWeb Project; History of California;** and **Search CAGenWeb.**

To search for documents within the counties of California, click on **Search CAGenWeb.** The traditional search box will appear. You may choose to match **ANY** or **ALL** of the search terms in the box, and there is a pull-down menu of the counties available to the right. (If you have any trouble with the search, scroll down and there are helpful directions to aid the user. Once again, this help section may not be found on all Web sites since different volunteer workers create the sites.) We put in the name *Pike*, chose to match **ALL** the search terms, and pulled Los Angeles County from the menu. We didn't receive any documents, so we performed a wider search by using the **ALL counties** in the pull-down menu. We were given two documents as a result. They displayed showing the best matches first. Both results were cemeteries and links to death records.

Our View: USGenWeb is an extremely useful start for any investigative research you might be conducting. For instance, because there are links to every state and county, the user would be assisted in a search for a missing person or for an individual's death records. And the states do really vary tremendously. We took a peek at Arkansas—their home page offered twice the links that California did.

Searching with a Date of Birth

Sometimes, you need to supply a date of birth along with a person's name when you search various databases. Instead of having to pay for using a database or go through the time and expense of ordering a birth record, you might be able to find it at Birthdatabase.com or at a site created by Stephen Morse (**http://stevemorse.org/birthday/birthday2**

.html). Although Morse obtains his data from Birthdatabase.com, his site has a better search engine.

Birthdatabase.com

http://www.birthdatabase.com

Purpose: To find birthdays.

Content: Over 20 million birthday records gathered from public records. Besides the date of birth, it displays a city and ZIP code for each name.

Our View: As noted above, this is a great little free service when you need to find a birthday. However, there is no documentation as to where the birthday information comes from, but we think it may be voter registration rolls. When we looked up Carole Levitt's birthday, it showed two records that belonged to her, but the ZIP codes were different (one was from her childhood home and the other from her current home). To locate birthdays, we'd like to see birthdatabase.com adopt two features from AnyBirthday.com (a site that is no longer available), which allowed you to add a ZIP code to your name search and e-mailed you a reminder of your spouse's (or anyone's) birthday.

Tip: Since so many people share the same name, it's best to add in the person's estimated age if you know it—this will improve your chances of finding the correct person. As noted above, Stephen Morse has taken the data from birthdatabase.com and created a better search engine at **http://stevemorse.org/birthday/birthday2.html**. We recommend trying this site when you know enough about a person that you could add in any of the following to your search to narrow down the search: a middle initial; a range of possible birth dates; an estimated age plus 3 years; a city (full or partial); a state; or a ZIP code (full or partial). In addition to the above optional criteria, a full first and last name are required.

Searching for Classmates (and More)

Classmates

http://www.classmates.com

Purpose: Multipurpose—everyone has a reason . . . but let's just say for finding people.

Content: Classmates includes 200,000 schools located in the United States and Canada, and also American and Canadian schools located overseas. Forty million people are listed. If you don't want to pay to become a member, you can still use a portion of the site by registering (free). To become a registered user, you must give your contact information and list where you attended high school. Once registered, you can search the entire database, not just your high school, but the amount of information you can view is very limited: the person's name, high school name, date of graduation, and possibly a woman's married name. A paid "Gold" membership allows you to see more complete information (that is, if the person has added any information), such as a person's profile and biography, which could include the name of someone's college, their employment history, their military history, and even personal information such as their marital status and number of children. As a paid "Gold" member, you can also send e-mail, post to message boards, and post photos. The "Gold" membership is priced at $39 for one year (or $59 for 2 years or $15 for 3 months). Use the **Advanced Search** to refine your person's name search by adding one or more of the following: school name, city, state, or graduation year.

Our View: Lots of private investigators have joined and claim they successfully locate people on this site. The search functions have improved—you no longer must know someone's exact name. Partial name searching is now permitted. For a partial name search, place an asterisk after the first few letters of a name to serve as a "wildcard." For example, search sus* if you are looking for susan or susie or suzi.

Tip: Tabs on the left side of the home page labeled **College** or **Workplace** allow one to find a list of people who attended a specific college or worked at a specific workplace. These searches can be useful when you need to locate a witness about an incident at a specific company or college. We were able to test out all the features of the site by signing up for a guest pass (however, we did not see this offer when we returned to the site a few weeks later). If you are adverse to pop-up ads and spam, you'll want to avoid registering.

Verifying Current Military Status

Have you tried to sue or subpoena someone and gotten no response? With the recent wars in Iraq and Afghanistan, you need to consider that they might be in the military and thus legitimately unavailable. How to verify whether someone is on active duty is a question we are frequently asked. The answer is the Defense Manpower Data Center (DMDC) Military Verification service.

Military Service People

**Defense Manpower Data Center (DMDC)
Military Verification Service**

https://www.dmdc.osd.mil/scra/owa/scra.home
(Once you have a password, you search here)

Purpose: To verify if someone is currently serving in the military.

Content: You can search to verify if an individual is currently on active military duty. You must enter at least a Social Security number to conduct a search. You can also add last, first, and/or middle name, as well as birth month and/or year. When you conduct a search at this site, you will obtain written documentation that the individual is in the military and it will contain the Department of Defense seal and a signature. For information about the site see **http://www.dod.mil/dfas/**

Our View: Originally, access to this database required registration, and a phone or fax request for an account and password. At that time, many users described it as a "bureaucratic mess" and used a pay service such as **www.military-search.org**. Others warn that there are many scam pay sites claiming to be able to access the Military Verification database for you. The DMDC website is provided as a public service for the Defense Manpower Data Center and the Department of Defense. The site is now available without registration and states that the Information is considered public information and may be distributed or copied.

GI Search

http://www.gisearch.com

Purpose: To locate current and/or former military personnel.

Content: GISearch is a self-reporting database for people who wish to get keep in touch with others with whom they served in the armed forces. The site offers a database searchable by as little as a last name. Additional search criteria include: maiden name, nickname, and home state.

Our View: Like Classmates.com, all of the information contained in the GISearch database has been supplied by the individual. The site's database is by no means comprehensive, but it can be a good place to start a search. The search results also include a **Contact Me** link to send a message to the individual whose record you are viewing. (Note that their e-mail address is not revealed to you.)

Tip: This resource could also be useful if you are looking for acquaintances of an individual who has served in the military. It would be necessary to know at least one location where your individual had been stationed and when they were posted there, however.

The site also encourages civilian employees of military installations and the (now-grown) children of military personnel to enter information about themselves into the database.

You can search the site and see if it contains information on your target individual without registration. To view any information your subject has reported, you must join the site.

Backgrounding Attorneys, Judges, and Parties Through Reported Opinions

When we talk about "backgrounding," we typically are referring to gathering background information about a client, the opposition, an expert, a company, or a product. However, there are times when you need to gather background information on a lawyer or a judge. While all the backgrounding tips offered in Chapters 7-11 apply equally as well to lawyers and judges, one other source for backgrounding them is to learn about the types of cases with which they've been involved. LexisONE.com provides the opportunity to do this type of backgrounding—if you know the "trick."

Lawyers and Judges

lexisONE.com

http://www.lexisone.com/

Purpose: To research full-text case law primarily, but also useful to gather background information about cases where a certain attorney, judge, or party was involved.

Content: lexisONE.com is a free, full-text case law database. The coverage goes back to 1790 for U.S. Supreme Court cases, but only back the last five years for state cases and federal appellate cases. If you want to search for reported cases involving a specific lawyer of record, use the **Judges** and **Counsel** search boxes, but if they do not work, the "trick" to gathering this background information is to IGNORE the search boxes at the bottom of the screen that are labeled **Judges** and **Counsel** and instead use the **Search by Keywords** search box to conduct a field restrictor search. Type the word "counsel" into the **Search by Keywords** search box and then enter the lawyer's name (in parentheses) after the word counsel. Be sure to use a proximity connector between the first and last name (e.g., use the proximity connector "w/3" so the first name is within three words of the last name). We use a proximity connector because we never know whether someone uses a middle name or initial. Your search would look like this:

Counsel (lloyd w/3 levitt)

To search for opinions written by a specific judge, use the *opinionby* field restrictor, and to search for opinions where a specific judge was on the panel but did not author the opinion, use the *judge* field restrictor. Your searches would look like one of these:

Judge (gary w/3 wade)

Opinionby (gary w/3 wade)

To search by party name, use the *name* field restrictor. It's best to use the most unique plaintiff and defendant name listed in the case caption if there is more than one party involved. Never use the "vs" or "versus" or "v." as your keywords. A search for *Brown v. Board of Education* would look like this:

name (Brown w/5 "Board of Education")

If you get no results, try expanding the proximity connector to w/10 or w/20 or use the "and" Boolean connector between the plaintiff and defendant names.

Our View: Although free is always good, there are some downsides to the free *lexisONE.com* search: (1) you are limited to the past five years only for state cases and federal appellate cases; (2) federal district cases are not part of the database; (3) if there are more than 100 results, you are shown nothing and asked to revise your search and (4) the **Judges, Counsel** (and **Party**) field restriction search boxes do not always work as expected, which is why we show you the "work-around" of creating a field restricted search in the **Search by Keywords** search box. The only way to make use of these search boxes is if you ALSO add a keyword to the **Search by Keywords** search box.

In the past, we had used the **Judge, Counsel,** and **Party** field restriction search boxes to search by a specific judge, counsel, or party name, without adding a keyword into the **Search by Keywords** search box, but this feature was apparently disabled a few months ago and not divulged. (Now it appears to have been re-enabled, but we are unsure if that will last.)

Tip: If there are more than 100 results, you are shown nothing and asked to revise your search. In that case, use the date restriction search boxes toward the bottom of the menu and try searching year by year or in six month chunks. If you are focusing on a specific type of case involving a specific judge or lawyer, you can narrow your search down using keywords instead of dates. For example, you could search for a judge's opinions about Sarbanes Oxley. Your search would look like this:

Judge (gary w/3 wade) and "Sarbanes Oxley"

Validating Social Security Numbers

U.S. InfoSearch

http://www.free-ssn-id-verification.usinfosearch.com

Purpose: For Social Security number validation.

Content: This search shows whether a Social Security number is valid and whether it belongs to someone alive or deceased. To use this site, enter a Social Security number into the search box and then enter your e-mail address. Results will be e-mailed to you almost instantly.

Our View: This site's service is limited because it does not tell you who is linked to the number. Nevertheless, it has some value because it does tell you if someone is using a deceased person's Social Security number or an invalid (made-up) number, indicating that someone is concealing his true identity. But, if someone is misusing a live person's actual number, then this site is of little value since it doesn't show names.

Tip: Since this service is free, it's useful as a preliminary check because it can show that the Social Security number is invalid or belongs to a deceased person. If the number is valid, you'll need to search a pay database sooner or later to verify that the Social Security number belongs to the person who is claiming it or you can register for free use of the Social Security Business Services Online (BSO) service (**http://www.socialsecurity.gov/ bso/bsowelcome.htm**). The BSO offers two options to verify that employees' names and Social Security numbers match their Social Security records. Online verification of up to 10 names and SSNs is the first option for those who wish to receive immediate results. Uploading batch files of up to 250,000 names and SSNs is the second option. Results are typically provided the next day. Both services are available to all employers but may only be used to verify current or former employees and only for the purpose of wage reporting (Form W-2) purposes (**http://www.ssa.gov/employer/ssnv.htm**).

Over the phone verification is also another option but there is a limit of 5 names/SSNs. Call toll-free for phone verification at 1-800-772-6270. The hours are weekdays only, from 7:00 a.m. to 7:00 p.m. EST. You must provide: your company name and EIN and the employee's SSN, last name, first name, middle initial, date of birth, and gender (**http://www.ssa.gov/employer/ssnv additional.htm**).

Banks

There is no database of where people bank. Sometimes this information can be gleaned from a public record, such as a lien or a mortgage, or even from the unclaimed property database. (See Chapter 8 for Web sites that may help you to obtain these types of records.) However, if you need to trace a bank routing number, the next site will assist you.

RoutingTool.com

http://www.routingtool.com/

Purpose: Routing Tool's site allows you to search their database using only a U.S. routing number to identify bank names, locations, and their phone numbers for funds verification and account validation.

Content: If all you possess is a routing number, then, in a sense, you will need to investigate "backwards." In the upper-right side of Routing Tool's home page, click on the box that reads "Online Routing Tool FREE." You will be asked to register your full name and e-mail address. Upon receiving a confirmation e-mail, you will then be able to access their system but not until you provide more contact information. Once you are fully registered, click on "Perform Single Routing Lookups Here." You may enter either a bank name or the nine-digit routing number.

The results are displayed to you with the following information: Routing number; bank name; address; city, state, and ZIP code that the number was assigned in; and phone number.

Our View: This site worked very simply, keeping clutter down to a minimum. There is a demo on the home page that diagrams where the routing number begins and ends in regards to the account and check numbers next to it.

After you've exhausted your thinking-outside-the-box avenues, try searching public records and pay databases (see the Chapter 8, "Accessing Public Records"). There are also many other techniques for finding and backgrounding people that you can learn about in Chapter 9, "Finding and Backgrounding Expert Witnesses;" Chapter 10, "Company Research;" and Chapter 11, "Competitive Intelligence Research."

*CHAPTER*EIGHT

Accessing Public Records

Using Public Records for Factual Research

Public records are chock-full of facts. Because of their content, they can be used for all kinds of fact-finding research, from finding and back-grounding people and companies, to locating patents and trademarks. The original purpose of public records, of course, was not for fact finding, but very often that's what legal professionals use them for. For example, the original purpose for maintaining real estate records was to enable the free transfer of property and to protect property owner's rights. But these very same records are also useful to lawyers for such fact-finding missions as locating someone's whereabouts or determining a person's assets, clearly not the intended purpose of the records.

The following are some of the purposes for which lawyers use other public records (some fall within their intended purpose and some do not):

- Skip-trace, whether it's to find a missing child, witness, or heir, or to serve a complaint
- Find assets
- Conduct due diligence (on a person or a company)
- Identify registered agents for service of process
- Locate liens, judgments, and Uniform Commercial Code (UCC) Filings
- Unearth criminal records
- Access court dockets and pleadings
- Obtain vital records (birth, marriage, divorce, and death)

- Verify or find Social Security numbers
- Uncover bankruptcies
- Find terrorists (government lawyers might use the records for this purpose)

What Are Public Records?

Public records can be loosely defined as anything filed with a government agency, and are typically open for public inspection. The records can vary from someone's divorce decree filed at the courthouse to their property records filed at the assessor's office. These treasure troves of government-held data must be made available to the public in order to advance commerce, give notice to the public, and to protect the public. For example, let's look at why bankruptcy records have been deemed to be public records. First, making them public gives notice to the public that someone they are dealing with may be financially unreliable and this protects the public (from extending credit to the person or going into business with him). Second, making the records public also advances commerce by offering some protection to the claimants.

Simply because a record is filed with a government agency does not necessarily mean the record is always subject to public scrutiny. Even though federal agencies are required under the Freedom of Information Act (FOIA) "to make their records promptly available to any person who makes a proper request for them," many records are exempted or excluded from provisions of the Act (**http://www.usdoj.gov/oip/foi-act.htm**). Thus, many records are not open to public scrutiny (or not to be shared between government agencies). Examples of such records are an individual's tax return or the FBI's National Crime Information Center's database. Obviously, these types of records would be rich sources of data that could be used to find people and find out about people—if they were available to the public.

For copies of FOIA request forms, see **http://www.usdoj.gov/04foia/att_d.htm**. Because FOIA only applies to federal agencies, different procedures must be followed for state FOIA requests. The National Freedom of Information site provides links to state FOIA information (**http://www.nfoic.org/web/index.htm**).

The Definition of a Public Record Varies by Jurisdiction

Every jurisdiction has its own definition of public records and policies for access to them. State, local, and federal governments differ greatly on what is and is not considered public. What's public today may be private tomorrow (and vice-versa). The information in drivers licenses, for instance, shifted from public to private. While many states used to consider driver's license records to be public, others, over time, shifted to deeming them to be private records. In 1994, federal legislation was enacted and they were deemed private (pursuant to the DPPA—the Driver's Privacy Protection Act of 1994, 18 U.S.C. 2721 et seq). However, it wasn't until 2000 that the U.S. Supreme Court settled the controversy between state law and federal law, declaring drivers license records to be private records (*Reno v. Condon*, 528 U. S. 141 (2000), available at **http://caselaw.lp.findlaw.com/scripts/getcase.pl?court=us&vol=000&invol=98-1464**). However, there are exceptions to the DPPA and the records may be accessible in some instances. See the section, "Drivers License Records and Driving History Records" in this chapter for more information.

An example of a record that was private before but is now considered public (to the government) today, is the record of the books you have checked out from your public library, due to the 2001 U.S.A. Patriot Act (Public Law No. 107-56, available at **http://frwebgate.access.gpo.gov/cgi-bin/getdoc.cgi?dbname=107_cong_public_laws&docid=f:publ056.107**). For revisions to the Act, see the USA Patriot Act section later in this chapter. The specific section of the Act that allows the government to peer into your library records (and other business records) is found at 18 U.S.C. Sec. 2703 and is available at **http://uscode.house.gov/uscode-cgi/fastweb.exe?getdoc+uscview+t17t20+1105+0++%28records%29**. "USA Patriot Act" stands for "Uniting and Strengthening America by Providing Appropriate Tools Required to Intercept and Obstruct Terrorism."

Every jurisdiction also has its own definition of access. Sometimes access to online public records is free, making them more accessible to more people. Other times, there is a fee for access, making the public record less accessible to fewer people. Some public records have not been digitized, so they are only accessible by in-person public inspection of the print record. For those public records that have been placed on the Web, access to the amount of information displayed may be limited. The limitations are based upon privacy concerns. However, if a record found on the Internet only displays part of the information, it is possible that the print version would show the excluded information. Thus, there are varying levels of access to the amount of information in a public record, depending on whether the record is found on the Internet or in-person at a government agency.

Thanks to the Internet, Public Records Are Now More Public

It's been accepted that public records are available to anyone who takes the time to go to the appropriate venue to ask for them (or resorts to a FOIA request if needed), or who has a paid subscription to commercial public records databases. However, when the very same records are being made publicly accessible (for free or for a low cost) over the Internet, privacy advocates (and even some non-advocates) are not so accepting. The E-government Act of 2002, 44 U.S.C. 3601,Public Law 107-347, which was enacted "To promote use of the Internet . . . to provide increased opportunities for citizen participation in Government" is just one of the many pieces of legislation causing privacy advocates consternation (**http://frweb gate2.access.gpo.gov/cgi-bin/waisgate.cgi?WAISdocID=978675260992 +0+0+0&WAISaction=retrieve**). With this ease of access from the comfort of home or the workplace, public records have truly become public, and so has the personal, private, and sensitive information found within the public record. This concern about privacy has been referred to as the doctrine of "practical obscurity," a term the U.S. Supreme Court used in 1989 when it held that a person's rap sheet was not subject to a FOIA request and should remain in practical obscurity (*U.S. Dept. of Justice v. Reporters Committee*, 489 U.S. 749 1989). As more and more courts are requiring electronic filing and more and more court files are thus becoming accessible over the Internet, it is becoming more difficult for the government to ensure that certain records remain in practical obscurity. Chief Judge D. Brock Hornby, chair of the Judicial Conference Committee on Court Administration and Case Management, to the Conference for Chief District Judges, commented, "This 'practical obscurity' ends when the court records become easily accessible and searchable electronically from remote locations—anywhere in the world and at any time of the day or night. This end of 'practical obscurity' for court records raises a number of policy issues . . . One policy issue is created by the very nature of the Internet." (See **http://www.uscourts.gov/ttb/june00ttb/internet.html**.) With the demise of practical obscurity, lawyers need to carefully consider what, if anything, needs to be redacted from court records. For more information about redaction, see the section later in this chapter on Federal Dockets and Redaction.

For those who advocate for access to public records as part of our open, democratic tradition and our free speech rights, nothing short of full access to public records via the Internet (public, personal, and sensitive information included), is acceptable. On the other hand, those in favor of the right to privacy want all of the information (public, personal and sensitive) taken off the Internet, especially in light of the ever-growing identify theft and stalking cases.

What's in a Public Record?

Public records can include personal, private, or sensitive information. Often these labels overlap, but we'll try to draw some distinctions.

Personal Information

Personal information can be found in public and private records. Personal information is that which personally identifies you—such as your Social Security number, your address, your phone number, and so on. This is also sometimes referred to as sensitive information.

Sensitive Information

Sensitive information can be found in public and private records. Sensitive information can be that which personally identifies you, as noted above under **Personal Information**. There are also two other definitions of sensitive information: (1) information found in a public record that is personal or private, and if released could cause harm, bias, or embarrassment (for example, a medical disability listed on your driver's license); (2) information that is private, or personal information found in a public record about a person who is in a protected group and if released could cause harm, bias, or embarrassment. For example, minor children are a protected group—even their names are protected. If their names (or anything about them) can be gleaned from a public record (such as a divorce decree), this information is considered sensitive and might be redacted from an online record (where anyone could easily access it). An adult's name found in the same divorce decree would not be considered sensitive because they are not in a protected group. The minor's name might or might not be redacted in the paper record.

Private Information and Private Records

Private information is what you consider to be for your eyes only—and for those you've given permission to view it. Your medical records contain private information, but you have given your doctor permission to view them (and if you want to be reimbursed by your health insurance company, you've given them permission too). Your private information in your private records is not subject to general public inspection or a FOIA request.

Although you probably consider what you paid for your house to be private information, the information is considered public nevertheless.

The information is found in real estate records, and real estate records are deemed to be public records, as noted earlier.

Public Records May Contain Personal, Sensitive, and Private Information

In a public divorce decree, personal and private information can also be found. Personal information such as the Social Security numbers of the divorcing couple may appear. Private information, such as tax information or their yearly income, might appear in the public record. Bankruptcy filings also include personal and private information, such as the debtor's Social Security number, credit card numbers, bank name and account numbers, and so on. Some of this personal and private information found in court records is now being protected from public scrutiny. For instance, according to new federal bankruptcy court guidelines, only the last four digits of an individual's Social Security number is displayed. Recent federal and state legislation and court opinions have also limited the access to personal and private information found in public records.

"Publicly Available" Information

"Publicly available" information must be distinguished from public records. Publicly available information does not come from a government agency. It is that information (whether it be private, personal, or sensitive) that you voluntarily provide to a private entity. For example, you provide your phone number and address to the telephone company or your ZIP code to the person who checks you out at a department store register. That information is now publicly available and may be (and usually is) sold to marketing companies or public record database companies (whose databases also include a mix of public records and publicly available information). As noted in Chapter 7, "Finding and Backgrounding People," the Internet contains loads of publicly available information such as anything you say in an online community or on your own Web site, or the information you provide to a site like Classmates.com (such as your place of employment and marital status).

Privacy and Information on the Internet

Right-to-privacy advocates and right-to-access advocates have always been at loggerheads over access to public records, but even more so after two unrelated events: the advent of the Internet and the aftermath of September 11, 2001.

With the advent of the Internet came easy, anonymous, and often free access to public records. The Internet made public records, in essence, even more public. The Internet also made access to publicly available information easy. With easy access to both came the problem of identity theft, which is now growing at an unprecedented rate.

In the aftermath of September 11, the right-to-privacy versus the right-to-access debate is taking another direction. While the privacy concerns centering around the advent of the Internet focused more on individuals invading other individuals' privacy (and stealing their identity or stalking them, for example), now the privacy concerns have shifted to the government invading an individual's privacy. The government, in a quest to ferret out terrorists, is looking more closely at background information about people. They are doing this in two ways: (1) more searching of commercial databases (such as ChoicePoint at **http://www.choicepointonline.com**, Accurint at **http://www.accurint.com** and Merlindata at **http://www .merlindata.com**) that compile and consolidate public records, non-public information from credit headers and publicly available information; and (2) passing legislation, such as the U.S.A. Patriot Act, Public Law No. 107-56 (2001) (18 *U.S.C. Sec. 1 et seq.,* **http://frwebgate.accessgpo.gov/cgi-bin/ getdoc.cgi?dbname=107_cong_public_laws&docid=f:publ056.107)** and the USA Patriot Improvement and Reauthorization Act of 2005 (**http:// thomas.loc.gov/cgi-bin/query/F?c109:6:./temp/~c109UegzKT:e14909:**) that allows the government to obtain private information about people from private and public entities.

The U.S.A. Patriot Act and Privacy

The 2001 U.S.A. Patriot Act's original scope was broad enough that the FBI could demand, without any prior governmental authorization, to see records about an individual from private and public entities, such as video rental stores or even libraries to discover an individual's video viewing, Web-surfing, and reading habits. And in fact, the government (primarily the FBI) did visit libraries requesting to see patron's circulation and Internet records (see **http://alexia.lis.uiuc.edu/gslis/research/civil_ liberties.html**). Some libraries complied with FBI requests, some did not, and some even shredded the records in order to avoid the issue (such as the Santa Cruz Public Library in California). However, when the Patriot Act was reauthorized in 2005, revisions to the act tempered the FBI's unfettered reach into people's records by requiring the director of the FBI (or the Deputy Director or the Executive Assistant Director for National Security) "to make an application for such an order involving library circulation records, educational records, or medical records containing information that would identify a person." The Act also now requires that the application for such an order "(1) include a statement of facts showing that there are reasonable grounds to believe that the tangible things sought are relevant to an authorized investigation; (2) include an enumeration of minimization procedures adopted by the Attorney General that are applicable to the retention and dissemination by the FBI of any tangible things produced; and (3) describe the tangible things to be produced with sufficient particularity to permit them to be fairly identified."

The U.S.A. Patriot Improvement and Reauthorization Act of 2005, Public Law No: 109-177, **http://thomas.loc.gov/cgi-bin/query/C?c109:./temp/ ~c109Mtdbdo**.

The Video Privacy Protection Act

In the first edition of this book, the authors stated, "Although there is legislation protecting privately held data in random niches, including the Robert Bork-inspired Video Privacy Protection Act [18 U.S.C. 2710], which protects from public scrutiny the lists of videotapes we rent, most private data is protected only by the discretion of the private entities which possess it." While the Video Privacy Protection Act also shielded the public from government scrutiny of our video rental list (with some exceptions) and still shields us from the general public's scrutiny of that list, those very same lists are now more open to government scrutiny as a result of the U.S.A. Patriot Act noted above.

The Privacy Act of 1974

The Privacy Act, 5 U.S.C.§ 552a, was enacted to protect against the disclosure of information that government agencies keep about individuals. The fear was that without this act, there was nothing to prevent the government from compiling dossiers about a person—going from agency to agency to collect the data. Recently, the government has reportedly paid $50 million annually to the commercial database company Choice-Point (also marketed as AutoTrack, KnowX, and ScreenNow) to search through what amounts to data that can be used to create dossiers about individuals—from both public records and publicly available information. ChoicePoint's records can vary (depending on each state's policies), but often include motor vehicle records, automobile and boat registrations, liens, deeds, military records, bankruptcies, UCCs, judgments, Social Security numbers (limited access as of 2005), phone numbers, and addresses, and so on. Another commercial database company also used by the government, Accurint, has records that show the following about a person: relatives and associates, past work and home addresses, phone numbers (from up to twenty years back), Social Security numbers (limited access as of 2005), and so on. Privacy advocates are up in arms regarding the government's heavy reliance upon commercial companies' databases to access the very types of information that the Privacy Act of 1974 seemingly prohibited.

Pending Privacy Laws:

As a result of several data breaches at ChoicePoint and Accurint (among others), numerous bills concerning identity theft and protecting the privacy of individuals were introduced in Congress during 2005 and 2006. One of the bills being considered is "The Personal Data Privacy and Security Act" (S.1789 at **http://thomas.loc .govcgi-bin/bdquery/z?d109:s.01789:**), sponsored by committee Chairman Arlen Specter and Senator Patrick Leahy. It would require database vendors to allow U.S. residents to correct personal data in the databases and require vendors to perform risk assessments and implement data-protection policies if they had personal data on over 10,000 U.S. residents in their databases. Businesses that do not implement security plans could be fined up to $35,000 a day if found in violation of the requirement. The Judiciary Committee bill would allow companies that suffer data breaches to avoid notifying consumers if they determine the breach poses "no significant risk" of identity theft or other data fraud. Further, the bill does not require companies who detect a breach to inform individuals in their database if the company determines there has been no risk; however, they must inform the Secret Service (who can then conduct an investigation).

Public Records Web Sites
Public Records Metasites

Access to federal, state, and local agencies' public records varies from jurisdiction to jurisdiction and agency to agency. Some don't place them on the Web at all, some place them on the Web for free, and some charge a fee.

There are several excellent free and low cost metasites that link to those agencies that do place their public records on the Web. While the links on these metasites point primarily to free government sites, they also point to nongovernment sites such as universities, nonprofits, and commercial database companies, that have created searchable databases from public records derived from (or purchased from) the government. Some of the links may also point to publicly available data and not just public records per se. The following are the top metasites for beginning your public record quest:

- Search Systems at **http://www.searchsystems.net**
- Portico at **http://indorgs.virginia.edu/portico**
- BRB Publications at **http://www.brbpub.com/pubrecsites.asp**
- State and Local Government on the Net at **http://www.statelocal gov.net**
- Pretrieve at **http://www.pretrieve.com/**

Search Systems

http://www.searchsystems.net   **$**

Purpose: To link (for a small fee) to free and pay sites that contain public records and publicly available data.

Content: Search Systems (which became a pay site in 2006 after many years of being free) links to over 35,000 mostly free searchable public record databases covering U.S. federal (or nationwide), state, and local records; U.S. territories; Canada (nationwide and provinces); foreign countries, and Outer Space (current news from NASA).

At the state level, links point to databases that provide public record information about businesses (such as secretary of state corporate records), licensing (such as dentists), criminal records, inmates and offenders, missing children, unclaimed property, trade names and trademarks, state employee and department lookups, UCC filings, and state codes.

At the city and county levels, links are provided to local civil, criminal, probate, family, and traffic court records; birth, death, and marriage records; assumed and fictitious business name filings; recorded documents; county and city inmates; and tax information. The site also offers subject-oriented categories for Corporations, Birth, Deaths, Marriages, Inmate, Sex Offender, Real Property, UCC, and Unclaimed Property resources.

Our View: The following are the features we find extremely useful: (1) next to each link is a description to inform you about what the site contains to help determine if it's worth a visit, and (2) next to each link is a notation of free or pay, warning you in advance if you need to get your credit card out.

Offsetting these useful features, however, were two major mid-2005 and 2006 changes to Search Systems.

In 2005, Search Systems instituted a 15-second delay before you were forwarded to the resource that you originally clicked. The delay was for a promotional page that announced Search Systems' "Direct Pass" subscription service. It informed you that for $4.95 per month (or $48.90 per year), the "Direct Pass" service cuts out that 15-second delay and delivers continued "Direct access to thousands of databases containing billions of records."

In 2005, Search Systems ceased displaying the URL of the resources linked to. They are now displayed in a Search System "frame" that masks the direct URL of the site.

The owners of Search Systems implemented these changes to thwart individuals who, according to Search Systems, had copied their database of links and created their own online services for which they were charging subscription fees.

Then, in 2006, free access ended and Search Systems moved to a subscriber-only service.

Search Systems, aside from providing links to free public record sites, now offers access to pay sites to help users search across state lines—something not possible using free sites. See pages 333–334 for details about Search Systems' "Premium" pay databases.

Tip: Instead of browsing by jurisdiction, use the **Public Record Locator** feature at the top of the home page to search by keywords that describe the type of public record sought (such as marriage records) or to search by jurisdiction (such as Cook County) or to search by a combination of the two types of keywords. To search by jurisdiction, type in the name of a city for links to that jurisdiction's Web public records. To search by type of public record, type in a category of records (such as death records) and a list of death and cemetery records in various jurisdictions is displayed. Or, type in the name of a county (Cook County) and the category of public records you are seeking (death records) to discover if Cook County has their death records free on the

Figure 8-1. Search Systems lists thousands of public records sites, notes if they are free or pay, and offers a detailed description of the site before you link to it. This is a screen shot of their New York state page.

Web. Use the **Advanced Search** option for more search functions.

Pretrieve.com

http://www.pretrieve.com/

Purpose: To find public records pertinent to a business, address, phone number, or person.

Content: Unlike Search Systems, which links to sites where you can access public records, Pretrieve works as a meta-search site that actually searches numerous public records databases simultaneously. Its home page is simple and straight to the point. You can either choose to search by person, business, address, or phone number—with the boxes below waiting for the information terms.

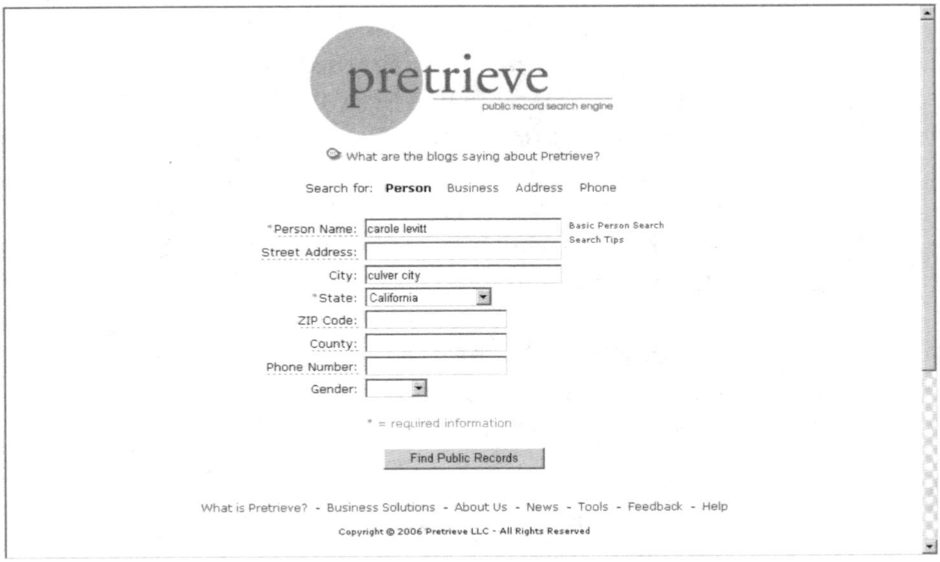

Figure 8-2. This is Pretrieve's advanced search page. Pretrieve searches a name through a host of public record databases.

A red star indicates those criteria that are required to conduct the search. If you are searching for a person and click on **Advanced Person Search**, located to the right side of the first box, it will allow you to narrow your search. For example, we searched for "Carole Levitt in California" (a name and state are required criteria). But after clicking on the **Advanced Person Search**, we could narrow down the search more specifically by ZIP code, county, phone number, or gender. The same would apply for business and address searches (phone searches do not have an advanced option), although they all differ slightly in the advanced search criteria you can add. (For the advanced search, the default on the home page is **Advanced Person Search**. When you click on **Business**, the link name changes to **Advanced Business Search**, and so on.) (You can enter a ticker symbol into the **Business** Search.)

On the top of the results page, Pretrieve shows you the number of results found in your particular query. In our case, Carole Levitt's name brought up 38 public records links. Pretrieve will organize these links under "tabs" which you can then click on to access the information they cover. The "tabs" for a **Person** search were as follows: **Property Information, Criminal, Court, Financial, Professional, Local Info,** and **Miscellaneous**. Each of these links allows the user to delve into further information about the person that they are searching. The same is true for the other search categories, although their "tabs" might be slightly different.

Our View: We long thought this type of meta-search function would be a great addition to Search Systems. While Pretrieve is easy to use and returns results in an easy to use format, it doesn't say how wide or deep its Web site access is, so it's hard to know whether you would be getting all the facts. For example, for searches conducted of Nevada information, Pretrieve does not return data from the searchable database of Clark County (Las Vegas) marriages. Considering the number of people who get married in Las Vegas, this is a pretty glaring omission.

Considering how new it is, though, there is still hope that Pretrieve will grow to include more sources. For now, though, it is a welcome, useful addition to our "Public Records Search Toolbox."

Portico

http://indorgs.virginia.edu/portico

Purpose: To provide, free of charge, links to public record and publicly available information.

Content: Portico is arranged topically, and then broken down by state. Topics covered include personal property, stocks, salaries, obituaries, occupations, and more.

Our View: While we prefer Search Systems, sometimes we find a topical approach is what we need and Portico fits the bill.

Tip: If you need information other than public records, such as salary surveys, calculators, and various other reference resources, take a look at Portico's directory for links.

BRB Publications Inc.

http://www.brbpub.com/pubrecsites.asp

Purpose: To provide, free of charge, links to over 1,400 state, county, city, and federal sites where public record information is free. Also, BRB has a pay site with links to 26,000 government agencies that store public records at **http://www.publicrecordsources.com**.

Content: BRB now contains links for state occupational licensing boards. Its online Public Records Research System (PRRS) offers annotated links to over 26,000 government agencies, county courts, county recording offices, and federal courts that house public records.

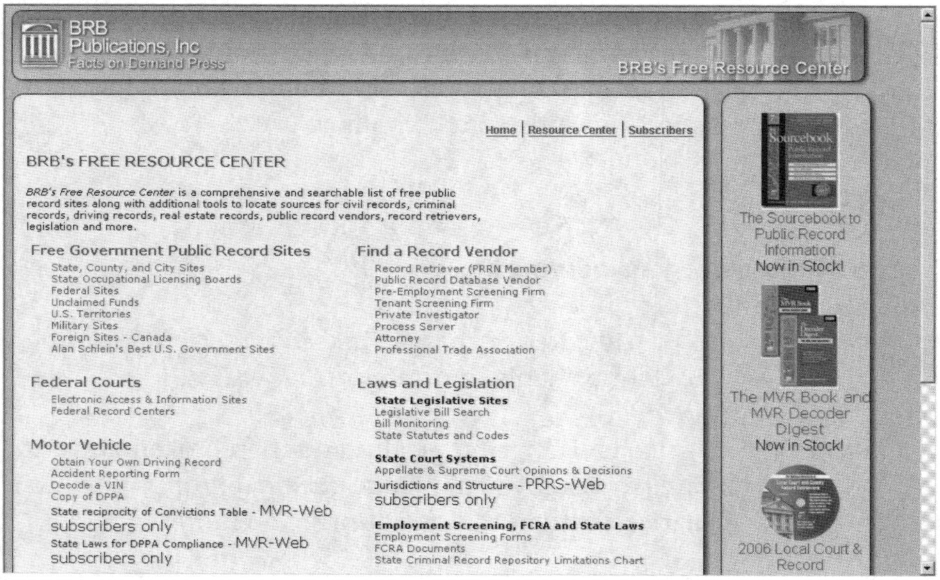

Figure 8-3. BRB offers links to: state, county, and city public records Web sites, public record retrievers, courts, and legislatures.

Our View: With 26,000 links, it may be worth the annual fee of $119 (for two users) to subscribe to PRRS, especially because of the detailed annotations. For instance, a search of "Anchorage accident report records" displays contact information and the following details: "Records are available from seven years. Only legal representatives and insurance agents of the participants, or the participant him/herself may obtain copies. The lawyer or legal representative must have a notarized request, an insurance agent a signed request with reason." PRRS also provides a directory of over 630 local court and county record retrievers.

Tip: For links to PRRS-approved local document retrievers, search firms, preemployment and tenant screening firms, trade associations, PIs and process servers, see **http://www.brbpub.com/prrn/**. To find a document retriever, select a state from the drop-down menu and click **Submit**. Then, select a county from the pull-down menu and click **Submit** again. The results show the name and phone number of the retrieval company and also a grid displaying (1) from which courts the company will retrieve and (2) what type of records the company will retrieve.

State and Local Government on the Net

http://www.statelocalgov.net

Purpose: As the name implies, to link to over 11,000 official state and local government sites.

Content: There are links to state, territorial, tribal, county, and city—broken down by branch of government. There are also links to federal and multi-state sites, but we do not find these as useful (or comprehensive) as the state and local links.

Our View: There are two ways to search the same data, which we find a bit odd. The first option is to choose from one of the three drop-down menus on the left side of the home page (labeled **Select State** or **Select Topic** or **Local**

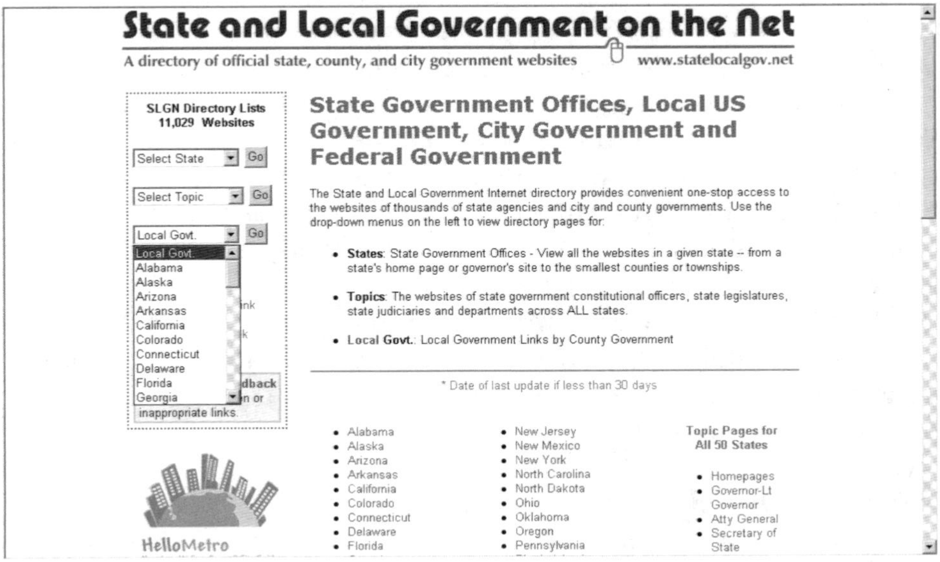

Figure 8-4. Browse for government sites at **State and Local Government on the Net** or use the drop-down menus to select a state, topic (such as Education or Legislature), or local government.

Government). The **Local Government** menu only brings you County results while the **Select State** menu brings you County, City, and more. Do not try to choose from more than one drop-down menu at a time. At first glance we thought this type of combined search would work, but each drop-down menu is a separate search function. We like that a date next to each state name tells us when links were last updated. If there is no date, this means it was updated within the last month.

Tip: If you don't find what you're looking for, visit the individual state's home page (as the site suggests); though State and Local Government on the Net's pages are updated frequently, they may not be as up-to-date as the various government's official home pages.

Vital Statistics: Birth, Death, Marriage, and Divorce

Vital statistic records are typically found at the local level, but there are some national and statewide records. Every jurisdiction has different access policies.

Some vital statistic records are available online for free at government Web sites. Some jurisdictions offer online ordering for a fee. Some jurisdictions sell their records outright to fee-based databases that then compile the government information and make it available for a fee. And finally, some public records may be found online at local historical society Web sites, local library Web sites, or even at genealogy sites (use Ancestry.com or RootsWeb.com to locate these types of sites). However, because of identity theft and confidentiality laws (especially for birth and death records), many jurisdictions, such as California, have ceased online ordering altogether or have begun restricting access to "authorized" requestors. As of July 1, 2003, a new California law designates who is an "authorized" requestor and requires a notarized Certificate of Identity and a completed application form signed under penalty of perjury by the authorized requestor for all mail orders.

To Order Certified Copies for a Fee

If you are unable to easily find and order vital statistics, or if the jurisdiction doesn't offer online ordering, there are private companies that can expedite the process for you. For example, VitalChek (**http://www .vitalchek.com**) handles over twenty-five thousand certified vital records on a weekly basis. Their processing fees vary from state to state (and county to county) and also depend on your required turnaround time (for example, the cost is $18.50 for a three-to-five-business-day turnaround in Montana, but in California it is $23.50). Add to this the state or county's fees also when calculating costs. Search Systems will direct you to a similar company, CourthouseDirect.com (**http://www.courthousedirect .com**), where you can order vital statistic documents.

RootsWeb

http://searches.rootsweb.com

Purpose: To provide links to free and pay state and local vital statistic public records sites and publicly available data.

Content: RootsWeb links to selected state and county vital statistics public records and publicly available data (from historical and genealogical societies and libraries). It also includes a

Figure 8-5. RootsWeb links to free state and local vital statistic public records (including the SSDI) and publicly available data from historical societies and libraries.

free national death records database based on the Social Security Death Index (SSDI). (See the separate entry below for details on SSDI searching). RootsWeb is supported by Ancestry.com (see the next entry) and some of the data overlaps, such as the SSDI. Strangely enough, while the SSDI is free at Rootsweb, it's not free at Ancestry. State death records are available only for California (9,366,786 records from 1940 to 1997), Texas (death records from 1964 thru 1998), Kentucky (2,921,383 records from 1911 through 2000) and Maine (401,960 records from 1960 through 1997). To access those four states' death records (or the national SSDI), go to **http://searches.rootsweb.com** and scroll down to **Records from Federal and State Resources**. To view other state and county records, go to **http://www.rootsweb .com/~websites/usa/index.html** and select a state from the list. After selecting a state you can also scroll down and select a county (not all counties are included) to drill down to the county level.

Our View: This is a useful site to discover what state and county public records and publicly available records are online. It's very hit or miss, of course.

Tip: Avoid filling in any of the search boxes on the home page of RootsWeb; you will more than likely find yourself being led to a pay database or a page asking you to subscribe to Ancestry.com.

Ancestry.com

http://www.ancestry.com/search/rectype/vital/main.htm (\$) \$ ▤

Purpose: For genealogy research primarily, but useful for those who need access to a variety of public records, such as census records and "publicly available" information such as family trees. Private investigators use this site. They find the census records useful for "quiet title" research when they need to identify siblings, for instance.

Figure 8-6. Enter your ancestor's name and click **Search** for a list of possible links. You can narrow a search by entering a birth or death year or by clicking on the drop-down menu to select the country of birth or death. To view any of the results at Ancestry.com, though, you'll need to register.

Content: Ancestry.com contains over 3 billion names and 4,000 searchable databases relating to family history information and various historical records such as census data. If you register (free) you can search and view summary information free, but any time you choose to view the entire record you are taken to a paid subscription page. Some of the same databases that are free at RootsWeb .com as noted above cost $79.95 annually to access from this site. Linking to these records used to be free.

Our View: Even though the same SSDI, California, Maine, Kentucky, and Texas death records found at Ancestry.com for a fee are free at RootsWeb, we have included Ancestry.com because we wouldn't be surprised if it stopped supporting RootsWeb at some point. If that occurs, RootsWeb might cease being free (or even cease to exist), at which time you'll need to know about Ancestry.com.

Tip: After the September 11, 2001, terrorist attacks, Califor-
                nia's governor requested that the death and birth
                records found at Ancestry.com and RootsWeb be taken
                down due to security concerns that public records were
                (or could be) used by terrorists to obtain new identities.
                That request was complied with at first. Now, however,
                the death records are back up. While the California
                birth records are still down at those two sites, they are
                up at others (such as Vitalsearch.com). Texas birth and
                death records have been taken off the Texas Depart-
                ment of Health page, but they are still available at
                Ancestry.com and RootsWeb.

The VitalSearch Company Worldwide, Inc.

To search: (🚫$)   To view records: 📄   To search by more criteria: **$**

http://www.vitalsearch-worldwide.com

Purpose: To verify deaths or births by a person's last name or other
                criteria (such as mother's or father's last name). Discover
                someone's mother's maiden name (sometimes).

Content: VitalSearch has birth, death, marriage, and divorce
                records for nine states (including California, Oregon,
                and Texas); dates and types of records vary for each
                state. On the home page, a state chart shows what
                records are available for various states. For example,
                VitalSearch offers access to over 12 million name entries
                for California birth and death records from 1905 to
                2000. These are the same records no longer available for
                free at Ancestry.com. To access these records is another
                story. Several steps are involved:

                First choose a state. We chose California. We were then
                taken to a page with flashing ads. Ignore these and click
                on **Continue Loading the California State Portal**.
                More ads appear but notice a white box on the left side

underneath **For California Specific Data**. In this box, you can then select a database to search (**Birth, Death,** or **Marriage**) and then click on the **Go** button. However, as soon as we selected **Birth Indices** we learned that registration as a guest is required if you are not already a Premium (paid) subscriber. Click **You will need a free guest pass**. After filling in a brief form and submitting it, a user name and password was emailed back to us within seconds. At this point we can now click on **All Other Searchers Enter Here** and enter our new user name and password. A huge ad appears for Net Detective. Ignore this and scroll down the page and click on **Begin Search** located on the bottom right. In the **Birth Indices** for California, we learn that Guest Users can only perform a surname search (Premium searchers have more choices). We entered a surname and were rewarded with the person's full name, mother's maiden name, and date and place of birth. In the death index, Premium Searchers obtain more details than the Guest Searcher, such as the cause of death.

Our View: Though the site has useful information, there are innumerable ads and pop-ups that can get in the way of even beginning a search.

Tip: After just a few minutes of searching for free, the site had opened about ten new windows on our PC. A premium membership is worth the fee of $57.95 per year or $24.95 per quarter to avoid this. See **http://www.vital search-ca.com/gen/premregm.htm**. Do not click on the message **Those Entering This Database For The First Time Should Click Here** once you arrive at the search screen of the Birth Index because you will only be routed to an ad.

Death Records

Lawyers often need to verify deaths for many reasons. Recently, a lawyer trying to locate an heir asked for our assistance. Before doing any extensive investigating, we first check to see if a missing heir (or witness) is deceased. National death records can be found in the Social Security Death Index (SSDI), searchable at several free sites, such as Ancestry.com (**http://www.ancestry.com**) and RootsWeb (**http://ssdi.rootsweb.com**). There are also other death indexes found at the state and local level.

RootsWeb SSDI Search

http://ssdi.rootsweb.com

Purpose: For genealogy research primarily, but useful to verify a death in the Social Security Death Index (SSDI) and to link to other public records.

Content: The site contains death records for over 76 million deaths occurring after 1962 that were reported to the Social Security Administration. The index is updated monthly. The records show the decedent's name, birth and death dates; last known address; and Social Security number and place of its issuance. Because RootsWeb is

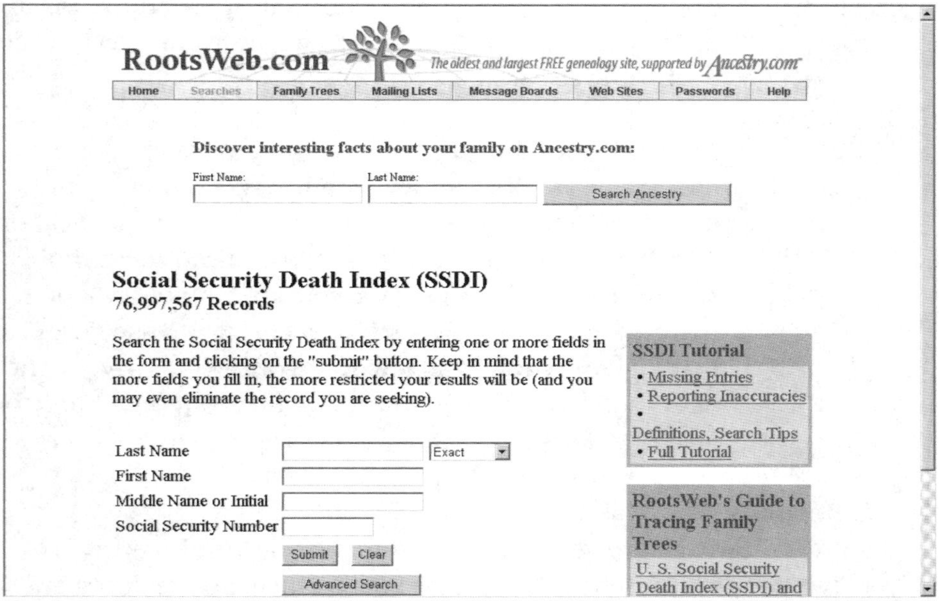

RootsWeb.com *The oldest and largest FREE genealogy site, supported by Ancestry.com*

| Home | Searches | Family Trees | Mailing Lists | Message Boards | Web Sites | Passwords | Help |

Discover interesting facts about your family on Ancestry.com:

First Name: Last Name: [Search Ancestry]

Social Security Death Index (SSDI)
76,997,567 Records

Search the Social Security Death Index by entering one or more fields in the form and clicking on the "submit" button. Keep in mind that the more fields you fill in, the more restricted your results will be (and you may even eliminate the record you are seeking).

Last Name [   ] [Exact ▼]
First Name [   ]
Middle Name or Initial [   ]
Social Security Number [   ]
[Submit] [Clear]
[Advanced Search]

SSDI Tutorial
• Missing Entries
• Reporting Inaccuracies
•
Definitions, Search Tips
• Full Tutorial

RootsWeb's Guide to Tracing Family Trees
U. S. Social Security Death Index (SSDI) and

Figure 8-7. Unless you have the subject's Social Security Number, be sure to click on the **Advanced Search** button on this page where more search options are provided to assist you in pinpointing the correct person.

supported by Ancestry.com, they have some similar data. Although there are many ways to access the SSDI from the RootsWeb home page, the easiest and most direct route is to avoid going to the home page and use the URL noted above. Do not enter any information into the **Discover Interesting Facts About Your Family** query box. It's simply a diversion. Some summary results will be displayed and then an offer to sign up for Ancestry.com's pay service will be offered. Also, don't enter the decedent's name into the search boxes displayed underneath. Instead, click on **Advanced Search** and then search by any of the following criteria, or combinations of them: name (for the last name you can choose exact, or if unsure of the spelling, choose soundex, which is the "sounds like" feature); last residence; last place benefit was sent to; Social Security number; birth date; and death date.

Our View: Although RootsWeb and Ancestry.com have similar data, including the SSDI, we prefer RootsWeb because it does not require registering (Ancestry.com does) and some of the same data that is fee-based at Ancestry.com (some state public records) is free at RootsWeb.

Tip: Once you locate the record, you may decide that you want a copy of the decedent's original Social Security application for further background information. To do this, click on **Letter**. The decedent's information is automatically placed into a letter to the Social Security Administration, which you can print out and mail with a $27 check to obtain a copy of the application. The following valuable information will be found once you receive a copy of the decedent's original application: full name; full name at birth (including maiden name); present mailing address and current employer's name and address (at the time of application); age at last birthday; date of birth; place of birth (city, county, state); father's full name (regardless of whether living or dead); mother's full name, including maiden name (regardless of whether living or dead); sex; race; whether the decedent ever previously applied for a

Social Security number or Railroad Retirement; date signed; and the applicant's signature. If you require additional records, such as birth, death, marriage, or divorce, click on the shopping cart icon in the **Order Record?** column. This will take you to VitalChek—a pay service.

Although we usually suggest that you enter as much information into a database about a person in order to narrow a search, if you receive no results from the SSDI (or any database, for that matter), start backing out information. Not all records contain the person's middle name, Social Security number, or place of death, for instance.

Gravesites and Obituaries

For those who haven't found the decedent's records in the SSDI, see Chapter 7, "Finding and Backgrounding People," to learn other ways to verify someone's death, such as by locating a gravesite or obituary notice.

Marriages and Divorces

Jurisdictions vary widely as to whether marriage and divorce records are online. While most counties do not provide online access, it's more likely that marriages will be online than divorces, judging by a search in Search Systems' Public Record Locator (1,110 results for marriage versus 91 results for divorce). On the other hand, it is possible that the record of a divorce may be chanced upon in a county civil docket database along with myriad other civil cases.

Marriage records are useful for skip tracing in several ways. First, the record shows a birth year of the subject and this can narrow down a search if you are given the option of adding the year of birth to a name search. With so many people sharing the same name, adding the year of birth can better target your intended subject. Also, some databases require a birth year to even conduct the search (see Rapsheets.com, where a $19.95 national search of over 140 million criminal records requires a date of birth along with the name). Second, this is another resource to discover a woman's maiden name: A maiden name can be used to try to track the subject through her relatives or to track her directly by her maiden name if she is now divorced and has gone back to using it. Third, the county where the marriage took place may also be the current location of the subject, or at least can serve as a starting point for further research. For example, searching that county's real estate assessor's records may be a good idea in case the couple settled down in the same county in which they married. Or, you might find relatives with the same name in that county who can be of assistance.

Figure 8-8. Searchsystems.net displays two results (although they are to the same site) for the search "clark county nevada marriage."

Using Search Systems (**http://searchsystems.net**), type the word "marriage" and the name of the county and state (for example, Clark County Nevada) into the Public Record Locator search box or use BRB (**http://www.brbpub.com/pubrecsites.asp**) and click on State/County/City Sites to browse through the list of links. The results from both BRB and Search Systems provide links to Clark County (Las Vegas) marriage records, but running a similar search at Ancestry.com does not. Therefore, it's always best to check a few metasites (and the jurisdiction's site too) before concluding that the records are not on the Web or are not free. Other states and even countries are also available at Ancestry (see **http://ancestry.com/search/rectype/default.aspx?rt=34** and scroll down to the list of databases beginning with Aberdeen, Scotland).

Records of all marriages taking place after 1984 in Las Vegas are freely searchable by bride's name, groom's name, or marriage certificate number at the Clark County government Web site **(http://www.co.clark.nv.us/ recorder/mar_srch.htm)**. Considering how many people get married in Las Vegas, Clark County is a good starting place to search for a marriage record when uncertain of the place of marriage. (Clark County divorce records are not online but they may be available at Wiznet, a pay civil docket database at **http://documentaccess.wiznet.com/pages/login.jsp** or at one of the other commercial docket databases discussed later in this chapter.)

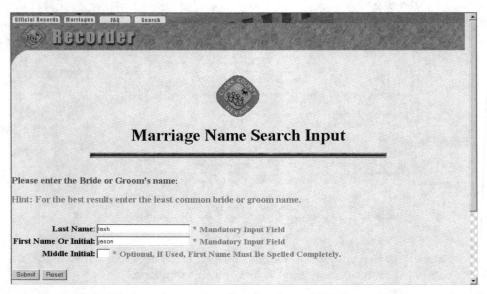

Figure 8-9. Marriages are indexed online from 1984 through the present, and are updated daily.

Texas marriage records for 1850-1900 can be found at a pay site, Genealogy.com (**http://www.genealogy.com/398facd.html?priority= 0000900**). For Texas marriage records from 1966-2002, Courthouse Direct offers a free user-friendly searchable database (**http://www.courthousedi- rect.com/TexasMarriageSearch.asp**). In addition, they also offer Texas divorce records from 1968-2002 in a free user-friendly database at **http:// www.courthousedirect.com/TexasDivorceSearch.asp**.

While the State of Texas offers free marriage and divorce records, they are not in a user-friendly searchable database. The records must be down- loaded and then opened in Excel. The state seems to have more up-to- date records than Courthouse Direct (e.g., the state offers 2003 records while Courthouse Direct offers 2002 records). The state divorce records are at **http://www.dshs.state.tx.us/vs/marriagedivorce/dindex.shtm** and their marriage records are at **http://www.dshs.state.tx.us/vs/marriage divorce/mindex.shtm**. Earlier records may be found at county Web sites since marriage and divorce records were not filed at the state level until 1966 and 1968, respectively).

Professional and Trade Licensing Boards

Use a metasite, such as Search Systems, BRB, or Portico to link to national and state licensing boards. If you do not know what profession or trade the subject is in, a good solution is to enter their name into Pretrieve (**http://www.pretrieve.com**). Pretrieve will then run the name through many licensing databases and display the results.

Portico (Occupations page)

http://indorgs.virginia.edu/portico/occupations.html

Purpose:	To link to various licensing boards throughout the country, arranged by occupation.
Content:	Occupations listed (with links) range from architects and brokers to lawyers, judges, doctors, and more.
Our View:	License verification for occupations such as contractors or doctors will typically be found on a government site, but we often find it quicker to search Portico, BRB, or Search Systems rather than a state government's home page because most of the government pages have too much data to wade through. (And, if the licensing informationis not located on the government site, but resides at a professional association's site instead, you'll spend a lot of time spinning your wheels at the government site. For example, a lawyer license database is often found at a bar association site and not at a state site.)
Tip:	The professional association sites might also include disciplinary or biographical information, while goverment sites often do not.

Medical Doctors

There is no public access to the Practitioner Data Bank—the federal government's database of malpractice judgments and disciplinary actions taken against practicing physicians. Only hospitals, HMOs, and state medical boards can access the site. See Chapter 12, "Medical Research," for information on finding medical doctors' licenses or certifications, or search Portico's list of occupations (noted above).

Court Records and Dockets

See the separate section later in this chapter, "Court Dockets and Pleadings."

Criminal Records

There are various types of criminal records: (1) arrest records (booking logs), (2) charges filed with the court, and (3) incarceration records. There are also various entities that maintain criminal records, from the federal government, to the state, to the county, and the city. Gathering all these various records from all these various jurisdictions into one central database has not happened. The only criminal record database that even comes close to being comprehensive is the FBI's National Crime Information Center (NCIC) database, which, unfortunately, is unavailable to us mere mortals. There are some exceptions, based upon Public Law 92-544, which authorizes the FBI to "conduct a criminal history record check for noncriminal justice purposes" (see **http://www.fbi.gov/hq/cjisd/backgroundchk.htm**). The FBI's database relies, in part, on the various jurisdictions to report charges and dispositions, but the system is imperfect and many charges fall through the cracks. A searcher who wants to conduct a so-called comprehensive criminal record search will find the going laborious. A mix of fee-based searching, free Web searching, and in-person searching is probably necessary. Additionally, local, state, and federal criminal records need to be searched separately.

If you plan on searching on your own, you can try using Portico or Search Systems for links to the various criminal record sites. In addition, we recommend *The Criminal Records Book* by Derek Hinton (**https://www.brbpub.com/books**), one of the best books (practical and detailed) for searching criminal records. Rapsheets.com (profiled below) might ease some of the burden of criminal record research with its low-cost state and local criminal record database, but it too is not complete. Even though some of the records found at Rapsheets.com can also be found free by visiting the specific state or county incarceration or booking log sites, or court docket sites, it might be quicker to use Rapsheets.com.

Pay Databases for Criminal Records

Rapsheets

http://www.rapsheets.com   **$**

Purpose: To find individual criminal records

Content: Rapsheets claims to cover almost the entire U.S. (see
https://www.rapsheets.com/business/default.aspx and
**https://www.rapsheets.com/business/info/aboutdata
.aspx**) but does not necessarily include every county in
every state. Results typically display the defendant's
name, date of birth, race, sex, offense date, offense

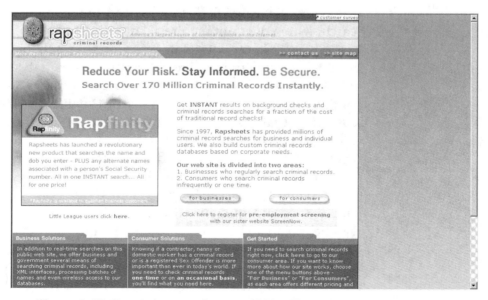

Figure 8-10. Rapsheets.com has over 170 million criminal records from various counties in 35 states.

description, case number, disposition, disposition date, county of disposition, and the sentence (these results can vary from jurisdiction to jurisdiction). Rapsheets has over 170 million records. Subscribers can perform a $19.95 "national" search but must also enter a date of birth along with the name. The database is easy to use.

Our View: If you conduct criminal records research often, it's worth the monthly subscription of $14.95 plus a per search fee. Otherwise, opt for the nonmember arrangement, but be prepared to pay more per search. Another option for nonmembers is to use SearchSystems' Premium service at **https://premium.searchsystems.net** (see below for more details).

Tip:
- Rapsheets also provides some noncriminal searching (click on **Other Searches**) to verify a name, a Social Security number, or a residential address. These searches cost from $1 to $4.
- Rapsheets doesn't work using the AOL browser.
- To find a date of birth that is required for the national search above, try first performing a state or regional search, which does not require a date of birth. You would have to know what state or region to search, but if you found their criminal record it might show a date of birth. You can also try to locate a date of birth by conducting a name search at the free birthdatabase .com. If that fails, visit a pay database such as Accurint, Choicepoint, or Merlindata.
- If you perform these types of criminal records searches infrequently and want to avoid the monthly account maintenance fee, see the Search Systems listing on page 333 for information on accessing Rapsheets searches on an ad hoc basis.
- The "Rapfinity" search runs the subject's SSN through a third-party database to locate all aliases and addresses associated with the SSN and then searches the Rapsheet database with all the names found associated with the SSN (and the date of birth that the searcher entered).

Pay Databases for Criminal Records

At a recent conference, a speaker warned the audience (consisting of private investigators) that when they conducted criminal record searching in Rapsheets, the criminal was sent notification. We were astonished to learn this and decided to do some digging around. While the speaker's statement was true (in the strictest sense), we found that the whole story was a bit different.

Notification is not simply a policy created by Rapsheets.com and other third-party background-checking services, but is regulated by the Fair Credit Reporting Act (FCRA), 15 U.S.C. Sec. 1681d.

Rapsheets and other third-party background-checking services only notify a criminal that you are conducting a search of their records if you are an employer who is conducting a background search of an employee or job applicant (or volunteer), and, in the course of using a third-party background-checking service (e.g., Rapsheets, ChoicePoint, etc.), you discover adverse (criminal) information about the person. This is where the FCRA requires that the subject of the search be notified.

Notification is not required if the third-party background-checking service has verified the accuracy of the information during the thirty-day period ending on the date on which the background report is furnished. It does not appear that Rapsheets and other third-party background-checking services are offering to do this thirty-day verification.

However, under FCRA, you may not be required to notify the employee, job applicant, or volunteer that you have uncovered adverse information about them, if you are gathering data directly from public records without using a third-party agency. However, check to see if there are any labor laws or privacy laws in your state that would then apply.

If a lawyer is conducting background research about a witness or the opposition, for example (and not conducting a background search of an employee, job applicant, or volunteer), and finds adverse (criminal) information, notification would probably not be necessary under FCRA.

Thus, the above law and the notification requirements only apply to lawyers who, as employers, conduct a background search of an employee or job applicant (or volunteer).

Search Systems Premium Search Services

https://premium.searchsystems.net **$**

Purpose: To find criminal records using a "pay as you go" database.

Content: In addition to the over 34,000 links that the public records directory Search Systems has compiled, the site also offers "pay as you go" criminal record database searches as part of its Premium Services. These are the same searches available to subscribers of Rapsheets (see above) but without the monthly account maintenance fee. Subscribers to Search System's Direct Pass service, explained on page 312, receive a discount off the posted search rates.

Pricing is as follows, with Direct Pass subscriber pricing indicated in parentheses:

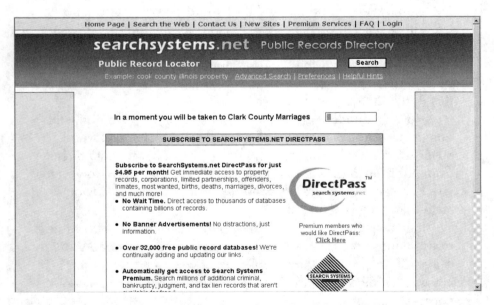

Figure 8-11. Before you are forwarded to the Web site that you originally clicked, you will be delayed by this promotional page that announces Searchsystems' "Direct Pass" feature. By subscribing to "Direct Pass," you would bypass this delay screen.

- Nationwide Criminal Records—$29 ($19)
- Regional Criminal Records—$15 ($13)
- Statewide Criminal Records—$9 ($7)
- Bankruptcies, Judgments, and Tax Liens—$10 ($8)
- Nationwide Sex Offenders—$5 ($4)

Remember that for a variety of reasons—e.g., not every law enforcement agency digitizes its records—there are no true statewide, regional, or national criminal record databases. Search Systems is very up-front about these limitations (click on **Our Databases** at the top of the page to learn about the date range and scope of each state's criminal records database).

It is necessary to open a Premium Services account (free) with Search Systems before you can begin utilizing these searches.

Our View: Even though Search System's per search charges for its Premium Search services are a bit higher than those for the same searches conducted directly at Rapsheets, ($10 vs. $15 for a Regional Criminal Records search), Search Systems offers a useful alternative to a Rapsheets account if you do not perform a lot of criminal records searches.

Tip: A Nationwide (all states plus the District of Columbia) Sex Offender search can be conducted for free at the Department of Justice's National Sex Offender Public Registry (**http://www.nsopr.gov/**—see page 340 in this chapter).

Criminal Records

We've all read about victims who were never apprised of their perpetrator's release from prison and who were later murdered by their perpetrator after the perpetrator's release from jail. VineLink was created in Jefferson County, Kentucky, in response to this type of tragedy. Twenty-one-year-old Mary Byron was murdered in 1993 by a former boyfriend, who was out on parole. He had previously been charged with rape and assault of Ms. Byron. She had not been notified of this man's release.

Criminal justice officials in Jefferson County contracted with Appriss to create a system that would provide victims (or anyone) with rapid notification of the release date of an offender. One year after Mary Byron's death, Jefferson County, Kentucky, introduced the first VineLink system.

VineLink.com

http://www.vinelink.com/index.jsp

Purpose: VineLink obtains information about criminal cases and when the offenders are arrested, released, or scheduled to appear in court.

Content: Appriss provides the technology and the data network that allows VineLink access to more than 1,400 criminal justice agencies across the U.S. and processes more than 13 million transactions every month. From the homepage, VineLink asks you to choose a state and then a **Search For Offender** form pops up. Every state page is different. For example, in Montana, only the State Department of Corrections can be searched, while in Illinois, you may choose to search the State Department of Corrections and/or the county jails. The first name (full or partial) and last name of the offender must be entered into the search form, and if known, their date of birth or age range can be entered.

The inmate search results show date of birth, the offender's identification number, custody status, agency, race, and gender. After selecting a result, you can ask to be notified when the custody status of the inmate changes. Victims, or any citizen, can ask to be phoned or e-mailed in either English or Spanish. To complete the phone registration, you are asked for a PIN number. This number needs to be entered upon receiving the phone call.

Free State and Local Criminal Records

Some state and local law enforcement agencies have placed records of inmates, criminal docket sheets, driving-while-intoxicated (DWI) history, delinquent parents, sex offenders, and booking logs on the Web for anyone to search for free. At Corrections Connection, you can view a list of various state and local agencies that have free Web searching of booking logs or inmate records. Use the State Links page (**http://www.corrections .com/links/viewlinks.asp?cat=30**) as a source for links to inmate locators in all 50 states. The Inmate Locator links page at **http://www.corrections .com/links/viewlinks.asp?cat=20** offers another collection of links to searchable inmate locator databases in selected states across the country. Some states and some counties provide free access over the Internet to criminal dockets, while others may charge a fee. For example, in California, criminal dockets are available free at the California Supreme Court and Court of Appeals Web site (**http://appellatecases.courtinfo.ca.gov**), while Los Angeles County charges a small fee ($4 to $4.75) to access its criminal dockets database (**https://www.lasuperiorcourt.org/online services/criminalindex/**). For more information on criminal dockets, see the section in this chapter, "Court Dockets and Pleadings."

Free Inmate Locator

http://www.inmatesplus.com/

Purpose:	To locate public records about prison inmates nation-wide, free of charge.
Content:	While Inmatesplus.com does not offer an all-in-one search of all states' inmate records, it does present direct links to the inmate locator databases of the 32 states that offer them online. Additionally, the site presents a link to the Federal Bureau of Prisons' Federal Inmate Locator database. For those states that do not yet offer online inmate locators, Inmatesplus.com offers direct links to the states' Department of Corrections Web sites. Users should note that each state uses a different search criteria and methodology for retrieving data.
Our View:	With its alphabetical list of state inmate locators, the site is easy to use and might be described as the "Yahoo!" of inmate locators.
Tip:	We have not tested, nor are we recommending, any of the pay aspects of this site or its affiliates (such as the link to **Inmate Record Search** that brings you to the **Surefire Detective** membership page or the **Inmate Penpals** service).

State DWI Offender History

New Mexico recently made its DWI Offender History Application available free on the Internet (**http://traffic.nmcourts.com/offender History/ohSearch.jsp?NAME**). While it does not contain all DWI charges processed by the courts, searching by full name or by Social Security number for those that it does contain, retrieves the full docket.

State and Local Sex Offender Registries

Wonder if your new neighbor is a sex offender? Sex offender registries have been one of the more litigated areas of free public records on the Web. A recent U.S. Supreme Court case just declared Alaska's Sex Offender Registration Act to be constitutional and compared the Web access to the registry to be "more analogous to a visit to an official archive of criminal records . . . The Internet makes the document search more efficient, cost effective, and convenient for Alaska's citizenry." (*Smith v. Doe*, No. 01-729 [U.S.], **http://supct.law.cornell.edu/supct/html/01-729.ZO.html**.)

Still, every state and county handles the logistics of access differently (for example, some sex offender Web registries are searchable by offender's name while others permit searching by a tattoo or by the offender's proximity to a specific library or school). A keyword search at Search Systems (such as "sex offender clark county Nevada") might link you to your county's sex offender registry if it is online. To link to statewide sex offender databases, see the FBI's site or the DOJ site (below).

As of this writing, there are several bills pending in Congress to make the National Sex Offender Registry available to the public on the Internet (e.g., see S.B. 792 in the 109th Congress (**http://thomas.loc.gov/cgi-bin/ query/C?c109:./temp/~c109JpGp9v**). However, the beginning of what will become a national database is already available to the public at the Department of Justice's (DOJ) site at **http://www.nsopr.gov/** (see below for details). The DOJ database contains records from all states and the District of Columbia, all of which can be searched simultaneously.

National Sex Offender Public Registry

http://www.nsopr.gov/

Purpose:	To track sex offenders in all states and the District of Columbia (D.C.) simultaneously.
Content:	The National Sex Offender Public Registry offers users the ability to conduct a single search through the public sexual offender registries of all states and D.C. by click-

ing the **National Search** tab. The other search option is to click on the **Show State List** to conduct a search of one jurisdiction only or more than one (but less than 49). The search menu offers a search by name, county, city, or ZIP code.

Our View: The search menu choices are misleading since not every state registry offers each one of the search criteria listed (and some states offer other search criteria—such as searching for offenders who live near a particular school or library). Nevertheless, this is a useful site when you don't know where the offender is registered.

Tip: A **National Search** requires that the searcher enter both an offender's last name and first initial of his or her first name. The site cautions searchers to visit the state where the offender is listed to verify the information. Each listed offender in the results list is hyperlinked back to the host state.

FBI State Sex Offender Registry Websites

http://www.fbi.gov/hq/cid/cac/states.htm

Purpose: To search for state information on sex offenders.

Content: This site provides links to the sex offender registry of each state that has placed records online that identify individual sex offenders. You can also locate information on crimes against children investigated by the FBI, such as kidnappings and online child pornography, on this Web site.

Our View: Unfortunately, the public cannot access the FBI's national database. Data in the FBI National Registry of Sex Offenders, established in 1996 under the Lychner Act, 42 U.S.C.14072, may only be released for law enforcement purposes to federal, state, and local crimI-nal justice agencies. However, there is an exception:

Figure 8-12. By clicking on "National Search" from the home page of the National Sex Offender Public Registry, choices for regional and "national" (48 states plus D.C.) will pop up (see the bottom of the screen).

public notification will be made if it's necessary to protect the public, and, as noted earlier, a public national database is now available at the DOJ's site.

Other Local Criminal Records

Booking Logs

Local law enforcement agencies vary as to whether they place booking logs or other local criminal records online. There's no central index for local booking log records. Each local entity's site must be searched. Once you're in jail, privacy, of course, goes right out the window, but in Arizona's Maricopa County privacy went right out the window and into a Web cam, until suit was brought against Sheriff Joe Arpaio. For a time, anyone could view Maricopa County inmates in holding cells, search cells, and pre-intake areas via the jail's Web cam.

The Los Angeles Sheriff's Inmate Information Center (booking log), containing six months to one year of historical data, is available free on the Internet (**http://app1.lasd.org/iic/ajis_search.cfm**). Search by an arrestee's name and the following information will unfold: full name, gender, race, age, date of birth, weight, hair color, eye color, reason for arrest, bail amount, and housing location. Placing this free on the Internet should raise some privacy concerns. Even if the arrest is later found to be unwarranted, simply being in a booking log can taint a person's reputation.

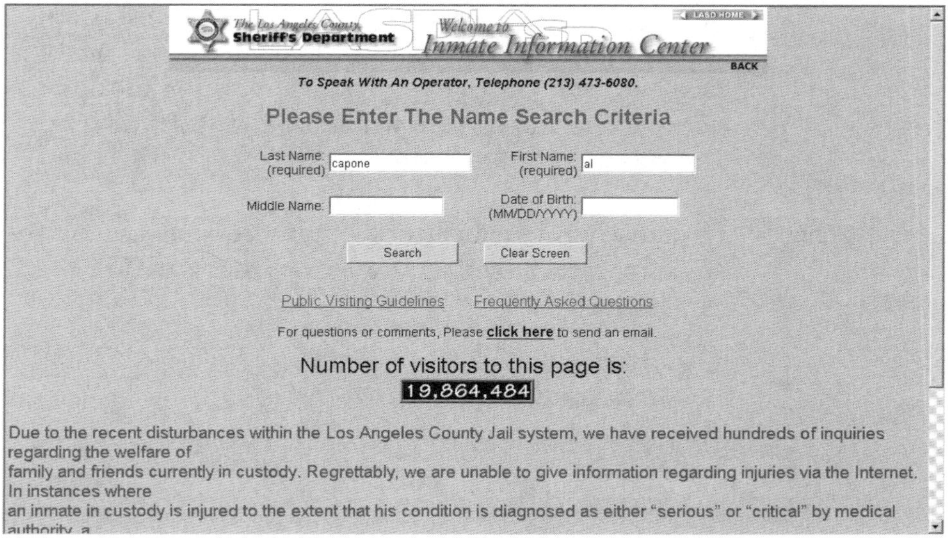

Figure 8-13. The Los Angeles County Sheriff's booking log is available free on the Internet. Visitors to the Web site can search by name for individuals who have been booked into custody.

Delinquent Parents

Access to a list (with pictures) of deadbeat dads (and moms) is available at Los Angeles County's Most Wanted Delinquent Parents site (**http://childsupport.co.la.ca.us/dlparents.htm**). This site announces to the world the name of the county's most delinquent parents, and provides the following details: amount owed, date of birth, race, height, weight, hair and eye color, number of children, and where last seen. When we visited, the most delinquent parent owed more than half a million dollars, and was last seen in Beverly Hills.

Outstanding Arrests

Florida Department of Law Enforcement Wanted Persons Search Page

http://www3.fdle.state.fl.us/fdle/wpersons_search.asp

Content: The Florida Department of Law Enforcement (FDLE) offers a free searchable database of outstanding criminal warrants in the state. Not every locale reports to the FDLE when they issue warrants, so the database is not comprehensive. Returned warrant results include full name, photo (if available), nature of offense, reporting agency, agency case number, date of warrant, warrant number, date warrant entered, date of birth, race, sex, hair and eye color, scars, marks or tattoos, occupation, and last known address (at least the city and state).

Our View: Of course we'd prefer a comprehensive database. But the ability to search by so many possibilities is useful. You can search by:

- Last name
- First name
- Middle name or initial
- Nickname
- Race
- Sex
- Date of birth or age

Tip: Searches can be performed with as little information as just a last name or nickname. (A minimum of the first two characters of the last name or the exact nickname must be entered.)

Federal Inmates

The Federal Bureau of Prisons maintains a free database of all federal inmates from 1982 to present.

Federal Criminal Records

Federal Bureau of Prisons Inmate Locator

http://www.bop.gov

Purpose: To locate federal inmates.

Content: Records of all federal inmates from 1982 to present are contained here. The record shows name, age, race, sex, and date released. To find inmates released before 1982

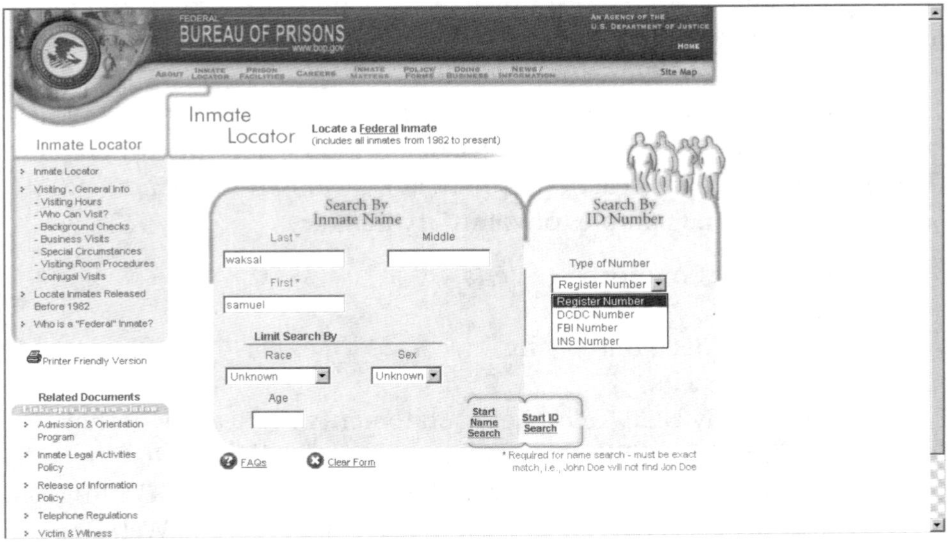

Figure 8-14. The BOP site contains all federal inmates from 1982 to the present.

researchers must contact the Federal Bureau of Prisons (for details see **http://www.bop.gov/inmate_locator/ inmates_b4_1982.jsp**).

Our View: Click on **Inmate Locator** listed in the left column or go directly to the database by using this URL: **http:// www.bop.gov/iloc2/LocateInmate.jsp**. This is an easy-to-use database, with many search options. You can search the database using the **Inmate's Register Number, Detailed Case Data Component (DCDC) Number, FBI Number, Immigration Number,** or just by using the inmate's first and last name. The search can be narrowed by entering an age into the **Age** query box or by making selections from the drop-down menus labeled **Sex** and **Race**.

Tip: You can't search by last name only. A first name is required.

Liens, Judgments, and UCCs

Besides providing information about a person's background (such as whether he failed to pay taxes, has had a judgment entered against him, and so on), these documents are also just one more place to find some-one—because most of the documents include addresses and possibly other personally identifying information.

There are two categories of liens: voluntary and involuntary. Voluntary liens are placed against a property or a person when the owner voluntarily pledges property (real or personal) as consideration for a mortgage or other obligation. Examples of voluntary liens are

- Deeds of trust or mortgage liens
- Notes
- Builder's or mechanic's liens
- Contracts for sale
- UCCs (usually UCC-1 Financing Statements.) To learn whether a state offers UCC filing online or access to a searchable UCC database, select a state from the drop-down menu at the UCC Filings page of the National Association of Secretaries of State Web site **(http://www.nass.org/busreg/uccfilings.html**).

Involuntary liens are referred to as adverse filings. In this case, the person or company did not pledge something as consideration. Instead, there has been an adverse judgment filed against the person or his property if (1) he defaulted on an obligation to pay a lender or a governmental entity, such as a failure to pay taxes, or (2) he was on the losing side of a lawsuit and a judgment was filed against him. Examples of involuntary liens are

- Federal or state tax liens
- Mechanic's and materialman's liens
- Abstracts of judgment

Liens, judgments, and UCCs can be filed at the federal, state, or county level, so you need to search in many different places. For example, there are both federal tax liens and state tax liens, and county judgments and state judgments. Using SearchSystems.net, you can type in the word "liens" or "UCC" or "judgment," for example, and get a list of Web sites where you find documentation. Another search strategy is to use Search Systems' directory and view by state or county to discover whether liens, judgments, or UCCs are online at a particular jurisdiction. Some of the sites listed are free and some are pay. Some are searchable by document number only, while others allow for name searching (or other search criteria). Some provide limited information, while others provide the image of the original filing. Lexis, Westlaw, and other pay databases allow you to search liens, judgments, and UCCs in one fell swoop and across jurisdictions using the subject's name.

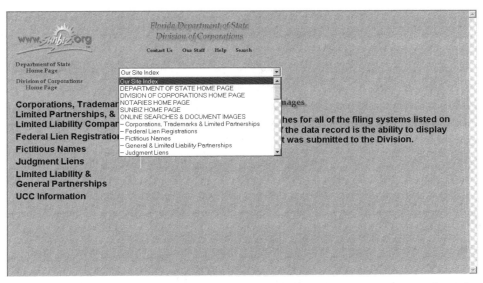

Figure 8-15. Users can search federal liens, UCCs, judgment liens, trademarks, corporate records, limited liability and general partnerships, limited partnerships, limited liability companies, and fictitious names at Florida's Sunbiz portal.

By using Search Systems' directory, we clicked on **Florida** and were pointed to the Sunbiz government site (**http://www.sunbiz.org/ corpweb/inquiry/search.html**), where we learned that the following documents can be searched in Florida at the state level: federal liens, UCCs, and judgment liens. Through Sunbiz, one can also search trademarks, corporations, limited liability and general partnerships, limited partnerships, limited liability companies, and fictitious names. You can view summaries of the documents and the actual images of the original filings. Searching was very flexible and could be done by name or docket number. We searched the Judgment Lien database by debtor name and found the following information about a specific lien: (1) name and address of judgment creditor and debtor, (2) amount of lien, (3) amount of interest, (4) case number, (5) document number, (6) name of court, and (7) dates relating to the file date, date of entry, and expiration date. To determine if a writ of execution on a final judgment was docketed with a sheriff, you are instructed to click on the docket number to view the filing image.

Bankruptcies

See the section "Court Dockets and Pleadings" later in this chapter.

Locating Assets

Real Property Records

When lawyers need to discover who owns a certain property, or discover its assessed value, or simply use the record to locate someone's address, Portico (**http://indorgs.virginia.edu/portico/personalproperty.html**), Search Systems (**http://www.searchsystems.net**), or the Tax Assessor Database (**http://www.pulawski.com**) can be used to quickly locate links to county assessors' offices that are free on the Web. The Tax Assessor Database site provides ratios of assessed value to market value by state and county as well as a phone number for each assessor's office.

There is no consistency in the varying states' and counties' policies regarding free access to real property records or the amount of information listed on the record once it's been found. Most free sites only permit address searches, but some do permit owner name searches. As an example of the varying policies between counties within one state, we'll use California and as an example of a standard policy among all counties, we'll use Tennessee. In California, all but five county assessor offices have placed some information on the Web (**http://www.pulawski.com/california.html**), and in Tennessee at the Comptroller of the Treasury's Web site (**http://170.142.31.248**), ninety of ninety-five counties are searchable through the same interface (but one must still search county by county) and four of the counties have separate interfaces that can be linked to from the Comptroller's site. In Los Angeles County, free searching by an address or assessor number is possible, but searching by a person's name is not (**http://assessormap.co.la.ca.us/mapping/viewer.asp**). Even after conducting an address or assessor number search at the Los Angeles County Assessor's site, the property owner's name is still not shown. In sharp contrast to Los Angeles County, California, Tennessee property records can be searched free by owner name. For prices of home sales (some back to 1987), see Domania.com (**http://www.domania.com**). Searching is by address only. Not all states and not all counties are in the database. Owner names are not shown.

Searching Pay Databases for Real Estate Records

Go directly to a pay site for real estate records in the following situations:

- After checking one or more of the sites that link to real estate assessors' offices (noted above), you learn that the jurisdiction does not have its real estate assessors' records online free

- When a county or state's free database only permits address searching but you only have a name
- When a county or state's free database permits address searching and you have the address, but the record does not display the owner—which is what you are seeking
- When you need to conduct a statewide (more than one county) or multistate real property search to marshal someone's real estate holdings

The cost to search property records in a pay database varies from database to database and the pricing even within one database can vary, depending on the type of search (for example, a search through a single state's records will cost less than multistate searching in some of the databases). So, do some comparison-shopping first. While all fifty states are represented in most of these databases, not every county is represented for each state. Some counties also include tax assessor deed transfer records in addition to mortgage records.

The following is a list of pay databases that include real estate records online:

- Accurint at **http://www.accurint.com** (now owned by Lexis)
- Merlin at **http://www.merlindata.com**
- ChoicePoint at **http://www.choicepoint.net**
- FlatRateInfo.com at **http://www.flatrateinfo.com/fri/public/**
- Lexis at **http://www.lexis.com**
- Westlaw at **http://www.westlaw.com**

The first four are probably the least costly to search—but this could vary depending on an individual's contract with the database vendor. Also, some of the vendors will run batches of records for you overnight if you are dealing in high volume public record searching (we have done this through Accurint in the past). The other databases noted below require an approval process and some also require a subscription fee. The cost for some searches can be as low as twenty-five cents. We'll discuss two database vendors as examples: Lexis (**http://www.lexis.com**) and FlatRateInfo.com.

To use Lexis you must first have a subscription. Property records can be searched by county, by state, or by all states, using the property owner's name or address. If you only know a partial name or address, you can use all of the special Lexis search features (Boolean connectors and wild cards) to try to find the record. For those who do not have an annual subscription to Lexis (or an annual subscription to any other databases),

Lexis was one of the few vendors that provided access to real property records on an ad hoc basis by using a credit card. Unfortunately, all public record searching by credit card has been disabled. See the full story in the LexisONE entry later in this chapter.

FlatRateInfo.com (**http://www.flatrateinfo.com/fri/public/**) as the name implies, offers a flat rate (as do some of the other databases listed below), so depending on the level of your use, it may cost less than going with a database that charges per search.

Personal Property

In a search for assets, lawyers should not overlook assets that the subject himself has overlooked, such as unclaimed personal property. A lawyer who was owed money by a client (a lot of money!) found $32,000 by running the client's name through the California unclaimed personal property database. You can guess what the lawyer's next step was . . .

Unclaimed Property

Unclaimed.org

http://www.unclaimed.org

Purpose:	To link to each state's unclaimed property database.
Content:	Unclaimed.org provides links to each state's unclaimed property database. Each state's database differs from the next. In some states the database record shows the amount of unclaimed property that the state is holding and in other states you'll need to contact the state by mail to find out. The property is usually money left in an old bank account, but it could be stocks, bonds, or safe-deposit contents. The site is sponsored by NAUPA (National Association of Unclaimed Property Administrators).
Our View:	Searching for unclaimed money can be a laborious search if the person left a trail of unclaimed property throughout the U.S.—because you must search state by state in the free databases. On the other hand, every time we offer hands-on seminars, one or more people in

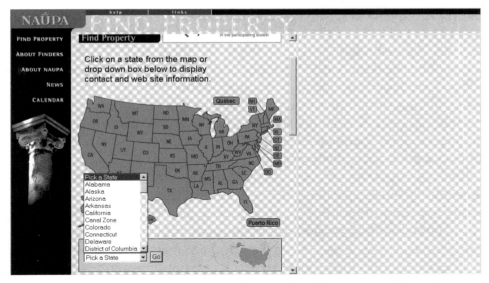

Figure 8-16. Search for money you (or your clients) forgot about. Unclaimed.org links to the custodian of unclaimed property in all fifty states.

the class find money they forgot they had by just searching one or two states (usually those states where they have lived in the past) to hit pay dirt.

Tip:

- NAUPA also sponsors a free multistate searching database, MissingMoney.com; it covers about thirty-two states, the District of Columbia, and Puerto Rico. (For a list of states covered by MissingMoney.com, see **http://www.missingmoney.com/Main/StateSites.cfm**. About twenty states were added in just the past two years, so check back regularly to learn which states have been added.) Some of the pay databases, such as FlatRateInfo.com, also search multiple jurisdictions.
- Ignore those e-mail messages offering to search through unclaimed personal property databases in exchange for a percentage of anything found. The databases are public record, freely accessible on the Internet.

Boats and Airplanes

See Chapter 18, "Transportation Research," for public record information about boats and airplanes.

Drivers Records

There is much confusion over access to an individual's driver's records. The first reason for confusion is that there is confusion as to what is meant by the term "driver's records." Is it one's driver's license record, or one's driving history, or the records about one's motor vehicle—the motor vehicle registration record? These various record types are often referred to as if they are one and the same, but they are not. The second reason is there is both federal law (Driver's Privacy Protection Act (DPPA), 18 U.S.C. 2721) and state law governing access to these records. And, to complicate matters even more, the various states interpret the federal law differently from each other. Thus, one state may provide different types of access than another state, or even no access at all. The third reason is the law (DPPA) itself is confusing because it carves out numerous exceptions as to who may have access to the records (permissible users) and whether authorization from the licensee is required or not. The fourth reason for confusion is that the same record type, such as driving history records, is accessible from more than one governmental agency depending on the whether the driving history record relates to accident reports, which may be held by the Department of Motor Vehicles or the driving history relates to traffic tickets or DWI records, which may be held at a local court (and even available free online at the court's Web site).

The most restrictive access to driving records applies to one's driver's license record. DPPA, 18 U.S.C. 2721(b)(1)-(12). In 1994, the Driver's Privacy Protection Act (DPPA), 18 U.S.C. 2721, placed many restrictions upon states' right to disclose or resell a driver's personal information without the driver's consent. Personal information under the DPPA is defined at 18 U.S.C. 2725(3) as "an individual's photograph, Social Security number, driver identification number, name, address (but not the 5-digit ZIP code), telephone number, and medical or disability information" but does not include "information on vehicular accidents, driving violations, and driver's status." (As noted earlier in the "Criminal Records" section of this chapter, New Mexico, for instance, has placed DWI history for free on the Internet since this information is not considered private.)

The following are a few of the exceptions to when one may access driver's license records under 18 U.S.C. 2721(b):

> (4) For use in connection with any civil, criminal, administrative, or arbitral proceeding in any Federal, State, or local court or agency or before any self-regulatory body, including the service of process, investigation in anticipation of litigation, and the execution or enforcement of judgments and orders, or pursuant to an order of a Federal, State, or local court.

(6) For use by any insurer or insurance support organization, or by a self-insured entity, or its agents, employees, or contractors, in connection with claims investigation activities, antifraud activities, rating or underwriting.

(8) For use by any licensed private investigative agency or licensed security service for any purpose permitted under this subsection.

Despite the passage of the DPPA in 1994, the state of South Carolina, up until the year 2000, considered driver's license records to be public and would hand them over the counter, for a fee, to anyone who wanted to see someone else's record. The only restriction was that the information could not be used for telephone solicitation. Selling motor vehicle information was big business for states; the state of Wisconsin used to receive approximately $8 million annually from the sale of motor vehicle information. During this same time frame, the state of California considered driver's license records to be private records. Finally, in 2000, the U.S. Supreme Court (*Reno v. Condon* at **http://caselaw.lp.findlaw.com/scripts/getcase .pl?court=us&vol=000&invol=98-1464**) deemed them to be private under the DPPA, but as noted above, the DPPA does allow access to driver's license information, in specified instances, without the licensee's consent.

While there are state databases and commercial databases that provide license and motor vehicle records, there are restrictions as to who can subscribe.

Insightamerica.com's DriverData.com database (**https://www.e-driverdata.com**) contains driving records from thirty-nine states and links directly to those states' motor vehicle records. But access is available only to those who meet DPPA's exceptions. Insightamerica.com makes its Colorado motor vehicle and driver information records available to lawyers in a database called FastMVR.com (**http://www.fastmvr.com**). Records are updated daily.

For more information about automobiles, see Chapter 18, "Transportation Research." How to access driver's license information, driving histories, VIN, and registration information for vehicles and vessels in the U.S.(on a state-by-state basis), Guam, Puerto Rico, the Virgin Islands, and Canada, is explained in *The MVR Book*, published by BRB (**https://www .brbpub.com/books/**).

DMVonline.com

http://www.DMVonline.com

| *Purpose:* | To locate links to Department of Motor Vehicle information in all fifty states |

Content: DMVonline.com presents a set of links to the Departments of Motor Vehicles in all fifty states. You can access the site's **DMV Guide** for each state by clicking on the map in the upper right-hand side of the home page, or selecting the state from the alphabetical list. These **DMV Guides** offer links to more DMV information (e.g., driving records, and vehicle registration information) for the state you selected. Before you can get to the specific state's DMV site, these links lead to another internal page that offers a description of the specific, relevant information about driving records or vehicle registration information found at the state DMV site, and (finally) a direct link to that information on the state's DMV site.

     The homepage also offers a list of topical links (e.g., **Driving Records, DMV Forms, Manuals**). These links lead to a page on which you can select the state you're interested in from a drop-down menu. Those selections lead you to another internal page that has a direct link to the information on the desired state's DMV site.

     Mailing addresses and phone numbers for the DMVs are available by clicking the **DMV Addresses** link near the top of the home page.

Our View: Even though the amount and type of DMV information available online is extremely limited, the site is a useful collection of links to (eventually) take you directly to the specific DMV you're looking for. Additionally, it can be helpful if you're looking for information in a state other than your home state. DMVOnline's direct links can cut down the amount of time you'd spend sifting through other states' Web sites and DMV sites by directly delivering to you the type of information you need.

     All of that said, the site is filled with sponsored links and ads that clutter the main page and each of the more detailed pages contain links to more specific information. It can be tedious to drill down through the site's own pages until the link to the desired DMV site is actually offered up. Also, users should be careful to read all of the information on a page to be certain you're linking to a state's official DMV site and not an information vendor offering to sell public record information.

Other Assets

For the following public records that can be used to marshal assets or to locate people, see Chapter 19, "Entertainment Industry Research and Intellectual Property":

- Trademarks
- Patents
- Copyrights

For the following public records that can be used to marshal assets or to locate people, see Chapter 10, "Company Research":

- Stocks
- Security and Exchange Commission filings
- Corporate filings (registered agents)
- Fictitious business names

What's Your Political Persuasion (and Where Do You Work)?

An example of a database created by a nongovernment sponsor who uses data derived from government public records is Politicalmoneyline.com.

Political Money Line

http://www.politicalmoneyline.com

Purpose:	Jury consultants use this database to determine potential jurors' political persuasions (assuming they have made contributions to candidates and haven't changed their political allegiance). This site also works for finding people, especially work addresses or employer names.
Content:	This site has gathered federal political contribution public records (from individuals who contribute over $200) back to 1980 and created a free searchable database for the public to search by donors' names. You can also

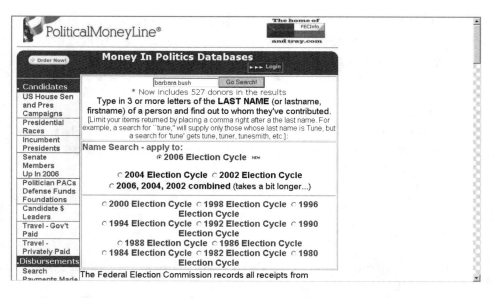

Figure 8-17. Search PoliticalMoneyLine.com to determine someone's political persuasion—if they've made a political contribution.

search by ZIP code, employer, or occupation, and for out-of-state donors. There are various additional services for subscribers, such as enhanced searching and downloading capabilities ($99 to $2,500 annually).

Our View: Up until recently, it was a bit laborious to search each election year separately. We're happy to report that a combined search, which does take longer, is now available for election years 2006, 2004, and 2002.

Tip:
- If you have been unable to serve someone at a home address, this is a great place to identify someone's workplace because donors are supposed to list a mailing address and an employer and occupation. To reach this information, click on the **Image** link after pulling up a subject's record.
- To search by partial names, type in three or more letters of the last name (or last name, first name). This won't work with the first name. To limit your search to the exact name as typed, place a comma after it. For example, a search for *gold,* will rule out *Goldstein,* while a search for *gold* will include it.

- Some states have state political contribution records online. To see if a state's election board has a database available, check your state's home page or visit the Campaign Finance Information Center (CFIC) (**http://www.campaignfinance.org/linksstate.html**) for their list of free links to the forty-four states that provide online databases. The CFIC's purpose is to assist journalists in following the campaign money trail (using a pay database). In Alaska, for instance, this data is searchable at the Alaska Public Offices Commission (**https://webapp.state.ak.us/apoc/searchcampaign disclosure.jsp**) and click on "Contributor."

Court Dockets and Pleadings

When you think about uses for court dockets and pleadings, you probably think about their use as legal research tools. But, they also can be used for all types of factual research by lawyers, legal administrators, law librarians, paralegals, or members of the firm's marketing or recruiting departments. What used to require a trip to the courthouse to retrieve the docket sheet (and then usually a return trip to copy the chosen pleadings off the docket sheet) now has become an easier task because of Internet access to docket sheets and in some cases even the full text of some of the pleadings. The following are some of the uses of dockets for factual research.

Using Dockets for Research

Using Dockets for Backgrounding
Dockets are useful for backgrounding people. Enter the name of a prospective client (or the opposing party, and so on) to learn

- How litigious the person is
- What type of suits the prospective client has been involved in
- Which lawyers the person has retained in the past
- Whether a prospective client has filed any lawyer malpractice lawsuits
- Whether a prospective client has been sued for lawyer's fees

Dockets can be used to research judges, although this only works with docket databases that have a field for searching by judge. Enter the name of a judge to learn

- What types of cases he or she typically hears
- How the judge typically ruled in the past on specific matters or issues (such as summary judgment motions, motion for new trials, and so on)

Dockets can also be used to research lawyers, although this only works with docket databases that have a field for searching by lawyer. Enter the name of an opposing lawyer (or even a lawyer you want to recruit) to learn

- What types of cases the lawyer typically handles
- Who the lawyer typically represents

Using Dockets for Conducting Due Diligence

Protect yourself by researching dockets to discover if a prospective client or partner has been involved in a bankruptcy or any type of fraud. Also, protect a current client who seeks your advice about whether to go into business with someone—by backgrounding the potential business partner through docket searching. Search bankruptcy dockets in particular.

Using Dockets for Current Awareness and Client Development and Retention

Dockets can help you answer the following questions:

- Who is suing whom?
- Who is representing whom?
- Is it time to shift your area of practice to the hot practice areas? Review the types of cases being filed to figure this out. Learn which lawyers are handling the hot practice areas (for recruiting purposes).
- Is a current or former client being sued and doesn't know it? Review local dockets regularly to keep clients apprised.

Using Dockets to Locate Pleadings

Dockets can be used to help you draft pleadings by providing sample pleadings from cases similar to yours. For example, in a recent instance, a firm needed to file a motion to freeze assets (the day before the New Year's Eve holiday). Since time was of the essence, the firm wanted to locate a similar motion to pattern theirs after instead of drafting one from scratch. Knowing of a similar case, the firm was able to pinpoint a useful motion with a quick check of that case's docket online. A messenger was then sent to the courthouse to make a copy of the motion for use as a sample.

Search docket sheets online to identify a pleading missing from your file. If the court has placed the pleading on the Internet for immediate download, you can even avoid sending a messenger to the courthouse to retrieve it.

Which Courts Have Placed Dockets on the Internet?

First of all, no blanket statement can be made as to the ready availability of dockets on the Internet. Every court is different and the rules are constantly changing. Some courts are currently

- Providing free access
- Providing free access, but requiring a password
- Charging a fee for access
- Providing no electronic access at all
- Allowing access to both civil and criminal dockets
- Limiting access to civil dockets only
- Placing images of the pleadings online for immediate download

Privacy Concerns

Courts limiting the type of dockets and pleadings placed on the Internet are basing their decision on the need to protect a litigant's privacy in general, to protect privacy in specific types of cases such as family law where minors' names are given, or to comply with confidentiality laws (for example, in juvenile law cases). Courts are also concerned with identity theft. The federal and state courts are each drafting their own access rules, typically differentiating between the three access points to court records: (1) in-person access to the paper copy at the courthouse; (2) in-person access to the digital records via public computers located at the courthouse; and (3) remote access to digital records via the Internet.

While some courts place documents online that others would not, they might attempt to at least insure privacy for the more sensitive information found in the documents by allowing the litigants to redact the information (but in the electronic file *only*). Sensitive information (which the federal courts label as personal data identifiers) refers to Social Security numbers, dates of birth, financial account numbers, and names of minor children.

Federal Court Privacy Policy on Case Files

Civil and Bankruptcy Dockets

In 2001, the Judicial Conference of the United States' Committee on Court Administration and Case Management issued its Report on Privacy and Public Access to Electronic Case Files (**http://www.privacy.uscourts .gov/Policy.htm**). The Committee recommended that "documents . . . should be made available electronically to the same extent that they are available at the courthouse with . . . one change in policy." The one change was that the personal identifier data (Social Security numbers (SSNs), dates of birth, financial account numbers, and names of minor children) should be redacted from any federal case files to which the public has remote electronic access, and that criminal case files not be placed on the Internet at all. The Committee explained that a "case file" (whether electronic or paper) means the collection of documents officially filed by the litigants or the court in the context of litigation, the docket entries that catalog such filings, and transcripts of judicial proceedings" (**http://www.privacy.uscourts.gov/Policy.htm**).

Criminal Dockets

In March 2002, the Judicial Conference adopted two modifications to their prohibition on remote public access to electronic criminal case files: (1) allowing high-profile cases to be remotely accessed by the public where demand for copies of documents places an undue burden on the clerk's office, and if the parties have consented, and the judge finds access is warranted; and (2) creating a pilot project to allow some courts to return to the level of remote public access that they provided prior to the Conference adoption of the policy restricting access.

Then, in March 2004, the Committee stated that criminal case filings would be treated similar to civil and bankruptcy case filings (**http://www .privacy.uscourts.gov/crimimpl.htm**). This was more in line with the 2002 E-government Act, Public Law 107-347, which was enacted to "promote use of the Internet . . . for citizen participation in Government" and with Section 205 of the Act, 44 U.S.C. 3601, which promoted public access to federal dockets and made no attempt to differentiate between civil and criminal dockets (**http://frwebgate.access.gpo.gov/cgi-bin/useftp.cgi?IP address=162.140.64.21&filename=publ347.107&directory=/diskc/wais/ data/107_cong_public_laws**). However, to comply with the E-Government Act of 2002 (44 U.S.C.101 et seq.), a document in a criminal case that contains "personal data identifiers" may be filed without any redactions, if filed under seal and then retained by the court. The court may require a redacted copy be filed for the public file (44 U.S.C. Sec. 3501).

Redaction for All Federal Dockets

The redaction policy is not retroactive, so neither the courts nor lawyers are required to redact any "personal data identifiers" from earlier filings. However, Florida's Manatee County Circuit Court has purchased software from Extract Systems, a Wisconsin company, that will automatically redact "personal data identifiers" from earlier filings **(http://www .bradenton.com/mld/bradenton/12412418.htm?template=content Modules/printstory.jsp)**, so we wouldn't be surprised if the federal government eventually followed suit.

Redaction and SSNs

The Committee instructed lawyers that SSNs only had to be partially redacted and instructed them to redact the first five digits only. Commercial databases are now also partially redacting SSNs, but they have chosen to redact the last four digits of the SSN and to display the first five digits. Thus, one might be able to ascertain a subject's SSN by piecing together the first five digits of the SSN from a commercial database and the last four digits from PACER. This would only work if the subject had a bankruptcy docket on file at PACER because SSNs are usually only reflected on bankruptcy filings (if at all).

Even though a full SSN will no longer be displayed at PACER (or on commercial databases unless one obtains a higher level of security from the commercial database vendor), the full SSN can still be used to perform searches in the databases.

Finding Dockets and Pleadings

To discover which courts' docket sheets, pleadings, and case records are available online, use docket metasites such as the free LLRX.com site or the fee-based Legal Dockets Online (LDO) site.

LLRX Court Rules, Forms and Dockets

http://www.llrx.com/courtrules (click on "Dockets")

Purpose: To discover which courts' dockets are available on the Internet.

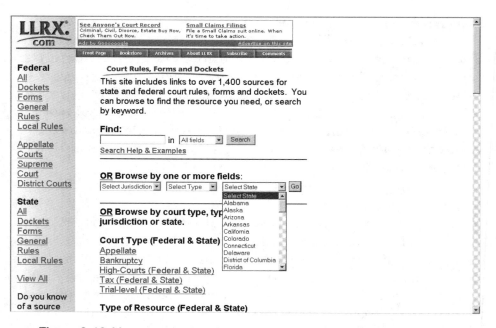

Figure 8-18. You can search or browse for court rules in a variety of ways, such as by jurisdiction or court type **http://www.llrx.com/courtrules/**.
© Law Library Resource Xchange, LLC.

Content: Search and link to all federal, state, and local dockets available on the Internet either by using keyword searching or browsing by court type (such as tax court), by jurisdiction (federal or state) or by state (choose a specific state to view a list of all federal and state courts located in that state). Links are annotated with useful information. For example, for federal courts you are told which docket system each uses (Web PACER, RACER, CM/ECF) and for state courts you are told if document images are available for immediate downloading.

Our View: We find the annotations useful, such as "Search by case number only." We also like the various search functions and the price: free.

Tip: This court docket database also includes links to court rules and court forms available on the Internet (for a total of over fourteen hundred sources).

Legal Dockets Online (LDO)

http://www.legaldockets.com

Purpose: To discover which courts' dockets are available on the Internet.

Content: While LDO's links are browsable by state only, they also include the same types of annotations as LLRX (such as noting the type of docket system each federal court uses, and if state court dockets provide images for immediate downloading). Depending upon the number of subscribers, the cost ranges from $199 (for 1–2 subscribers) up to $699 (for 19 subscribers) per year, while an entire firm is charged $1,200 per year. (A free one-week trial is available at **http://www.legaldockets.com/FreeTrial.html**.)

Our View: Although LDO is a pay site and LLRX is free, there are two functions we like about LDO that may prompt you to subscribe: (1) subscribers receive an e-mail alert each time LDO finds a new online docket site, and (2) LDO immediately alerts you to the free sites (saving time and money) by its **FREE** notation in the left margin, in all caps and red type.

Tip: LDO also links subscribers to case information, calendars, new filings, inmate databases, and Stanford University's Securities Law database. Law schools can receive a free annual subscription to LDO by sending a request on their official letterhead (**http://www.legal dockets.com/FreeforStudents.html**).

Between LLRX and LDO, which of these sources would we use? We'd probably use both since each one offers some information that the other doesn't. However, even taken together, neither one is 100 percent comprehensive. For instance, we did not find the Los Angeles County Bar Association Civil Register database at either site when we searched in 2003 but did find it at LDO when we searched in 2005.

Federal Dockets and Case Records

PACER (Public Access to Court Electronic Records) is the federal government's pay docket site. The PACER Service Center serves only as the judiciary's centralized registration, billing, and technical support center, which you need to contact for a login name and password (issued free). From the PACER homepage (**http://pacer.psc.uscourts.gov**), you can log onto an individual court's site by clicking on **Links to PACER Web sites** or search multiple courts simultaneously by clicking on PACER's **U.S. Party/Case Index** (discussed later in this chapter). Once logged on, there is a link to a chart showing the dates of coverage for each court.

PACER is in the midst of being replaced by the Case Management/ Electronic Case Filing (CM/ECF) system. Whether a court is using PACER or CM/ECF, one can log onto either system from the PACER homepage. By late 2006, the switch to CM/ECF should be complete. At that time, assuming all courts participate, we will have a national docket lookup. See **http:// www.uscourts.gov/Press_Releases/pacer.html** for details. CM/ECF was developed in January 1996 by the Administrative Office of the U.S. Courts. In addition to immediate access to all case information (docket sheets and imaged documents such as complaints, etc.), it offers electronic filing over the Internet. Currently, eighty-five district courts, ninety-one bankruptcy courts, the Court of International Trade and the Court of Federal Claims use the CM/ECF system (for a list of the specific courts using CM/ECF, see **http://pacer.psc.uscourts.gov/announcements/general/ecfnews.html**). While no federal appellate courts have been able to implement CM/ECF as of yet, they too are expected to be part of the system by late 2006. To use the CM/ECF system to search for dockets, a PACER password is required. To use the system for electronic filing, a separate password is required. Not all federal courts participate in the PACER program. To link to courts that participate in PACER or CM/ECF, see **http://pacer.psc.uscourts.gov/psco/ cgi-bin/links.pl**. Notice the **IMG** icon next to the PACER courts; it indicates that imaged documents are available. Imaged documents are available over the Internet on all courts using CM/ECF.

The following courts do not participate in PACER or its U.S. Party Index, nor the new CM/ECF system:

District Courts:

- New Mexico

U.S. Courts of Appeal:

- 2nd
- 5th
- 7th
- 11th

Review the list at **http://pacer.psc.uscourts.gov/cgi-bin/miss-court.pl** periodically to learn if a court has been taken off the Index's nonparticipating list.

Some federal courts still offer free dockets, including

- U.S. District Court for the Southern District of Indiana (civil cases filed before June 1, 2002, and all criminal cases)
- U.S. Bankruptcy Court for the Western District of Oklahoma
- U.S. Supreme Court
- U.S. Court of Appeals for Veterans Claims
- U.S. Tax Court

PACER (Public Access to Court Electronic Records)

http://pacer.psc.uscourts.gov　**$**
(PACER home page; use this to register)

http://pacer.psc.uscourts.gov/cgi-bin/links.pl (the list of Web PACER courts, what system they use, and whether they have images for immediate download)

Purpose:　PACER allows access to federal case and docket information (and sometimes images of the documents themselves) in all approved federal judiciary electronic public access programs (PACER, RACER, CM/ECF, and the U.S. Party Case Index). It covers U.S. district, appellate, and bankruptcy court dockets.

Content:　Most dockets include
- A list of all parties and participants (including judges and lawyers)
- A list of case-related information (e.g., for civil cases: the cause of action, nature of the suit, and the dollar demand)
- A list of all events entered into the case record, by date
- Appellate court opinions
- Judgments or case status

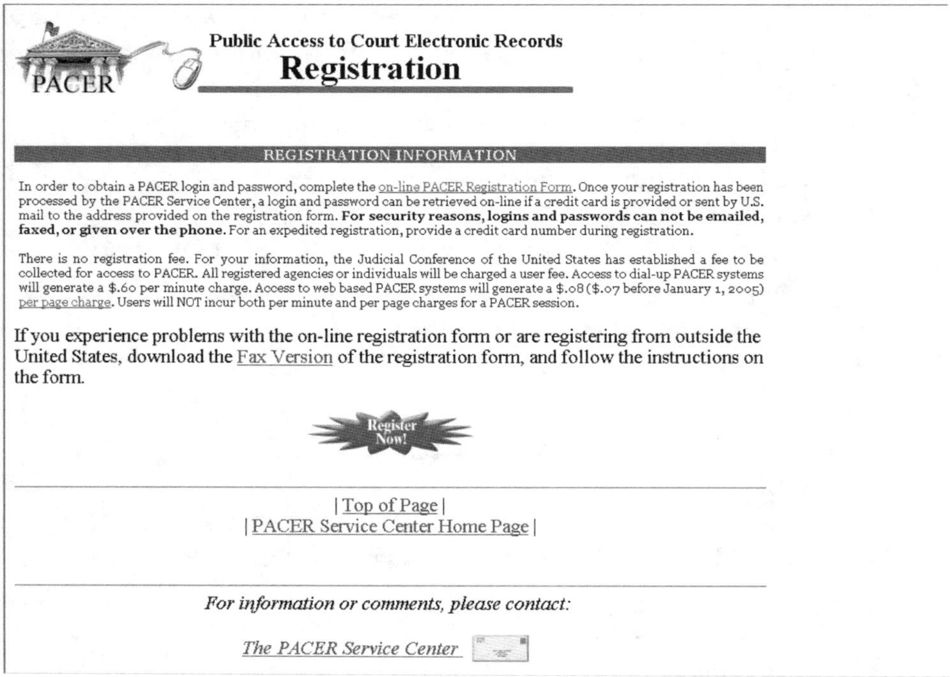

Public Access to Court Electronic Records

Registration

REGISTRATION INFORMATION

In order to obtain a PACER login and password, complete the on-line PACER Registration Form. Once your registration has been processed by the PACER Service Center, a login and password can be retrieved on-line if a credit card is provided or sent by U.S. mail to the address provided on the registration form. **For security reasons, logins and passwords can not be emailed, faxed, or given over the phone.** For an expedited registration, provide a credit card number during registration.

There is no registration fee. For your information, the Judicial Conference of the United States has established a fee to be collected for access to PACER. All registered agencies or individuals will be charged a user fee. Access to dial-up PACER systems will generate a $.60 per minute charge. Access to web based PACER systems will generate a $.08 ($.07 before January 1, 2005) per page charge. Users will NOT incur both per minute and per page charges for a PACER session.

If you experience problems with the on-line registration form or are registering from outside the United States, download the Fax Version of the registration form, and follow the instructions on the form.

Register Now!

| Top of Page |

| PACER Service Center Home Page |

For information or comments, please contact:

The PACER Service Center

Figure 8-19. Visit PACER's Service Center to set up a subscription for access to federal court dockets.

For bankruptcy dockets, see the Bankruptcy entry on page 371.

Some PACER dockets also provide immediate access to the documents listed in the docket sheet (this will be indicated if the number adjacent to the docket entry is underlined). All courts using the CM/ECF docket provide access to the documents listed in the docket sheet (click on the circle adjacent to the document).

There is no annual charge to subscribe to PACER; you are billed quarterly for your transactions, but no fee is owed until a user accrues more than $10 worth of charges in a calendar year.

Fee changes: Fee changes for PACER took affect on January 1, 2005. The new fees are:

- 8¢ per page to view, print, or download court data (or 60¢ per minute for dial-in access) with the following exceptions:

(1) the maximum charge for any document, docket sheet, or case-specific report will not exceed the fee for thirty pages, which is $2.40; (2) transcripts have no cap; (3) each attachment in a CM/ECF site is considered a separate document, so the cap applies to each attachment over thirty pages; (4) there is no charge to obtain the court's written opinions; (5) attorneys of record and parties in a case (including pro se litigants) receive one free electronic copy of all documents filed electronically, if receipt is required by law or directed by the filer; and (6) the summary list of results is 8¢ regardless of how many pages long it is.

Registration: Beginning January 5, 2004, PACER began offering instant registration and delivery of passwords over the Internet to those who provide credit card information. Up until then, passwords were sent via postal mail and that process could take up to two weeks. To register instantly, users can visit the PACER Service Center web site at **http://www.pacer.uscourts.gov/**—and click on the **Registration** icon.

Billing: New PACER subscribers who provide their credit card information will automatically be enrolled in the automatic billing program. (Existing customers can also set up automatic billing.)

Lost Passwords: Another new feature is the ability to retrieve a lost password online.

Our View: PACER is the most economical docket database; at 8¢ per page, you can't beat the price. So even though it can sometimes be cumbersome to use (because each court maintains its own internal electronic case management system and its own unique URL (or in some unfortunate cases, a modem number for dial-in access only), you might start your search here before using any of the pay docket databases.

Tip: • For those who bill their clients, a client code of your choosing can be entered each time you log into PACER.
    • Use pay databases when you need more user-friendly search options and to set up automatic alerts. (Infor-

mation about fee-based databases is discussed later in this section.)

- Because some courts do provide case information on the Internet without support by PACER, check the individual court's home page at **http://www.uscourts .gov/links.html**.
- Aside from each individual court's docket database, PACER also includes the U.S. Party Case Index (see the next entry), which might be your first step if you want to do a broad search to find a party's dockets in more than one court.

PACER U.S. Party Case Index

http://pacer.uspci.uscourts.gov   **$**

(Log on to the index by clicking on the large blue box that says **U.S. Party/Case Index** or by clicking on the very small **Enter U.S. Party/Case Index** link directly under the blue box.)

Purpose: To search federal filings "nationwide" and to link to various types of courts.

Content: Though the Index is labeled a "nationwide" locator index of federal filings, we place nationwide in quotation marks because, as noted above, not all courts participate in the Index. The U.S. Party/Case Index has five different search pages: (1) All Court Types; (2) Appellate; (3) Bankruptcy; (4) Civil; and (5) Criminal. The Index displays the party name, court, case number, and filing date.

You can search all courts by an individual's name (enter the last name first and the first name second with a comma in between (Brown, David) or by a business name (David Brown Engraving). You can also limit the **All Court Types** search by date filed or you can change the **All Court Types** search to search by a region or state. For example, selecting a specific circuit from the **All Court Types** drop-down menu will bring back results from the Circuit Court of Appeals (if that circuit's Court of Appeals is on PACER—see the earlier list of

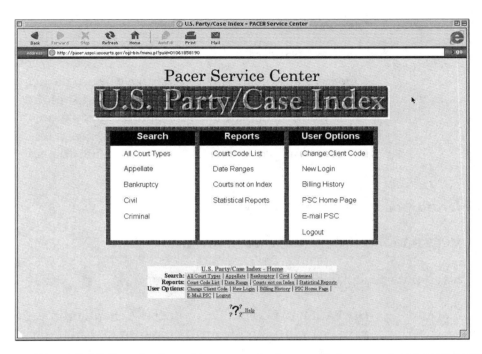

Figure 8-20. Search all court types or select a specific type, such as bankruptcy.

non-participating courts) and all district courts from all states in the circuit. Selecting a specific state from the **All Court Types** drop-down menu will bring back results from that one State's District Courts and the Circuit Court of Appeals for that state (if that circuit's Court of Appeals is on PACER—see the earlier list of non-participating courts).

Our View: Although it's not a truly national index, it's the best we've got.

Tip: As noted above, although they might participate in PACER or CM/ECF, the following courts do not participate in the **All Court Types** section of the Index:

U.S. Courts of Appeal:

- 2nd
- 5th
- 7th
- 11th

District Courts:

- New Mexico

To learn if any of the above courts have begun participating in the Index, periodically review the list of the Index's nonparticipating courts at **http://pacer.psc .uscourts.gov/cgi-bin/miss-court.pl**. In some states, all federal courts participate in the Index (California, for example).

Federal Dockets: Bankruptcy Courts

PACER Bankruptcy Case Information

http://pacer.uspci.uscourts.gov (select Bankruptcy) **$**

Purpose: Use PACER to find out if a prospective client, prospective partner, or the opposing party has filed for bankruptcy in the past, and to monitor the progress of a bankruptcy. There is no need to know in advance the jurisdiction in which someone declared bankruptcy: simply use the U.S. Party Index and click on **Bankruptcy** after you log in and you will be able to search nationwide.

Content: Search the nationwide bankruptcy index by party name (person or company), Social Security number, case number, or tax identification number (TIN). You can also narrow your national search to one state (to search all districts if the state has more than one Bankruptcy District) or to district (to search just one district if the state has more than one Bankruptcy District). You will be able to view case information; names of parties, lawyers, and judges; claims; schedules and deadline information; and docket entries. Personal data identifiers (Social Security numbers, dates of birth, financial account numbers, and names of minor children) might show on older records (or even on new records if the attorney failed to redact).

There have been some changes to the PACER Bankruptcy database. First, all bankruptcy courts are now participating in PACER (or CM/ECF).

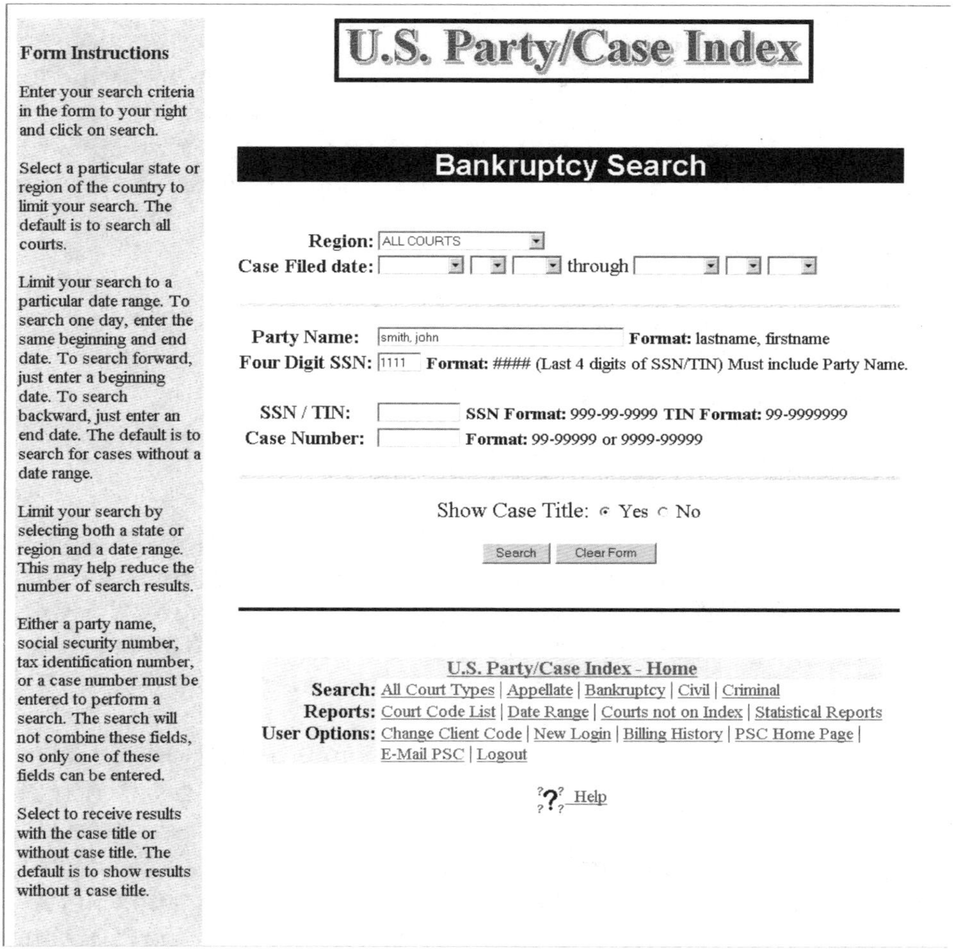

Figure 8-21. Search by a name, Social Security number, or docket number to discover bankruptcies in any bankruptcy court.

Second, a new search function has been added to the **Bankruptcy** search portion of the U.S. Party/Case Index: this function allows you to search by the last four digits of a party's Social Security number combined with the party's last name (or last name/first name).

Our View: We are thrilled that all Bankruptcy Courts now participate, making this a truly national bankruptcy index.

Tip: There are sample PACER Bankruptcy Case Information dockets to view at **http://pacer.psc.uscourts.gov/**

bksamples/bkcase.html. Even though the full SSN is shielded, searching by the full SSN is still an option. So if you have the full Social Security number (or Tax Identification Number), you should search with it since it is a more precise search than a name search or a search with the last four digits/name combined search.

Federal Dockets: Appellate and District Courts

PACER Appellate Courts

http://pacer.uspci.uscourts.gov **$**

(Select Appellate to search the circuit courts.)

Purpose:	Use the PACER Appellate Courts site to find U.S. appellate cases and dockets by party name or docket number. The appellate courts are also searchable by NOS (nature of the suit). The NOS search can be useful for client development and current awareness.
Content:	You can search all circuits (which actually includes only the First, Third, Fourth, Sixth, Eighth, Ninth, Tenth, and District of Columbia Circuits) or you can search an individual circuit. You can search by name (last name, first name, or last name only) or case number, and you can also limit the search by date filed. For the appellate and civil district courts only, you can conduct a NOS search or a combined party name-NOS search (see below for more NOS search details).
Our View:	It may be hard to know if you have the correct party since so many people share the same name. Therefore, if you have the docket number, search by number rather than party name. If you don't have a docket number, try to limit the party search by selecting a specific circuit or a date.
Tip:	To search only Civil Appellate cases or only Criminal Appellate cases, click on the **Civil** or **Criminal** link (see next entry). A page offering a drop-down menu is

presented from which one can select a specific Circuit Court of Appeal (or a District Court).

PACER Civil and Criminal District and Appellate Courts

http://pacer.uspci.uscourts.gov **$**

(Select **Civil** to search civil district or civil appellate court cases or select **Criminal** to search criminal district or criminal appellate court cases.)

Content: There are four geographic ways to search Civil only or Criminal only cases. From the **Region** drop-down menu you can either select: (1) **All Courts** (to search all appellate and district courts together); (2) A specific circuit (1st–11th); (3) A state to search all federal district courts in that state (if that state has more than one district court); or (4) A specific federal district court within the state (if that state has more than one district court). Note that the "State" searches are not state level court searches. They are federal district court searches within that state.

The Civil and Criminal search screens both offer searching by: name, docket number, and date filed but NOS searching is only offered on the Civil search screen.

Tip: To search all civil and criminal district court cases simultaneously, you will need to use the **All Courts** U.S. Party/Case Index (though the results will also include appellate, if they participate, and bankruptcy cases.)

(Remember that all appellate courts do not participate, so when you are conducting a circuit search in a circuit where the appellate court does not participate, you will be searching only the district courts of all the states located within that circuit.)

Federal Dockets: NOS Searching

PACER Nature of Suit Codes

http://pacer.psc.uscourts.gov/natsuit.html   **$**

Purpose: NOS searching is useful for topical current awareness or to find other cases like yours for sample pleadings—for instance, a personal injury lawyer specializing in airline crashes can search NOS code 310 (airplane) to keep abreast of every personal injury suit filed involving airplanes or to locate samples of pleadings for a current lawsuit.

Content: PACER allows you to search the Federal Appellate and District Courts and the Civil Indices for cases by their NOS code, a subject matter categorization of federal civil cases. There is no NOS searching in the following Indices: Criminal, Bankruptcy and All Courts. Categories and codes are listed at **http://pacer.psc.uscourts.gov/natsuit .html** and also on the Appellate and Civil search menu page (click on the **Detailed NOS listing** link to review and select an NOS topic). One can conduct an NOS search, with or without a date limitation, or a combined party name-NOS search (with or without a date limitation). An NOS search can be limited to one NOS topic only, to a range of NOS topics or to multiple NOS topics.

Our View: The site is easy to use, but not all lawsuits are categorized the way you might think they should be, so you might miss something useful.

Tip: While NOS searches must be conducted manually at the government's free PACER site, they can be set up to run automatically at some of the pay sites such as Westlaw's CourtEXPRESS (**http://courtexpress.westlaw .com/**) or CourtLink, which is accessible through LexisNexis (see **http://www.lexisnexis.com/courtlink/online/ default.asp**).

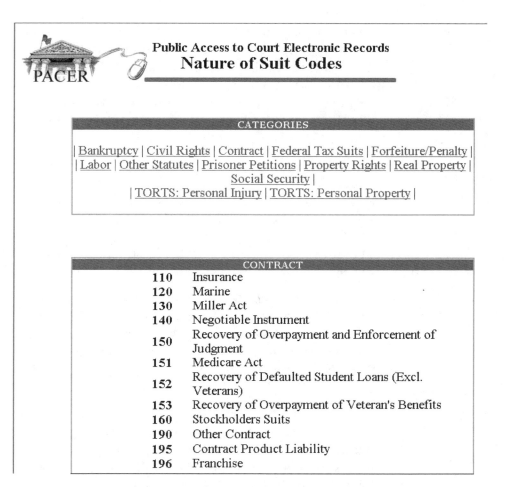

Figure 8-22. A federal docket search at the Pacer site can be limited to a specific type of lawsuit, such as a contract lawsuit based upon the Miller Act. Use this list to find the nature of the suit code and enter it into the search box.

Exemplaris.com

https://www.exemplaris.com/federal/content/login.asp

To search: **($)** To access and download full transcripts:

Purpose: Use Exemplaris to search, locate and purchase transcripts from civil, criminal, and bankruptcy proceedings tried in federal district courts.

Content: The home page allows for free searching of federal trial court transcripts by case name or number only. Information returned for these searches includes Case Name, Case Number, and a brief section of text from the transcript containing your search term—with the search term highlighted. Clicking on any returned result yields more information about the case/transcript, including

- Case Name
- Case Number
- Case Type
- Nature of Suite
- Case Status
- Plaintiff
- Defendant

- Transcript Date
- Volume Number
- Judge
- Court
- Expert Type
- Billable Pages

Only those who create a (free) user account, however, can access the more full-featured **Advanced Search**. The **Advanced Search** adds the option to also search for **Case Type** (e.g., Civil, Bankruptcy), **Nature of Suit**, **Judge Name**, and **Expert Type**, among other criteria.

Transcripts are paid for online via credit card and downloaded. The cost is approximately $1.25 per page. (Court reporters receive their court-mandated $1 per page fee—minus payment processing fees.) Transcripts are downloaded in the RealLegal E-Transcript format.

Also on the home page are **Breaking** and **Industry** news sections with links to high-profile transcripts of interest.

Our View: Exemplaris claims a database of over 10,000 federal trial court transcripts. However, it is up to the individual court reporters to set up their own accounts with Exemplaris in order to upload their transcriptions. Transcripts available are for the trial court only. There are no options for searching the courts of appeal.

Setting up an attorney user account is free and easy. It does require downloading and installing the Real Legal E-transcript viewer.

One drawback is that Exemplaris requires Microsoft's Internet Explorer Web browser (version 5.5 or higher). Users of any other browser, including the newest releases of the popular Firefox browser, receive the following error message: "Netscape is not supported by the Exemplaris application; please update your browser to Microsoft Internet Explorer 5.5 or higher."

U.S. Supreme Court Dockets

U.S. Supreme Court Dockets

http://www.supremecourtus.gov/docket/docket.html

Purpose:	To retrieve current Supreme Court dockets.
Content:	The U.S. Supreme Court is not part of the PACER system. Although the documentation on the site states that only the current and prior term dockets are archived, we have found cases further back (e.g., in 2005, we found cases back to 2002).
Our View:	The database has good search functionality. Search by docket number (the Supreme Court or lower court), by case name, or by any word or phrase (such as a lawyer's name).
Tip:	For more background information about the facts of a case or the parties, see FindLaw's Supreme Court Center to view briefs back to 1999 (**http://supreme.lp.findlaw .com/supremecourt/resources.html**).

Court Dockets and Pleadings: Foreign Dockets

Most foreign courts do not have electronic access to dockets, with the exception of Canada. Several courts in Canada have Web sites that allow searching by party and case number, such as the Canadian Supreme Court. CourtExpress can search some individual courts of various foreign countries.

Canadian Dockets

Supreme Court of Canada Information on Cases

http://209.47.227.135/information/scc_case/index_e.asp

Purpose: To search for Supreme Court of Canada case information.

Content: If you know it, enter all or part of the five-digit Supreme Court of Canada case number and then click on **Search**. You can also use the lower court number; otherwise, search by:

- All Parties
- Crown
- Attorney General
- First Name
- Last Name
- Institution
- Reference

You can limit the search by **Province of Origin** (use the drop-down menu to select the province) or check off **Federal**.

Our View: Searching is straightforward, but once you click on a case and the docket is displayed, be sure to notice the **Parties** and **Counsel** links in the left-hand column. Click on **Parties** for a list of all parties and the case status (e.g., active/closed), and click on **Counsel** to view full contact information for the lawyers. There is no documentation on dates of coverage.

Tip: Court records are not online. However, copies of documents can be obtained for 50¢ per page (add $5 for a closed file). Contact the court records office at (613) 996-7933 or by e-mail at **records-dossiers@scc-csc.gc.ca**.

Commercial Docket Databases

Why use a commercial service if you have free or low-cost access to federal and state court dockets at some of the courts' Web sites or on

PACER? Although the commercial databases obtain the dockets from the courts, they then create user-friendly searchable databases, with extra functions, instead of merely providing a gateway to the court site. (Note that these searchable databases are typically available only for federal dockets). This allows you to search by more options than the official court sites, which usually allow searching only by docket number (although some do allow party name or lawyer name searching). The major commercial docket vendors are CourtLink (Lexis), and CourtExpress (purchased by Westlaw as of January 1, 2006). Courthouse News Service, while not a docket database, *per se*, does offer access to new complaints filed in numerous federal, state, and local courts.

The following are some of the reasons to use pay docket sites:

- Better search functions: besides party name and docket number, search by lawyer name, judge name, subject, or keyword
- Alert functions: set up automated case tracking of a specific case or any case involving a specific party, lawyer, judge, NOS, and so on
- Older archives: at some of the commercial sites, dockets are not taken off line, so you may be able to find a docket that has already been taken off of the courts' official site and archived off line by the court
- Document ordering: you can order copies of documents from commercial sites (they can be mailed, sent by Federal Express, e-mailed, or faxed)

Using the Alert Function on Commercial Docket Sites

Setting up an automatic alert with a commercial docket vendor to track specific cases, clients, types of cases (using the NOS), or all new complaints filed in specific courts, can assist you with your business development efforts and in maintaining ongoing client relations. For example, a NOS alert can help you with your business development efforts by alerting you to who is being sued in specific practice areas or to alert you to hot practice areas that the firm might want to develop. Setting up a new complaints alert allows you to warn ongoing clients about any complaints filed against them—but not yet served. Alerts can be set up with the various pay docket vendors profiled below.

Commercial Docket Vendors

CourtLink (part of LexisNexis)

https://courtlink.lexisnexis.com **$**
(for those with a Lexis account, use **http://www.lexis.com**)

Purpose: To access dockets for current awareness, business and client development, client retention, backgrounding people (judges, lawyers, clients, opposition), conducting due diligence (in particular to search for past bankruptcies), and to put your hands on missing pleadings or locate sample pleadings in similar cases

Content: The site provides online access to dockets in over forty-seven hundred courts, covering ten to twenty years' worth of cases, from federal district courts (civil and criminal), bankruptcy courts, U.S. Courts of Appeals, U.S. Claims Court, and online real-time access to all or parts of twenty states. CourtLink does not offer online access to U.S. Supreme Court dockets (CourtExpress does) or the U.S. Tax Court. CourtLink also offers "Assisted search access" (courts that are not online via CourtLink but to which CourtLink representatives have online access) to over 500 additional courts. Also, CourtLink has a "runner network"—people who can retrieve, in person, docket sheets (and any document from the docket sheet) from 16,000 courts (federal and state). CourtLink claims to go back further in time than other services (because, unlike Pacer, it does not purge older dockets) and to have more state and local coverage. CourtLink offers transactional and subscription pricing. CourtLink downloads federal dockets each evening and creates a searchable database, so the searcher is not using CourtLink as a gateway to PACER. For the state and local courts some searchable databases have been created and for others CourtLink dials into the courts and users search by docket number (or party name, depending on how the court has set up their database). In April 2005, the interface for CourtLink was completely redesigned and is now much easier to use. More courts were added and new features such as simultaneous searching through multiple courts or all courts and searching Patent complaints were added. From the home page, the new interface displays seven tabs that offer various services.

Tab 1 is **My CourtLink** and is used to monitor the searcher's recent (seven days) activity and any tracks or alerts that the searcher has set up.

Tab 2 is **Search**, which is used to begin a docket search. After clicking **Search**, three tabs are displayed: a **Docket** tab to search by docket number (a link for **Formatting Rules** should be clicked to be sure the docket number is entered in that court's required format), a **Patent** tab to search by patent number and another **Search** tab. From here, the searcher must first select a court (or multiple courts) from the drop-down menus. Not all courts are online, so there is a drop-down menu labeled **Runner Court** that must be selected for those courts. One can search by the following criteria in many courts (but not all criteria is available at every court so search criteria will vary from court to court):

(a) subject matter
(b) litigant's name (there are separate templates for personal names and business names)
(c) lawyer's name
(d) judge's name
(e) bankruptcy debtor's name
(f) class actions
(g) bankruptcy chapters (such as a search for all Chapter 7 filings).

Tab 3 is **Dockets and Documents** which is used to order any document that is not immediately downloadable (select delivery by e-mail or Federal Express) and to track the progress of the orders. Documents can also be ordered while viewing the docket sheet.

Tab 4 is **Track** which is used to track a specific case by its docket number.

Tab 5 is **Alert** which is used to track cases by a variety of criteria.

(1) all new filings in all courts or selected courts
(2) new filings limited to:
    (a) a specific state or federal subject matter
    (b) litigant's name
    (c) lawyer's name
    (d) judge's name
    (e) bankruptcy debtor's name

(f) class actions

(g) bankruptcy chapters (such as a search for all Chapter 7 filings).

After setting up an **Alert** or **Track**, the searcher can request to be notified by e-mail when a new filing matches the search criteria or the searcher can simply check for new information by clicking the **My Courtlink** or the **Alert** or the **Track** tabs located at the top of CourtLink's homepage.

Tab 6 is **Strategic Profile**, used to develop historical background information about cases involving a specific litigant, firm, attorney, judge, court, or subject (NOS). The searcher can limit the search to a specific date range. For instance, a searcher who is considering adding a new practice area could research how many antitrust cases were filed in a specific court in the last year or an attorney who wants to assess an opposing lawyer's experience back to 1999 could search for all cases involving the opposing attorney from 1999 to date.

Tab 7 is **My Account**, used to manage billing matters.

Pricing:

Searching dockets: Pricing to search dockets varies from court to court. For instance, to search U.S. District Courts (civil and criminal) is $8 and to immediately view the docket is $4. To update the docket is $4. For U.S. Bankruptcy Courts, docket searching is $8 and to immediately view a summary of the case is $1; to view the full docket, per name, is $9.

Tracking: Pricing for tracking varies on the frequency of notification and the court chosen. For example, tracking a specific state case can cost from $5.75 to $18.50 and tracking a specific federal district court case will cost $5.50 per day (it had been $5 in 2003), $7.50 per week or $10 per month, while tracking a bankruptcy case is $18 per month.

Alerts: Pricing for Alerts varies from court to court, from 15¢ to $6.50 per case found that matches one's criteria.

Strategic Profile: Strategic Profile Pricing ranges from $25-$150, depending on the court and type of profile.

Documents: To immediately download a U.S. District Court document would cost $5 per document but if one has to order a document from a "runner court" fees range from $78-$95 per document, depending on the court, plus: copying fees of 50¢-$1.50 per page and delivery fees of $1 per page with a $35 maximum for e-mail (Federal Express is also a delivery option). There is a $25 rush fee (**https://courtlink.lexisnexis .com/Help/Pricing/DocumentRetrievalPricing.pdf**).

Our View: When we first reviewed the site it was not always intuitive. That has now changed with the new interface that we described above and we're pleased to say it is now very intuitive, but there is still room for improvement in a few areas. For instance, nowhere are the phrases "online courts" or "runner courts" defined. Also, it would be useful if it was easier to find a list of prices for searching the docket database (and for retrieval of documents) and a list of included courts. (We were sent these URLs by CourtLink: for a list of federal courts see **http:// www.lexisnexis.com/literature/pdfs/FederalinWord 2005_11_03.doc** and for a list of state courts see **http:// www.lexisnexis.com/courtlink/online/StateinWord 2005_12_19.doc**.) Setting up, editing, and deleting alerts and tracks is a very simple process.

Tip: • The online training modules (**http://www.lexisnexis .com/courtlinktraining/**) are excellent and we recommend you take the time to view them. They are broken down by topic (e.g., how to set up an alert, how to set up a track, etc.). Each topic is presented in a short, easy to follow manner. There is also a downloadable user's guide with screen shots.
  • More courts and features are added all the time, so check back frequently at **http://www.lexisnexis.com/ courtlink/online**.

Westlaw CourtExpress

http://courtexpress.westlaw.com/ **$**

Purpose: To access dockets for current awareness, business and client development, client retention, or backgrounding people (judges, lawyers, clients, opposition); to conduct due diligence; to put your hands on missing pleadings; or to locate sample pleadings in similar cases

Content: A few years ago, West began building a docket database, WestDockets (to compete with Lexis' purchase of the CourtLink docket database). WestDockets lacked many of the features of CourtLink, such as downloadable pleadings and document delivery.

However, in 2005, Westlaw purchased CourtLink's competitor, CourtExpress, replete with all the missing services of WestDockets. CourtExpress was then merged into Westlaw's fold, but was still accessible at courtexpress .com. As of January 1, 2006, however, CourtExpress is no longer accessible directly at courtexpress.com. Instead, users now need to obtain a Westlaw password and access the database at Westlaw.

CourtExpress has docket content and services somewhat similar to CourtLink in that they have dockets from the following courts: federal district courts (civil and criminal) in a searchable database, gateways to the bankruptcy courts (note that CourtLink has a database for the bankruptcy courts), U.S. Courts of Appeals, and U.S. Claims Court. In addition, CourtExpress also searches a few courts that CourtLink does not: the U.S. Supreme Court (by docket number only), the U.S. International Trade Commission, and the U.S.Tax Court. Aside from the federal courts, CourtExpress has direct access to twenty-seven state courts (and select county courts within each state) and indirect access to 3,500 state and local courts. For indirect access, although the searcher enters the search online, a CourtExpress help desk employee actually runs the search by dialing into the court. After you enter a search, you can continue on with your usual multitasking and you will be notified by e-mail when the search is complete. Document delivery and research are also available.

Database Interface:

There are several choices listed at the top of the screen with the first one labeled **Search for Dockets**. After clicking on it, a list of courts from which dockets are available are displayed. Federal courts are listed first, then state courts. A plus sign to the left of the court name indicates there are dockets available from multiple courts within that jurisdiction. Clicking on the plus sign reveals them in a drop-down list. There is an Information icon (the letter "I" with a circle around it) to the right of each court name. Clicking on this icon provides very detailed information about the court's dockets, from dates of coverage, pricing, content, additional functions (such as links to attorney profiles), to how to search the dockets. To select a court, click into the box to the left of the court name and then click the **Next** button that is to the right of **Select federal and/or state courts to search** (this step is not that apparent—you're supposed to somehow know it's the next step). After selecting a court to search for dockets, a field search template is presented. (The option to search full-text is also available by clicking on the link on the top right of the field template that is labeled **Go to a keyword search page**.) The templates will vary depending on which court is selected. For example, the Bankruptcy Court template is the only one that offers a **Chapter** field box. This is used to enter the specific bankruptcy chapter which a filing was based upon, such as Chapter 7.

More search choices can be added to the template by clicking on **View more fields for searching** or **Add a date restriction to this search**. While the Bankruptcy Court basic template offers searches by **Party** or **Attorney Name**, **Docket Number**, and **Chapter**, more field search boxes, such as one for **Debtor Name** and one for **Creditor Name**, will appear by clicking on **View more fields for searching**.

Once a specific docket has been selected and viewed, one MUST click on **Update** to view *all* the information (such as the full docket sheet, the attorney's name, etc.). We are mystified as to why the information in the **Update** isn't just part of the initial search results.

Aside from entering information into templates, one can also search with traditional Westlaw search functions (terms and connectors) if one wants to search multiple fields. For example, to locate all negligence cases where Michael Pressman was the attorney of record, click on **Go to a keyword search page** from the template page and then type in the following search: at(pressman) & ctp(negligence) "At" is the abbreviation for the attorney field and "ctp" is the abbreviation for case type.

The cost for an "initial" docket search is:

- $7 for any of the following: a single State Court, all Bankruptcy Courts, all Courts of Appeal or all District Courts
- $75 for all State Courts combined
- $30 for an all Federal Courts combined
- $100 for all State and Federal Courts combined

For any of the above searches, add in $2 for an update to the initial search and $5 per document displayed. There is also an extra charge to order any of the documents listed in the docket sheet (e.g., a complaint). To order, click on the link labeled, **Order document for later delivery**. Dates of coverage vary from court to court but may go back as far as the 1980s.

CourtExpress offers alert and tracking services for various courts. Delivery options can be tailored to your needs. For example, an attorney can decide how often to be notified, how to be notified, when to end the service, and whether to be notified when there are no results. Click the **Docket Alerts and Tracks** tab and then:

- **Track a Docket** allows you to track specific cases by court and case number (courts that can be searched are the U.S. Supreme Court, U.S. Circuit Courts of Appeals, U.S. District Courts, U.S. Bankruptcy Courts, and selected state courts).

- **Create a New Case Alert** allows you to choose up to ten courts from which to be alerted to either (1) all new cases filed or (2) all new cases filed that match specific criteria that you indicate such as the name of a party, attorney, or judge or a case type for state courts (and Nature of the Suit for U.S. Circuit Courts of Appeals and U.S. District Courts). NOS and case type searches are useful to prospect for clients in your practice area.

Our View: Searching for dockets online, and then being able to order the underlying documents online from the same company is convenient to rushed researchers and also to their billing departments, since the charge is bundled in one invoice. Another added convenience is being able to track the order online much like you can track the status of a UPS delivery. Order directly from CourtExpress's **OrderTrack** document ordering and online tracking order service. The document will be e-mailed as a PDF or delivered by Federal Express, fax, or messenger (usually within one day), or you can request a phone call first before deciding on the delivery method. The cost is $79 per document plus 75¢ per page for photocopying. About 30 of the 130 courts on CourtExpress make PDFs of their documents available online for immediate download. In that case, CourtExpress informs you of this capability and you can immediately download the document via CourtExpress for 25¢ per page instead of ordering a hard copy of the document. Except for a few steps at the beginning that could have been more clearly marked, using Westlaw CourtExpress should be very easy for long-term Westlaw users (or really for anyone; we found the searching very easy). Westlaw users will already understand how to create searches using terms and connectors and fields. We would prefer if all search fields, date fields and keyword searching options were displayed in one search menu at the beginning of a search.

The purchase of CourtExpress was a smart move—West needed to keep up with Lexis and its purchase of CourtLink. Building a docket database from scratch would have been a lot of work.

Tip:

Do the math! For those who wonder how CourtExpress' document delivery fees compare to working directly with a local retrieval service, everyone needs to do their own math. Barry Berkowitz, president of Now Legal Services in Los Angeles, reported that the cost to retrieve a document from the downtown Los Angeles courthouse is $35 per hour, plus 57¢ per page to copy, plus $1 per mile to deliver the document. For delivery via fax or e-mail, the charge is $1 per page. Thus, the cost could fluctuate widely each time you need a document, depending on the length of the document, the degree of difficulty in obtaining the document (fifteen minutes is the usual time frame, but it could be more if the document is not yet available), and where the document needs to be delivered.

Users of traditional Westlaw.com can access dockets by clicking the **Court Docs** tab.

Courthouse News Service

http://www.courthousenews.com

Purpose:

To track newly filed complaints for business and client development and to maintain ongoing client relations by warning ongoing clients about any complaints filed against the client, but not yet served

Content:

Courthouse News Service is partially free and partially fee-based. The service provided by Courthouse News differs from CourtExpress and CourtLink because it is not a full-blown docket database. Instead it is a legal news wire and an alert service for complaints only. It is staffed by local correspondents who write daily summaries about new rulings, legislation, and complaints. Some of this information can be read free by visiting the site, while other information is for paid subscribers only (click on the **Subscribers** link on the top right of the screen). The other paid portion of Courthouse News is its alert service, which consists of daily e-mailed summaries of new complaints. The report also includes a link to immediately download (for an additional fee) selected complaints. The e-mail is referred to as a "Report." Subscribers can choose to subscribe to various federal, state, or county courts. For a complete list of specific courts covered by Courthouse News see **http://www.courthousenews.com/subinfo.html**.

The price to subscribe to a report, such as the Nevada Report, is $100 a month but half-price for firms with ten lawyers or less.

An additional service, called a "dinger," comes free with each report that one subscribes to. The dinger can be set up on Courthouse News' web site to track new filings by the name of a (1) plaintiff or defendant; (2) plaintiff or defendant law firm; (3) plaintiff or defendant lawyer; or (4) keywords. One can also exclude a keyword. To receive a dinger for a nonsubscribed court would cost $10 per case.

At Courthouse News' home page, clicking on **Subscribers** takes one to a page listing various courts. After choosing a court, a list of complaints in reverse chronological order is displayed. There are two pricing levels for downloading a complaint. If a firm already has a subscription to that court's report, the cost is $35. If a firm does not have a subscription to that court's report, the cost is $50.

Subscribers can also search a database of the complaint summaries free (but the most recent two weeks' worth of information is not accessible for any reports that are not subscribed to). The summary of complaints can be searched by the following methods (if you select **Advanced Search**): (1) by case number; (2) by the name of a plaintiff, defendant, law firm, lawyer, or judge; or (3) by keyword.

The e-mailed summary report includes the case caption, a brief description of the issues and facts involved, and the name of each party's lawyer. If the complaint is available for immediate download, this will be indicated in the report. It can be downloaded by clicking the link on the report or it can be downloaded from the Courthouse

News Web site. If it's not available, it can be ordered by contacting the local reporter whose name and phone number is provided in the report. Some reporters fax the complaint while others scan and e-mail it.

Our View: If your court is one of those included, you'll find this a useful alert service. Many large law firms use this service. However, this would be a better service if its "Search" of complaint summaries provided access to the full text of the complaints and not merely a list with summary information about the complaint.

Tip: At the site's home page, there are several free features: First, there is a legal blog, On Point. The topic varies daily. Second, there is an editorial column (on the left side of the homepage), where you'll often find some humorous law-related topic. Third, there is a link to **Federal Appellate Summaries** (top right-hand corner).

Do You Need Access to All the Docket Databases?

In a recent law library online community posting, it was made apparent that we still need access to all the docket databases out there. Case in point: In a search to download a bankruptcy court pleading from the Delaware bankruptcy court, a librarian found the docket on PACER, but could not (for unknown technical reasons) download one of the pleadings listed on the docket sheet. Every time she clicked on the hypertext document number she was rewarded with only a blank page. She then proceeded to CourtEXPRESS, found the docket, but did not see any indication that she could download the pleadings. Finally, she proceeded to CourtLink and had success. Why? The answer is that CourtLink downloads dockets and pleadings every evening to create a searchable database, and is not dependent on PACER (except for same-day dockets and pleadings); thus, even though PACER was not working correctly, CourtLink came through since their system didn't have to dial in to PACER. Had the librarian needed a docket or pleading filed that day, she would not have succeeded at CourtLink either. The reason she had no luck at CourtEX-PRESS is because CourtEXPRESS does not download bankruptcy dockets and pleadings into a searchable database—only federal district dockets and pleadings. So, if the PACER bankruptcy court system is not working correctly, then neither would CourtEXPRESS. This is not to say that CourtLink always comes through and CourtEXPRESS never does! The

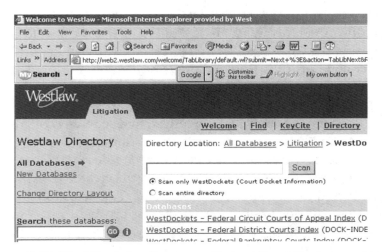

Figure 8-23. West Dockets offers many Federal Court Dockets and is continually adding State Court dockets.

librarian stated that in similar situations she has found that sometimes PACER is the winner, other times CourtEXPRESS is the winner, and other times CourtLink is. In the final words of the librarian, "It seems you have to maintain all three so they can back up one another." And, a final word of caution: most courts have disclaimers on their docket databases that the database is "for information purposes only" and that only the clerk's transcript is the official transcript.

State and Local Court Dockets

Many state and local courts are placing their dockets online. The state courts are not bound by the rules and policies promulgated by the Federal Judicial Conference of the United States' Committee on Court Administration and Case Management regarding access to electronic court documents discussed earlier. Instead, the National Center for State Courts and the Justice Management Institute (at the behest of the Conference of Chief Justices and the Conference of State Court Administrators [CCJ/COSCA]) produced a model policy, "Developing CCJ/COSCA Guidelines for Public Access to Court Records: A National Project to Assist State Courts" (see **http://ncsconline.org/WC/Publications/Res_ PriPub_GuidelinesPublicAccessPub.pdf**) The policy, which seeks to provide a consistent way to access electronic court documents in each state, advocates access to electronic court records. However, it seeks to limit access to any information in court documents that is not already accessible to the public pursuant to federal or state law, court rule, or case law.

The policy was endorsed by CCJ/COSCA on August 1, 2002. In October 2005, a follow-up report was issued, "Public Access to Court Records: Implementing the CCJ/COSCA Guidelines Final Project Report" (**http:// www.ncsconline.org/WC/Publications/Res_PriPub_PubAccCrtRcrds_ FinalRpt.pdf**).

The follow-up report "allowed a group of the original *CCJ/COSCA Guidelines* drafters and committee members to discuss a set of additional philosophical and practical concerns and developments relating to implementation of some aspects of the *Guidelines*." While no new policies were created, a lengthy (and useful) FAQ template was created to assist each state court to add to its Web site its jurisdiction's policies about public access to electronic documents. Also, a discussion about issues surrounding public access to family law matters, and especially juvenile hearings, ensued.

While the State Court's follow-up report discussed that individual state courts have differing public access policies, they did not provide a survey of each state's policies in the follow-up report because even though a national survey was one of their original objectives, funding was never provided.

To ascertain whether a court has its dockets online, use LLRX.com or Legal Dockets Online (both described earlier in this chapter) or FindLaw's state directory (go to **http://www.findlaw.com/11stategov**, choose a state, and then click on **Courts**).

While all sixty-two counties in New York have online dockets searchable from a unified system for free (see the New York E.Courts site described below), not all Texas county courts are even online, and some Texas counties that are online charge a fee to search dockets (such as Dallas County). In California, it's every county court for itself—there's no unified docket site, so the parameters of docket searching vary from county to county. For instance, in Los Angeles County the court does not permit anything but docket number searching at their free site at **http:// www.lasuperiorcourt.org/civilCaseSummary/index.asp?CaseType=Civil** (they do, however, now offer a pay site for party name searching—use the above URL and then click on **Party Name Search** in the left column). Some of the other counties in California allow party name searching free, such as San Francisco at **http://www.sftc.org/scripts/magic94/Mgrqispi 94.dll?APPNAME=IJS&PRGNAME=CaseSearch&ARGUMENTS=-A**. In addition to New York, the following states have a unified docket system that can be searched on the Internet: Alabama, Arizona, Colorado, Connecticut, Iowa, Missouri, Oklahoma, Rhode Island, Utah, Virginia, Washington, and Wisconsin.

New York E.Courts

http://e.courts.state.ny.us

Purpose:	To background judges, lawyers, and parties by searching dockets (and online decisions) using names as your search terms.
Content:	At the New York E.Courts site, you can look up Supreme Court civil court case information in all sixty-two counties, search the Supreme Court calendars, and search for the next court appearance in a criminal case. You can also track specific cases online and be automatically notified of any change in a case. Case information is updated four times daily and is searchable by:

- Firm or lawyer name
- Index number
- Plaintiff
- Defendant
- Supreme court calendars (by justice)
- Supreme court calendars (by part—choose a county first)

The following is just some of the data displayed once a case is selected to view:

- Names of lawyer or firm (and contact information), justice, plaintiff, and defendant
- County
- Index number
- Appearance date
- Activity count

In some counties, cases can even be filed on the Internet.

Our View:	We're impressed by a unified system like this where all counties in the state are participating. Although we are also impressed with the robust search engine, better examples are needed to explain search parameters. Review the search instructions (**http://www.nycourts.gov/ dot/fcas/cmsinstructions.html**) to learn, for instance, how proper names should be searched (last name first

and first name last). Unfortunately, plaintiff and defendant searching is limited to the first named plaintiff and defendant only. The court explains that this limitation was implemented to speed up searching through 60 million records.

Tip: Over 146,000 Supreme Court civil decisions from twenty-nine counties back to 2001 and over 6,000 decisions from thirteen Supreme Criminal Court and other criminal courts are online (**http://portal.courts.state.ny.us/ pls/portal30/CMS_DEV.DECISIONS_NDAWCASE.show_ parms**). They can be searched by (1) docket number (and a county can be chosen as a limiter), (2) key words (for search tips, see **http://www.courts.state.ny.us/search/ ixtiphlp.htm**), or (3) natural language.

When to Use Investigative Pay Databases That Compile Public Records, Non-Public Personal Information, and Publicly Available Information

While most of the data in this book is about information found at free sites, we are including investigative pay databases because, as we noted earlier in Chapter 1, pay databases have their place in research. If you have a lot of clues about a person or if the person has a unique name, you can probably begin your research with free public record databases. If this is not the case, it's best to begin with a pay investigative database. Beginning your search with a pay investigative database is also best when you need to conduct a national or multistate search, or when you need to gather various types of records. Another reason you might use pay databases over free public record databases is to have access to the extra data they have compiled from publicly available information and non-public personal information and (for a definition of "non-public records," see the "Credit Reports and Credit Headers" section later in this chapter).

The investigative pay databases described in the remainder of this chapter below are geared to collection agencies, lawyers, and law enforcement agencies who are involved in skip-tracing (whether to locate a missing witness, heir, debtor, or criminal suspect), backgrounding people and marshalling assets (such as a divorce lawyer who needs to search for real property records, boats, planes, patents, trademarks, and so on).

Some of these database companies are the ones with which lawyers are already familiar because they use them for legal research, such as Lexis and Westlaw, while others may not be as familiar, such as ChoicePoint, Accurint (now owned by Lexis), Merlin, FlatRateInfo, Knowx.com, and Rapsheets.com, to name a few. Some of these databases cover a narrower compilation of records or have chosen to focus more on publicly available information than public records or vice-versa. For example, Rapsheets.com focuses almost completely on criminal public records, while the other databases are more broad and focus on publicly available information and non-public personal information (current and past addresses, phone numbers, relatives and associates, and so on) and public records, such as real property and bankruptcy records.

Where Pay Databases Get Their Data, and How to Become a Subscriber

Before we examine some of these databases, a word about how to gain access to the databases and where they get their information. To gain access, one must become a subscriber and go through an application process and prove that one has a legitimate use of the database. This entails filling out an application and faxing one's business license and law license. Most lawyers would be approved subscribers, but see the "Credit Reports and Credit Headers" section below to learn about the need to attest to a permissible purpose each time you use the database. While much of the data in investigative pay databases comes from public records or publicly available information (such as phone directories), some of the information comes from non-public personal information found in credit headers. (See the section "Credit Reports and Credit Headers" below to learn about credit headers.)

Credit Reports and Credit Headers

Some of the "freshest" information on someone's address and phone number comes from the credit applications they fill out each time they attempt to obtain credit from a financial institution. Information from the applications is reported to credit bureaus (such as Experian, Trans-Union, and Equifax). These bureaus compile the information into a consumer credit report that contains financial information, such as the account type, the opening date of the account, the credit limit, the account status, and the payment history. It also contains nonfinancial, personal information such as a person's address and phone number, and drivers' license number, employment information, date of birth, and Social Security number. There are two federal laws to protect people's financial and non-financial privacy. The first law is the Fair Credit Reporting Act (FCRA), which regulates credit reports. (See Chapter 7 for the text of FCRA.) 15 U.S.C. 1681 et seq, **http://www.law.cornell.edu/uscode/html/ uscode15/usc_sec_15_00001681----000-.html**. To access them, one must obtain consent from the subject of the report or fall within one of the exceptions to FCRA. (See "Credit Reports" in Chapter 7.) Although obtaining a missing person's credit report would be useful in trying to locate a person, this is not one of the exceptions to access.

The second law is the Gramm-Leach-Bliley Act (GLBA), 15 U.S.C. 6802, which prevents financial institutions (which includes credit bureaus) from disclosing (and selling) *financial* information to third parties. However, they can extract the *nonfinancial* personal information from credit reports to sell to the investigative pay database vendors. This allows lawyers who subscribe to investigative pay databases to access some of the nonfinancial information (name, address, date of birth, and in some cases, the Social Security number) found within credit reports.

> The nonfinancial personal information is commonly referred to as "credit headers" because the data is found at the "head" of a report. GLBA refers to this information as "non-public personal information."

The vendors aggregate the credit header data with data from other sources, such as public records and publicly available information. Together, this data is used to create, more or less, a dossier about a person.

Access to "non-public personal information" is regulated by the Gramm-Leach-Bliley Act (GLBA), 15 U.S.C. 6802(e). Each time a lawyer wants to access a pay database that contains non-public personal information, the lawyer must check off one of the GLBA permissible uses listed on the search screen. If a search does not fall within a GLBA permissible use, one must check off "no permissible purpose." The lawyer can still use the database, but information from credit headers is not displayed. However, if the same information has been found within public records or publicly available information sources, it will be displayed. The only caveat is that it might not be as fresh as information from a credit header. Lawyers using a pay database usually come within one of the GLBA exceptions in Section 6802(e)(3)(A)-(E), available at **http://www.law.cornell .edu/uscode/html/uscode15/usc_sec_15_000**

GRAMM LEACH BLILEY ACT

15 U.S.C.§ 6802. Obligations with respect to disclosures of personal information

(a) Notice requirements
Except as otherwise provided in this subchapter, a financial institution may not, directly or through any affiliate, disclose to a nonaffiliated third party any nonpublic personal information, unless such financial institution provides or has provided to the consumer a notice that complies with section 6803

(e) General exceptions
Subsections (a) and (b) of this section shall not prohibit the disclosure of nonpublic personal information—

(1) as necessary to effect, administer, or enforce a transaction requested or authorized by the consumer, or in connection with—
   (A) servicing or processing a financial product or service requested or authorized by the consumer;
   (B) maintaining or servicing the consumer's account with the financial institution, or with another entity as part of a private label credit card program or other extension of credit on behalf of such entity; or
   (C) a proposed or actual securitization, secondary market sale (including sales of servicing rights), or similar transaction related to a transaction of the consumer;
(2) with the consent or at the direction of the consumer;
(3) (A) to protect the confidentiality or security of the financial institution's records pertaining to the consumer, the service or product, or the transaction therein;
   (B) to protect against or prevent actual or potential fraud, unauthorized transactions, claims, or other liability;
   (C) for required institutional risk control, or for resolving customer disputes or inquiries;
   (D) to persons holding a legal or beneficial interest relating to the consumer; or
   (E) to persons acting in a fiduciary or representative capacity on behalf of the consumer

Relational Investigative Pay Databases

Merlin (**https://www.merlindata.com/**) and Accurint (**http://www
.accurint.com**) are "relational" investigative pay databases. A relational
database tries to link people to their neighbors, associates, and relatives—a useful tool for contacting someone who might know the whereabouts of a person who has gone missing. With that said, the relational
database is not as powerful as we'd like to see it because it only links people who share the same name and address (or different names but same
address). For example, one of the authors of this book who shares the
same last name as her parents and brothers, but who hasn't shared an
address with them in about thirty years, is not linked to them on her so-
called complete Accurint or Merlin report. However, her former father-
in-law shows on her report because they owned real property together
from 1983–1985.

Pricing and Access to Investigative Pay Databases

Pricing varies among investigative databases. Some offer flat-rate pricing while others offer a per search fee. Some demand a monthly subscription while others don't. Accurint used to offer a per search price and did
not require a monthly subscription. All that changed when Lexis acquired
Seisint Inc., Accurint's parent company, in 2004 (and paid $775 million in
cash for it). We waited for a price increase and, sure enough, in 2005,
Lexis instituted a monthly subscription fee for subscribers who are frequent users and wants a discounted per search fee. (Fees vary depending
on one's contract.) In addition, Lexis clamped down on access to its database and to full Social Security numbers (as did other vendors). For access
to Accurint (and most any investigative pay databases) these days, a fairly
extensive application and approval process is required to ensure that the
vendor is not selling information to identity thieves. To add to the
approval process, many vendors (e.g., Merlin and Accurint) have added
another requirement for those who need access to full Social Security
numbers and not just the truncated numbers: a site visit. While Merlin
charges $60 for the site visit (because it's outsourced), Accurint does not
charge (because it uses a local Lexis representative). According to some
lawyers we've spoken to (and this was later confirmed by Accurint),
Accurint only approves full Social Security number access to those lawyers
whose primary function is collections work. Merlin, on the other hand,
does not have this stringent limitation.

Merlin Information Services

http://www.merlindata.com   **$**

Purpose: Merlin is a relational investigative pay database, useful for skip-tracing, marshalling assets, and backgrounding people.

Content: Merlin has information from public records, credit headers, and publicly available information. Merlin includes such information as addresses, phone numbers (including a reverse unlisted phone number feature and cellular phone numbers), bankruptcies, secretary of state records, fictitious business records, dates of birth, criminal records, real property records, motor vehicle records, UCCs, neighbors, relatives, credit headers (live, in contrast to Accurint—which are a month behind) and more (depending upon the jurisdiction). It covers national

Figure 8-24. Merlin charges only per search fees, with no monthly subscription fee, for access to all its skip-tracing, assets searching, and people backgrounding search tools.

data and all states. In addition, it has a heavy California emphasis.

Our View: Merlin has long been the private investigator's database of choice for investigative searching, but for some unknown reason has not been the law librarian's first choice. Law librarians typically use Lexis, Westlaw, ChoicePoint, KnowX, or Accurint. We think Merlin is worth a shot because it doesn't require a monthly subscription fee or any monthly minimum usage, but you do have to fill out a detailed seven-page application and make an initial deposit of $100 to open a debit account (that Merlin will deduct $10 (monthly) from whether you use the service or not).

Another reason Merlin is worth a shot is that Merlin's access to full Social Security numbers policy, which, unlike Accurint's, does not rule out attorney access (but lawyers must still meet GLBA and FCRA requirements). We also like that Merlin allows you to sort the columns in your results page to create a customized report. Merlin's **Link to America** feature is a skip-tracing tool that costs 25¢ per search. The Merlin report most similar to Accurint's **Comprehensive Report** is Merlin's **Link to America Pro** report, which costs $7.50 (if you have the higher security clearance it also will include live credit headers, full Social Security numbers and dates of birth). A noteworthy feature in Merlin is its "drill-down feature" that allows the searcher to learn the source behind each record and the date it was last updated. Merlin's other databases vary in price. For instance, if you purchase reports from all the databases found in its **California Ultimate Weapon** database, the cost is $20 while a national **Investigator's Background Report** is $3.50.

Tip: Merlin has some proprietary databases that others may not have (especially for California). For instance, California marriage records from 1960–1985 are online at Merlin—records that the State of California no longer sells. Another unique database is its **Western States Evictions** database, covering evictions in all counties in California, Nevada, Oregon, and Washington. Merlin has created a **National Fictitious Business Name** search with over 10 million records—saving you the time of a county-by-county search in each state.

Accurint

http://www.accurint.com **$**

Purpose: To search using more-sophisticated search techniques than the free public records sites offer. Accurint is useful for skip-tracing, marshalling assets, linking people together through its "relational" database (informing us about a subject's possible associates, neighbors and relatives, for example) and to discover aliases.

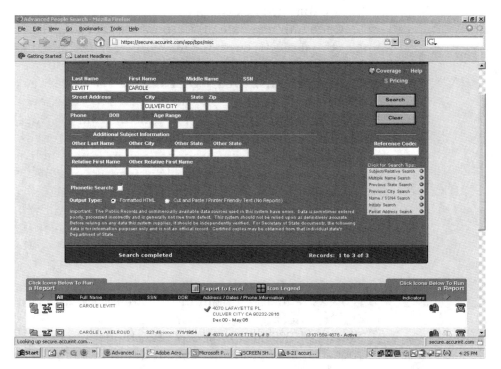

Figure 8-25. Accurint is one of the few databases that allows you to narrow a search by adding in the subject's age range. This is useful if you don't have a birthdate or enough other clues about the subject.

Content: Now that Lexis owns Accurint, expect to see Lexis and
                    Accurint's public record and publicly available informa-
                    tion databases to be integrated over time. Accurint was
                    the least expensive investigative pay site to use, with a
                    basic search costing 25¢ and a full report about $6.50.
                    After Lexis purchased Accurint, prices rose. There are
                    various pricing options available, from a "pay as you
                    go" option that offers "per search" fees of $1 per basic
                    search and $8.50 per full report, to a "subscription"
                    option that offers discounted "per search" fees but a set
                    monthly service fee. Its database has more than twenty
                    billion records from four hundred sources. Search with
                    any clues you have about the person such as last name,
                    first name, middle name, current address or phone
                    number, old address or phone number, Social Security
                    number, or any combination of these. The **Compre-
                    hensive Report** displays a person's current name (or
                    names), any aliases (AKAs), property ownership, date of
                    birth, Social Security number, current and historical
                    addresses dating back twenty to thirty years, current
                    telephone number, date of death, names of others liv-
                    ing at the subject's current address, associates, and
                    relatives. Property and bankruptcy records are also
                    included. The **Instant Identification** database is a
                    validation and verification tool endorsed by the Ameri-
                    can Bankers Association as a non-documentary verifica-
                    tion of a consumer's identification. After you enter all
                    the information you know about the consumer, such as
                    his or her name, address, and Social Security number,
                    the information is searched through numerous data-
                    bases to be sure it is valid information—that is, in the
                    correct format. It then assigns a verification score of
                    1 to 50 to the consumer.

                    New Accurint features include:
                    • People's cellular phone numbers can now be searched.
                      On December 6, 2005, Tamara Thompson, in her PI
                      News Link blog (**http://yourpinews.blogspot.com/
                      2005/12/accurint-unveils-unlisted-and-cell.html**),
                      reported that Accurint and IRB (IRB signed a letter of
                      intent to merge with Merlin on May 31, 2006) now
                      offer unlisted and cell phone number directories.

Thompson said, "Take a look at the Phones Plus search added to the array of people finder tools offered by Accurint and IRB. Here's the official announcement, somewhat short on details":

> When traditional phone sources are not enough, Phones Plus provides a new alternative. Access over 50,000,000 phone numbers not typically published, such as non-Electronic Directory Assistance records, including cell phone and unlisted numbers.

Thompson explained how she tried out the new directory: "I conducted a search entering the first and last name of my subject, with the state and county. The results returned three telephone numbers, one of which was an active Verizon cell phone in another state. The cost to you is 50 cents, plus your monthly fee."

- A relational feature "Relevint" that helps you to visualize relationships between people and their possible relatives and associates (and vehicles, property, and even businesses) by allowing you to create diagrams. Relavint costs $2 per diagram.
- Accurint now provides access to its records via wireless hand-held devices (such as the Palm, Pocket PC, and BlackBerry), without any extra charge—but only to law enforcement subscribers.
- More criminal court and arrest records or logs from more states and counties have been added to Accurint.
- A new "Phone batch" feature allows you to search for phone numbers in a variety of ways (fees vary depending on the "level" chosen): For example, if you want only directory assistance phone numbers, choose level one, but for a broader search that will attempt to return a "possible" current phone number, choose level four. If you want only the newest phone number, select the **Return Different Phone** option (this is a lower price option).
- The **People at Work** feature has added 30 million new records so you can now search for business links for more than 132 million individuals.

Our View: We assume that Accurint stands for "accurate" and "current." Is it accurate and current? According to a librarian at Bryan Cave, the answer is "yes" as to whether it is current; she finds it's the most up-to-date people-finding site. As to accurate, we'd say "yes and no." It is as accurate as the public records and other sources upon which it depends are. Its "relational" ability, which attempts to show relationships between people, can sometimes be inaccurate or incomplete. For instance, a search of Carole Levitt's record linked her to her current husband (but labeled him a mere "associate"). It then linked her to her former husband and his entire family but as noted earlier, missed her parents and brothers entirely. A search by one of her old phone numbers did not work; however, searching an old address worked like a charm, as did searching by Social Security number. Users must subscribe and be approved in advance. The subscriber application requires such information as your bank name and account number, your business license, your law license, and so on. Expect a phone call (or two) to verify your information.

Tip:

- When dealing with a common name, it helps to have a date of birth. If you don't have that, but are able to estimate the subject's age range, add this information into the **Age Range** field to narrow down the search.
- When uncertain of a subject's address, use the **Radius** search box on the search query menu. For example, after you type the subject's suspected address into the **Address** search box, you can type "10" into the radius search box, and the search engine will display addresses within 10 miles of the address you've entered.
- Besides home addresses, Accurint will sometimes display work addresses—always a difficult bit of data to locate.
- Basic information about any person found in your subject's report is made available for the price of the original report. You can also link directly to any person listed in your subject's report if you need more information from their separate report (which you will be charged for, of course).

In March 2005, Reed Elsevier's LexisNexis unit sent notices to approximately 30,000 people advising them that unauthorized individuals may have accessed their personally identifiable information via LexisNexis' recently acquired Seisint subsidiary and its Accurint database. As of early April, LexisNexis said in a press release, "No individual has advised of having experienced any form of identity theft." (See **http://www.lexis nexis.com/about/releases/0789.asp**.)

Also, in March 2005, LexisNexis performed an in-depth audit of data search activity on Accurint covering the past two years. That review found fifty-nine incidents in which "unauthorized persons, primarily using IDs and passwords of legitimate Seisint customers, may have acquired personal-identifying information, such as Social Security Numbers (SSNs) or Driver's License Numbers (DLNs), of individuals in the U.S." (See **http://www.lexisnexis.com/presscenter/SanfordTestimonyJudiciary.pdf**.) These findings led LexisNexis to notify an additional 280,000 people (approximately) whose information may have been compromised in those newly identified incidents.

Like the ChoicePoint data breach discussed on page 268, there was apparently no "hacking" or other method of electronic eavesdropping or "breaking and entering" into the Accurint database. LexisNexis claims that, "The substantial majority of instances involved IDs and passwords stolen from Seisint customers that had legally permissible access to SSNs and DLNs for legitimate purposes, such as verifying identities and preventing and detecting fraud." (See **http://www.lexisnexis.com/about/releases/0789.asp**.) So, unlike the ChoicePoint situation where nefarious individuals set up valid accounts using false business identification, the breach at Accurint was caused by the theft (or misuse) of the user name and password information of legitimate Accurint account holders. LexisNexis has advised those customers whose user names and passwords were compromised

In response to these breaches, LexisNexis is invoking more restrictive access to SSNs for Accurint users. "This included truncating SSNs displayed in non-public documents and narrowing access to full SSNs and DLNs to law enforcement and a restricted group of legally authorized organizations, such as banks and insurance companies," the company said in a press release (see **http://www.lexisnexis.com/presscenter/SanfordTestimonyJudiciary.pdf**.). Law firms are not on the list of client categories that can view full SSNs unless the firm's practice is in collections. We have already heard angry comments from lawyers who can no longer view these SSNs. For lawyers who still need access to full SSNs, see the entry on Merlindata.com.

"Practical Points"

The Accurint situation illustrates an extreme example of improper user name and password usage. Any service or technology that requires a user name and password can be compromised in the same way—this goes for everything from your e-mail and voice mail to the logon password for your computer.

    To help insure the security of your (and your clients') information, it is important for lawyers to use hard-to-guess passwords and to change them regularly, so that unauthorized individuals do not have access to your information.

Lexis

http://www.lexis.com **$**

Purpose:	To search using more-sophisticated search techniques than the free public records sites offer. Lexis is useful for skip-tracing, marshalling assets, and backgrounding people.

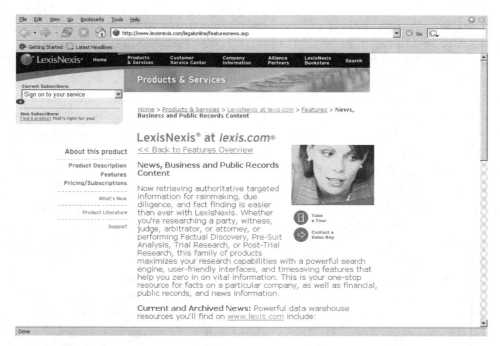

Figure 8-26. The Lexis Web Site offers the ability to search numerous different types of public records. Reprinted with the permission of LexisNexis.

Content: Now that Lexis owns Accurint, expect to see Lexis and Accurint's databases integrated over time. From assets to verdicts, the Lexis database contains information garnered from public records, publicly available information, and proprietary sources (for example, D & B credit reports for companies). For a complete list of public records available at Lexis, scroll down the page at **http://www.lexisnexis.com/sourcelists** and click on the **Public Records** drop-down menu. For non-U.S. public record data (Canada, France, UK, and Russia), see **http://www.lexisnexis.com/sourcelists/pdfs/ nonus.pdf**.

Our View: The major advantage of Lexis is the ability to conduct multistate and nationwide public record searching and **All Records** searching (searching through a diverse group of records).

Tip: If you want to find as much information as possible about an individual, it may be worth the money to run an **All Records-All States** type of search instead of running several individual searches in selected states or agencies. Lexis also has all types of **People Finder** databases covering 146 million individuals. The data varies from state to state but could include driver's license information, marriage, divorce and death records, voter registration records, and more.

FlatRateInfo.com
(owned by InsightAmerica)

http://www.flatrateinfo.com   **$**

Purpose: To search using more-sophisticated search techniques than the free public records sites offer. FlatRateInfo is useful for skip-tracing, marshalling assets, and backgrounding people. Directed at those who do a high volume of people searching and prefer a flat rate.

Content: After your application is approved, you can access:

- Twenty-seven national databases
- Two national people locators (but access to one of them, the QI National People Locator database, is offered on a limited basis) containing over 600 million records from most U.S. residents, including Social Security numbers, current and previous addresses, real-time phone numbers, relatives, dates of birth, and aliases
- National bankruptcies, judgments, and liens
- National real property records
- National fictitious business names
- Social Security Death Index (SSDI)
- Criminal records

Our View: For those who do a high volume of people searching, such as collection laywers, FlatRateInfo may be the way to go. Contact the company for pricing.

Tip:

- See the parent company site, InsightAmerica at **http://www.insightamerica.com/**, which was recently acquired by a public company, Acxiom (**http://www.acxiom.com/**), for access to other databases such as a multistate unclaimed property database (**http://www.insightamerica.com/gateways/uprop.html**) for about forty-five states and drivers records discussed earlier in this chapter.
- Colorado lawyers should also take a close look at InsightAmerica's databases—they have several Colorado specific databases, such as a real-time court records databases (**http://www.cocourts.com/**) and a Colorado Department of Motor Vehicles database that is updated daily, noted earlier in this chapter.
- Although some of FlatRateInfo's databases, such as the SSDI, can be accessed free at RootsWeb.com, they have been placed here simply for the customer's convenience (with the flat rate, in essence, it is free).

Westlaw

http://www.westlaw.com **$**

Purpose: To search using more-sophisticated search techniques than the free public records sites offer. Westlaw is useful for skip-tracing, marshalling assets, and backgrounding people.

Content: Westlaw offers online access to national and state public records, from courthouses to government agencies and more. Records relate to searching for people, assets, and adverse filings. Search for executive affiliations, environmental records, and more.

Our View: For those who have a flat-rate Westlaw contract (and if access to public records is part of it), it may be cost-effective to use Westlaw. Like Lexis, Westlaw offers multijurisdictional and multiagency searching, and many people and business finder and locator databases.

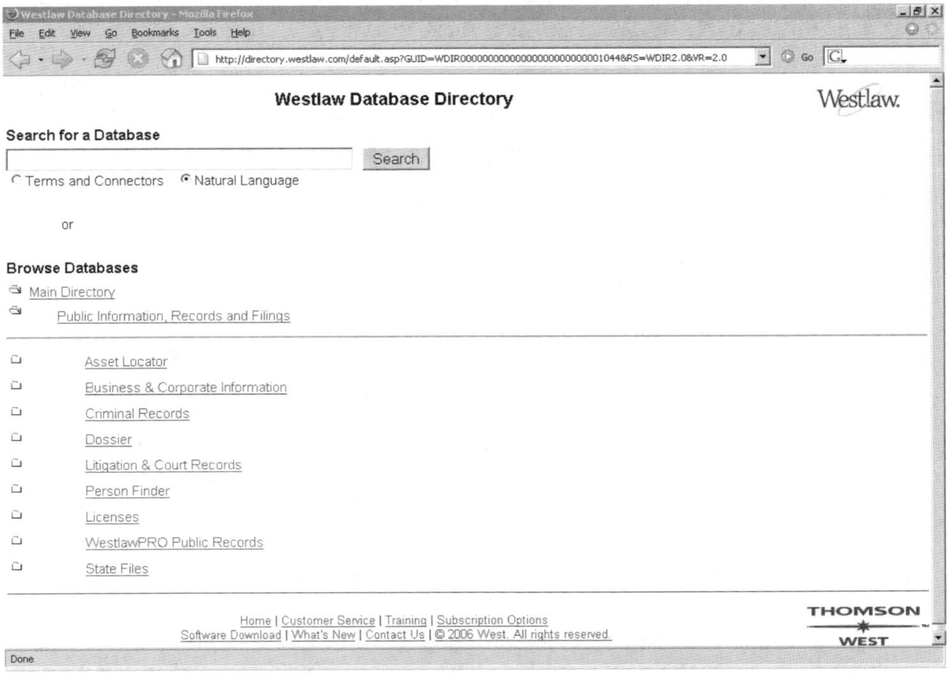

Figure 8-27. Only Westlaw subscribers can access the searchable multijurisdictional and multiagency databases available through the Westlaw.com Web site.

Tip: Nonsubscribers cannot use Westlaw for public record searching. Use any one of the other fee-based databases in this section if you are an occasional public record searcher.

ChoicePoint

(formerly CDB Infotek; also marketed as KnowX, Auto-Track, and ScreenNow)

http://www.choicepoint.net

Purpose: To search public records using more-sophisticated search techniques than the free sites offer; useful for skip-tracing, marshalling assets, and backgrounding people

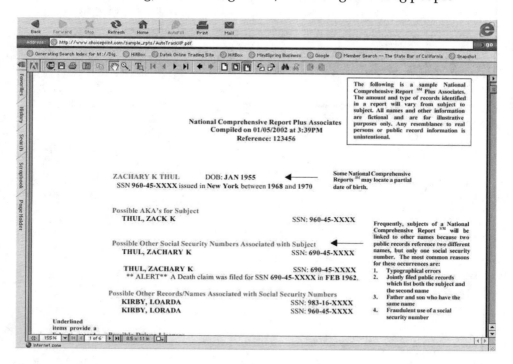

Figure 8-28. Combined, ChoicePoint's databases contain over 19 billion records. A subject's name, partial DOB, and partial SSN are displayed on the first page of a **National Comprehensive Plus Associates** report. ChoicePoint and the ChoicePoint logo are registered trademarks of ChoicePoint Asset Company.

Content: ChoicePoint provides Internet access to over 19 billion records on individuals and businesses, by way of public and proprietary records. Information includes relatives and associates, corporate information, real property records, and deed transfers. Users must subscribe and be approved in advance. The subscriber application requires such information as your bank name and account number, Social Security number, two credit references, your business license, your law license, and so on. As of March 4, 2005, ChoicePoint stopped selling "sensitive consumer data" (SSNs and DLNs) to many of its customers, unless they meet one of three tests:

- Support consumer-driven transactions where the data is needed to complete or maintain relationships such as insurance, employment and tenant screening or to provide access to their own data;
- Provide authentication or fraud prevention tools to large, accredited corporate customers where consumers have existing relationships. For example, information tools for identity verification, customer enrollment and insurance claims; or
- Assist federal, state and local government, and criminal justice agencies in their important missions.

This probably rules out attorney access to "sensitive consumer data" via ChoicePoint.

Our View: Aside from individual records, one can also retrieve comprehensive reports about people by using the **Info-Probe** or **Discovery PLUS** features. The **Discovery PLUS** report shows an individual's current and previous addresses, relatives, assets, corporate involvement, derogatory information, and vehicle identification number. The **InfoProbe** report searches millions of records simultaneously and shows a list of databases containing records matching your search criteria. From the list, you choose which databases to view and regardless of the number of records viewed, the charge will never exceed $100 per search. The **National Comprehensive Report**, provided through ChoicePoint's AutoTrackXP database, searches national and state databases for a subject's assets (e.g., real property and deed transfers and vehicles), professional licenses, current and past addresses and phone numbers, drivers license information, UCCs, bankruptcies, etc. An **Associate** search can also be added to the report, which includes names of neighbors, relatives, and anyone else linked to the subject's addresses.

Tip: If you anticipate that there could be reams of information about your subject, consider an InfoProbe search instead of conducting various individual searches; it might save you time and money.

KnowX

(launched in February of 1997 as Information America, and merged with ChoicePoint Inc. in May 2000)

http://www.knowx.com

Purpose: To search public records using more-sophisticated search techniques than the free sites offer; useful for skip-tracing, marshalling assets, and backgrounding people.

Content: KnowX searches national and state databases for a summary of assets, driver's licenses, professional licenses, real property, vehicles, liens, business entity filings, lawsuit information, marriage records, birth and death records, and more (associates, relatives and others linked to the same addresses as the subject and neighbors). Registration with a credit card is required and searches cost anywhere from $1.50 to $129.50 for a comprehensive report (for the full-price list see **https://www.knowx .com/statmnts/priceinfo.jsp#corp**).

Our View: For the occasional user, this may be a better choice than ChoicePoint because you need not fill out such a personal application and wait to be approved. Also, you can save some money by purchasing a 24-hour, 30-day, or annual subscription for selected databases, instead of

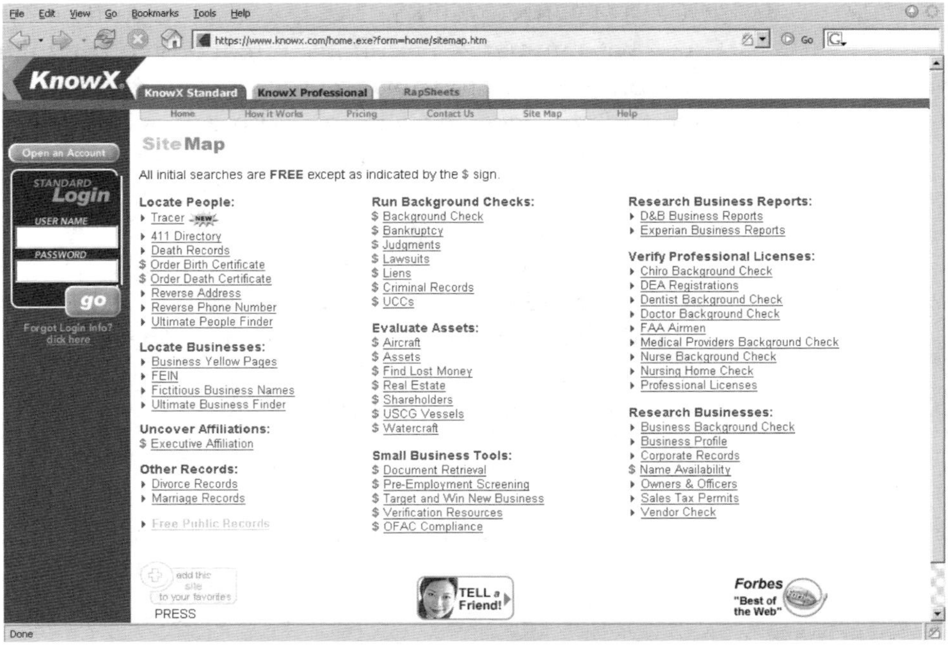

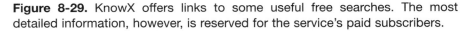

Figure 8-29. KnowX offers links to some useful free searches. The most detailed information, however, is reserved for the service's paid subscribers.

paying per search. KnowX obtains its information from "official records" which we assume means public records. They are probably also obtaining information from "publicly available" information which the individual voluntarily provides such as when they order telephone service and place their phone numbers in the telephone book. Thus, KnowX is not offering the general public access to the "sensitive, personal information" found in credit headers. This means that the information may not be as "fresh" as that found in the databases described above. However, as explained earlier, data from credit headers may not be available to lawyer users either—unless they come within the FCRA and GLBA requirements.

Tip: Some KnowX searches are free (but the results are very summarized). Check the price list noted above to discover which ones are free.

Even though the free results are very summarized, sometimes that's all you need! For example, a free corporate record search for "Coastal Printworks" returns the result

"COASTAL PRINTWORKS, INC. is a business entity in CA." That summarized result just might be good enough if you only wanted to know whether they were registered to do business in California. Those in need of a mailing address and registered agent, however, will need to pay for a more detailed record from KnowX ($6.95), which is why KnowX offers "free" searches. A savvy searcher can take advantage of the free search by using KnowX to conduct this national corporate record search free and then taking the information (that the company is registered in California) to visit the Secretary of State site in California, where the full information will be supplied free.

Intelius

http://find.intelius.com/   **$**

Purpose: To search public records using more-sophisticated search techniques than the free sites offer; useful for skip-tracing and backgrounding people.

Content: Intelius, like KnowX, is geared more to the general public. It searches its database of public records and publicly available information to provide the following information about people: address, phone number, real property ownership, selected lawsuit information (bankruptcies, marriage and divorce records, criminal records, tax liens, and judgments), licenses, birth and death records, and names, addresses, and phone numbers of neighbors and also of associates, relatives, and others linked to the same addresses as the subject. There are no business records in this database. Registration with a credit card is required and the cost to search begins at $7.95 for a **People Search** results displaying first name, middle initial, last name, address, city, state, ZIP code, phone number, age, date of birth, average yearly income, and average house price).

Our View: We included Intelius because you will often find links to their pay database when you use various free telephone directories discussed in Chapter 7. For example, if you look up a phone number at Infospace.com you are linked to Intelius when you click on **Background Check**. The cost is $49.95, which is steep compared to using other data broker vendors such as Accurint, Merlin, or ChoicePoint. However, like KnowX, Intelius may satisfy the occassional user who doesn't want to fill out an application and get approved by the above data broker vendors.

Tip: Intelius also has a 24-hour pass, volume discounts, and batch searching.

CHAPTER**NINE**

Finding and Backgrounding Expert Witnesses

There are plenty of low-tech traditional ways to find experts, such as telephoning colleagues or one of the numerous brokerages (not unlike Hollywood talent agencies) that represent experts. These companies can pump résumés and curriculum vitaes (CVs) through your fax machine to satisfy every esoteric expert need you can think of. They also often charge fees in advance of providing any expertise. You'll find scads of ads for these companies, as well as for individual experts in the back pages of most legal periodicals, especially those targeted at trial lawyers. Usually, these companies charge a representation fee in addition to the fee you'll pay to the expert. Another low-tech way of searching is to look through an expert witness directory (in print). This is time consuming and often means a trip to a library. Also, the print directory's arrangement is not always helpful. If you want to search for an expert by both location and expertise, but the directory is only arranged by expertise, or only by location, or only by expert's name, you'll be out of luck.

The Internet, however, has expedited the traditional searching for expert witnesses by providing easy and free access to so many resources, from online expert witness directories to online library catalogs, periodical indexes, and databases that contain full-text articles (to satisfy your search for articles or books relevant to the subject or authored by the expert).

The Internet also lends itself to creative ways to find experts (and to help you learn enough about the subject matter and the expert to be able to make an informed decision about the qualifications of a potential expert). These creative ways vary from taking advantage of the professional association community, to reviewing jury verdicts, to finding mailing-list postings and the like, to searching through the expert's own site. Many of the traditional searches and creative searches can be done on the Web and usually for free.

War Story: Enhanced Collaboration

Insurance defense lawyer Jim Walter relates this collaborative use he made of a free online expert witness directory, JurisPro:

"In one case, we needed to find an expert witness who could testify regarding premises liability issues. From the JurisPro Web site, I downloaded the expert's full curriculum vitae, reviewed the expert's background as a witness, (including the number of times they have testified, and whether it was for the plaintiff or defense), and read their articles that discussed their expertise. Most impressively, I was able to get an idea how the various experts *presented* themselves—by viewing their photos and hearing them speak through streaming audio on the site. I then got on the phone with the insurance adjustor and we simultaneously reviewed the qualifications of potential experts online on JurisPro. JurisPro allowed my firm and the company to agree to hire an expert witness in one telephone call. We did not have to fax résumés back and forth, play 'phone tag' for several hours or days on potential hires, or have an adjustor simply rely on my judgment in hiring a witness. The hiring process was easy and fast, allowing both of us to make a decision swiftly and move on to other cases."

Checklist for Finding and Verifying Experts

❑ 1. Develop a working knowledge of the expertise by reading books and articles. This can also lead you to the experts in the field or help verify credentials for the experts you already have.
❑ 2. Review the expert's writings.
❑ 3. Search free expert witness directories.
❑ 4. Use online directories to find trade or professional associations.
❑ 5. Find the expert's conference presentations.
❑ 6. Join an online community to find experts' postings or to learn about the topic.
❑ 7. Review the expert's own Web site.
❑ 8. Determine if the expert has ever been disciplined.
❑ 9. Find experts via jury verdict reporter databases.

❏   10. Find the expert's deposition testimony.
❏   11. Find briefs and cases that refer to the expert.
❏   12. Locate academic experts through university sites.
❏   13. Find government experts through government reports.
❏   14. Use pay referral sites.

Checklist Item 1: Develop a Working Knowledge of the Expertise by Reading Books and Articles

Before seeking an expert, it's useful to first familiarize yourself with the area of expertise by reading an article or two, or scanning a book on the topic. Searching a library's catalog (via the Internet, of course) by subject can lead you to some of the literature in that area of expertise. A comprehensive listing of public library Web sites can be found at Libweb (**http://sunsite.berkeley.edu/Libweb**). As you browse through the book titles, you may spot certain authors who have written several books on that specialty and this may assist you in identifying some of the top experts in the field to contact. In addition to sifting through online card catalogs for books, you should also conduct an online search for articles; articles tend to be more current than books and are certainly easier to digest than a lengthy book. This search for books and articles can also assist you in finding materials authored by an expert you have already been referred to.

Online Library Catalogs

Libweb

http://sunsite.berkeley.edu/Libweb

Purpose: To find library URLs to search their online catalogs.

Content: Use Libweb to link to all types of libraries' home pages in 135 countries by browsing by location or type of library, or by keyword searching using the library name, a location, a type of library, or a combination of these. From the library's home page, link to the catalog and search by author, subject, or title.

Our View: It's useful to begin with your public library in case you want to borrow the book or have them arrange an inter-library loan for you.

Tip: However you do a thorough search, don't overlook the mother of online library catalogs—the Library of Congress (**http://catalog.loc.gov**). Finally, don't discount online bookstore catalogs such as Amazon (**http://www.amazon.com**) or Barnes & Noble (**http://www.barnesandnoble.com**) to find leading authors in a subject area. Results at those retail sites may include a synopsis, the author's name, table of contents, a note from the publisher about the work, and, in many cases, reviews of the book.

Has the Expert Been Published?

Although someone may have provided you with a name of an expert, it's your job to independently verify the expert's expertise. One way to do this is to discover if the expert has been published in his or her area of expertise. You will need to uncover the expert's authored materials (and not by just by reading the materials featured on the expert's own Web site). Reading authored material will also show you the expert's opinions and help you to discover any inconsistencies. Uncovering the opposition's expert's authored materials is also in order—for the very same reasons. This research will assist you to better prepare for direct or cross-examination.

Checklist Item 2: Review the Expert's Writings

You cannot depend on experts to have posted all of their published works on their Web sites, and therefore an independent literature search is in order. To conduct a nationwide search of newspaper or periodical articles written by (or about) your expert, pay databases such as Lexis, Westlaw, or Ingenta are best, especially for scholarly articles. Ingenta is useful for those who do not have a subscription to Lexis or Westlaw because you can search, at no cost, the summaries of articles from over 25,000 publications and purchase the full text online. To obtain consumer magazine articles, at no cost, use FindArticles.com, where you can search a database of full-text articles from over 300 magazines and journals back to 1998. For more specialized topics, such as toxic mold and stachybotrys, a search through medical literature at the government's National Library of Medicine (NLM) gateway site is in order (**http://gate way.nlm.nih.gov/gw/Cmd**). See Chapter 12, "Medical Research," for more information on the NLM.

Online Periodical Indexes and Full-Text Articles

FindArticles.com

http://www.FindArticles.com

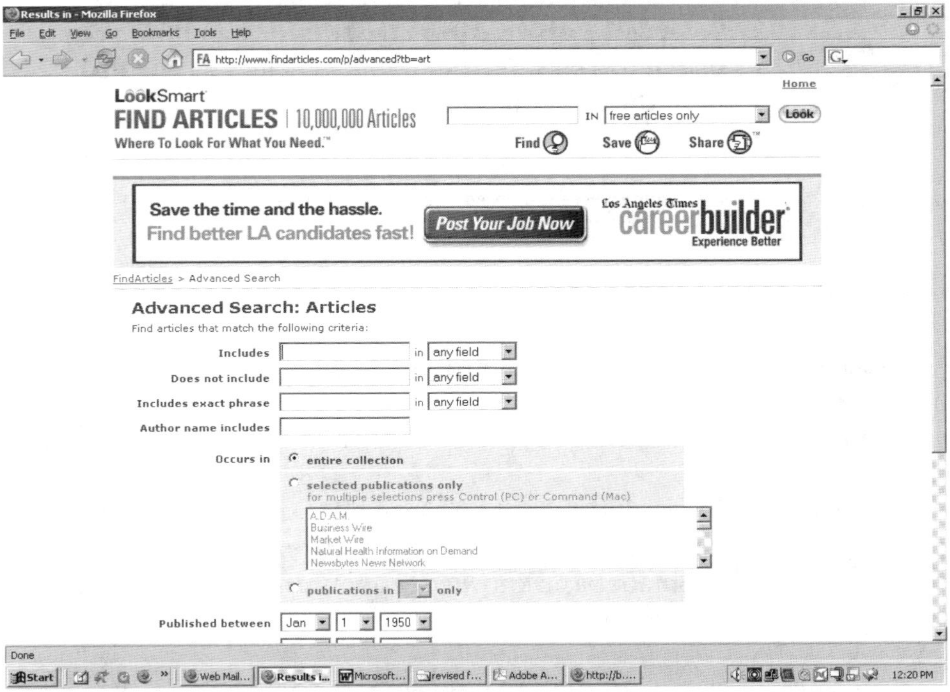

Figure 9-1. FindArticles is useful to conduct a literature search for the articles written by (or about) an expert, or to search by expertise to learn about the subject or to identify leading experts in the field. The Advanced Search page offers more search options.

Purpose: To conduct a literature search for the articles written by (or about) an expert to ascertain their expertise and their opinions; to obtain basic knowledge about the subject before hiring an expert.

Content: FindArticles.com is a database of published articles that can be searched for free. It is continually updated, and contains articles back to 1984 from "thousands of resources."

Our View: Being able to read and print the full text of an article at no cost is very useful, especially if you need an overview of a topic or need to find an expert. Many of the articles contain quotes by experts.

Tip: Use the **Advanced Search** to search by keywords, phrases, or author's name. You can limit your search to a particular magazine by selecting the **Occurs in Selected Publications Only** button or limit your search to a specific timeframe by selecting the **Published between** option.

Ingenta

To search: To view and print full text:

http://www.ingenta.com

Purpose: To conduct a literature search for the articles written by (or about) an expert to ascertain expertise and opinions; to obtain basic knowledge about the subject before hiring an expert.

Content: Search 20,100,219 articles from 29,909 academic and professional publications and read the abstracts—for free.

Our View: Being able to read abstracts and purchase the full text of the articles online without having to figure out which library may carry a specified article is very useful when time is of the essence. If time is not important, you might be able to locate the article for free at a local library because Ingenta provides the complete citation.

Tip:
- Be sure to click on **advanced search** to refine or narrow your search.
- You can e-mail the entire list of results to someone so he can choose the articles he wants.

Check the Library

Before paying for an article, check your library's online databases to see if the full text of the article is offered there for free (see the section "Free Internet Access to Library Databases and Catalogs" in Chapter 5, "General Factual Research"). Also, run the article title through a search engine in case it has been posted free on someone's Web site (such as the author's).

If you need to only access an individual newspaper or magazine, the Internet is a perfect source. For information about sites that link to thousands of publications from around the world, such as CEOExpress (**http://www.ceoexpress.com**), see the section "News, Periodicals, and Broadcast Media" in Chapter 5, "General Factual Research."

Many trade associations publish online newsletters, and some provide either full-text articles or extracts. For example, the Accident Reconstruction (ARC) Network (**http://www.accidentreconstruction.com**), a professional organization for those in the accident reconstruction industry, has a monthly newsletter with expert's articles. This site also has an active discussion forum that includes opinions posted by various accident reconstructionists.

Use Dictionaries and Encyclopedias

Sometimes you just need a brief introduction to a subject area and an encyclopedia article or dictionary will do the trick instead of a book or journal article. Check out Refdesk.com for links to medical and drug dictionaries, technology encyclopedias, and more (**http://www.refdesk.com**). There's even an Ask an Expert section.

War Story: Finding an Expert—Fast

Ben Wright (Ben_Wright@compuserve.com) is a lawyer in Dallas, Texas and an expert on digital signatures and electronic contracts. He described how Julian Ding, a lawyer in Malaysia, arranged for his expert services.

Julian Ding needed to find an electronic commerce expert—fast. Julian is a partner in Zaid Ibrahim & Co., a large law firm in Malaysia, a developing country determined to leapfrog itself into leadership on the information highway. The Malaysian Parliament was in the process of adopting digital signature legislation, and Julian's firm wanted to convene a public seminar to examine the topic. To add the requisite cachet, the firm invited the Minister of Energy, Telecommunications and Post to open the seminar.

Unfortunately, the Minister could only confirm the invitation rather late due to his busy schedule. That left Julian in a bind. He was forced to organize the seminar in thirty days, and he needed to find, among other experts, a foreign lawyer having special experience with digital signatures. So, he turned to Yahoo! (**http://www.yahoo.com**) and searched for "digital signature," which yielded the Web page for Ben Wright's book, *The Law of Electronic Commerce* (**http://wright.safeshopper.com**). Ben obviously knew the skinny on digital signatures because his Web site contained several articles about it. Julian dashed off an e-mail invitation to Ben, and the two soon negotiated an arrangement for Ben to be present at the event.

Finding an Expert's Book

Had Ding searched Barnesandnoble.com for the key words "electronic and commerce and law," Wright's book would have come up as the first result if sorted by best match. Tip: to find the most recent books, sort results by date. Wright's book showed up as the eighth-most recently published book on the topic (out of 186 books). You can also search by the best-selling books, but you might not see the best matches (those most closely related to your search words) listed at the beginning.

Checklist Item 3: Search Free Expert Witness Directories

There are many expert directories on the Internet. While most of them charge experts to be listed, they provide free search access to everyone. All the directories are searchable by expertise, while many are also searchable by expert name, geographic location, and a few other methods. The directories that offer geographic searching are useful, especially when a lawyer wants to hold down travel expenses by finding a local expert. The directory listings vary from the very brief to the very complete.

Lawyer Jim Robinson founded the JurisPro Expert Witness Directory (**http://www.JurisPro.com**) after experiencing frustration over trying to locate expert witnesses for his cases. "There are a lot of 'white page telephone' types of expert witness directories that just include an expert's contact information, with very little information about their background, noted Robinson. Attorneys rely on experts to make them look good to the client; therefore, attorneys want to be as comfortable with that expert as possible. We have not met an attorney yet who said they want to know *less* about the expert they were going to hire. We designed the features of JurisPro from an attorney's point of view. Attorneys want to know the expert's full range of experience within their field of expertise, and their background as an expert witness. They want to be able to read the expert's actual résumé (not just some blurb), and know how the expert presents him or herself. They also wanted to be able to find out this information from a place that was free and convenient to use, Robinson explained. With this in mind, we set up JurisPro as a free, content-based directory for finding and researching expert witnesses."

Free Expert Witness Directories, Searchable by Keyword, Name, and Location

Jurispro.com

http://www.jurispro.com

Purpose:	To find experts, view their pictures, listen to their audio, and read their CVs and articles.
Content:	Search for an expert witness by name or area of expertise, or by selecting from a list of expert categories. As each expert is displayed, you will first see a narrative summary of the expert's background, contact information, photo, and an audio clip to listen to his or her voice. Then, select any of these tabs for more data: **Background** (in the form of questions and answers), **CV, Articles, References, Web Page,** and **E-mail.**

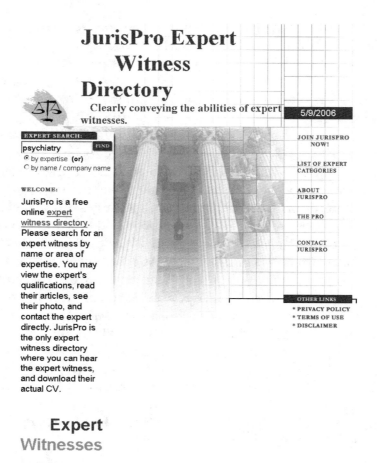

JurisPro Expert Witness Directory

Clearly conveying the abilities of expert witnesses.

5/9/2006

EXPERT SEARCH:

psychiatry   FIND

⊙ by expertise **(or)**
○ by name / company name

WELCOME:

JurisPro is a free online expert witness directory. Please search for an expert witness by name or area of expertise. You may view the expert's qualifications, read their articles, see their photo, and contact the expert directly. JurisPro is the only expert witness directory where you can hear the expert witness, and download their actual CV.

JOIN JURISPRO NOW!

LIST OF EXPERT CATEGORIES

ABOUT JURISPRO

THE PRO

CONTACT JURISPRO

OTHER LINKS
* PRIVACY POLICY
* TERMS OF USE
* DISCLAIMER

Expert Witnesses

WHY REGISTER WITH JURISPRO?

REGISTER NOW

EXPERT LOG IN

JurisPro is a Better Business Bureau Company

Figure 9-2. JurisPro provides lawyers with an invaluable tool by allowing them to see the experts' pictures and listen to their audio clips.

Our View: A jury survey found that jurors sided with one expert over another because one expert more clearly communicated her expertise. JurisPro provides lawyers with an invaluable tool by allowing them to see the experts' pictures and listen to their audio clips. If it sounds like the expert can clearly communicate his expertise on the audio clip, this helps lawyers decide whether to even bother phoning the expert in the first place.

Tip: Once you pull up a list of results, you can further refine the search by selecting a state.

Experts.com

http://www.experts.com

Purpose: To find experts and consultants.

Content: Search by clicking on the **search** tab at the top and then search by keywords, category, name, company, address, or a combination. You can also browse by clicking on the **directory** tab and then choosing a category (some will have subcategories). To refine the directory

Figure 9-3. Search the National Law Journal's Expert Witness directory by area of expertise, or by name of expert or company.

search, choose **Categories** or **Experts** from the pull-down menu on the Directory page, then type in a keyword and click on one of the directory categories. Results will display a summary of the expert's background and a link to the expert's e-mail and Web site. Some experts have their picture displayed.

Our View: An interesting feature is the ability for the lawyer to let the experts know he's interested in hearing from them by placing check marks next to the experts' names and clicking the **SynapsUS** online inquiry button at the bottom of the page.

Tip:
- You have a choice of refining your search on the Search page by choosing **all words**, **is exactly** or **any words**.
- Experts.com members are entitled to a discount at the MDEX Daubert Tracker database (**http://www.mdexonline.com**).

ALM (American Lawyer Media) Experts

http://www.almexperts.com

Purpose: To find experts and consultants.

Content: ALM has a directory with over 15,000 experts, expert witnesses, investigators, court reporters, and consultants in more than 3,300 categories. Search by area of expertise, or by name of expert or company. While free to users, experts who wish to list themselves in the database pay for inclusion. Users can search by keyword, area of expertise, or company name to find a list of national experts. Users can also choose to browse through the directory of expert categories. Once an expert is selected, the site makes it easy to determine if the expert has posted a Resume, Profile, Image, Web Site, or E-mail link.

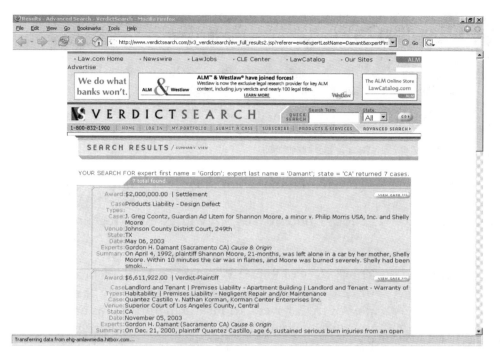

Figure 9-4. ALM's Experts.com site links to Verdict Search, where summaries of cases in which the expert testified are displayed (the full text of a case can be purchased at Verdict Search's site).

Our View: A very useful feature is the link (on the left-hand side of the expert's listing page) that allows you to check **Verdict Search** for cases involving the expert you've selected. A summary of the verdicts is displayed, and you can buy them for $9.95 each (see Verdict Search later in this chapter or at **http://www.verdictsearch.com** for more information). We like the handy chart that appears with the resulting list of experts. If you can't figure out what the icons stand for, just hover over them—they indicate whether the expert has an online profile, photograph, or CV; a Web site; or an e-mail address.

Tip: Click on the **Advanced Search** link to further refine your search by state or keywords.

See Expert's Prior Cases

The ALM Experts directory provides a useful feature: links to a pay site that displays the expert's prior cases.

Society of Expert Witnesses

http://www.sew.org.uk/database/database_index.htm

Purpose: To locate potential expert witnesses in the European Union.

Content: The Society of Expert Witnesses provides a browseable directory of what the site describes as only "a small sample" of their "over a thousand members," as only those members who request it are added to the online database. Database categories range from "Accident" to "Woodworm" specialists. Of most interest to U.S. lawyers will probably be those categories related to international business (e.g., contracts, valuations, taxation, pensions, etc.). The Society is a private, non-profit membership organization run by and for expert witnesses, established to "promot[e] training for expert witnesses and those aspiring to become expert witnesses."

Our View: The alphabetical list of areas of expertise is easy to browse. The clickable links take you directly to contact information for each expert listed, including their e-mail and Web site addresses (where applicable), in addition to their postal mail address and phone number.

The National Directory of Expert Witnesses is a very extensive print directory of experts and a free searchable online database of 2,000 technical, scientific, and medical experts arranged into 400 categories (**http://national-experts.com/Members2/search.html**). It is published by the Claims Providers of America and is designed to be used by law firms and insurance professionals. Search by keywords (partial or complete), phrases, category, name of expert, or name of company. To limit the search to a certain state, use its postal abbreviation, followed by an ampersand (for example, "IL&"). You can also e-mail this site and ask for a referral (for free) to an expert in a specified field.

Hieros Gamos's database lists experts in nearly 1,200 categories. It is searchable by company name, state or province, country, or any keyword in the firm's description (**http://www.hgexperts.com**). Even though there is no expert-name field, you can search for an expert's name in the description field. The database is also browsable by subject.

Free Expert Witness Directories, Searchable by Category Only

Yearbook.com
(formerly Yearbook of Experts, Authorities and Spokespersons)

http://www.expertclick.com

Purpose:	A very extensive searchable database of experts designed primarily for journalists, but anyone can search it for free.
Content:	Once a search is conducted for a particular area of expertise, you can read a summary about the expert, link to the expert's site, and link to press releases posted by the expert.
Our View:	This site also makes it easy to search for experts and to access additional information about them. The **Contact this Expert** link, on the left-hand side of the listing page, is a useful shortcut that will help you get a message or question to the expert quickly. In some cases, you will be informed that you must be a registered journalist. However, you can easily contact the expert on your own—from the information listed on the profile or by linking to the expert's site.
Tip:	• By clicking on **View Releases** you can read the expert's press releases. But remember—this is what the expert wrote, not what an objective third party wrote.
	• Some expert listings include a **View Daybook** link to view the expert's calendar of events (such as seminars).

- A PDF version of the site's print directory is available for download at **http://pages.zdnet.com/biswire/yearbookpdf**.

Free Expert Witness Directories, Searchable by Category and Location

Expert Pages ⑧ is one of the oldest online directories of expert witnesses (**http://www.expertpages.com**). Experts are arranged by hierarchical categories and subcategories of expertise. The information for each listing is very brief, but includes links to the expert's Web site, e-mail, or phone number.

Findlaw ⑧ , like Expert Pages, has an online directory searchable by category (**http://marketcenter.findlaw.com/expert_witnesses.html**). The results might include listings of individual experts or links to some of the referral sites we note below. The expert listings offer a bit more information than those at Expert Pages, and include descriptions of services offered and full contact information.

Finding an Expert in Your State

Although several sites allow the user to narrow down the expert witness search to a particular state, it should be noted that no matter what state is chosen, the results may still include experts from outside your requested state. This is because experts can ask to be listed in states other than the one in which they reside.

Pay Directory of Expert Witness CVs with Free Links to Experts' Sites

The Expert Witness Network $ allows lawyers to access a database that includes 2,000 CVs for $99 per year, or $25 per session (**http://www.witness.net**). Also on this site is a free Expert Witness Links database (click the **Expert Links** link on the left-hand side of the page) where you can browse an alphabetical collection of experts, brief directory listings, and then link to the expert's own Web site. Experts pay to be included in the Expert Witness Network. Sites on the **Expert Links** list are included for no fee.

Does Your Bar Association Have an Expert Witness Database?

When you need to keep expenses to a minimum, but still need an expert, it's helpful if you can target local experts. To do this, consider turning to your local bar association's Web site to see if they have created an expert witness directory. For instance, in Los Angeles, lawyers can consult the Los Angeles County Bar Association's online expert database, Expert4law.org (**http://www.expert4law.org**), and lawyers in the Bay area can consult the Bar Association of San Francisco's online directory of expert witnesses (**http://www.sfbar.org/register/**).

Checklist Item 4: Use Online Directories to Find Trade or Professional Associations

Lawyers who need an expert in an uncommon field or who simply do not know where to begin their search for an expert should consider consulting with an association that deals with that particular field. According to the American Society of Association Executives, there are over 147,000 associations in the United States (127,340 local, state, or regional; 20,285 national; and 2,409 international associations headquartered in the United States). One easy way to find an association's Web site is to simply enter its name into a Web search engine (like Google); however, this assumes you know the name of the association. If you don't know the name, you can enter a descriptive keyword and the word "association." Another easy way to find an association's Web site is to access one of the free online association indicies or directories.

Lawyers very often need to find translators or interpreters. A useful site for finding one is the American Translators Association's site (**http://www.atanet.org**). Like many association sites, it includes an online directory searchable by name, language, location, and various other criteria.

War Story: Chewing Gum Expert

There are associations for nearly every profession and interest group, as we learned when recently asked to find a chewing gum expert (for a personal injury case). The case involved a plaintiff who slipped and fell on a hard piece of chewing gum and the issue was one of notice, which could only be answered by figuring out how long that piece of chewing gum was on the floor. This, in turn, called for a chewing gum expert who could tell us how long it takes chewing gum to become hard. We knew it would be a waste of time to search a traditional expert witness directory and immediately thought of the Encyclopedia of Associations (also called Associations Unlimited). Seconds after logging into my public library's Web site, and locating the free Associations Unlimited remote database, we found the Association of Chewing Gum Manufacturers. We turned the contact over to the lawyers.

The Encyclopedia of Associations is free to use only if your public library provides remote access to it (otherwise, it is a pay database). If your library does provide access, you are in particular luck because it is one of the largest of the association directories. It indexes and provides detailed information on more than 155,000 organizations worldwide, and has Internal Revenue Service (IRS) data on 300,000 nonprofit organizations with 501(c) status. The Encyclopedia provides numerous search functions—keyword, acronyms, location, subject, and more. If the Encyclopedia entry for the association has a URL listed, go there to scour the site for a list of research links to learn more about the topic. Also, take note of the executive director's name or the names of any of the association's officers. Typically, their e-mail addresses or a link to them will be included. Lawyers can then contact the director or one of the officers for a referral to an expert. If you don't have access to the Encyclopedia of Associations, see below for some free alternatives. For more information on remote online resources offered by public libraries, see the "Free Internet Access to Library Databases and Catalogs" section of Chapter 5, "General Factual Research."

Online Directories of Associations

The Internet Public Library Associations on the Net

http://www.ipl.org/div/aon

Purpose:	To browse or search for information about prominent organizations and associations.
Content:	The Internet Public Library provides this collection of over 500 descriptions and links to associations on the

Internet. Categories include "Arts & Humanities,"
"Business & Economics," "Computers & Internet,"
"Entertainment & Leisure," "Health & Medical Sci-
ence," "Law, Government & Political Science," and
"Science & Technology."

Our View: The descriptions are helpful in determining if a particular association will yield useful information before linking to the association's Web site.

Tip: To perform a keyword search of this Associations list,
select the **Advanced Search** option from the drop-
down menu underneath the search box in the upper
right-hand corner of the page and then click the
Search button. On the subsequent page, check the
Association on the Net box and enter your search
terms before clicking the **Search** button.

GuideStar

http://www.guidestar.org/search $ $ (circled $ crossed out) [Registration Form icon]

Purpose: To search for data on nonprofits; geared to donors,
grantors, and nonprofits.

Content: GuideStar provides annual reports and IRS Form 990s
filed by about 1.5 million nonprofit organizations, and
also provides direct links to nonprofits' Web sites. The
free "GuideStar Basic" registration allows users to search
organization name, keyword, city, or state. Users who
opt for the paid "GuideStar Select" membership ($30/
month or $300/year) have more search options, includ-
ing ZIP code searching and a "starts with" option for
searching by organization name. The "GuideStar Premium" ($100/month or $1,000/year) membership offers
even more search options, including city and income
range.

Figure 9-5. GuideStar provides annual reports and IRS 990 forms filed by about 1.5 million nonprofit organizations, and also provides direct links to the non-profits' Web sites.

Our View: If you are looking for financial data on a specific organization (and you know the organization's name), the free, Basic registration will get users much of the information they need. However, if you're looking for data on organizations using more general search criteria (e.g., organization type, ZIP code, or income range) it'll be necessary to opt for one of the fee-based subscriptions.

Tip: If you don't find the charitable organization that you are looking for, check the list of charitable organizations in IRS Publication 78, Cumulative List of Organizations, and its Addendum. To search this list, type "Publication 78" into the **Search Forms and Publications for** query box at **http://www.irs.gov**, or go to **http://apps .irs.gov/app/pub78**. You can search by full or partial organization name, city, or state. Returned results include only the name of the charity, its city and state, and its IRS deductibility code.

Be sure to also check the alphabetical addendum to the list at **http://www.irs.gov/charities/article/0,,id= 96291,00.html**. The addendum is not searchable.

The Foundation Finder

http://lnp.fdncenter.org/finder.html

Purpose: To search for information about nonprofits.

Content: Search the Foundation Finder—a listing of 86,000 private and community foundations in the U.S. Other information on this site includes a list of the top funders by type or state (hover over **Find Funders** at the top of the home page and then select **Top Funders** from the drop-down menu that appears).

Our View: It's an easily searchable database, and one more source for PDFs of each organization's filled-in and filed IRS

Figure 9-6. Search the Foundation Finder by foundation's name (or partial name) or its EIN, and add a city, ZIP code, or state to narrow the search.

Form 990. The additional statistics available by clicking on the **FC Stats** link can be very useful in evaluating various organizations. This information is not as readily available at other sites.

Tip: Lawyers looking for grants need to subscribe. Click the **More Search Options** link to get the most flexible search options.

Specialized Association Directories

While the above directories cover a wide spectrum of areas, there are directories that are more specialized. For example, in the health care industry, the Joint Commission on Accreditation of Healthcare Organizations has a site that includes a database of more than 15,000 health care organizations. Searchable by ZIP code or organization name, the database includes ambulatory care facilities, assisted living facilities, behavioral health care facilities (such as chemical dependency centers and developmental disabilities organizations), HMOs, home care organizations, hospitals, laboratories, long-term care facilities, and office-based surgery facilities (**http://www.qualitycheck.org**).

Reliability and Relevance of Experts

Harold J. Bursztajn, MD, is an Associate Clinical Professor of Psychiatry at Harvard Medical School. He also has broad courtroom experience as an expert witness in civil and criminal litigation. In his forensic practice, he has consulted to plaintiff and defense counsel and to state and federal agencies as an expert in medical-legal decision-making and forensic psychiatry. Dr. Bursztajn's Web site (**http://www.forensic-psych.com**) focuses on the nexus of forensic psychiatry, medicine, and the law. He offered the following insights regarding using the Internet to find medical experts:

"With its emphasis on judicial discretion, and the judge as 'gatekeeper' for admitting expert testimony, *Daubert v. Merrel Dow Pharmaceuticals, Inc.* 509 U.S. 579 (1993), has been slowly but steadily transforming how lawyers seek experts. With the increasing likelihood that an expert's testimony will face judicial scrutiny, the reliability and relevance of an expert's analysis and evaluation needs to be established long before trial, ideally prior to retaining an expert. While the specific guidelines enumerated by the Supreme Court for scientific testimony are most often used to evaluate the quantitative sciences, the more general criteria of reliability and relevance are increasingly used by judges to evaluate the admissibility of applied science-based expert medical opinion. One of my most common forensic consultations is to evaluate another 'expert's' opinion. When I analyze it as unreliable or irrelevant on medical-decision analytic grounds, the lawyer or court which has retained me can rapidly move to dismiss either the questionable testimony or the claim or defense as a whole which is founded on such testimony (*Mayotte M. Jones v. Metrowest Medical Inc.* [CA-96-10860-WD]).

"By researching via the Internet, a lawyer seeking an expert can avoid both false starts and subsequent disappointments. The Internet offers the following advantages for evaluating the potential usefulness of a medical expert in light of the general principles of *Daubert:*

"1. *Reliability:* The medical expert needs to be both a practicing physician who consults to other physicians and patients, and well published in refereed medical journals. This information can be gleaned from the expert's Web page more easily than from the CV alone. The Web page will often include not only a complete CV, but also selected case citations and authored publications. Moreover, the expert with a resource page on the Web is more likely to be able to do computer-aided literature searches. Such research can provide the foundation for the reviews and analysis needed to corroborate the reliability of another expert's opinion. In addition, such research can identify alternative opinions in the medical community.

"2. *Relevance:* The medical expert needs to show ability to teach not only other medical professionals but also an ability to teach other professionals and educated laypersons, e.g., judges, lawyers and jurors. The lawyer can have some sense of how the expert teaches in a public context by reviewing the expert's Web page. The fact that an expert has a content-filled, yet user-friendly Web page, can itself be an indication that an expert has the competence, confidence, and sensitivity to present work in a public context with authority rather than arrogance, and in a relevant and meaningful manner."

Daubert on the Web

See Peter Nordberg's site, Daubert on the Web, to read the *Daubert* decision and hundreds of post-*Daubert* cases—indexed by circuit and by area of expertise (**http://daubertontheweb.com**). Nordberg is a shareholder in the Philadelphia-based Berger & Montague, specializing in complex and environmental litigation.

Checklist Item 5: Find the Expert's Conference Presentations

To locate an expert in a specific area of expertise, enter the search term "expert witness" (in quotation marks) along with any other search criteria, such as "child custody," into a search engine. Searching a known expert's name through a search engine is a way to capture any extra nuggets of information—such as links to the expert's personal Web site, discussion group messages sent by the expert, or any references to the expert on a discussion group or a Web site other than his or her own.

It is often important to learn if an expert's opinion has been consistent in public forums, such as conferences. An expert's conference papers can sometimes be found on the Web by typing the expert's name into Google. Very often, experts post their own papers, or the conference host might post them. To limit your search to an expert's PowerPoint presentations only, go to Google and click on **Advanced Search**. Enter your search term (the expert's name) and then select **Microsoft PowerPoint (.ppt)** as the file format.

PowerPoint Presentations

FirstGov.gov also indexes PowerPoint presentations that have been posted, but they are limited to presentations on government Web sites only.

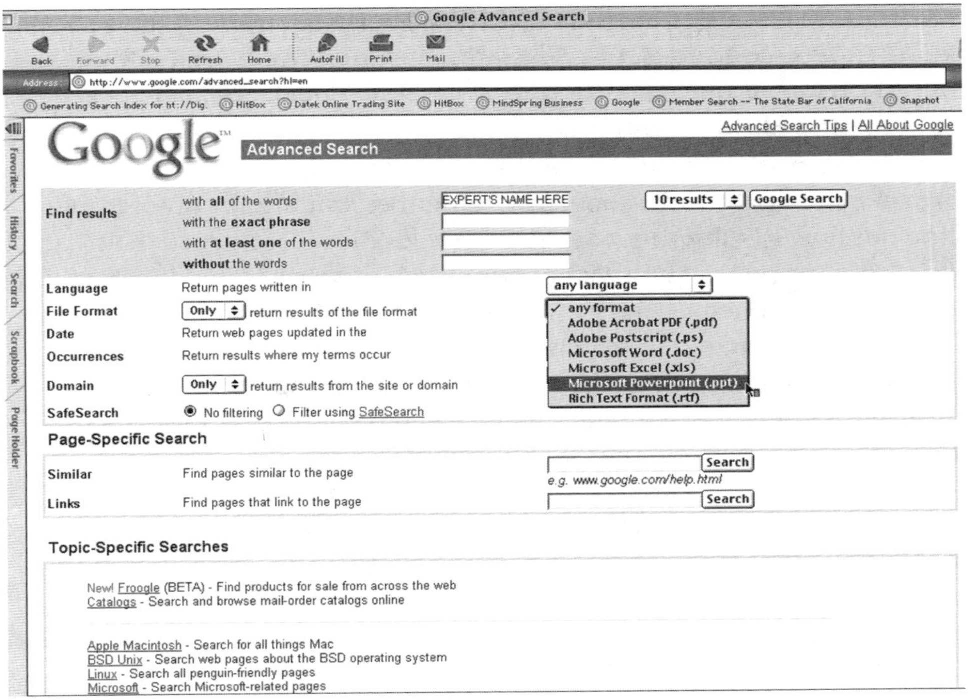

Figure 9-7. Using Google's Advanced Search page, you can limit a search to a PowerPoint presentation by clicking in the file format drop-down menu. Google™ is a trademark of Google Technology Inc.

Checklist Item 6: Join an Online Community to Find Experts' Postings or to Learn About the Topic

As noted in the "Thinking Outside the Box" section found in Chapter 7, "Finding and Backgrounding People," online discussions can take place in a variety of places on the Internet: in Usenet newsgroups, mailing lists, forums, blogs, and message boards. Though very hit and miss, searching through online communities' current discussions and archives can sometimes be excellent tools for identifying and contacting experts. For any topic you can imagine, there is an online community discussing it.

Some online communities require that you subscribe in order to participate, and some limit their subscriptions to those with particular credentials. But many lists have no subscriber limitations at all. Once you locate an appropriate community, the best thing to do is lurk around a bit. In other words, read the postings prior to submitting your own, or simply browse through the archives. In this way, you may come across an expert or another lawyer you wish to correspond with. You can then send private e-mail messages to individuals, rather than letting all subscribers know your intentions. If the community has an archive, search it for your expert's name or the expertise you are seeking (not all archives are keyword searchable, however).

To determine whether an online community in a particular subject area exists, or to find out about any subscriber limitations, or to simply find out how to subscribe, consult a LISTSERV list directory such as Cata-List (**http://www.lsoft.com/lists/listref.html**) or a newsletter directory like the one maintained by Topica (formerly Liszt) (**http://lists.topica.com**). At Topica, you can either search by keywords or browse categories and subcategories to find the right group. Browsing through the category Health & Fitness, we found many subcategories and chose Diseases & Conditions, then Autoimmune & Immune Disorders, and then CFS (Chronic Fatigue Syndrome). Just by reading some of the current posts, we found one that included the name, e-mail address, and mailing address of a staff member of the National CFIDS Foundation, Inc., and a reference to a case involving long-term disability benefits for a plaintiff suffering from chronic fatigue syndrome. It would be easy to contact her for follow-up.

The PSYLAW-L mailing list is a well-trafficked and excellent place to post a request for psychological experts. You can join this group by sending an e-mail message to listserv@unl.edu and by typing "SUBSCRIBE PSYLAW-L" (without quotation marks) into the Message field (not the Subject field). To review some of the archived postings, go to **http://crcvms.unl.edu/htbin/wa?A0=PSYLAW-L** and click on any of the months and years listed.

EXPERT-L is an Internet mailing list for those individuals engaged in expert witness activities associated with litigation. It was inspired by the need for experts to communicate with each other about issues related to the expert witness profession and for networking between experts and lawyers. For example, a search in the archives (where you can search without subscribing) found a request from a lawyer for an "expert in tensile strength and fractile characteristics of cast metal machinery components" (**http://lists.digilogic.com/archives/expert-l.html**). To subscribe, visit **http://lists.digilogic.com/cgi-bin/wa.exe?SUBED1=expert-l&A=1**.

Using Google Groups to Find or Background an Expert

As discussed earlier, Google Groups (**http://groups.google.com**) allows for anonymous searching through over 1 billion postings of the archives of thousands of Usenet newsgroups dating back to 1981. For a thorough discussion on how to use Google Groups, see the "Thinking Outside the Box" section in Chapter 7, "Finding and Backgrounding People." Searching Google Groups by keyword, you may come across an expert who is relevant to the matter at hand. Searching by an expert's name, you may come across a posting made by your own expert or your opponent's expert. This is an excellent way to attempt to undermine the opponent's expert and to evaluate your own expert.

To find the expert's postings, users should conduct a few different types of searches on Google Group's Advanced Groups Search page (**http://groups.google.com/advanced_group_search**). First, search for the expert's name in the **Return only messages where the author is** field. However, keep in mind that some people surf anonymously by using pseudonyms, so you may find nothing.

Second, search for the expert's e-mail address in the **Return only messages where the author is** field. Since many people share the same name, searching by a unique e-mail address will help you verify that you've found the correct person. Because some people have more than one e-mail address, try to discover all of them to conduct a complete search of a person's postings.

The third search method is to search for the expert's name in one of the keyword fields of the Advanced Groups Search page (either in the **with all of the words** field or **with the exact phrase** field). This may

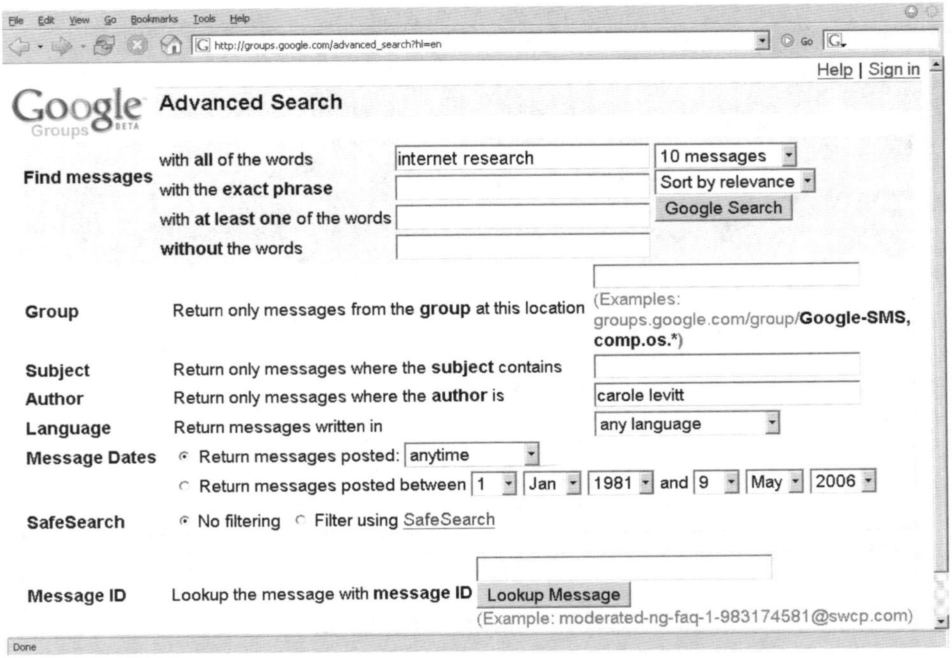

Figure 9-8. Search for the expert's name in the **Return only messages where the author is** field in Google Groups. Google™ is a trademark of Google Technology Inc.

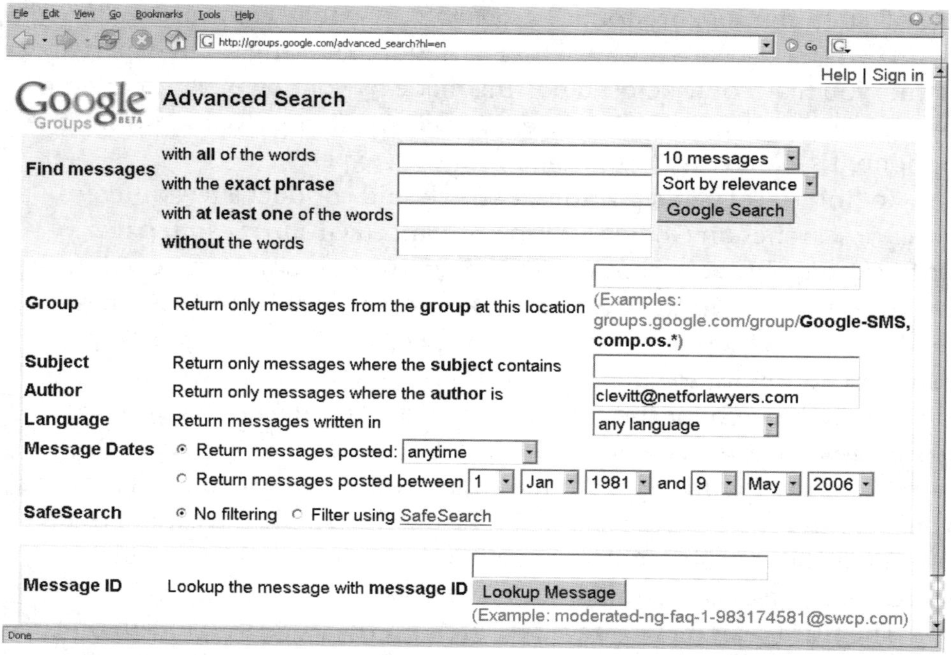

Figure 9-9. Search for the expert's e-mail address in the **Return only messages where the author is** field. Google™ is a trademark of Google Technology Inc.

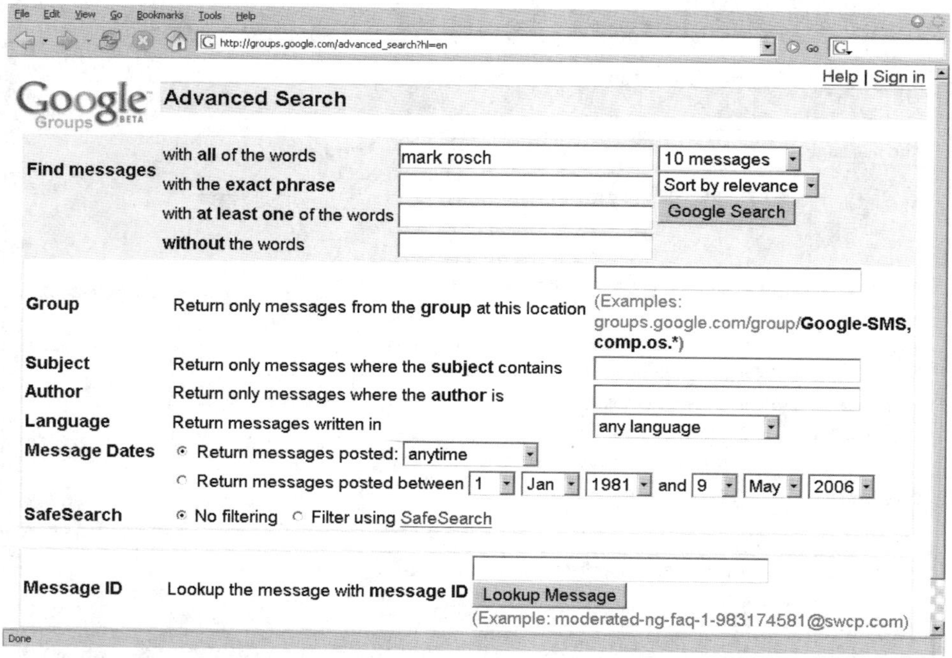

Figure 9-10. Search for the expert's name in one of the keyword fields of the Advanced Search page. Google™ is a trademark of Google Technology Inc.

disclose other people's postings that contain their opinions about the expert.

Fourth, Google Groups can also be used to search by topic to find experts in a certain specialty when you don't already have a name of an expert. For example, if you are representing a client who was seriously injured when the treads of his Firestone tires separated, causing his vehicle to overturn, entering "Firestone tires" into Google Groups as a search phrase might lead you to an expert who has testified in prior tread-separation lawsuits. Also, the same search may identify people who have also been seriously injured when the tire treads on their vehicles separated. They might mention their expert's name or their lawyer's name (which can be a lead for you), or they may express their opinion about the expert.

Checklist Item 7: Review the Expert's Own Web Site

An expert's own Web site should be carefully reviewed prior to retaining him or her. If a search engine did not locate the expert's Web site, try simply entering the expert's name or company name followed by .com (expertname.com). Many experts post their full CV, prior litigation experience, speaking engagements, references, memberships and professional organization affiliations, and articles and newsletters on their Web sites. When reviewing an expert's Web site, keep in mind that opposing counsel can do so as well. Be aware that experts' Web sites are sometimes little more than self-promotion, so tread carefully. Is there anything embarrassing or contradictory on the site? Does the expert pronounce that he or she is "the leader in the industry" or put forth similar bravado that could affect how the jury perceives the expert? Imagine how the jury would react if the pages of the expert's Web site were displayed as exhibits at trial—because they very well could be.

Checklist Item 8: Determine If the Expert Has Ever Been Disciplined

It is also important to determine if an expert has been reviewed or disciplined by their jurisdiction's licensing boards. You may be able to find this discipline information by conducting a free public records search (see Chapter 8, "Accessing Public Records") if this type of information is public record. Although not a free search site, Idex.com has created a searchable database of experts who have been reviewed or disciplined by their jurisdiction's licensing boards (**http://www.idex.com/about/ index.html#discipline**). To access this database, you must be an Idex member and a defense lawyer (or work on behalf of a defense lawyer). It is also worthwhile to check with any voluntary or mandatory membership professional organizations of which the expert is a member to gather this information.

Checklist Item 9: Find Experts via Jury Verdict Reporter Databases

Another way to find experts is by way of jury verdict reporters. While most lawyers search jury verdicts to assess the worth of a case, the astute lawyer knows that jury verdicts are useful in finding experts who testified in specific types of cases. By searching for an expert's name in a jury verdict reporter, you may discover whether the expert has given opposing opinions in similar cases, appears more often as a defense witness, or has usually testified for the winning side. The lawyers involved in the cases are also listed in the jury verdict database. You might consider contacting them for information about their experience with their own expert or the opposition's expert (for example, how the opposition's expert came across during cross-examination). Free online jury verdicts (and settlements) can be found at MoreLaw.com. Lexis and Westlaw offer pay jury verdict databases, as do NASJVP and VerdictSearch.com.

Free Jury Verdict Reporter Databases

MoreLaw.com

http://www.morelaw.com

Purpose: To find experts by way of jury verdict reports.

Content: MoreLaw.com is a free online legal information resource with a jury verdict reports database (where experts can be found), a lawyer directory, and an expert witness database. MoreLaw.com's verdict database has over 25,000 verdicts, all hand selected and summarized by Tulsa, Oklahoma lawyer Kent Morlan, who reviews verdicts by searching Google, legal newspapers, and 125 appellate court Web sites. The database is searchable by keywords describing the expertise involved, by the facts of the case, or by lawyer, expert, or party name.

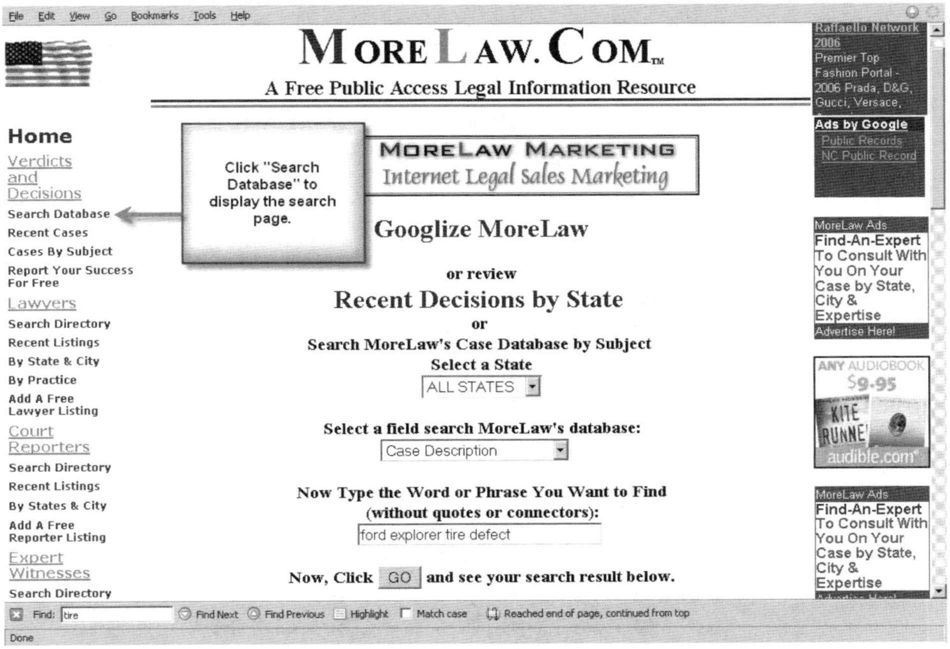

Figure 9-11. To search for verdicts at MoreLaw.com, click on **Search Database** (under "Verdicts & Decisions" in the left-hand column) on the top left side of the site's pages. Click on the **Select Field to Search** drop-down menu, and enter your keywords or a person's name into the search box.

Our View: This might be the only free verdict site you'll find. It's a useful site for searching for experts; you may discover whether the expert has given opposing opinions in similar cases, appears more often as a defense witness, or has usually testified for the winning side. The lawyers involved in the cases are also listed in the verdict database and may provide you with information about their experience with the expert if you contact them directly.

Tip: • We have found experts through MoreLaw.com's jury verdict database who did not list themselves on the expert witness database. Check both.
   • To begin searching verdicts, first click on **Search Database**, (under "Verdicts & Decisions" in the left-hand column) then click on the drop-down menu titled **Select Field to Search**. Select **Case Description** as the field to search if looking for a case similar

to your case and then enter your keywords. If you are looking only for cases where a specific expert served as a plaintiff's expert (or defendant's expert), select the **Plaintiff(s) Expert(s)** or **Defendant(s) Expert(s)** field and enter the expert's name into the search box.

Pay Jury Verdict Reporter Databases

VerdictSearch.com

http://www.verdictsearch.com   **$**

Purpose:	To find verdicts and settlements in order to identify experts.
Content:	VerdictSearch is a product of the *National Law Journal's* Litigation Services Network and its database includes jury verdicts from the VerdictSearch National, VerdictSearch California, VerdictSearch Florida, VerdictSearch Illinois, VerdictSearch New Jersey, VerdictSearch New York, VerdictSearch Pennsylvania, VerdictSearch Texas, and New York Judicial Review of Damages, among other sources.
Our View:	This is a useful service for those who frequently need to find experts and want to read about the cases that the experts were involved in. The cost for an annual subscription is dependent upon the size of the firm, with solo lawyers paying $1,195 and larger firms up to $1,795 (there is a limit of 250 cases e-mailed and/or viewed within any 24-hour period). A 24-hour subscription for $195 has a limit of 100 cases e-mailed and/or viewed within the 24-hour period. A free limited subscription is also available.
Tip:	Instead of subscribing to VerdictSearch, the occasional user might try searching the expert or expertise at the ALM Expert Directory site (**http://www.almexperts.com**). Then, from the NLJ Expert Directory, a user can link to that expert's list of cases at VerdictSearch and purchase a single verdict for $9.95. (See the above section, "Free

Expert Witness Directories," for more information about NLJ).

National Association of State Jury Verdict Publishers (NASJVP)

http://www.juryverdicts.com **$**

Purpose:	To find experts via jury verdict or case testified.
Content:	The NASJVP site offers an alphabetical listing of 40,000 experts. It includes their expertise and the name of the jury verdict publication where they are referenced.
Our View:	Although users can search free at NASJVP, after clicking on the expert's name, they are simply referred to the third-party company that has published the verdict related to that expert (e.g., VerdictSearch) where the user can obtain detailed information about the verdict, for a fee.
Tip:	If you don't have the luxury of time, you'll probably be better off using one of the pay databases where the verdicts are readily available online and full text.

Checklist Item 10: Find the Expert's Deposition Testimony

Reading an expert's deposition testimony can provide an abundance of information about how the expert may perform. Currently there is no free, centralized database for expert witness transcripts, but there are several commercial sites and professional association sites that gather this information for members.

Deposition Testimony Databases

TrialSmith

http://www.trialsmith.com (formerly known as DepoConnect) **$**

Purpose: For plaintiff lawyers only—to find expert's deposition testimony to determine possible performance.

Content: TrialSmith is an online database with more than 277,000 depositions, and other documents that include briefs, pleadings, seminar papers, verdicts, and settlements. It also includes an expert witness database and e-mail discussion lists where lawyers discuss and recommend experts.

Our View: If you're a member of one of the dozens of "partner" trial lawyers associations to which TrialSmith offers free "Basic" memberships, there's no reason not to sign up. (Free members pay $49 per document to print or save a transcript.) Even the paid annual subscription beginning at $299 per year and $30 per transcript seems reasonable. Lawyers may find the private discussion groups useful for sharing information about experts.

Tip: Paid subscribers can instantly view or download any transcript.

While TrialSmith is for the plaintiff's bar, the Defense Research Institute (DRI) site, as its name implies, is only for defense lawyers who are DRI members. Also for defense lawyers is Idex (www.Idex.com). Idex has built its database of deposition transcripts (and trial testimony by experts) by submissions from its own members. Electronic versions of some documents can be viewed and downloaded directly from this site at a reduced price. According to its Web site, 6,000 records are added each month to Idex's database of over 900,000 records of expert involvement.

ATLA

Also see the **Exchange** section of the Association of Trial Lawyers of America (ATLA) site at **http://www.atla.org**, which makes available to its members a database of over 10,000 expert witnesses, and over 15,000 searchable transcripts. This database is developed by submission from its members. ATLA posts the contact information for the member who provided information about that expert.

Defense Research Institute (DRI)

http://www.dri.org **$**

Purpose: To find expert's deposition testimony to determine possible performance.

Content: DRI offers a searchable database to the complete text of expert witness testimony from trial courts around the country (and briefs, pleadings, motions, affidavits, orders, verdicts, judgments, and jury instructions). The DRI Expert Witness Database includes over 65,000 plaintiff and defense experts and CVs for selected experts.

Our View: The annual subscription of $195 per year seems quite reasonable, even when compared to the free "Basic" membership at TrialSmith, because all documents downloaded or requested via e-mail are free to DRI members. Only documents requested in either CD-ROM or hard copy format are charged a per document handling fee. (Contact DRI for further details.)

Tip: The DRI has other member benefits, such as a magazine, a newsletter, and seminars.

Checklist Item 11: Find Briefs and Cases That Refer to the Expert

Briefs

Experts may also be referred to in briefs. All types of briefs can be found at Brief Reporter (**http://www.briefreports.com**). Searching (by keywords) is free and so is viewing an abstract of the brief (which includes the case name, court, docket number, and/or citation). A search for "tires" resulted in seventy-five briefs. Subscribers who pay a $35-per-month access fee can download documents for $10 each. Nonsubscribers can download briefs for $40 per brief.

BriefServe.com has searchable briefs from 117,220 cases from all United States Courts of Appeals from 1981 to the present, the U.S. Supreme Court from 1984 to the present, New York appellate courts, and

California Supreme Court and appellate courts (**http://www.briefserve .com/home.asp**). Pennsylvania state court briefs are promised soon. Briefs are searchable by party name or docket number and cost $25 to download, with a two brief minimum (abstracts are viewable for free). Briefs for some courts are free at other sites (such as U.S. Supreme Court briefs at FindLaw), but they are not keyword searchable. You must search by year and party name.

Ask a Lawyer for Help

An alternative to joining one of these associations in order to search their deposition transcripts would be to contact lawyers directly to see if they will supply you with transcripts of the experts. You would either have to know of a case similar to yours to do this (which you might through your case law or jury verdict research), or you might find that the experts themselves have listed, on their Web sites, the names of the lawyers with whom they have worked in the past. Of course, you can simply ask the expert for a list of lawyer references and case names. Most lawyers keep their own expert witness transcripts, and would be willing to share (provided, of course, the favor is returned some day).

Case Law

An expert's name may also appear in a reported opinion. Fortunately, many reported opinions can be searched for free (see LexisOne at **http://www.lexisone.com** or FindLaw at **http://www.findlaw.com**). To conduct retrospective or nationwide searches, you'll usually need to use a pay database such as major players Lexis or Westlaw (which both also have a variety of other tools for finding experts, including expert witness directories and jury verdicts), or some of the newer case law sites such as LoisLaw or VersusLaw. Searching for experts in reported decisions is similar to the technique used in a general search-engine search for experts as noted above. To find cases using a known expert's name, type in the name alone; if their name is common, add keywords that describe the expertise. If trying to locate an expert in a specific area of expertise, type the word "expert" along with the expertise sought, using relevant keywords.

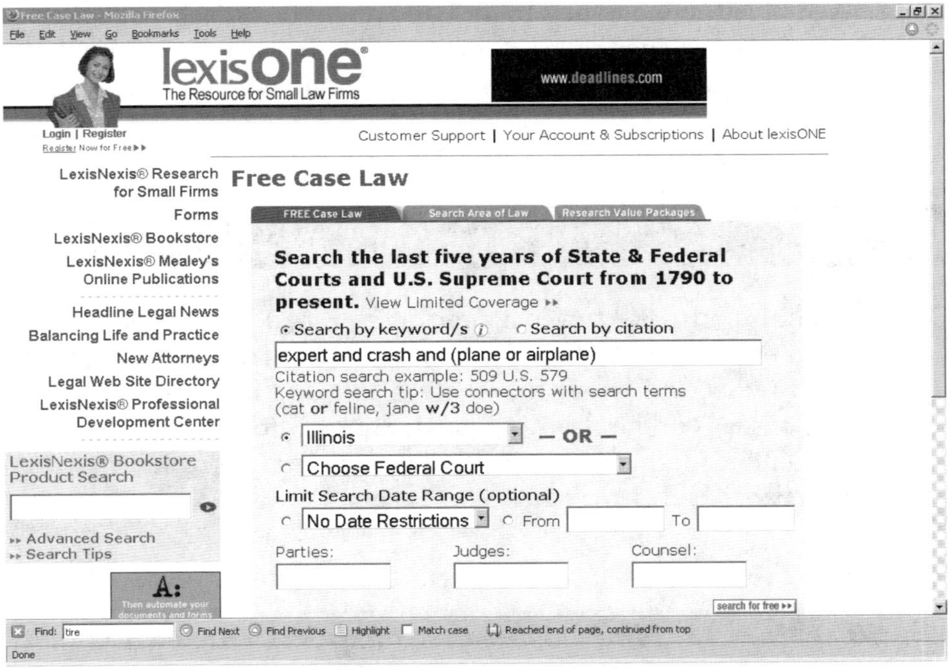

![Screenshot of the lexisONE Free Case Law web page in Mozilla Firefox. The page header shows the lexisONE logo with "The Resource for Small Law Firms" and a banner for www.deadlines.com. The left sidebar lists: LexisNexis® Research for Small Firms, Forms, LexisNexis® Bookstore, LexisNexis® Mealey's Online Publications, Headline Legal News, Balancing Life and Practice, New Attorneys, Legal Web Site Directory, LexisNexis® Professional Development Center, LexisNexis® Bookstore Product Search, Advanced Search, Search Tips. The main area shows "Free Case Law" with tabs FREE Case Law, Search Area of Law, Research Value Packages, and a search form "Search the last five years of State & Federal Courts and U.S. Supreme Court from 1790 to present." with a keyword search box containing "expert and crash and (plane or airplane)".]

Figure 9-12. Type the word "expert" along with the expertise sought using relevant keywords that describe the expertise (e.g., plane crash). Reprinted with permission of LexisNexis.

Checklist Item 12: Locate Academic Experts Through University Sites

If you plan to hire or depose experts who happen to be professors, go to the university's Web site for a look at their CV, courses they've taught, and articles or books they have published. Links to college and university home pages can be found at the American Universities site, described below.

American Universities

http://www.clas.ufl.edu/CLAS/american-universities.html

Purpose: To locate for academic experts who are teaching in universities and colleges.

Content: The site provides an alphabetical list of links to Web sites of universities and colleges in the Unites States.

Our View: Having to link to individual schools college by college, and then search for faculty who may make good experts at each one can be time consuming.

Tip: Start out with institutions nearby.

USC Experts

USC Experts Directory is a directory provided by the University of Southern California of over a thousand USC scientists, scholars, administrators, and physicians who are able and willing to comment on issues in the news. Although primarily for the media, this could be another avenue to find academic experts. See **http://www.usc.edu/uscnews/experts/**.

Checklist Item 13: Find Government Experts Through Government Reports

Former government employees may make good experts and so may nongovernment experts who have testified before a Senate or House committee hearing, or have been quoted in a Senate or House report. Current government employees may be able to answer your questions or point you to a former government expert. But, it can take time to cut through the layers of government to find the right person. If you persevere, you're likely to be rewarded with someone who understands exactly what you're talking about. A good starting place to locate potential experts is at a government agency's Web site because it often includes personnel directories. To find a specific state government agency's Web site, see State and Local Government on the Net (**http://www.statelocalgov.net**). To browse through an alphabetical list of all federal agencies, a visit to FirstGov.gov is in order (**http://www.firstgov.gov/Agencies/Federal/All_Agencies/index.shtml**).

FirstGov.gov can also be searched using keywords to locate testifying experts by name or by the specialty you are interested in (**http://www.firstgov.gov**). FirstGov.gov indexes millions of Web pages from federal and state governments, the District of Columbia, and U.S. territories. Most of these pages are not be available on any commercial Web site.

To search House and Senate committee reports, full text back to 1995, use Thomas (**http://thomas.loc.gov/home/thomas.html**). At the state level, the legislative history of a bill may include references to government and nongovernment experts. Use FindLaw (**http://www.findlaw .com/casecode/#statelaw**) to link to any state's legislative information.

Here is an example of how we found experts by searching California legislative history. We searched the bills for the keywords "seat belt and school bus and safety and children." This led to a 1999 bill requiring that seat belts be installed in school buses by 2002 (**http://www.leg info.ca.gov/bilinfo.html**). The Analyses (California's equivalent of legislative history) section of the bill listed several committee reports. We reviewed the Senate committee report from July 12, 1999 and its staff comments and learned that "this bill is the latest in a series of efforts . . . [that] have been largely unsuccessful . . . [A] study to determine the appropriateness of requiring lap belts . . . determined that the existing research . . . weigh(ed) *against* new lap belt policies for . . . school buses." Listed in these staff comments were specific references to several studies, the names of associations in opposition to the bill, the name of the chair of the committee, and the name of the consultant for the study. Contacting any of these people or groups could be fruitful in finding an expert to testify that requiring lap belts in school buses is unsafe.

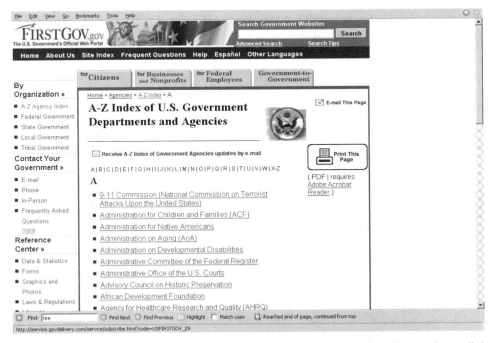

Figure 9-13. Browse through FirstGov.gov's alphabetical list of agencies to link to one that deals with the subject area for which you are seeking an expert.

Checklist Item 14: Use Pay Referral Sites

If you haven't had luck finding the appropriate expert with any of the above sources (or if you want someone else to do the legwork for you), consult a referral site.

The California-based ForensisGroup (**http://www.forensisgroup .com**) provides referrals to 500 technical, engineering, medical, scientific, and environmental experts. While you can view short blurbs about selected experts (by clicking on **Expert Profiles**), you'll need to contact this referral company to retain that expert or to learn of other experts in that field.

For referrals to medical experts who will review a case or testify in all types of health-care related malpractice, personal injury, and other tort litigation cases (and criminal law), go to medQuest (**http://www.med questltd.com**). It provides referrals to testifying medical experts (physicians, dentists, osteopaths, podiatrists, chiropractors, optometrists, nurses, pharmacists, therapists, and others) in every region of the country. There are no profiles for you to preview as there are at ForensisGroup.

TASA (**http://www.tasanet.com**), a site with more than 10,000 areas of expertise represented, is one of the best known of the expert witness referral companies. When you search TASA's online Directory of Expertise you are offered many categories to choose from, plus subcategories. Once you make your selection, the number of experts in the selected field and their geographic locations are shown. Users are then required to call or e-mail TASA for the experts' names and contact information. If an expert is engaged, there is a one-time (per-case) $125 fee payable to TASA (in addition to the expert's fee).

*CHAPTER***TEN**

Company Research

Company research is one of the subjects that ought to be taught in law school. There are endless bits of information that lawyers need to know about companies in order to serve clients. Understanding what information is available and how to access it efficiently can make all the difference, whether you're bringing suit, seeking to help your client acquire a company, or representing shareholders. Competitive Intelligence, a close relative of company research, is another subject they should teach in law school. (See Chapter 11, "Competitive Intelligence Research," for more information.)

Company research can help both litigators and transactional lawyers. For example, in a litigation matter, where your client has been injured by an improperly designed garage door, you need to do company research to learn more about the manufacturer of the door and any other company that was involved in its design, distribution, or installation in order to answer the following questions:

- Who is the proper defendant: the manufacturer, the installer, the retailer, or all of them?
- Is your target the manufacturer who is identified on the product (the door)?
- Is the manufacturer the parent corporation, or merely a subsidiary?
- Where is the company headquarters? In Delaware or the UK?
- Who's the registered agent for service of process?

You also need to learn more about the product, so you continue on with your company research by visiting the manufacturer's Web site or even competitors' sites to find out:

- If the specs for the door are listed on any of the Web sites so you (or your expert) can:
  1. Compare their designs
  2. Ascertain whether they were manufactured in a like or different manner
- If there are any claims, warranties, or admissions on the company site

Transactional lawyers, such as counsel to shareholder groups or a business lawyer counseling a client who is seeking to acquire a business, may use company research to:

- Access corporate press releases
- Locate all of the target's recent Securities and Exchange Commission (SEC) filings
- Locate corporate annual reports
- Locate sales figures
- Conduct general due diligence

The Internet can help with all these tasks.

Financial Information

Company research often involves finance, another topic not always taught in law school. Getting up to speed on financial and business terms can be accomplished rather quickly by finding just the right Web site. Investorwords.com and Professor Campbell R. Harvey's Hypertextual Finance Glossary, detailed below, are just those sort of sites.

InvestorWords.com

http://www.investorwords.com/

Purpose:	To define company-related financial and investment terms.
Content:	InvestorWords.com is a glossary of 6,000 definitions, with new terms added frequently. The site also claims to include more than 20,000 links between related words and terms listed by subject. Terms are retrievable by

entering the word or phrase you wish to define into the **Search for a Term** box on the home page and clicking the **Search** button. You can also browse the entire word list by selecting the letter with which your term begins from the **Browse by Letter** list.

Tip: If you're looking to improve your business vocabulary, you can sign up for the site's free "Term of the Day" newsletter that delivers a new term and definition to your e-mail inbox each day.

Professor Campbell R. Harvey's Hypertextual Finance Glossary

http://www.duke.edu/~charvey/Classes/wpg/glossary.htm

Purpose: To define common and obscure business terms.

Content: Campbell R. Harvey, a professor of international business at Duke's Fuqua School of Business, has compiled a list of more than 8,000 entries covering common and obscure business terms and acronyms. Definitions are arranged in a traditional dictionary fashion, with links to take you to terms, acronyms, etc., that begin with each letter of the alphabet.

Our View: Even though the clickable links to each letter of the alphabet are easy enough to use, a keyword search would make the glossary even easier to use. This list is more inclusive than Harvey's 2,500 entry glossary maintained by the *New York Times*.

Checklist for Finding Company Information

- ❑ 1. Locate the company's Web site by finding its URL.
- ❑ 2. Review the company's Web site to discover the company structure, to find specifications for its products, and so on.
- ❑ 3. Google the company using both the Google search engine and Google Groups.

❑   4.   Use company directories (covering public and private companies) for third-party opinions.

❑   5.   Use Web-based phone directories to locate the company.

❑   6.   Use product directories to learn about the company and its products.

❑   7.   Locate public-company financial information, such as SEC filings, annual reports, stock prices, and set up SEC-related E-alerts.

❑   8.   Order credit reports over the Internet for both public and private companies.

❑   9.   Search for current and archived news about the company, its executives, and products, and set up news E-alerts.

❑ 10.   Review secretary of state records and county business records to find registered agents and fictitious business names.

❑ 11.   Consider using pay databases to find information about the company.

❑ 12.   Find reported decisions, dockets, verdicts, and settlements involving the company, its executives, and products.

❑ 13.   Ascertain which federal or state agencies regulate the company's products or industry. Search government Web sites for any mention of the company or products, especially product recalls.

❑ 14.   Think outside the box. (See Chapter 11, "Competitive Intelligence Research;" Chapter 7, "Finding and Backgrounding People;" and Chapter 8, "Accessing Public Records.")

Checklist Item 1: Locate the Web Site's URL

If you do not know the company's URL and have not been able to guess it by adding .com to the company name (such as Nike.com), there are many ways to find a public or private company's URL. For instance, to find a company's URL you can enter a company's name into a company directory Web site such as Hoover's (see below). Often the URL will be noted in the directory's company profile.

You can also type the company name into any search engine (such as Yahoo! or Google—see below). If you search a company name using Google or Yahoo!, typically the company's Web site will often be the first one in their results list.

Checklist Item 2: Review the Company's Web Site

Company Web sites are often the simplest starting points for company research. Company Web sites often begin where a company's printed literature leaves off. Companies may take the printed literature and transform it into an expanded electronic dossier, offering more insight into products and activities. Thus, locating a company's Web site should be the first step you take to learn about the company. By using a company's own site, you'll be able to obtain information that you would normally have to spend hours compiling from other sources. Company sites may provide their SEC filings, press releases, background information about company executives, other financial information (annual reports, stock quotes and history), and even some information not available anywhere else on the Internet (such as job openings and salaries). Some of this information will only be found if the company is public (such as SEC filings). After discovering what the company has to say about itself, you can then search the Internet for outside information about the company in order to compare the data and draw your own conclusions.

Figure 10-1. Some companies' Web sites include detailed information regarding their stock. Reproduced with permission of Yahoo! Inc. © 2006 by Yahoo! Inc. YAHOO! and the YAHOO! logo are trademarks of Yahoo! Inc.

Checklist Item 3: Google the Company

Enter the company name into the search box on Google's home page and click on the **I'm Feeling Lucky** or **Google Search** buttons. This will usually bring up the company's Web site. Also run the company name, executives' names, and product names through

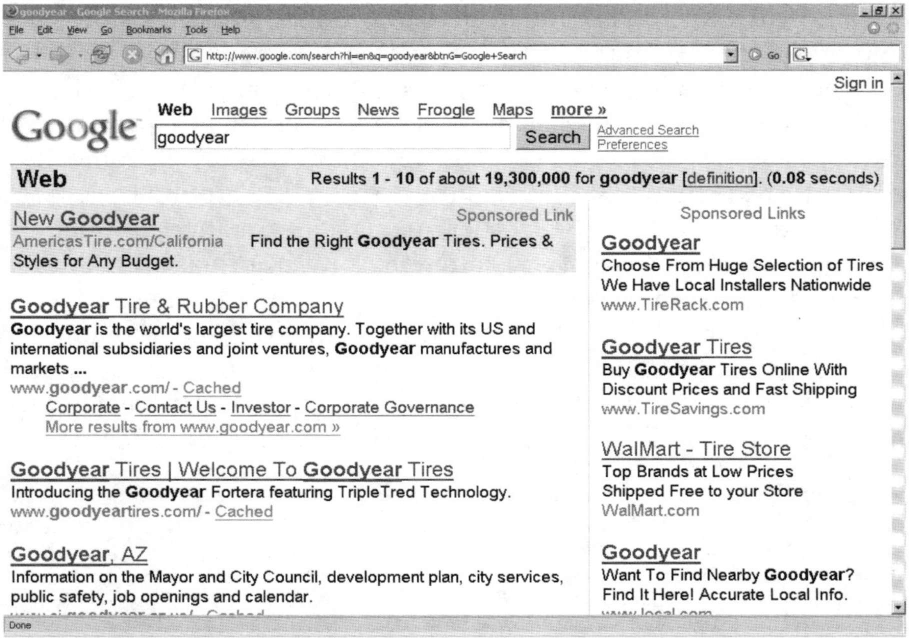

Figure 10-2. If you search a company name using Google.com, typically the company's Web site will often be the first one in the results list. Google™ is a trademark of Google Technology Inc.

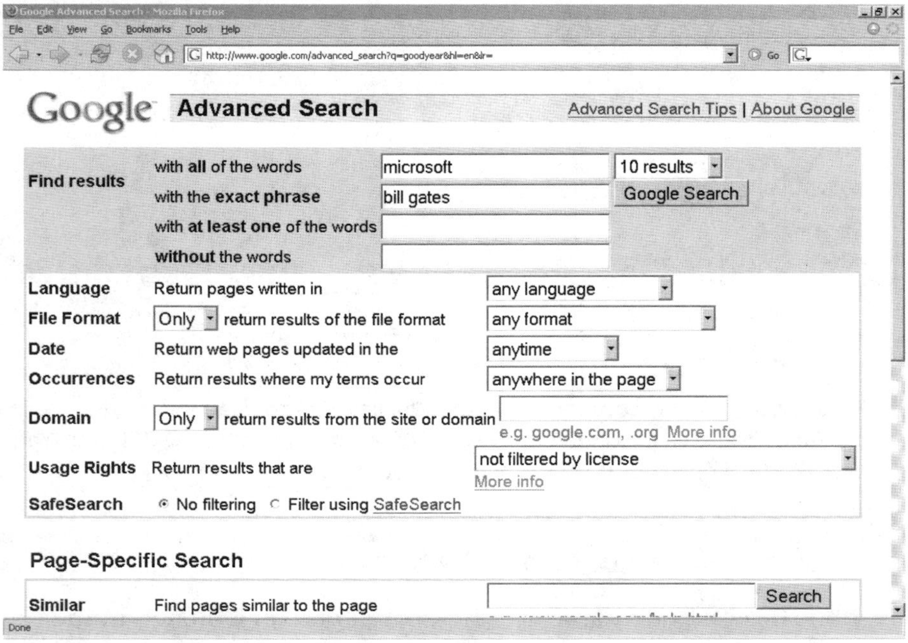

Figure 10-3. Using the Google Advanced Search page, enter both an executive's name and the company's name to search for extra nuggets of information. Google™ is a trademark of Google Technology Inc.

Google.com (**http://www.google.com**) and Google Groups (**http://groups.google.com**) just to see if you come up with any interesting nuggets of information.

For more details on Googling and searching for information in on-line communities, see the "Thinking Outside the Box" section in Chapter 7, "Finding and Backgrounding People."

Checklist Item 4: Use Company Directories

An important distinction to make when setting out to conduct company research is whether the target of your search is public (meaning shares in the company are traded on a public exchange) or private (meaning that shares of the company are not publicly traded). There's significantly more credible information available about public companies than private. Public companies are regulated by the SEC, and are therefore required to make certain public filings, many of which are easily retrievable on the Internet for free via the EDGAR database (discussed later in this chapter—see **http://www.sec.gov/cgi-bin/srch-edgar**).

Even if you know a company is public, rather than going directly to the company's public SEC filings, we suggest going first to a company directory site for a more objective look at the company. And, if you don't know whether a company is public or private, these directory sites usually indicate that. (More public companies than private companies appear in these company directory sites.)

Company directory sites compile background information about companies from many sources to create a profile that gives an overview of the company. These sites also link you to secondary sources about the company (such as news articles, stock quotes, and research analyst reports), in addition to linking you to the company's Web site and its SEC filings. If you're searching for a company's address, but you're uncertain how to spell the company name, there are Internet directories that enable you to search based on the type of industry and the state where the company is headquartered. If you are trying to ascertain name availability, such directories can also be used to quickly determine whether your client's proposed company name is in use anywhere in the country. Some of the company directory sites are free, and some are partially free (basic information is free, but there is a fee for detailed information). Those that charge a fee do so by subscription or on a pay-as-you-go model (or both).

The following are examples of some excellent company directory sites. Some include only public companies and some include both public and private. See also the later section, Checklist Item 8, "Private Company Directories." While known primarily for their private company data, some Private Company Directories also include public companies.

Public Company Directories

Yahoo! Finance Company and Fund Index

http://biz.yahoo.com/i 🚫$

Purpose: To find public-company background and financial information.

Content: Search 35,403 companies and funds by name or browse an alphabetical list. Your results offer you links to news, message boards, insider trading, stock quotes, and for 9,000 public companies out of the list of 35,403 companies and funds, a profile. The profile is provided by Capital IQ. It lists the following information: contact information; business summaries; employee information and officer information (including key executives' pay); sector and industry classifications; business and earnings announcement summaries; and financial statistics and ratios. There are also links to the company home page, stock price, and SEC filings.

Yahoo!'s company profile database also has a corporate governance rating system, called the Corporate Governance Quotient (CGQ®), which is provided by the company Institutional Shareholder Services (ISS). ISS rates over 7,500 worldwide companies to evaluate the corporate governance practices and board of directors of companies—an important indicator in this post-Enron era.

We ran a company profile for Yahoo! and learned that its CGQ is better than 40.5 percent of companies in its index group (S&P 500 companies), and better than 92.4 percent of industries in its S&P peer group (Software & Services companies). We then ran a company profile on Yahoo!'s main competitor, Google, and learned that its CGQ is better than 6.8 percent in its index group (Russell 3000 companies) and better than 15.6 percent of industries in its S & P peer group (Software & Services companies).

Our View: This is an easy-to-use site chock-full of information.

Tip: If you click on **SEC** from the profile, you will only be shown recent filings. If you click on **Full Filings at EDGAR Online**, you will find yourself at a pay site offering you a two-week trial. Instead of using the pay site, try one of the free EDGAR sites discussed later in this chapter.

Public and Private Company Directories

Hoover's Online (a subsidiary of D & B since 2003)

http://www.hoovers.com

Purpose: To find private and public company information and to link to their sites.

Content: The database contains 12 million companies, with in-depth coverage of 40,000 of them. To search, enter a word or name into the search box and then select one of the following options: Company Name, Ticker, Industry Keyword, Executive Name, News/Press Releases, or Reports. On the search results page, you will find a very brief "Overview" about the company with the following free information: the company's address, phone number, fax number, and a link to the company's Web site. As you scroll down the page, the following is displayed: key numbers (sales, growth, company type [private or public], number of employees, and so on); key people (names only—you must be a subscriber for biographies and for more people); rankings; and names of a few top competitors and subsidiaries or affiliates (for complete lists, you must be a subscriber). On the left side of the Overview page, you can click on the **News** link to find links to very current news (for free) about the company from various sources. There is also a link to the company's press releases. The **Industry Watch** link provides free video interviews with expert analysts and business leaders in the industry. Most of the other links bring you to a subscriber page. If you scroll down the page, there are links to **Related Products From Our Trusted Partners** (pay databases where you can buy information on an ad-hoc basis with a credit card). One can also browse a company index at Hoover's.

Our View: When Hoover's became a subsidiary of D & B, the amount of free information was reduced. The "Overview" became much shorter. However, it is a useful site for those who need basic company information and those who only occasionally need detailed information and are willing to pay for it. We can't comment on how it compares price-wise to other sites that have like information because subscriber rates are not posted; you must make an individual inquiry. Pricing depends upon the number of users and the plan chosen—the Pro Premium, Pro Plus, and Pro Subscribers plans. Subscribers also have access to the "Boneyard" (see below).

Tip: • A paid subscription to Hoover's is useful for gathering competitive intelligence (see Chapter 11, "Competitive Intelligence Research"), because in addition to the detailed company and financial information, it offers e-mail alerts and the ability to search extensive databases and create custom reports and lists.
     • Hoover's also sponsors IPO-Central; some information is free and some is restricted to subscribers only (**http://www.hoovers.com/global/ipoc/index.xhtml**).

Historical Company Information

Hoover's Boneyard

**http://www.hoovers.com/free/burn.xhtml?dest=%2
Ffree%2Fco/boneyard%2Fdir.xhtml**

Purpose: To locate information about companies that have merged, been acquired, or are no longer actively covered by industry experts.

Figure 10-4. Enter a word or name into the search box and then select one of the following options: CompanyName/Ticker, Industry Keyword, Executive Name, News/Press Releases, or Reports.

Content: Hoover's Business Boneyard contains historical information about more than 2,000 companies that are no longer actively covered by Hoover's. This historical data is available only to Pro Premium, Pro Plus, and Pro Subscribers. Data available for those companies include: History, Key People, Key Numbers, Location and Subsidiaries, Products/Operations, and Competitors. To get information from the Boneyard, users browse an alphabetical directory, clicking on a company's name. Subscription prices vary depending on the level and volume of access, number of users on an account, among other criteria.

Our View: Hoover's Boneyard is a good way to gain historic perspective into businesses that are no longer active and their industries. The ability to analyze company records, whether they are merger, acquisition or closure contents, gives you an edge in your own business dealings.

Public Company Directories for U.S. and Foreign Companies

Corporate Information
(merged with Wright Research Center)

http://www.corporateinformation.com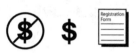

Purpose: To search for information on public companies, both U.S. and foreign.

Content: This site has created 31,000 private and public company reports and its search engine links to 350,000 public company profiles found at other sites. There is a search box in the top left corner of the site for searching by company name or ticker symbol. The results either provide a free Company Snapshot from the 31,000 reports created by Corporate Information (with links to purchase reports) or the results display a free Company Profile found at other sites (without links to pay reports). Information found in the Profiles varies, but the Company Snapshot information is consistent for each of the 31,000 companies. It includes a brief description about the company and shows its: ticker symbol; exchange; annual sales; currency; fiscal year end; share type; country; major industry; sub industry; number of employees; market capitalization; total shares outstanding and number of closely held shares. The pay reports, for those needing more detailed information, can be purchased for $24.95 or $39.95 (or a monthly subscription is offered for $59.95). No information is shown for the annual subscription pricing, but there are three levels (corporate, individual, and student).

     There are also more search boxes down the middle of the page that allow you to search the 31,000 reports by country, state, or industry. The first search box down the middle, however, allows you to search the Web for the other 350,000 companies.

Our View: The site is confusing because it fails to make clear the difference between reports for the 31,000 companies and profiles for the 350,000 companies. We do like the fact that it shows samples for the various pay reports and that registration is no longer required to access the free data.

Tip: For those viewing a Company Profile, use the Currency Converter to convert a company's financials into any currency, such as U.S. dollars, into Columbian pesos, or vice versa, so you will be able to evaluate the company's financials in any currency you prefer.

High-Tech Company Directories

CorpTech.com

http://www.corptech.com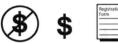

Purpose: To find and obtain information about United States and foreign private and public companies and also government labs and non-profits that manufacture, develop, or provide services related to high-tech items.

Content: Those who registered as guest members used to be able to search over 95,000 companies by company name or ticker symbol and view a capsule profile of that company for free. This free guest membership is no longer offered. Instead, a one-day trial subscription is offered and then, should one decide to subscribe, be prepared to pay $500 per month or $5,500 annually for the Unlimited Gold package. The subscription includes: a 2-user license; unlimited downloading from the Web and a print directory. Additional users are assessed $175 monthly. The Silver package pricing is $300 per month or $3,300 annually and includes: 40,000 downloads from the Web; a print directory; and a 2-user license. Additional users are assessed $100 monthly. The paid subscription provides an extended profile of the company that includes company name, address, telephone, fax, home page, ownership, year formed, sales revenue, employees, primary industry, CEO name and background, and names of other executives and their backgrounds. Subscribers are offered the ability to query the database by thirty search criteria, such as SIC code, number of employees, revenue, state, ZIP code, product line, and so on.

Our View: Unless your clients are in the high-tech arena, you might find the subscription fee too steep.

Tip: • This is useful for client development since you can create all types of reports based upon any of the thirty criteria you select.
• Check your local library's remote access databases (see the section "Free Internet Access to Library Databases and Catalogs" in Chapter 5, "General Factual

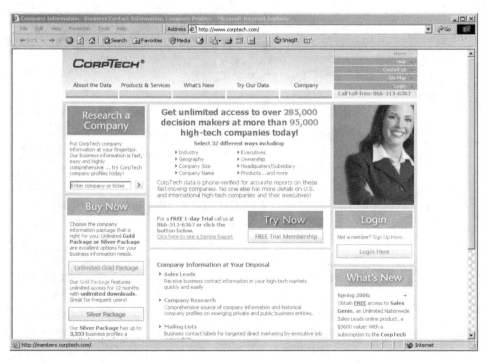

Figure 10-5. Use CorpTech to search over 95,000 companies related to the high-tech industry and view company profiles.

Research"), because your library may offer free access to a database with similar information (such as Gale Business Resources or REF USA).

Checklist Item 5: Use Web-Based Phone Directories

Another type of directory that shouldn't be overlooked is the Web-based phone directories, both White Pages and Yellow Pages. (See Chapter 7, "Finding and Backgrounding People," for more information.) While the existence of a company with the same name your client plans to use for a new venture or product does not necessarily bar its use, a quick, free Internet search through Web-based phone directories may give you enough information to decide if an expensive trademark or trade name search is in order. Such directories also allow you to search at your own pace through the nation's business phone books, a luxury previously available only to those willing to spend time in the rare library that keeps current phone books for the nation, or those willing to pay the cost of a national phone book directory on CD-ROM.

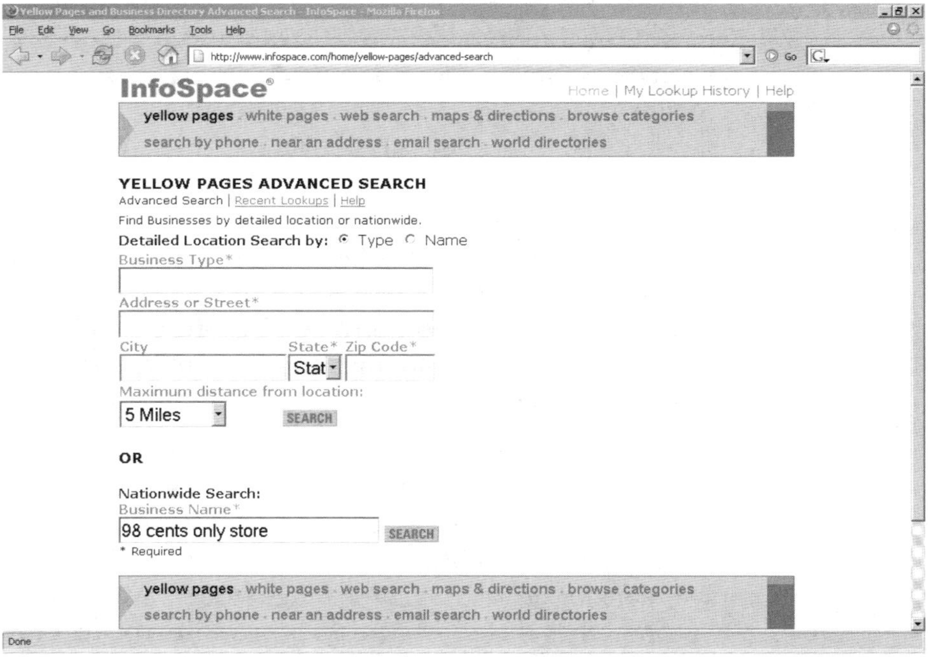

Figure 10-6. If you are uncertain where a specific business is located, use Infospace's Yellow Pages Advanced Search to search nationwide by business name. You can also search by type of business (e.g., restaurant) in a geographic area, if you don't have a specific business name in mind.

Checklist Item 6: Use Product Directories

A products liability lawyer who needs to find out who manufactured a product that injured a client or who needs to find an expert witness about a certain product would be advised to search ThomasNet (formerly the Thomas Register) by product name to find a list of companies that manufacture that product.

Product Directories

ThomasNet

http://www.thomasnet.com/

Purpose:	To retrieve United States and foreign company profiles and contact information, by searching not only by a known company name, but also by product name, service name, or brand name.
Content:	**Search:** The search is conducted by first clicking on tabs at the top of the screen labeled **Product/Service**, **Company Name**, **Brand**, or **Industrial Web** (to obtain information from industrial supplier Web sites, product catalogs, and CAD drawings). Then, one enters keywords into the search box and uses the pull-down menu labeled **Provinces/States** to select **All States (U.S.)/Provinces (Canada)** or to choose an individual State or Province. Registration (free) is not required but is recommended to those who want to store search results, contact multiple companies, or create customized news feeds.
	Browse the Directory: For those who prefer browsing rather than entering keywords into a search box, there is a directory, located in the middle half of the home page, which lists 17 broad categories that are available for browsing. These range from a wide variety of topics that include **Adhesives & Sealants**, **Chemicals**, **Materials Handling**, **Plastics & Rubber**, to **Other** (with more in-depth topics listed beneath each of the 17 categories).

Our View: One of the best improvements recently made to the site is the addition of an international section—the Thomas Global Register (see below). The earlier rendition of the site focused only on U.S. and Canadian companies. We also like the **Modify Results** feature on the left side of the results page, which allows you to narrow your search results to a ZIP code, a company type (e.g., manufacturer, distributor), or ownership (e.g., woman-owned or minority-owned), to name a few.

Tip: **Additional Resources:** Do not overlook the **Additional Resources** found on the bottom of the ThomasNet home page, with such offerings as **Thomas Global Register**, **Product News**, **Business Service Center**, and **Manufacturers Directory**. The Thomas Global Register is a directory of 700,000 distributors and manufacturers from 28 countries and is classified by 11,000 service and product categories. Its purpose is to bring sellers and buyers together to facilitate the purchasing process by offering detailed product and company information. This global arm of the company can search in 11 different languages, including Japanese (traditional and simplified Chinese to be added soon).

Product News offers access to current industrial product news releases on various issues.

The **Business Service Center** gives ThomasNet users special offers on many business-related fields such as financing options, discounts for books (we saw a Barnes and Noble ad), competitive quotes on dental and medical benefits, freight services, etc.

The **Manufacturers Directory** is an alphabetical list of industrial suppliers, products, and services available for browsing on ThomasNet.

Another site for searching 600,000 European companies by company name, product, or service, is Europages (**http://www.europages.net**). You can limit the search to a specific country or to a region within the country. Though not as detailed as Thomas, it provides contact information, including an e-mail address and map, and sometimes a link to a Web site.

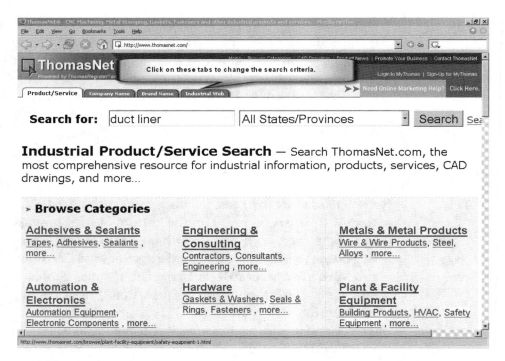

Figure 10-7. Use ThomasNet to search by Product/Service, Company Name, Brand Name, or Industrial Web.

Checklist Item 7: Locate Public-Company Financial Information and Set Up SEC E-alerts

SEC Filings

As of May 6, 1996, all domestic public companies, with some exceptions, were required to make their SEC filings on the SEC's EDGAR (Electronic Data Gathering and Retrieval) site. Because the requirement to file electronically was on a rolling schedule, beginning in 1994, only some companies' files on EDGAR go back that far. While annual 10-Ks, 10-Qs and a variety of other filings are filed on EDGAR, annual reports to shareholders are not, since they are not required to be filed at all; however, some companies do file them (see the section on "Annual Reports" later in this chapter to learn where to obtain them). Searching for filings can be done for free at the SEC's official site, EDGAR, and other sites (some free and some fee-based). EDGAR has finally stepped up to the plate with much better search capabilities, such as full-text searching, as of June 2006. For information on SEC E-alerts, see "SEC Related E-alerts" on page 477.

War Story: Finding a Casino Deal

When Daniel T. Hardy from the Madison, Wisconsin firm of Axley Brynelson asked his law librarian, Clare L. Winkler, to find a casino management agreement between nontribal companies and Native American tribes, she found samples by using EDGAR. However, since she couldn't full-text search using EDGAR (it was pre-June 2006), she first did some newspaper sleuthing where she found articles that identified names of companies that had struck these kinds of deals. While surfing the Internet, she also ran into the National Indian Gaming Commission (NIGC) Web site which proved helpful as well (**http://www.nigc.gov/nigc/index.jsp**). As Winkler relates, "From here, I searched EDGAR filings [by company name] and found a contract as an exhibit in a company's 10-K. I then used the Find feature on my Internet browser to locate casino management agreements within the very large company filings." At our suggestion, Winkler tried some of the full-text SEC filings databases noted below. Although she's sure that using the full-text database would've been helpful in pinpointing an agreement by searching for the phrase "management agreement," a certain amount of sleuthing would still have been necessary in order to find the actual document because the phrase "management agreement" is mentioned quite frequently in casino management company filings. In deference to its official status, we'll look at EDGAR first and then review other sites.

Full-Text SEC Searches

Have you ever been asked to draft an executive compensation agreement for a client? Instead of starting from scratch, use one of the full-text search SEC filing sites (such as the government's free EDGAR site (new as of June 2006) SEC Info, 10k Wizard, FreeEdgar, Westlaw, EdgarScan, Global Securities Information's LIVEDGAR, or LexisNexis's EDGARPlus). They offer searching by ticker symbol, person's name, date, type of form, and—more importantly—full-text searching with Boolean connectors. Using one of these databases, you can limit a search to your client's industry (or use the SIC code) and type in the keywords "executive compensation." You'll be rewarded with agreements that you can use as examples.

There are a variety of other ways to customize your search when using a full-text SEC database. To name just a few, you can search by a key executive's name, an insider's name, or an event such as a bankruptcy. While some of these sites are free, the sites with the most robust search engines (as we'll point out below) are only partially free: they are free to search, but to view the filings, you must have a subscription. When FreeEdgar and 10k Wizard ceased being completely free, there was a flurry of e-mail postings on a law librarian list querying what to use now for free, full-text, real-time access to SEC filings. A law librarian answered, "No question about this one, SEC Info.com." (This was before June 2006, when the government's EDGAR site was not full-text searchable.) For those who don't want to pay for a subscription, but still want to take advantage of the robust search engines of the partially free SEC databases, you can do so by using a two-step process: (1) search the more robust database (free) and make a note of the company name, the type of filing, and date of the filings that seem relevant; (2) take your results to EDGAR, where you can view and print for free. (Although EDGAR is now full-text searchable, this two-step process is still necessary for filings before June 2004 because the full-text capability only goes back two years at EDGAR.)

EDGAR

http://www.sec.gov/edgarhp.htm

Purpose: To search for public company filings (U.S. companies as of May 6, 1996, and foreign issuers as of November 4, 2002).

Content: The content includes filings. Help aids should be explored before beginning a search. First, look at the tutorial for an overview of what's available on EDGAR and for search tips. Then, click on **Descriptions of SEC Forms** to help decide what type of form will answer your question. Although you can search all types, it's better to limit your search if you can. For instance, if you only want information on material events or corporate changes that are too recent to be in a 10-K or 10-Q, limit the search to an 8-K. Click on **About EDGAR** to learn which forms are not required to be filed electronically and which are optional (for example, Form 144, notice of proposed sale of securities, is optional). To begin searching, click on **Search for Company Filings** (or go directly to **http://www.sec.govedgar/searchedgar/company search.html**). At the EDGAR site, you can search by com-

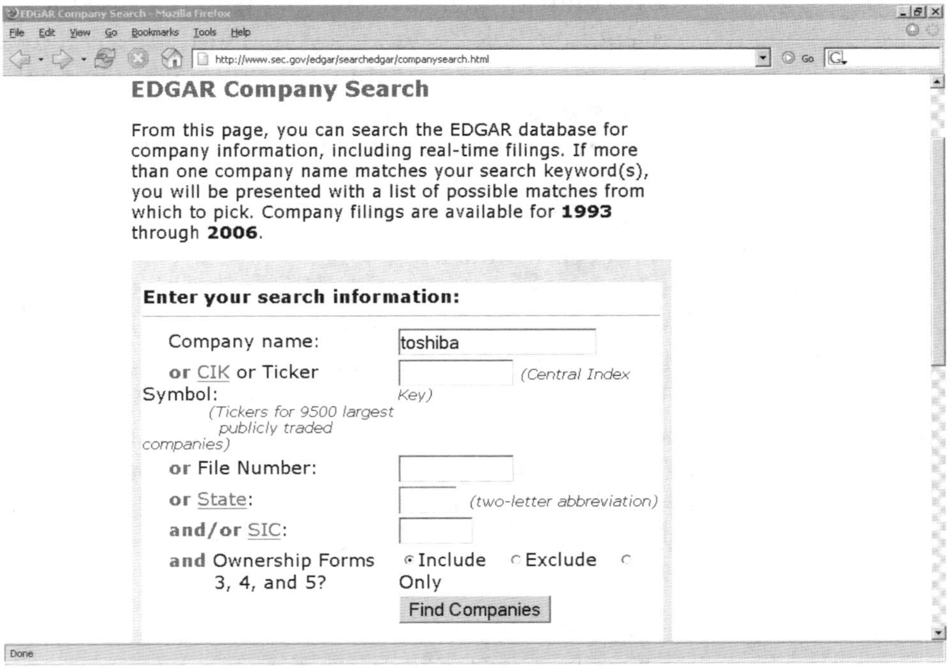

Figure 10-8. At the EDGAR site, search by company name, file number, state, SIC code, or CIK.

pany name, state, SIC code (Standard Industrial Classification—identifying the business type), CIK (Central Index Key—a unique number assigned by the SEC's computer system to individuals, funds, and corporations who file), and as of June 2006, full text. Be sure to review the FAQ (**http://searchwww.sec.gov/EDGARFSClient/jsp/ EDGAR_MainAccess.jsp**) before beginning a full-text search. There you will learn, for instance, that Boolean connectors must be in all caps. You can also search by clicking on **Latest Filings** to view the most recent real-time filings, or on **Current Events Analysis** to view filings from the previous one to five business days.

Our View: Free EDGAR is by far one of the richest collections of information available concerning U.S. public companies. The site has improved over the years by offering real-time filings and full-text searching. The full-text searching is in beta and only goes back to the past two years of filings, so you may still need to access pay databases for earlier filings.

Tip:
- Many companies have similar names, but each one has a unique CIK. As soon as you identify the CIK (by using the CIK lookup feature at **http://www.sec.gov/edgar/searchedgar/cik.htm**) for your subject company, always search by that number to pinpoint the company.
- Search by SIC code when you want samples of filings from specific industries.
- If you search at a site that offers free full-text searching, but charges to view the document, you can return to EDGAR to view and print free. The downside is that you won't have your search terms (from the full-text search database) highlighted and will have to use the "Find" function to locate the terms. (see Figure 2-1 on page 43). For regular SEC searchers, a subscription to a fee-based service may be a better option.

SEC Info (registration is required)

http://www.secinfo.com

Purpose: To search for U.S. SEC filings and Canadian Securities Administrators (CSA) SEDAR (System for Electronic Document Analysis and Retrieval) databases—with more search functions than EDGAR.

Content: The following search options are provided: name, industry, business, SIC code, area code, topic, CIK, accession number, file number, date, ZIP code, and state of incorporation. There are easy-to-view lists of: most recent filings, future events, form types, insider trading, IPOs, tender offers, and so on.

Our View: There's a lot to like about this site:

- The way it displays information (for example, it makes use of a table of contents so you can click either on the document or on any of the exhibits).
- Its useful download and print options.

- Its inclusion of Canadian filings (it is one of the few sites to search the Canadian filings exchange).

But, because SEC Info encourages searching by one or two words only, searchers can't construct as complex a search as at the other SEC filing sites noted below. For example, there is no phrase searching or combination searches (such as company name and keyword). It is unclear how long you can use the site for free. A warning states it can be used for free "until you exceed a usage threshold" (at which point you will be offered a subscription). We haven't reached our threshold yet, so we're not sure at what point you reach it or what the subscription price is. There is no indication as to the benefits of registering. We were able to use the site and view full documents without registering.

Tip:
- Forms can be downloaded into several formats of your choice (Word, rich text, plain text, XML, and so on).
- You can print one page only.
- Once you open a document, use the internal hyperlinking (for example, if you click on the by-laws link in Exhibit 3.1, you are then taken to Exhibit 3.2, where the bylaws are found).
- There is a free e-mail alert service.
- An internal "find" function appears at the top of the screen once a document is opened.

Even though it's no longer free to view or print filings, you can still take advantage of 10k Wizard's search engine—which is still free and real time (**http://www.tenkwizard.com**).

10k Wizard

To search: 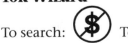 To view and print: 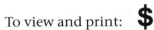 **$**

http://www.10kwizard.com

Purpose: Don't be misled by 10k Wizard's name; this site provides real-time access to all forms filed with the SEC (not just 10-Ks), and offers full-text searches.

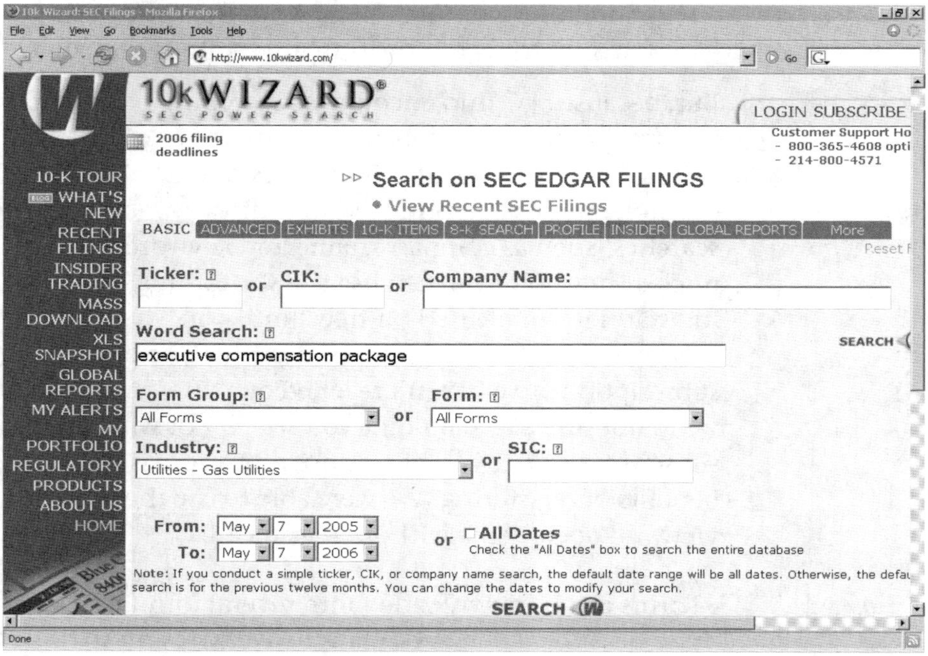

Figure 10-9. With 10k Wizard, you can search by any of the following (or a combination): company name, ticker, CIK, industry, SIC code, date, form group, and keyword (words and phrases with Boolean or proximity connectors).

Content: Search by any or a combination of the following: company name, ticker, CIK, industry, SIC code, date (specific, a range, or all), form group or specific form (or all forms), and keyword (words and phrases with Boolean or proximity connectors).

Our View: This site has excellent search functions. After performing a search, the results list presents you with company names, type of filings, and the dates filed. Paid subscribers can then select documents to view in full. Non-subscribers (occasional users) should see our Tip below.

Tip: For the occasional user, take advantage of 10k Wizard's robust search engine to pinpoint the information you are seeking and then take your findings to EDGAR to view and print for free. For the more frequent user, the $199 per year subscription fee is probably well worth the cost (this is a $100 increase since the last edition of this book). There are several other annual subscription packages, ranging up to $2,395 (which includes foreign companies and other features such as mass downloads, alert portfolios, industry comparisons, and more (see **https://secure.10kwizard.com/subscribe.php**).

Also recommended by a number of librarians as a replacement for FreeEdgar is EdgarScan, provided by the ABAS Technology Group of Pricewaterhouse.

EdgarScan

http://edgarscan.pwcglobal.com/servlets/edgarscan

Purpose:	To search for company information and annual reports and to create interactive financial charts.
Content:	It offers full-text searching with keywords and phrases (and Boolean connectors), and if you use the advanced search, field searching is available. There is also an IPO lookup by date, company name, and industry.
Our View:	Lawyers primarily interested in the financials of a company or how its financials compare to others will like EdgarScan for the following reasons:

- When EdgarScan pulls filings from the SEC's server, it automatically locates key financial tables and creates a common format across companies
- It also has a Benchmarking Assistant to perform graphical financial benchmarking interactively
- Tables showing company comparisons can be downloaded into Microsoft Excel
- Registered users can store company portfolios for future benchmarking

Tip:	Some things to be aware of:

- The site is not real-time—there is usually a 24 to 48 hour delay in adding new filings.
- Only 10-Ks and 10-Qs are indexed, and only back to 1999.
- The key word searching function isn't as good as other SEC sites discussed—for example, a search for

the word "pension" also returned filings with the word "suspension."

SEC Related E-alerts   **$**

For those who want to set up e-alerts for new SEC Filings, pay sites such as Global Securities Information's LIVEDGAR (**http://www.gsionline.com/livedgar/alerts.html**) and LexisNexis' EDGARPlus (**http://www.lexis-nexis.com**) are two options.

Annual Reports

Annual reports are chock-full of interesting company information, all shaped and supplied by the companies themselves. You'll usually find a message from the chief executive, a discussion of new initiatives begun in the past year, a list of company executives, and extensive company financials. Anyone can get a copy of a company's annual report by simply calling the corporation's investor relations department. However, there are times when you might not want the company to know you're gathering information about them, in which case calling the investor relations department is out of the question. Or, there may be times when you need instant access to the report and don't have time to wait for a mailed print copy. Fortunately, there are several ways to obtain the reports via the Web.

Many companies post their annual reports on the Internet. While you can do a general search-engine search to determine whether a particular company has an annual report on the Internet, beware of too many results; a search for "Microsoft" and "annual report" returned 137,000 results. A better option is to check the company's site first.

When you need a foreign company's report or an older domestic report no longer posted on a company's Web site, you might try one of the many annual reports archival sites (see Global Reports below for both of these services). These sites might also be helpful if you need to access more than one company's report (see PRARS below), or if you want to search by industry, SIC code, or other options (see all annual report sites below, with the exception of ReportGallery).

Annual Reports for U.S. Companies

IRIN (Investor Relations Information Network)

http://www.irin.com/cgi-bin/main.cgi

Purpose: To search for recent annual reports of corporations (the past one or two years).

Content: IRIN supplies free access to online versions of more than 12,500 current and historical annual reports of more than 4,100 public companies that users can download as a PDF file (some are available in HTML). In addition to the annual report, each entry includes delayed stock quotes, an image of the annual report, and links to additional company information (basic contact information, charts, and graphs). One can either browse an alphabetical list of companies or search by: (1) **Company name**; (2) **Symbol** (ticker); or (3) **Keyword** (enter a word or phrase, person's name, or product).

Our View: We were pleased to learn about the keyword search feature (noted above), which was added sometime after we first visited the site in 2003, but we are displeased that two other handy features were eliminated: the ability to search by SIC code to create a list of companies in the same industry and forwarding to a company your request that a print copy of their annual report be mailed to you.

Tip: Downloading the PDF of the annual report can take a bit of time unless you have a high-speed connection. If you don't need to view the annual report in color and with all the graphics, it's quicker to open the HTML version, if available.

Some other free sites offer different features than IRIN. If you need annual reports from many companies, and want to avoid filling out a request for each company, use PRARS (the Public Register's Annual Report Service) at **http://www.prars.com**. PRARS allows you to add multiple company-report requests to your virtual shopping cart (for free) to request that annual reports be sent to you via postal mail, anywhere in the U.S., for no charge. Also, a handy feature at PRARS (which is not available at IRIN) is a search by industry or state. There is a link from PRARS to Annual Report Service (**http://www.annualreportservice.com**) to view annual reports and 10-Ks online. Registration is required and one's contact information is forwarded to the company whose filings one reviews. Search by ticker symbol or browse by state, industry, or company name. For those who prefer a site where registration is not required for viewing annual reports (and sometimes 10-Ks) online free, see **AnnualReports.com**. Search by company name or by ticker symbol or browse by company name, exchange, industry (e.g., auto parts) or sector (e.g., financial). Whether reports are in HTML or PDF varies from company to company. Some companies also offer a link to order a hard copy.

Global Reports

If you don't find what you want on the free sites, or need foreign annual reports and you're willing to pay, check out Global Reports below (they recently purchased Annual Reports Library).

Annual Reports for U.S. and Foreign Companies

Global Reports

http://www.global-reports.com

To search: To view and print: **$**

Purpose: To search for current and retrospective annual reports.

Content: Global Reports has a collection of full-color annual reports from over 22,000 companies in more than seventy countries, going back at least three years for many, and back to 1996 for some. E-Alerts can be set up to notify you whenever new filings are made by your subject companies. A full-text search offers users the capability to search by words or phrases across the entire annual report database.

Our View: This is one of the few services where you can download more than current annual reports. The search options are very useful—search by company name, ticker symbol, country, exchange, index, report type (annual, interim, or IPO), and report year.

Tip: You can search free to find out whether the site's archive contains annual reports for the company in question and which years it has available but you must be a paid subscriber to download the reports. Contact the company for pricing.

Stock Quotes

Current Quotes

For a while, Yahoo! offered free real-time quotes, but it went to a pay scheme priced at $9.95 per month for streaming real-time quotes (**http://finance.yahoo.com**). Most free stock quote sites are delayed by 15 to 20 minutes. For those that still offer free access to real-time quotes, you'll find that you typically need to register. One example is Reuters (**http://www.investor.reuters.com**). Most sites require you to search for quotes by ticker symbol, but they usually provide a convenient company name lookup to find the ticker. See the next entry for a way to search for stock quotes without registering.

Free Current Stock Quotes (Sometimes)— Without Registration

Google's Stock Quotes

http://www.google.com/

Purpose:	To get stock quotes and information without having to visit a stock quote Web site—some even in real time.
Content:	To search for stock quotes on Google's home page, just enter the ticker symbol into the box and click Search. If the stock ticker symbol you entered is recognized, Google will show you a list of results including the latest stock price, an intra-day chart, the daily high and low, and other information. As with most free stock quote sites on the Internet, a 15-minute delay for NASDAQ and a 20-minute delay for AMEX and NYSE is normal. Some results also show real-time quotes from RealTime ECN. They are clearly marked.
Our View:	This is one of the few stock quote sites that doesn't require registration, which is a step we're sure everyone

is happy to skip. Google was also able to get results back quickly. We conducted two searches—one for MSFT (Microsoft) and one for TWX (Time-Warner)—and they both yielded results in .07 seconds. The only thing missing here that you would find on most other stock sites is the ability to look up a ticker symbol by a company name. Google won't find your stock quote if it doesn't recognize the ticker symbol, so you need to be accurate when entering your search terms.

Tip: To find the ticker symbol, enter the company name you are searching for and the words "ticker symbol" into the Search box. The results generated will be links to sites that can offer you the assistance you need.

Historical Quotes

Yahoo! Finance Historical Prices

http://finance.yahoo.com/q/hp?s=GE

Purpose: To find historical U.S. stock quotes (back to 1962 for some stocks).

Content: Results show the open, high, low, volume, and close, in addition to splits and dividend distributions of historical data of U.S. stock quotes.

Our View: This is great free service for those who need to know what a stock was priced at in the past. Before the Internet, access to this information was from an expensive pay database. You'll appreciate that you can create a weekly, monthly, or daily chart. Additionally, you can limit the search results to dividends only.

Tip: • Although quotes are not adjusted for splits or dividends, in the **Adjusted Close** column the close price is adjusted for all splits and dividends.
   • Click on the **Download Spreadsheet Format** link at the end of the Historical Prices table to download into a Microsoft Excel spreadsheet.

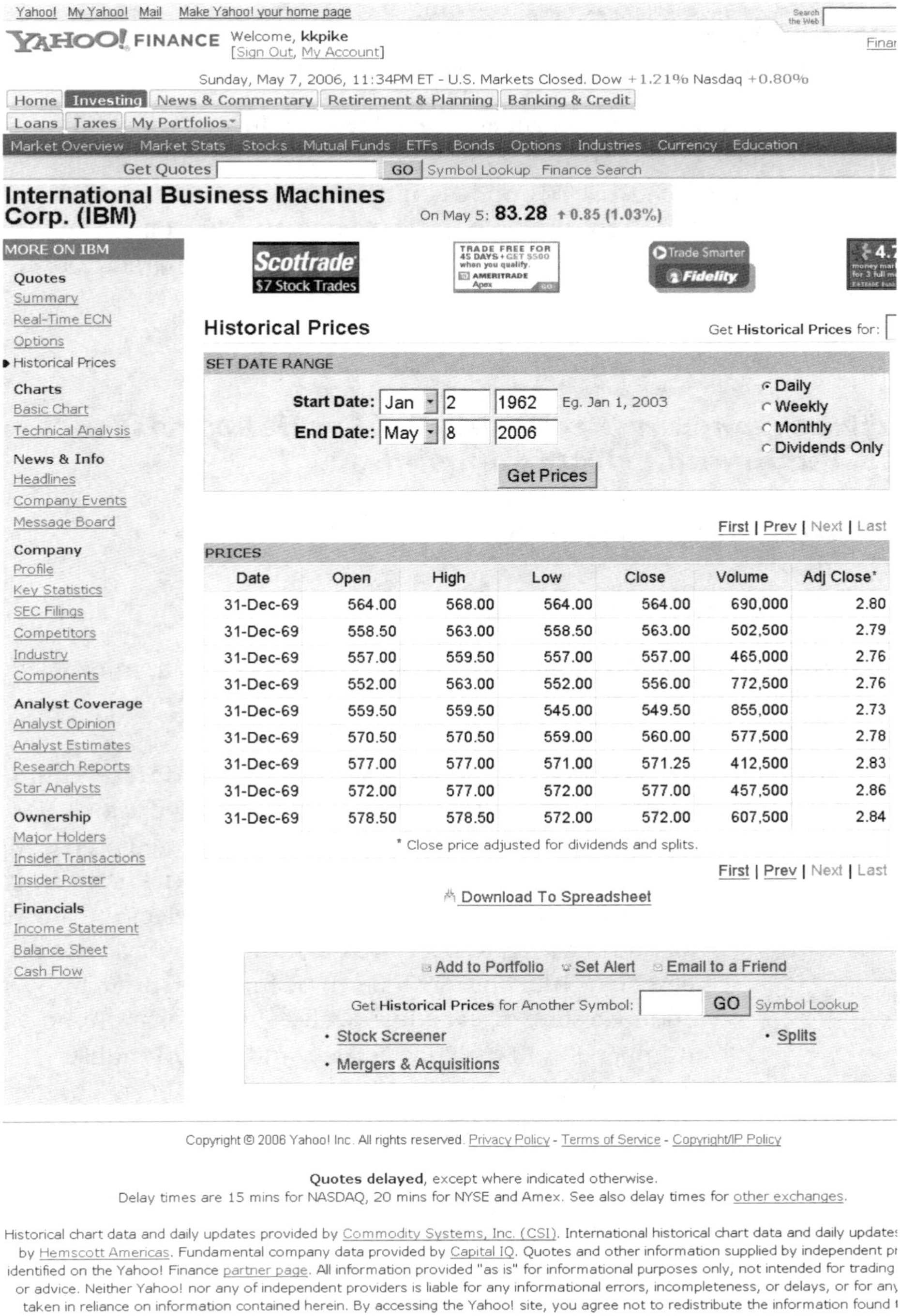

Yahoo! My Yahoo! Mail   Make Yahoo! your home page

YAHOO! FINANCE   Welcome, kkpike
[Sign Out, My Account]

Sunday, May 7, 2006, 11:34PM ET - U.S. Markets Closed. Dow +1.21% Nasdaq +0.80%

Home | Investing | News & Commentary | Retirement & Planning | Banking & Credit
Loans | Taxes | My Portfolios

Market Overview   Market Stats   Stocks   Mutual Funds   ETFs   Bonds   Options   Industries   Currency   Education

Get Quotes [   ] GO Symbol Lookup   Finance Search

International Business Machines Corp. (IBM)

On May 5: **83.28** +0.85 (1.03%)

MORE ON IBM

Scottrade $7 Stock Trades

TRADE FREE FOR 45 DAYS + GET $500 when you qualify. AMERITRADE Apex

Trade Smarter Fidelity

Quotes
Summary
Real-Time ECN
Options
▶ Historical Prices

Historical Prices

Get **Historical Prices** for: [   ]

Charts
Basic Chart
Technical Analysis

SET DATE RANGE

Start Date: Jan ▾ 2 1962   Eg. Jan 1, 2003
End Date: May ▾ 8 2006

⦿ Daily
○ Weekly
○ Monthly
○ Dividends Only

News & Info
Headlines
Company Events
Message Board

Get Prices

First | Prev | Next | Last

Company
Profile
Key Statistics
SEC Filings
Competitors
Industry
Components

Analyst Coverage
Analyst Opinion
Analyst Estimates
Research Reports
Star Analysts

PRICES

Date	Open	High	Low	Close	Volume	Adj Close*
31-Dec-69	564.00	568.00	564.00	564.00	690,000	2.80
31-Dec-69	558.50	563.00	558.50	563.00	502,500	2.79
31-Dec-69	557.00	559.50	557.00	557.00	465,000	2.76
31-Dec-69	552.00	563.00	552.00	556.00	772,500	2.76
31-Dec-69	559.50	559.50	545.00	549.50	855,000	2.73
31-Dec-69	570.50	570.50	559.00	560.00	577,500	2.78
31-Dec-69	577.00	577.00	571.00	571.25	412,500	2.83
31-Dec-69	572.00	577.00	572.00	577.00	457,500	2.86
31-Dec-69	578.50	578.50	572.00	572.00	607,500	2.84

Ownership
Major Holders
Insider Transactions
Insider Roster

* Close price adjusted for dividends and splits.

First | Prev | Next | Last

Financials
Income Statement
Balance Sheet
Cash Flow

⊟ Download To Spreadsheet

⊟ Add to Portfolio   ⊽ Set Alert   ⊟ Email to a Friend

Get **Historical Prices** for Another Symbol: [   ] GO Symbol Lookup

· Stock Screener
· Mergers & Acquisitions

· Splits

Figure 10-10. Yahoo! Finance offers access to historic stock quote information that was once only available at a (high) price. Reprinted with permission of Yahoo! Inc. © 2006 by Yahoo! Inc. YAHOO! and the YAHOO! logo are trademarks of Yahoo! Inc.

Checklist Item 8: Locate Private-Company Information in Directories and Credit Reports

It can be very difficult to get accurate, timely information about private companies. Private firms are not bound by SEC filing requirements that result in the rich trove of public-company data available on EDGAR. One of the most common sources of private company data (and one that you must pay for), the D & B company report, is composed largely of self-reported data. This makes it hard to know whether the data is completely accurate.

Private Company Directories and Credit Reports for U.S. Public and Private Companies

Zapdata (owned by D & B)

http://www.zapdata.com

Purpose:	To find public and private company contact information.
Content:	Thirteen million public and private United States companies can be searched in the company lookup search box (click on the **Company Lookup** link located on the top blue bar of the home page). Enter a company name into the **Company Name** search box. Then select the down-arrow on the State query box to either choose a state or **Nationwide**. Your search can be further refined by adding a state, street address, city, ZIP code, or phone number. Results include address and type of industry, and show whether a company's headquarters is a branch or whether it is a single location only.
Our View:	This site is useful not only for general contact information, but also when you need to find out what type of entity the company is—in preparation for serving a complaint. For example, a search for "24 Hour Fitness" returned 150 results. Scanning the list, it was easy to separate the headquarters from the branches and single locations and to identify clubs connected to 24 Hour Fit-

ness that used different names (for example, Scottsdale Club showed 24 Hour Fitness USA Inc. as its parent).

Tip: For $5, you can order a very basic D & B report. Additional data can be ordered, such as contact names (at 40¢ per name).

Private and Public Company Listings and Credit Reports for U.S and Foreign Companies

D & B

http://www.dnb.com/us

Purpose: To find information (free) on 100 million private and public companies from 214 countries, and to order various business and credit reports (fee-based).

Content: 80 percent of its U.S. company database is comprised of businesses with 10 or fewer employees. Search by company name and country or state or select **Nationwide** and the results will show a list of companies with that name. There is also an **advanced search** where you can add the following criteria to refine a company name search: address, city, or ZIP code. One may also reverse telephone number search to learn which company is linked to the number (for U.S. only) and one may search by DUNS number. Each entry provides only two pieces of free information: the company's address and business entity type (single location, branch, or headquarters). All other information, from the comprehensive report to the company profile report, is fee based. The comprehensive report shows the background of each executive (and even includes names of their former companies), an executive summary about the company, a credit score, financials, and details about judgments, liens, UCCs, bankruptcies, lawsuits, and so on.

Our View: Unfortunately, this site no longer offers one crucial piece of contact information: a phone number. However, this site does offer more-detailed reports than the $5 Zapdata report. Order a comprehensive report for $39.99 or a credit report for $29.99 (various other reports are also available such as a company profile for $9.99).

Tip:
- If you don't know in which state the company is located, select a **Nationwide** search.
- Click on **See Sample** to get a good idea of what type of information each D & B report offers.

Private Company Directories for U.S. Companies

Vault

http://www.vault.com

Purpose: To provide an insider's view of a company.

Content: The site covers over 4,000 public and private companies. Enter a company name and a results page is displayed. Click on the company name link and you can read, for free, some basic contact information, the name of the company president, and a "Snapshot" of the company from an insider's viewpoint. Click on the **Message Board** link to read the messages. For more-detailed information and to pose questions and provide answers to the message board, however, requires a paid membership is required (see below). Recently, Vault Asia and Vault Europe were added.

Our View: A search of E! Entertainment Television brought up a company profile that was very sparse but gave an idea of the work conditions and attitudes. There was a link to Vault's unofficial E! company message board where you could read the questions posed, but to answer or view answers older than 60 days, you would have to join Vault (for $3.95 per month—the cost of a basic membership. A Gold membership is available, but pricing was not shown).

Tip: Search for your client companies every now and then to see what people are saying.

Private Company Directories for Foreign Companies

Kompass

http://www.kompass.com/kinl/en/

Purpose: To search information about 23 million products and services and 1.9 million companies in 70 countries.

Content: You begin by selecting one of the tabs at the top of the page search, either **Products & Services**, **Company Names**, **Trade Names,** or **Executives**. (Note that the fifth tab—the **Advanced Search** option—is only available to subscribers.) The search interface for each tab includes three search boxes to fill in on the home page. The first box, the **Search Text** box, is where users enter the company name, keywords, terms, or names (as applicable) they're interested in. The second box, which is the **Region** selector in which you can choose a region (such as Africa) or a specific country (such as Nigeria) where you want to locate information. In the last box you can indicate the language in which you want to search for results (ranging from English to Svenska).

Only the most basic information is available free for most companies. This includes address, phone, fax, and e-mail link. More detailed profiles are available for those companies that have chosen to advertise on the Kompass site. These enhanced listings are listed first in the results list and are indicated as "Premium Suppliers." Their listings include information about the companies' products and services, executives, and in some instances, financial information. Access to more detailed information is available in 50 "unit" increments—starting at $127 for the first 50 units. Credits are then debited from your account per search (in varying amounts, depending on the type/volume of information you choose to access).

Our View: Being able to search through nearly 2 million companies worldwide, by a wide variety of search criteria, makes this a good starting point even though non-subscribers only get basic contact information for many of the companies.

Checklist Item 9: Search for Current and Archived News and Set Up News E-alerts

Company directories can quickly get outdated, so we also recommend running the company name and its executives' names through a few major newspaper databases to verify information and to find the most current information. We've found that Hoover's is very up to date (it makes changes on the same day), while Vault is not. A few business-oriented news site are noted here, but for more information about searching newspapers, see the section "News, Periodicals, and Broadcast Media" in Chapter 5, "General Factual Research."

CEOExpress (**http://www.ceoexpress.com/**) has an extensive list of business news resources, arranged topically. Some of its topics are **Quotes, Banking and Finance,** and **International Business**. For local and regional business news from business journals (in over forty local markets throughout the United States), check out the American City Business Journals free (registration required) site at **http://www.bizjournals.com**. You can search current news and archives back to 1996 by headline, byline, or full text. You can also request e-mail news alerts from a list of markets or industries. Additionally, you can set up a search watch about any topic, company, or person, from any or all of the markets.

Setting Up Alerts for Company News

Yahoo! Alerts

http://alerts.yahoo.com

Purpose:	Yahoo! Alerts sends you up-to-the-minute news, stock information, weather, and more to your e-mail or Yahoo! Instant Messenger accounts—or even to your cell phone or pager.
Content:	Unlike Google's alert service, Yahoo! requires that you set up an account (free) before being allowed access to the feature. However, if you already have a Yahoo! e-mail

account, then you are set to go and can skip this step. Once logged into your Yahoo! account, you will be asked to choose the type of alert you want. There are twenty alert categories listed, ranging from **News**, **Sports**, **Weather**, **Children**, **Music**, **Health**, and **Best Fares** (travel).

We chose a News alert and were then given the option of choosing **Breaking News**, **Keyword News**, or a **Daily News Digest**. **Breaking News** gives brief up-to-the-minute updates; **Keyword News** allows the user to create custom news searches in their topics of interest; and **Daily News Digest** provides summaries of top news stories in your choice of categories. Each category allows you to view a sample alert, and within each category are icons that indicate what delivery forms that alert is available in (e-mail, Instant Message, or mobile device).

Clicking the box for **Keyword News** leads to a page where you can add keywords to your alert search, or modify your search by excluding keywords (by adding them to the **Do not include** box). Yahoo! offers fewer delivery frequency choices (**Once Daily** or **As they happen**) than Google. However, Yahoo! offers more options for where it delivers its alerts: users can choose to receive the alerts via e-mail, Yahoo! Instant Messenger, a separate, free Yahoo! service, or delivered to a text-message-enabled cell phone or pager. To specify whether one wants to receive Yahoo! alerts **Once Daily** or **As they happen**, users must click the **Change Delivery Options** link near the bottom of the alert set-up screen. Yahoo! Alerts can be edited by clicking on the **My Alerts** tab.

Our View: It is unfortunate that Yahoo! does not allow you to set up a Web search alert using your own search terms as Google does. Rather than create a unified alert service across all of its properties, it appears as if Yahoo! has cobbled together functions of various Yahoo! sections to create this "service." Because of this, there is a lack of consistency in the twenty different categories that Yahoo! Alerts offer and this creates some confusion. For instance, if you click on Music, your alert options are given in pull-down menus (instead of the check-box selection method offered on the News page). But if you look closely, most of the options listed aren't actually for alerts, they are just links to other Yahoo! music areas. For example, the user can search for music videos either by genre or by clicking on the "Top 100" or "New videos" link. The results listed are content oriented.

News/Reviews/Interviews is one exception (listed under Artists), but it only offers the ability to get a very general alert from a news source such as E! Entertainment or AP Online. Other categories are simpler in design and ability, but still dissimilar enough in look to be confusing. Yahoo! Alerts definitely needs some work in streamlining the process.

Tip: This service is most flexible (and useful) for creating News alerts. Because Yahoo! and Google do not monitor the same exact sources (especially for news), it is useful to set up an E-alert on both.

Setting up e-alerts to keep updated about public companies can be done *free* at The Scannery (see below) or at various pay sites.

The Scannery

http://www.thescannery.com ($) Registration required to subscribe to Alert Service

Purpose: An investor's search engine that covers over 36,000 public companies from 120 countries around the world. The Scannery's database can be searched manually or, better yet, can be set to automatically track a watch list of keywords and search phrases that you set up. The results are then emailed to you.

Content: Scannery's home page offers a five-step search process: Step 1: Select a **Content Set** (e.g., **Companies, Government, Political**). Step 2: Select **Function** (e.g., **Watch List** to set up an e-alert). Step 3: Select a regional or topical category in which to search from the **Where** list (either a category such as **S & P Global 1200** or a country such as **Argentina**). Step 4: Select an **Industry** from the pull-down list (e.g., select **all**, **unspecified**, or select a specific industry such as **Energy**). Step 5: **Search Options**: select one or more options including **Phonic** (search for words that sound like your search term), stemming, or finding synonyms. You can also specify your search type (e.g., phrase or Boolean) and how you would like your results sorted (e.g., **Score** [relevancy], **Date**); type of search; number of results; and how to sort results). A list of results is displayed and you can select any of the results to view full text. Scannery also allows users to set up a **Watch List** to automatically search for keywords/phrases you define every time the Scannery database is updated. You will get an e-mail message when they have new information to share with you. **Watch Lists** require a (free) registration. To create a **Watch List**, select **Watch List** from the **Function** drop-down menu.

Another way to search is to go to the home page and click on **My Scannery** (in the upper right-hand corner) and you will be provided with **Passive Searching**, an automated way to search the database. You will need to register (it's a free subscription) and log in. Once you enter your keywords and phrases, you can sit back and relax. **My Scannery** will automatically search every time they update their database. You will get an e-mail message when they have new information to share with you.

Our View: The Scannery offers many ways for you to get the information you seek. We especially liked the variety of searches available. The knowledge provided is lengthy and the free automated services are a definite plus. Put your keywords in and let someone else do the digging for once!

Tip: E-alerts, specifically for new SEC filings, are available at pay sites such as Global Securities Information's LIVEDGAR (**http://www.gsionline.com/livedgar/alerts. html**) and LexisNexis' EDGARPlus (**http://www.lexis-nexis.com/**).

Checklist Item 10: Review Secretary of State Records for Registered Agents and Fictitious Business Names

To serve the correct party, lawyers need to discover a corporation's (or limited partnership's or limited liability company's) registered agent. If the company is not a corporation, but a sole proprietorship with a fictitious business name (FBN), then lawyers need to identify the owner to know who to serve. Many states and counties have made these business records available for free on the Internet. These records can also be used if a lawyer simply needs to know where the company is incorporated or whether the corporation is registered to do business in a particular state or states.

If you need to serve a complaint or contact, for other reasons, a general partner or an individual doing business using an FBN, this can be difficult. The difficulty of identifying general partners is that in some states they are not required to file with the secretary of state. The difficulty of identifying sole proprietors is twofold: (1) in states where they file by county, you would first have to know in which county they filed; and (2) even in states that require statewide filing, it's possible a sole proprietor has failed to file a fictitious business statement at all. InfoSpace (see Chapter 7, "Finding and Backgrounding People") may be useful if you know the business's phone number or address because you can do a reverse search on the phone number or address. The name of the person who is connected to that phone number or address may be displayed. For example, an InfoSpace reverse phone search for the phone number connected to Levitt & Levitt showed the names of both lawyers connected to that phone number.

The depth of information in a secretary of state or county clerk business record posted free on the Web varies. The record may be a full reproduction of the actual documents filed with the secretary of state (as in Florida), or merely a list of company names incorporated in the state (with no contact or registered agent information), or a mere acknowledgment that the FBN is being used (as in Los Angeles county). Some states allow you to search only by the corporation or FBN. Others also allow you to search by the name of the registered agent, an officer, or fictitious business owner. Most allow for partial company name searching. Some states, such as New Jersey and Delaware *can* be searched free, but there is a fee to view some, but not all, of the documents. For instance, at the New Jersey State Business Gateway Service site (**https://accessnet.state.nj.us/home.asp**) there is a $5 charge for an online status report and a $40 charge to place an order for a standing certificate.

Multistate corporate record searches can be conducted only at pay databases (noted in Chapter 8, such as LexisNexis®, Westlaw®, Choice-Point, Merlin, and Accurint). Although the pay databases all indicate that an "all state" corporate search is available, this is not completely accurate, except for ChoicePoint (**http://www.choicepoint.com/**). Lexis and Westlaw, for example, do not include Delaware in their "all state" corporate search. Instead, Delaware must be searched separately and Lexis does not include New Jersey at all. For a state-by-state list of where to locate registered agent information, both on the Web and off, see ResidentAgent Info.com (**http://www.residentagentinfo.com**).

Secretary of State Sites

Resident Agent Info

http://www.residentagentinfo.com

Purpose:	To link to online secretary of state sites that contain registered agent records.
Content:	The site has links to states that have registered agent data online.
Our View:	We like the simple straightforwardness of this site, and that it takes you directly to the page on the site that contains the database for searching the corporation records.
Tip:	• This site is also useful to get contact information for those secretaries of state that are not online. Contact information for states that don't post registered agent records online, but that do have a Web site, can also be found at the NASS (National Association of Secretaries of State) site (**http://www.nass.org/sos/sos.html**).
	• To learn what other records (such as UCCs) or information are available at a secretary of state's office, you can also use the NASS Web site to link to each state's site.

Delaware Corporate Records

Although Delaware probably has the highest number of incorporations of any state, it was one of the last to make its database freely available. See the next entry for details on the State of Delaware's Division of Corporations Web site.

State of Delaware: Division of Corporations

http://www.state.de.us/corp/onlinestatus.shtml

Purpose: The State of Delaware's Division of Corporations provides a free database of general information about active and inactive corporations, including the name of their registered agents. One can view more details (such as status) by paying a fee.

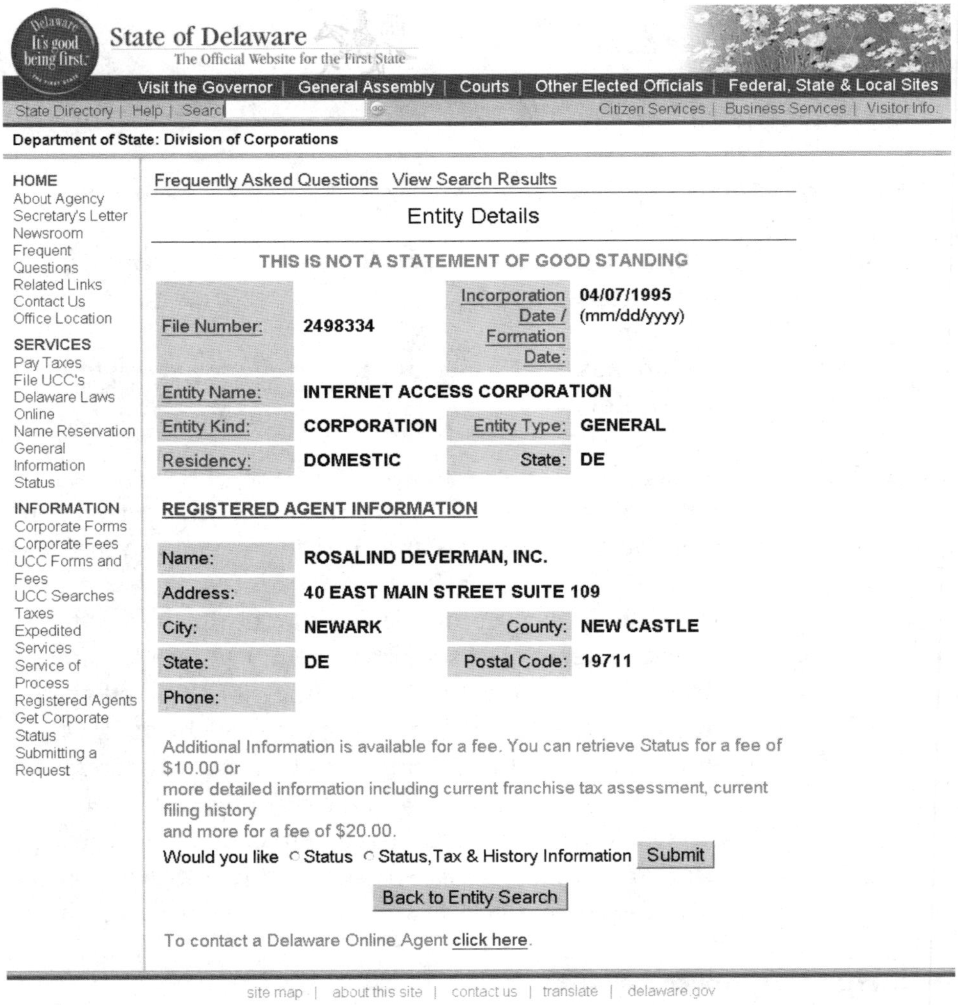

State of Delaware
The Official Website for the First State

Visit the Governor | General Assembly | Courts | Other Elected Officials | Federal, State & Local Sites

State Directory | Help | Search

Citizen Services | Business Services | Visitor Info

Department of State: Division of Corporations

HOME	Frequently Asked Questions View Search Results
About Agency	
Secretary's Letter	**Entity Details**
Newsroom	
Frequent Questions	**THIS IS NOT A STATEMENT OF GOOD STANDING**
Related Links	
Contact Us	
Office Location	

SERVICES
Pay Taxes
File UCC's
Delaware Laws Online
Name Reservation
General Information
Status

File Number:	2498334
Incorporation Date / Formation Date:	04/07/1995 (mm/dd/yyyy)
Entity Name:	**INTERNET ACCESS CORPORATION**
Entity Kind:	**CORPORATION** Entity Type: **GENERAL**
Residency:	**DOMESTIC** State: **DE**

INFORMATION
Corporate Forms
Corporate Fees
UCC Forms and Fees
UCC Searches
Taxes
Expedited Services
Service of Process
Registered Agents
Get Corporate Status
Submitting a Request

REGISTERED AGENT INFORMATION

Name:	**ROSALIND DEVERMAN, INC.**
Address:	**40 EAST MAIN STREET SUITE 109**
City:	**NEWARK** County: **NEW CASTLE**
State:	**DE** Postal Code: **19711**
Phone:	

Additional Information is available for a fee. You can retrieve Status for a fee of $10.00 or
more detailed information including current franchise tax assessment, current filing history
and more for a fee of $20.00.
Would you like ○ Status ○ Status, Tax & History Information   Submit

Back to Entity Search

To contact a Delaware Online Agent click here.

site map | about this site | contact us | translate | delaware.gov

Figure 10-11. The Delaware corporate record displays general information about a corporation and its registered agent. More details, such as status, can be ordered online for $10. Certified copies must be requested in writing.

Content: To conduct a **General Information Name Search**, click on **Click Here**, located in the first paragraph on the home page. A simple search box asks you to enter an entity name. We chose to search for an entity name beginning with the word "Internet." The results page displayed two columns—the left-hand side had a file number, and the right-hand side had the corporations' full name, with all of the names starting with the word "Internet." There were 882 matches found, but only 15 displayed. The database asks that you narrow your search by typing more of the entity's name into the search field before any more results appear.

We chose to investigate Internet Acquisition, Inc. When you click on the company's name, you find the following information: **Incorporation Date**; **Entity Kind**; **Entity Type**; **Residency**; **State** and **Registered Agent Information**. Other additional information can be viewed online for a small fee. The first additional information choice is **Status** (for $10), and the second is **Status** together with **Tax** (franchise tax assessment) and **History** (current filings) information ($20). Clicking on the bubble underneath one of the choices leads you to a registration page, and then to payment options.

Our View: Because more corporations incorporate in Delaware than any other state, finally having free access to general corporate information about Delaware corporations and low-cost access to **Status**, **Tax**, and **History** is big news. The functionality of the database has been greatly improved compared to the database Delaware offered via Lexis, Westlaw, and other commercial databases. For example, access is now 24/7 instead of 9:00 A.M. to 5:00 P.M. EST, and searching by partial name is now allowed. Even the fee-based portion of the site is now priced lower. We look forward to the day when all Delaware corporate information is online (see below for what is missing), even for a fee.

Tip: Be aware that the free **General Information** Web result does not constitute an official Certificate of Good

Standing and one will not be generated even in the fee-based portion of the site. A Certificate of Good Standing can only be obtained by submitting a request in writing along with a fee (see **http://www.state.de.us/corp/ reqguide.shtml**). For those who need Officer and Director names and addresses, the only place they are maintained is in each corporation's annual report, which must be ordered by calling 302-739-3073.

County Fictitous Business Name Records

As noted above, if a county has placed its FBN records on the Web, you'll find that each county differs widely (even in the same state) as to how much information is included in the Web record. Also, the search functions of each county's FBN database varies. A case in point is California: in San Francisco, you can perform an FBN search using either the FBN or the owner's name (**http://services.sfgov.org/bns/start.asp**), but in Los Angeles county you can search only by the FBN (**http://regrec .co.la.ca.us/fbn**), and the record, once located, fails to even identify the owner.

To discover whether a county has placed its FBN records on the Web, use State and Local Government on the Net (see below) to link to all on-line counties.

State and Local Government on the Net

http://www.statelocalgov.net 🚫$

Purpose:	To find links to FBN listings or databases at state, city, or county Web sites.
Content:	To link to a state, city, or county's FBN Web site, click first on the state to learn if the state registers FBNs. If they don't, then scroll down to **County** or **City** and select from those lists.
Our View:	Once you reach a county's or city's Web site, you might need to do a lot of searching around to find the part of the site that contains the FBN records (if they are online at all). It's usually the county or city clerk's or the county or city recorder's page that you are looking for.

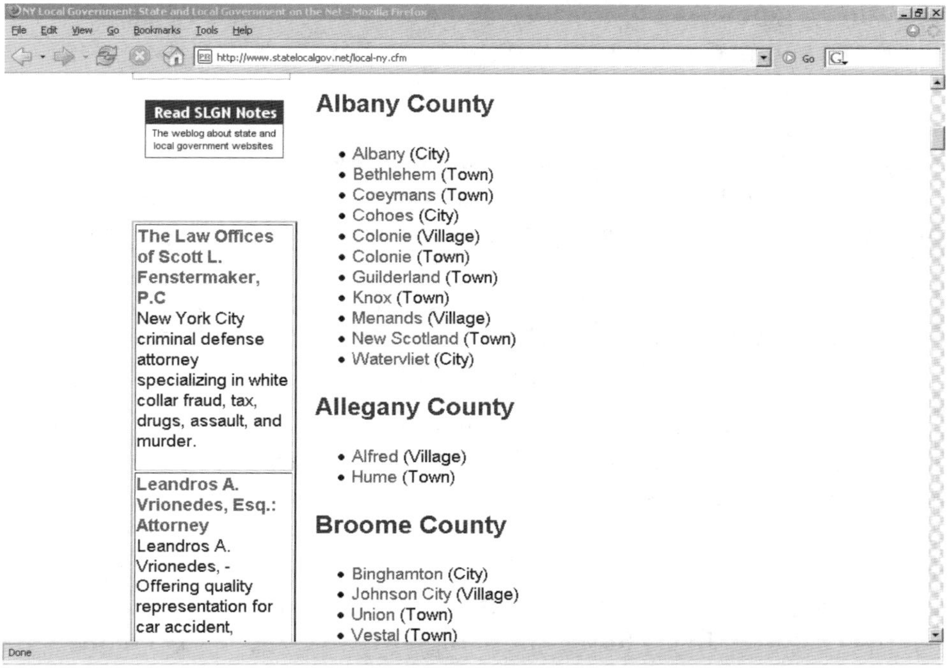

Figure 10-12. To link to an FBN Web site using the State and Local Government on the Net site, click first on the state and then scroll down to County or City if the state does not register FBNs.

Tip: • If you don't know in which state, county, or city a business has registered its FBN, use a pay database (such as Lexis, Westlaw, Accurint, or Merlin) to conduct a statewide or multistate search.

Checklist Item 11: Consider Using Pay Databases

Using a fee-based database is the better choice if you need to locate a corporation's registered agent in more than one state, or if you don't know in which state a company is registered to do business. Fee-based sites are also useful when you need to search for an FBN but don't know the state, city, or county. At the free sites, you have to search state by state (or county by county or city by city, for FBNs), while at a fee-based site, you can run a single multijurisdictional search (such as in Lexis.com's **All States** business record database). Don't be misled by the term **All States,** though. It really means only the states that are online, and not every state is. Also, some states, such as Delaware, have opted out of the **All States** database. Delaware corporate records must be searched separately at Lexis and Westlaw (and in other fee-based services) because the state of

Delaware requires a separate search and a separate fee. See the earlier section on Delaware Corporate Records to learn how to search the official site for corporate records.

Nonprofit Organizations and Associations
See Chapter 9, "Finding and Backgrounding Expert Witnesses," for information about locating nonprofit organizations and associations.

Checklist Item 12: Find Reported Decisions, Dockets, Verdicts, and Settlements

Information about companies, their executives, and their products might be found in reported case decisions. If there was no reported decision (because the case was dismissed or settled, for instance), then checking through dockets and through settlements (using jury verdict reporters) can shed some more light on a company's legal activities.

To find reported decisions about a company, it's best to use a pay database because they offer a more comprehensive search. If you only need to search one jurisdiction and primarily current years only, then try the free LexisONE (**http://www.lexisone.com**) or FindLaw (**http://www.findlaw.com**) sites. For information on how to search these sites and how to search for verdicts and settlements, see Chapter 9, "Finding and Backgrounding Expert Witnesses." For information on how to search dockets, see Chapter 8, "Accessing Public Records."

Checklist Item 13: Ascertain Which Agencies Regulate the Product or Industry

Search government Web sites for any mention of the company, its products, or the industry it falls within. Often, there will be separate Web pages on a government agency's site that gather all documents relating to a specific legal issue concerning a specific industry or company. For example, information about the Bell Atlantic/GTE Merger and various supporting documents can be found at the Web site of the agency that regulates telecommunications—the Federal Communications Commission (FCC) (**http://ftp.fcc.gov/ba_gte_merger/**). Documents on the site range from the 226-page Memorandum Opinion and Order for approval to transfer licenses and lines from GTE to Bell (**http://ftp.fcc.gov/Bureaus/Common_Carrier/Orders/2000/fcc00221.pdf**), to FCC Statements to the Spinoff Fact

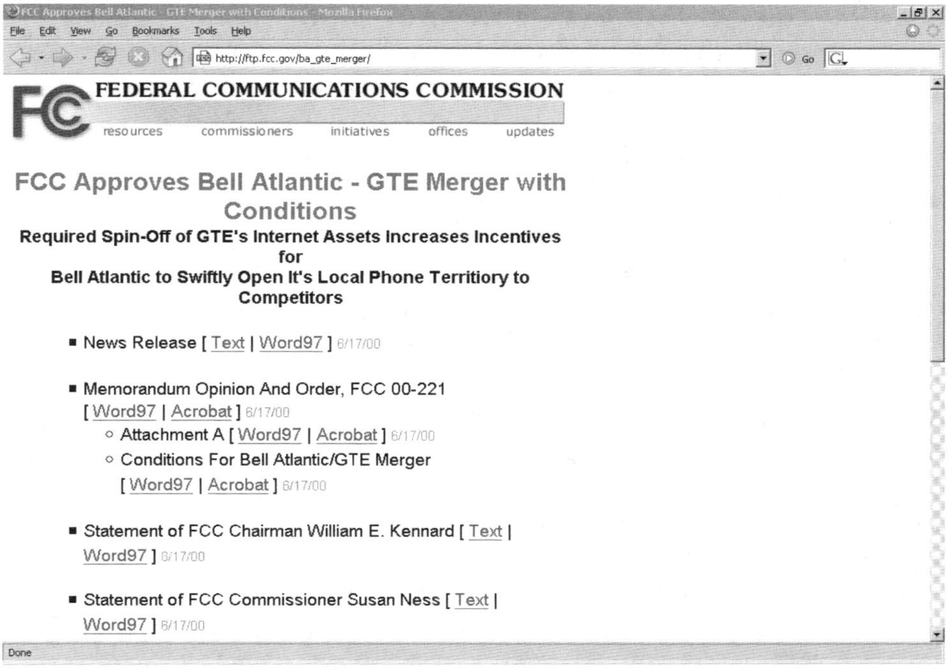

Figure 10-13. The FCC provides detailed information about the companies and industries it regulates.

Sheet. See Chapter 9, "Finding and Backgrounding Expert Witnesses," for information about using FirstGov.gov (**http://www.firstgov.gov**) to either locate government Web sites by agency name or to use FirstGov's Advanced Search page for full-text keyword searching of company names, products, or legal issue through multiple government agencies simultaneously.

Checklist Item 14: Think Outside the Box

Many of the same thinking-outside-the-box research strategies discussed in other chapters in this book also work well with company research, especially searching through postings in online community archives. For information and examples for how to search online communities, see Chapter 7, "Finding and Backgrounding People;" Chapter 8, "Accessing Public Records;" Chapter 11, "Competitive Intelligence Research;" and Chapter 9, "Finding and Backgrounding Expert Witnesses."

Thinking Outside the Box with Online Communities

For example, in Chapter 9, "Finding and Backgrounding Expert Witnesses," we used a scenario where you are representing a client who was seriously injured when the treads of his Firestone tires separated, causing his vehicle to overturn. We noted that searching the online community Google Groups (**http://groups.google.com**) with the keywords "Firestone tires" might lead you to experts, lawyers, or other plaintiffs who were involved in similar lawsuits. But what if you were representing Firestone? You might also think about keyword searching Google Groups to learn (in advance) what people are saying about your client and its product. A useful search might include the following keywords: "firestone tires treads accidents roll-overs or separation." Our Firestone tires search not only brought back messages from people who were having serious tire separation long before the media began reporting the problem, but also brought back a picture showing the shredded treads on someone's Firestone tire.

Also, search with company executives' names through Google Groups, just as you searched with an expert's name. If you are Firestone's in-house counsel (or their retained lawyer), you might consider doing these types of searches on a regular basis to keep apprised of any other problems concerning the company's products that are being discussed in online communities. It's better to be proactive than reactive.

Aside from searching through all postings in all groups at Google Groups, you can also try to narrow down your search to a specific group or groups. There seems to be a group for everything. There are ways to identify the most relevant group (or groups) and then either join the group or search postings only within that group. For instance, by searching with the keywords "explorer tires" at Google Groups, we were able to identify the group rec.autos.4x4 as we read through many postings about Firestone tires and Ford Explorers. You can do the same thing with the companies you represent and once you find postings that are on point, you can determine what group they are coming from (by looking at the heading of the e-mail). You can then choose to follow that group's discussions by entering its name into the Google Groups search box as if it were a keyword, or entering its name into the **Return only messages from the newsgroup** search box found on the Google Groups Advanced Search page, or entering specific keywords (or names of people or companies) into the keyword search boxes on the Google Groups Advanced Search page and then entering the group's name into the **Return only messages from the newsgroup** search box.

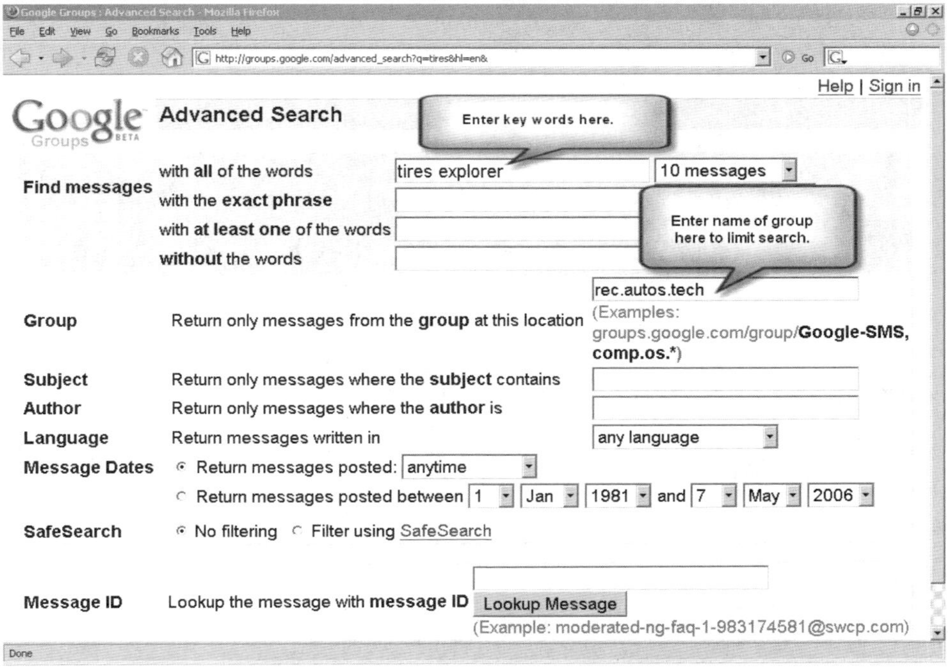

Figure 10-14. Enter keywords or names into the keyword search boxes and then enter the group's URL into the **Return only messages from the news-group** search box to limit your keyword search to one group. Google™ is a trademark of Google Technology, Inc.

To find other online communities to join or to search, aside from Google Groups, visit CataList (**www.lsoft.com/lists/listref.html**), a directory and search engine of nearly 75,000 public LISTSERV lists, which can be searched by keywords found in the list name, list title, description, or host name, or browsed by host country, country, or by number of subscribers. Another site to visit to find the right group is Topica, a directory and search engine that you can either keyword search or browse by categories and subcategories (**http://lists.topica.com/**). (Details about using these sites can be found in Chapter 7, "Finding and Backgrounding People.")

Also, remember to search through blogs and podcasts (See Chapter 20) for "outside the box" information about companies, products, and executives. While many of the blogs and podcasts at these sites will be posted by company outsiders, others might be posted by company insiders or by the company itself.

CHAPTER*ELEVEN*

Competitive Intelligence Research

What Is Competitive Intelligence?

Whether it's referred to as Competitive intelligence (CI), or synonyms such as business intelligence or competitor intelligence, CI can be used to assist lawyers or their clients in making external or internal business decisions. The cliché definition of competitive intelligence involves corporate spies who hoodwink rival executives into revealing trade secrets. While corporate espionage does occur, CI is, generally, not cloak and dagger. Rather, it is a recognized and growing field focused upon "the legal and ethical collection and analysis of information regarding the capabilities, vulnerabilities, and intentions of business competitors," according to the Society of Competitive Intelligence Professionals (SCIP) (**http://www .scip.org/about/index.asp**). CI is aimed at understanding the competitive environment, and as further noted by SCIP, "to help . . . companies achieve and maintain a competitive advantage." Such understanding of the competitive environment can alert you and your clients to potential threats and opportunities. Used wisely, CI can give you the information necessary to help you make a decision based upon your understanding of those threats or opportunities. The decisions to be made may revolve around whether a client should sell or buy a business, whether the lawyer should accept a new client or matter, and so on. The type of information gathered can identify new products planned, the percentage of annual revenue spent on computing, or the hiring or layoff trends of select competitors. Good competitive intelligence acts as a filter to sift through the ocean of available information to identify and analyze the most relevant facts. CI enables businesses to move beyond merely accessing and accumulating information and into acting on the intelligence they've gathered.

Cloak-and-Dagger CI Tactics

Not long ago, a Swedish firm accused a Reuters reporter of employing cloak-and-dagger tactics via the Internet when the reporter published the company's as-yet-unreleased earnings report. The company, Intentia International, was scheduled to release its third-quarter earnings on October 24, but Reuters beat it to the punch by locating it on Intentia's Web site. Reuters asserted, "This information was not accessed from a private or password-protected site, but from the public Internet." Although Intentia had placed the report on the Internet, they had not posted a link from their home page to it. They were going to add the link to the home page once the information held in the earnings report was officially announced to the public. How did the reporter find this seemingly "inside" information? He simply took an educated guess as to the URL he thought Intentia would use to post the report. The guess was based on deciphering the naming system Intentia had used for all previous reports.

Metadata

While most CI does not require "cloak-and-dagger" tactics, an astute researcher might be able to uncover "hidden" information stored within electronic documents.

When you create a document using a computer application (such as Word, WordPerfect, Excel, PowerPoint, or Adobe Acrobat), information about the document (e.g., the author of the document, the date the document was created, changes made to the document, and so on) is automatically inserted behind the scenes. This information is called "metadata" or "hidden" data.

In and of itself, there is nothing sinister about metadata. In fact, it can be useful to the author of the document. For example, before using an older document as a starting point for a new document, the author can ascertain whether it is current enough to use for the new purpose by viewing the metadata that shows the last edit date.

The problems with metadata arise when it is accessed by someone other than the document's original author for some unintended purpose.

Imagine that a lawyer is preparing a demand letter on behalf of a client. Through the drafting and revision process, the description of the facts of the matter are fine-tuned and the terms for which the client will settle are edited and altered. Once the lawyer and the client are in agreement, the lawyer e-mails the final version of the demand letter to the opposition.

An opposing lawyer who has some rudimentary knowledge of computer applications can easily view the metadata that Word or WordPerfect have added to the document without the author's knowledge. In this example, the lawyer who receives the final draft of the demand letter from the original lawyer might be able to view prior drafts of the letter or learn who authored the revisions, all without the knowledge or consent of the sending lawyer, simply by viewing the metadata.

The sending lawyer might face ethical charges for leaving the metadata in the document (and could even face a malpractice suit if the metadata harms the client's case). The receiving lawyer (in New York and Florida) would also face ethical charges for surreptitiously viewing the metadata (**http://www.netforlawyers.com/metadata-ethics.htm**).

Thus, metadata can quickly turn damaging or sinister. For this reason, it is important for lawyers to remove as much of this metadata as possible before sending electronic documents outside of their office. To avoid any ethical or malpractice issues (or any embarrassment), removing metadata is advisable before e-mailing a document. Microsoft's free "Remove Hidden Data add-in" tool claims to remove hidden metadata, but only from Word 2003/XP, Excel 2003/XP, and PowerPoint 2003/XP files, and, according to many experts, it doesn't remove all hidden data.

The better solution is to download a commercial stand-alone "analyze and remove/clean" utility that can analyze documents to determine whether metadata is evident and then remove the metadata. Some choices are Payne Consulting's Metadata Assistant (**http://tinyurl.com/4ykyn**), WorkShare (**http://www.workshare.com/products**) or Kraft Kennedy & Lesser's ezClean (**http://www.kklsoftware.com/**).

Competitive Intelligence and Knowledge Management

Competitive intelligence has traditionally focused on collecting and analyzing external data and information in order to make decisions. However, in more recent years, companies have also been focusing on collecting and analyzing their own internal data and information (and knowledge) to make decisions. This is commonly referred to as Knowledge Management (KM).

CI Departments at Corporations

Of the 1,000 U.S. and European companies surveyed by the CI firm of Fuld & Co. in 2002, about half had an organized CI program, and 45 percent of the U.S. firms that didn't have one said they planned to within the year. Their in-house CI departments commonly save them millions per year. But sometimes it's not just about money. For example, CI can help a company prepare for any kind of change in the marketplace by monitoring any industry or company rumors that could affect them. A case in point is Visa's quick reaction when MasterCard merged with Europay in 2001. Visa's head of market intelligence assigned one of his two staff people to troll the Internet for two hours daily to learn about Master-Card and its other competitors. When MasterCard merged with Europay, Visa had been tracking the impending merger for months. When it was finally announced, Visa already had prepared a letter to their board members on Visa's take on the situation and how it would affect them. The letter was sent within an hour of the merger announcement. Many corporate executives consider such efforts imperative to survival, especially in the global economy.

CI Departments at Law Firms

While many smaller companies either think that they can't afford CI or, more likely, are not savvy enough to recognize its benefits, the lawyer who perceives the worth of CI and takes the time to develop CI research skills can provide immense value to clients. The even savvier lawyer recognizes that CI can benefit the firm's own business development. And the savviest lawyer recognizes the need to develop a CI department in house, just as the larger corporations have. Some firms use their marketing staff and library staff as *de facto* CI staff.

In a 2005 survey of 119 U.S. law firms, Fuld and Company found that "more than three-fourths of the responding firms say they use competitive intelligence in some form." (See **http://www.fuld.com/bin/f.wk?fuld.doc .gen+@TYPE=LS2005**.) The survey also found that more than two-thirds of the firms responding to the survey are using CI data "to make decisions about expanding business and practice areas," despite the fact that 69 percent of the responding firms "don't even have a formal CI budget."

Leonard Fuld, company president, noted in a press release announcing the survey's findings (**http://www.lexisnexis.com/about/releases/ MH-LMASurvey.asp**) that, "these firms are by-and-large [only] using pieces of competitive intelligence techniques. They have begun to grasp the importance of monitoring competitors, but they are still doing that in the context of marketing activities like business development. They tend not to engage in the depth of analysis—such as via the building of early-warning systems, or conducting war games or competitive analysis exercises—that would indicate a more strategic commitment to competitive intelligence."

Other firms have a more complete picture of the role of CI. The law firm of Kilpatrick Stockton, a national firm with about 500 lawyers, designated one of their former law librarians, Donna Cavallini, as their Director of Competitive Knowledge (**http://www.kilstock.com**). Aside from providing CI to the lawyers in her firm (who then use it to assist their clients to make business decisions), she also provides CI to the firm itself to assist them to develop firm business. This can range from keeping the firm informed about competitor law firms (and the legal industry in general), to looking for new legal markets to service, to any other information that helps the firm make sound business decisions. Cavallini makes use of both external sources (such as databases, the Internet, and books) and internal sources (using the in-house knowledge management systems that might include documents and client-contact information). Thus, the title of Director of Competitive Knowledge does best describe her position since her work includes both traditional CI and the less traditional knowledge management.

Why Use the Internet for CI Research?

It is incumbent on lawyers to ensure that their business advice considers all the relevant facts, some of which are discoverable only through careful and comprehensive competitive intelligence research, including use of the Internet. The Internet has quite simply become one of the primary tools in any research strategy that aims to pull data from all relevant sources.

As those who have ventured online can attest, the Internet contains a vast collection of information, some of it fascinating and uniquely valuable, and some of it useless. But the sheer volume of data testifies to the Internet's value for competitive intelligence research. The mere size of the data collection demands attention by CI researchers. The Internet simply can't be ignored.

The emergence of the Internet as a critical business (and therefore legal) information tool parallels the rise of CI as an essential offensive as well as defensive strategic weapon. Both the Internet and CI grew from the need for the U.S. to address global issues. While the Internet was created by the U.S. Department of Defense to provide sustained communication in a catastrophic war, CI's use by domestic corporations rose in response to foreign competitive threats and the need to penetrate overseas markets. Deregulation of various industries in the U.S. and elsewhere has also increased competitive pressures and fueled the need for companies to increase their use of CI.

The parallel development of the Internet and CI suggests a certain symmetry that makes the Internet a natural CI tool. For example, due to its nonproprietary nature and widespread public accessibility, the Internet is perceived as a source of and place to provide "free" information. Perhaps because of this non-ownership, many government bodies, domestic and foreign, have chosen to use the Internet medium as a very low-cost distribution mechanism. Among the information distributed on the Internet are many national databases that are perfectly suited to investigating competitive companies. In the U.S., the Securities and Exchange Commission database known as EDGAR (Electronic Data Gathering, Analysis, and Retrieval system at **http://www.sec.gov/edgarhp.htm**) is one of the best examples of this trend. EDGAR is a source of data on domestic public companies that contains the 10-Ks, 10-Qs, and shareholder proxy statements filed by every publicly held firm. These documents provide a wealth of financial, operational, and strategic information.

As the Internet has grown up along with the discipline of CI, so has the increasing importance of technology in business. As a result, most major companies have established Web sites that are rich with all sorts of information that companies previously did not make easily accessible to the public. For example, some companies post their internal employee directories and company newsletters. Employee directories can be used to identify the caliber of competitor's staffs, while company newsletters may disclose job openings that could indicate the areas in which a competitor is planning development.

Not only does the Internet provide a wealth of CI source data, it also provides access to sources that exist only on the Internet, such as the online communities discussed in the "Thinking Outside the Box" section found in Chapter 7, "Finding and Backgrounding People." For example, if you represent a firm that plans to hire a particular acoustic engineer to develop a new technology or to serve as an expert witness, and you are charged with investigating how this individual represents herself and whether she can be trusted with trade secrets, you might search Google Groups to find a group focusing on acoustic engineering (**http://groups**

.google.com). If you did this, you would find the archives of the alt.sci.physics.acoustics newsgroup (**http://groups.google.com/groups ?hl=en&lr=&ie=UTF-8&group=alt.sci.physics.acoustics**), where you could search by her name or e-mail address for evidence of her past online discussions and behavior. Instead of searching for a specific group, you can simply search the entire Google Groups archive using the expert's name or e-mail address. This is the type of information that is not available anywhere but on the Internet. Another reason to use the Internet for CI is that doing so can avoid data collection liability. Since the Internet is a publicly accessible source, finding information on it may defeat a claim of data theft, privacy violation, or anticompetitive behavior. For example, a company that acquired a competitor's pricing or market share data might be charged with trade-secret theft. However, if that information was found on freely available pages of the competitor's Web site (e.g., not password protected), the defense might argue that one can't steal what's been given away for free. In fact, such a case occurred recently. Although the client insisted he obtained the pricing sheet of his former company from the company's own Web site, the lawyer was unable to locate it . . . until he searched for the page's URL at Archive.org, where he found the pricing sheet. Indeed, it had once been posted by the company, but the company had recently taken it off their site in an effort to claim that the competitor was engaged in "theft of trade secrets."

Anonymous CI Researching

Your IP Address

The Internet is an almost perfect place for a CI researcher because your use of the Internet for research, in most instances, cannot easily be traced back specifically to you. Therefore, if you are viewing data on a rival's Web site, the rival would not be easily tipped off. But, every time you use your browser to visit a Web site, your browser does leave a record of your Internet Protocol (IP) address on that site's Web server. Your IP address is merely a series of numbers (like a telephone number) and is in no way connected to your e-mail address. In general, every Web site you visit can obtain the following information about you in addition to your IP address: (1) your Internet Service Provider (ISP), (2) what country you are from, (3) what Web browser you are using, (4) what operating system you are using, and (5) possibly what domain name you are using. Therefore, while it is not easy to precisely identify a specific visitor to a Web site via an IP address, if the IP address leaves behind the domain name this might give a clue that someone from your company has visited a site. Additionally, a site owner could block a specific IP address, or a range of IP addresses, in an effort to block access to their site from a specific competitor.

Tracking an IP Address

The Webmaster of a site you have visited could use an online IP tracker, such as those found at TraceRoute.org (**http://www.traceroute.org/**) to determine the ISP to whom an IP address (as recorded in their traffic log) is assigned. In theory, the ISP could match that IP address to a specific user by reviewing its own log-in records. The target site's owner could then figure out that you visited them, but it is unlikely that an ISP would turn over any identifying information without a court order. But, for researchers who want to be certain they are leaving no identifying trail at all, there are ways to do so by using third-party providers to conduct research and send e-mails anonymously.

Surfing Anonymously

A number of services exist that allow you to conduct research anonymously. By using a service such as Anonymizer (**http://www.anonymizer .com**), you can anonymously access any Web site—leaving behind the IP address of the Anonymizer server rather than your own. To use Anonymizer's free cloaking service, just type the Web address (URL) of the site you wish to visit into the "free private surfing" box in the upper right-hand corner of the Anonymizer.com home page. The current version of the service has even downplayed the advertisement for the pay version of Anonymizer that is displayed at the top of each site visited while using the free service. A no-ad version, with additional security features, is available for $29.99. The Cloak (**http://www.the-cloak.com**) offers similar free and pay services.

For an example of how this all works, let's say we are conducting Internet research about IBM from a computer at our company, Internet For Lawyers. Our Internet access is provided by the ISP Earthlink, the world's second-largest ISP, and is configured much like your non-networked home (DSL or dial-up) account. If we point our Web browser to IBM's company Web site (**http://www.ibm.com**), the Webmaster at IBM can review IBM's site's traffic logs to learn that a Web user who had been assigned our specific IP address has visited IBM.com. They cannot easily discern, however, that we were the specific individual who visited IBM.com, only that someone (or even something, since robot programs commonly visit Web sites) assigned to our specific IP address (at that precise moment) visited. Using a Trace Route service, IBM could determine that the IP address was controlled by Earthlink. With our IP address (and a court order) they could request that Earthlink identify us.

Let's look at an example of how we can trace a domain name. The IP addresses of some corporate networks (and this includes some law firms) might broadcast more identifying information regarding their users than an ISP does, such as their domain name. We know this because when we review the traffic logs of our own Web site (**http://www.netforlawyers .com**) we readily see the domain names of specific institutions' computers whose users accessed our site. Recent examples include Gibson, Dunn & Crutcher; Pillsbury Winthrop; Jefferies & Co. (an investment bank); IBM; UCLA; and the U.S. Navy, among others. We cannot, however, determine the precise identity of the individual visitors by reviewing our traffic logs (short of that court order).

Sending E-mail Anonymously

There are also free online services that can hide your identity when sending e-mail. These free, anonymous re-mailers allow you to send anonymous messages via e-mail. Web-based versions offer you a form in which to input the destination e-mail address, subject, and message. Clicking the **Submit** button sends the message to the address you entered. The delivered message contains no information that identifies you as the sender (unless you include it in the body of the message). Additionally, most of these re-mailers claim not to retain any data regarding the IP address of the sender. One example of a re-mailer can be found at **http://www.anon-remailer.gq.nu**. Because these re-mailers can disappear from the Internet as fast as they appear, visit the Open Directory for a list of links to many such sites (**http://dmoz.org/Computers/Internet/E-mail/ Anonymous_Mailers**).

Cookies Can Reveal Your Precise Identity

One way that a Web site can discover your exact identity is when another site has left a cookie on your computer and this cookie includes your identity. Basically, other sites can sneak a peek at the cookies already saved on your machine by other Web sites to determine your identity. Cookies (with such identifying information as your name, e-mail address, password for a specific Web site, or a combination of this information) can be accessed and deciphered by Web site servers other than the site that originally generated the specific cookie. They can then track your Internet usage—identifying sites you've visited and perhaps even your password and user name for those sites. (Newer versions of Netscape Communicator and Internet Explorer can be configured to warn you before cookies are added to your computer. This gives you the option of allowing the cookie to be placed on your computer or not.)

Protecting Yourself

There are many software programs that are cookie-killers (and more) that you can use to protect your privacy on the Internet. One of the more popular ones is called Window Washer, available from Webroot Software (**http://www.webroot.com**). The company Web site explains that Window Washer will "Wash away all traces of your PC and Internet activity and improve system performance." It also explains that the program handles both browser cleaning (it clears out your cookies, cache, history, mail trash, drop-down address bar, auto-complete forms, and downloaded program files) and PC cleaning (it clears out your recycle bin, registry streams, Windows run and find lists, history, scandisk files, recently viewed pictures, locked index.dat files, recently opened documents list, and Windows temp files folder).

ZoneAlarm (**http://www.zonelabs.com**) is a PC firewall that "keeps your personal data and privacy safe from Internet hackers and data thieves." The basic product protects against worms, Trojans, and spyware, and 47 types of malicious e-mail attachments, while ZoneAlarm kills cookies, and blocks ads.

Where Does CI Information Come From?

CI comes from the same Internet resources that we've already discussed for researching experts, companies, public records, and people. CI can come directly from competitors themselves (such as their Web sites and their government filings) or it can come from external sources such as industrial reports, periodical articles, directories, financial industry data, association materials, and various databases. And, we start CI research the same way we do other factual research: by gathering information from basic and traditional sources on the Internet that often have evolved from print materials (like phone and business directories) and expanding toward creative sources (such as online communities like Google Groups, eBay, blogs, and so on) that are unique to the Internet.

Web Sites for CI Research

Starting-Point Sites for CI

A useful site to get you started on the use of CI is the Web site of Fuld & Company, one of the preeminent research and consulting firms in this field (**http://www.fuld.com**). Its founder, Leonard Fuld, has placed selected chapters from his book, *The New Competitor Intelligence,* on his site for review (**http://www.fuld.com/Tindex/CIbook/chap01.html**).

To find specific URLs that will assist you in your CI endeavors, refer to Chapter 10 in this book, "Company Research." Because you often need to focus on specific industries when conducting CI, you'll find the following two sites' links useful: (1) the Internet Intelligence Index, provided by Fuld & Company (**http://www.fuld.com/Tindex/I3.html**), and (2) the business research resource guide developed by the Business Librarians at the Rutgers University Libraries (**http://www.libraries.rutgers.edu/rul/rr_gate way/research_guides/busi/business.shtml**). And, because CI has a lingo all its own, you might also find Fuld's Intelligence Dictionary of some use (**http://www.fuld.com/Tindex/IntelDict.html**).

Using Search Engines for CI Research

The first step in using the Internet for CI is to conduct a broad search to find the most obvious sources. Start with keyword searches in various search engines (Google, Yahoo!, AltaVista, Alltheweb, FirstGov.gov, and so on) to see what turns up. Among the most obvious sources (and easiest to use) that you will find with a search engine are competitors' Web sites. The next basic source to study is company directory sites, in order to find more objective information than what's found at a company's own Web site.

News, Alerts, and E-newsletters

News is a natural place to find out what competitors are up to or what potential clients who you plan on pitching are doing. Many companies put news releases on their home pages. Read these when looking for insight about what the company has to say about new products, new hires, and so on. You can search for press releases (for free) by country, company, organization name, or keywords at PR Newswire (**http://www.prnewswire .com/news**). If you click on **advanced search** you can also tailor your search by choosing **All Releases** (in the past 30 days), **News by Company** (by company name, plus an archive search back to at least 1996) ,

Topical Search (by industry, state, company name, or subject), or **Keyword Search** (last three days or last thirty days).

But, for more current (and objective) insights, review newspaper and magazine articles about companies. For the most current news, use the News tabs on Google, Yahoo!, and AltaVista's home pages. To cast a wider net for news, try NewsDirectory (**http://www.newsdirectory.com/web**), an index of 20,400 English-language media links (from newspapers, magazines, and television stations to colleges, visitor bureaus, and governmental agencies). Also, refer to the following chapters in this book for more news and magazines sources: Chapter 5, "General Factual Research;" Chapter 9, "Finding and Backgrounding Expert Witnesses;" and Chapter 10, "Company Research."

Just as the Visa CI department relied on old-fashioned manual trolling of the Web to learn about the MasterCard-Europay merger (rather than just relying upon automated alerts), so does Donna Cavallini of the law firm Kilpatrick Stockton. Her explanation is that sometimes events or concepts are stated in a much different way than she had anticipated when she originally chose the keywords for her automated alerts. However, she still uses some automated alerts, especially if they are free (Westlaw's Clips offers free alerts to headlines to its subscribers), but she manually scans about 400 e-newsletters, most of which are free (but might require registration). Some of the newsletters that Cavallini scans relate to the firm's current clients, while others may provide the firm with leads for new business, especially financial-related newsletters such as those from Financial Times (**http://news.ft.com/home/us**). From this information, you might be able to target potential clients. She also subscribes to newsletters offered by Forbes and Tech Wire.

Using Industry Watchdogs

Thinking like a researcher in the context of CI involves thinking about who would monitor or care about the target subject. Who would want to catalog such information? Where would they catalog it? Combine this thought process with the basic and creative sources available on the Internet and elsewhere. Industry watchdogs such as unions, government regulatory agencies, and professional or trade associations may be monitoring your target company or industry. Therefore, you might find it fruitful to search through information found on their Web sites.

Government Regulatory Agencies as Industry Watchdogs

Regulatory agencies at all levels collect information on companies. Often, vital product and plant intelligence, as well as records of complaints and investigations and any action taken as a result will be found in these Internet data warehouses. Knowing how to get around amid government data is a specialty unto itself, now made a bit easier with FirstGov.gov. It's an excellent starting point for government research because it indexes over 50 million state and federal government documents (see Chapter 6, "Government Resources Online," for more information). And, since FirstGov.gov covers all agencies, you don't need to try to figure out which agency or agencies are regulating a certain industry, company, or matter. Simply use FirstGov.gov to search with the keywords that describe the industry, company, or matter at hand, or search by a specific company or executive's name to search across multiple agencies, commissions, boards, etc., simultaneously.

A potentially useful government regulatory agency site, if you are aiming to identify a competitor's weak points, is the Occupational Safety and Health Administration (OSHA) at **http://www.osha.gov**. It provides, among many other valuable free resources, Hazard Information Bulletins identifying manufacturers whose products have caused injury and death (**http://www.osha-slc.gov/dts/hib/index.html**). These monthly OSHA bulletins can make a sharp impression.

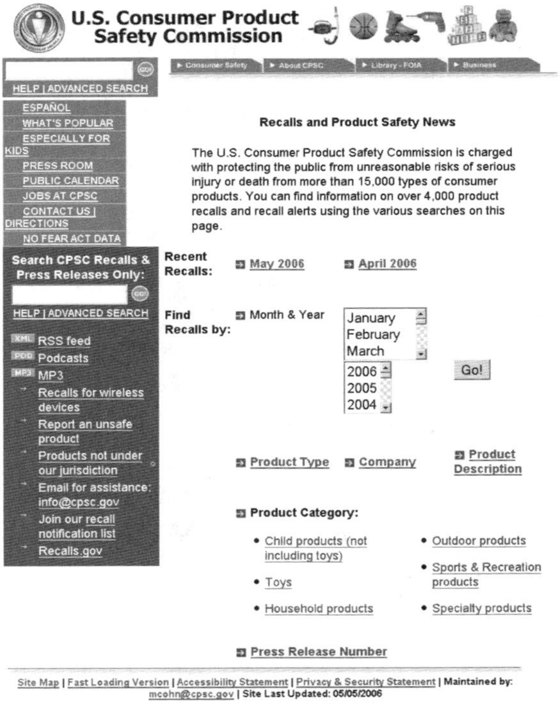

Figure 11-1. The U.S. Consumer Product Safety Commission's Recall database can be searched by date of recall, by product type, company, product description, or product category.

Finding Associations, Public Interest Groups, and Unions that Serve as Industry Watchdogs

To find associations, use Yahoo!'s extensive professional association list (**http://www.yahoo.com/Business_and_Economy/Organizations/ Professional**), and see the section on associations in Chapter 9, "Finding and Backgrounding Expert Witnesses" in this book. To find union sites, see the AFL-CIO Web site (**http://www.aflcio.org**), which provides links to numerous other unions (**http://www.aflcio.org/aboutunions/unions**) and links to sites that cover corporate accountability. Public interest groups can be found by using a search engine and searching for words that describe the industry (or situation) and adding the phrase "public interest groups" or the word "advocacy." For example, if your firm represented an oil company, you'd want to keep apprised about what the public was saying about the oil industry (or your company). To do this, we searched for "public interest groups" and oil. One of the results was a site with a list of public interest groups on the topic of oil and the environment, one of which was the Offshore Oil and Gas Environment Forum (**http://www .oilandgasforum.net**), whose mission is to "[T]o learn more about these potential impacts and what we can do [about] oil exploration and production operations [that] have the potential for a variety of impacts on the environment."

AFL-CIO's PayWatch

http://www.aflcio.org/corporateamerica/paywatch/

Purpose: The AFL-CIO Web site offers myriad articles on CEO income and allows users to search its database to learn specific CEO incomes and pay packages.

Content: Just one part of the AFL-CIO's large and multifaceted Web site, the Executive PayWatch database has links to several different articles covering the "disproportionate share of the wealth" CEOs are paid. On the left side of the page, you can quickly access articles such as "2004 Trends in CEO Pay" and "What Is Wrong with CEO Pay?" Under those articles are more in-depth examinations of the business practices of Wal-Mart, Enron, and others.

There is also a Top 10 of 2004's most highly paid CEOs in the county located in the middle of the page (Yahoo!'s Terry Semel heads the list). To access the site's company database for other CEO information, scroll down and click on *The CEO and You*. The first page will describe the information you will be able to access. Clicking on **Database** in the middle of the resulting page will give you an alphabetical index listing of the companies (simply click on a letter to get to that section faster). Once you have located the company (e.g., Abercrombie & Fitch, Co.), you can click on the name to view detailed information on the CEO's compensation and stock options. On the right-hand side of the *The CEO and You* home page, you can also search for a specific company by name or ticker symbol, as well as by industry or dollar amount of total compensation.

Other information available for each CEO includes: *How You Compare, How Other Workers Compare, CEO Fact Sheet*, and *The CEO Shopping Cart.*

Our View: AFL-CIO's CEO PayWatch database provides an easy way to determine the total compensation for the CEO of a particular company, or an industry. The AFL-CIO's agenda is to expose the "travesty" behind multimillion dollar CEO paychecks. Their articles and most of the links listed above in the database section are all skewed toward showing the "injustice" to workers that this kind of CEO compensation creates. Regardless, the database still provides the user with valuable competitive intelligence (or perhaps just interesting knowledge) with which to arm yourself or your clients in business.

Using Government Agencies to Find Business Information

The U.S. Department of Commerce (DOC) (**http://www.commerce .gov**) provides reams and reams of business-related information via the Internet. The number of bureaus and agencies that fall within the DOC's jurisdiction is staggering. There's testimony, export schedules, and regulations, and it goes on and on.

The SEC's EDGAR system (**http://www.sec.gov/edgarhp.htm**) is also among the most useful federal government sites for public company CI because a company's filings can provide significant insight into its operations. In addition, since these filings are required by law, they have a certain amount of assumed accuracy. (See Chapter 10, "Company Research," for detailed information about searching EDGAR and other SEC databases that permit full-text searching of filings.)

Researching with SIC Codes and NAICS Codes

The government's Standard Industrial Classification (SIC) system (**http://www.sec.gov/info/edgar/siccodes.htm**) and the North American Industry Classification System (NAICS) (**http://www.census.gov/ epcd/naics02/naicod02.htm**) classify all businesses into categories, from very broad categories to very narrow categories, using descriptive words and numerical codes. For example, businesses relating to the agriculture, forestry, fishing, and hunting industries are assigned the broad NAICS category code 11, while the narrow category of soybean farming is assigned code 11111. The codes can be used to search various databases that allow SIC or NAICS searching. The codes are the key for accomplishing all kinds of CI research because they allow you to create lists of specific companies

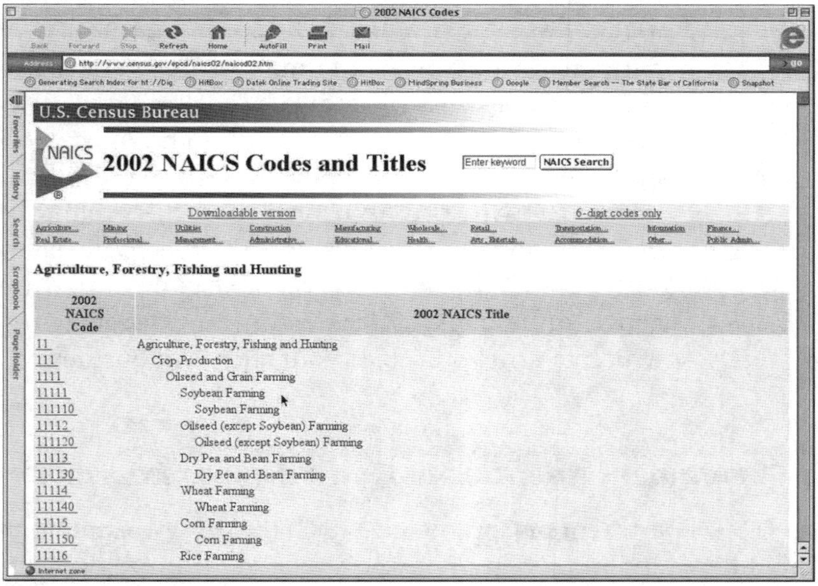

Figure 11-2. Note that agriculture, forestry, fishing, and hunting are assigned NAICS code 11, and are then broken down into more specific sectors, such as soybean farming (code 11111), wheat farming (code 11114), and so on.

within a specific industry. For instance, if you wanted to create a list of a client's competitors or you wanted to create a list of specific companies in an industry the firm wanted to service, you would use the SIC or NAICS codes.

NAICS was developed jointly by the U.S., Canada, and Mexico to be able to compare business activity statistics across North America. Although NAICS was to replace the SIC system, you still see references to SIC as you research. Many business directories (such as the subscriber side of Hoover's) and online databases (such as EDGAR and other SEC databases discussed in Chapter 10, "Company Research") allow searching by SIC code (and sometimes by NAICS code). Some databases also allow you to further refine the SIC and NAICS searches by geographic location, number of employees, and revenues. Gale's Company and Business Resource Center (a company directory database noted in the "Free Internet Access to Library Databases And Catalogs" section of Chapter 5, "General Factual Research") also allows for this type of refined searching (for free). Some of the databases also can generate mailing labels from your custom-designed SIC list.

The NAICS codes are found at the U.S. Census Bureau's site (**http://www.census.gov/epcd/naics02/naicod02.htm**). They can be browsed numerically or can be keyword searched. There are also tables that show how the NAICS codes correspond to the older SIC codes. There are various places to find the SIC codes, but not all have searchable keyword indexes (EDGAR has a numerical list only). For an easy-to-use searchable keyword index, see **http://www.osha.gov/pls/imis/sicsearch.html**.

Locating Researchers in a Targeted Field

Another good approach for researching industry developments is to find companies and universities that conduct research in that field. For example, if you need to find chemical industry developments, use a search engine or directory to find your way to chemical companies, research organizations, and academic departments that make information available online.

Locating CI About Private Companies

Some company reports, such as D & B reports, can be purchased (**http://www.dnb.com**). (See Chapter 10, "Company Research," for a detailed profile of D & B's content.) They contain self-reported data from each company being researched (usually private companies). The information is not required to be reported by law (as public company information is). It's fair to say that a good researcher is a skeptical researcher, especially when the data is self-reported in this manner. Whenever possible, get independent verification for all information you need to depend on.

The following are some of the reasons D & B gives for ordering a comprehensive company report:

- To identify companies that have slow payment experience, which might indicate the company is undergoing financial stress
- To use business ratios to help make sure a company has enough assets to pay you
- To compare a company to others in the same industry, locally or nationally
- To background a company's owners or executives
- To discover how many times a company has moved and where— and even how well it functioned under natural disasters or fires
- To see if any suits have been brought against the target company

Using Creative Sources for CI Research

Since the Internet is a newer medium, it lends itself very well to creative research, or what we referred to as "thinking outside the box" in Chapter 7, "Finding and Backgrounding People." Virtually every sector of society, including government, nonprofits, public and private companies, and religious and secular organizations, are all looking for ways to take advantage of the Internet's multimedia, interactive, and international features. As a result, there's a lot of different sorts of information provided on the Internet, which you can turn to your research advantage.

For example, the many classified and job advertisement sites on the Internet are excellent places to scope out competitors. You may find that a competitor is trying to fill new positions in a brand-new business area. Alternatively, a rival might be trying to fill key positions that have recently been vacated (although no public announcement was made). To find out about job opportunities that indicate a change in a company, you can visit the following Web sites: the local newspaper, where classified are often included; a job database site such as Monster.com; or simply visit the targeted company's Web site.

Let's say you represent a telecommunications company that competes with MCI. In the course of your representation, you want to know what sort of new initiatives MCI is undertaking. While scouring the MCI site for clues, you discover the **Career Center** page that MCI uses to recruit new employees and you notice that the job openings are searchable by job category and by state (**http://careers.mci.com/careers/us/ index.phtml?pagename=jobsearch**). It so happens that your client is particularly concerned about a suspected new research and development facility being built by MCI in northern California. In your research, you discover that in fact, MCI has posted numerous ads for exotically skilled engineers in Sacramento, thereby lending credence to your client's concerns. You also notice that MCI is hiring commercial law lawyers (and you weigh the possibilities).

E-mailing the Experts

Another creative intelligence gathering technique is the use of e-mail. E-mail is an easy way to communicate with experts, reporters, analysts, insiders, educators, and players in specific industries and markets. You can use e-mail to solicit opinions, explanations, comments, and even rumors. You might use e-mail to contact journalists who are writing company profiles or researching new markets. To identify and locate experts, see Chapter 9, "Finding and Backgrounding Expert Witnesses."

Conducting a Links Search

One of the completely unique-to-the-Internet techniques you can try is to find out what Web sites link to your competitor's page. This technique may alert you to previously unknown strategic alliances or may open up a market for your client's products that hadn't been foreseen. Use the **Links Search** function at Google.com (which we explained in the section "Credibility Checklist" in Chapter 1, "Using the Internet for Factual Research"). For example, if you type the URL of a company into the **Links** search box, you will be able to see how many pages point to your target company. This may indicate alliances or may otherwise provide you with insight about the company.

Using Online Community Postings

Another way to leverage the Internet's uniqueness is to take advantage of the "off the beaten track" information (such as rumors or public opinion) found in various online community postings about a company, product, or executive. For example, you might post a message in one of these online communities, such as ones found at Google Groups (for detailed information about using Google Groups, see the discussion on "Thinking Outside the Box with Online Communities" in Chapter 10, "Company Research"), asking a question about your client's competitor (or even about your own client) to determine what's being said about them and their products or services. You'll need to join the group to do this. Then, sit back and monitor the responses. You can join a group that is very narrow in its scope, like banking in Britain (uk.finance), or you could try broader discussion areas, like business (alt.business), import-export business (alt.business.importexport), or international marketplace (biz.marketplace.international).

The following are sites where you can locate all types of relevant on-line communities (whether you want to lurk, join, or search the archives, if available):

- Google Groups for Usenet postings (**http://groups.google.com**)
- Boardreader for message board postings (**http://www.boardreader .com**)

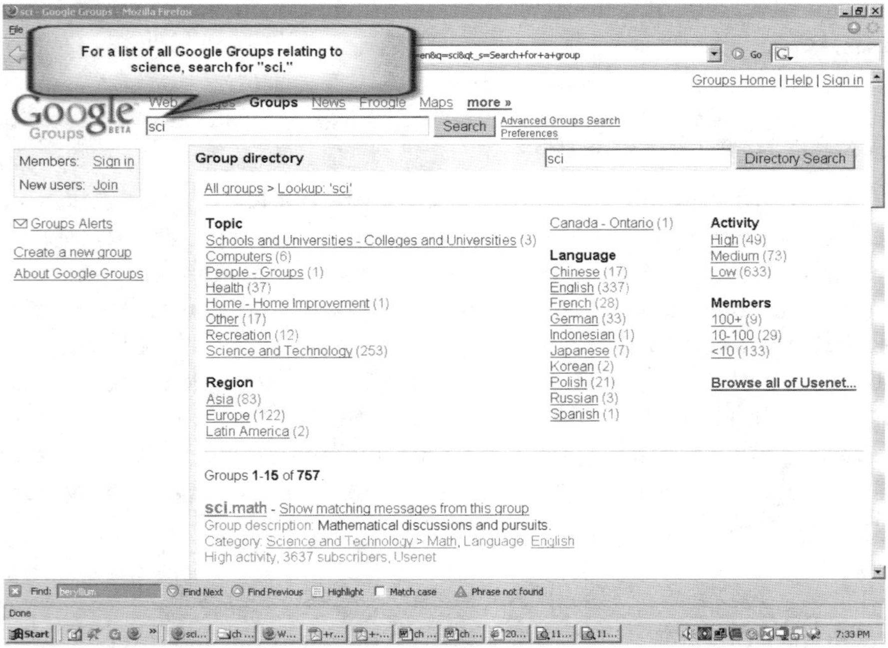

Figure 11-3. This is a sample of all the various science-related groups available for joining (or lurking or searching the archives) found in Google Groups. Google™ is a trademark of Google Technology Inc.

- CataList for LISTSERV lists (**http://www.lsoft.com/catalist.html**)
- Daypop for blogs (**http://www.daypop.com**)

For detailed information on these resources, see the section on on-line communities in Chapter 9, "Finding and Backgrounding Expert Witnesses," and in Chapter 20, "Weblogs, RSS Feeds, and Podcasts."

Cloaking in a Group

For more clandestine research, you can search a group's archives without joining the group. If you do want to participate, however, you usually need to join. In either case, you'll probably want to mask your identity by using one of the cloaking sites discussed earlier in this chapter.

Searching Opinions, Briefs, Complaints, and Settlements

Besides searching case law databases (free or pay) for lawsuit information about a company or person whom you are researching, see the Delaware Corporate Law Clearinghouse site. Posted here are selected opinions, briefs, complaints, settlements, motions, and other documents filed in business law matters in the Delaware Court of Chancery, from March 1999–December 2001. From January 2002 until March 2004, the court continued to send opinions to the Clearinghouse. (These opinions are still available from the Widener site by clicking on the "Recent Opinions" link on the left-hand side of the home page. An up-to-date collection of opinions is available from the Chancery Court's own Web site (**http://courts.delaware.gov/Courts/Court%20of%20Chancery/**). To access the opinions, hover over the **Opinions** button near the top of the page and select **Chancery** from the drop-down menu (**http://corporate-law.widener.edu/case.htm**).

Finding Confidential Company Information on the Internet

Is someone posting the "confidential" internal memos of your firm, your client's company (or the opposition's) on the Internet? Inter-nalMemos.com offers nearly 2,500 internal memos from companies ranging from General Electric and WorldCom to AOL TimeWarner. It is free to browse the abstracts of available memos (in chronological order—back to

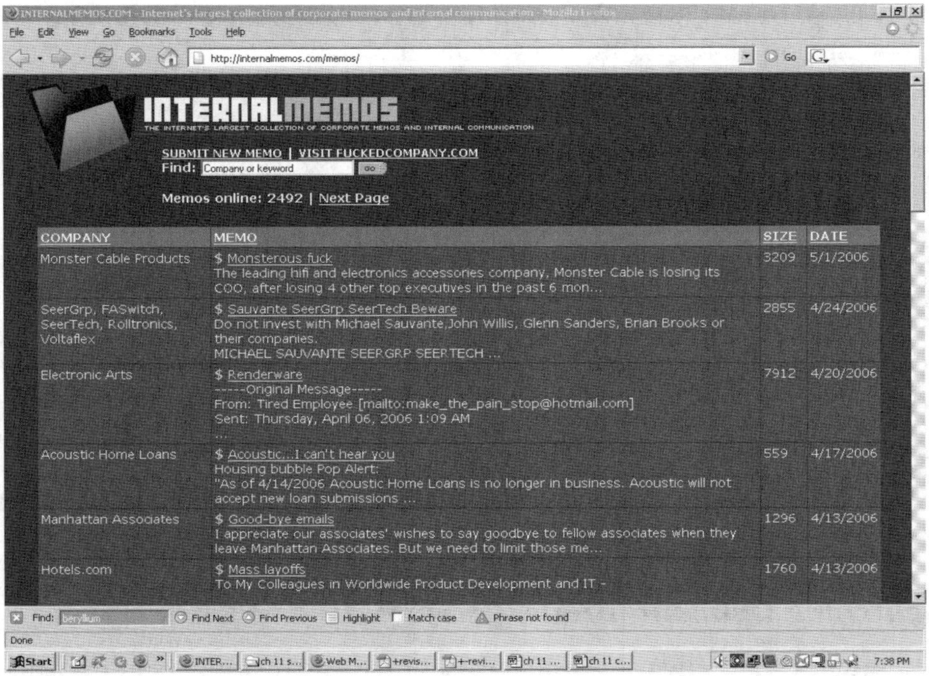

Figure 11-4. You can access the internal memos of numerous public and private companies at InternalMemos.com.

1998) or search by company name or keyword. However, only some memos may be viewed for free; the majority require a paid subscription to view. A $45 monthly or $180 annual subscription buys unlimited viewing of the premium memos. InternalMemos.com solicits additions to its database via a form on the site. Visitors can cut and paste the contents of internal e-mails, or type text from hard copy documents into the Internet form for posting on the InternalMemos.com site (**http://www.internalmemos.com**).

Using CI for Law Firm Business Development

To learn what your rivals are doing and saying, try the free LawKT (Law Knowledge Tools) service (**http://www.lawkt.com**). This site allows you to quickly browse by category (e.g., "Adverse Interest," or "Negligence, Compensatory"), full-text search over 60,000 Web-based publications (such as client alerts, newsletters, and articles) from hundreds of the world's leading firms. Previously, this service carried an annual subscription fee of $750.

LawKT.com also offers an expanded "premium" service that is also free called Nextaris (**http://www.nextaris.com/**). It combines a Web-based search engine with easy-to-use tools to capture images, save clips or files, publish the information you've located, and notify others where they can share your information. Nextaris users can create separate folders to save and categorize the materials they find in their searches so that only they can access the saved data, or they can activate the **Publish** feature and select which of those folders they wish to share in an online blog format with other Internet users.

Free subscription users get 100MB of storage space for the information they find, upgrading to a paid $49/year membership includes a total of 250 MB of storage.

Docket research is particularly useful for business development as we noted in the section on "Court Dockets and Pleadings" in Chapter 8, "Accessing Public Records." For example, NOS docket research can identify hot areas of practice that the firm might want to shift to. Searching dockets by a lawyer's name and a practice area might help you target someone you'd like to recruit to develop a certain practice area for the firm.

Also useful for recruiting (or for obtaining background information about specific lawyers) is Martindale-Hubbell's law directory online (**http://www.martindale.com**) or FindLaw's directory (**http://lawyers.find law.com**) because they allow for practice area searching.

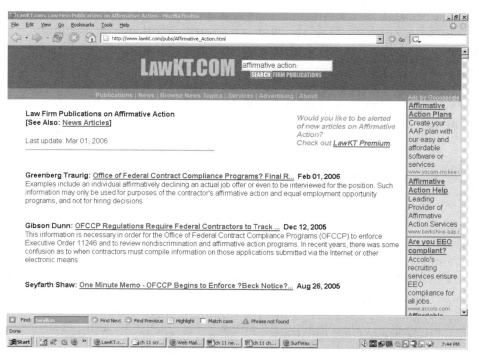

Figure 11-5. Using LawKT.com, Web-based lawyers can full-text search over 60,000 publications from hundreds of law firms, in addition to searching major law, news, and other Web sites.

Using Public Records for CI

Review Chapter 8, "Accessing Public Records," for links to public record databases. Some of the public records you might want to search for your CI endeavor include bankruptcies, liens, court dockets, real estate records, patents, trademarks, and so on.

Searching with Pay Databases

When researching CI, using pay databases is in order. Cavallini recommends Dow Jones' VentureSource (**http://www.venturesource.com**) to track venture capital sources or find information about executives and their past affiliations, Hoover's (**http://www.hoovers.com**) when you need company executive biographies (it covers more executives than other company directories), and D & B (formerly known as Dun & Bradstreet, **http://www.dnb.com**) for private companies (although it seems they are no longer providing annual revenues for most of the companies), to name a few.

Cookie Lewis, president of Infomania, a legal and business research company based in Los Angeles, is a proponent of using LexisNexis for CI because she believes it has the largest amount of industry-related publications. She also uses it when she needs to search nationally for public records and for docket searching (through the LexisNexis-owned CourtLink). Other databases also have industry-related publications, such as Westlaw and Dialog, and many of them have CI databases that compile company dossiers.

War Story: An Industry-Trend CI Search

Cookie Lewis relates the following CI project she recently began. A client hired her to help him decide whether to sell land to a time-share developer. The land was located in a highly desirable area—just off the Strip in Las Vegas. To assist her client, Lewis first ran a search for magazine and news articles indexed in LexisNexis, focusing her search on the time-share industry in general and also zeroing in on the time-share industry in Las Vegas. Her choice of keywords for her search, in addition to the word "time-share," are illustrative of what a typical industry-trend CI search would be. Lewis searched for the word "time-share" within fifteen words of the following: "forecast OR statistics OR report OR trend OR Las Vegas." (She also ran a more-focused search by using the Lexis real estate articles news database.) By choosing search terms that included the word "report," Lewis would be likely to locate reports (if there were any at all) that had already been written about the time-share industry. The smart CI researcher first looks for reports that have already been written on the intended topic to save the client the expense involved in writing a new report. The next step in her CI plan was to focus on the time-share developer, to learn about his background and to ascertain his track record in time-share developments. Was he litigious? How many other time-shares had he developed? Did he have solid financial backing for his other developments? How much property did he own?

To answer these questions, Lewis knew public record searching would be in order. Lewis ran a UCC search (through Lexis) to find out who was lending the developer the money to finance his projects. The search showed her that his financers were solid. She also ran his name and the company's name through CourtLink to learn about any lawsuits filed by or against him and his company. What she found led her to ascertain that he was litigious. Putting that fact together with his financial worth (ascertained by a property record search, among other searches), it became obvious that he was willing and financially able to litigate in the face of any conflict. She alerted her client to these facts and explained that they indicated that the client might find himself being sued by the developer if he and the developer ever had a conflict over the sale or the terms. And, given the developer's worth, it might be too expensive for the client to defend himself.

Finally, as she read articles about the time-share industry in Las Vegas, she got wind that there was some Las Vegas City Council activity about it. What she learned was that the hotel industry, in their quest to fight off time-share developers from taking over the market, were getting into the time-share market themselves. The next step Lewis took was a trip to the Internet to visit the city's Web site. There, she tried to discover if the City Council's minutes were on the site (or their taped hearings). Her final step was to compile a list of time-share competitors in Las Vegas and pull their permits (approved and pending). She did this for several reasons: to benchmark the price her client should seek for his land, to identify other potential buyers to seek counter offers, and to forecast time-share development in Las Vegas for five years out.

As you can see, CI specialists like Cookie Lewis and Donna Cavallini know where to look for the information (in pay and free sites) and know how to piece the information together to assist clients to draw legally and financially sound conclusions. The clients can then take action based upon this solid information.

Parting Recommendations of a CI Expert

Cavallini recommends that you bookmark everything you find while surfing the Internet, even if you have no present use for it. She also notes, as we have earlier, that you might not find your answer on the Internet, but you may find a lead to it there. Also, she regularly takes advantage (as we do) of the remote library databases that library card holders can access for free. As a prime example of using these last two tips, Cavallini tells about the time she was searching for biographical information about an executive of a small company. She used the Master Index of Biographies (one of those valuable free, remote library databases), and although the biography was not on the Internet, the index provided a lead by showing that there was a biography of the target executive in the 1992 print edition of the Directory of Corporate Affiliations. A quick post to a mailing list resulted in someone sending a copy of the biography to her from the 1992 print edition. Finally, she recommends that you leave no stone unturned, as the following war story illustrates.

War Story: CI at Amazon.com

A client (a venture capital group) had hired a president for one of their companies. He had come from a big accounting firm. After two years of steadily losing money (and hiring his son in an executive position), the client asked the firm to do some background checking, in the hope of finding a reason to fire him. After searching the NASD database (which showed no actions had been filed against him) and finding nothing else damaging after completing a thorough search of the Internet and pay databases, Cavallini searched Amazon.com using his name. She found that he had written a book, but because it was unrelated to his profession, she nearly brushed it off. But, applying her leave-no-stone-unturned mantra, she clicked over to it, and noted that someone had left a scathing review—not of the book, but of the executive himself! It gave a long account of how the "reviewer" had been defrauded by this executive and referred to a book that had chronicled the fraud (and the pending investigation). Cavallini obtained the book and turned it over to the lawyer she was working with. It proved to be the smoking gun and gave the client grounds for firing the executive for failing to be forthcoming about his past and failing to disclose that he was currently under investigation.

Failing to conduct CI research is a mistake. To quote Cookie Lewis's mantra, "It's what you don't know that can hurt you." CI research can help you discover what you don't know. Armed with all the facts, you can then make sound business and legal decisions.

CHAPTER**TWELVE**

Medical Research

Why Do Medical Research?

Successful personal injury and medical malpractice actions usually require a fair amount of general medical information regarding the condition, in addition to the testimony of medical experts. The opinions of experts with direct clinical experience, for example, can provide invaluable perspective on the client's specific situation. However, a familiarity with the medical issues involved will help you keep in control of the case. Gathering your own medical background information can give you the edge in the case. Whether it's in cross-examining the opposition's expert, or even on redirect with your own expert, an awareness of the specific medical issues in question is essential.

Continuous change in the ever-more-complex health care industry has resulted in new sources of work for lawyers. In response to the rising cost of health care, new types of organizations, jobs, equipment, procedures, and intensified patient-privacy requirements under the Health Insurance Portability and Accountability Act (HIPAA) are changing the profession on a regular basis. These changes can result in legal disputes, for example, pitting the quality of care against health care company interests in making a profit. Recent issues include the responsibilities of managed care companies; the displacement of traditional jobs (like nurses) by new, often less-experienced workers; and pharmaceutical company liability. As the industry evolves, so will the nature of disputes and contracts handled by lawyers who practice in the health-related fields. Lawyers will need to understand the new issues and arguments relative to hospitals, physicians, corporate liability, and standard treatment guidelines for common conditions. The Internet is an excellent reference source for gathering information on these issues.

War Story: Heart Center Online

Melissa L. Gray, of Fix Spendelman Brovitz & Goldman, P.C. in Rochester, New York, tells this story:

"We had a client who suffered a heart attack while visiting his father in the hospital and underwent bypass surgery a few weeks later. We alleged that the surgery caused him to have a stroke from which he incurred permanent severe injuries.

"The defense alleged that his injuries were caused by a blood clot rather than from a blocked vein that was used in his bypass surgery. I searched the Internet to research blood clots and their effects and found www.heartcenteronline.com. That site educated me on everything from the causes of a stroke and a heart attack to the procedure for bypass surgery and even had illustrations and animated videos showing what happens to the heart and brain during both.

"The site even described different procedures that could have been used in the surgery, such as the insertion of an intra-aortic balloon, to ensure that the patient's blood would freely flow to and from the heart after surgery. HeartCenterOnline is a resource that I use every time I have a medical question about the heart and a tool that saved our firm a lot of time and money."

Starting-Point Web Sites for Medical Research

The medical research materials available for free on the Internet are both broad and deep. Available resources include the entire physician database from the American Medical Association (listing over 690,000 physicians in the United States), glossaries to help you navigate through medical jargon, and detailed collections of resources covering anatomy and medical procedure that can provide what you need to understand the facts of medically related legal matters.

There are many collections of medical information on the Internet organized by body part, disease, or area of medicine, which function quite well as introductions and as general starting points for medical research on the Internet. Listed below are some of the metasites that link you to these online resources.

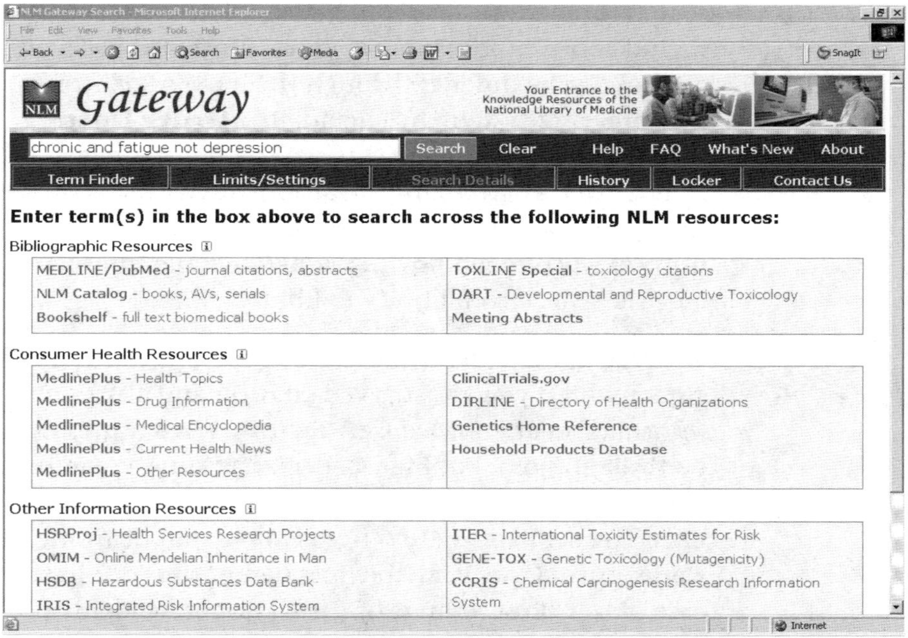

Figure 12-1. The National Library of Medicine's Gateway offers a searchable database of millions of medical journal articles, books, clinical trails, conference abstracts, and other medicine-related resources dating back to the 1950s.

NLM Gateway (National Library of Medicine)

http://gateway.nlm.nih.gov/gw/Cmd

Purpose: To locate abstracts and citations from medical journal articles, books, conference notes, and other written materials on a variety of medicine-related topics.

Content: The NLM provides this one-stop shop to search and retrieve abstract and citation information for over 12 million medical journal articles, books, conference notes, and other written materials back to the mid-1950s, from multiple sources, including MedLine/PubMed, OLDMedline, ClinicalTrials.gov, and consumer health publications, among others.

Our View: Because of the breadth and the depth of the material covered by the NLM Gateway, it is a good place to start a search for medical-related literature. The search results include only citation and abstract information. The full articles can be ordered through the NLM's Loansome Doc ordering system, by clicking the **Order Documents** button. Utilizing this service requires registration, as well as arranging a relationship with a Loansome Doc member library. (For more details, see **http://www.nlm.nih.gov/services/ldwhatis.html**.) Article prices vary from library to library.

You may be able to retrieve a free copy of a journal article for which you've retrieved citation and abstract information at PubMed Central (**http://www.pubmed central.nih.gov**). PubMed Central contains a searchable, full-text archive of more than 200 medical journals. The available date ranges vary by publication, but some journals are available for their entire run. In the case of the "Proceedings of the National Academy of Sciences of the United States of America," that's back to January 1915.

To locate information, enter your keywords in the search box at the top of the screen. Each result also includes a link to related articles that could lead you to additional related information regarding your search topic.

You can create a list of the citation and abstract information of the articles in your search that interest you most, using the site's **Locker** function. (Using the **Locker** requires free registration.) To hold the selected information in the **Locker**, check the box on the left-hand side of the article's title, then click the **Send to Locker** button above the list of search results. You can add as many as 500 items to the **Locker**. Those items will remain in the **Locker** until you delete them.

To view the items in the **Locker**, select the **Locker** button near the top of the page. While viewing the list in your **Locker**, you can select individual articles for which to format information to save to a file on your computer, to print out, or to e-mail to yourself or someone else. To do so, click the check boxes next to the articles whose information you want to save and click the **Download or Display** button at the top of the list. On the next screen, you can choose the depth of the details (brief, expanded, or complete) and the destination (display in browser, display for printing, save to file, or send via e-mail), among other options. (You can also utilize the **Download** or **Display** function from your search results list.)

You can also view a history of your searches during your current session by clicking the **History** link near the

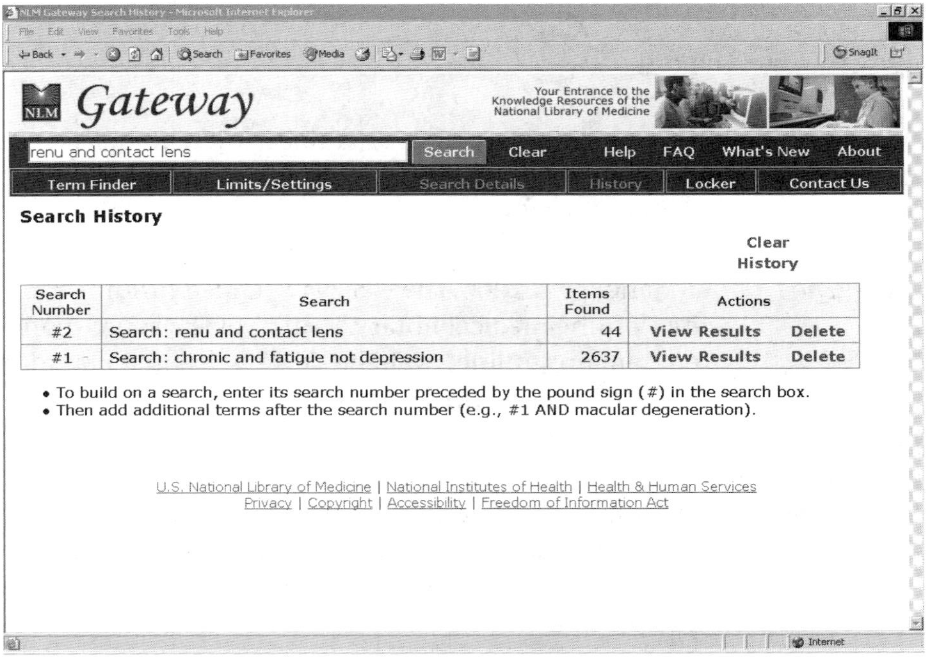

Figure 12-2. By clicking on the **History** tab, the **Search History** page appears, allowing you to review the searches you have conducted during your current session.

top of the page. A description of each of the searches you've conducted is shown with the number of results per search and a link to get back to that search.

Tip:
- You can pay to access Medline on LexisNexis and Dialog, or you can search it for free on the Internet. The choice is yours.
- Click on **Term Finder** to use the NLM Gateway as a medical dictionary.
- If you want an e-mail alert each time a new PMC journal is added to the archive or each time there has been a major update to the archive, sign up for the PMC News list.

Virtual Naval Hospital

http://www.vnh.org

Purpose:
To locate links to practice manuals and textbooks related to the prevention, detection, diagnosis, and treatment of numerous diseases and conditions.

Content:
On January 1, 2006, the U.S. Navy ended funding for this "online medical library." Much of the source content remains online, available from is original providers. The VNH site is currently maintaining links to that source material.

Our View:
This remains an excellent source of information when looking for diagnosis, treatment, and management information for a wide range of diseases, conditions, and injuries.

Tip:
The site can be especially helpful in locating information for certain types of Naval-specific injuries, such as those related to deep-sea diving and high-altitude and aerospace activities.

MedWeb

http://www.medweb.emory.edu/MedWeb

Purpose: To locate links to medical information, journals, and textbooks on the Internet.

Content: The staff of Emory University's Health Sciences Library maintains this large index to biomedical and health related Web sites.

Our View: The site is set up as a drill-down index, so you can select the category you're interested in and click through to the specific information you need. Some subcategories include a **Focus Further** link that lists even more subcategories from which to choose. A search engine is also available to keyword search the index. Note that the search engine supports word-stemming, so searching for "canc" would return results that include the words "cancer" and "cancerous."

Tip: Check the **New Sites** link (on the left-hand side of the home page) that lists the newest sites added to the index in the preceding thirty days. These often reflect sites about cutting-edge, news-making medical topics. (In a recent month, they added more than 200 new resources to the index.)

Hardin Meta Directory of Internet Health Sources

http://www.lib.uiowa.edu/hardin/md

Purpose: To locate medical sources on the Internet.

Content: This site from the University of Iowa links to thousands of other medical information sites on the Internet. The links are arranged in more than two hundred alphabetical categories (from ADHD:Adult to Yellow Fever).

Our View: This site uses a logical drill-down method to locate resources on a particular topic. First select the main category where your information is likely to be found (such as Appendicitis), then select the topic you prefer (such as Understanding Appendicitis—The Basics).

Tip: The site also contains links to pictures of medical ailments, skin lesions, and so on. Use the **Medical Pictures** link at the top of the home page.

Martindale's Health Science Guide

http://www.martindalecenter.com/Medical.html

Purpose: To locate medical sources on the Internet.

Content: Prodigious online list maker Jim Martindale has assembled these links to more than 2,000 journals, textbooks, and tutorials. This is an extremely comprehensive medical index, with links to thousands of other sites and documents. (There's even a dental and veterinary index.)

Our View: The amount of information accessible through these pages is staggering, but getting to it can be a bit trying. The site offers a long list of the sites to which it links. There's no search engine. If you scroll down four or five screens, you'll find a subject index (Anatomy to Womans Health [sic]) with internal links to the portion of the list covered by the specific subject heading you choose. It's worth clicking through to get to the large number of resources Jim Martindale has compiled on this page.

Tip: Don't miss Martindale's list of medical dictionaries online at **http://www.martindalecenter.com/Medical D_Dict.html**

Other useful medical information metasites include the sites below.

U.S. Department of Health and Human Services

http://www.dhhs.gov

Content:	The department oversees hundreds of programs covering a wide spectrum of health related activities. Its site contains links to resources related to many of them in a topical index. Top-level categories include **Diseases & Conditions, Families & Children** (includes Vaccines), and **Resource Locators** (includes a physician locator), among others.

U.S. Food and Drug Administration (FDA)

http://www.fda.gov

Content:	The FDA provides regulatory guidance to the medical industry. The site includes lists of approved drugs and news concerning new medical procedures and devices, among other topics.
Tip:	Note the **A-Z Index, Search,** and **product-related** links located on the left-hand side of the screen.

Healthfinder

http://www.healthfinder.gov

Content:	This government portal presents links to medical information sites in six primary categories: **Health Library, Just for You, Health Care, Online Check-ups, Health News,** and a directory to **Organizations.**

Our View: While much of the information available at this site is useful, the **Medical Errors** topic in the **Health Care** category will no doubt be of great interest to some lawyers.

HealthWeb

http:www.healthweb.org

Content: This site offers links to other Internet medical information resources arranged in nearly 70 browsable categories. An internal search engine allows you to search the site's collection of links.

Getting Well (also called PDRHealth)

http://www.gettingwell.com

Content: Written in plain English, this is a consumer targeted site from the publishers of the *Physicians' Desk Reference* (PDR). It offers medical-related information in three categories: **Drug Information, Clinical Trials** and **Treatment Option Tools.**

Our View: Even though this site is targeted at consumers, it still contains a great deal of information—particularly in the **Drug Information** category. The plain-English approach of the site is Treatment Option Tools section can also be helpful in demystifying complicated procedures for jurors, mediators, and arbitrators. (The online version of the PDR offered only to medical professionals is available at **http://www.pdr.net** and requires registration.)

Palm Medical Dictionary

For mobile lawyers, *Dorland's Pocket Medical Dictionary,* an abridged version of the print book, is available to purchase and load onto your Palm, Pocket PC, or BlackBerry handheld computer for $39.95.

For more information, see **http://www.handango.com**. A search for "dorland" will find the dictionary. (A free searchable database of medical abbreviations is also available for the Palm.)

Dictionaries and Glossaries

Health care professionals, like lawyers, have a language all their own. Some of the most respected and comprehensive medical references, such as *Dorland's Illustrated Medical Dictionary* (see **http://www.netforlawyers .com/dorland**), are available for free on the Internet. Some of the glossaries are specific to areas of medicine, and some are general. Following are a few resources to help you locate them.

General Medical Dictionaries and Glossaries

There are a number of useful metasites that will point you to many different medical dictionaries and glossaries on the Internet. One of the largest is Jim Martindale's Virtual Medical Center list of links to medical dictionaries located at **http://www.martindalecenter.com/Medical D_Dict.html**.

Direct links to some of the medical dictionaries available online include the sites listed below.

Dorland's Illustrated Medical Dictionary

http://www.mercksource.com/pp/us/cns/cns_health_library_frame. jsp?pg=/pp/us/cns/cns_hl_dorlands.jsp?pg=/pp/us/common/dor lands/dorland/dmd_a-b_00.htm&cd=3d

Purpose: To define medical terms.

Content: The site contains definitions of thousands of medical and medicine-related terms. To locate the term you're looking for, navigate through the site using the links to each letter of the alphabet near the top of page. Then browse through the list of terms until you find the one you want.

Tip: Use **http://www.netforlawyers.com/dorland** to be redirected to this resource and avoid typing in the entire URL.

Stedman's Online Medical Dictionary

http://www.stedmans.com/section.cfm/45

Purpose: Locate definitions of medical terminology.

Content: The publishers of Stedman's Medical Dictionary offer this online, searchable, browseable version of their 27th Edition. You can search by keyword or by definition. You can also use the site's alphabetical directory to drill down through the alphabet, and if you're not certain of the complete spelling of a word, search by wildcard.

Our View: Searching and browsing are easy. If the page display looks odd when you visit, or some paragraphs seem "cut off," click the **Search** button near the top of the page. This will take you to a page with an **Online Medical Dictionary** search box. You can enter your term in that box (and press the **Go** button) to perform a simple search. To conduct a more-advanced search (as described below, just click the **Go** button without entering a search term. This will take you to the properly formatted search/browse page (as described above).

Tip: You can use the asterisk wildcard at the end of a word or character string to substitute for one or more characters. For example, a search for "ang*" returns listings for definitions of "angina," "Angelman Syndrome," "abdomi-

.nal angina" and numerous other medical terms that include the character string "ang." It is interesting to note that a search for "angina" returned only one listing for the exact term "angina" and none of the results for other terms that include the word "angina" that were returned in the previous search using the wildcard.

MedicineNet

http://www.medterms.com/script/main/hp.asp

Purpose: To define medical terms.

Content: The doctors of MedicineNet, who also authored *Webster's New World Medical Dictionary,* Second Edition, also offer this free online medical glossary of more than 16,000 terms. It is no longer possible to keyword search only the glossary. All searches retrieve results from all areas of the site, including definitions. If you know how to spell the term for which you seek a definition, you can click on the letter with which the term begins and browse until you find the term. If you're not certain how to spell your term, you can use an asterisk ("*") as a wildcard to stem a word. For example, a search for "asp*" will return listings for "aspirin," aspartame," and "asperger."

Medical Information Management
Approved Abbreviations for Medical Records

http://medicine.osu.edu/currentstudents/support/MIMabbrev/

Purpose: To decode medical abbreviations and symbols.

Content: This site from the Ohio State University College of Medicine and Public Health offers a useful, browseable glossary of medical abbreviations and another browseable list of abbreviations used only in hospice care situations. It also includes a list of common medical symbols (the kind included in medical charts and prescriptions) as a PDF document.

Foreign-Language Medical Glossary

Multilingual Medical Glossary

http://allserv.rug.ac.be/~rvdstich/eugloss/language.html

Content: This site from the Heymans Institute for Pharmacology in Belgium offers glossaries of medical terms in seven European languages, in addition to English.

Medical Textbooks and Encyclopedias

Medical encyclopedias can be good sources for getting up to speed with an unfamiliar or complex medical situation. Generally, they provide broad (yet detailed enough) descriptions of diseases and procedures. Just as with legal information, the more recent the book the better, but even older books can be of value if you are able to fill in with more recent information from scholarly journals or consumer publications.

For a large list of links to medical textbooks, organized by topic, see Emory University's MedWeb at **http://www.medweb.emory.edu/ MedWeb**. (For more information about this site, see its listing earlier in this chapter.) Jim Martindale's Virtual Medical Center page (**http://www .martindalecenter.com/Medical.html**) also includes links to a number of online medical textbooks.

MEDLINEplus A.D.A.M. Medical Encyclopedia

http://www.nlm.nih.gov/medlineplus/encyclopedia.html

Purpose: To locate information about diseases, tests, symptoms, injuries, and surgeries.

Content: The National Library of Medicine offers the popular
A.D.A.M. illustrated medical encyclopedia. The site has
over 4,000 articles about diseases, tests, symptoms,
injuries, and surgeries, along with extensive illustrations
to accompany many of them.

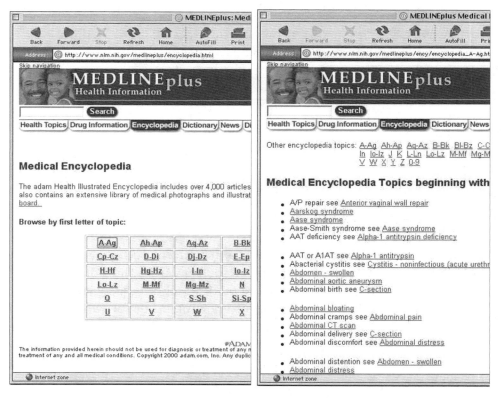

Figure 12-3. Selecting an alphabetical range from the A.D.A.M. Medical Encyclopedia (left) brings up a page of medical terms that fall within that range (right). Clicking on the name brings up a detailed entry about the term you've selected.

Our View: The site is easy to navigate, but unfortunately there's no
search function just for the encyclopedia. You have to
browse the topic headings alphabetically, by selecting
the alphabetical range in which your word or
term appears, and then scrolling through the list of
entries to find the one you need. Each entry includes
information in a number of categories, including its definition, alternate names and terms, illustrations, causes,
symptoms, tests, prevention, treatment, and so on. The
entries also include cross-referenced links to associated
terms.

Tip: Use your browser's **Find** function to locate the term you
              need in the alphabetical list of topics, rather than scroll-
              ing down the page on which it's located. (See the sec-
              tion "Browsers and Favorites" in Chapter 2, "Internet
              Tools Protocol," for more information on this browser
              feature.)

              The site's search box returns results from Medline and
              outside medical-related sources.

Martindale's Anatomy Center

http://www-sci.lib.uci.edu/HSG/MedicalAnatomy.html

Content: Jim Martindale's done it again with this extensive col-
              lection of links to anatomy atlases, anatomy animation
              and image databases, and anatomy tutorials arranged by
              body parts or systems (such as cardio-pulmonary, diges-
              tive, and so on) from medical schools, associations, and
              other organizations from throughout the world.

Human Anatomy Online

http://www.innerbody.com

Content: This site offers interactive medical drawings and non-
              interactive color (drawn) animations of selected body
              structures and functions. The drawings feature a
              series of interactive identifier markers (multicolored
              diamond shapes). Hovering your cursor over those
              points pops up the name of the structure at that point
              on the body (for example, hovering over a diamond on
              the chest might pop up the label "sternum"). If a lateral
              view or close-up of the body part is available, a Magnify-
              ing Glass icon accompanies the label. Click the icon to

see the alternate view. Additionally, there are noninteractive drawings (click on the **Images** button at the bottom of the page) and noninteractive animated images (click **Animations** in the left-hand column).

The Digital Anatomist Project

http://www9.biostr.washington.edu/da.html

Content: The Department of Biological Structure at the University of Washington provides two-dimensional and three-dimensional views of various organs reconstructed from cadaver sections, MRI scans, and computer reconstructions. There are also a small number of downloadable animations of some body structures available in the AVI format.

Armed Forces Institute of Pathology—Autopsy Diagrams

http://www.afip.org/Departments/oafme/diagrams.html

Purpose: Locate diagrams of various body structures.

Content: The Armed Forces Institute of Pathology presents links to a set of nearly two dozen Medical Examiner autopsy diagrams covering bodily structures such as the complete skeleton (front and rear view) to the cerebellum and spinal cord sections. The diagrams are presented in a single, well-labeled list. The JPEG files are easily printed.

Our View: These line drawings can be useful additions to your client intake process for detailing the locations of bodily injuries.

Sites About Diseases and Procedures

The Merck Manual of Diagnosis and Therapy, 17th Edition

http://www.merck.com/pubs/mmanual/sections.htm

Purpose: Locate descriptions and recommended treatments/procedures for various diseases.

Content: The Merck Manual is a primary source of information on any disease. It is available full text on the Internet. It describes symptoms, common clinical procedures, laboratory tests, and virtually all the disorders that a general internist might encounter. Current therapy is presented for each disorder and supplemented with a separate section on clinical pharmacology. You can use the search

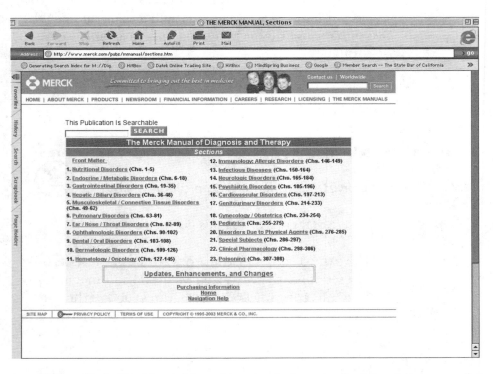

Figure 12-4. *The Merck Manual* is a trusted source for information regarding diseases and disorders. The Internet version is updated regularly, and can be more up-to-date than the print version. From *The Merck Manuals*. Copyright 2003 by Merck & Co., Inc. Whitehouse Station, N.J.

engine to locate a specific disorder (such as angina) or you can browse through topical chapters covering diseases and disorders (such as **Cardiovascular Disorders**) to find the information you need.

Our View: There are two big advantages to the online version of the Manual versus the print edition: (1) the online version is full-text searchable, and (2) the online version is more up-to-date than the currently circulating print version. Changes and additions (to be made in the next print version) are continually added to the online version. Therefore, an expert relying on a print copy may be using out-of-date information.

Tip: While the changes are not noted in the text of the online entries, you can see where changes have been made to the online version when compared to the current print edition. Click the **Updates, Enhancements, and Changes** link under the **Table of Contents** to see if there were any important changes made regarding the disorder you're researching. To compare the changed text to the original, download the PDF document found at the bottom of the **Changes** page. The dates of changes and additions are not noted on the page or in the PDF.

Centers for Disease Control and Prevention (CDC)

http://www.cdc.gov/az.do

Content: The CDC provides an alphabetical list of diseases (and other health-related topics) that link to fact sheets, pronunciation guides (to be certain that you're pronouncing the terms correctly in trial, or at deposition), and other background and treatment information.

Virtual Hospital

http://www.vh.org

Content: Like the Virtual Naval Hospital (see page 538) the Virtual Hospital site also went offline as of January 1, 2006. Similarly, it is also keeping links to some of its source material available online.

Mayo Clinic Patient Information

http://www.mayoclinic.org/patientinfo

Purpose: To locate information regarding various diseases and conditions and their treatments.

Content: The prestigious Mayo Clinic has compiled a list of more than 150 diseases and conditions and recommended treatments. The list is browseable by clicking on the letter of the alphabet, at the top of the home page, with which the term you wish to define begins. Entries include:

- Disease name
- Synonyms
- Detailed explanation of disease/condition (including variant forms)
- Treatment options (including drug and surgical options)
- Links to related articles, news releases, or other informational resources on the Mayo Clinic Web site (when applicable)

Our View: While the list is meant as an informational resource for those considering treatment at the Mayo Clinic, it can also be a good source of information for lawyers whose cases involve any of the diseases/conditions treated by

Mayo. Because the Clinic is known for its cutting-edge treatment options, it can also be a good source of information about emerging treatments for the diseases/conditions listed.

Tip: You can also retrieve information about these diseases/conditions by using the site's search box located in the upper right-hand corner of every page of the Web site. Returned results will include the description from the "Patient Information" center (discussed here), but also additional material on the subject contained on the Mayo Clinic Web site in the following categories:

- Medical Services
- Research
- Medical Education
- News Releases
- Mayo Publications
- Jobs
- Other (uncategorized content)

Cancer and Oncology

National Cancer Institute (NCI)

http://www.cancer.gov/

Purpose: To locate information regarding various types of cancers and their treatments.

Content: The National Cancer Institute has compiled an exhaustive collection of information about dozens of types of cancers. Links to information on some of the most common forms of cancer (e.g., breast, colon, and lung) are listed alphabetically in the center of the home page. Additionally, there is an **A to Z List of Cancers** containing links to information regarding (what must be) every conceivably known type of cancer. Information available regarding each specific type of cancer includes:

- Treatment
- Prevention, Genetics, Causes
- Clinical Trials
- Cancer Literature
- Research & Related Information
- Statistics

Self-explanatory tabs along the top of the site's pages lead directly to "Cancer Statistics" (including the NCI's "Annual Report to the Nation," a glossary of cancer statistics and cancer profiles by state) and cancer-related news.

Our View: If you're looking for information regarding (seemingly) any type of cancer, the NCI site should probably be your first stop.

Tip: Don't miss the link to the site's dictionary, located under the **Quick Links** heading on the left-hand side of every page. The NCI also publishes a weekly newsletter titled "NCI Cancer Bulletin." Visit **http://www.cancer.gov/ ncicancerbulletin** for information on beginning a free subscription via e-mail. Links to back issues are also available at this page.

OncoLink

http://cancer.med.upenn.edu

Content: The University of Pennsylvania Cancer Center provides a wide variety of information regarding numerous forms of cancer. The information ranges from the general to the specific. Click the **OncoLink Library** link on the left-hand side of the screen to access journal articles and additional background information on specific forms of cancer. Information is provided on pediatric and adult cancers, descriptions and stage explanations of disease, and treatment options. Click the **Cancer Treatment Information** link on the home page, and then the

Clinical Trials link on the resulting page for information regarding new treatments under evaluation. The site also includes a search engine.

Heart Disease and Cardiology

HeartCenterOnline

http://www.heartcenteronline.com

To search: ($) To read entries: [Registration Form]

Content: This site contains detailed information regarding many cardiopulmonary conditions and diseases ranging from high cholesterol and high blood pressure to arrhythmia and coronary artery disease. To locate the information you need, you can either use the search engine to locate specific terms or diseases, or click the **Conditions & Diseases** or **Procedures & Tests** buttons at the top of the page. After clicking the entry that interests you, you'll notice many key terms are highlighted (in blue). You can click these terms for more detailed explanations.

Our View: This is a good resource for background information on heart-related medical conditions and for keeping up to date regarding those conditions. You can track news regarding a particular disease or disorder by registering (free) for the site's weekly newsletter (see the **Free Newsletter!** link at the top of the page). You can customize the newsletter with up to ten cardiac related topics relevant to your cases. Registration also allows you to post questions to the site's patient discussion boards. (See the War Story at the beginning of this chapter for one lawyer's success story using this site.)

Tip: Don't bother clicking the **Healthcare Professionals Site** tab on the site's introduction page. That section is primarily meant as a practice management and development tool for doctors. You can access all of the disease and disorder related news and information from the **Patient Site** area.

Medical Journals and Articles

Journal articles are an excellent way to learn about current medical thinking, and possibly pick up information on more up-to-date treatment techniques than the opposition (or their experts) are aware of. One excellent source is the National Library of Medicine's MedLine databases discussed at the beginning of this chapter. Other good sources include the site listed below.

University of Houston Libraries' Scholarly Journals Distributed Via the World Wide Web

http://info.lib.uh.edu/wj/webjour.html

Purpose:	To locate links to medical, scientific, legal, and other journals.
Content:	The librarians of the University of Houston have compiled an alphabetical list of over 150 peer-reviewed journals that are available for free on the Internet.
	Users can access a list of links to journals by clicking on the link to that letter. For example, clicking on the **C** returns links to "Cancer Control: Journal of the Moffitt Cancer Center," "Cornell Law Review," and "Current Research in Social Psychology," among other journals.
Our View:	A search function for the collection of journal links would be useful. The search box at the bottom of the page and the **Research a Topic** link on the left-hand side of the page apparently do not search through the journal collection at all.
	Even though the only way to find a journal would be to already know its name, or browse through each letter of

the alphabet looking for a journal on the topic you need to research, the collection is still useful. At about 150 entries, the entire list of titles can be browsed in a minute or two.

Medscape

http://www.medscape.com

Purpose: To locate abstracts and citations from selected medical journals.

Content: Medscape's online library offers full-text access to selected articles from nearly 100 medical journals.

Our View: For the most comprehensive search of the site's collection of journal articles and news stories, click the **All** button underneath the search box at the top of the page. The site's search recognizes the Boolean connector AND as well as the use of quotation marks for exact phrase searching.

To access the list of journal titles, click the **Library** link at the top of the home page. You can browse the journal list and tables of contents without registration, but reading the articles requires (free) registration. It's important to note that not all articles from each issue of these journals are available.

Tip: The site also has **Resource Centers** focusing on individual diseases and conditions, as well as its **Drug Reference** database of prescription drug uses, precautions, and side effects, among other information. **Drug Reference** is searchable by drug name or disease name (to find drugs recommended for use to treat that disease).

Public Library of Science—Medicine

http://www.plosmedicine.org

Purpose: To locate current medical journal articles on conditions and diseases.

Content: PLoS Medicine is a free peer-reviewed medical journal published by the Public Library of Science (PLoS), a nonprofit. It is published monthly, online and in print simultaneously. All articles are available free online, full text, to be "read, download[ed], redistribute[d], include[d] in databases, and otherwise use[d]—subject only to the condition that the original authorship is properly attributed." Individual articles are presented in "full text" (HTML); a screen resolution PDF; and a higher resolution printable PDF.

The **Advanced Search** page, accessible by clicking the link near the upper right-hand corner of the site's home page, allows you to search numerous fields for the information you need. For example, you can search by an author's last (or first) name, or you can search for all articles written by individuals affiliated with a specific institution that you define. Additionally, you can full-text search the title, abstract, references or figures and tables fields, or the entire document at once, for your keywords or phrase. (Each field search offers a drop down menu from which to choose "with all the words," indicating the Boolean "AND" connector; "with any of the words," indicating the Boolean "OR" connector; and "with the exact phrase.")

Our View: Articles in recent issues cover medical issues ranging from research into a vaccine to produce tumor-killing T-cells to the drug industry's use of celebrities to market new drugs. The PLoS' medical journal, only launched in October 2004, is still building its library of articles.

The Advanced Search page will look familiar to anyone who uses the advanced search functions of Google or Firstgov.gov.

Tip: For information on general scientific subjects, see the
               main Public Library of Science discussed on page 589.

American Medical Association Journals

http://pubs.ama-assn.org   (\$) \$ [Registration Form]

Purpose: To locate abstracts, citations, and articles from AMA
               medical journals.

Content: In addition to its well-known *JAMA*, the AMA also pub-
               lishes a number of specialized medical journals. These
               include *Archives of Internal Medicine*, *Archives of General
               Psychiatry*, and *Archives of Facial Plastic Surgery*, among
               others. The AMA makes the full text of most articles
               available online for free (generally for 12 months after
               the publication date). For older material, only article
               abstracts are offered for free, with the full text available
               for purchase for $15–$45. In the instance of the oldest
               years (generally before 1974) only the tables of contents
               are available online.

Our View: From the publications page you can search a database of
               all the available journals, or select a specific journal and
               search only that one.

There are a number of other journals that make some of their content
available online at their own Web sites (such as the *New England Journal of
Medicine* at **http://www.nejm.org**), or smaller collections of journals,
where they may offer full-text or partial-text access to their articles. Some
may require free registration. Some of these include:

- University of Buffalo Health Sciences Library metasite at **http://
  libweb.lib.buffalo.edu/ft/hslejournal.asp**
- Emerging Infectious Diseases at **http://www.cdc.gov/ncidod
  /EID/index.htm**
- A collection of links to journals offering free content at **http://
  freemedicaljournals.com**

Hospital Sites

The American Hospital Directory (AHD)

http://www.ahd.com

Summary data on specific hospitals: 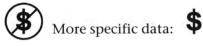 More specific data: **$**

Purpose: To locate hospital management and care statistics.

Content: The AHD provides select data for over 6,000 U.S. hospitals online. Summary data provided free includes the following (from the American Hospital Association Annual Survey data):

- Address
- Phone
- Number of beds
- Type of business organization (for-profit, non-profit)
- General description of services offered (from the federal Centers for Medicare and Medicaid Services [CMS, formerly HCFA] data)
- Medical services provided (by category, with numbers of Medicare patients served)
- Statistics for the most common Ambulatory Patient Classification (APC) codes
- Financial data

More-detailed information in each of these categories is available to paid subscribers. Subscriptions are $395 for a single user per year. Discounts are available for additional users from the same organization.

Our View: The AHD database is a good resource to develop an overview of a particular hospital's services, caseload, and finances. It is built from Medicare claims data, cost reports, and other public use files from CMS. The directory also includes AHA Annual Survey data.

Tip: If you ever need to decode Diagnosis Related Group (DRG) codes, you can do it here. When reading a hospital report, clicking on any of the categories of service provided (such as cardiology or urology) reveals the DRG codes in that category used to identify specific diagnoses.

Find a Hospital

http://apps.nlm.nih.gov/medlineplus/directories

Purpose: To help you find any hospital in the United States by name, ZIP code, city, or the specialty needed.

Content: This straightforward search engine enables you to search for a hospital by (1) name (a state must be chosen); (2) ZIP code (with a choice of broadening your request to hospitals within 10 to 200 miles of the ZIP code entered); and (3) city (a state must be chosen). Within the ZIP code and city searches there is the possibility to refine further by hospital specialty or service. "Specialties" include Cancer, Rehabilitation, Heart, and the like, while "Services" include Patient Education Center, Nutrition Programs, Geriatric, and the like. After selecting your criteria, a hospital list is displayed that matches your criteria.

Our View: MedlinePlus is an easy way to find a hospital anywhere in the U.S. Its uncomplicated process is a breeze to use. However, it would be a more powerful tool if one could search by name only or by city only—without having to know the state. Also, we are a bit unclear as to the difference between "Specialties" and "Services." For example, "Rehabilitation" is listed under "Specialties," but it seems it could just as well be a "Service."

Tip: After clicking on the hospital of your choice, you can discover more about that institution besides its address and phone number by selecting the link titled

Details, map, and directions. This leads you to information about the hospital such as type, system, amount of beds, accreditation, services provided, and more. There is also a visual map and the ability to search directions to the hospital from any location.

New Medical Development Sites

Medical Breakthroughs

http://www.ivanhoe.com

Content: This site, maintained by a news-gathering and production company that supplies medical reports to local television stations around the country, tracks medical breakthroughs in nearly two dozen categories.

Click on any topic on the left-hand side of the home page to see the latest headlines for that topic. You can also sign up for free e-mail updates on the latest breakthroughs.

Reuters Health

http://www.reutershealth.com

Content: While this site is designed primarily as a sales tool for Reuters to offer its medical coverage to other news and Internet outlets, the wire service does present current headlines of breaking medical news and feature coverage of medical research, breakthroughs, and industry-related news.

Nonsubscribers can search the archive of stories, though it has its limitations. For instance, in a search for the keyword "asthma," we were informed that there were 6,737 results, but as nonsubscribers we were limited to viewing only the first page of results and only some included links to the full text. On the upside, the one page of displayed results was for the more current articles.

Our View: With its clickable headlines to the full text of the current stories, and the limited search ability, the site is best used for keeping up-to-date with current information, but is not useful for historical research.

For another source of information regarding medical breakthroughs, also see the entry for GettingWell.com later in this chapter.

Medical Device Sites

The U.S. Food and Drug Administration (FDA) Center for Devices and Radiological Health (CDRH) at **http://www.fda.gov/cdrh** oversees the

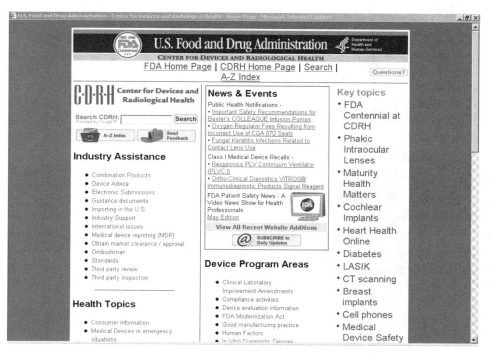

Figure 12-5. The FDA's Center for Devices and Radiological Health (CDRH) maintains numerous databases regarding medical devices and reported failures of those devices.

safety and effectiveness of medical devices as required by the Medical Device Amendments to the Federal Food, Drug and Cosmetic Act of 1976. The Center maintains a number of subsites containing information about medical devices that have been reported to have malfunctioned, or caused serious injury or death. For example, the Center maintains a database of information regarding recalls of medical devices at **http://www .fda.gov/cdrh/recalls**.

Use the following sites maintained by the CDRH to search for other types of detailed information regarding devices and device failures.

Medical Device Reporting Database

http://www.accessdata.fda.gov/scripts/cdrh/cfdocs/ cfmdr/search.CFM

Content: This searchable database contains information regarding medical devices reported to have malfunctioned or caused a death or serious injury during the years 1988 through 1996.

Manufacturer and User Facility Device Experience Database (MAUDE)

http://www.accessdata.fda.gov/scripts/cdrh/ cfdocs/cfMAUDE/Search.cfm

Content: This searchable database contains information regarding medical devices reported to have malfunctioned or caused a death or serious injury since 1996.

Device Advice Medical Device Tracking

http://www.fda.gov/cdrh/devadvice/353.html

Content: These pages contain information regarding mandatory medical device tracking and the types of devices that require tracking.

There are also a number of nongovernmental sites that offer free information regarding medical devices and manufacturers. Some of these are listed below.

Medical DeviceLink

http://www.devicelink.com

Purpose: To locate news, and contact information regarding the medical device and pharmaceuticals industries.

Content: This site contains numerous links to medical device manufacturers and suppliers, news, and other information related to the medical device industry.

Our View: Maintained by Canon Communications, publisher of more than a half-dozen medical device and pharmaceutical industry publications, this site offers searchable databases of:

- North American medical device manufacturers
- European medical device manufacturers
- Medical electronics suppliers
- Industry consultants
- Suppliers of packaging materials
- In vitro diagnostic suppliers (IVD)

These are accessible using the pull-down menu beneath the search box in the upper left-hand corner of the home page. Select **Entire Site** to search all of these databases at once.

On the home page, the site also features medical, pharmaceutical, and medical device news stories. Hover over the **News & Research** tab, then select **News** from the subsequent drop-down menu to view all the current headlines. Click any headline to read the full story. Near the top of the page displaying the headlines is a pull-down menu that allows you to request the headlines that appeared on the page on any particular day of the last thirty days.

Additionally, the site also has discussion forums on a variety of industry-related topics, which are available only after (free) registration. None of the other features discussed here requires registration.

Tip: Many of the company's print magazines are available full text. Use the **MDL News Search** box in the upper left-hand corner of the news story headline display page to search all of their publications at once.

MDRWeb

http://www.mdrweb.com

Purpose: To locate information regarding medical devices and manufacturers.

Content: Maintained by the publishers of the *Medical Device Register*, this site offers a searchable database of nearly 18,000 medical device manufacturers worldwide and 82,000 products. Listings include e-mail and Web site links, where available. The database costs $399 for one year of access for an individual user.

Our View: This is the *Martindale-Hubbell* of the medical device industry. Any device manufacturer can receive a free listing. You can search by more than a dozen criteria, including company or product name, geographic location, company revenue range, product keyword, registered trade name, or product distribution category, among others.

Tip: Paid subscribers also receive new product and recall alerts via e-mail.

Click the **510(k) Database** link in the left-hand column to access the site's collection of FDA 510(k) premarket notification filings dating back to (at least) 1977.

AdvaMed (The Advanced Medical Technology Association)
(formerly the Health Industry Manufacturers Association HIMA)

http://www.advamed.com

Content: This site is maintained by the largest professional association representing the medical device industry. It includes news releases, white papers, and fact sheets addressing issues facing the industry and information regarding its lobbying activities. The organization's daily "SmartBrief" newsletter is also available, with archives back to February 2006.

Pharmaceutical Sites

ClinicalTrials.gov

http://www.clinicaltrials.gov

Purpose: Locate information regarding clinical trials of experimental drug treatments.

Content: Developed by the National Library of Medicine, this site features a database of approximately 27,000 ongoing clinical trials of experimental drug treatments. It offers up-to-date information for locating federally and privately supported clinical trials for a wide range of diseases and conditions. While most studies included in the database are conducted in the United States, it contains information on studies in over 90 countries.

You can keyword search the database or browse by disease, sponsor, or geographical location. The site's simple search engine (featured on the home page) recognizes the "AND," "OR" and "NOT" Boolean connectors (the connectors must be entered in ALL CAPS) and the use of parentheses to indicate a phrase. The **Focused Search** allows you to narrow your keyword search—searching by:

- disease name
- experimental treatment
- age group
- study phase
- geographical location
- sponsor (e.g. government, university, private, etc.)
- NCT or study ID

Our View: Aside from the extensive database of studies, the site also offers easy-to-understand definitions of terms commonly associated with these studies, (e.g., "protocol") and different types of clinical trials by clicking on the "Resources" link at the top of each page. Searching and browsing are easy. You can browse by condition, sponsor, status, or map.

Tip: Click the "What's New" link at the top of the home page to view clinical trials added to the database within the past 7 or 30 days.

PDRhealth

http://www.gettingwell.com/drug_info

Content: This is a consumer-oriented index of drug indications, drug interactions, and other information from the publishers of the *Physician's Desk Reference* (PDR). The database includes information on prescription drugs, over-the-counter drugs, herbal medicines, and nutritional supplements. On the **Clinical Trials** page is a subtopic, New FDA Drug Approvals, that offers a year-by-year list of drugs approved. Grouped by type of disease the drug is approved to treat (such as **Neurology, Pulmonary**, and so on), lists are available back to 1995.

RxList

http://www.rxlist.com

Content: This is a consumer-oriented index with a list of the drugs most commonly prescribed, or most-often searched on RxList. The site contains cross-referenced links to:

- Descriptions
- Side effects & Drug interactions
- Indications & Dosage

You can search for information on over 1,000 drugs by prescription name, generic name, imprint (on the pill or capsule), or NDC (National Drug Code) number.

MedicineNet

http://www.medicinenet.com/medications/alpha_a.htm

Content: This consumer-oriented site also features an A-to-Z list of hundreds of prescription drugs. You can search by brand or generic name or browse the alphabetical list. When searching, you can use an asterisk (*) as a wild card to replace letters at the end of a drug name if you're not sure how to spell the name correctly. For example, "acet*" would return "acetaminophen," among other drugs that include that string of letters.

Tip: At the bottom of the results page is a link, **Visit eLibrary to find more information about <search term> in Newspapers and Magazines**. Clicking here takes you to an eLibrary.com (**http://www.elibrary.com**) page displaying results from its database for the drug you searched for. Even though access to eLibrary costs $19.95 per month or $99.95 per year, you can get a free seven-day trial during which you can access the full text of any articles in the site's database.

MEDLINEplus' Drug Information: The National Library of Medicine

http://www.nlm.nih.gov/medlineplus/druginformation.html

Purpose: Locate information regarding prescription and over-the-counter drugs.

Content: The National Library of Medicine offers information on thousands of prescription and over-the-counter medications. The information is compiled from two respected sources: the American Society of Health-System Pharmacists' (ASHP) "MedMaster™," and the United States Pharmacopeial Convention's (USP) "USP DI® Advice for the Patient®: Drug Information in Lay Language."

Our View: Unfortunately, there's no search function for the drug information. You have to browse the drug names (either generic or brand names) alphabetically, by selecting the alphabetical range in which your drug will appear, and then scrolling through the list of entries to find the one you need. Each entry includes information in a number of categories, such as: **Brand Names** (U.S. and Canadian), **Category** (e.g., analgesic, antipsychotic, etc.), **Description** (e.g., usages and methods of administration), **Before Using This Medicine, Proper Use of This Medicine,** and **Side Effects of This Medicine,** among others.

Tip: Use your browser's "Find" function to locate your search term in the alphabetical list of topics, rather than scrolling down the page on which it's located. (See the "Browsers & Favorites" section of the "Internet Tools" chapter for more information on this browser feature.)

New Medicines in Development

http://www.phrma.org/medicines_in_development

Content: The Pharmaceutical Research and Manufacturers Association (PhRMA) provides a searchable database (by disease, indication, or drug) of new drugs in development.

Clinical Pharmacology

http://www.clinicalpharmacology.com $

Content: Geared toward medical professionals, this site offers in-depth information regarding dosage, usage, FDA-approved off-label uses, and mechanisms of action for "all U.S. prescription drugs, hard-to-find herbal and nutritional supplements, over-the-counter products and new and investigational drugs." It also provides extensive resources for identifying drugs by size, color, markings, and ingredients, and for comparing drugs based on brand name, ingredients, and so on. A single-user annual subscription to the online service costs $435. Site licenses are also available for firm-wide access if needed.

Also see the entry on Medscape in the "Journals and Articles" section earlier in this chapter for information on its **DrugInfo database**.

———————————

The Doe Report

http://www.doereport.com/   **$**

Purpose: Locate graphics, models, etc. as demonstrative medical evidence.

Content: The Doe Report contains more than 8,000 proprietary medical-legal illustrations, videos, and other materials that can be used as exhibits at arbitration, mediation or trial.

The materials can be browsed by type (e.g., **Medical Exhibits, Medical Animations,** etc.) **Medical Specialty,** or **Body Region** (e.g., **Abdomen, Head & Neck,** etc.) or keyword searched (either by similar topical criteria, or through all topical categories).

Prices start at $119 for basic 8 1/2" x 11" exhibits (that you print yourself from a provided .PDF file) to $419 for a 30" x 40" print shipped to you by Doe. Prices for custom graphics are quoted based on a base/flat charge of $119 plus a $125/hour fee.

Our View: The browsing and searching capabilities make it easy to locate resources about the specific condition or injury you need.

Tip: (1) You can search the Doe materials for resources specifically related to your client by typing (or pasting) text from a medical report (up to 32,000 characters) into the site's **Advanced Search** function. Click the **Advanced Search** button on the left-hand side of the home page to access this feature.

(2) Click the **Free Samples** link at the top of the page to view and request copies of selected medical exhibits. Recent samples included "Instability of the Knee with Reconstruction of the Support Ligaments," "Cesarean Delivery with Entrapment of the Head," and "L4-5 Disc Herniation and Anterolisthesis with Nerve Root Impingement." (You will have to give the Doe Report your contact information before you receive your electronic copy of the free sample exhibit.)

(3) DRI and ATLA members receive a 10 percent discount.

Health Professions Sites

Physician Directories

AMA Physician Select

http://www.ama-assn.org/aps/amahg.htm

Content: The AMA provides the primary physician directory available to the public. For information on individual doctors, choose **Search for a Physician**. All 690,000 accredited doctors (MDs and DOs) in the U.S. are represented. You can search by the doctor's name, specialty, or only for doctors available for an online consultation. Information provided includes address, phone number, specialty, where degrees were obtained, where residencies were served, and American Board of Medical Specialties certifications. No discipline information is provided.

Tip: Of course, we'd all rather have access to the government's National Doctor Index. Start lobbying.

● Use the asterisk (*) as a wild card when uncertain of a doctor's first name spelling (for example, to search for Jeffrey Smith, search for "J* Smith" in case "Jeffrey" is spelled "Jeffery" or in case the doctor goes by "Jeff").

- You can also perform a sounds-like search (click the **sounds like** box under the ZIP code entry field) if you're not sure how to spell the doctor's last name. Note that this only works for last names, not first names.
- Deceased physicians will not be found online, but contact the AMA—they keep some limited history.

---

eCare UPIN Lookup

http://upin.ecare.com

Content: Federal law provides for the creation of a Unique Physician Identification Number (UPIN) for every doctor who provides services for which payment is made under Medicare, and requires the publication of a directory of those numbers. At this site, you can search for a doctor's UPIN, or determine a doctor's name if you only know the UPIN. For each physician, the database provides medical specialty, state, ZIP code, and identification number only. For a full address, you will have to use the AMA database noted above.

Physician Licensing and Disciplinary Action Sites

Many states make their professional licensing databases available for free on the Internet. Access to these databases and the amount of information provided varies from state to state. One site that allows you to search the records of many states is the Administrators in Medicine (AIM) DocFinder (**http://www.docboard.org/docfinder.html**). DocFinder also links to discipline records, if available. New York provides both licensing and discipline information. For information on other metasites that will link you to licensing records on the Internet (if they are available), see Chapter 8, "Accessing Public Records."

Federation of State Medical Boards

http://www.fsmb.org/directory_smb.html

Purpose: To locate links to U.S. medical licensing boards.

Content: The Federation of State Medical Boards has compiled a collection of seventy-one links to its member medical licensing boards in all fifty states and numerous commonwealths and protectorates. Data include mailing addresses, Web site addresses, and phone numbers.

Our View: The list is presented in alphabetical order (by the name of the jurisdiction). Links at the top of the list allow users to jump to various portions of the alphabet. The list is also easily browseable or searchable using the Web browser's "Edit" and "Find" features.

Tip: If accessing this site via the home page, the link to the state medical examining boards is difficult to find. First, hover over **Public Services** on the home page's left-hand side, and then click the **Directory of State Medical Boards** link to access the list.

New York State Department of Health

Office of Professional Medical Conduct

http://w3.health.state.ny.us/opmc/factions.nsf

Content: New York is one of the states that offers a searchable database of its physician discipline database. On the left-hand side of the page, you can choose to view lists of the disciplined doctors arranged by:

- Physician name
- License number

- License type
- Effective date

You can also search for a specific doctor by clicking the **Physician Search** button in the center of the page.

Once you've located the doctor you're looking for, clicking on the name returns an abstract about the discipline.

Tip: At the bottom of the page is the juiciest information—a link to the full **Board Order**. This order contains all of the hearing information regarding the discipline, saved as a PDF document. These can make very interesting reading.

Medical Board of California Physician Lookup (Update)

http://www.medbd.ca.gov/Lookup.htm

Purpose: To allow public access to a physician's licensing and disciplinary records.

Content: The Board's home page stresses the importance for the public to know what is and is not available when reviewing a physician's records and features a concise list of what is considered public and nonpublic information. Once this data is read, you may click on the **Continue Search** link. Search fields include name, license number, and city or county where in practice. Search results appear as a list of names and addresses. Once you've chosen your doctor, their individual information will be listed. This includes their license number, type, date originally issued, expiration date, status, etc. On the lower portion of the page all public disclosure disciplinary actions are listed. At the very bottom, medical school and graduation year information is also given.

Our View: We like the clear and concise manner in which The California Board presents the search results. Unfortunately (or perhaps fortunately?), we were unable to find a physician with disciplinary records when testing the site.

Tip: If your physician is an osteopath, a link is provided on the licensed physician's search page that leads to a separate searchable database of osteopaths to conduct your search. (Considering that the URL for the osteopath database is **http://www2.dca.ca.gov/pls/wllpub/ wllqryna$lcev2.startup?p_qte_code=GEN&p_qte_pgm_ code=8510**, it's easier to use that provided link, or the one on the CD included with this book, rather than trying to type all that in yourself. Discipline information is also included in the osteopath's database.

Other Health Profession Sites

Here are some sites for more health profession associations:

- American Chiropractic Association at **http://www.amerchiro.org**
- American Dental Association at **http://www.ada.org**
- American Health Lawyers Association at **http://www.health lawyers.org**
- American Nurses Association at **http://www.ana.org**
- American Optometric Association at **http://www.aoanet.org**
- American Physical Therapy Association at **http://www.apta.org**
- American Psychiatric Association at **http://www.psych.org**
- American Academy of Nurse Practitioners at **http://www.aanp.org**

*CHAPTER***THIRTEEN**

Scientific Research

While few of us are trained scientists, there are still instances when we need to find information on a science-related subject. Sometimes it may be related to medicine (also see Chapter 12, "Medical Research"), while other times it might have to do with some sort of chemical reaction or an issue concerning forensic evidence. Starting your search in a consumer publication or educational resource can be a good way to locate background and introductory information before moving on to more detailed (and technical) journal articles. These introductory sources can also help you explain difficult or advanced concepts to jurors at trial.

Starting-Point Web Sites for Scientific Research

MadSci Library

http://www.madsci.org/libs/libs.html

Purpose:	To locate information and resources regarding numerous scientific topics.
Content:	The MadSci Library is one portion of Washington University School of Medicine's (St. Louis) Young Scientists program aimed at improving science literacy among school-aged children. It contains links to numerous arti-

cles, Web sites, and other online resources related to many different areas of science.

Our View: Don't dismiss this site just because it's geared toward helping K-12 students gain a better understanding of science. It includes introductory information on many advanced scientific principles such as biochemistry, clinical microbiology, immunology, chemistry, and physics, among other topics.

The site offers a list of topics in the left-hand frame, with the accompanying resources and links appearing in the right-hand frame after you click a topic.

The left-hand frame also has a **USENET** link pointing to specific discussion groups or forums where you can pose a question.

Tip: For hard-to-locate facts, or continually puzzling questions, click on the **Ask-A-Scientist** link to find a scientist to whom you can pose your question via e-mail.

Zeno's Forensic Site

http://forensic.to/forensic.html

Purpose: To locate links to information regarding forensic science and investigative methods, including forensic medicine, psychiatry, and psychology.

Content: The site provides an extensive collection of links to forensic science resources in nearly two dozen categories including such topics as **General Web Sites, Associations and Societies, Arson, Entomology,** and **Computer Investigation**—all in a drill-down directory. Click through the selections until you find the information you need.

Our View: Compiled and maintained since 1993 by Dr. Zeno Geradts, a forensic scientist in Amsterdam, this site covers a lot of bases. Dr. Geradts clearly knows his stuff and has taken the time to assemble a comprehensive set of links across a number of different categories. (He is employed in the Digital Evidence section of the Netherlands Forensic Institute of the Ministry of Justice, where he handles forensic [video] image processing.) The site is updated regularly. (The site had last been updated less than three weeks before our most recent visit.)

Tip: The site also features a search engine (at the bottom of the page) to keyword search the links.

TNCrimLaw Forensic Science Resources

http://www.tncrimlaw.com/forensic

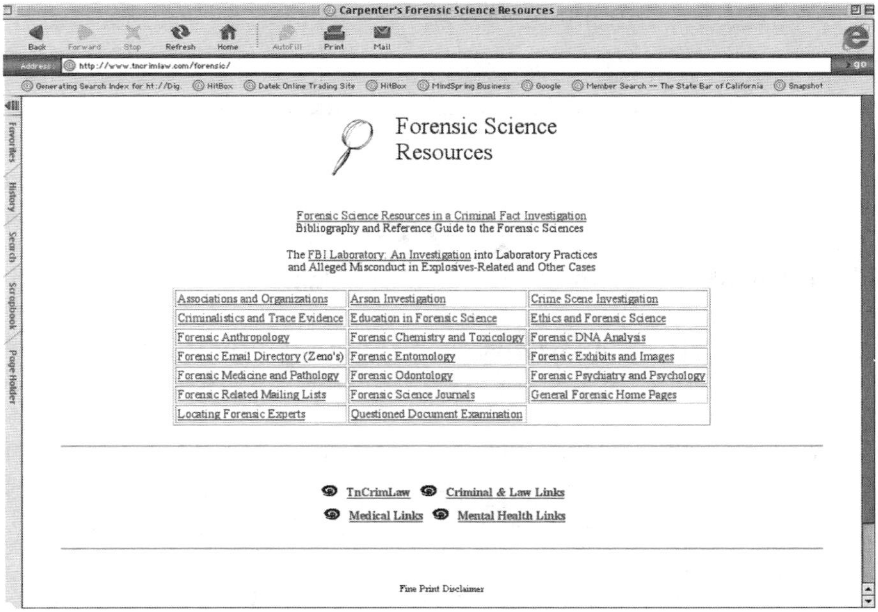

Figure 13-1. The TNCrimLaw.com Forensic Science Resources page provides links to forensic science resources valuable to lawyers in any state.

Purpose: To locate links to information regarding forensic science and investigative methods.

Content: The site provides links to forensic science resources in nearly two dozen categories including **General Forensic Home Pages, Associations and Organizations, Forensic Odontology,** and **Questioned Document Examination**.

Our View: Despite the name, this site is not just for Tennessee lawyers. The site features a drill-down directory of forensic science topics. At the top of the page is a link to **Forensic Science Resources in a Criminal Fact Investigation**, which is a bibliography of online and off-line sources for information (arranged topically). When available, bibliography entries include a link to the online version of the article, otherwise the print citation gives you enough information to find the book from a library or bookstore source.

Tip: Don't miss the links at the bottom of the page to other TNCrimLaw resources, including medical and mental health resources.

Scirus

http://www.scirus.com $ $ Registration Form

Purpose: To locate science-related information via this science-only search engine.

Content: The site provides a free search of more than 250 million science-related pages, including text, PDF and PostScript formatted files. Scirus also claims to search "access controlled sites" and deliver "more peer-reviewed articles than any other search engine." Scirus returns both free and fee-based resources in its results.

Our View: Users are given the option of a **Basic Search** or **Advanced Search** to keyword search.

                 Results are broken down into 3 categories: **Other Web Results, Journal Results,** and **Preferred Web Results**.

While the other **Web Results** are usually available free, the **Journal** and **Preferred Web Results** are available for a fee from a variety of partners including BioMedNet/MEDLINE, ChemWeb.com, and Science-Direct, among others. Charges for these articles vary.

In a column to the right of the search results is a list of suggested words and phrases to help refine your search. If you do not want to use one of their suggestions, at the bottom of the list is a search box where you can enter your own word or phrase to refine your search.

Scirus, owned by Elsevier Science, is powered by FAST Search, a search engine from Norway-based Fast Search & Transfer, the company which originally developed the popular Alltheweb search engine.

Tip: Use **Advanced Search** to narrow down your search by time frame, information type (abstracts only, articles, books, company Web sites), file format, subject areas, and more.

Refdesk's Science Information Resources page at **http://www.refdesk .com/factsci.html** contains descriptions and links to over 150 other sites containing information on scientific topics ranging from biology and chemistry to forensic science. (For more information about the Refdesk site, see its entry in Chapter 5, "General Factual Research.")

Popular Science

http://www.popsci.com

Purpose: To locate news and feature articles regarding the application of science to our everyday lives.

Content: The site features selected articles and features from the current (and past) editions of *Popular Science* magazine.

Our View: The site arranges articles into seven topical categories:

- What's New
- How 2.0
- Science
- Computers & Electronics
- Aviation & Space
- Technology
- Automotive Tech
- Medicine

Links to the full text of select current articles are listed on the site's home page. You can click on any of the category names (along the left-hand side of the screen) to see the available current articles from the most recent issues for that topic. A keyword search is also offered to locate available articles (see the Tip below for search techniques). An e-mail newsletter is available with (free) registration.

Tip: Like most search engines, the site's internal search engines defaults to the AND Boolean connector; phrases are indicated with quotation marks. Make sure to add your Boolean connectors (in all caps) to your search. A search for "steering wheel" produced 66 results back to early 2002. Be sure to uncheck the **include web results** box under the search box if you only want to see articles from the Popular Science archive. Unfortunately, even then, the results include **Sponsored Results** that will be marginally relevant to your search.

European Organization of Nuclear Research (CERN)

To search and view selected articles: $\varnothing$ To purchase articles: **$**

http://library.cern.ch/electronic_journals/ej.html

Purpose: To locate scientific journals by topic.

Content: The CERN library provides links to nearly 3,000 journals covering numerous physics, chemistry, and engineering topics.

Our View: You can view the list by subject, or as a browsable, alphabetical list. Some are available online free, in full text, while others are available only by online subscription or on a pay-per-view basis. (Some sites allow you to pay a fee to access a single article for twenty-four hours. You may or may not be able to print the pay-per-view article, depending on the site.)

Tip: Despite repeated attempts and varied search terms and syntax, we could not get any results from the "**Query online e-journal catalogue**" search engine when attempting to locate keywords that might appear in an article's abstract.

MIT Technology Review

http://www.technologyreview.com

Purpose: To locate news and feature articles regarding scientific innovations.

Content: The site features articles, columns, and features from the current (and past) editions of the *MIT Technology Review* magazine.

Our View: The site arranges information into seven topical categories:

- Biotech
- Biztech
- Nanotech
- Infotech
- Magazine
- Blogs
- MIT News

Links to the full-text current articles are accessed by clicking on the **Magazine** tab at the top of the site's home page. Most are available to read for free. (A subscription to either the digital or print version costs $19.97 for six issues.) You can click on any of the category tabs (along the top of the screen) to see the most recent articles for that topic.

A keyword search is also offered to locate specific articles (see the Tip below for search suggestions). An e-mail newsletter is available with (free) registration, by clicking the **Subscribe** link at the bottom of any page.

Tip: Unfortunately, the search seems to use the Boolean connector OR as a default, so a search for the phrase "computer forensics" (without quotation marks) returns articles with the word "computer" or the word "forensics"—a pretty long list to be sure. Put search phrases in quotation marks, and add a plus sign next to search terms to force the search engine to include both of them (for example, search for "+computer +forensics"—without quotation marks—to find articles that contain both of those words).

Stetson University College of Law's National Clearinghouse for Science, Technology, and the Law

http://www.ncstl.org/

Purpose: To locate links to scientific, technological, and associated legal resources.

Content: On the home page, users must select a version—**Flash** (high bandwidth), **HTML** (low bandwidth), or Section 508 (low bandwidth). Clicking the **Search Database** button on the top of the home page brings you directly to a search page containing both a basic search box and advanced search functions to access the Clearinghouse's collection of conference papers, cases, dissertations, magazine articles, newspaper articles, law review articles, etc. Results are displayed in a list with an abstract describing the resource and a link to the full document. Until recently, the more powerful advanced search functions were reserved for registered members of the site. Now, the advanced searching functions are available without registration, but other tools are still reserved for registered members.

Click on the **Members** button on the top of the home page to bring up the registration page. The free membership requires only your name, e-mail address, a username and password. Previously, there was a fee-based membership ($50 per year), but there was no description of the difference between it and the free membership. On our most recent visit to the site, the paid membership option was gone.

After you've signed in as a member, you can enter your search terms in the **Search Keyword(s)** box of the **Advanced Search** section and also add terms to exclude in the **Excluding Word(s)** box. After entering your search terms, clicking on the **Pre-Search** button displays the number of **Matching Records** in the upper left-hand corner of the search page, but no abstracts or links. To access the materials, it's necessary to click on the **Submit Advanced Search** button.

The advanced search page also offers a series of **Actions** buttons (including **Add, Edit,** or **Remove**) to the left of the keyword search boxes that allow you to search any of the specific "Topics" (e.g., **Biometrics, DNA,** or **Digital Evidence**), or "Resources" (e.g., **Agencies, Internet Articles** or **Radio/Television**). Limiting your search to specific **Topics** or **Resources** will greatly reduce the number of results you will receive. Other **Actions** buttons allow you to save your search or initiate a new search. You can access saved searches and your last ten searches by clicking on the **Members** button at the top of the page. These features are available only to registered users of the site.

Our View: While the site offers access to a wide range of useful documents and links to other sources (see the "Tip" below), it lacks documentation.

This site is still a work in progress, judging from its lack of documentation, list of products that are "still in production," and help topics labeled "under construction." It's still useful, but the developers might have been better off calling this a public beta until all the elements were fully developed.

Tip: Clicking the **Related Links** button at the top of
                   the home page displays links to nearly 200 criminal,
                   forensic, medical, judicial, and general scientific Web
                   sites.

ChemIDplus

http://chem.sis.nlm.nih.gov/chemidplus/chemidheavy.jsp

Purpose: To identify an unknown chemical using information
                   that is known, or to get more information on a known
                   chemical substance or drug.

Content: This National Library of Medicine site allows users to
                   identify unknown chemicals using known information
                   in six distinct categories: **Substance Identification,
                   Toxicity, Physical Properties, Locator Codes,
                   Structure** and **Molecular Weight**. You can also use
                   the **Name/Synonym** search in the **Substance Iden-
                   tification** category to locate more information on a
                   drug or chemical when you know the name.

                   Each criteria has a separate area to input search terms,
                   an information icon to further explain the use of the cri-
                   teria and a reset button to clear your entry in the sec-
                   tion. Results are drawn from NLM sources such as MED-
                   LINE, CANCERLIT and its Household Products
                   databases, as well as other government and non-govern-
                   ment resources available on the Internet.

                   On the top of the page are links to other NLM Web sites:
                   Toxicology and Environmental Health, ToxNet and
                   ChemIDplus Lite.

Our View: Although the homepage is a bit overwhelming to look
                   at, the information it provides in this new advanced ver-
                   sion is impressive. You may now search for chemicals
                   using such limited information as the part of the body
                   the chemical may act on, such as the heart or liver, or

retrieve detailed information about a substance if you know the name (e.g., Vioxx).

The **Help** screens guide you through the searches in a clear and concise manner, making the site more useful for the non-medical researcher.

Tip: The less-advanced "lite" version of this search tool is available by clicking the link on the top of the page which says simply **Lite**. There you can perform a chemical name or registry number search only. It is particularly useful in cutting through the clutter of the search page if you already know the name of the chemical or drug for which you need more information.

Public Library of Science (PLoS)

http://www.plos.org

Content: PLoS is a nonprofit organization working to create a free archive of scientific journal articles available online. Currently, the site offers links to over seventy-five journals covering biological, medical, and other scientific research that offer their full contents online for free.

Public Library of Science—Biology

http://www.plosbiology.org

Purpose: Free access to scholarly biology-research related journal articles.

Content: PLOS Biology publishes the latest in peer-reviewed articles covering biology- (and medicine-) related research findings.

Our View: While highly technical, the journal's articles can be a good source of cutting-edge medical information. They can be extremely useful in relation to medical malpractice, standard of care or birth defects, among other issues. Full-text searching is available via the **Search** box in the upper right-hand corner of the site. The default Boolean connector is **and**.

Tip: Sign up for the free e-mail **Content Alerts** to receive the Table of Contents for each month's journal via e-mail.

Science News

http://www.sciencenews.org

Purpose: To locate news on scientific and technological advances.

Content: This site offers free access to selected articles from the print version of *Science News*, an eighty-plus-year-old weekly chronicle of scientific developments.

Our View: Published since 1922, the print magazine covers important research and development in all areas of science. The Web site provides free access to some of these articles. Recent free articles have covered the cholesterol level of eggs, bacterial infections, and possible links between estrogen and cancer and blood clots, among other topics. The Web site offers an online archive of back issues to 1996 and selected articles available full text back to 1994. Click **Archives** to browse the issues by date. A full-text archive of all the magazine's stories is available to paid subscribers of the print magazine (which costs $54.50 per year). Click **Search** to perform a keyword search. The site also offers a free newsletter.

Tip: For older articles, you can also contact *Science News* by e-mail to search their print archives.

Science @ NASA

http://science.nasa.gov

Purpose:	To locate background information on how NASA programs and experiments affect scientific research on Earth.
Content:	This site provides informative articles on NASA's scientific initiatives and how the agency's experiments can, or will, be practically applied. Articles are arranged by topic, including:

- Space Science
- Astronomy
- Earth Science
- Biological & Physical Sciences

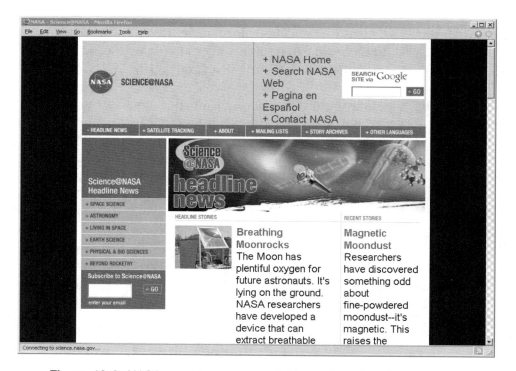

Figure 13-2. NASA provides news, updates, and explanations of how space program experiments affect scientific research on Earth.

Recent articles have discussed research on antibiotics, bone implants, and weather research, among other topics.

Our View: The site has replaced its internal search engine with one powered by Google, making it much easier to locate articles because it uses AND as its default Boolean connector. Previously, its internal search engine used OR as a default Boolean connector (without bothering to mention it anywhere on the site). The results list used to include a lot of off-topic results, but that problem has been rectified. An e-mail newsletter is available with (free) registration.

ScienceDaily

http://www.sciencedaily.com

Purpose: To locate breaking science and research news.

Content: This site aggregates information from various academic and corporate research sources to list new announcements in scientific, medical, and technological research.

Our View: The site summarizes and posts news releases gathered from universities and other research institutions. (Contributors can actually post the news releases to the site themselves.) You can view the news either by topic, by headline, or by headlines with abstracts. The site's **Search Archive** internal search engine uses OR as a default Boolean connector. Here, a search for the phrase "nano tube" (even in quotation marks) nano AND tube, as well as +nano +tube, returned articles with the word "nano" or the word "tube"—ending up with a lot of off-topic results. While the site does not offer any critical analysis or peer review, it can be helpful in keeping up with new announcements.

Thankfully, the site has also added a search option powered by Google to locate relevant articles in its archive. It returns much more relevant results.

Tip: You can also view headlines from the preceding day or
                  week by scrolling to the bottom of the page.

Kroll Ontrack

http://www.krollontrack.com/legalresources/

Purpose: To locate articles, case law, and statutes related to com-
                  puter forensics and electronic discovery.

Content: The lawyers of computer forensics and digital evidence
                  consulting firm Kroll Ontrack have compiled a list of
                  links to:

- Articles written by Kroll lawyers and consultants
- Case law (organized by jurisdiction and topic)
- Kroll newsletters (**http://www.krollontrack.com/
  newsletters/**)
- Law review and journal articles
- Rules and statutes (federal and local, arranged by
  jurisdiction)

The site also contains a glossary of digital discovery and
computer forensics terms.

Our View: The lawyers and consultants of Kroll Ontrack write
                  extensively and often on the subjects of computer foren-
                  sics and digital discovery. The articles included on the
                  site are current and easy to read. The material accessible
                  here can be helpful whether you're defending a client
                  whose computer has been seized by law enforcement or
                  has been subpoenaed, or you are working to subpoena a
                  computer from the opposition.

A number of other practitioners also offer useful resources. The Web
sites of Computer Forensics, Inc. (**http://www.forensics.com/html/
resource_articles.htm**l) and Mares and Company (**http://www.dmares**

.com/maresware/articles.htm) both offer numerous informative (though sometimes very technical) articles on the subject of conducting computer forensics analysis. Additionally, the U.S. Department of Justice's Cyber-crime Web site (**http://www.cybercrime.gov**) offers an online version of the department's manual *Searching and Seizing Computers and Obtaining Electronic Evidence in Criminal Investigations*, located at **http://www .cybercrime.gov/s&smanual2002.htm**.

*CHAPTER*FOURTEEN

Environmental Research

Obviously, every lawyer does not have an Erin Brockovich to dig up local records regarding environmental issues. Whether it's locating facilities that use hazardous materials within a certain radius of a housing development, or identifying "brownfields" near a school, it's lucky for the rest of us that there is a wealth of sources for environmental information on the Internet.

Even though the first thing that pops into most of our minds when we think of environmental information is probably air pollution or hazardous waste, a case could be determined by an environmental condition as common as the weather. Was it really a "dark and stormy night" on the night in question? In this chapter you'll learn how you can find out for yourself.

War Story: Weather Information

Bernard P. Weisel, a lawyer in Beverly Hills, California, tells this story:

"I represented a gentlemen who was being sued for damages based upon a contract that the plaintiff said my client signed on a February day in Los Angeles. My client denied signing that contract and claimed that the plaintiff fabricated the contract by using my client's signature from another contract that the plaintiff had access to. During discovery the plaintiff said the contract in question was signed at a meeting between he and my client on a beautiful sunny day outdoors on the patio of a coffee shop. Prior to the arbitration hearing I researched the weather history of Los Angeles for the day in question and for two days before and two days after and discovered that it had rained all five days! Needless to say I impeached the plaintiff's testimony with this information.

"The look on the arbitrator's face was priceless! The arbitrator found for my client."

War Story: Sunset Time

Matthew J. Webb, a lawyer in Oakland, California, had this story to tell:

"I once had a case where a woman was the victim of a stray bullet, fired from across the street. The shooting took place at 7:10 p.m., in January, and the woman testified that she could see her assailant clearly. I went on line to the U.S. Naval Observatory Web site, www.usno.navy.mil, to establish that sunset occurred at 5:22 p.m., while civil twilight ended at 5:50 p.m., [and] successfully argued that the judge take judicial notice of this fact."

Starting-Point Web Sites for Environmental Research

EPA Envirofacts (Environmental Protection Agency)

http://www.epa.gov/enviro

Purpose:	To locate information about environmental activities in a particular area.
Content:	Envirofacts provides access to several EPA databases that provide information about environmental activities that can affect air, water, and soil quality anywhere in the country. You can use the **Quick Start** search (in the lower left-hand side of the home page) to enter a ZIP code, city and state, or county and state into the query

box. The search returns information on facilities in the area regulated by the EPA, including:

- Waste (hazardous waste)
- Water (water treatment)
- Toxics (chemical release)
- Air (air pollutants)
- Radiation (radiation releases)
- Land (brownfields)
- Other
- Maps (showing the locations of any facilities that fit in the above categories)

From the results page you can also access the EPA's **Windows To My Environment** service that presents federal, state, and local information about environmental conditions and features in an area you designate.

Our View: The **Envirofacts Quick Start** search and the information from the **Windows To My Environment** link

Figure 14-1. At the EPA Envirofacts site, you can search for information about environmental activities that can affect air, water, and soil quality anywhere in the country, by ZIP code or other criteria.

make for a comprehensive (quick) snapshot of the environmental state of your target area.

The date coverage is also pretty good; some of the data retrieved in a **Quick Start** search regarding toxic waste treatment and removal dated back to 1987.

Tip: Data from the various databases accessed by **Envirofacts** is updated regularly. Some databases are updated nightly. Click the **Data Update** link on the left-hand side to view the update schedule, and date of last update, for each database included in its searches.

To keep up to date regarding EPA activities, you can subscribe to the Agency's mailing lists to receive news and information in these categories: Compliance, Civil Enforcement, CleanupNews, Environmental Justice, Federal Facilities, and the National Agriculture Compliance Assistance Center (Ag Center) (see **http://www .epa.gov/compliance/resources/newsletters**).

Natural Resources Defense Council (NRDC)

http://www.nrdc.org

Purpose: To locate information on environmental issues from a protectionist point of view.

Content: The site offers concise (as well as in-depth) explanations of dangers facing the environment in ten categories:

- Clean Air & Energy
- Global Warming
- Clean Water & Oceans
- Wildlife & Fish
- Parks, Forests & Wildlands
- Health & the Environment
- Nuclear Weapons, Waste & Energy

- Cities & Green Living
- U.S. Law & Policy
- International Issues

Each category offers a brief and an in-depth discussion of the topic at hand. If a topic includes subtopics, each subtopic has its own discussions. Each topic also features links to other Web sites related to that topic.

Our View: The discussions related to each topic are good starting points to learn more about topics you may not be familiar with. Even if you already have a familiarity with a topic, the accompanying links will give you additional resources to locate still more information.

Tip: To access a glossary of environmental terms, click on **Reference/Links**, in the lower left-hand side of the site's home page. Then select the letter your search term starts with under the **Glossary of Environmental Terms** near the top of the page.

Directory of Best Environmental Directories

http://www.ulb.ac.be/ceese/meta/cds.html

Purpose: To locate links to environmental resources.

Content: The site contains an alphabetical list of links to more than 600 sources for environmental data on the Internet.

Our View: For a more worldwide view of environmental resources, see this page maintained by Bruno Kestemont, a scientific adviser and former researcher with Belgium's Centre for Economic and Social Studies on the Environment. Each entry has been descriptively categorized by subject, and those categories are listed in alphabetical order (from Accounting to World Wildlife Fund). The setup makes it easy to find sources on the subject you need.

Tip: The site points to numerous non-English (French, German, Japanese) sites.

EarthTrends (World Research Institute)

http://www.earthtrends.wri.org

Purpose: To locate environmental information for countries around the world.

Content: The World Research Institute has collected environmental data from multiple sources around the world and created a single browsable (drill-down) database offering detailed information in ten categories for countries around the world. The categories are

- Coastal and Marine Ecosystems
- Water Resources and Freshwater Ecosystems
- Climate and Atmosphere
- Population, Human Health and Well-being
- Economics, Business and the Environment
- Energy and Resources
- Biodiversity and Protected Areas
- Agriculture and Food
- Forests, Grasslands and Drylands
- Environmental Governance and Institutions

Our View: To find the information you're looking for, select one of the categories listed above, and then drill down, selecting a more specific information subtopic, e.g., **Maps, Country Profiles, Data Tables**. The date range of available information varies from topic to topic; in some categories, the data was available back to 1995. While this might give you a general sense of the environmental picture, you'll find more recent domestic information from the other sites discussed in this section.

Tip: Use this site primarily for information pertaining to foreign countries.

ECHO (Enforcement and Compliance History Online)

http://www.epa.gov/echo

Purpose: To locate current and historical enforcement and compliance information about EPA-regulated facilities.

Content: The EPA's ECHO site provides compliance and enforcement information for approximately 800,000 EPA-regulated facilities around the United States. The site includes information regarding permits, inspections, violations, enforcement actions, and penalties covering the past two years. The site also includes information regarding facilities regulated as Clean Air Act stationary sources, Clean Water Act direct dischargers, and Resource Conservation and Recovery Act hazardous waste generators or handlers.

Our View: Like the **Quick Start** search discussed in the description of the Envirofacts site above, at ECHO you can enter a ZIP code or other location information to get a quick sketch of EPA-regulated facilities in that area. ECHO offers a more sophisticated advanced search, labeled **All Data Search** on the site's home page. It is located at **http://www.epa.gov/echo/compliance_report.html**. From here, you can sort and analyze data in many ways.

The **Advanced Search** page allows you to specify additional search criteria such as asking for information on only those facilities that have had a Formal Enforcement Action taken against them, or facilities that have had a penalty levied against them within a time frame you specify (within the last two years). You can also search for facilities with clean records—ones that have not had actions or penalties levied against them.

Clicking on the name of a facility in the search results brings up a page with more information on the facility, including compliance, enforcement, and penalty information (including dollar amount) for the past three years. The data is updated monthly. (Previously, the site offered a **Map Returned Facility** feature to render a map of the area you had searched for, with all EPA-regulated facilities marked, and the location of the one whose information you are viewing marked with a star. This feature is no longer available.)

Tip: Using the ZIP code box for searching only returns larger facilities in your search results. To include smaller facilities, use the **Advanced Search** page and check the **Include Minor Facilities** box at the bottom of the form. Additionally, you can download the returned data as a comma-delimited text file which can be viewed in Microsoft Excel. (You might need to right-click and select **Save Target As** to save the data to your hard drive.) Checking the **Search Logic** box at the bottom of the **Advanced Search** page displays the (lengthy) search string the database generated to produce your results, at the bottom of your results list. Knowing this will not help your search in anyway.

DOE (U.S. Department of Energy) Environmental Policy & Guidance

http://www.eh.doe.gov/oepa

Purpose: To locate information regarding environmental compliance issues related specifically to DOE installations.

Content: The Office of Environmental Policy assists with environmental compliance issues for DOE installations. This Web site includes some of the environmental data and reports the Office compiles regarding DOE sites' environmental compliance.

Our View: Click on the **Environmental Data & Reports** link to access PDF versions of some of the Office's output, including "Estimate of Potential Natural Resource Damage Liabilities at U.S. Department of Energy Sites" and "Disposal of Low-Level and Mixed Low-Level Radioactive Waste During 1990," as well as links to selected EPA online databases.

Tip: Click the **Search** link on the left-hand side of the home page to access a database of Federal Register notices related to the EPA, back to January 1995. Selected DOE Environmental Policy and Guidance documents are also searchable from that page.

RTK NET (Right to Know)

http://d1.rtknet.org/doc

Purpose: To locate historical docket information for civil cases filed on behalf of the EPA.

Content: The Right to Know database contains docket information for civil cases filed by the Department of Justice with regard to EPA violations. *It has not been updated, however, since October 18, 2000.*

Our View: The database is searchable by a number of criteria, including defendant or facility name, case type (such as Clean Air Act or Clean Water Act), or specific violation (such as spill or asbestos). While the data has not been updated since 2000, the search can still be worthwhile in determining if individuals or businesses have been prosecuted for violations back to 1971.

Tip: The EPA has a searchable database of its enforcement cases back to (fiscal) 2001 at **http://www.epa.gov/echo/ compliance_report_icis.html**.

Lawrence Berkeley National Laboratory Air Pollution Resource

http://www.lbl.gov/Education/ELSI/pollution-main.html

Purpose: To find background information regarding air pollution and its effects.

Content: This site offers explanations and background information regarding the causes, types, and effects of air pollution.

Our View: An index of topics is listed on the left-hand side of the screen. Click any topic for more information on that subject.

Tip: While designed as a teaching module for middle school and high school teachers, the material contained in this site presents a useful basic overview.

Rainforest Web

http://www.rainforestweb.org

Purpose: To locate rainforest-related information and resources.

Content: The site includes extensive links to other resources containing information about the world's rainforest regions.

Our View: While this site has a conservationist bent, its links are useful for anyone. The links are classified into headings such as **What's happening in the rainforests?** and **Why are rainforests important?** Each topic has a variety of subtopics. To find the information you need, just click through the appropriate topics and subtopics.

Tip: Be careful not to inadvertantly click on a link to an outside Web site, rather than an information subtopic. Subtopics are listed near the top of each page, outside links are directly below them.

For additional information on hazardous materials spills while the material was being transported, see the description of the Department of Transportation's TranStats site in Chapter 18, "Transportation Research."

Locating Environmental and Ecological Organizations and Agencies

University of Denver College of Law's Natural Resources Weblinks

http://www.law.du.edu/naturalresources/weblinks/default.cfm

Purpose: To provide quick access to Web links to natural resources reference and research information.

Content: Developed by the University of Denver's Sturm College of Law, the home page features a large selection of topics to start your search. In the left column, **Countries, Subjects, Journals,** and **Organizations & Associations** are listed. On the right, you may choose from **Legislation, Treaties, Reference,** and **Careers**. The last option, **Comprehensive Sites,** is shown toward the bottom of the site's home page. When you roll your computer's cursor over these selections, a detailed description is given for each category. You can choose to "drill down" through the categories and sub-categories until you locate the sites where you will find the information you're looking for, or you can use the keyword search function for quicker access to information.

For example, if you needed to locate information on water law in Mexico, you could click on **Countries** and choose Mexico from the drop-down list. You will then be presented with a list of links organized by environmental subject (e.g., **Energy, Forestry, Gas & Oil,** and **Water**). The title of each Web link and the language in which the site is written are offered in addition to a link to the site. Clicking on the link takes you to the selected Web resource.

To find a database or Web site by topic, click on **Legislation** or **Treaties** from the Web site's home page. Links to sites related to that topic are then displayed along with the sites' titles and the language in which they are written.

Our View: Offering numerous **Subjects** to explore (i.e., constitution, energy, environmental, forestry, indigenous peoples, mining and minerals, investments and trade, legal databases, oil and gas, sustainable development, and water), the information is easy to find. This is another excellent starting point for anyone needing information on environmental research topics. Note that not every **Subject** is included for every country.

EnviroLink

http://www.envirolink.org

Purpose: To locate regional and local environmental groups by the issues they address.

Content: This site contains an index of thousands of environmental organizations around the world, organized by the specific environment-related issue they address.

Our View: Issues range from **Agriculture** to **Wildlife**, with subcategories for each main issue. To locate the organization you want, click through the issues and subtopics until you find the ones that suit your needs. Click the **advanced search** link at the top of the home page to define numerous criteria for your search (such as ZIP code, city, topic) through the database.

Weather Information

Weather Underground

www.wunderground.com

Purpose: To locate current and historical weather information.

Content: Enter a city, state, ZIP code, or country name in the search box and click the "magnifying glass" button at the top of the home page to return the usual current weather conditions and five-day forecast.

Figure 14-2. WeatherUnderground.com offers free historical weather data (accessible by ZIP code) back to 1935. Attorneys can also get more detailed historical weather information for a specific location for a fee. By providing a longitude, latitude, time of day and date, you can obtain weather data for three surrounding locations (including radar data). (Click on **Contact Us** for more information regarding this paid service.)

The first phase of searching for historical weather data goes back to 1970. Select a date (back to 1970) at the bottom of the list of current weather conditions to view the weather for the location you selected on that date.

Results are reported from standard weather reporting stations (often airports). A sample search for historical weather in Culver City, California returned accurate reporting from the nearest reporting station (in Santa Monica), less than five miles away.

To get to the second phase of date searching, use the pull-down date menu on the results page where you have retrieved historical weather back to 1970. You can once again choose a date for which to retrieve historical weather data—this time back to 1935 (dates vary by location).

Our View: While there are numerous sites that offer current weather conditions and forecasts of coming weather, Weather Underground is one of the few we've found that offers easily accessible historical weather information, too. However, the site hides the fact that historical data goes back to 1934 because retrieving data from 1934–69 is a two-step process (as noted above).

Tip: Use this site to locate historical weather data before you try to use the NOAA site listed later in this chapter. For the importance of historical weather data in litigation, see "War Story: Weather Information" at the beginning of this chapter.

The Old Farmer's Almanac

http://www.almanac.com/weatherhistory/index.php

Purpose: To locate historical weather information

Content: The online version of *The Old Farmer's Almanac* offers historical weather data back to 1973 for thousands of locations in the U.S. and Canada, but it doesn't cover every location for every date.

To retrieve historical weather data, select a date from the pull-down menu, then enter a ZIP code or a city and state (or province), and then click the corresponding **Search** button. Alternatively, you can click on the desired location on the posted map of the United States.

Results are available from the weather reporting stations closest to the ZIP code or city you entered (usually airports). A search for historical weather data for "Culver City, CA" offered results from five airport reporting stations ranging from five to twenty miles from the selected city.

Returned data include:

- Maximum Temperature
- Mean Temperature
- Minimum Temperature
- Mean Sea Level Pressure
- Mean Dew Point
- Total Precipitation
- Fog
- Snow
- Rain

- Hail
- Thunder
- Tornado
- Visibility
- Snow Depth
- Mean Wind Speed
- Maximum Wind Gust
- Maximum Sustained Wind

Our View: This is a good site to retrieve weather information for a general area, although it is less useful if more precise targeting of weather information is needed.

Tip: Historical weather data for a specific location (down to latitude and longitude) is available for a fee from **http://www.wunderground.com/**.

National Oceanic and Atmospheric Agency (NOAA)

To search: ($) To purchase historical weather data: **$**

http://www.noaa.gov

Purpose: To locate accurate current and historical weather and other in-depth weather-related information.

Content: NOAA conducts research and gathers data about the global oceans, atmosphere, space, and sun. Its National Weather Service is the primary supplier of weather forecasts in the country. The site offers current weather conditions, 24-hour satellite image loops, and historical weather information.

Our View: Current weather data from anywhere in the country is easy enough to get. The site also offers in-depth information on weather and oceanography from **Air Quality** to **Volcanoes**. Use the pull-down menu on the left-hand side of the home page to select a topic for more information and links to additional resources.

Unfortunately, there is no easy way to search or access the historical weather data available from NOAA—and it is not available for free. Historical weather data are retrievable (very easily) from the Weather Underground site listed above for the location at which you're interested. To determine if historical data are available from NOAA, visit **http://hurricane.ncdc.noaa.gov/CDO/cdo** and select a **Country, Geographic Region**, etc. in which to locate data. You can also select a data set (daily, monthly, annual, and so on) to narrow down your results. After selecting the region or precise weather station and the date range for the data you wish to retrieve, the site confirms the availability of the data and informs you of the cost. (Prices are dependent on the size of the data file you request. Data for a single month begins at $6.) Click the **Add to Shopping Cart** button to purchase the data as a downloadable text file.

Tip: The site also has a **People Locator** to locate NOAA employees.

Sunrise and Sunset Information

U.S. Naval Observatory

http://www.usno.navy.mil

Purpose: To determine sunrise and sunset times for any date at any location.

Content: Click the **Sun Rise/Set** link on the left-hand side of the screen to input a date and location for which you want to know this information. Using **Form A**, you can retrieve this information by entering a date, city or town name, and selecting the state from a pull-down menu. Using **Form B** (scroll down to access), you can retrieve information for any point on the globe by entering latitude and longitude coordinates.

Our View: This site allows you to easily find the sunrise, sunset, high noon, or other sun and moon information for any place and any time in the U.S. The available city and state list for the country, based on U.S. Census Bureau data, contains more than 22,000 places. While the site does not list a limit as to how far back it can supply data, recent searches returned data for dates as far back as 1900.

For the importance of this data, see "War Stories: Sunset Time" at the beginning of this chapter.

Tip: Click **What time is it?** on the site's home page to locate a page containing the current time (wherever you are in the U.S.) according to the Observatory's atomic clock.

*CHAPTER*FIFTEEN

Foreign and International Research

Even though most of the research we do centers on information and sources from this country, there are a number of professional and personal situations where you might need information from, or about, foreign sources.

Could you ever have to solve one of these problems?

- Your client wants to open an office in Asia, and is asking your advice regarding the best markets and most stable governments.
- Your client is traveling in Eastern Europe and has scheduled a conference call for next Tuesday, at 3:00 P.M. his time. What time should you call in?
- Your client is being sued for trademark infringement in Argentina, because the Spanish-language name for his product is the same as an existing product in that country. How will you find competent local counsel?
- You're going on a tour of China and Central Asia and want to find out in advance where the U.S. Embassy is in each country you're visiting.
- You're being sent to the firm's Singapore office for a six-month project—and you don't know a yen from a yuan. Will the *per diem* they're offering be enough?

The solutions to all of these problems, and many others, can be found for free on the Internet. After all, they don't call it the *World Wide Web* for nothing . . .

For information on international news sources, see the "News, Periodicals, and Broadcast Media" section in Chapter 5, "General Factual Research." For information on online language translators, see the "Standard Reference Resources" section of that same chapter. For information on foreign companies, see Chapter 10, "Company Research."

Information About Other Countries

CIA World Factbook

http://www.cia.gov/cia/publications/factbook/index.html

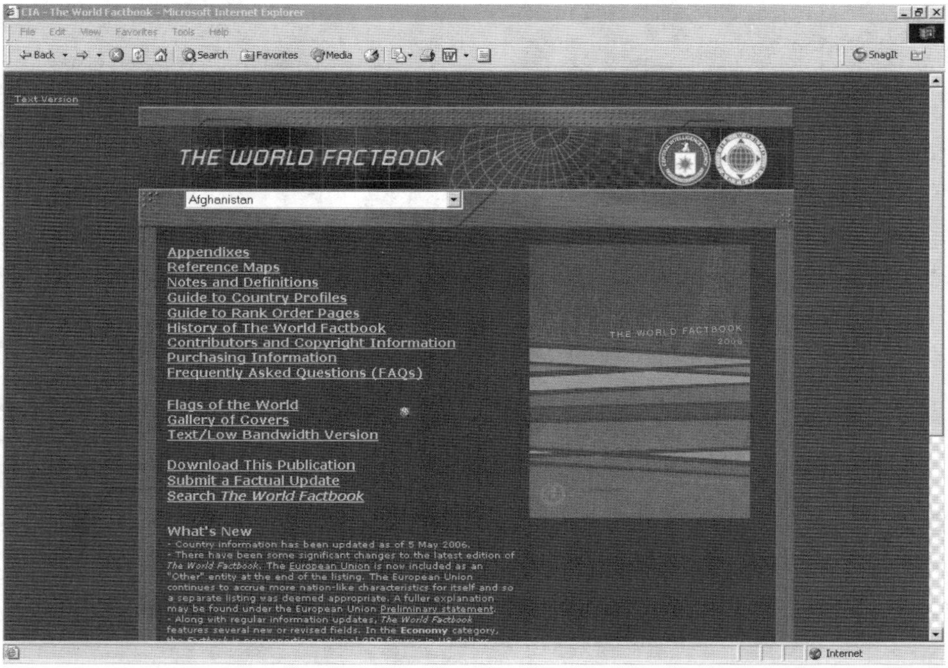

Figure 15-1. Can you think of a better source for information on foreign countries than the CIA? Its *World Factbook* contains information on over 200 countries.

Purpose: To find facts and statistics on foreign countries.

Content: This site contains myriad facts regarding over 200 countries around the world. Since 1975, the Central Intelligence Agency (CIA) has made its printed *World Factbook* available for purchase by the public. It is now available for free online, or for download.

Detailed information is presented for each country in nine categories:

- Introduction
- Geography
- People
- Government
- Economy

- Communications
- Transportation
- Military
- Transnational Issues

There are numerous subcategories within each of these categories.

Our View: Who better than the CIA to ask about information regarding foreign countries, cities, and organizations? Select a country from the pull-down menu, or click on **Flags of the World** to access the core data for each country.

Appendix F (access it by clicking Appendixes on the Fact book home page) is invaluable if you have a geographic name (city or town) but do not know what country it is in. This appendix offers a browsable, alphabetical list of places in all the countries covered in the book. It also includes phonetic equivalents of place names in local languages (for example, *Al Imarat al Arabiyah al Muttahidah*—the local name for the United Arab Emirates).

Tip:
- Use the book online rather than downloading it. The entire book is over 30 megabytes when compressed! You shouldn't attempt to download this book unless you have a high-speed Internet connection—or you have a lot of free time. For those with lower-speed connections who must download the book, the CIA has broken it up into 24 smaller files that can each be downloaded separately. Also, once uncompressed, the Factbook requires over 80 megabytes of disk space on your computer. Be sure you have enough available disk space before you download it.
- Note: for some reason, in the alphabetical list of countries, Taiwan is listed near the end of the list—after Zimbabwe and before the European Union (which is the last entry).

CIA's Chiefs of State Directory

http://www.cia.gov/cia/publications/chiefs/

Purpose: To identify government officials of foreign countries.

Content: The CIA's Chiefs of State and Cabinet Ministers of Foreign Countries database contains the names of government officials for nearly 200 countries around the world, including:

- Chief of State
- Second-in-Command
- Cabinet Ministers
- Head of the Central Bank
- Ambassador to the U.S.
- Permanent Representative to the United Nations

Governments are listed in alphabetical order according to the most commonly used version of each country's name. The spelling of the personal names is approximated as closely as possible—following transliteration systems generally agreed upon by U.S. Government agencies (unless officials have stated a preference for alternate spellings of their names). The list is updated weekly.

Our View: This list offers even more detailed information about the members of individual governments than does the CIA's World Factbook. The standardized presentation (in a table) makes the entries easy to read.

Tip: Be sure to click the "Key to Abbreviations" link near the top of the page to decipher less common abbreviations used in the listings such as "Cdte." (Commandante).

Infoplease

http://www.infoplease.com/countries.html

Purpose: To find information about countries.

Content: Infoplease has information on more than 200 countries. Each profile includes information on:

- Geography
- Maps
- Flag
- History
- Current ruler
- Population
- Capital

- Largest cities
- Languages
- Ethnicity and race
- Religion
- Literacy rate
- Economy
- Government

Our View: While much of the information is the same as is covered in the CIA's *World Factbook*, some may find the layout of Information Please's Countries of the World page easier to use.

Tip: Handy lists of capitals, currency, ethnicity and race, languages, and religions— listed alphabetically by country—are also available. Other useful information not included in the CIA site include countries with nuclear weapons, world cities' average daily temperatures, and air distance between world cities, among others.

Country Studies Program (Library of Congress)

http://memory.loc/gov/frd/cs/cshome.html

Purpose: To find information on specific foreign countries.

Content: Formerly known as the Army Area Handbooks program, the Library of Congress developed a set of handbooks to help inform U.S. Army personnel about locales where they might be deployed. This information is now available to us online. There were 102 countries included in the handbook series, but as of this writing only 49 had been converted to this new format. These are accessible by clicking the **Choose a Country Profile** link. Notable countries missing include Canada, France, Great Britain, Italy, and numerous other Western and African nations.

Our View: You can keyword search on one country, or across any combination of countries. Additionally, you can browse the alphabetical list of included countries to select the region you are interested in. The individual country entries include extensive coverage of the country's history, as well as background on the social, political, and economic climates. While covering many smaller countries (for which information may be difficult to find), information in these handbooks might only be as current as 1988. (The date the data was gathered is clearly noted on each page.) However, the in-depth historical information remains valuable.

Tip: Use these handbooks for in-depth historical background on a country. Use the CIA's *World Factbook* for more current demographic, political, and economic information.

Use the **List of Countries** link or the **Choose a Country Study** drop-down menu to access information on the larger list of 102 countries.

Weidenbaum Center on the Economy, Government and Public Policy (Washington University, St. Louis)

http://wc.wustl.edu/parliaments.html $\oslash$

Purpose: To locate links to the rule-making bodies of foreign governments.

Content: The site offers links to the parliaments, national assemblies, and other legislative bodies of over 150 countries around the world—from Albania to Zimbabwe.

Our View: The site presents an alphabetical list of links all on one page. It is very easy to navigate.

Embassy World

http://www.embassyworld.com

Purpose:	To locate embassies and consulates around the world.

Content: This site claims to have "absolutely all of the world's embassies in a searchable database." That claim is equally difficult to prove or disprove, but suffice it to say that the list seems comprehensive. (There are thirty-four pages just for the embassies of foreign countries within the United States.)

Information available includes:

- Type of office (embassy, consulate, mission, high commission, and so on.)
- Street address
- Phone number
- Web site address (if applicable)
- E-mail address

Our View: Embassy World allows you to browse in just about any combination imaginable (through a series of a browsable directory pages):

- By country (such as all embassies of Kazakhstan)
- U.S. Embassies in other countries
- Embassies of other countries in the U.S.
- Permanent Missions of the United Nation

You can also search by clicking on **Find Your Embassy** after selecting from two drop-down lists, **Whose Embassy?** and **In What Location?**

Tip: Starting out with the search engine can save time over drilling down through the directory.

Information About Foreign Travel and Business

Travel Warnings & Consular Information Sheets from the U.S. Department of State

http://travel.state.gov/travel/cis_pa_tw/tw/tw_1764.html

Figure 15-2. The U.S. State Department issues Travel Warnings regarding unsafe travel conditions in specific countries.

Purpose: To get current information regarding specific foreign countries.

Content: **Travel Warnings** advise U.S. citizens to avoid traveling to specific countries or regions. **Consular Information tion Sheets** provide practical information regarding specific countries. This page provides a chronological list of all the current U.S. State Department **Travel Warnings** (back to "Philippines, 3/23/2005") and a link to the up-to-date **Consular Information Sheets**.

While the content of the **Travel Warnings** is pretty self-explanatory, the **Consular Information Sheets** provide concrete information about traveling to the specific countries discussed. This includes:

- Entry and Exit Requirements
- Safety and Security
- Crime
- Information for Victims of Crime
- Criminal Penalties
- Medical Facilities

- Medical Insurance
- Traffic Safety and Road Conditions
- Customs Regulations
- Currency Issues
- Photography Restrictions
- Children's Issues
- Locations of Embassies

Our View: Because the State Department is constantly updating its information, this is probably the best source for detailed current information on a specific country.

Tip: You can get State Department Travel Warnings e-mailed to you directly by joining their DOSTRAVEL mailing list. The online subscription form for this and other lists, podcasts, and RSS feeds is available at **http://www .state.gov/misc/52620.htm**.

EUROPA

http://europa.eu.int/index_en.htm

Purpose: Styled as the "Gateway to the European Union," this Web site is meant to educate everyone, from the layperson to the professional, about the European Union.

Content: With over 1 million documents, this site has a wealth of information on anything EU. The information on EUROPA is organized into six main headings located in the center of the page. The first two headings are **In the Spotlight** and **The EU Day by Day**, and they focus on current international events. The other four headings are: **Activities, Institutions, Documents**, and **Services**. On the left side of the page, an additional list of links gives more information concerning life in the EU.

Our View: This is a very thorough site that offers an amazing range of information. Lawyers can use it to find certain EU documents (including summaries of EU legislation and case law) or access a library or court, but it also offers information at the other end of the spectrum, such as how Europe is "fun for the young." Or, if you want to work or live in Europe and need to learn your rights, this is the place to start your search.

Tip: If you can't find what you need by clicking on the various topical links, you can type your keywords into a search box or click on the **Advanced search** link for more tailored searching. These tools are located on the right side of the home page. Our search for "olympics" found 2,184 matches out of the 1,548,097 documents on the site. By using the "Advanced search" feature, you can narrow down your search by excluding words, limiting your keywords to the title of a document, and so on.

If you still can't locate your information by searching the site, you are given the opportunity to either e-mail, telephone, or use Web assistance to get answers to your questions by clicking on **Your Direct Line** (located on the left navigation bar on the home page under "Interact with the EU").

U.S. Government Export Portal

http://www.export.gov

Purpose: To find country and industry market research.

Content: This site presents comprehensive information on doing business with countries around the world, including:

- Broad country information
- Agricultural market research (click **Market Research** in the left-hand column)
- Tariff and tax information
- Trade agreements

Our View: This is an excellent one-stop shop that aggregates content from numerous other government agency Web sites.

Tip: You can access a wealth of non-agricultural market research data at **http://www.export.gov/market_research**.

Consular Affairs Bureau (Canadian Department of Foreign Affairs and International Trade)

http://www.voyage.gc.ca/consular_home-en.asp

Purpose: To locate current information regarding specific foreign countries.

Content: The Consular Affairs Bureau's **Current Issues** notices advise of potentially dangerous situations when traveling to specific countries or regions; click on the **Travel Updates** link to see them. **Country Travel Reports** provide practical information regarding specific countries.

Our View: While covering much of the same ground as the U.S. State Department site, the Canadian point of view can occasionally be different enough to prove additionally enlightening.

Tip: Use this site in conjunction with the U.S. State Department Travel Warnings page.

Information from Other Countries

Search Engine Colossus

http://www.searchenginecolossus.com

Purpose: To locate search engines around the world.

Content: From the Aaland autonomous region of Finland to Zimbabwe, the Search Engine Colossus offers links to hundreds of search engines from over 200 countries and territories around the world. The list is in alphabetical order by country.

Clicking on a particular country brings up a list of search engines that index content in, or related to, that particular country. Many of these sites search and return results in English. (Instructions on the site's home page and the list of countries covered are also available in French and Spanish.)

Our View: The quality and relevance of the results can be hit or miss depending on the actual source you select. Clicking on the listing for Bangladesh brings up a list of 13 search engines and directories that index information related to that country. These include the English language Prantor Bangladeshi Web directory, as well as the Bangla version of the popular search engine Google. Although Google's search page is in the Bangla language, a search for the term *government* returns results in English, however the Google Bangla results were more international than the results at Google's English language search page (and none of the results listed on the first three pages was related to Bangladesh).

Finding Lawyers in Other Countries

Martindale-Hubbell

http://www.martindale.com

Purpose: To find lawyers in other countries.

Content: Martindale-Hubbell is arguably the world's largest lawyer directory, and the online version contains listings for untold numbers of lawyers around the world.

Our View: It's easy to find the lawyer you're looking for—wherever he or she may be located. The process of locating foreign lawyers is the same as for locating lawyers in this country. To locate a specific lawyer, fill in the name and select the country in which the lawyer practices. Clicking the **Search** button brings up the Martindale listing for that individual.

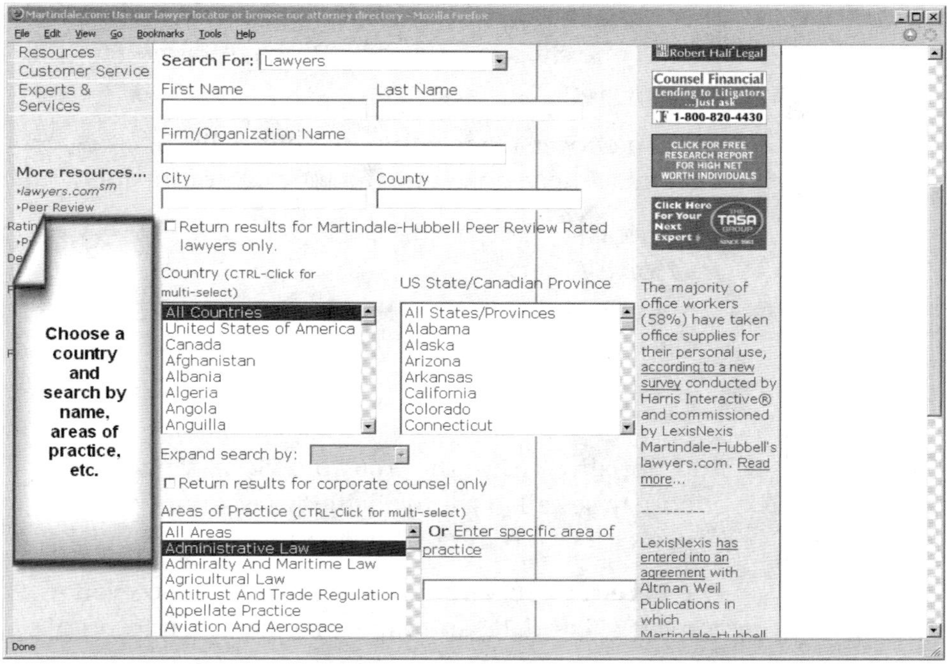

Figure 15-3. You can use Martindale-Hubbell online to search for lawyers in foreign countries.

Tip:	You can also find lawyers and firms that specialize in certain practice areas by using the **Advanced Search**, which brings up a page with enough search criteria to allow you to search for specific listings, such as law firms that practice business law in Argentina and have someone who speaks English (for the record, there were 210). Results can be sorted by city or last name.

Other Related Useful Information

The World Clock

http://www.timeanddate.com/worldclock

Purpose:	To answer the question "What time is it in . . .?"
Content:	The site presents a grid of local time in (up to) 550 cities around the world.

Our View: This site is very useful whether you need to know the time in one city, or you need to track the time across an entire region.

You can choose to view the site's entire list of cities, or customize the view to only include one of the following:

- Africa
- North America
- South America
- Asia
- Australia/Pacific
- Europe

Additionally, within these custom views, you can also choose to see all of the available cities, or only the largest cities, or only the capital cities.

The **Fixed, Past, Future Time** option allows you to convert a day, date, and time for a particular location into the day, date, and time for any city in the list. This is useful for planning an upcoming event, such as a phone conversation.

Tip: The list of cities can be sorted by city, country, or time zone. Cities observing Daylight Savings Time (or Summer Time as it is known in some parts of the world) are clearly marked with an asterisk (*).

Country Calling Codes

http://www.countrycallingcodes.com

Purpose: To determine the proper telephone dialing code for a country or city.

Content: This site contains the country codes for more than 250 countries and countless more cities within countries that require additional dialing codes.

Our View: Self-explanatory drop-down menus allow you to choose where you are calling from, and where you are calling to. Clicking the **Submit** button returns a page with the proper codes to use with the phone number you wish to call. For larger countries with multiple city codes, the results page includes another drop-down menu for selecting the city you are calling. Clicking the **Submit** button on that page returns the full country and city dialing code string.

Tip: Don't be fooled by the **Quick Reference Phone Book** link on the left-hand side of the page. It is only an alphabetical list (by country) of the corresponding dialing codes. It is not an international phone directory search.

U.S. Department of the Treasury Office of Foreign Asset Control (OFAC) Specially Designated National (SDN) List and Blocked Persons List

http://www.ustreas.gov/offices/enforcement/
ofac/sdn/index.html

Purpose: To determine if the assets of potential clients or their business have been frozen or blocked by the Department of Justice (DOJ).

Content: This section of the Treasury Department site contains the (very large) list of foreign nationals and companies that have had assets frozen by the U.S. government. This more than 200-page list is provided "to assist the public in complying with the various sanctions programs administered by OFAC."

Our View: A searchable database version of the list would be useful. The easiest way to use the list is to download the PDF version, and use Acrobat Reader's search function (click on the Binocular icon in the toolbar) to search for par-

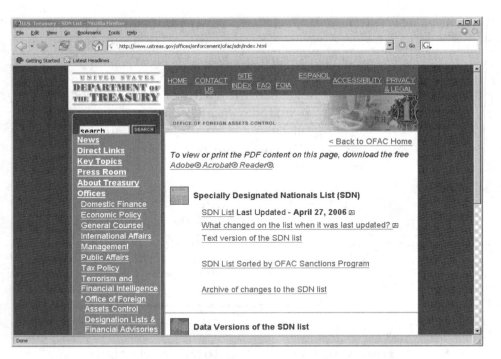

Figure 15-4. The U.S. Department of Justice's Office of Foreign Asset Control (OFAC) maintains a list of foreign nationals and companies that have had assets frozen or blocked by the DOJ.

ticular individuals or companies you suspect might be on the list.

Tip:
- The list is updated approximately every two weeks, and actions of the OFAC are also listed in the Federal Register, so check back often.
- The list also warns that "the latest changes may appear [on the list] prior to their publication in the Federal Register, and it is intended that users rely on changes indicated in this document that post-date the most recent Federal Register publication ... New Federal Register notices with regard to Specially Designated Nationals or blocked entities may be published at any time. Users are advised to check the Federal Register and this electronic publication routinely for additional names or other changes to the listings."
- A compendium of changes to the list, organized by date, can be found by clicking the **What Changed on the list when it was last updated** link.

Bloomberg.com Currency Calculator

http://www.bloomberg.com/analysis/calculators/
currency.html

Purpose: To serve as a currency converter.

Content: Select a currency to convert and a currency to change it
into, enter an amount, and click **Calculate**. It's that
easy.

Our View: The site offers more than 200 currencies to choose from.
Also, because Bloomberg is in the financial information
industry, they update their exchange rates throughout
the day.

XE Interactive Currency Table

http://www.xe.com/ict

Purpose: To obtain historical currency exchange rates.

Content: This site allows you to generate a table of exchange rates
for the currency you select from a list of approximately
80 major world currencies on a specific date (back to
November 16, 1995).

CHAPTER SIXTEEN

Law Practice Management and Professional Development

"Law practice management" is which of the following?

   A. The day-to-day management of a case load
   B. Firm calendar, docketing, and conflict management
   C. Staff management (human resource and personnel issues)
   D. Financial management (billing and receivables)
   E. Office management (physical space, equipment, and technology)
   F. Image management (marketing and networking)
   G. All of the above

Running a successful law practice means more than just doing a good job for your clients. The most successful lawyers also do a good job for themselves. In his popular *Attorney and Law Firm Guide to the Business of Law,* Second Edition (ABA General Practice, Solo and Small Firm Section, 2002), law firm management consultant Edward Poll posits that in order to survive and grow, all businesses (law firms included) must be proficient in what he has labeled "the three competencies": marketing (getting clients), technical (doing good work), and financial (getting paid).

Therefore, to insure a successful practice, lawyers must take the time to focus on the business of practicing law in addition to the mechanics of properly handling cases for their clients. The following checklist, adapted from Poll's book, outlines the principles he deems inherent to a successful law firm.

The successful law firm:

❏ Pays attention to the needs and desires of their clients

❏ Communicates their awareness of and sensitivity to the client's wishes

❏ Delivers their services at a price that does not offend the client

❏ Knows how to run the business of their practice

It is easy to see, then, that the correct answer to the question posed at the beginning of this chapter is "G: All of the above."

There are a number of resources readily available online to help you focus on some of these important business aspects of practicing law.

The American Bar Association's (ABA) Law Practice Management (LPM) section (**http://www.abanet.org/lpm**) offers a wide range of resources covering all areas of running an efficient practice, including implementing technology that works, quality of life, e-lawyering, alternative billing methods, and other ways of serving your clients more effectively.

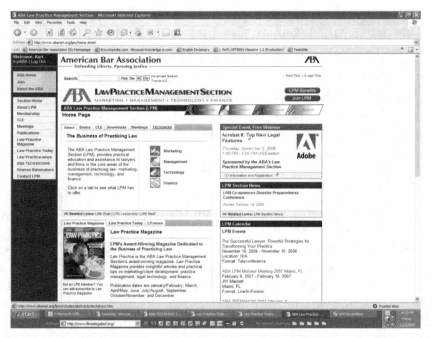

Figure 16-1. The ABA's Law Practice Management Section offers a number of free resources on its Web site to members and nonmembers alike, including *Law Practice* magazine and Law Practice Today.

Two excellent (free) resources also available to non-ABA members include the online version of the long-time favorite print publication, *Law Practice* magazine (**http://www.abanet.org/lpm/magazine**) (eight issues per year), and the new online publication *Law Practice Today* (**http://www.lawpracticetoday.org**). Full text of both publications is available online to section members and nonmembers alike.

Bar Cat

http://67.29.152.234/dbtw-wpd/barcat.htm

Purpose: Think of Bar Cat as a serials and treatise database for anyone involved in bar associations (whether as a paid staff person or a volunteer lawyer who happens to be their local bar's president) or anyone with law practice management questions (e.g., what is the best billing software, etc.). More precisely, Bar Cat is the online catalog of DBS, a division of the Bar whose function is to serve as a link between the ABA and other bar associations and to provide education, training, and management support services for bar leaders. Bar Cat allows keyword searchable access to all types of bar association publications, many of which are also geared to helping any lawyer with the management of his or her law practice.

Our View: This site does offer a wealth of information in a friendly and easy to use manner. The popular searches save time and energy. The search assistance icon (question mark on the home page) helps you learn how to search online. It's too bad that materials in the DBS' collection can no longer be borrowed, though.

Content: Bar Cat provides the user easy access to more than 15,000 holdings of the DBS Information Clearinghouse and also to full-text *Bar Leader* articles from 2000 to the present. Bar Cat's home page offers the usual way to search, by **Keyword** or by **Title**. In-depth search methods, using Boolean connectors, are explained on the site. A lawyer who is not interested in bar leader-type information but who is searching for information about which billing software to purchase can enter a search for "billing and software." But if you are unsure of where to start, there is also a **Browse** button for **Subject**, **Publisher**, and **Bar Type**. Also offered is a short list of **Popular searches** such as "Long Range Planning," which is a good example of the type of information a bar leader would be interested in. An example of a "Long Range Planning" result is the "Long Range Planning [Information Background Kit]" published by the American Society of Association Executives and including case studies and sample plans. Once you complete your search, the results are posted, and it's an easy scroll to discover if you want to delve further.

Tip: The **Add to Cart** button that accompanies each result is for saving that particular record to your "want list." Once you finish gathering all the information needed, you simply submit an online request form. Items can also be requested by e-mail or by telephoning the DBS Clearinghouse, identifying the materials by title.

If you search by selecting a Subject from the **Browse** list, you may select as many subject headings as needed to lend precision to your results. The number in parentheses indicates how many Clearinghouse documents have been assigned that subject classification.

ABA Section members also receive discounts on registration for the ABA Techshow and LPM books (like this one), and can access special section meetings and educational programs around the country.

Another free resource that covers a wide range of law office management and technology topics is FindLaw's *Modern Practice* magazine (**http://practice.findlaw.com**). This monthly online publication's articles cover the issues of client retention, effective marketing materials, knowledge management, and software selection and use, among other subjects.

Additionally, many state bar associations have robust LPM sections. Space does not allow us to list or review all of the useful resources offered by these organizations, but a selection of those providing a broad range of information include:

- California at **http://www.calbar.org/lpmt**
- Florida at **http://www.flabar.org**

- Maryland at **http://www.msba.org/departments/loma/**
- New York City at **http://www.nycbar.org/SmallFirmCenter/index.htm**
- Oklahoma at **http://www.okbar.org/members/map/services.htm**

If it is not listed here, also check with your state and local bar associations to see what resources they offer.

Financial Resources

As if practicing law wasn't time-consuming and difficult enough, once the work is done, lawyers must deal with getting paid. Positive cash flow is essential to any business, but the legal profession brings along its own set of difficulties tied to pricing, billing, accounts receivable, and collections. These sites offer some general (and law office specific) information on business finances.

Small Business Administration (SBA)

http://www.sba.gov/index.html

Purpose:	To find information on building and maintaining a profitable business.
Content:	The SBA provides information on starting, financing, and managing your business.
Our View:	The site offers a plethora of information, as well as links to external sources regarding business management, finance, and accounting.
Tip:	In the left-hand column of the home page, click on **Training** for links to online presentations covering cash flow, accounting, budgeting, and other finance basics.

LawBiz

http://www.lawbiz.com

Purpose: To find information on building and maintaining a profitable practice.

Content: The site is a mixture of free articles, newsletters, and links to purchase law firm management consultant Ed Poll's informative books, or subscribe to his monthly podcast (free).

Our View: Poll, a nationally recognized law firm management consultant, covers effective methods for law firms to ensure business success, including pricing, invoicing and collection techniques, maintaining positive cash flow, reaching and maintaining profitability, and how Sarbanes-Oxley effects law firms, among other topics.

Tip: Select the **Blog** or **Published Articles** links from the **Resources** tab at the top of the page to access the site's free content.

Figure 16-2. The LawBiz site offers articles on managing and marketing your practice, as well as a free e-mail newsletter.

A number of other law firm management consultants also offer articles and background information on cash flow and collections, including Kohn Communications (**http://www.kohncommunications.com**—select **Articles** and then **Management Articles** at the top of the page) and the Centurion Consulting Group (**http://www.centurionconsulting.com**—select **Articles** at the top of the page).

Marketing Resources

Too often people think only about brochures, paid advertising, and (occasionally) their Web site when the topics of marketing and business development are discussed. There are a number of other online resources than can be used to develop new business, such as creating lists of targeted potential clients and dossiers about those potential clients. Additionally, you can put together fact books about your competitors to track their growth and (possibly) predict trends in your practice area.

As a brief example, you might use the Thomas Register (**http://www.thomasnet.com/**) to locate information on companies that manufacture a certain type of product. You could then use Hoover's (**http://www.hoovers.com**) or Vault (**http://www.vault.com**) to find specific information (such as contacts or financials) about those individual companies. With that information you could determine if there are any potential problems with the companies' products (via complaints in newsgroups or message boards), litigation against competitors, or any other industry trends that might affect that company.

American Lawyer Media draws on its database of surveys to create the numerous database products and reports offered for sale on its ALM Research Web site (**http://www.almresearchonline.com**). Reports include industry rankings (by size or revenues), trends (such as revenue per partner, firm diversity, and mergers and acquisitions) and surveys (such as firm diversity, *pro bono* statistics and lateral partner surveys). Reports on individual law firms are also available. Prices vary depending on the report, but as an example, a searchable, electronic spreadsheet version of the company's AmLaw 100 is offered for $250.

For more-detailed information on conducting marketing and competitive intelligence research, see Chapter 10, "Company Research;" Chapter 11, "Competitive Intelligence Research;" Chapter 7, "Finding and Backgrounding People;" Chapter 9, "Finding and Backgrounding Expert Witnesses;" and Chapter 5, "General Factual Research."

These resources can be used to prepare presentations to potential clients or to proactively service existing clients. These techniques can also help you spot potential problems for clients and quash them before they become major, or to be prepared to deal with them when they do.

Figure 16-3. Many law firm consultants, such as Kohn Communications, offer articles and tips for marketing and developing your practice.

Additionally, there are a number of sites that focus on more traditional and Internet-based areas of law firm marketing. These include:

- Lawyer Marketing Tips at **http://www.lawyermarketing.net**
- Justia at **http://www.justia.com**
- Next Client at **http://www.nextclient.com**
- Consultwebs at **http:www.consultwebs.com**
- FindLaw at **http://marketing.lp.findlaw.com**
- Kohn Communications at **http://www.kohncommunications.com**
- Law Biz at **http://www.lawbiz.com**
- Law Marketing Portal at **http://www.lawmarketing.com**
- Legal Marketing Association (LMA) at **http://www.legalmarket ing.org**
- LexiWebs at **http://www.lexiwebs.com**

Technology Assessment and Purchase Research

ABA Legal Technology Resource Center (LTRC)

http://www.lawtechnology.org

Purpose:	To locate the latest information regarding law office hardware and software.
Content:	The LTRC offers articles about, and reviews of, the latest law office hardware and software. Topics include:

- Calendaring and docketing
- Conflict checking
- Document scanning, management, and retention
- Time and billing
- Internet connectivity
- Handheld computers
- Networking (wired and wireless)

Our View:	The LTRC articles vary in depth from overviews that give a sketch of available options to in-depth product reviews and comparisons. Whether you're just beginning to think about adding something new, or looking for guidance to make a final decision, the LTRC can help.
Tip:	Telephone or e-mail research and assistance is available to ABA members seeking information on practice technology. Nonmembers have access to the Web site that is updated often, so check back regularly.

Law Technology News

http://www.lawtechnews.com

Purpose:	To keep up to date on law office hardware and software.
Content:	This monthly print magazine covers a wide range of technology subjects applicable to lawyers in any size practice.

Our View: Each issue features dozens of short items about the latest hardware and software releases. In-depth articles focus on product reviews and comparisons and technology trends.

Tip: You can either register for a free print subscription or access the articles and news online (also requires registration).

Law Office Computing

http:///www.lawofficecomputing.com

Purpose: For keeping up to date on practice management and technology tools.

Content: This bimonthly magazine offers news coverage, in-depth articles, and product reviews about the latest developments in law office hardware and software.

Our View: Online access to the articles is for paid subscribers of the print magazine only. Annual subscriptions are listed at $39 when you subscribe at the magazine's Web site. If you want to be billed for the subscription, the price is $49.

Tip: Those who pay for a new subscription by credit card get instant access to the articles online.

The State Bar of California Law Practice Management & Technology Section

http://www.calbar.ca.gov/lpmt

Purpose: For keeping up to date on practice management and technology tools.

Content: The site features free access to selected articles from the section's bimonthly print newsletter the *Bottom Line*, covering new developments in law office-related hardware and software, as well as practice management strategies.

Our View: While the newsletter is meant for section members, it is a valuable resource to lawyers anywhere. Most articles are not limited in scope to California, so they are applicable to practices just about anywhere in the country. A subscription to the print version of the newsletter is available to any legal professional (membership is $65 per year for lawyers and $60 for non-lawyers).

Tip: Subscribe to the print version of the *Bottom Line* newsletter for useful technology and practice management tips.

ESQLawtech Weekly

http://www.mylawtips.com

Purpose: For keeping up to date on practice management and technology tools.

Content: ESQLawtech Weekly is a free weekly e-zine covering law office technology tips, tools, and tricks.

Our View: This site "comb[s] the Internet, and written publications to provide you with a consolidated view of law office technology information." Its aggregation can save you time locating the information elsewhere.

Pocket PC Legal

http://www.pocketpclegal.com

Purpose: To locate information regarding use of handheld computers in the practice of law.

Content: The site contains feature articles and news dealing specifically with the Pocket PC platform of handheld computers. The coverage focuses on how lawyers can use the handheld devices in their practice.

Our View: The site offers a good primer on using the Pocket PC for more than a calendar and notepad. It outlines how you could (almost) replace your laptop on some trips.

Tip: See the site's pages comparing different Pocket PC models.

Other general-interest computer print publications also offer free online access to some (or all) of their recent articles. They are excellent sources for news of new software and hardware releases, and product reviews. See:

- *PC World* at **http://www.pcworld.com**
- *PC Magazine* at **http://www.pcmag.com**
- *Macworld* at **http://www.macworld.com**
- *pdaJD* at **http://www.pdajd.com**
- *Handheld Computing* at **http://www.pdabuzz.com**
- *Pocket PC Magazine* at **http://www.pocketpcmag.com**

Some publications (*PC World, PC Magazine, Macworld,* and others) also offer free e-mail newsletters covering some of the same topics included in their print publications.

Apex Digital Glossary of Television/DVD-related Terms

http://www.apexdigitalinc.com/glossary.asp

Purpose: To define terms related to the latest TV, digital video, and DVD player technology.

Content: Definitions of terms related to the latest TV, digital video, and DVD player technology, including:

- DVD Terms
- TV Terms
- Digital Camera Terms
- Home Theater Terms

The list includes a wide range of input and output formats (e.g., "DVI" vs. "S-Video" or "Component Video" vs. "Composite Video"), as well as file formats (e.g., "MPEG," "MPEG-1," and "MPEG-2"). All of the glossary's terms and definitions are presented as a long list, all on one page.

Our View: Whether you're buying new equipment for your conference room, or need to arrange to play back video at trial, this glossary can help decode some of the myriad new terms associated with audio-visual electronics. The definitions are (mostly) written in plain English and are easy to understand.

Tip: Some sort of search feature would be helpful, but because the list of terms and definitions is not overwhelmingly long, it is easily browsable. Although the glossary is not necessarily comprehensive, it will help make sense of all the terms and acronyms the salespeople throw at you.

For a detailed glossary of computer and technology firms, see the Glossary that begins on page 757 of this book.

Human Resources: Recruiting, Retention, and Personnel Management

The first step in using the Internet for recruiting lawyers and staff to join your firm should be posting information about the available positions on the firm's Web site. A recruiting section on the site can help focus potential employees' attention on the pertinent information regarding the firm and available positions.

Logically dividing available positions by category is also helpful in targeting potential hires. Categories might include

- New associates
- Laterals
- Partners
- Associates
- Summer associates

- Staff
- Paralegals
- Secretaries
- Other support

Additionally, it is helpful to potential hires for the site to include information on the firm culture, its management style, and other pertinent information regarding life at the firm.

In addition to using the firm's own Web site to recruit new hires, many job search sites allow employers to post job openings on the Internet. Each of those sites mentioned below allows firms to directly post their job openings in the sites' respective databases and browse the qualifications of available candidates who have registered at those sites. Check with each of the sites for their respective fees.

A number of law firm management consultants offer information on their Web sites regarding evaluating your firm culture and hiring and retaining the right people. Altman Weil offers downloadable PDF versions of some of its reports (see **http://www.altmanweil.com**). Older material is replaced as newer data is added. Click the **Articles, News & Resources** tab at the top of the page to access these reports. There, you'll also get access to some of the company's law firm management articles.

Figure 16-4. Legal consulting firm Altman Weil offers free access to some of its reports and articles on its Web site, as well as offering a free newsletter.

Ida Abbott, author of *Developing Legal Talent: Best Practices in Professional Development for Law Firms* and other books advising firms how to attract, develop, and retain employees, offers a free newsletter and access to recent articles she has written at her Web site (**http://www.idaabbott. com**—click on the **Books and Resources** link on the left-hand side of the home page to access these). Abbott also offers free access to PDF versions of diagnostic tools (questionnaires) that you can use "to help you assess your firm's performance and identify areas where improvement is needed." (Click on **Resources: Free Assessment Tools** to access these.)

Rigorous pre-employment screening has become a regular part of doing business for many companies. Law firms (large and small) are not immune to the factors that have made pre-employment screening a fact of business life. While there are a number of companies that specialize in conducting these types of investigations, you can (depending on where you are located) find some of the same information yourself for free on the Internet.

See Chapter 7, "Finding and Backgrounding People"; Chapter 8, "Accessing Public Records"; and Chapter 4, "Search Tools" for detailed information on the types of information available, including:

- Current and previous employment
- Licensure
- Education
- Criminal background
- Civil litigation
- Other public records
- Select online activities (such as personal Web sites, blogs, and online discussion groups)

Not all of this information is available in every jurisdiction. For example, Texas (**http://records.txdps.state.tx.us**) charges to access its Criminal History Conviction database while Florida (**http://www3.fdle. state.fl.us/fdle**) provides free access via the Internet to searchable databases of outstanding warrants, while most other states do not.

Additionally, some lawyer oversight organizations such as the Illinois Attorney Registration & Disciplinary Committee (**http://www.iardc.org**) and the State Bar of California (**http://www.calbar.ca.gov**) have a fully searchable database of their members available free on the Internet. These sites can be very handy in helping to determine whether a candidate has ever lost the privilege of practicing law or been otherwise disciplined. Available information varies from state to state. Not all states provide this search.

As with any searching, locating this information on the Internet does not necessarily constitute a thorough background investigation, but it can be a good place to start.

The Work Number

http://www.theworknumber.com **$**

Purpose: For employment and salary verification.

Content: This site provides out-sourced employment verification services for hundreds of employers, including banks, city, state and federal agencies, and corporations of varying sizes. Its database covers more than 100 million employee records from over 1,000 organizations nationwide. The database is updated directly from the employer's payroll records every pay period to provide the most recent employment information. Employers have signed up with the Work Number to relieve their human resources departments of the task of taking and handling all of the employment verification requests they receive. Pay-as-you-go employment verifications are $11.50–$13 and income verifications are $14–$16 per verification, billed to your credit card. Lower per search fees are available for volume users.

Our View: Even though you have to know the name of the company a prospective employee had worked for to verify employment, the service can still be a worthwhile timesaver. (That company must have contracted with the Work Number to handle its verifications for you to be able to get the information from the Work Number database.)

Tip: Click on the **Enter Verifier Section** and then **Verification Demo** for more information on how to order employment or income verifications. You can also order verifications by phone at 800-367-5690. There is no charge for attempting a verification for an employee not in the Work Number database.

Association of Corporate Counsel (ACC) (limited information is free)

(restricted membership) $

http://www.acca.com/

Purpose: The Association of Corporate Counsel (ACC) helps its members with legal, technological, and management issues. However, ACC restricts membership to corporate counsel "who are engaged in the active practice of law on behalf of organizations in the private sector and do not hold themselves out to the public for the practice of law."

Content: If you click on the tabs at the top of the home page, drop-down menus appear with more selections. The first tab is **Networks** and links mostly to member-only information such as a member directory, a jobline, and a database to find members in a specific geographic area who are experts in a specific area of law. The second tab is **Legal Resources**, which includes ACC's magazine, *Docket* (nonmembers can view the front page only); a Virtual Library that can be keyword-searched for articles, briefs, sample forms, and more on a plethora of topics (nonmembers can search, but only members can view the full text); and Stats and Surveys (nonmembers can view the full text of some of the information). The third tab is **Advocacy**. Nonmembers can view the full text of much of the information in this tab, which includes amicus briefs and information about multi-jurisdictional practice (MJP).

Our View: Although you need to be a member to access all the information on the site, there is some free information that any lawyer would find useful. For example, information about one of the hottest topics in law practice, MJP, is provided in a chart that outlines each state's rules (**http://www.acca.com/admissionRules/index.php**).

Information regarding Multi-Disciplinary Practices can be found at **http://www.acca.com/practice/mdp.php**.

Tip: For those corporate counsel who have yet to join ACC, visit the site if you need help in deciding. In between the *Virtual Library* found in the **Legal Resources** section of the site and the virtual networking found in the **Networks** section of the site, this is a membership site any corporate counsel could benefit from. For those who are already members of ACC, be sure to visit the site.

Information about MJP can also be found at the ABA's site at **http://www.abanet.org/cpr/mjp-home.html**.

For new or growing businesses that do not yet have a procedure manual or standard set of forms, the Internet can be a valuable resource in building such a collection. Usually, the form letters found on the Internet are nothing fancy and are a bit on the general side, but they can be a good starting point for creating your own targeted letters. See FormsGuru.com (**http://www.formsguru.com**) and Office Depot's Business Center (**http://www.officedepot.com/renderStaticPage.do?context=/ content&file=/BusinessTools/forms/default.jsp**—or visit **http://www.officedepot.com**, click on **Business Center** and then click on **Free Business Form Templates**) for sample forms pertaining to:

- Business finance
- Compensation and benefits
- Employee management (recruiting, hiring, and termination)
- Excessive absenteeism
- No open employment positions
- Office space sublet agreement

While the Office Depot forms are all free, only some of the forms offered at FormsGuru are. Others, clearly marked by a dollar-sign icon ($), range in price from $8.99 to $25 each.

LexisOne's forms library (**http://www.lexisone.com/lx1/store/ catalog?action=main** or click on **Forms** on the left-hand side of the LexisOne home page) offers a variety of transactional, court and administrative forms. Forms are keyword searchable. You can click on the

Advanced Search link to narrow your search further by state. This offering is mainly meant to leverage LexisNexis' ownership of the HotDocs document assembly sotware—with many interactive forms available for sale and download in the HotDocs format (most are in the $10–$15 range.). However, many of the forms are available as a free download (as PDF documents) that you can print out and fill in by hand or typewriter. (You can also create your own interactive versions if you have the full paid version of Adobe Acrobat.) Still other documents are available in a free, online HotDocs Interactive version that allows you to enter variables (names, addresses, etc.) into a series of form boxes. At the end of the process, you can then print out the completed form. You cannot save this completed version of the form however.

Law-Related Job Search Sites for Employers and Employees

As it has done in so many other areas, the Internet has added a new dimension to the job market. Whether you're a lawyer looking for a new job in your current hometown, or relocating to another part of the country, or your firm needs to hire a new tax associate, there are a number of Web sites that list law-related jobs. While the general employment sites such as Monster and HotJobs include many legal jobs, and should not be discounted, a legal professional seeking a new position (or a firm attempting to fill open positions) could benefit more from sites that specialize in legal employment but still feature the advanced search functions of the general employment sites. Although the specialty sites are not as well known as the general ones, no legal professional should leave them out of a search.

Legalstaff

http://www.legalstaff.com

Purpose: To conduct a job search.

Content: Legalstaff offers thousands of searchable job listings around the country. You can post a résumé, choosing to show your name or post anonymously. You can also search for employers or recruiters by location.

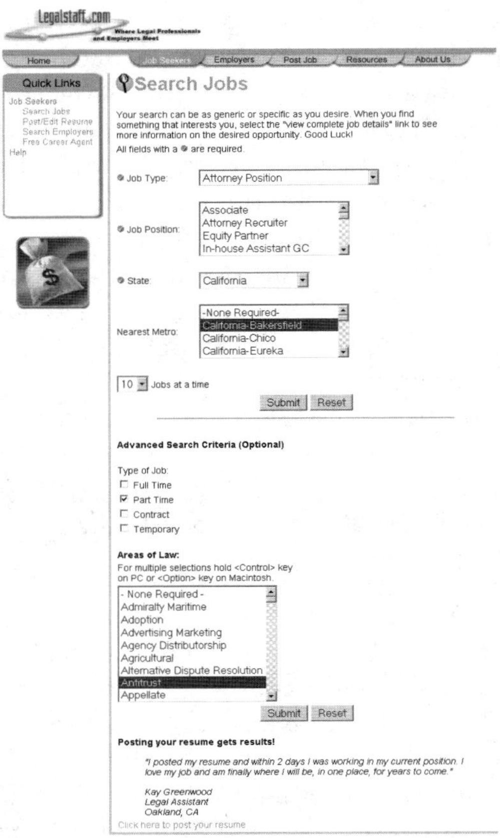

Figure 16-5. LegalStaff.com provides free online access to thousands of law related jobs around the country.

Our View: Legalstaff has one of the most targeted free legal job searches available on the internet. You can search by:

- Job type (such as lawyer or staff)
- Position (associate, partner, in-house)
- State
- Nearest metropolitan area (for example, there are nineteen cities listed for Texas, eighteen for California, and twelve for New York)

The **Nearest Metro** criteria allows you to search for jobs only in cities in which you're interested—either where you live, or where you'd like to relocate.

Legal Staff also offers a free **Career Agent** (registration required) that e-mails you when jobs are posted that fit certain criteria you select. For example, you could request an e-mail notice if a position for a full-time associate position, with three to nine years' experience, was posted by a law firm in Chicago.

Tip: Use the free **Career Agent** to keep up to date with new job listings of interest without having to keep checking for new postings.

FindLaw Career Center

http://www.careers.findlaw.com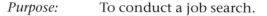

Purpose: To conduct a job search.

Content: FindLaw's career center includes listings for thousands of available jobs around the world. FindLaw also offers an employer and recruiter directory, searchable by name or location. Two of the resources that set FindLaw apart are

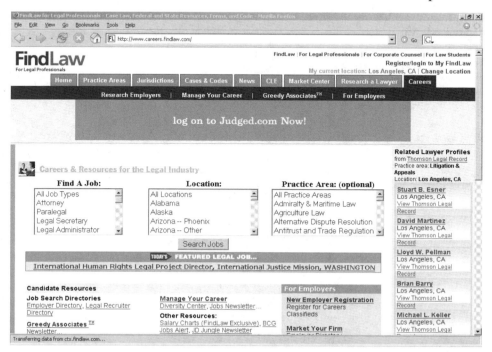

Figure 16-6. FindLaw's Career Center includes salary charts and insider information about firms, in addition to listings for thousands of available law related jobs.

- Salary charts (listing first-year through eighth-year salaries for law firms by city or region).
- Greedy Associates message boards (offering anonymous postings from lawyers discussing internal firm politics, salaries, and so on, by city or region). These boards are free to read and require free registration (anonymous) to post.

Our View: FindLaw also offers flexible and targeted searching of its nearly 3,000 job listings. You can search by:

- Job (such as lawyer or paralegal)
- Practice area
- Location (many states are broken down into metropolitan regions)

Tip: Definitely use the salary charts and Greedy Associates message boards to collect background information on firms you may be interested in working for.

LawJobs

http://www.lawjobs.com

Purpose: To conduct a job search.

Content: LawJobs lists thousands of available positions around the country. The listings are a combination of classified advertisements placed in American Lawyer Media publications (owner of LawJobs' parent, Law.com) and positions posted directly to the site.

The site's **Advanced Search** function offers a very flexible search of its listings. This includes:

- Boolean searching
- narrow or broad geographical restrictions
- entire state
- individual ZIP Code
- single city
- within 10-125 mile radius of a selected city
- single employer

You can also choose to receive listings only from employers, only from recruiters, or both. The results include more-detailed information regarding the position and links to more information about the employer or recruiter.

You can also create a free job-seeker user profile by clicking the **My LawJobs Log-in** link on the upper left-hand side of the home page. This allows you to create, post and manage your résumé and cover letter online; apply for posted jobs online; receive job alerts for new listings that match criteria you define; track and organize all your online job applications and responses; and save and store job searches and e-mail alert results.

Our View: The site offers a good mix of tools for the job searcher. In addition to the searchable job postings, the site also has a page of law firm recruiting links to more than 40 top law firms, a browsable list of recruiters and headhunters by location, and links to legal temporary staffing agencies if you're looking for a short-term position. (See the **Resource Directories** links in the lower left-hand corner of the home page.)

Tip: While these tools are all helpful, they are not necessarily comprehensive in their depth. Use the LawJobs site in conjunction with other sites discussed in this section.

Emplawyernet

http://www.emplawyernet.com

Purpose: To conduct a job search.

Content: Emplawyernet features thousands of legal jobs across the country. To access them you have to pay a membership fee of $14.95 per month or $125 per year. (Law students pay only $7.95 per month.) The free membership (registration required) allows you to post a profile in the

Emplawyernet database. The profile, built from a series of fill-in-the-blank fields and menu selections, becomes a *de facto* online résumé that employers can search when they have positions to fill.

Our View: While posting a free profile in the Emplawyernet database can be useful to a job search, we'd search through the free listings at other sites before signing up for paid access to their database.

Tip: You can register your profile (for free) anonymously. This way potential employers can review your qualifications and Emplawyernet will contact you if any express interest. This will keep you from "bumping into yourself" if you have already applied for a position you found elsewhere, or you wish to test the waters for a job change. If you do choose to sign up for a paid membership, see if a discount is available to members of your bar association. Emplawyernet offers discounts to ABA members and Los Angeles County Bar Association members and alumni of numerous law schools, among others.

General Job-Search Sites

Monster

http://www.monster.com

Purpose: To conduct a job search.

Content: Monster boasts over 500,000 member companies. While they're not all law related, its job search engine allows you to specify a geographical region (Texas is divided into twelve regions) and a job category (legal). You can further customize the search by including a keyword, such as a practice area. A sample search for legal jobs in Dallas yielded 160 listings for positions ranging from associates to Judge Advocate General (JAG), as well as legal secretaries, paralegals, and court clerks. Refining the search further by adding the keywords "tax" and "lawyer" returned 12 results—most of which were for tax lawyers, however, there were a number of listings returned for secretaries, paralegals, and non-tax-law-related attorney positions.

Our View: You can search and view the listings without registration, but if you do register (free), you can post your résumé, apply for jobs online, and have jobs e-mailed to you based on criteria you select.

Tip: You can refine the search even further by using the site's ZIP code function.

HotJobs

http://hotjobs.yahoo.com

Purpose: To conduct a job search.

Content: HotJobs lists thousands of jobs in nearly thirty categories. Here you can search for jobs by job category, keyword, location, or any combination. Our sample search for legal jobs in Dallas yielded 199 listings for positions ranging from associates to real estate specialists, as well as legal secretaries, paralegals, and firm administrators. Refining the search further by adding the keywords "tax" and "lawyer" returned just one result. (While the posting included the keywords "tax" and "lawyer," it was not for an actual tax lawyer.)

Our View: Registering for your own personalized **myHotJobs** account can help you organize your job search. It also allows you to post your résumé online, allows access to statistics about the number of times an employer or recruiter reviewed your résumé, and keeps a complete history of cover letters and résumés you have sent. The site also offers a personal job search agent (requires free registration) that e-mails jobs to you that match criteria you select.

Tip: Based on the results of our sample search (compared to similar searches at other sites) it's probably a wise idea to use HotJobs in conjunction with some of the other sites discussed here, and not rely on it solely.

A natural inclination for any legal job seeker might be to check out the job listings at a well-known legal directory like Martindale-Hubbell (**http://www.martindale.com**). While searching Martindale's jobs database did return large numbers of results, the site only allows you to narrow your search down geographically to the state level—and not a city or ZIP code. Also, most of Martindale's listings seem to come from one recruiter. A search for job openings in **All Practice Areas** in California returned 809 results, only four of which were from individual firms and not from this one recruiter. A similar search in Texas yielded 100 overall results, only five of which were from individual firms and not from that same recruiter.

While the Internet has added a new dimension to job hunting and recruiting, online job seekers should not forget old-fashioned methods such as going directly to the source. LawJobs, which supplies job listings to the Martindale site, aids this type of search by offering direct links to the recruiting sections of more than 40 top firms (**http://www.lawjobs .com/firms.asp**). You can also find a firm's Web site by conducting a search for the firm name using the Martindale-Hubbell Web site, or the Google search engine. (See Chapter 4, "Search Tools," and Chapter 3, "Search Strategies," for further details on effective Google searching.)

A visit to a targeted employer's Web site can be the beginning of a profitable information-gathering campaign. Many firms make job openings, compensation information, and benefit information available in a recruiting section on their sites.

Another old-fashioned method with an online twist is finding and registering with a traditional recruiter or headhunter. While a number of national recruiters post their openings at some of the employment sites noted above, you might also find smaller local or regional recruiters that do not post on these sites. Working with a recruiter might not be for everyone, so getting referrals from colleagues is also a good idea. Online, you can search the recruiters' listings noted in the sites above, or you might also check some of these sites listed below.

Hieros Gamos

http://www.hg.org/rec_sel.html

Purpose: To locate listings of hundreds of legal recruiters around the world.

Content: Companies range from large national recruiters such as Major Linsay & Africa (**http://www.mhasearch.com**) to regional and local recruiters such as Southern California's Attorney Network (**http://www.attorney-network.com**). You can search for a specific firm if you have their name, or you can search by location.

Our View: While the large national recruiters have the highest number of job listings, the local recruiters may have access to more jobs in their respective cities, or closer relationships with the firms listing the jobs. You can create a list of recruiters to contact (either on the Web, via

Figure 16-7. Hieros Gamos offers a list of hundreds of legal recruiters around the world.

e-mail, or by phone) using Hieros Gamos' recruiter search. To pull up the largest list of local recruiters, select your state from the pull-down menu and click **GO** to return the list of recruiters listed from that state.

Tip: Adding a city can narrow your search too much, since the search will not return recruiters from nearby cities (for example, results for Los Angeles will not include recruiters in nearby Santa Monica). Since links are not provided to most recruiters' Web sites, you'll have to infer the Web address from the e-mail address given for particular companies (for example, the Web site for mrosch@netforlawyers.com would be **http://www .netforlawyers.com**).

Robert Half Legal (formerly The Affiliates)

http://www.affiliates.com

Purpose: To conduct a job search.

Content: Robert Half Legal lists thousands of jobs across North America. To access the most flexible search functions, ignore the **Find a Job Now box** on the home page's left-hand side, and instead, click the **Jobs** tab at the top of the page. The company breaks down its listings of legal (and other) jobs into logical categories (attorney, licensed, 10+ years experience; attorney, licensed, 0-3 years experience; file clerk; and so on). Their database is searchable by location, category, and keyword.

Our View: A search for jobs for "attorney, licensed, 0-3 years experience" returned more than 85 results, including Seattle, Washington; Dallas, Texas; and Ottawa, Canada. These included mostly full-time positions as well as temporary and contract lawyer positions. A more targeted search for "attorney, licensed, 0-3 years' experience" in Los Angeles with the added keyword "litigation" produced only two results. However, utilizing too narrow a search could eliminate worthwhile results. Removing the keyword "litigation" returned 17 listings, including one seeking "a 3+ year litigation associate."

Tip: Leave keywords out of your search for more results.

Legal job seekers can also use the Internet to research salaries, firm culture, and the outlook for employment in different geographic and practice areas. Salary information from a wide variety of firms in California is provided at the FindLaw Career Center site (**http://careers.findlaw .com**—click on **Salary Charts**), for example. Data are obtained from the recruiting pages of the law firms' own sites as well as from lawyers who are, or were, associated with the firms they write about. Monster.com also offers a **Salary Wizard (http://content.salary.monster.com/)** that leads you through a few general questions regarding the job you're seeking (e.g., type, location, level) in order to deliver a general report on the range of salaries to expect (or to ask for).

Continuing Legal Education Sources

Online continuing legal education (CLE) comes in a variety of styles. As audio and video on the Internet have become easier for users to access, state and local bar associations have moved into the business of providing online (recorded) versions of their live seminars for CLE credit. Other providers offer an online version of the article and quiz format that is familiar from its use in any number of legal print publications. Whatever the format, online CLE offers you the opportunity to acquire new, useful information (and satisfy your state's CLE requirement) at a time and place that is convenient to you. This convenience is slowly catching on. The ABA's 2004–5 Legal Technology Survey found that more of lawyers have tried online CLE, reporting that "live webcasts are increasing, up to 27% this year, from 18% in 2003 and 13% in 2002. Archives of live webcasts are also gaining in popularity, up to 12% this year from 5% in 2002 and 2003."

Just like live seminars, online CLE programs cover a wide spectrum of topics—from general law office management and research skills to reviews of the latest substantive legal or legislative developments. Below are some of the best-known multistate providers of online CLE courses. You might also want to check with your own state and local bar associations to see if they offer CLE courses online.

CLE Now!

http://www.abanet.org/cle/clenow

Content: The ABA's CLE Now! offers topics covering a wide range of law practice management and litigation-related subjects. The programs are presented as RealAudio streams (requiring the RealOne player, a free download). The free programs vary in length from 41 to 84 minutes long. The ABA also offers CLE online in a variety of other media formats. Most of those programs are not free (though some of them are discounted to ABA members or members of certain ABA sections).

Cost: Free for ABA members; though some are free to all site visitors.

ABA Connection

http://www.abanet.org/cle/connection.html#previous

Content: Recorded versions of the ABA's monthly mandatory CLE (MCLE) teleconferences are available via the Internet.

Cost: Free for ABA members.

Internet For Lawyers

http://www.netforlawyers.com/online_mcle.htm   **$**

Content: The site offers text-based quizzes covering a total of 16 hours of general, legal ethics, substance abuse education, and law practice management credits. The quizzes combine a comprehensive article with locating material from outside Web sources.

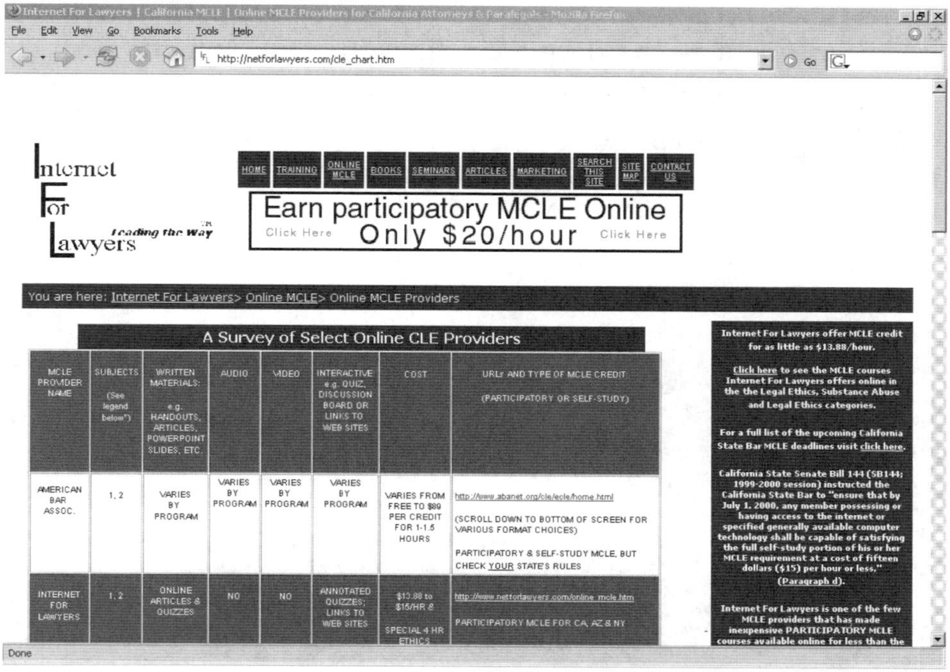

Figure 16-8. Internet For Lawyers provides an online chart comparing approximately one dozen local and national providers of online CLE (**http://www.net forlawyers.com/cle_chart.htm**).

These quizzes lead you through the functions of other Web sites where you can find important free resources useful to your practice while also satisfying your CLE requirements.

Cost: Credit can cost less than $15 per hour when submitting all 16 hours ($20 per hour when submitted separately).

Law.com

http://www.clecenter.com   **$**

Content: Law.com offers a combination of streaming audio or streaming video, from a variety of program producers around the country (mostly local and state Bar associations, seminar companies and law firms). Many

Law.com courses also include "library documents" to enhance the presentation (often the written materials distributed at the live presentation of the same course.)

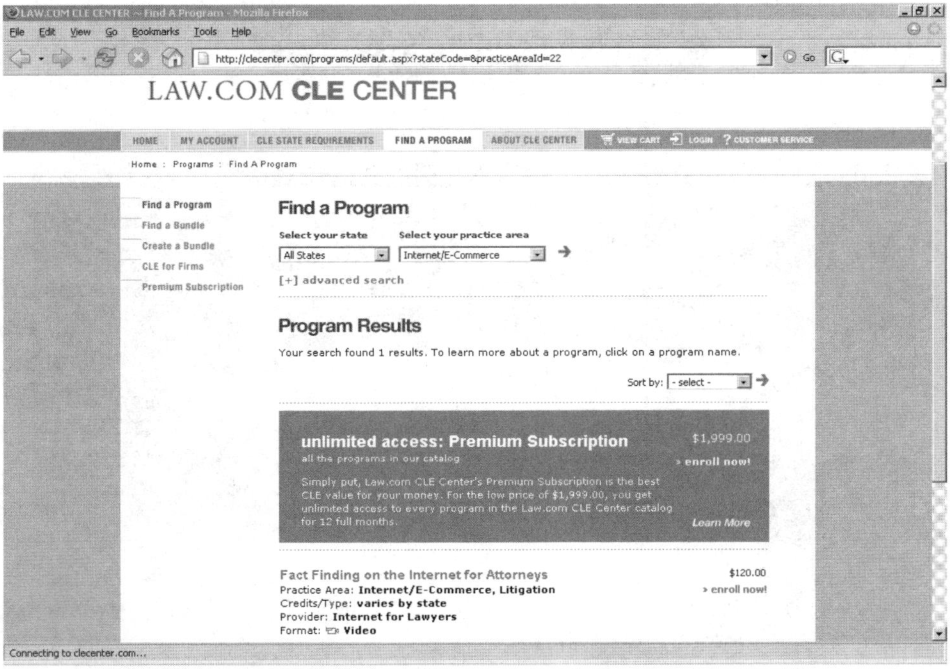

Figure 16-9. Law.com offers online CLE in a variety of formats, including streaming audio, streaming video, and e-mail panel discussions.

Cost: Prices range between $60 to $205 for courses lasting .75 to 5 hours. Preset bundles (offered on a state-by-state basis) can bring the price down under $30 per hour. Group pricing is also available for blocks of 100 or more hours.

West LegalEdCenter

http://www.westlegaledcenter.com/   **$**

Content: West LegalEdCenter offers live webcasts, in addition to a combination of pre-recorded streaming audio and video

CLE courses from a variety of program providers around the country, similar to Law.com's CLECenter.

Cost: Prices range from $50 to $610 for programs from 1 hour to 4 hours and 15 minutes in length.

Taecan

http://www.taecan.com   **$**

Content: Taecan has teamed up with more than two dozen state and local bar associations and private MCLE providers to deliver streaming audio and video versions of programs that the providers have previously presented live.

Cost: Fees per seminar range from $25 to $50 per hour (depending on the provider). Discounts are available to individuals who purchase multiple hours or to firms purchasing large blocks of seminars.

Legalspan

http://www.legalspan.com   **$**

Content: Legalspan has teamed up with more than three dozen state and local bar associations and private MCLE providers to deliver streaming audio and video versions of programs that the providers have previously presented live as well as live webcasts.

Cost: Prices vary depending on the provider. Most courses cost approximately $25 to $30 per hour. Once paid for, the courses can be accessed for three months.

Figure 16-10. Legalspan offers CLE programming from numerous state and local bar associations.

ABA Online CLE

http://www.abanet.org/cle/ecle/home.html $

Content:	The ABA cosponsors online audio and video seminars (some with slides) with a variety of partners, ranging from ABA sections to outside groups. Questions and exercises are mixed throughout the audio and video programs. Written materials are also available for download. The programs are searchable by topic or browsable by title.
Cost:	Most courses are priced at $59 for 1 to 1 $1/_2$ hours. Pricing is in two tiers: the highest price for non-ABA members, ABA members pay only $49. Many courses are available for free.

Practising Law Institute (PLI)

http://www.pli.edu

Content: PLI offers streaming audio and video online versions of their live programs, as well as live webcasts of seminars as they are being presented. They also include links to related written materials from PLI, other non-PLI Web-based resources, and an online discussion group.

Cost: The streaming video of previously-presented programs are mostly priced at $750, but can go up to $1,299 for a two-day seminar. Streaming audio programs are priced lower—mostly $129 for one-hour programs, with downloadable MP3s priced at $49.99 per hour. Prices for webcasts of live events are occasionally higher, up to $2,095 for a two-day seminar. Some 1-hour programs may be priced as low as $80, and PLI has occasionally offered a program for free.

CHAPTER**SEVENTEEN**

Statistical Research

Various organizations compile statistics on an unimaginable number of topics. Depending on the types of matters you handle, you can use statistics to prove (or disprove) an argument or better illustrate a point. As the oft-quoted American humorist Evan Esar defined it, the science of statistics is "the only science that enables different experts using the same figures to draw different conclusions."

Statistics Metasites

From the Census Bureau to the FBI, this country's most prolific gatherer of statistical information is probably the U.S. government. The first stop for federal statistical information has to be FedStats at **http://www.fedstats.gov**. You can search by topic, keyword (click on **Search across agency websites**), or by agency name. Searches can also be limited to regions. The choice of topics appears limitless, from **Abortion** to **Women-Owned Businesses**. See below for more information on selected statistics data available on the Internet.

For nonfederal statistics, your first stop should be the University of Michigan Documents Center site, Statistical Resources on the Web (**http://www.lib.umich.edu/govdocs/stats.html**).

The University of Michigan Documents Center site categorizes its links into a broad array of nearly 300 topics ranging from **Abortion** to **World-Village**. Additionally, the site offers an **Experimental Statis-**

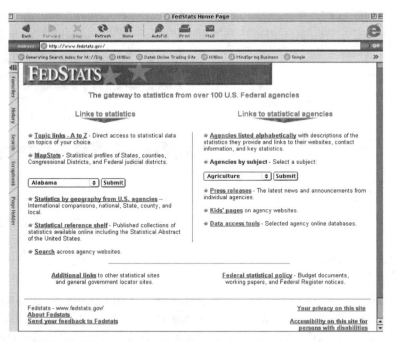

Figure 17-1. FedStats links to the statistical databases from more than seventy federal agencies.

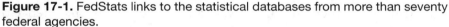

Figure 17-2. The University of Michigan Documents Center, Statistical Resources on the Web, links to state, local, and foreign governmental statistical databases, as well as to many nongovernmental databases, such as private nonprofits.

tics Database (the link is in the center of the home page) that may still need a bit of work. For example, a search for documents containing "work" and "injury" in the title or description returned no results, while a search for just "injury" returned two results for two documents from two different government agency Web sites; however, neither of the links to those documents was still accurate. Try some sample searches of the experimental database for yourself, but you may have your best results browsing the extensive list of topics.

Judicial Statistics Sites

Federal Court Management Statistics

http://www.uscourts.gov/fcmstat/index.html

Purpose:	To locate information regarding the U.S. District Courts and Courts of Appeals.
Content:	This site offers statistical information regarding the operation and caseloads of all the U.S. District Courts and Courts of Appeals. After clicking on **District Courts** or **Courts of Appeals** for a particular year, you can pick the court about which you want more information (such as Ninth Circuit or Texas Northern). Results are returned in a spreadsheet format in your browser window.
	Information returned includes "Overall Caseload Statistics," "Actions per Active Judge," and "Median Time" from notice to disposition, among other useful data. The report also includes comparative data in each category back five years from your year of inquiry.
Our View:	For the courts of appeals, you can view information for a single circuit or all twelve. For the district courts, you can request information for one district, or aggregated data for all of the districts. There is no way to pick and choose the districts to compile an original report for multiple districts of your choosing. Only aggregated

information for the courts is available. No judge-specific information is offered.

Tip: To view results in your browser, do *not* check the **Open in spreadsheet format** option beneath the court name. Checking this option allows you to save the data to your computer, but you must open the file using Excel, or some other spreadsheet software.

U.S. Sentencing Commission (USSC) Annual Reports

http://www.ussc.gov/annrpts.htm

Purpose: To locate statistics on the application of the federal sentencing guidelines.

Content: Each year the U.S. Sentencing Commission compiles its annual "Sourcebook of Federal Sentencing Statistics" containing data on the application of federal sentencing guidelines on a national level, as well as statistics broken down by district and circuit. The report's other statistics (arranged nationally—by offense, by district, or by circuit) include:

- Demographic information on offenders
- Guilty pleas
- Average length of sentence
- Sentencing appeals

Our View: The Sentencing Commission has broken down the information far enough that you can get a pretty good picture of what your client might expect to face in the courts. For example, selecting the Illinois Northern district court link in Appendix B of the 2005 report, you can learn that of the 323 offenders brought before the court on drug offenses during the reporting period, 320 received prison time—with 188 of those receiving more than 60 months. Two of the 320 received probation only, and none received a sentence that combined probation and confinement.

Tip:　　　Note that the 2001 "Sourcebook of Federal Sentencing Statistics" contains a *major* typographical error. Repeatedly, throughout the document, it states that it covers the period from October 1, 2001, through September 30, *2001* instead of October 1, 2001, through September 30, *2002.*

Note that in 2004, the sentencing Commission began splitting the reports in Appendix B into two parts, each covering half the fiscal year.

Federal Justice Statistics Resource Center (FJSRC)

http://fjsrc.urban.org/noframe/wqs/q_intro.htm

Purpose:　　To locate information regarding offenders in the federal justice system.

Content:　　The site contains "comprehensive information describing suspects and defendants processed in the Federal criminal justice system" compiled by the Bureau of Justice Statistics (BJS). Specific data sets for the most recent available year include:

- Executive Office for U.S. Attorneys (EOUSA)—suspects in matters received and concluded by the U.S. Attorneys office
- Administrative Office of the U.S. Courts (AOUSC)—ongoing and completed cases in the U. S. District Courts
- U.S. Sentencing Commission (USSC)—defendants sentenced
- Federal Bureau of Prisons (BOP)—inmates entering and exiting the federal prison system, and total inmate population at fiscal year end

To query the database you must:

- Select a year
- Select a data set
- Select a variable
- Check one or more value boxes

- Click the **Go** button
- Click **Frequency**

To view a list of the searchable variables in each of the data sets, and a description of each, click the **Data Dictionary** link on the left-hand side of the screen. Then select a **Year** and **Data Dictionary** and click the **Submit** button. Then select a specific data set for which to retrieve the list of variables and their explanations, and click the **Submit** button.

Our View: There is a lot of useful information contained in the FJSRC data sets, but it's not that easy to get at. Each source, each dataset, and each subcategory must be queried separately. It is much easier to retrieve information from the USSC (see the listing above).

Tip: Check the site's list of **Easy Query** questions at **http://fjsrc.urban.org/noframe/wqs/easy_q.cfm** for the answers to some of the more frequently asked questions. These questions and their answers also serve as a *de facto* tutorial for searching the individual datasets. Along with the answers to the questions, this page also delivers instructions on how you could have constructed the search yourself.

Federal District Court Civil Trials

http://teddy.law.cornell.edu:8090/questtr7900.htm

Purpose: To determine detailed (nonidentifying) information about completed civil trials in the federal district court system for 1978-2000.

Content: Two professors at the Cornell University School of Law, Theodore Eisenberg and Kevin M. Clermont, have developed a search interface for federal district court civil case information. The data are gathered by the Administrative Office of the United States Courts, based on forms completed by the clerks of each court for each completed case.

Our View: You can narrow your search to particular types of cases by selecting numerous criteria (you can make more than one selection per criteria by holding down the *Ctrl* key while clicking the selection):

- Category (such as real property or torts)
- Year (1978-2000)
- District
- Jurisdictional basis (such as federal question, U.S. defendant)
- Route to court (such as original proceeding, removal from state court)
- Trial type (judge only, jury)
  From those criteria, you then choose the type of information you want to know about those cases:
- Frequency
- Duration
- Judgment
- Amount demanded
- Amount awarded
- Basis for aggregation (such as case category, district, trial mode [judge versus jury])

For example, for all civil Racketeer Influenced and Corrupt Organizations Act (RICO) trials in 2000 in the Central District of California (CACD) resting on a particular jurisdictional basis, you can determine the total number of such cases, the length of time they were on the docket, and information about the amount of monetary awards to successful plaintiffs. This data can give you a feel for the amount of time a case may take to make it through the courts.

Tip: You might compare result of jury trials against results from judge trials to help decide which might better serve your client.

California (**http://www.courtinfo.ca.gov/reference/3_stats.htm**), Illinois (**http://www.state.il.us/court/AppellateCourt/CaseloadStat_default. htm**), and New Jersey (**http://www.judiciary.state.nj.us/mcs/mcstats.htm**) are some of the states that also provide access to this type of statistical information regarding their courts. A Google search for the terms "court" and "statistics" and the name of your state should return a link to the site containing the data if it is available. Also see the entry regarding Syracuse University's TRACfed Web site (**http://tracfed.syr.edu**), and the federal judicial statistics available there, in Chapter 6, "Government Resources Online."

Crime Statistics Sites

FBI Uniform Crime Report (UCR)

http://www.fbi.gov/ucr/ucr.htm

Purpose: To locate information regarding serious crime in the U.S.

Content: This site provides access to the FBI Uniform Crime Reports back to 1995. The UCR program was initiated in 1929 to collect information on serious crimes in the following categories:

- Homicide
- Forcible rape
- Robbery
- Aggravated assault
- Burglary
- Theft
- Auto theft
- Arson

Additionally, the program collects information on hate crimes and on persons arrested for twenty-two other less-serious crime categories. Hate crime offenses cover incidents motivated by race, religion, sexual orientation, and ethnicity or national origin.

Our View: It would be easier to utilize the UCR's data if the FBI would come up with a standard interface in which to present the reports from year to year. Some overview information can be found in the **Report Summary** section. However, see the Tip below for one trick to getting at "top line" trend information faster.

The raw data (number of occurrences in each category per city) are included in an alphabetical list of cities and towns (of over 10,000 population) in a separate PDF document (for 2004, click **Offenses Report**, then **Offense Tabulations** and then **Table 8**).

Tip: Each year's UCR data offer a comparison to the data from the previous year, and you can download UCR data from earlier years (back to 1995) and chart your own, longer-term trends for the cities and offenses covered in the reports.

For an overview of the data contained in any specific year's UCR click on the **For the News Media** link to locate the press release announcing the release of the UCR. It will include a capsule description of trends in the data, etc.

Demographic Statistics Sites

U.S. Census Bureau

http://www.census.gov

Purpose: To locate information regarding people and business in the U.S.

Content: Every ten years the Census Bureau collects data about the people and economy of the United States. Additionally, the Census Bureau, along with the Bureau of Labor Statistics, conducts a monthly Current Population Survey that collects data from 50,000 households.

Our View: The Census Bureau has sliced and diced its data on the U.S. population in myriad useful ways.

Information on people is available in nearly forty categories ranging from **Age** to **Working at Home**, in addition to general population profiles and projections. (Click **People & Households** on the site's home page to access these.)

For more information on business and economic data from the Census Bureau, see the entry on its Economic Census below.

Tip: For detailed state-by-state demographic data (or county-by-county), see **http://quickfacts.census.gov/qfd**. For example, selecting **California** from the pull-down menu in the upper left-hand corner returns a page of data for the state. You can further target the data by selecting a county from the pull-down menu on the left. All the data are also downloadable as Microsoft Excel files, or as raw data.

U.S. Census Bureau's Statistical Abstract of the United States

http://www.census.gov/statab/www

Purpose: To locate information regarding people and business in the U.S.

Content: This site is an online version of the *National Data Book,* which contains a collection of statistics on social and economic conditions in the United States. Selected international data is also included.

Our View: Even though there is no search engine available for the *Data Book,* it is still fairly easy to use. The book is divided into thirty sections detailing various segments of the U.S. population, culture, and economy. Topics covered range from the **Population** and **Vital Statistics** (birth, death, mortality) to **Banking** or **Entertainment**. The topics are presented in numerical order (as organized in the print edition of the book) with links to PDF versions of the corresponding data in the two most recent editions.

Tip: Also see the Guide to State Statistical Abstracts (**http://www.census.gov/statab/www/stateabs.html**), the County and City Data Book (**http://www.census.gov/statab/www/ccdb.html**), and USA Statistics in Brief (**http://www.census.gov/statab/www/brief.html**).

Business, Economy, and Labor Statistics Sites

U.S. Census Bureau's Economic Census

http://www.census.gov/econ/census02/

Purpose: To locate information and trends related to business in
the U.S.

Content: Every five years the Census Bureau profiles the economy
of the United States at the national and local levels. Survey forms are sent to 5 million businesses, and the data
is available at this site.

Our View: You can view economic status reports by NAICS code
(the North American Industry Classification System
that has replaced the older Standard Industrial Classification [SIC] system), at nearly any level. You can
retrieve data for the entire nation, down to a single ZIP
code (depending on the size of the locale you're interested in), or by Industry Sector.

The next survey is scheduled for 2007.

Tip: Download the PDF files and print them yourself, rather
than paying the Bureau's print-on-demand fee (which
ranges from $25 to $150, depending on the report
requested).

U.S. Department of Labor Bureau of Labor Statistics (BLS)

http://www.bls.gov

Purpose: To locate information and trends related to business and
labor in the U.S.

Content: The BLS offers myriad statistics related to consumer
spending; employment and unemployment; and wages,
earnings and benefits.

Our View: Like the Census Bureau, the BLS has analyzed its data in
dozens of useful ways. Reports range from state-by-state
reviews of wages, earnings, and benefits to labor and
productivity costs for employers across the country.

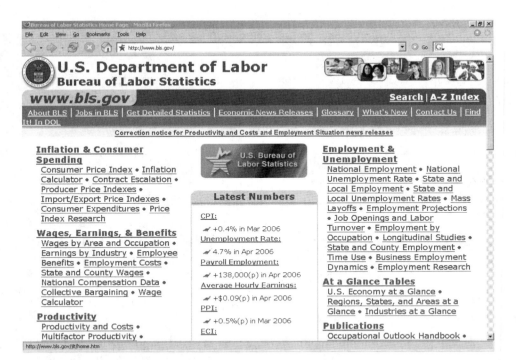

Figure 17-3. The Bureau of Labor Statistics Web site offers business and economical statistics in dozens of categories.

The topics are arrayed on the home page in broad categories, as noted above. Each broad category carries clickable subheadings of specific data available pertaining to that topic.

Tip:
For workers' compensation or other workplace injury cases, search for specific reports, such as "Injuries, Illnesses and Fatalities in Construction, 2004" (**http://www.bls.gov/opub/cwc/sh20060519ar01p1.htm**), that may help support your case (or refute the opposition's). Click **Search** in the upper right-hand corner of the home page to conduct keyword searches of the entire site to locate such materials.

Foreign and International Statistics Sites

U.S. Census Bureau International Database Summaries

http://www.census.gov/ipc/www/idbsum.html

Purpose: To determine population information regarding foreign countries.

Content: The site offers a database of population information summaries, viewable by country.

Our View: Selecting a country from the scrollable list brings up a summary of population data for that country that includes births and deaths, life expectancy, and a breakdown by age and gender.

Tip: In addition to current population data, the reports also include information back to 1950 and projections to 2025.

U.S. Census Bureau Foreign Trade Statistics

http://www.census.gov/foreign-trade/statistics/index.html

Purpose: To determine import and export activity and volume.

Content: The site offers a database of merchandise shipments to and from the U.S. Data is collected from import and export declarations filed with U.S. Customs and other government agencies.

Our View: You can retrieve data regarding the value of commodities shipped to and from the United States for the most recent five years. Select **Country/Product Data** at the top of the page, and then **Imports** or **Exports** (beneath **End-Use**) to view an alphabetical list of countries doing business with the U.S. Selecting a specific country displays a chart containing the dollar values of materials, ranging from **Wheat** to **Military Apparel**, sent to or from the U.S. (depending on whether you've selected exports or imports respectively).

Tip: Select **State Export Data** on the site's home page to view tables of exports from each state either by the country exported to or the commodity exported. (Data is shown for the top twenty-five export countries or top twenty-five export commodities only.) More in-depth data regarding which states exported which commodities to which countries is not available here.

For additional foreign and international statistics, see Chapter 15, "Foreign and International Research."

Transportation Statistics

For auto, aircraft, and train accident statistics, see Chapter 18, "Transportation Research."

CHAPTER**EIGHTEEN**

Transportation Research

Lawyers of many different disciplines can find a wealth of transportation-related information to help them in specific cases.

For example, a worker's compensation, personal injury, or insurance defense lawyer might use auto, plane, and train accident statistics and trends to bolster certain cases.

A products liability, class action, or personal injury lawyer could help make his case (or weaken the opposition's) with information on the number of other, similar complaints filed regarding a particular model of car.

A family law lawyer might wish to determine if the client's spouse owns any major personal property that the client is not aware of, such as a plane, boat, or luxury or sports car. (While airplane registration is available online for free, pleasure boat registration is handled at the state level in a manner similar to motor vehicle registration. Like car registration and licensing records, boat registration records are covered under the Driver's Privacy Protection Act [DPPA]. For more information on accessing motor vehicle records at the state level and the DPPA, see Chapter 8, "Accessing Public Records.")

Starting-Point Web Sites for Transportation Research

TranStats (U.S. Department Of Transportation's [DOT] Intermodal Transportation Database)

http://www.transtats.bts.gov

Purpose: To locate transportation data and statistics for air, road, and rail transportation.

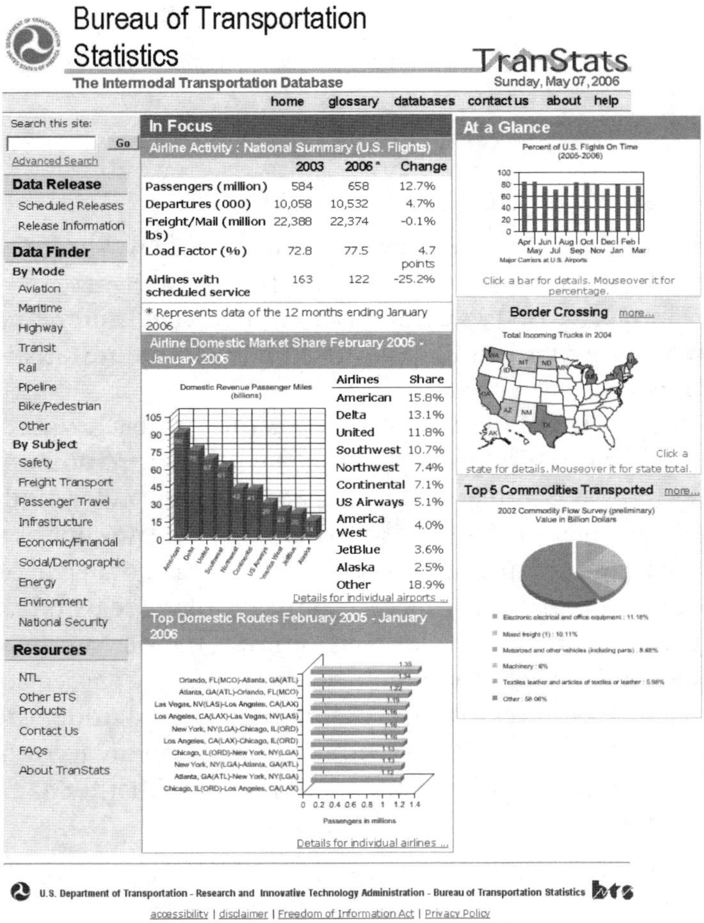

Figure 18-1. The U.S. Department of Transportation's TranStats database contains information regarding planes, trains, automobiles, and even oil and gas pipelines.

Content: TranStats is a metasite of government agencies and Web sites containing information on all conceivable modes of transportation, including:

- Aviation
- Maritime
- Highway
- Rail
- Bike and pedestrian
- Pipeline
- Transit

The site also has a number of preset **Explore by Subject** listings:

- Safety
- Freight transport
- Passenger travel
- Infrastructure
- Economic and financial
- Social and demographic
- Energy
- Environment
- National security

Our View: TranStats is an excellent one-stop shop for transportation data. For example, clicking on **Highway** brings up a number of data sets related to over-the-road transportation (for cars, trucks, and buses). The available data cover a wide range of topics from the **Commodity Flow Survey** (data on commodity shipments by industry, including hazardous materials) to the **Hazardous Materials Incidents Reporting System** (which includes information on hazardous materials spills occurring during transit). For a description of the data held in each of the listed sources, click on its name. For a more in-depth description of the government program responsible for collecting the data, click the **Profile** link. To actually view any information from the databases, you must click the **Download** link for that database. Then you can select the fields you want to include (using check boxes), and select locations, date ranges, and other limiters (from pull-down menus at the top of the database download page). Data is downloaded and saved in the .csv (Comma Separated Values) file-format which can be opened using Microsoft Excel or other spreadsheet or statistics software.

Tip: Click **Glossary** at the top of the page for a dictionary of transportation-related terms.

Center for Transportation Analysis (CTA)

http://www-cta.ornl.gov/Index.html

Purpose: To locate information on intermodal (air, road, and rail) transportation.

Content: The CTA conducts research and develops new methods for "the efficient, safe and free movement of people and goods in our Nation's transportation systems." The site links to various publications and research information produced by the CTA, dealing with the interstate highway system, traffic safety, air safety and air traffic management, military transportation and distribution, and highway security, among other areas.

Our View: Click on **On-Line Tools** to access surveys and reports such as:

- The National Household Travel Survey
- Nationwide Personal Transportation Survey
- Projecting Fatalities in Crashes Involving Older Drivers

Tip: Of particular interest is the **Intelligent Transportation System (ITS) Deployment Tracking** Web site, which tracks the implementation of the ITS initiative in seventy-eight major metropolitan areas. The ITS uses "the latest in computers, electronics, communications and safety systems . . . to better manage and improve how transportation providers such as governments, transit agencies and truckers offer services to the public." These include electronic traffic monitoring on highways and major streets, electronic toll collection, and so on. Progress is tracked through periodic surveys. The survey results, along with charts and other data, are available here, as well as blank and completed survey forms.

Transportation Acronyms

Bureau of Transportation Statistics Transportation Acronym Guide

http://www.bts.gov/publications/ transportation_acronym_guide/

Purpose: To decode transportation-related acronyms.

Content: The site offers a searchable and browsable list of hundreds of transportation related acronyms.

Our View: After clicking on **Search TAG**, you can either enter the acronym you're trying to decode in the **Acronym** box, or the full word or phrase into the **Definition** box. The acronym and its definition are returned, along with the guide's source for the information. Clicking any of the sources takes you to the **Source Index** where you can decode those Agency names.

Tip: (1) When searching for acronyms, be sure to click the **Search** button, *do not* press the <ENTER> key on your keyboard. Pressing <ENTER> will return an error message, even for valid acronyms.

(2) This guide might come in handy as you access some of the other sites discussed in this section. The agency also maintains a glossary of transportation expressions at **http://www.bts.gov/publications/ transportation_expressions**.

Airplanes

Bureau of Transportation Statistics Airline Information

http://www.bts.gov/oai

Purpose: To locate traffic, market, and financial statistics about specific airlines and the airline industry as a whole.

Content: This site provides access to numerous reports regarding the air transportation industry, ranging from financial statistics and fuel costs and consumption to on-time performance and number of employees per carrier.

Our View: If you're looking for general information on the state of the airline industry, or financial information on specific airlines, this is the place for you.

Tip: For Information on flight delays, click on **Causes of Flight Delay by Carrier.**

Transportation Security Administration (TSA)

http://www.tsa.dot.gov/public

Purpose: To locate information regarding airport security requirements and special considerations for air travelers.

Content: This site offers a clearinghouse for information related to the rapidly evolving policies of this nascent federal agency. It also provides administration news, tips on travel preparedness (such as packing and security screenings), links to U.S. Code sections related to the administration's operation, and claim forms for items lost or damaged as a result of TSA screening, among other information.

Our View: Here you'll get the definitive answer to the question, "Do I have to take my shoes off before going through the metal detector?" among others.

Tip: The clickable subject links near the top of the Web site's home page are too broad to really help locate the information you may need (**Travelers & Consumers, Law & Policy,** and **Security & Law Enforcement**, among others). Clicking on **Site Map** makes it easier to find the information you're looking for.

U.S. Aircraft Ownership and Pilot Registration

FAA Aircraft Registry Inquiry

http://registry.faa.gov/aircraftinquiry

Purpose: To locate aircraft assets and owners via registration information.

Content: The FAA database site offers ten different ways to search for aircraft information, including:

- Ownership (by name)
- N-Number (registration number)
- Serial number

Our View: The FAA site contains information not included in the Landings.com database (below). Recent searches at the FAA site turned up information on re-registered N-Numbers and additional owner names that were not included in search results conducted at Landings.com (see below). For example, a search for an old airplane registration number turned up information that the plane had been exported to Australia. The search also provided the name and address of the last U.S. owner before the plane was exported.

Tip:
- A name search to determine if an individual is a licensed pilot is not included at the site. Up-to-date pilot licensing data is available for download as a *large* data file from the FAA at **http://faa.gov/licenses_ certificates/airmen_certification/releasable_airmen_ download**. The data is updated monthly.
- Use this site in conjunction with the Landings site.

Landings

http://www.landings.com

Purpose: To locate aircraft assets and owners via registration information.

Content: The site maintains databases of aircraft (airplanes and helicopters) and pilot registrations in the United States (and nine other countries around the world). It also provides links to the registration databases of another twenty countries.

The four most useful searches are

- Licensing (by name)
- Ownership (by name)
- N-Number
- Serial number

To search this site's databases, click on **Databases** at the top of the home page.

Our View: This site is particularly useful for uncovering assets, if you suspect someone might own an aircraft, or when you are trying to locate someone who you know does own one, or is at least a registered pilot. While the information contained in the site's databases comes from the FAA, there is additional information included in some search results at the FAA site that is not found when conducting similar searches at the Landings site.

Tip:
- Landings allows you to construct fairly sophisticated searches using numerous search operators (wild cards, anchors, and so on). Click on the **Unix style regular expression link** on the Owner Search page to read more about them.
- Use in conjunction with the FAA site above.
- Clicking on the **Calculators** link brings up a list of links to many useful applications that supply the dis-

tance between two airports and distance between two locations. The latter requires you enter the exact longitude and latitude coordinates, which you can determine utilizing a Global Positioning System (GPS) device.

Tracking Planes In Flight

Flight Explorer Flight Tracker

http://www.flightexplorer.com
(use the **Flight Explorer FastTrack** tool on the right-hand side of the home page)

Purpose: To track commercial flights while they're in the air.

Content: Flight tracking software developer Flight Explorer offers a unique flight tracker that gives the real-time location of any airborne North American commercial airliner.

Our View: You can locate the flight you're interested in by entering the airline and flight number in the boxes provided.

Available information includes:

- Location (superimposed onto a map of the U.S.)
- Altitude
- Speed
- Equipment (type of plane)
- Distance remaining
- Time remaining

Tip: If you do not know the flight number or airline, select **More** from the airline list to reach an advanced search page where you can search if you, **know the airline and the departure and arrival airports** or retrieve a flight number if you, **know the departure and arrival airports and times**.

Locating U.S. Airports

AirNav.com

http://www.airnav.com/airports

Purpose: To find information on general, commercial, and private airports.

Content: AirNav offers a searchable and browsable list of general aviation, commercial, and private airports and heliports in the U.S.

Our View: It's not necessary to know the airport's official designation (LAX, JFK, and so on) to retrieve information. You can enter a city name in the site's search box, or click on **Browse by U.S. State** to view an alphabetical lists of all of the facilities in each state.

Tip: Click on **Advanced Search** to locate airports within a radius you select of any city, town, or latitude and longitude coordinates you specify.

For an explanation of the three-letter coding system used to identify airports, see the informative article "Airport ABCs: An Explanation of Airport Identifier Codes," (**http://www.skygod.com/asstd/abc.html**) written by Dave English and originally published in the *Journal of the Air Line Pilots Association.*

U.S. Aircraft Safety and Accidents

National Transportation Safety Board (Aviation)

http://www.ntsb.gov/aviation/aviation.htm

Purpose: For detailed information regarding aircraft accidents.

Content: This site provides access to aviation accident statistics, information on major accident investigations, and a searchable database of the synopses of over 140,000 U.S. aircraft accidents dating back to 1962.

Our View: Accident statistics are available for the period 1983-2005, broken down by numerous criteria (such as airlines, nonscheduled service, fatalities only). Statistics are also available for the current month and year to date.

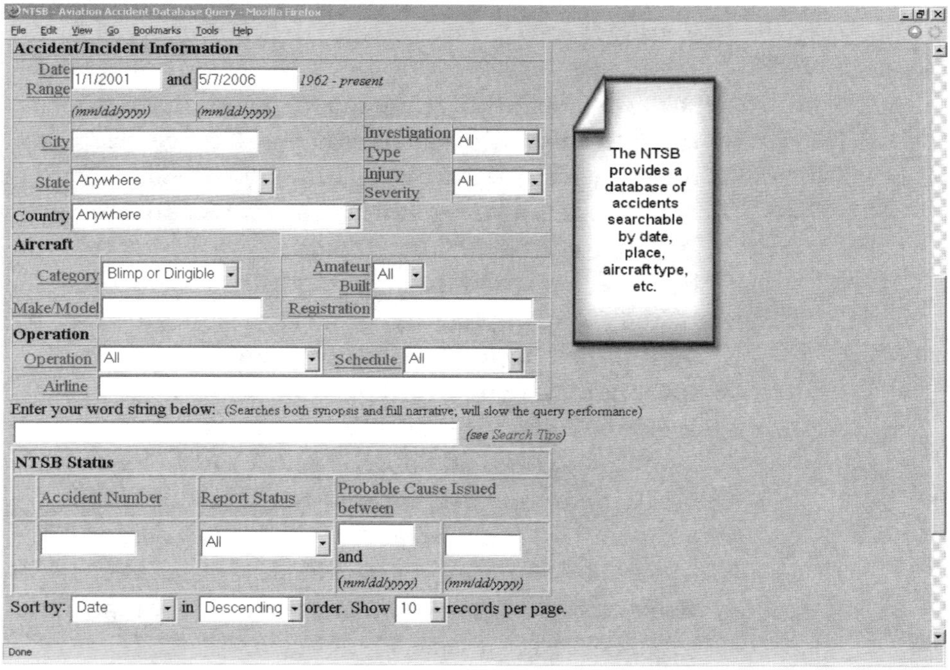

Figure 18-2. The Aviation section of the National Transportation Safety Board's Web site includes detailed information regarding plane accidents since 1962, and information regarding the agency's investigative procedures, among other useful information.

From the link marked **Accident Database & Synopses,** you can search for information on specific accidents using a variety of data fields, including a date range, city, state, aircraft category, severity of accident, and so on. You can also browse lists of accidents, listed month-by-month, back to 1962. Links are also provided to the preliminary or final reports on the accident as they are available. Additionally, by clicking on the **Completed Investigations** link, you learn which cases are expected to have additional information released in the near future.

The individual records for each aircraft accident can hold quite a bit of narrative information. Even the preliminary reports contained on this site contain more information than the preliminary reports contained on the FAA Office of Accident Investigation (OAI) Web site (see below).

Tip:
- Review all details in these reports carefully, and verify them from multiple sources when possible. Each preliminary record carries the following disclaimer: "This is preliminary information, subject to change, and may contain errors. Any errors in this report will be corrected when the final report has been completed." And apparently for good reason. One recent preliminary accident report indicated in two places that there were no injuries, while in the narrative of the same report, it stated that both occupants of the aircraft had been "fatally injured." Another recent NTSB preliminary report indicated that a particular accident had occurred at "1200 Alaska Daylight Time" (noon), "80 miles northwest of Skwentna, Alaska," while the FAA OAI (see below) preliminary report indicated that the same accident occurred at "2000 hours . . . 10 miles east of Farewell, Alaska." (Although it is not noted anywhere on the site, or in the reports, the FAA OAI site apparently utilizes Greenwich Mean Time to make note of times.)
- While the month-by-month chronological list of accident information (**http://www.ntsb.gov/ntsb/month.asp**) is listed as being updated daily, more complete information on recent aircraft accidents can be found at the FAA Office of Accident Investigation (OAI) site below.

FAA Office of Accident Investigation (OAI)

**http://www.faa.gov/data_statistics/accident_incident/
preliminary_data**

Purpose: For preliminary information regarding recent aircraft accidents.

Content: Information is available for the most recent ten days only.

Our View: The grid of dates for the past ten days indicates the number of incidents on each day. One confusing and annoying feature about the grid is that the date indicated is the **Date Reports Entered**, which in most cases is not the date that the accident took place. (The date the report was entered is usually the day after the accident took place, but can sometimes be later.) The grid further breaks the information down by fatal and nonfatal accidents. You can also view the accidents occurring in fixed-wing aircraft (planes) or rotorcraft (helicopters) by manufacturer. (Reports marked with an asterisk [*] signify updates to the reports since they were first filed.)

Another confusing and annoying feature of these reports is that the FAA apparently uses Greenwich Mean Time to denote the time of day these accidents occur (although they don't bother to tell you that on the site).

Tip: • For a copy of the FAA publication *Aircraft Accident and Incident Notification, Investigation and Reporting,* click the **Policies & Forms** link on the left-hand side of the site's home page.
• For additional information regarding specific accidents (or any accident more than ten days old), the FAA suggests contacting the NTSB. (For more information on aircraft accident information available online from the NTSB, see above.)

- For a *Tip* regarding inconsistencies in the data held in these preliminary reports, see the entry for the NTSB Aviation Web site above.

FAA Airworthiness Directives

http://www.faa.gov   (\$)

(click on **Airworthiness Directives** under **Regulations & Policies** tab near the top of the home page.

Purpose:	To locate FAA-issued safety notices for specific aircrafts or parts.
Content:	Like automobile recalls, the FAA issues Airworthiness Directives ordering the repair, replacement, or alteration of specific aircraft parts or mechanisms. This database contains the FAA's current Airworthiness Directives in a searchable and browsable format. You can:

- Conduct full text searches
- View emergency directives (issued in the last ten days)
- View new directives (issued in the last sixty days)
- Browse by manufacturer name or directive number

Our View:	Determining the airworthiness of an aircraft could hold the solution if the aircraft has caused damage or injury. If a directive had been issued and the aircraft's current (or previous) owner had not made the mandated repairs, negligence might also be involved. The FAA regularly issues these directives, and they remain in force until they are superceded by a subsequent directive. Some directives have been in force since the 1940s, according to the FAA site.
Tip:	Use the keyword search function. Click on **Search Help** for information on Boolean, phrase, and wild card searching.

**Aircraft Owners & Pilot's Association (AOPA)—
Air Safety Foundation, Accident Analysis**

http://www.aopa.org/asf/safety_db.html

Purpose: To locate information and statistics related to small, general aviation aircraft accidents.

Content: The AOPA's Air Safety Foundation (ASF) has taken the aircraft accident information made available by the National Transportation Safety Board (NTSB), for fixed-wing aircraft under 12,500 pounds, broken it down, and presented it in useful ways.

To search the database of accidents involving fixed-wing aircraft (no helicopters) under 12,500 pounds, back to 1983, click on the **ASF Accident Database** link on the home page and then click on the **Search the ASF Accident Database** link. You can search by date (entering a date range), the plane's tail (registration) number, NTSB investigation number, make, model, and the state in which the accident occurred (including protectorates).

Click on the **Popular Database Searches** on the home page and then **Night VFR Accident** to access a list of fatal accidents that occurred at night under generally good weather conditions between 1993 and 2002. Each entry includes the date and location (city/state) of the crash, the make, model, and registration number of the aircraft involved, and the NTSB accident number. Clicking on the Accident Number retrieves the NTSB narrative report of the accident. The list is presented in reverse chronological order. Clicking any of the column headings (e.g., "Make," Model," "City," or "State") reorders the list sorting by the criteria you have clicked. This way, for example, you could determine all of the night VFR accidents in a particular city, or for a specific make and/or model of airplane.

VFR refers to the Visual Flight Rules applicable when aircraft fly using visual navigation. Most small aircraft operate under VFR as they do not have the equipment necessary to operate under the more restrictive Instrument Flight Rules (IFR).

Clicking on **Popular Database Searches** and then **Collisions at Towered Airports** returns a similarly formatted list of collisions at airports with control towers between 1993 and 2002.

Our View: The ASF does a good job of interpreting and presenting accident data made available by the NTSB.

Plane Crash Info

http://planecrashinfo.com

Purpose: For background information regarding past plane crashes.

Content: This site contains a database of nearly 4,000 plane crashes from the first airplane fatality on September 17, 1908 (in which Orville Wright suffered several broken bones) to the present. Accident information can be browsed by:

- Date
- Airline and operator

The latest accidents are featured on the front page, with photos and details (as available).

Our View: The site's statistics can be helpful in getting an overview of air fatalities, and more.

Tip: The transcripts and audio of air traffic control dialogue and cockpit voice recording from selected crashes (in the aptly named **Last Words** section) is both disturbing and morbidly fascinating.

Trains

Federal Railroad Administration

http://www.fra.dot.gov

Purpose: To locate information regarding railroad safety, accidents, and rail lines.

Content: The site contains passenger and freight railroad accident and safety data, along with a railroad library covering the history of railroad development.

Our View: To access summary and detailed reports of train accidents and casualties, as well as searchable databases of train accidents and accident trends, click on the **Safety** link on the left-hand side of the home page.

Tip: View and download accident trend graphs and charts (1975 to the last fiscal year) for use at settlement, mediation, or trial. To access the searchable database (after you click the **Safety** link on the home page), click the **Accident/Incident Data** link near the bottom of the subsequent page and then the **Query** tab on the page that is displayed after that.

Amtrak

http://www.amtrak.com

Purpose: To locate information related to the Amtrak rail line.

Content: Set up much like an airline Web site, the site offers train schedules, routes, and the ability to make and pay for reservations.

Our View: This site is set up to serve the Amtrak clientele, and attract new riders.

Tip: Use the **Stations** tab to input a city name or ZIP code to find the closest Amtrak train stations. You can also use the **Train Status** feature to determine if a specific train has left or will arrive at its destination on time.

Automobiles

VehicleIdentificationNumber.com

http://www.vehicleidentificationnumber.com

Purpose: To locate information regarding Vehicle Identification Numbers (VINs)

Content: The site contains extensive information related to vehicle registration and VINs, including:

- **VIN decoding links**—Find vehicle identification decoders for numerous makes and models of cars, trucks, and motorcycles
- **Department of Motor Vehicle**—Links to all 50 states' DMV sites
- **State Transportation Web sites**—Links to all 50 states'Departments of Transportation
- **VIN Code Law**—Vehicle identification code law from the National Highway Traffic Safety Administration and Department of Transportation
- **VIN History**
- **VIN Glossary**—Vehicle identification dictionary
- **VIN and Auto Theft**—Use your vehicle identification numbers to help prevent stolen car parts or make theft report

Our View: This site is a good resource for vehicle registration, and state DMV and Department of Transportation information. It also offers a good explanation of the VIN system, from its origins to deciphering the number scheme and its meaning.

Tip:	While it also contains a large amount of information for deciphering VINs, if you know a vehicle's VIN, it is easier to verify the make and model using Carfax.com.

National Highway Transportation Safety Agency (NHTSA) Office of Defects Investigation

To search:
To request information not included in the free searches: **$**
http://www-odi.nhtsa.dot.gov

Purpose:	To locate information regarding automobile recalls, service bulletins, or ongoing investigations of potential vehicle defects.
Content:	The site offers searchable databases of:

- Consumer complaints (since 1995)
- Defect investigations (since 1972)
- Vehicle and equipment recalls (since 1966)
- Technical service bulletins (since 1995)

	Each of the databases is searched in the same way. Rather than entering search terms, you drill down by selecting the type of information (such as vehicle, tires, or equipment), year, make, model, and component (such as airbag or parking brake). If you do not select a component, all of the records related to the vehicle you selected will be displayed. For example, a search for consumer complaints regarding the 2000 Ford Taurus returned 612 complaints. Selecting the component **Vehicle Speed Control: Accelerator Pedal** returned ten results dealing specifically with that component of the car.
Our View:	Copies of many service bulletins and complaints can be accessed for free by clicking the **Document Search** button under the record you're interested in. If it is available, a new browser window will open with a link to a PDF version of the document. (Most identifying infor-

mation on complaints has been redacted, although a dealer name, location, or vehicle identification number [VIN] may remain.)

If documents are not available free online, you can request them from the National Highway Transportation Safety Agency's (NHTSA) Office of Defects Investigation (by clicking the **Request Research** button). Charges are $38.30 per hour for searching and copying time and 10¢ per page for copying.

Tip: Even if no recall or investigation has been launched, a search of the complaints database could turn up problems similar to those of a client experiencing problems with a vehicle.

NHTSA National Center for Statistics and Analysis State Data System

http://www-nrd.nhtsa.dot.gov/departments/nrd-30/ncsa/SDS.html

Purpose: To locate motor vehicle crash statistics from selected states.

Content: The National Center for Statistics and Analysis (NCSA) State Data System (SDS) provides motor vehicle crash data from seventeen states between 1990 and 1999. The states are California, Florida, Georgia, Illinois, Indiana, Kansas, Maryland, Michigan, Missouri, New Mexico, North Carolina, Ohio, Pennsylvania, Texas, Utah, Virginia, and Washington. (As of December 2004, 27 states had joined the SDS.)

Our View: The statistics are presented in a twenty-three-section document. General information can be found in sections 6 to 8, **Crashes, Vehicles,** and **People,** respectively. Other sections focus on accident causes (such as alcohol or speeding), vehicle actions and types (such as

rollovers, motorcycles, or large trucks) and a breakdown by driver's age. Each section is available as a separate PDF file. For people who might use the information often, or want a personal copy, downloadable
versions of the report's sections are also available from
this page.

Tip: Because the sample is only for seventeen states, the SDS
warns that the data are not representative of the entire
country, but only of the states for which data is
included.

NTSA NCSA Fatality Analysis Reporting System

http://www-fars.nhtsa.dot.gov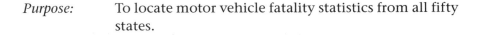

Purpose: To locate motor vehicle fatality statistics from all fifty
states.

Content: The Fatality Analysis Reporting System (FARS) collects
data on fatal motor vehicle traffic crashes from all fifty
states, the District of Columbia, and Puerto Rico. This
information is gathered from police accident reports,
death certificates, and coroner and medical examiner
reports, among other sources. Available information
includes times of day, contributing factors (such as
weather or alcohol), vehicle types, and so on.

Our View: The statistics are presented in five reports:

- Trends
- Crashes
- Vehicles
- People
- States

Each report has various subsections that further divide
the information. For example, in the **Vehicles** report,

you can view data for passenger vehicles only, for small trucks only, or for all vehicles. Similarly, in the **People** report, you can view statistics for fatalities to driver only, passengers, or pedestrians (among other categories), or view all categories in one report.

Tip: While the default view for each report is for the most current edition of data for the entire country, pull-down menus on the right side of the screen allow you to view any combination of states and years (back to 1994).

Insurance Institute for Highway Safety (IIHS)

http://www.iihs.org

Purpose: To locate crash test results for various cars by model and category.

Content: Data for the following IIHS tests are available back to 1992 for most cars:

- 40-mph offset frontal crash
- Side impact
- Head restraint

Click on **Vehicle Ratings** at the top of the home page to access the data.

Our View: The IIHS are the folks who made crash test dummies famous for performing crashworthiness evaluations of automobiles, and who issue safety ratings based on those test results. You can view the results for a particular model of automobile by selecting it from the alphabetical pull-down menus. You can also view the results of vehicle categories (such as large luxury car, midsize moderately priced cars, and so on)

Clicking **Research & Statistics** at the top of the home page and then **Show Topic List** (under the **Topical Index** heading) on the subsequent page gives you access to background information on a series of automobile-related topics, such as daytime running lights and red-light running, among others.

Tip: Was your client's car yielding to oncoming traffic or making a left turn when the other driver hit them? You may be able to prove (or disprove) that a collision your client was involved with occurred in a certain manner by comparing your accident scene photos with "control" photos of known collision damage from the Institute's tests. (Check with the IIHS regarding copyrights and usage permission before utilizing any of their photos for presentations.)

JustAuto.com

To search and access limited amounts of content:

To read and download reports: **$**

http://www.just-auto.com

Purpose: This site provides all the latest automotive news, analysis, and research from around the globe.

Content: Just Auto's homepage is broken down into 12 different sections that offer quite a bit for free consumption. **Latest News & Comments, Report in Focus** (as well as previous Reports and Features), **Latest Industry Announcements** and **Jobs** are all available for viewing in varying limited format. Even portions of the Member's Newsletter can be read for free. The only area immediately blocked from entry is the Discussion Forum, where you are asked to register first.

If you decide to become a member of JustAuto.com, go to the **Membership** link on the bottom of the page. Cost is $250 per year, with the first month free. They also offer a money-back guarantee within the first 30 days if you are unsatisfied. Benefits include a 5 percent discount on all reports and information bought through the site. Prorated memberships are sometimes available after the beginning of the calendar year.

Once you click on a particular report, there are two ways to purchase the information. Multiuser license agreements allow you to share the document with colleagues and make any copies you like. The single-user license agreement does not allow any sharing or copying of the information. The prices duly reflect the differences in the options and vary from report to report.

Our View: JustAuto.com is an excellent resource offering a tremendous amount of information, much of it available for free. Membership costs are relatively low and some of the advantages (email alerts, article archive) are really helpful. Anyone who has clients involved in the auto industry would find this site valuable.

Tip: The site's managing editor, Dave Leggett, offers commentary on his own experiences in the global automotive industry and also writes about events, people, and suggested topics in the "Dave's Blog" feature linked from the home page. If you have a hard-to-answer question, Dave might be the person to steer you in the right direction.

A free newsletter is also offered and edited by Leggett (go to the **E-mail alert** link on the top of the home page). Just Auto touts it as the best e-zine covering the auto industry and boasts a following of 40,000 subscribers.

Kelley Blue Book

http://www.kbb.com

Purpose: To determine the value of a used car (and other new car information).

Content: Going far beyond the scope of the old-faithful print version of the *Blue Book*, the site offers:

- Used car and motorcycle prices (buying and selling)
- New car prices
- New car reviews
- Side-by-side comparisons (new and used)

Our View: The site is easy to navigate and clearly labels the links and functions. To find out the value of a car if sold to a private party, click **Private Party Value.** To get the trade-in value likely to be offered by a dealer, click **Trade-In Value.** Once you select the pricing you want to retrieve, menu-driven pages ask for specific information on the car (such as year, make, and model) before offering up the value.

The site also allows you to compare features and options between two or more cars (new or used) by selecting the **Compare New Cars** or **Compare Used Cars** links on the home page.

Tip: If you have the VIN for a particular car, you can also order a CarFax vehicle report (see below) for additional information.

Other sites offering new and used car pricing and side-by-side comparisons include Edmunds (**http://www.edmunds.com**) and Vehix (**http://www.vehix .com**).

CarFax

Instant record check: Ⓢ⃠   More-detailed record check: **$**

http://www.carfax.com

Purpose: To determine used car vehicle history.

Content: CarFax's database contains more than 4 billion unique vehicle records compiled from thousands of data sources (such as state vehicle registrations, state inspections, and fire departments).

Our View: CarFax's vehicle history reports can confirm a clean title history or identify serious problems with a used car, including salvage history, odometer fraud, flood damage, or theft. Reports are available via the CarFax Web site for $19.99 for a single report, or $24.99 for two months of unlimited reports. Just enter the VIN into the designated box on the home page.

Tip: The site also offers a free instant record check (which returns year, make, model, engine type, and body type), lemon check, and recall check. The results page of each of those searches is also an effort to sell you a full report on the vehicle.

NHTSA Uniform Tire Quality Grading

http://www.safecars.gov/Tires

Purpose: To decode the letters and numbers on tire sidewalls.

Content: Uniform Tire Quality Grading (UTQG) is a tire information system designed to help buyers make relative comparisons among tires. Under UTQG, tires are graded by the manufacturers in three areas: tread wear, traction, and temperature resistance. The grades are molded into the sidewalls of the tire. This site identifies the meanings of the various codes and shows their relative locations on the tire.

Our View: Click **Tire Labeling** on the left-hand side of the home page and then **Passenger Vehicle Tires** on the ensuing page to access a diagram page giving a good illustration and explanation of what each of the codes on the tire represents. For a more-detailed description of the tread wear, traction, and temperature resistance grades, see the additional links on the left-hand side of the page.

Boats

As we mentioned in the beginning of this chapter, in many states, registration of recreational (and smaller commercial) boats is handled by the department of motor vehicles. (In others, it's handled by the department of fish and wildlife.) Regardless, as with driver licensing information, many states have limited the accessibility of this information to the public (such as Texas SB 95-72). Therefore, none of the states makes this information available on the Internet.

U.S. Coast Guard National Vessel Documentation Center

http://www.uscg.mil/hq/g-m/vdoc/nvdc.htm

Purpose:	To locate ownership information regarding domestic commercial vessels.
Content:	Vessels of five net tons or more used for fishing or "coastwise trade" (the transportation of merchandise or passengers between points in the U.S., or tow boats and tugboats operating in the U.S.) must be registered with the Coast Guard. Title abstracts can be ordered from this site.
Our View:	To order an abstract, click the **Order Abstracts of Title Online** link on the left-hand side of the screen. This brings up the site's **Storefront**. Select **Abstract of Title Payment** on the ensuing page to access the search page. On the search page you can enter the **Vessel ID** and click **Add to Cart** to request the Abstract of Title. Once completed, click the **Checkout** button on the left-hand side of the page to access the Order Page. On the order page, enter your contact and credit card information. Title abstracts cost $25 each and can be paid for online by credit card or automatic bank debit

(an electronic check). Copies of a ship's certificate of ownership (not available online) are $125.

Tip: These documents cannot be requested anonymously. Requesters must provide a valid credit card or bank account to pay online, or a Social Security number or taxpayer identification number when requesting these documents by mail.

Recently, a lawyer working on a reconstruction of a boat accident needed an aluminum Roughneck boat manufactured in 1997 that had to be about 17 feet long and hold a 125 hp outboard motor. The lawyer contacted the manufacturer, searched the Internet, searched eBay for potential sellers, and contacted companies that rent boats, but was still unable to locate this type of boat anywhere. One possible source that the lawyer could have tried is BoatTraderOnline.com.

BoatTraderOnline.com

http://www.boattraderonline.com/

Purpose: To search for used or new boats offered for sale. Useful for a lawyer who needs to find a boat for accident reconstruction purposes or for a lawyer who just wants to indulge in some smooth sailing!

Content: On the day we searched, there were 105,475 boats, yachts, and personal watercraft available for sale. The site claims to have over 1,710,000 visitors every month. You can search by (1) new and new or pre-owned; (2) manufacturer; (3) year range; (4) length; (5) boat type (e.g., power, sail); (6) price range; (7) ZIP code/distance, state, province, Caribbean, area code, region; and (8) keyword (e.g., name of boat).

Our View: We ran a search at BoatTraderOnline.com for "Roughneck" as a keyword and added "1997" into the date search box. We got two results, but not the 17-foot-long model the lawyer was searching for. They were close—18- and 19-foot long and all the other criteria matched up. This site is affiliated with TraderOnline.com, where you can search for a vast array of vehicles, from RVs, collector and specialty vehicles, motorcycles, ATVs, and trucks to aircrafts.

Tip: The **Advanced Search** offers even more choices that allow you to narrow your search even further, but you'll need to scroll all the way down to find the link. In addition to the criteria noted above, you can also search by: (1) type of fuel; (2) hull type; (3) engine type; and (4) model. There are also more choices for how you'd like to display your search results: (1) photos and (2) date in either descending or ascending order.

CHAPTER**NINETEEN**

Entertainment Industry and Intellectual Property Research

That's Entertainment: Locating Entertainment Industry Sites

What is entertainment? Depending on who is asked, the question elicits a variety of answers. For some it means attending the theater, a concert, a sporting event, the opera, or the ballet; to others it could mean watching a film or television show, listening to music (over the radio or the Internet), or playing video games. Ask a group of entertainment law lawyers to define entertainment law and their answers will be just as varied. Type "entertainment" into the Google search engine and 651 million results are listed, led by E! Online. Type "entertainment law" into Google and 1 million results are listed, with a Beverly Hills entertainment lawyer and a scholarly entertainment law review listed first and second, respectively.

When asked which resource she uses most in her entertainment law practice, Susan Kaiser, a lawyer who has represented network-owned radio and television stations, and negotiates and drafts agreements and contracts, replied, "Probably the resource I use most is Google.com to search opposing counsel, talent names, potential clients, and law firms." Searching Google makes sense when a lawyer is trolling for any and all information, since Google, which indexes more of the Internet than any other engine, casts such a wide net. It is not surprising then that her first line of research is a general search engine instead of an entertainment related site. However, if a lawyer is seeking background information about entertainment in general, especially people, the best place to start may be in consumer entertainment sites and entertainment trade publication sites.

Entertainment Research

Consumer Sites: Television and Film

E! Online

http://www.eonline.com

Purpose: For general entertainment news and background information on celebrities.

Content: The site content ranges from news, features, gossip, multimedia (for example, you can use keywords to find a clip), movie reviews, celebrity information, and information about shows on the E! network.

Our View: While it can sometimes be difficult to distinguish E! Online's news from its gossip, the site's full-text searching of its extensive Hollywood coverage and its hyperlink feature (see below) make the site worthwhile.

Tip: • A handy hyperlink feature allows users who are reading an article about a named celebrity, actor, musician, writer, or director to hyperlink to that person's biography, a chronology of the person's career, a credit list, links to other E! Online stories about that individual, online multimedia clips, and fan clubs.
                • Free membership entitles you to an e-newsletter and access to celebrity chats.

Entertainment Weekly (EW)

http://www.ew.com

Purpose: For online-only entertainment news on a daily basis, and information from EW's print magazine.

Content: EW offers the following content from its print magazine: reviews (movies, books, videos, film), some of its reporting, and an archive of all of the magazine's articles since its inception in 1990. EW's site also includes photo galleries, interviews, and video and audio clips.

Our View: It's useful that the archives include both EW's articles and the online content. However, we'd prefer a more advanced search menu than the simple search box on the site's home page.

Tip: Full access to the online content is no longer limited to print subscribers of the *Entertainment Weekly* magazine or AOL subscribers. Current news is also available via topic-specific RSS feeds.

Commercial Trade Databases

Law librarians at entertainment law firms are frequently asked to conduct background research on potential clients or opposing parties; at other times, they are asked to find contact information, perhaps to serve a complaint. To meet these queries, law librarians at entertainment law firms tend to favor two subscription sites: BaselineFT and the Internet Movie Database (IMDB) Pro.

Internet Movie Database Pro

http://www.imdb.com

Purpose: Internet Movie Database (IMDB) Pro offers access to more than 65,000 contact and agent listings, and international box-office statistics (as well as weekly and daily for the U.S.).

Content:	Nonsubscribers can access some information for free, such as IMDB's searchable archives back to 1997; celebrity news; box office information; reviews of movies, TV and videos; a picture gallery; and a film glossary. Subscriptions for individuals range from $12.95 (monthly) to $99.95 (annually). However, enterprise-wide subscribers need to contact the site for pricing.
Our View:	While nonsubscribers can view more detailed information if they register (free) at **www.imdb.com** site, they still can't access as much as the Pro pay subscribers (for example, they can't access the database of contact and agent listings). It's worth paying for a Pro subscription just to avoid wading through continual pop-up ads at the free site.
Tip:	Use **Power Searching (http://us.imdb.com/list)** when you have limited clues about what you're looking for (such as a movie with the word "Africa" for which the genre is adventure) or when you want to create a list (such as every horror film, in black and white, from Japan). For other sophisticated searches, go to **http://us.imdb.com/ search** and click on one of the **Popular Searches** or **Advanced Searches** (choose **people working together** to find movies in which certain people costarred).

Try the 14-day free trial to see if IMDB Pro's data contains the information you need.

BaselineFT

http://www.baseline.hollywood.com   **$**

Purpose:	Locate information regarding the entertainment industry.
Content:	BaselineFT's databases contain 1.5 million records with 8,000 biographies; credits for 1,100,000 actors, producers, directors, and crew members; and contact information for companies, executives, and talent.

Baseline also includes archives of Paul Kagan Associate's Motion Picture Investor database, the *Hollywood Reporter* (THR) and *Variety*. A daily e-mail provides updates about films and television programs in development and in production, and current entertainment news. Other information and statistics, such as the Star Salary Report, are available. Registrants pay a one-time sign-up fee of $49 or $99, which gets them access to the database and $49 or $149 in per-document-fee credits (respectively). The credits are only valid for 30 days however. Per-document fees can range from $1.25 for current weekly *Variety* stories to $79 for the Star Salary Report. Corporate and educational flat rates, as well as a "one time only" accessrate are also available.

Our View: This is a useful site for the following reasons:

- Its extensive database of biographies, credits, contacts, and hard-to-find information (such as the Star Salary Report)
- The ability to search THR back to May 1988 (which is three years further back than the archives at THR's own site)
- The ability to conduct simultaneous searches of the archives and current issues of the various databases, along with the Motion Picture Investor database

Tip: For those who do not have individual subscriptions to *Variety* or THR, one subscription to BaselineFT might be all you need (unless you need to go back further than 1988 for *Variety*).

Trade Publication Sites

Television and Film

The Hollywood Reporter (THR)

http://www.hollywoodreporter.com $

Purpose: For archives of past stories (back to early 1991) and continual updating throughout the day.

Figure 19-1. Search the Hollywood Reporter's archive of news, reviews, and features dating back to 1991 or search a separate database of reviews and columnists.

Content: Online viewers may find that the stories are longer than those found in the print version. The subscription portion of the site also includes the *Blu-Book Production Directory*, a news scroll, box office charts, production listings, and script sales.

Our View: With full access at $19.95 monthly or $229 annually (which includes the first ten full-text displays of news stories, archived items, and production listings for free), the site is a must for entertainment research. (Any displays beyond the first ten are charged at 10¢ to 25¢ each.)

Tip: The archives can be found by clicking on the **Advanced Search** link on the right side of the home page or by scrolling down and clicking on **Archives** on the left side of the page (under Resources). Search the archives by keywords, byline, or date. (Nonsubscribers have free access to parts of the site. For instance, they can read the headlines and abstracts of current articles (and the archives back to 1991), and the weekly box office charts (but not the daily charts). They have full access to PR Newswire.)

Variety

http://www.variety.com

Purpose: Locate entertainment industry news and information back to 1914.

Content: Visitors to Variety.com will find credits, classified ads, obituaries, and photos. On the media jobs pages, entertainment-law related jobs are posted free. Under the **Tools** heading on the left-hand side, nonsubscribers can read the headlines and abstracts of current and archived articles for free and sign up for various free RSS feeds with topics ranging from film news to box office numbers.

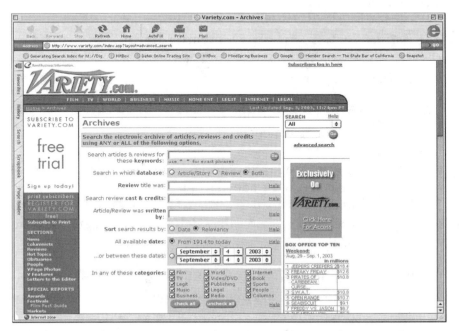

Figure 19-2. Search Variety.com for articles or reviews by keywords, cast and credit, title of review, or name of reviewer or article author. You can also limit by date.

Our View: While Variety.com has similar resources as THR, its archive goes back much further—to 1914—and has more search options.

With access to Variety's Web site free to print subscribers, and its deep archives back to 1914, this is also a must site for entertainment lawyers. The cost of an online-only subscription is $259 per year or $24.95 per month. Although more costly than THR, there is no per-display charge. A free 14-day trial subscription is also available. With access to RSS feeds of current news and access to a searchable archive, non-subscribers can find a wealth of useful information at this site.

Tip: Using the **Search Archives** function found on the left-hand side of the page, even non-subscribers can retrieve and read full-text articles back to (at least) 1993.

Television and Interactive Media

Television Week (formerly Electronic Media)

http://www.tvweek.com $ ⊘ [Registration Form]

Purpose: For coverage of broadcast and cable television, and the interactive media industry.

Content: Every Monday, top stories from the print edition of *Television Week* are added to TVWeek.com. The site is also updated every day with breaking news. Subscribers to the print version can search the Internet archives back to 1999. Subscriptions run $119 per year.

Our View: This is one of the few subscription sites where non-subscribers will discover that "more" actually means more. As of June 2006, non-subscribers reading news story abstracts at the site can click on the **Register for Free** link to create a free account giving them "full access to

TVWeek.com, including all stories, pages, and archives." Registered users can also sign up for TV Week's "First Look" and "!Extra Alert" newsletters.

This free access is labeled as being **For a limited time only**. The site also informs that free registrants "Will be notified by email when this special promotion expires."

Nonsubscribers can also avoid signing up and logging in by clicking the **Click Here** to get a Premium Pass. Articles are then displayed after a brief "commercial" is played.

Television and Radio

Broadcasting & Cable

http://www.broadcastingcable.com

Purpose:	For news and feature stories about broadcast and cable television, and the radio industry.
Content:	Full online access is available free for the current issue and archives back to April 2000. The Archives are browseable by date or full-text searchable.
Our View:	Between this site and TVWeek.com, nonsubscribers can get a good overview of current media news.
Tip:	The site also offers a free daily e-mail newsletter of the industries' top headlines with free registration.

Guild Information

Transactional entertainment lawyers spend a lot of time drafting agreements and searching for forms for both general business matters and entertainment-specific industry matters. Finding a good source of sample business forms and knowing where to find guild agreements, guild forms, and other guild information can speed up the process. For general business forms, The 'Lectric Law Library (**http://lectlaw.com/form.html**), a site with free and fee-based forms, is favored by an associate of the authors who is a cable television network vice-president for legal and business affairs. For entertainment-specific forms and agreements, the major Hollywood creative guilds' sites should be consulted (see below).

The Directors Guild (DGA)

Nonmembers and members:
Members only: (requires DGA membership)

http://www.dga.org

Purpose:	Locate information related to Directors and the Directors Guild.
Content:	The site has a **Members Only** section and a section for both members and nonmembers. It offers the full text of the guild's agreements (basic, commercial, documentary, and so on) and a variety of forms (such as deal memos, signatory compliance forms, and residual reporting forms) all available by clicking the **DGA Rate Cards** button on the left-hand side of the home page.
	Also available are the "minimums" (rate cards of directors' fees) to be paid by signatory companies to DGA members. Additionally, the site offers a searchable database of guild members and a browsable list of signatory agencies.
Our View:	This is a useful site that has recently added multimedia, links to member's Web sites (click on the **DGA Members Directory** button on the home page), and the DGA magazine. It will soon be adding members' demo reels and its Women and Ethnic Minority contact list (which is now on the members' part of the site but will soon be added to the public part of the site).

Tip: To link to different sections of the site, use the buttons on the left-hand side of the homepage. There is a DGA **Members Only** section of the Web site with information not available to the public (for example, an interactive calendar of events, committee meeting information, and so on) and a more-detailed version of the searchable database of members found on the public side of the site.

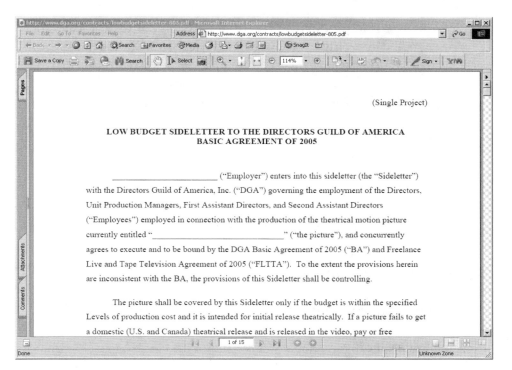

Figure 19-3. The DGA site links to a variety of contracts, from signatory documents, to rate cards, to residuals department forms. This is one of the signatory documents, the Low Budget Sideletter.

Writers Guild of America (WGA)

http://www.wga.org

(some material only available to WGA members)   **$**

Purpose: For resources for writers (and about writers), for members, and for producers.

Content: The site has its resources logically categorized by clickable tabs such as **If You're a Member** (committees, member news, constitution); **If You're an Employer** (this is where you'll find the contracts); and **Guild and Member Services** (including a searchable database of members for whom the Guild is holding money, but has no current address to send the funds). The WGA also offers a searchable database to determine whether a certain production was under a WGA contract, located by hovering over **Guild and Member Services** on the home page. Searchable by title only, the results do not include the name of the guild signatory that produced the work.

Our View: The site would be more useful if search results included the name of the guild signatory that produced the work.

Screen Actors Guild (SAG)

http://new.sag.org/sagWebApp/index.jsp

(some material only available to SAG members) **$**

Purpose: Locate information regarding actors, talent agents, and the Screen Actors Guild.

Content: The top tabs point you to news and events, SAG membership benefits, FAQs, information about SAG (such as its constitution), and contacts. On the right-hand side of the home page, the **Resources** drop-down menu includes links to **Contract Information, Signatory Information, Rate Information,** and **Talent Agent Information,** among other information. There are searchable databases in the **Talent Agent** and the **Signatory Information** sections. For example, you can search the signatory database by the title, keyword, or production ID of the film or television show to determine whether a certain production was produced under a contract from SAG.

Our View: The site is geared to SAG members and anyone who needs access to SAG's forms and contracts. Part of the site is password-protected and is for members only.

    The site has many useful forms, contracts, and information about signatories and agents, but like the WGA site, the signatory results do not include the name of the guild signatory that produced the work. It would be more useful if the results included the name of the guild signatory that produced the work.

Tip: SAG promises to have a "Locate a Performer" searchable database available to registered site users some time in the future. SAG has long made actor representation contact information (agents/managers) available via telephone, and now this information will be more readily available.

American Federation of Television & Radio Artists

http://www.aftra.org

Purpose: Locate information related to television performers and the AFTRA.

Content: Like other performer guilds' Web sites, the AFTRA site includes information on minimum payments due performers (covered by AFTRA contracts) in numerous categories (including forms, contracts, a list of franchised agents, and terms of AFTRA contract), information about the union and its executive staff, elected officers, and current news.

    The site also offers free access to full PDF versions of publications (AFTRA magazine, "Broadcast Bulletin," "Music Notes," and "Talent Agency Bulletin"—located by hovering over the **Press Center** link on at the top of the home page), and a list of franchised agents. While there is no searchable database of AFTRA members, information for requesting agent representation information for members is available by clicking on **Franchised Agents** then **Contact Agency Department**.

Our View: The site's home page offers very little suggestion of the information available, so go right to the Site Map by clicking on the **Site Map** link in the lower left-hand corner of the page.

The design of the Web site makes nearly all of its pages extremely slow to load, even on a broadband Internet connection.

Tip: The site also offers a list of performers for whom AFTRA or the American Federation of Musicians (AFM) is holding royalty checks. The names are maintained as one long list that can take some time to download on dial-up or broadband Internet connections. A searchable database is not offered. You can access the list directly at **http://www.raroyalties.org/unclaimedchecks_all.html.**

Well-Known Legal Site Reveals Its Hollywood Secret

A vice-president of legal and business affairs at a major cable television network lists a nonentertainment site as his first line of entertainment law research: FindLaw.com, and especially FindLaw's search engine, LawCrawler (**http://lawcrawler.findlaw.com**). And by digging deeper, he discovered FindLaw's "Hollywood secret": even though it's primarily a legal research site, it has a rather large entertainment and sports law and news component at its Entertainment and Sports Law page (see **http://www.findlaw.com/01topics/12entertainsport/index.html**). Lawyers can also subscribe to a free weekly entertainment law newsletter (**http://newsletters.findlaw.com/sample/elegal.html**) or a free sports law newsletter (**http://newsletters.findlaw.com/sample/sports.html**), each delivered via e-mail.

Music Industry Sites

Entertainment lawyers in the music industry can bookmark the following free sites to link to countless music publishing, U.S. copyright and licensing, songwriting rights, and music rights resources:

- The National Music Publisher's Association's music links page at **http://www.nmpa.org/links/index.asp**
- Kohn On Music Licensing at **http://kohnmusic.com**
- Worldwide Internet Music Resources at the Indiana University School of Music at **http://www.music.indiana.edu/ music_resources**

Performing rights organizations' sites, such as ASCAP (the American Society Of Composers, Authors And Publishers) and BMI (Broadcast Music, Inc.), have free lookup databases of licensed song titles with the publishers' contact data displayed. ASCAP's database can be searched by title, performers, writers, publishers, or administrators, and T-codes (**http://www.ascap.com/ace/search.cfm?mode=search**). BMI's free lookup database (**http://www.bmi.com/licensing**) may not be obvious to searchers. It can be found on the top right side of BMI's home page by clicking on the **Search** link. To begin, use the drop-down menu next to the **Search BMI's Repertoire** to select searching by artist, publisher, title, or writer.

Phoning Celebrities Overseas

Entertainment lawyers who regularly phone people (especially celebrities) outside the U.S. should bookmark the World Clock at Time-anddate.com (**http://www.timeanddate.com/worldclock**). A vice-president at a cable network that has offices worldwide touts this site because it saves him the embarrassment of waking someone up in the middle of the night. Besides mere embarrassment, we know someone who was promoted to his boss's job (after being at the company for just a few weeks) when his boss was fired for accidentally waking up a celebrity overseas in the middle of the night.

Entertainment Law Employment and Opportunity Sites

For those entertainment lawyers who are job seeking, a visit to Ifcome.com, an entertainment gossip site reporting on employment openings and "opportunities" (inferred from the gossip about who has left what job), is in order. Ifcome.com reports on business and legal affairs job openings and opportunities in television, entertainment, motion pictures, Internet, new media and dot-coms (**http://www.ifcome.com**). Lately, there have been more job listings than gossip.

The Truly Entertaining (in Other Words, Pure Gossip)

For truly entertaining information, check out these sites: FindLaw's FBI celebrity files (**http://news.findlaw.com/legalnews/entertainment/fbi**); Mugshots.org's postings of celebrity mug shots (**http://mugshots.org**), especially Larry King's mug shot (**http://mugshots.org/hollywood/larry king.html**); and the Smoking Gun (**http://www.thesmokinggun.com/backstagetour/index.html**) that "brings you exclusive documents—cool, confidential, quirky—that can't be found elsewhere on the Web." At the Smoking Gun site, read what stars demand in their contract riders: prune juice (Kansas), or an arrangement of tulips, roses, gardenias, and lilies (Janet Jackson).

Intellectual Property

A large component of entertainment law also deals with intellectual property (IP) law (especially copyright and trademark). But lawyers outside these two fields might also find a tour through the copyright, trademark, and patent databases fruitful. For example, a family law lawyer might use one of the databases to see if the other spouse has any intellectual property that may have some worth and be added to the marital estate.

Trademarks

For a basic trademark search, Susan Kaiser, a lawyer who has represented network-owned radio and television stations and negotiates and drafts agreements and contracts, searches the U.S. Patent and Trademark Office site (see the listing below). Although she wouldn't file a trademark application based only upon this search, she gets a sense of whether it's a good idea to then conduct a full-fledged search at a pay site, such as Thompson & Thompson (**http://www.t-tlaw.com/trademarks.htm**). Other pay sites for patents and trademarks are Thomson Derwent (**http://www.derwent.com**), which has subsumed the former free Delphion.com site, and LexisNexis (**http://www.lexisnexis.com/patent services/default.asp**).

U.S. Patent and Trademark Office (USPTO)

http://www.uspto.gov/main/trademarks.htm

Purpose: To learn about trademarks, to search trademarks, to file trademark applications, and to track the status of an application.

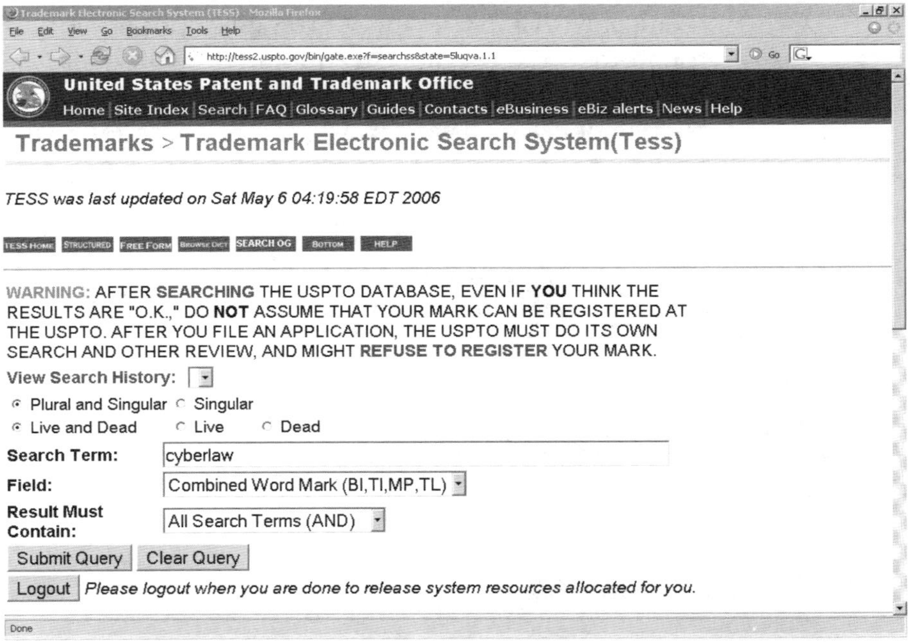

Figure 19-4. This is an example of a TESS basic search form. Enter your search terms; choose a field; and either choose the Boolean connector AND or OR, or search by an exact phrase.

Content: Users can view the *Trademark Manual of Examining Procedure* online to learn about trademarks. It contains specific rules and regulations for filing a trademark application. The Trademark Electronic Search System (TESS), which has over 4 million pending, registered, and dead federal trademarks, is used to search trademarks. There are several ways to search the TESS database: by using a basic form (enter search words and then select an option to search on all words, any word, or the exact phrase), a Boolean form (link search words with Boolean and proximity connectors, such as AND, OR, ADJ), or an advanced form (to link together search words with Boolean connectors and to restrict the search words to specific fields— such as the attorney of record field or owner field).

Our View: Trademark searching can be very tricky and TESS has done a good job at providing detailed help screens and sample searches to assist with the variety of search strategies, such as searching by truncating words, searching word patterns, or limiting words to their plural or singular format only, and so on. Some things to be aware of with TESS: it will not recognize phrases unless the words are surrounded by quotation marks, and TESS infers the OR connector unless the searcher uses another connector between each word (or uses quotation marks to show the words are to be searched as a phrase).

Tip: Take advantage of the **View Search History** link to view a record of all your searches done during your current session and then print them out for your files.

State Trademarks

States have their own trademark registration procedures. See the **State Trademarks** site (**http://statetm.tripod.com**) for links to the various state trademark offices.

International Trademarks

International Trademark Association

http://www.inta.org/

Purpose: The site states that its purpose is to advance the fair and effective use of trademarks in national and international commerce. It is geared toward lawyers, trademark professionals, students, and business owners.

Content: Lawyers will find the site useful for its articles about trademark and other IP topics and to explain to clients the purpose of both a U.S. trademark and an international trademark and how to obtain one as easily as possible. Hovering over **Information & Publishing** on the home page reveals a list of sections, including the **Reference Section**. There you'll find links to useful information like a **Glossary** (of trademark terms and language), **Acronyms** (of common companies), **Info by Topic** (from "Assignments" to "Valuation"), and **FAQs** (such as, "Is it mandatory to register a trademark?").

Our View: The INTA has done a good job of placing a large amount of information at your fingertips in a clear and concise manner. This makes your job easier when you are passing on that information to your client. Also, the "Trademarks Basics: A Guide For Businesses" pamphlet found by clicking the **Informational Brochures** link in the **Reference Section** can be a good resource for questions your clients may have.

Tip: Click on FAQs to find out the answers to INTA's most-asked questions. You won't have to worry about asking any "dumb" questions. They are all here, and the answers, too! In case anyone would like to research further, INTA provides the links to other categories of intellectual property-related Web sites as well. Just click on **Links** in the **Reference Section**. Some information, such as the **Trade Dress Image Library**, are limited to members only.

Patents

U.S. Patent and Trademark Office

http://www.uspto.gov/main/patents.htm

Purpose: To search for patents and published patent applications, to view the ***Official Gazette,*** to locate guides about the patenting process, to locate rules and laws about patents, to file patents and track their status, and so on.

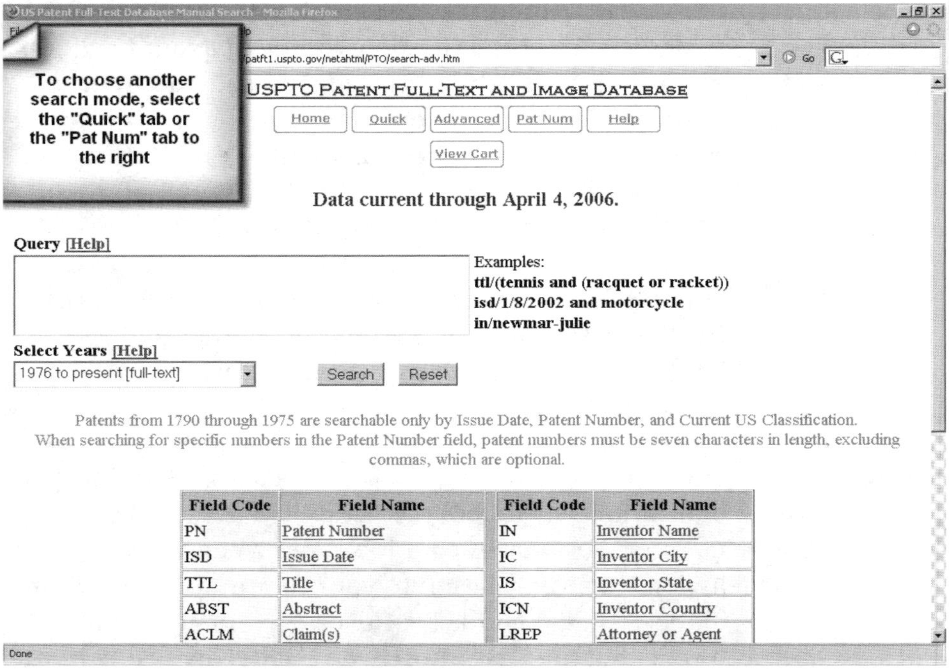

Figure 19-5. This shows the USPTO's advanced search query box and also provides an example of how to build your search. Click on **Pat Num** or **Quick** to choose another search mode.

Content: Patents from 1790 through 1975 are searchable by patent number and current U.S. classification only, while patents from 1976 to the present are full-text searchable.

Our View: There are plenty of help screens to make the searching easier. To search for patents or published patent applications, begin searching by choosing the range of dates, then enter your terms and select your fields (such as all fields, inventor name, and so on). Both the patents and published patent applications offer quick searching (using up to two terms and up to two fields) and advanced searching (using multiple terms and fields). Search patents by patent number and search patent applications by published application number or document number.

Tip: You'll need special plug-ins to view images of the patents.

U.S. Patent & Trademark Office Trademark Assignment Search

http://assignments.uspto.gov/assignments/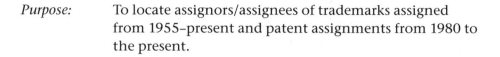

Purpose: To locate assignors/assignees of trademarks assigned from 1955–present and patent assignments from 1980 to the present.

Content: The USPTO has created a searchable database of trademark assignments back to 1955. You can search by a variety of criteria, including registration number, assignor or assignee name, applicant or registrant name, among others.

Our View: This relatively new searchable database is a boon to those needing up-to-date information on trademarks. While the USPTO TESS system has offered good online access to trademark filings, up until now, there has been no online access to recorded assignment information. Trademark assignment information had previously only been available on-site at the USPTO in Arlington, VA.

Tip: To access trademarks assigned before 1955 you'll have to visit the National Archives & Records Administration (NARA). **(http://www.nara.gov).**

U.S. Patent and Trademark Office

Trademark Application Document Retrieval

http://portal.uspto.gov/external/portal/tow

Purpose: To access more than 8 million document pages of information from nearly a half-million trademark applications.

Content: As of February 2005, the U.S. Patent and Trademark Office (USPTO) has made official trademark application files available on the Internet, including all decisions made by trademark examining attorneys and their reasons for making them.

The system, known as Trademark Document Retrieval (TDR), offers the public an advanced electronic portal to PDF viewing, downloading, and printing of an array of information and documents.

To access TDR, select either the **U.S. Registration number**, **U.S. Serial number**, **International Registration number**, or a **U.S. Reference Number** for the records you wish to retrieve—then click the **Submit** button.

Documents returned via a sample TDR search included copies of the file's jacket (folder), "Notice of Allowance," "Notice of Abandonment," and letters to interested parties from the examining attorney (as included in the file). Clicking on any of the links on the results page opens a PDF viewer in a new window. The viewer indicates the total number of pages in the document and the page you are currently viewing. Click the **Next Page** button to advance and the **Previous Page** button to go back.

Our View: A search by trademark name or owner would make the database even more useful.

Tip: You can find trademark serial numbers for specific trademarks or for all trademarks from a specific registrant using the USPTO's TESS search engine (**http://www.uspto.gov/**).

Copyrights

Those delving into copyright issues such as registrations and ownership documents will now find a Web-based alternative to the dreaded dial-up LOCIS Search System of the U.S. Copyright Office. The new Web-based system is called (aptly enough) Copyright Search.

Library of Congress Copyright Search

http://www.loc.gov/copyright/search

Purpose: Copyright Search has three databases: (1) a catch-all database for books, films, maps, music, and so on; (2) a serials database; and (3) a documents database (with legal records about transfers of copyrights, termination notices, statements about whether an author is alive or dead or about an erroneous name in a copyright notice, and documents identifying anonymous or pseudonymous authors).

Content: The databases go back to 1978, but it can take recent registrations several months to appear. The book database is searchable by author, title, claimant, or registration number, or by a combined search. The serials database is searchable by **Author**, **Title**, **Claimant**, or **International Standard Serial Number** (ISSN), while the documents database is searchable by **Title**, **Assignor**, **Assignee**, or **Document number**.

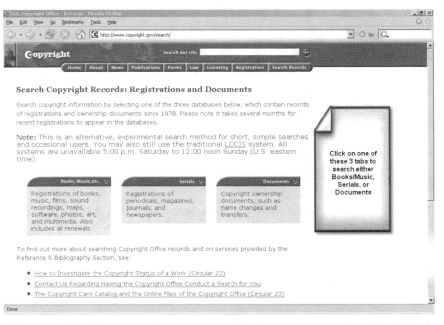

Figure 19-6. There are three separate databases to search at the U.S. Copyright Office Web site—depending on whether you want to search books and music, serials, or documents.

Our View: Because the database only goes back to 1978 and because it takes a few months for new registrations to be entered, lawyers who want to contact a live person for further inquiries can now e-mail or chat for free with the Library of Congress's virtual librarian at **http://www.loc.gov/rr/askalib**.

Tip: A vice president of legal affairs at a cable network explained that he also finds the **Library of Congress Online Catalog (http://catalog.loc.gov)** to be useful to see if there are any other details about a publication other than what the copyright search displays.

The Copyright and Fair Use site (**http://fairuse.stanford.edu**) was recently revamped by Tim Stanley (Justia and FindLaw's cofounder). It is a joint project of Stanford University Libraries, NOLO, and Justia. It includes an overview of copyright law and links to laws, cases, treaties, current legislation, articles, mailing lists, and more. It also offers (for free) Stanford's Fair Use Monthly Newsletter.

IP Web Sites

Aside from the "official" government sites for searching (and learning about) copyrights, patents, and trademarks, there are various non-governmental sites where you can learn about these areas of law. Many of the IP sites now are geared to the digital world, offering information about issues such as software, webcasting, and so on. Some useful free IP sites are listed below.

IP Litigation

Who's Suing Whom: Patent, Trademark & Copyright Edition

http://www.tlc-i.com/texis/tmp/litcases3 $\bigotimes$

Purpose: To determine if certain parties are involved in IP-related litigation.

Content: Southern California legal translation firm Interlingua sponsors this free searchable database of current and past patent, trademark, and copyright litigation. The database allows for as broad or narrow a search as you'd like to run. To start, you must select either a **Patent**, **Trademark**, or **Copyright** case search by filling in one of those "radio" buttons and filling in a party name (in the **Case Name** box). All of the other fields are optional.

You can choose to limit the search by entering an abbreviated court name in all caps (e.g., TXS for the Southern District of Texas, or CAC for the Central District of California), selecting a single state in which to search, or entering a date after which you want the database to search. Leaving these criteria blank, however, will give you the broadest range of results. For example, by not selecting a state, results are returned from all fifty states. Returned results include the Case Number, Case Name, Court, and the Date the case was filed.

While the searches are free, the site charges $25 for a copy of the docket sheet (per case) and another $25 for each supporting document from the case you wish to order. (See the Tip below for a lower cost alternative.)

Our View: You can use this database to quickly determine if a potential client has been sued (or is suing someone) for an IP issue. The search functions are easy to use and straightforward. While there is no documentation to speak of at the site, we were able to locate cases as far back as 1991 and as recent as within five weeks of our search. It can be a handy alternative, even if you already have a PACER account, because you can search for just IP cases by a specific party's name.

Tip: You can download these dockets from PACER for 8¢/page (up to a maximum of $2.40) per document. Additionally, many of the supporting documents might also be available via PACER for the same 8¢/page and $2.40 maximum/document fees.

IP Metasites

KuesterLaw, the Technology Law Resource (**http://www.kuesterlaw .com**), links to reams of technology law information, especially patent, copyright, and trademark law. There are links to leading IP cases and statutes, government sites, and various other IP resources such as law reviews and articles. According to site owner Jeffrey R. Kuester, the site is "reportedly the most linked-to intellectual property Web site on the Internet."

FindLaw also has many IP links (**http://www.findlaw.com/01top ics/23intellectprop**) and so does Hieros Gamos (**http://www.hg.org/ intell.html**). Hieros Gamos also links to many IP treaties.

IP Books

Digital Law Online (**http://digital-law-online.info**) is a full-text on-line version of the treatise *Legal Protection of Digital Information*, written by University of Utah School of Computing Professor Lee A. Hollaar. (Professor Hollaar was a technical consultant to the plaintiff states in the Microsoft antitrust litigation.) Updates to this treatise are also available at this site.

IP Articles

Although searching the Thomson Derwent site is not free, reading select articles about IP issues and trends is (**http://scientific.thomson .com/free**).

IP Blogs

I.P. lawyers J. Matthew Buchanan, Stephen Nipper, and Douglas Sorocco offer news and opinion on current developments in patent, copyright and trademark litigation and government notices.

Other IP blogs include:

- Bag & Baggage—**http://bgbg.blogspot.com/**
- The Invent Blog—**http://nip.blogs.com/**
- Promote the Progress—**http://www.promotetheprogress.com**

Links to more IP blogs (and blogs on numerous other law-related topics) can be found at The Blogs of Law (**http://www.theblogsoflaw.com**).

CHAPTER**TWENTY**

Weblogs, RSS Feeds, and Podcasts

Weblogs, known as "blogs" for short, are Web sites, but their content is more like a personal journal or diary—usually with an attitude. Blogs are typically made up of short, frequently updated posts that are ordinarily arranged chronologically—with the newest posts at the top of the page.

The contents and purposes of blogs vary with the personalities of the people who create them—known as "bloggers." Blogs contain everything from links and commentary about current events, to news about a specific topic or company. More personal blogs might constitute online diaries, and include photos, poetry, mini-essays, project updates, or fiction. Often blogs are no more than a chronicle of what's on the mind of the blogger at any given time. Their ease of development and updating make it extremely easy for anyone, even those with limited technical ability, to create, host, and update their own Web site.

Blogs give their owners an unfettered opportunity to express themselves, vent frustrations, espouse a particular point of view, discuss important issues, or spread rumors for their own purposes. Blogs can range from the off-beat humor of Davezilla (**http://www.davezilla.com**) or straightforward information sharing like TechForLawyers (**http://www.techfor lawyers.net**) to opinion, such as Stanford Law School Professor Lawrence Lessig's discussion of Internet Law (**http://cyberlaw.stanford.edu/lessig/ blog/**), and everything in between.

Law-related blogs are often referred to as "blawgs." Los Angeles intellectual property and appellate lawyer Denise Howell is generally credited with coining the term on her blawg (Bag & Baggage, at **http://bgbg**

.blogspot.com). Blawgs may cover a single legal practice area (such as intellectual property), or they may cover a broader topic, such as how to manage your practice. Many respected blawgs are maintained by lawyers who are experts in a particular area of practice and use their blawgs to track pertinent case law and legislative and regulatory developments, while others are maintained by journalists, librarians, or vendors with a particular area of interest or expertise. Ernest Svenson's Ernie the Attorney (**http://www.ernietheattorney.net**), Tom Mighell's Inter-Alia (**http://www.inter-alia.net**), Monica Bay's The Common Scold (**http:// www.thecommonscold.com**), and Sabrina Pacifici's beSpacific (**http:// www.bespacific.com**) are some of the more well-known blawgs. Each of these blawgs also has links to numerous other blawgs that their respective owners find useful. The news, information, and commentary provided by blawgs can provide informational support to lawyers who practice in the same areas of law. You can sample some of the most popular blawgs by visiting The Blogs of Law at **http://www.theblogsoflaw.com** or Blawg.org (**http://www.blawg.org**).

Figure 20-1. The Blogs of Law offers a list of law-related blogs arranged topically. The site can also be keyword searched.

Even if you do not have time to regularly visit blogs you find useful, you can arrange to have information on new posts delivered directly to you. Many blogs utilize Web feeds. The best known Web feed format is the RSS feed technology that allows you to automatically receive new information as it's posted to the blog. (RSS stands for "Rich Site Summary" or "Really Simple Syndication." See the Glossary for additional information.) RSS feeds are, essentially, an electronic update service that allows the blog to automatically deliver information directly to your desktop on a continual basis. Unlike a newsletter or other traditional online update service you may be familiar with, RSS feeds are not delivered via e-mail. To receive and read RSS feeds, users need to use specialized news aggregator software (see "RSS Readers" later in this chapter). A newer feed format is Atom.

By monitoring RSS feeds that are closely related to your areas of practice or interest, you can quickly keep up to date on any topic you choose. Because the RSS feed's information is automatically sent to you, you're freed from having to visit the sites from which the content originates. This can save you time that you might otherwise spend surfing to individual Web sites and waiting for their pages to download. RSS feeds allow you to control the intervals at which they receive updates and can even offer you continual updates without having to worry about missing a post or publication.

As a result of the rising popularity of RSS, established news Web sites such as CNN and the *Wall Street Journal* are also utilizing RSS feeds to distribute their information to readers almost instantly.

So, "How do blogs fit into my search for facts on the Internet?" you might ask yourself. For lawyers who represent companies that manufacture products or provide services to the public, periodic checking of certain blogs or subscribing to RSS feeds can also provide early warnings of product liability issues or shareholder unrest that could later lead to individual or class action lawsuits.

Many bloggers include links to breaking news, magazine stories, or other Web sites that interest them. Because blogs are updated often (e.g., throughout the day), they can be rich sources of current news or information on a specific topic.

A more personal blog might give you valuable information about the opposition or one of their witnesses—or even your own client. Have a look at a few of the diary-style blogs available at some of the sites mentioned below. You will probably be surprised at the volume and kinds of information people post about themselves on the Internet.

One provider of blogging tools, **Blogger.com**, suggests that "blogs are also excellent team/department/company/family communication tools. They help small groups communicate in a way that is simpler and easier to follow than e-mail or discussion forums. Use a private blog on an intranet to allow team members to post related links, files, quotes, or commentary."

Blogs and RSS feeds can be created easily. As a result, users can access feeds on a variety of topics—from criminal law to sports, travel, and technology. On the other hand, anyone can use a blog and an RSS feed to create what appears to be an authoritative Web presence. In short, it still takes a critical mind to evaluate and investigate the credibility of any information source, whether it is online or in print. With this caveat in mind, the increasing usefulness of blogs and RSS feeds promises to help make it easier for you to stay well informed.

Blogging Tools

There are a number of companies that provide creation tools and Web-hosting space for bloggers. Some of the best-known are

- Blogger—**http://www.blogger.com**
- JournalSpace—**http://www.journalspace.com/**
- Moveable Type—**http://www.movabletype.org/**
- My Blogspace—**http://www.myblogspace.net**
- Trellix—**http://www.trellix.com** (While business Web hosting provider Interland [**http://www.interland.com**] acquired Trellix in December 2002, Trellix continues to operate under the Trellix name.)
- Userland—**http://www.userland.com**

Locating and Searching Blogs

Searching blogs is almost like listening in on someone's phone conversation—except the blogger expects people to be listening. If bloggers are unhappy with a company, its financial performance, or the performance of its products, they may discuss it in their blog. Additionally, if someone was particularly upset, they might set up a blog devoted to bashing the company. Conversely, a blogger might offer praise for a company (it could happen). Regardless, numerous blog posts about a company or product could be a harbinger of greater unrest, or legal action, in the future. Knowing about it early, you can advise your client of steps to help minimize the damage or avoid the confrontation altogether. Locating the right phone line to listen to is easier than you might think. Blogs can be an excellent way to gauge consumers' perception of a client company or product.

As they first increased in popularity and numbers, blogs began to find their way into general purpose search engines such as Google. In February 2003, as a result of the popularity of blogs and the sheer volume of information they contain, Google purchased blog publishing pioneer **Blogger .com**. Blog results now regularly turn up in Google, Yahoo!, and Altavista Web search results.

TIP: You can help search engines focus on returning results from blogs by adding the word "blog" to your search. On Google, for example, a search for "blog intellectual property" (without the quotation marks) returns results that are almost exclusively from blogs that cover intellectual property issues.

As of this writing, only JournalSpace offers a search engine function to search across all of the blogs created through its service. With it, you can keyword search blog titles, blog keywords (owner assigned), and even search recent blog entries. Additionally, there are some search engines that focus primarily on returning results from blogs regardless of where they are hosted. Some other blog search engines are discussed below.

Google Blog Search

http://blogsearch.google.com/

Purpose: To locate information contained in blogs—using the search power of Google.

Content: Google has created a separate search engine to locate information posted to blogs. The interface will look familiar to anyone who is currently using the Google Web search engine. Google's blog search includes the familiar, standard search box with a link to the **Advanced Blog Search** appearing on the first page. Type the keyword(s) for which you want to search into the search query box and click the **Search** button. The Advanced search will allow users to define more specific criteria for their searches, including: the language, author, dates, and title of the blog they are searching for.

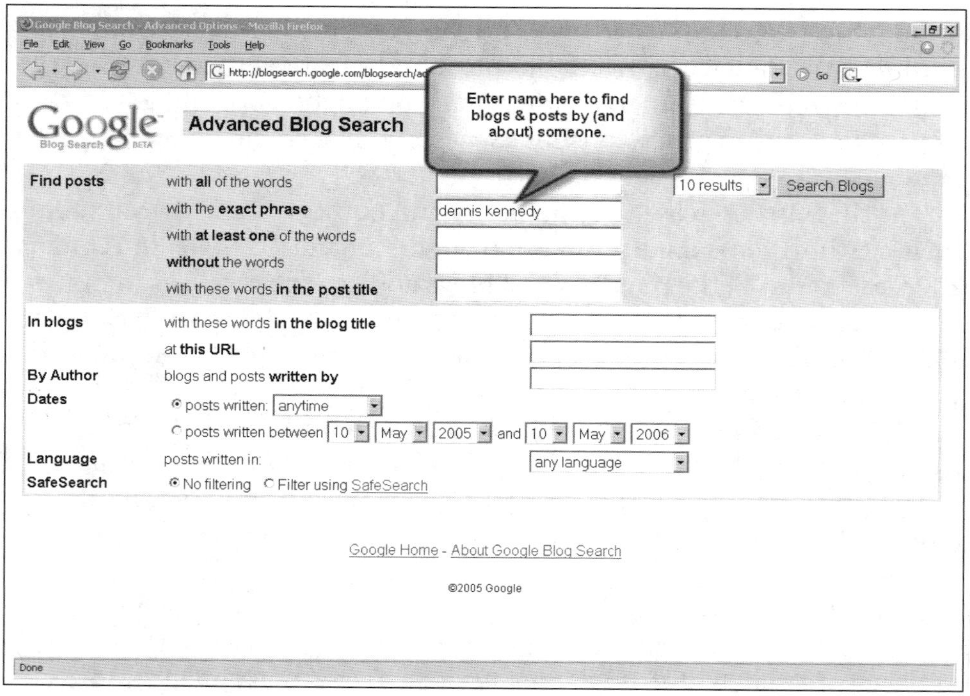

Figure 20-2. This is the Google "Advanced Blog Search" page where a more precise keyword or author search can be conducted. Google™ is a trademark of Google Technology Inc.

A **Safe Search** is available as well, which allows users to filter "explicit sexual content" from search results. The default display mode for results is **Sorted by Relevance**; users can also choose to **Sort by Date** by clicking on the **Sort by Date** link above the results list.

Our View: Google maintains that their index includes all blogs, not just those published through Blogger (the blogging service it owns). The Blog Search is continually updated. Blogs can be an excellent source of news (compiled from various sources by others), as well as commentary on hot topics, public opinion, or rumors regarding products or companies.

Tip: If you want to be automatically alerted to new blog postings related to your search terms, Google Blog Search also gives you the option of subscribing to either Atom or RSS feeds containing the continually updated results of your search. You can click on the link at the bottom of the results page that offers the top 10 or 100 results delivered to you via RSS. You will then be able to subscribe to them in the news aggregator of your choice and get updates whenever new postings are made that match your topic.

The Google Blog Search (like the Google Web search) allows users to limit their search with very specific criteria. For example, you can search for blog postings where your search term appears in the page's title by typing "intitle: search term" in the search box (without quotation marks). All of the other standard Google Search limiters are also supported in Blog Search. These include

- link:
- site:

Additionally, there are a number of search limiters that are new to the Blog Search service:

- inblogtitle:
- inposttitle:
- inpostauthor:
- blogurl:

Yahoo! Blog Search

http://news.search.yahoo.com

Purpose: To locate current information contained in blogs.

Content: In response to the blog-only search introduced by Google, Yahoo! added results from blogs to its news searches. There is no magic to getting blog results . . . just enter your search terms in the news search box and click the **Search** button. The blog results are displayed in a column on the right-hand side of the page, segregated from the results from "regular news" sources that are displayed down the center. The initial blog results list will include four to five blog listings. Click on the **More blog results** link to display only the list of all blog results related to your search—without any "regular news" results displayed.

Just like Google's blog search, Yahoo! offers you the ability to get constant updates on your search via an RSS feed. Yahoo! essentially runs your search continuously for you and alerts you when new results are added. You'll need an RSS reader application such as NewsGator or Pluck to receive and read these RSS feed updates. Yahoo! has also integrated RSS reader capabilities into its "My Yahoo!" personalized home page offering. "My Yahoo!" pages are available to anyone who registers (free at **http://my.yahoo.com**—see page 748).

Our View: One drawback is that Yahoo! offers no option for searching only blogs, (this is particularly annoying since Yahoo! does offer the option of searching **Yahoo! News Only** and omitting blog results). However, after displaying the news/blog results together, one can then display only the blog results by clicking on the **More blog results** link (as discussed above). On the plus side, blog searchers do have access to the full complement of the news search's **Advanced Search** features.

Tip: The owners of the ThreadWatch Web forum have rigged up a search box that will allow you to limit your Yahoo! search to blog results only. You can access it at **http://www.threadwatch.org/yahooblogs.html**.

Daypop

http://www.daypop.com

Purpose: A search engine for blogs and traditional news sources.

Content: Daypop offers a search engine covering 59,000 blogs, news, and other current events Web sites (more than 41,000 of these are blogs). Daypop crawls each of those sites at least once per day to index the newest additions. Major media sites, like CNN, are crawled every three hours.

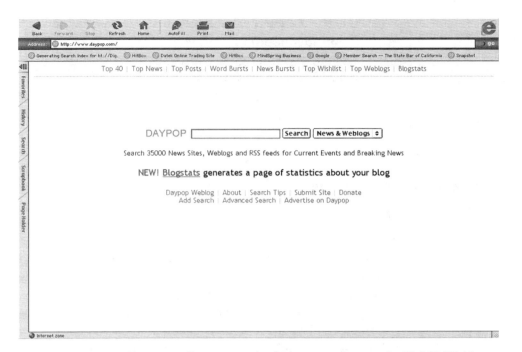

Figure 20-3. Daypop offers a search engine covering nearly 59,000 Weblogs, news, and current events Web sites.

Daypop allows you to keyword and phrase search all these sites at once. You can also use Daypop to track specific words or phrases that are currently appearing in many blogs (**Word Bursts**), view a list of the most-linked-to Web sites from the blogs Daypop monitors (**Top 40**), and examine the most-linked-to news stories from the blogs Daypop monitors, among other things. Because information from sites crawled by Daypop is available in search results immediately after those pages are crawled, Daypop essentially performs near-real-time analysis of this information. Additionally, you can limit your search to just **news, Weblogs, RSS News Headlines,** or **RSS News Posts**.

Our View: Daypop offers a number of powerful tools to make the search process more effective.

Tip: (1) Search for your clients' names and product names regularly to see what people are saying about them.

(2) Use the **Advanced Search** (**http://www.daypop .com/advanced**) to limit your searches to a particular country or language. You can also use the **Advanced Search** to specify a time range within which you want the blog posts in the results to have been created.

BlogStreet

http://www.blogstreet.com

Purpose: A search engine for blogs.

Content: The BlogStreet **Search & Directory** tool (on the right-hand side of the homepage) is a straightforward query box for keyword searching over 102,000 blogs. (See the "Tip" below for information on its **Advanced Search**.) Once you get your results list, each result will be followed by a **BlogRank** link. You can click on the main link and visit the blog page that contains your search terms or you can click first on the **BlogRank** link to learn more information about the blog that contains the search result. Among the information available is **BlogBack** (a list of other blogs that highly recommend the site containing your search terms) and **Neighborhood** (a list of other blogs that BlogStreet deems similar to the blog containing your search terms).

Our View: In addition to returning relevant results, the site's **Blogback** and **Neighborhood** information can help lead you to other blogs that might contain more information on the subject for which you're searching. One concern however, is the depth of the blogs that BlogStreet lists on any given topic. Despite claiming to include over 102,000 blogs, there are only 52 listed in the **Law** category of the site's directory (**http://www.blogstreet.com/ search.html#directory**). Other directories, like The Blogs of Law (**http://www.theblogsoflaw.com**), list hundreds of blogs in numerous practice-related categories.

Tip: Use the site's **Advanced Search** to limit your search to a specific date range or one particular blog.

Feedster Blog Search

http://blogs.feedster.com

Purpose:	A search engine for blogs.

Content: The Feedster blog search allows you to limit your search to the blogs in the Feedster index. The **Advanced Search** menu allows you to easily limit your search to a particular blog. The **Feedfinder** allows you to find all of the feeds emanating from a particular blog. The **Link Search** feature allows you to find which other blogs are linking to a blog, or blog post, of which you are already aware. At the top right-hand side of each search result page is an orange XML button. By dragging that button to your RSS reader (see below for more information about RSS Readers) you can automatically re-run your search (at intervals you prescribe) without actually having to return to the Feedster site. If you don't use an aggregator, then click the **get by e-mail button** near the top of the results page to have new results sent to your e-mail.

Our View: The **Advanced Search** page is well laid out, making it easy to use. The site defaults to the "AND" boolean connector, but allows use of the "OR" connector, or the "–" operator to omit a word. (Clicking the **Help** at the top or bottom of the **Advanced Search** page offers a quick tutorial to the site's search syntax.) Being able to find other blogs that link to a blog post that is of particular interest to you is a good way to help gather additional information on a topic or find others who are commenting about a client, for example. The ability to create an RSS feed of your search is also very useful to keep up to date with new developments related to your search.

Tip: (1) Use the site's "Advanced Search" to limit your search to a specific blog (or to omit a particular blog).

(2) Save time gathering information by "subscribing" to automatically receive results of your search on a regular basis through an RSS feed.

RSS Readers

In order to receive a blog's RSS feed, it is necessary to use an "aggregator" or "reader." These readers translate the XML programming language in which the feeds are created to a list of headlines and abstracts for each of the most recent articles added to a blog that you can easily read. There are a variety of news aggregator software products. Some are stand-alone programs, while others are add-ins that work with programs you might already have on your computer. Generally, they are available for download online (and must then be installed after they're downloaded). Most require a monthly service fee or flat usage fee, but some are free.

To find relevant RSS feeds, visit **Daypop.com**, **Feedster.com**, or **Syndic8.com**. **Syndic8.com** offers an extensive directory of over 26,000 news feeds, although only a few are law-related. (Click on **Categories** at the top of the Syndic8 home page to start browsing through the categories.) An advantage of using an RSS directory like **Syndic8.com** is that it automatically weeds out sites that don't contain XML capabilities.

Web sites that offer RSS feeds of their content usually announce this feature by means of a small orange button that reads "XML," "Atom," "RSS," or include this new RSS/news icon. To add a feed to a your news reader, all you usually have to do is click and hold on the orange button that appears on a page to which you want to subscribe and drag the button to your news reader.

Yahoo!

http://my.yahoo.com/

Purpose: An RSS news reader.

Content: Yahoo! has built a virtual RSS news reader into its *My Yahoo!* personalization service. This free Yahoo! service allows you to monitor RSS feeds in your browser by visiting a personalized *My Yahoo!* page. Accessing the *My Yahoo!* service requires signing up for a free Yahoo! account. Once you have established your account and logged in to your *My Yahoo!* page, clicking on the **Choose Content** link at the top of the page allows you to enter a URL for a specific RSS feed or conduct a key word search to retrieve, select, and display up to 50 RSS feeds. After the feeds are selected, each is displayed in its own box (labeled with the name of the feed) on the *My Yahoo!* page.

Our View: Because there is no software to download or install, this is a very good option for people uncomfortable with those tasks. Users might "graduate" to one of the readers discussed later in this section if they want to organize the feeds they have subscribed to or want to monitor more than 50 feeds at a time.

Tip: The topics and feeds suggested by Yahoo! are very general, so use one of the search engine strategies discussed in this chapter or a blawg directory (such as **http://www.theblogsoflaw.com**) to locate feeds that will be of interest to you.

Newsgator

http://www.newsgator.com

Purpose: An online RSS news reader.

Content: Newsgator offers a "Consumer Standard" version of its online RSS news reader for free (with registration), in addition to more-robust paid versions. Adding feeds is as easy as clicking on the **Newsgator Manager** tab and then clicking on **Add Feeds**. There you can select one of the feeds from their subject directory (there are about two dozen feeds in the law category) or click the **URL & Import** tab to add the URL of a feed you have found using another method.

Newsgator allows you to organize your feeds into folders so you can find them easily. The service allows you to rate each item you receive from any of the RSS feeds you subscribe to and the **My Clippings** feature allows you to save your favorite posts to a **My Clippings** folder for easy access later. Newsgator uses those clipping preferences and ratings to recommend feeds to you.

Newsgator's **Smart Feeds** allow you to conduct a keyword or URL search to retrieve RSS items that contain

Figure 20-4. Web-based RSS aggregator Newsgator's folder-within-folder hierarchy is similar enough to Microsoft Outlook that computer users of any level will feel comfortable using it.

specific keywords you assign. Newsgator also gives you the power to have e-mail sent to specific addresses converted to RSS feeds. (The free version only allows you to set up one of each of these searches.)

More features are available in the paid "Gold," "Platinum" and "Outlook" versions which add the ability to receive RSS feeds on a text-message-capable cell phone and in e-mail, among other features. Free 14-day trial versions are available for all for the paid versions.

Our View: The free Newsgator service could be a good "next step up" from the My Yahoo! aggregator, since it is easy to use, offers more organizational options, and does not require any installation. The e-mail conversion to RSS is especially useful for subscribing to mailing lists or for converting e-mail-based alerts to RSS. The RSS feed recommendations are a very helpful way of finding information you might not otherwise have ferreted out. One drawback, however, is that Newsgator does not seem to be compatible with a certain format of RSS feed—those bearing the ".RDF" extension (as opposed to those ending with ".XML" or ".RSS" extensions). Mac users will be pleased to know that because it is Web-based, they can also easily use Newsgator.

Pluck

http://www.pluck.com

Purpose: An RSS news reader.

Content: Pluck offers both a downloadable add-on that brings RSS reader capabilities to the Internet Explorer and Firefox Web browsers (for Windows) and a Web-based RSS reader service, similar to Newsgator (see above).

The downloadable add-in offers a robust set of customizable search and organization functions to locate, add, and create a steady stream of targeted information. Once installed, the Pluck Toolbar will auto-detect RSS feeds on any page you're viewing allowing you to subscribe with the push of one button. You can create a **Perch** (persistent search) to continually search Web pages for the terms in which you're interested—to be updated whenever your terms are added to those pages. You can use **Folders** to categorize, save, and view (1) related RSS feeds; (2) **Perches**; and (3) existing bookmarks (imported from your browser) all in the same folder. The tabbed browsing feature of newer Web Browsers allows you to view and manage the various items in a single folder simultaneously in different tabs. The **Publish** function allows you to post your collections of bookmarks, research, and RSS feeds on the public Internet for free, and also includes a function to invite others (via e-mail) to view those collections.

The Web version of Pluck includes many of the organizational and publishing features of the downloadable version, but does not include the **Perch** or auto-detect functions.

Our View: The **Perch** function of the downloadable version of Pluck is like having a research assistant who can continually monitor the sites and terms you define, immediately notifying you of changes, while the RSS auto-detect function keeps you from wasting time searching for the feed information if it's buried somewhere on a long Web page. The organizational features of Pluck are very useful. Also, the ability to easily publish link collections to the Web, to share with others, can be very handy for distributing information on news and articles to clients and co-counsel. The integration with the Internet Explorer and Firefox browsers in Windows is a useful way to keep your feeds handy while you're online. This Web-based service is also a good alternative for Mac users.

Newzcrawler

http://www.newzcrawler.com $

Purpose: An RSS news reader.

Content: NewzCrawler is a news reader compatible with the Atom, .RSS, and .RDF formats. It can also collect information from Usenet newsgroups and Web pages, all of which is displayed in a familiar, Microsoft Outlook-like interface.

Feeds can be easily dragged to NewzCrawler and arranged in Folders and Subfolders (just like e-mail messages in Outlook). The Folders reside in the program's left-hand frame. Clicking on a specific feed in the left-hand frame displays the headlines and descriptions of the most recent items from that feed in the upper center frame. Clicking on a specific item in the upper center frame displays the full item in the lower center frame.

NewzCrawler also has an embedded Web browser, so you can also visit links embedded in news items without leaving the NewzCrawler application. You can also choose to view a ticker of incoming headlines from your feeds at the bottom of your computer's desktop.

Newzcrawler is a separate program that must be down-loaded and installed on your computer before you can use it. It costs $24.95 to purchase a copy online, with a 30 percent discount for non-profit agencies and aca-demic institutions. A 14-day free trial is available.

Our View: The Microsoft Outlook-like interface will make NewzCrawler familiar for most Outlook e-mail users and thus easy to navigate. The organizational features are also very helpful.

ENewsbar

http://www.enewsbar.com

Purpose: An RSS news reader.

Content: ENewsbar allows you to monitor .XML and Atom news feeds in a continuously-running ticker that you can position on your computer's desktop. You can choose from pre-defined categories such as: **Tech, Entertain-ment, Sports, Health, Internet, Business,** and oth-ers, or input the URL for any specific feed you've found using other methods. ENewsbar requires a minimum of Internet Explorer Explorer 6.0 or recent versions of Fire-fox to click on the headlines and automatically have the browser open to retrieve the full story.

Our View: ENewsbar is a handy way to add feed information to an easy-to-access desktop ticker. It's good for monitoring a smaller number of feeds on one or two topics, but once you get beyond that, you probably would want the orga-nizational functions of NewzCrawler. One drawback is that ads are included in the ticker crawl of headlines—

the PC Way   MPAA training Dogs to Sniff Out DVDs   Sony's E3 booth tour   Why TVs Do Not Have Channel 1   Tag – You're a Criminal   Technology

Figure 20-5. Enewsbar lets you create custom lists of RSS feeds to monitor in its continuously scrolling text box on your computer desktop, or you can view content from preset lists.

but then again that's how they can keep the program free to use. At least the ads are displayed in a different color than the headlines.

Podcasts

Podcasts are the latest phenomenon in delivering audio content to listeners. You can think of it like "radio delivered via the Internet." Instead of listening to a live broadcast, however, listeners download audio files to their computers to play them back when it is convenient for them. Like other kinds of content available on the Internet, podcasts are relatively easy to create and cover a wide array of topics. Most podcasts are saved in the MP3 format, allowing maximum portability and flexibility in playing back those files. When we searched Google for *podcasts*, we received nearly 9 million results.

In the legal arena, some lawyers are creating podcasts for marketing purposes and to educate clients and potential clients on a variety of topics. (Legal podcasts are occasionally referred to as "plawdcasts," but the term has not yet gained the popularity of the term "blawg.") As listeners, legal professionals can use podcasts to get up-to-speed or keep up-to-date on numerous legal and nonlegal topics. Some even offer CLE credit.

Two ways to find podcasts are (1) to use an online directory of podcasts, such as **lpodder.org**, **TheBlogsofLaw.com**, or **Blawg.org** (click on the **Podcast** category) or (2) by simply using a search engine. For example, to find a podcast about using Google to conduct due diligence, we searched Google for *podcast, google,* and *due diligence,* which resulted in just over 4,500 results. One of the results was a podcast at the blog **Internet Cases.com**, maintained by Chicago IP attorney Evan Brown, who posts a new podcast every other week on various recent opinions related to Internet law, in addition to his regular text postings on the subject.

Once you have located podcasts you find useful (or entertaining), you can either check back with the host site frequently to download new installments, or many sites allow you to "subscribe" to the podcast via RSS using specialty RSS aggregators, often called "podcatchers." Similar to RSS feeds of text content (discussed earlier), podcast RSS feeds alert you automatically when new podcast content is available and even send the files to you automatically. Some of the more popular podcatchers include iTunes (**http://www.apple.com/itunes/**) for Mac and Windows; Juice (**http://juicereceiver.sourceforge.net/index.php**) for Mac, Windows, and Linux; and Jpodder (**http://jpodder.com/**) for Windows and Linux.

Even the Federal government has hopped on the podcast band-wagon. FirstGov.gov lists more than a dozen podcasts available from a wide range of U.S. government sources from "Air Force News" and the "Pentagon Channel" to "State Department Recent Stories" and the "White House Weekly Radio Address." The list is available at **http://first gov.gov/Topics/Reference_Shelf/Libraries/Podcasts.shtml**.

Even though podcasts have been around for more than two years, few lawyers are currently taking advantage of them either as "broadcasters" or listeners. Like any information on the Internet, it is important to carefully review the source of a podcast before relying on the information you hear from one.

Glossary

Note: Terms that are italicized within a definition are defined separately in this glossary.

A

Adware
A software application designed to display advertising banners, Web pages or other commercial content. Adware can sometimes be downloaded and installed onto users' computers without their knowledge. See also *Spyware*.

Archie
A software tool used to locate files that can be downloaded via *FTP*. Derived from the word archive.

Applet
A small program, written in *Java*, that can be included in a *Web page*. It is loaded by the Web *browser*, along with the Web page, and causes the user's computer to execute some function or action. Because applets operate within the Web browser, they are not *platform*-dependent. See also *Java*.

ARPA (Advanced Research Projects Agency)
U.S. Department of Defense agency that initially funded the development of the Internet's predecessor, ARPAnet. Now known as the Defense Advanced Research Projects Agency (DARPA).

ASCII
Short for American Standard Code for Information Interchange (pronounced "Ask-ee"). An international standard that assigns all numbers, letters, punctuation marks, symbols, and control codes a number from 0 to 127. ASCII is plain, unformatted text. It does not utilize style or font specifications. Most "plain text files" (.TXT) utilize the ASCII standard.

Atom
A specific format for automatically delivering information to users via *RSS* feeds, utilizing *XML*.

Attachment
A file that is sent along with an e-mail message, in addition to the main message. Any type of file can be sent as an attachment, including: word processing documents, PDFs, images, or executable programs.

Avatar
A digital representation of one's self (usually involving a graphic) used in an interactive, online, or virtual reality environment. Originally derived from a Sanskrit word meaning "descent" and related to Hindu mythology, the term's popularity in a technology-related context is generally credited to Neal Stephenson's novel *Snow Crash*.

B

Bandwidth
The amount of data that can be transmitted over a network over a specified amount of time. For computers and other digital devices, the concept is usually expressed in *bits* per second, (bps), or *bytes* per second.

Bit
Short for "binary digit," a bit is the smallest unit of information that a computer can hold. Abbreviated "b", a bit is a one or a zero, a true or a false, a "switch" or "flag" which is "on" or "off." Eight bits equal one *byte*.

Blawg
A law-related *blog*. Blawgs may cover a single legal practice area (such as intellectual property), or they may cover a broader topic such as how to manage your practice. Los Angeles intellectual property and appellate attorney Denise Howell is generally credited with coining the term on her blawg (Bag & Baggage, at **http://bgbg.blogspot.com**).

Blog
Web sites with content more like that of a personal journal or diary—often with an attitude. Blogs are usually made up of short, frequently updated posts that are ordinarily arranged chronologically—with the newest posts at the top of the page. Blogs are easily developed and updated. Even those with limited technical ability, can create, host and update their own blog.

Bookmark

(1) To save a "pointer" (in a Web *browser*) to a Web site you wish to revisit at a later time.

(2) The pointer that is created. Selecting the bookmark in the Web browser takes the user directly to the original Web site without typing in a *URL*. Also known as a "Favorite."

Bookmarklet

Like an *applet*, a bookmarklet is a small program, usually written in *Java*, that causes the user's computer to execute some function or action. Unlike applets which are loaded by the browser when a user visits a Web page, bookmarklets can be stored as a URL within a *bookmark* in most Web browsers, or within *hypertext* links on a Web page. Because bookmarklets operate within the Web *browser*, they are not platform-dependent.

Boolean Searching

The ability to connect search keywords and phrases with "logical operators," such as AND, OR, and NOT to establish relationships between the search terms.

Broadband

Generally used to identify different types of high-speed, high-bandwidth connections to the Internet, including cable and *DSL*.

Browser

A computer program that allows you to view pages on the Internet.

Byte

Short for "binary term," a byte refers to the size of a collection of data—measured in bits. For example, one byte equals eight *bits*, one kilobyte (KB) equals approximately 1,000 bits, one megabyte (MB) equals approximately 1 million bytes, one gigabyte (GB) equals approximately 1 billion bytes and one terabyte (TB) equals approximately 1 trillion bytes.

C

Cache

(1) Copies of Web pages you have visited that are automatically stored on your computer's hard drive after you've visited those pages. Your Web browser uses these "cached" copies to display those pages more rapidly if you make return visits to those pages.

(2) Copies of Web pages that are saved by a search engine (or other Web service) for later access or archive purposes—where the site storing the copy is not the original publisher/owner of the page.

(3) A specialized type of computer memory, usually used to store frequently accessed information or instructions. Similar to *RAM*, this cache is volatile—meaning that anything stored in this cache is lost when the computer is turned off. This is the place where your computer may store files as you are editing them—until you save them to the hard drive. That is why, if your computer freezes or otherwise loses power, all of your changes that have not been saved are lost.

Cascading Style Sheets.
See *Style Sheets*. Abbreviated as CSS.

Chat
A feature that lets you communicate, via typing, with computer users in real-time sessions. Messages typed into the chat software are displayed to all other users logged on to a particular chat session.

Client
Hardware or software necessary for users of the Internet, or any computer network, to query a remote host. Web *browsers* and e-mail software are examples of software clients. A home computer connected to the Internet is an example of a hardware client.

Cookie
A small piece of information written to the hard drive of a Web surfers' computer by a site they have visited. Intended as a means to expedite a user's return visits to favorite sites or personalize the information received from a site.

> *Example:* Amazon.com uses a cookie to identify returning visitors by name and to recommend products for purchase based on their prior buying history with Amazon.

CPU
Short for Central Processing Unit.

(1) This microchip is the electronic brains of the computer. Sometimes referred to as "the processor." The speed with which the CPU performs basic calculations is measured in Hertz (Hz). Pentium, Celeron,

and Opteron are examples of CPU models from different manufacturers.

(2) In a desktop computer, the term can also refer to the case that contains the *motherboard* and the microchip "brain."

Cyberspace
Used to describe the electronic space of the Internet. Data posted on the Internet is said to reside in cyberspace. The term was coined by author William Gibson in his 1984 novel *Neuromancer*.

D

DHCP
Short for Dynamic Host Configuration Protocol. A method by which *IP addresses* are automatically assigned to computers connected to a particular network. As new computers connect to the network, IP addresses from the available pool are automatically assigned to those machines. When a computer disconnects from the network, its IP address is put back into the pool of available addresses.

DHTML (Dynamic HTML)
Developed by theWorld Wide Web Consortium (W3C), DHTML is an extension of standard *HTML*. Dynamic HTML gives Web designers greater control over Web page layout. DHTML utilizes Java and Cascading Style Sheets (CSS) to deliver Web pages that can change based on user input without having to communicate with their host again.

Dial-up
Internet connection over standard telephone lines that requires users to dial in to a host computer to gain access to the Internet. Quickly being replaced by *broadband* connections.

Direct Connection
A "permanent" connection to the Internet via a dedicated phone line leased from a telephone company. Also known as a "leased line" connection.

Directory
A Web site containing a list of links to other sites, organized by topic. Top level topics are broken down into more detailed subtopics, which are bro-

ken down into more specific sub-subtopics (e.g., *Government >Law >Legal Research >Libraries*).

DNS
Short for Domain Name System. The numerous servers on this system translate domain names into the corresponding *IP addresses* where a domain name's Web site is hosted.

Domain Name
The portion of a Web address that follows "http://www." (e.g., for the Web site http://www.netforlawyers.com, the domain name is "**netfor lawyers.com**"). See also *URL*.

Download
To copy a file that is stored on another computer onto your own computer, via the Internet or other network connection. The opposite of *Upload*.

Drilling Down
The act of navigating through layers of information, as in the topics and more detailed subtopics of a *Directory*.

DSL
Short for Digital Subscriber Line. DSL allows for high-speed digital transmission of documents, voice and video files over regular telephone lines. DSL allows data and telephone traffic to travel over the set of copper wires simultaneously. See also *Broadband*.

Dynamic IP
An Internet protocol address that changes with each connection to the host computer (or Internet); usually assigned by *DHCP (Dynamic Host Configuration Protocol)*. The opposite of *Static IP*.

E

802.11
A set of wireless network connection standards developed by the Institute of Electrical & Electronics Engineers (IEEE). There are four distinct, commonly used standards: 802.11, which moves data at 2 Mbps (Megabits per second); 802.11a (which moves data at 54 Mbps); 802.11b (which moves data at 11 Mbps); and 802.11g (which moves data at 20 Mbps). Also known as Wi-Fi or WLAN.

Ethernet
The most widely-used method for connecting computers in a network. Ethernet utilizes eight-strand copper cabling (similar to telephone wiring) to transmit and receive data between computers at speeds up to 100 Mbps (Megabits per second). See also *Bit*, and *LAN*.

Expansion Cards
Additional devices than can be plugged into an *expansion slot* to increase a computer's functions or capabilities. Video cards, sound cards and internal *modems* were some of the first examples.

Expansion Slots
Locations on a computer *motherboard* where expansion cards are plugged in. NuBus, PCMCIA, PCI, and Compact Flash are all examples of different types of expansion slots.

Extranet
A private network available only to authorized users via the Internet. Access requires a username and password from the extranet's administrator. Lawyers can give select clients secure access to documents pertinent to their matters via an extranet.

F

FAQ
Short for Frequently Asked Questions. A feature commonly found on *Web sites*, FAQs are documents offering answers to commonly asked questions about the site, its products, or services.

Favorite
See *Bookmark*.

Firewall
A hardware or software security system designed to protect a computer network from unauthorized access.

Frames
A method for designing the layout of *Web pages* that divides the page into distinct sections (frames) each displaying *HTML* content from a different source.

Freeware

Software that is offered to the public for free by its author. While there is no license or registration fee, the user cannot make changes to it, as the author retains the copyright to the software. See also *Shareware*.

FTP

Short for File Transfer Protocol, this is a means of transferring files from one computer to another. It is the most common method by which Web pages are uploaded to a host computer. The term is also sometimes used as a verb to describe the act of transferring files using this *protocol*.

G

GB

Short for Gigabyte, a unit of measurement equal to approximately 1 billion bytes. See also *Byte*.

GIF

Short for Graphic Interchange Format, a common compression format for images. This format is popular for use on Web pages due to their small files sizes. Because of their low resolution and the fact that the GIF format only supports 256 colors, they are not recommended for images that are meant to be printed out. Originally developed by CompuServe, using compression technology from Unisys, usage of GIFs was covered under U.S. patent 4,558,302 until early 2003. While the technology described in the original patent has now entered the public domain, on its Web site Unisys claims to have "patents pending on a number of improvements on the inventions claimed in the above-expired patents." See also *JPEG*.

GUI

Short for Graphical User Interface. GUI refers to the front-end of a software application or operating system where users click on images and icons (e.g., Macintosh and Microsoft Windows Operating Systems) rather than entering text commands (DOS—Disk Operating System).

H

Home Page

The first page displayed in a user's Web *browser* when visiting a domain. The term can also refer to document displayed when you first open your Web browser.

Host

A computer, attached to a network, that sends and receives information to other computers on the network. See also *Client* and *Server*.

HTML

Short for HyperText Markup Language. HTML is the primary programming language used to create *Web pages*. *Web browsers* follow the directions of the HTML code to display a Web page as the designer intended it to look.

HTTP

Short for Hypertext Transfer Protocol. HTTP is the communications method used to send and receive requests for documents stored on the Internet.

Hub

Hardware that connects multiple computers. Hubs accept data from one device connected to it and distribute it to all of the other devices connected to it. Used in LANs. See also *Router* and *Switch*.

Hypertext

A method for accessing documents stored on a computer in a non-sequential fashion. Hypertext links serve as interactive cross references in electronic documents so the user can jump from one associated document to another—similar to the "See also" references in this glossary.

I

Inline Images

Graphical images embedded within a Web document along with the page's accompanying text. Images that are not "inline" are displayed in their own separate browser windows. In e-mail, inline images are included in the body of the e-mail message, as opposed to being sent as an attachment.

Interface

The point of meeting between two devices. The point where *RAM* chips plug into a computer's motherboard, and a simple electrical outlet and plug are examples of interfaces. When related to software, the interface refers to the method by which the user interacts with program. See also *GUI (Graphical User Interface)*.

Intranet

A private network available to authorized users within an organization such as a law firm or other company. Intranets are used primarily to share company information and computing resources among employees. Because of the shared nature of their information, intranets can also be used to foster collaboration among groups of employees, even if they are not physically located in the same office.

IP

Short for Internet Protocol. The IP is a set of communication standards that determines how information is sent and received via the Internet. See also *IP address*.

IP Address

An IP address is the number assigned by a host computer to any computer connected to the Internet or other computer network. The IP address acts like a phone number, so specific computers can be found on the network. Like phone numbers, no two computers on a network can have the same IP address. See also *Dynamic IP*, *IP,* and *Static IP*.

ISDN

Short for Integrated Services Digital Network. ISDN allows for high-speed digital transmission of documents, voice, and video files over regular telephone lines. See also *Broadband*.

ISP

Short for Internet Service Provider. A company that provides a connection to the Internet. ISPs can also provide hosting services for Web Sites. See also *Broadband* and *Dial-up*.

J

Java

A programming language, developed by Sun Microsystems, whose programs are automatically downloaded and run within a computer user's Web *browser*. Because Java programs operate within the Web browser, they are not platform-dependent. It is different from *JavaScript*. See also *Applet*.

JavaScript

A programming language, developed by Netscape Corporation, whose code is embedded into the body of a Web page. When the JavaScript code is loaded, it causes the user's computer to perform some action or function. Like *Java*, JavaScript operates within the Web *browser*, making it platform-independent. It is different from *Java*, though: Java's applets are downloaded to the user's computer before their instructions are activated.

JPEG

Short for Joint Photographic Experts Group. JPEG is an image compression standard used for color images and photos stored on computers. Even though JPEG supports more colors and higher resolutions than the *GIF* standard, JPEG produces files that can be as much as 95 percent smaller than the same uncompressed image. Some fine details may be lost when an image is compressed using JPEG. Most digital cameras save their images in this format. See also *GIF*.

K

KB

Short for Kilobyte, a unit of measurement equal to approximately 1,000 bytes. See also *Byte*.

L

LAN

Short for Local Area Network. A LAN is a computer networks confined to a relatively small area, such as an office or home. The opposite of a *WAN*.

Leased Line Connection

See *Direct Connection*.

M

MB

Short for Megabyte, a unit of measurement equal to approximately 1 million bytes. See also *Byte*.

Meta Search Sites

Internet search sites that utilize the searching power of other search engines to return results. Meta Search sites submit your query to multiple search engines simultaneously and display all of the results. Meta Search sites do not maintain their own index of other Web sites. Dogpile and Teoma are popular examples of Meta Search sites.

Metatag

A type of *HTML* code used to define keywords and phrases to describe a *Web page*. Metatags are added to Web pages during the development process, but can be edited at any time by a site's *Webmaster*. For many years, the meta "keyword" tag and the meta "description" tag were an important component used by search engines to determine search result rankings. Currently no major search engine relies on keyword tags when determining results. The meta "description" and "title" tags however, are still considered by some search engines. The "title" tag is often overlooked by *Web site* designers.

MIME

Short for Multipurpose Internet Mail Extensions. A messaging standard that allows e-mail users to exchange messages that include various types of graphics, video, or audio files via the Internet.

MODEM

Short for modulator/demodulator. Hardware that converts digital signals from a computer into analog signals that can be transmitted over phone lines. Modems also convert incoming analog signals into digital signals the connected computer can understand. Required for connecting to most *Wide Area Networks* (WANs).

Mosaic

Developed by the National Center for Supercomputing Applications (NCSA) at the University of Illinois, at Urbana-Champaign, Mosaic was the first Web *browser* capable of displaying text and graphical information contained in *Web pages*. Prior to Mosaic, browsers displayed only text.

Motherboard

The main printed circuit board of a computer, containing the computer's *CPU, RAM* chips, and *expansion slots*.

MPEG

Short for Moving Pictures Expert Group. MPEG is video compression standard that affords high picture quality from relatively small file sizes. Because of these qualities it is a popular format for video files on the Internet. Special software is required to view files of this type.

MP3

Short for *MPEG*-1 Audio Layer 3. MP3 is a popular format for audio files that creates smaller files sizes by compressing the data. Downloadable music and *podcasts* are often in the MP3 format.

N

Network

A group of computers connected together either by wires or wirelessly. See also *LAN* and *WAN*.

Noise Words

Common words such as "the," "if" and "an" that are ignored by many search engines when they are used as search keywords. You can force many search engines to search for these words if they are integral to your search (e.g., if you're searching for a particular quote). Google requires the addition of the "+" ("plus sign") symbol next to the word (no spaces) you want to force it to search for. For example, to search for the phrase "If I were a rich man," you would enter "+if +I +were +a rich man" in the Google search box. Other search engines have different methods for forcing them to search for these noise words. See their respective "help" screens for their individual requirements.

O

Operating System

A computer program that manages all of a computer's functions, as well as the functions of other programs the computer is running. Windows 98, Windows XP, Red Hat Linux, and Mac OS X are common operating systems. See also *Platform*.

OS

See *Operating System*.

P

PDF

Short for Portable Document Format. A file type created by Adobe Systems utilizing the *Postscript* printer description language. The free Acrobat

Reader software (available for numerous *operating systems*) is required to read PDF documents. Documents created in this format can be easily shared with others regardless of what operating system they are using.

Platform
A computer *operating system* such as Windows, Macintosh, or Linux.

Plug-in
An add-on or "helper" application that adds functions to your Web *browser*. Plug-ins allow you to view or display certain types of files (e.g., Quicktime video, Flash) that might be included as part of a *Web page*.

Podcast
The latest phenomenon in delivering audio content to listeners, you can think of podcasts like "radio delivered via the Internet." Instead of listening to a live broadcast, however, listeners download audio files to their computers to play them back when it is convenient for them. Most podcasts are saved in the *MP3* format, allowing maximum portability and flexibility in playing back those files. Though the term is derived from the popular "iPod" brand of portable digital audio players from Apple computers, podcasts can be played back on any portable audio player that can handle the format in which the individual files are saved. Podcasts are not directly related to the Apple players.

POP
(1) Short for Post Office Protocol. A communications standard used to send and receive e-mail messages. (This is the more common usage.)
(2) Short for Point of Presence. A location on a telephone network where other phone networks can connect to it. Also a location on a phone network where computer users can dial in to gain Internet access. (This usage is also referred to as a dial-in number.) See also *Dial-up*.

Postscript
A computer programming language used to create documents for printing. Postscript "describes" the document to be printed using a series of mathematical descriptions and geometric shapes which special Postscript printers interpret to recreate the document as it was intended to look. Because the Postscript descriptions are interpreted by the printer to create the documents, Postscript files can be shared between users of different computer platforms; however, the user must have a postscript printer in order to print a hard copy of the file. Postscript files were initially popular

for sharing documents on the Internet where formatting elements of the document needed to intact (such as in desktop publishing). More recently, *PDF* documents have supplanted Postscipt's popularity for this purpose. Like *PDF*, Postscript was developed by Adobe Systems. Postscript files usually carry the suffix ".PS" or ".EPS" after the filename.

PPP

Short for Point-to-Point Protocol. A type of Internet connection utilizing standard phone lines and a *modem*. See also *Dial-up*.

Protocol

A set of rules or standards defining how data is transferred between computers connected to a private network or the Internet. For example, the *HTTP* defines how Web *browsers* and Web *servers* communicate with one another and the *POP* defines how e-mail programs and e-mail servers communicate.

Q

QuickTime

A digital video format. While originally developed by the Apple Computer company, Quicktime viewing software is also available for other operating systems. Quicktime files usually carry the ".QT", ".MOV" or ".MOOV" extension after the filename.

R

RAM

Short for Random Access Memory. This is the place in a computer where the *operating system*, programs, and data currently in use are kept so that they can be quickly reached by the computer's *CPU*. Because the information stored on RAM can be accessed in any order (randomly), it is much faster to read from and write to than sequential types of computer storage such as a hard disk, floppy disk, or CD-ROM, that rely on the mechanical movement of a "head" to read or write data. RAM is volatile—meaning that anything stored there is lost when the computer is turned off. This is the place where your computer may store files as you are editing them—until you save them to the hard drive. That is why, if your computer freezes or otherwise loses power, all of your changes that have not been saved are lost. The amount of RAM a computer contains is measured in *Megabytes* or *Gigabytes*. See also *Cache*.

Robot

(1) A program used by *search engines* to automatically locate and classify other sites on the Web and create a searchable index of those other sites. It is from this index that the search engine returns its list of results when you enter your search terms into the search box. Sometimes also referred to as a *spider*.

(2) A program that automatically visits Web sites to collect of e-mail addresses for use by *spammers*.

Router

Hardware that connects two computer networks (usually a *LAN* to a *WAN*) that send data and instructions to the proper locations on those networks. Routers accept data from one source connected to it and distribute it only to intended devices connected to it. Routers can also provide firewall protection by limiting in-bound connections to a *LAN*. See also *Hub* and *Switch*.

RSS

Short for Rich Site Summary or Really Simple Syndication. An electronic update or notification technology that automatically delivers information from a *Web site* utilizing the technology to users who subscribe to receive the information. RSS feeds allow users to keep up to date with new information as it's posted to a Web site utilizing the technology without the user having to continually visit the site to check for new posts. To receive and read RSS feeds, users need to download RSS aggregator (or "reader") software. See also *Atom* and *XML*.

S

Search Engine

A Web-based search tool that uses automated *"robots"* or *"spiders"* to locate other sites on the Web and create a searchable index of the content on those other sites. It is from this index that the search engine returns its list of results when you enter your search terms into the search box. See also Meta Search Sites.

Server

A computer, connected to a network, that manages and delivers data such as documents, audio, video, or e-mail to other computers connected to the network. See also *Client* and *Host*.

Shareware

Software that is freely offered to the public by its author, where the author asks for a small donation to offset their time developing the software. There is no license or registration fee, however, these donations are completely on the honor system. Shareware developers will usually include language like, "If you found this program useful, please send $15 to . . ." Paying the fee usually entitles the user to receive updates of new versions or upgrades to the software.

SPAM

Unsolicited commercial e-mail. Also, generally compared to electronic junk mail—unsolicited e-mail messages that are trying to sell you something you probably don't want or need.

Spider

A program used by *search engines* to automatically locate and classify other sites on the Web and create a searchable index of those other sites. It is from this index that the search engine returns its list of results when you enter your search terms into the search box. Sometimes also referred to as a *robot*.

Spyware

A software application designed to monitor and record the users activities, often reporting back to the software's developer. Spyware is usually downloaded and installed onto users' computers without their knowledge, or it can be a clandestine component of some software that the user has knowingly downloaded and installed. See also *Adware*.

Static IP

A fixed *IP address* that identifies a specific computer on a network. Like a phone number, a static IP does not change. The opposite of *Dynamic IP*. See also *IP Address*.

Stop Words

See *Noise Words*.

Style Sheets

A set of instructions, defined by a *Webmaster* to control the look and design of a *Web site*. A single file is used to define fonts (size, color, and style), link color and underlining, background images, and other attributes for numerous pages of a single *Web site*. Also called *Cascading Style Sheets*.

Switch
Hardware that connects multiple computers. Switches accept data from one device connected to it and distribute it only to the device for which it is intended. Switches work more efficiently than hubs. Used in *LANs*. See also *Hub* and *Router*.

T

T-1
High-bandwidth, digital data line connection, operates at 1.54 Mbps.

T-3
High-bandwidth, digital data line connection, operates at 45 Mbps (roughly 28 times as fast as a T-1).

Tags
Formatting codes used in HTML documents. Tags define how various elements of a document will be displayed in a Web *browser*, including fonts (size, color, and style), link color and underlining, and background images. See also *HTML* and *Metatags*.

TCP-IP
Short for transmission control protocol/Internet protocol. A set of *protocols* that defines how data are transferred on computer networks, including the Internet.

TIFF
Short for Tagged Image File Format. A graphic file format that is widely supported by various programs in different operating systems. TIFF files usually carry the ".TIF" or ".TIFF" extension after the filename.

Thumbnail
(1) A small version of a larger image—often, literally about the size of a human thumbnail—usually linked to a larger version of the same image.
(2) A small version of a *Web page*, usually linked to the full-sized original.

Toolbar
(1) The row of icons below the Menu Bar of a software application. Clicking on an icon executes a common command.

(2) An add-in program to a Web *browser* that inserts a row of icons below the *Browser's* Address Bar. Toolbars are available from various sources, such as Google and Yahoo!. Like the example in definition (1), clicking an icon on one of these toolbars causes the browser to execute a command or initiate some action using the resources of the site that provided the toolbar. Multiple toolbars can be installed and active simultaneously.

Trojan

A program that appears to be useful or benign, but actually performs unauthorized operations on the user's computer, such as taking over the Internet connection to send *Spam*, or engage in detrimental data collection or even data destruction. See also, *Virus* and *Worm*.

Trojan Horse

See *Trojan*.

U

Upload

To send a copy of a file from one computer to another—usually from a *client* to a *host* via a remote connection. The opposite of *Download*.

URL

Short for Uniform Resource Locator. See also *Domain Name*.

User Interface

See *Interface* and *Graphical User interface (GUI)*.

V

Virus

A program or executable code that self-replicates itself, hiding itself in other programs or documents. Viruses are usually downloaded onto users' computers without their knowledge, or they can be a clandestine component of some software that the user has knowingly downloaded and installed based on its advertised usefulness. Viruses can be passed from computer to computer via infected e-mail attachments, or on discs that are shared between more than one computer. Virus activity can range from annoying (displaying pre-programmed messages) or malicious (hijacking your Web *browser* to display predetermined content) to destructive (deleting data). See also *Trojan* and *Worm*.

W

WAN

Short for Wide Area Network. A WAN is a computer network spread over a relatively large geographic area. The in-house computer network of a national law firm that allows all of their offices access to a central server and documents on that server is an example of a WAN. The Internet might be considered the largest WAN. The opposite of a *LAN*.

Wi-Fi

See *802.11*.

WiMAX

The popular name of the long-range, metropolitan area network standard being developed by the Institute of Electrical & Electronics Engineers (IEEE)—802.16. The 802.16 standard will have a greater range (up to 31 miles) than its home wireless standard cousin *802.11*. Where 802.11 replaces network wiring in a home or office, WiMAX replaces external cable or *DSL* wiring to provide wireless broadband access across its coverage area.

WLAN

See *802.11*.

Webmaster

The person in charge of administering a *Web site*.

Web Host

A company that provides server space to host *Web sites* to individuals or companies. See also *ISP*.

Web Page

A document, generally written in *HTML*, that is accessible via the Internet.

Web Site

A collection of *Web pages* that refer back and forth to one another (and other pages on the Internet) using *hypertext* links.

Wildcard

A placeholder used to represent a variable in a search term or phrase. It can be used to replace a letter (in a word) or a word (in a phrase) when searching. Words with any character (or phrases with any text) in the position of the wildcard may be returned in search results. The asterisk is a common wildcard.

Worm

(1) A program or executable code that self-replicates itself, hiding itself in other programs or documents. Unlike a *virus*, worms are self-contained and can exist without hiding in another file. Worms can be downloaded onto users' computers without their knowledge, or they can be a clandestine component of some software that the user has knowingly downloaded and installed based on its advertised usefulness. Worms can be passed from computer to computer via infected e-mail attachment, on discs that are shared between more than one computer, or they can transport themselves from computer to computer, across a Local Area Network (*LAN*), exploiting the network's own file transfer capabilities. Worm activity can range from annoying (displaying pre-programmed messages) or malicious (hijacking your Web browser to display predetermined content) to destructive (deleting data). See also *Trojan* and *Virus*.

(2) Short for Write Once/Read Many. Refers to computer media such as CDs and DVDs onto which data can be written only once, but data can be read from many times. (This is a less-common usage.)

WYSIWYG

Short for What You See is What You Get. Used to describe a document that is displayed on a computer screen in the same layout and format as it will appear when printed. Microsoft Word is a WYSIWYG document editor, because the document on the screen includes all of the fonts, boldface characters, paragraph and page breaks, etc. contained in the printed document.

X

XML

Short for eXtensible Mark-up Language. A programming language that allows information to be collected, transmitted and shared between applications or users.

Index

A

A Million and One World-Wide Videos, 218

A&M Records, Inc. v. Napster, 37–38

Abbott, Ida, 645

Abbreviations, 165, 177–78. *See also* Acronyms

Abbreviations and Acronyms of the U.S. Government, 165

Abebooks, 211–12

Academic Search Premier, 185

Accident Reconstruction (ARC) Network, 423

Accurint
  cellular telephones at, 259
  overview of, 398, 401–6
  privacy issues and, 309
  real estate records at, 349
  security breach on, 401–6

Acrobat Reader, 44, 114. *See also* .Pdf files

Acronym Finder, 166

Acronyms, 166–69, 685. *See also* Abbreviations

Acxiom, 408

Ad*Access, 219

A.D.A.M. Medical Encyclopedia, 546–48

Adams Golf Securities Litigation, 13

Addresses, 184, 248, 399. *See also* Maps

Adelstein, Jonathan S., 263

Adflip, 219

Administrative Office of the United States Courts, 671

Administrators in Medicine (AIM), 574

Adobe, 44, 113, 114. *See also* .Pdf files

Adsense, 105

AdvaMed, 567

Advanced Medical Technology Association, 567

Advanced Research Projects Agency, 751

Advanced searches
  cached links, 116
  domain searches, 70–71
  file format searches, 67, 112–15
  in pay databases, 29–30
  on FirstGov.gov, 225
  on Google, 65–66, 106–7, 115–23
  on Yahoo!, 112–15, 121–23
  overview of, 106–7

Advertising, 56–60, 105, 219

Adware, 757

Aerial images, 174–75

AFL-CIO, 520

Agence France Presse (AFP), 204

Agencies, 222, 227–29, 231–32, 234–35. *See also* individual agencies

Air pollution, 597

Air Safety Foundation, 695–96

Aircraft, 685–96

Selected Books from ...
THE ABA LAW PRACTICE MANAGEMENT SECTION

The Lawyer's Guide to Creating Persuasive Computer Presentations, Second Edition

By Ann Brenden and John Goodhue

This book explains the advantages of computer presentation resources, how to use them, what they can do, and the legal issues involved in their use. You'll learn how to use computer presentations in the courtroom, during opening statements, direct examination, cross examination, closing arguments, appellate arguments and more. This revised second edition has been updated to include new chapters on hardware and software that is currently being used for digital displays, and all-new sections that walk the reader through beginning skills, and some advanced PowerPoint® techniques. Also included is a CD-ROM containing on-screen tutorials illustrating techniques such as animating text, insertion and configuration of text and images, and a full sample PowerPoint final argument complete with audio, and much more.

The Lawyer's Guide to Adobe® Acrobat®, Second Edition

By David L. Masters

This book will show you the power of using the Adobe Acrobat system and how to utilize its full potential in your law practice. Author David Masters takes readers step by step through the processes of creating PDF documents and then working with these documents. In subsequent chapters, Masters covers adding document navigation aids, commenting tools, using digital signatures, extracting content from PDF documents, searching and indexing, document security, saving Web pages to PDF, plug-ins, display mode, e-briefs, using Acrobat in the paperless office, and more.

The Lawyer's Guide to Marketing on the Internet, Second Edition

By Gregory Siskind, Deborah McMurray, and Richard P. Klau

The Internet is a critical component of every law firm marketing strategy—no matter where you are, how large your firm is, or the areas in which you practice. Used effectively, a younger, smaller firm can present an image just as sophisticated and impressive as a larger and more established firm. You can reach potential new clients, in remote areas, at any time, for minimal cost. To help you maximize your Internet marketing capabilities, this book provides you with countless Internet marketing possibilities and shows you how to effectively and efficiently market your law practice on the Internet.

The Electronic Evidence and Discovery Handbook: Forms, Checklists, and Guidelines

By Sharon D. Nelson, Bruce A. Olson, and John W. Simek

The use of electronic evidence has increased dramatically over the past few years, but many lawyers still struggle with the complexities of electronic discovery. This substantial book provides lawyers with the templates they need to frame their discovery requests and provides helpful advice on what they can subpoena. In addition to the ready-made forms, the authors also supply explanations to bring you up to speed on the electronic discovery field. The accompanying CD-ROM features over 70 forms, including, Motions for Protective Orders, Preservation and Spoliation Documents, Motions to Compel, Electronic Evidence Protocol Agreements, Requests for Production, Internet Services Agreements, and more. Also included is a full electronic evidence case digest with over 300 cases detailed!

The Lawyer's Guide to Extranets: Breaking Down Walls, Building Client Connections

By Douglas Simpson and Mark Tamminga

An extranet can be a powerful tool that allows law firms to exchange information and build relationships with clients. This new book shows you why extranets are the next step in client interaction and communications, and how you can effectively implement an extranet in any type of firm. This book will take you step-by-step through the issues of implementing an extranet, and how to plan and build one. You'll get real-world extranet case studies, and learn from the successes and failures of those who have gone before. Help your firm get ahead of the emerging technologies curve and discover the benefits of adopting this new information tool.

Paralegals, Profitability, and the Future of Your Law Practice

By Arthur G. Greene and Therese A. Cannon

This is the essential guide to effectively integrating paralegals into your practice and expanding their roles to ensure your firm is successful in the next decade. If you're not currently using paralegals in your firm, the authors explain why you need paralegals and how to create a paralegal model for use in your firm—no matter what the size or structure. You'll learn how to recruit and hire top-notch paralegals the first time. If you are currently using paralegals, you'll learn how to make sure your paralegal program is structured properly, runs effectively, and continually contributes to your bottom line. Finally, eight valuable appendices provide resources, job descriptions, model guidelines, sample confidentiality agreements, sample performance evaluations, and performance appraisals. In addition, all the forms and guidelines contained in the appendix are included on a CD-ROM for ease in implementation!

The Lawyer's Guide to Marketing Your Practice, Second Edition

Edited by James A. Durham and Deborah McMurray
This book is packed with practical ideas, innovative strategies, useful checklists, and sample marketing and action plans to help you implement a successful, multi-faceted, and profit-enhancing marketing plan for your firm. Organized into four sections, this illuminating resource covers: Developing Your Approach; Enhancing Your Image; Implementing Marketing Strategies and Maintaining Your Program. Appendix materials include an instructive primer on market research to inform you on research methodologies that support the marketing of legal services. The accompanying CD-ROM contains a wealth of checklists, plans, and other sample reports, questionnaires, and templates—all designed to make implementing your marketing strategy as easy as possible!

The Lawyer's Guide to Increasing Revenue: Unlocking the Profit Potential in Your Firm

By Arthur G. Greene
Are you ready to look beyond cost-cutting and toward new revenue opportunities? Learn how you can achieve growth using the resources you already have at your firm. Discover the factors that affect your law firm's revenue production, how to evaluate them, and how to take specific action steps designed to increase your returns. You'll learn how to best improve performance and profitability in each of the key areas of your law firm, such as billable hours and rates, client relations and intake, collections and accounts receivable, technology, marketing, and others. Included with the book is a CD-ROM featuring sample policies, worksheets, plans, and documents designed to aid implementation of the ideas presented in the book. Let this resource guide you toward a profitable and sustainable future!

The Lawyer's Guide to Strategic Planning: Defining, Setting, and Achieving Your Firm's Goals

By Thomas C. Grella and Michael L. Hudkins
This practice-building resource is your guide to planning dynamic strategic plans and implementing them at your firm. You'll learn about the actual planning process and how to establish goals in key planning areas such as law firm governance, competition, opening a new office, financial management, technology, marketing and competitive intelligence, client development and retention, and more. The accompanying CD-ROM contains a wealth of policies, statements, and other sample documents. If you're serious about improving the way your firm works, increasing productivity, making better decisions, and setting your firm on the right course, this book is the resource you need.

The Successful Lawyer: Powerful Strategies for Transforming Your Practice

By Gerald A. Riskin
Available as a Book, Audio-CD Set, or Combination Package.
Global management consultant and trusted advisor to many of the world's largest law firms, Gerry Riskin goes beyond simple concept or theory and delivers a book packed with practical advice that you can implement right away. By using the principles found in this book, you can live out your dreams, embrace success, and awaken your firm to its full potential. Large law firm or small, managing partners and associates in every area of practice—all can benefit from the information contained in this book. With this book, you can attract what you need and desire into your life, get more satisfaction from your practice and your clients, and do so in a systematic, achievable way.

How to Start and Build a Law Practice, Platinum Fifth Edition

By Jay G Foonberg
This classic ABA bestseller has been used by tens of thousands of lawyers as the comprehensive guide to planning, launching, and growing a successful practice. It's packed with over 600 pages of guidance on identifying the right location, finding clients, setting fees, managing your office, maintaining an ethical and responsible practice, maximizing available resources, upholding your standards, and much more. You'll find the information you need to successfully launch your practice, run it at maximum efficiency, and avoid potential pitfalls along the way. If you're committed to starting—and growing—your own practice, this one book will give you the expert advice you need to make it succeed for years to come.

Flying Solo: A Survival Guide for Solo and Small Firm Lawyers, Fourth Edition

Edited by K. William Gibson
This fourth edition of this comprehensive guide includes practical information gathered from a wide range of contributors, including successful solo practitioners, law firm consultants, state and local bar practice management advisors, and law school professors. This classic ABA book first walks you through a step-by-step analysis of the decision to start a solo practice, including choosing a practice focus. It then provides tools to help you with financial issues including banking and billing; operations issues such as staffing and office location and design decisions; technology for the small law office; and marketing and client relations. Whether you're thinking of going solo, new to the solo life, or a seasoned practitioner, *Flying Solo* provides time-tested answers to real-life questions.

30-Day Risk-Free Order Form
Call Today! 1-800-285-2221
Monday–Friday, 7:30 AM – 5:30 PM, Central Time

Qty	Title	LPM Price	Regular Price	Total
_____	The Lawyer's Guide to Creating Persuasive Computer Presentations, Second Edition (5110530)	$79.95	$ 99.95	$_____
_____	The Lawyer's Guide to Adobe® Acrobat®, Second Edition (5110529)	49.95	59.95	$_____
_____	The Lawyer's Guide to Marketing on the Internet, Second Edition (5110484)	69.95	79.95	$_____
_____	The Electronic Evidence and Discovery Handbook: Forms, Checklists, and Guidelines (5110569)	99.95	129.95	$_____
_____	The Lawyer's Guide to Extranets: Breaking Down Walls, Building Client Connections (5110494)	59.95	69.95	$_____
_____	Paralegals, Profitability, and the Future of Your Law Practice (5110491)	59.95	69.95	$_____
_____	The Lawyer's Guide to Marketing Your Practice, Second Edition (5110500)	79.95	89.95	$_____
_____	The Lawyer's Guide to Increasing Revenue (5110521)	59.95	79.95	$_____
_____	The Lawyer's Guide to Strategic Planning (5110520)	59.95	79.95	$_____
_____	The Successful Lawyer: Powerful Strategies for Transforming Your Practice (5110531)	64.95	84.95	$_____
_____	How to Start and Build a Law Practice, Platinum Fifth Edition (5110508)	57.95	69.95	$_____
_____	Flying Solo: A Survival Guide for Solo and Small Firm Lawyers, Fourth Edition (5110527)	79.95	99.95	$_____

*Postage and Handling	
$10.00 to $24.99	$5.95
$25.00 to $49.99	$9.95
$50.00 to $99.99	$12.95
$100.00 to $349.99	$17.95
$350 to $499.99	$24.95

**Tax
DC residents add 5.75%
IL residents add 9.00%

*Postage and Handling	$_____
**Tax	$_____
TOTAL	$_____

PAYMENT

❑ Check enclosed (to the ABA)

❑ Visa   ❑ MasterCard   ❑ American Express

_____
Account Number   Exp. Date   Signature

Name _____ Firm _____
Address _____
City _____ State _____ Zip _____
Phone Number _____ E-Mail Address _____

Guarantee
If—for any reason—you are not satisfied with your purchase, you may return it within 30 days of receipt for a complete refund of the price of the book(s). No questions asked!

Mail: ABA Publication Orders, P.O. Box 10892, Chicago, Illinois 60610-0892
♦ Phone: 1-800-285-2221 ♦ FAX: 312-988-5568

E-Mail: abasvcctr@abanet.org ♦ Internet: http://www.lawpractice.org/catalog

About the CD

The accompanying CD contains a hyperlinked index of Web sites listed in the book (**Fact Finding on the Internet Index.pdf**), as well as the following checklists from the book: Internet Methodology Checklist (**Internet Methodology Checklist.doc**); Internet Source Credibility Checklist (**Internet Source Credibility Checklist.doc**); Search Strategy Checklist (**Search Strategy Checklist.doc**); and the Checklist for Finding Company Information (**Checklist for Finding Company Information.doc**).

For additional information about the files on the CD, please open and read the **"readme.doc"** file on the CD.

NOTE: The set of files on the CD may only be used on a single computer or moved to and used on another computer. Under no circumstances may the set of files be used on more than one computer at one time. If you are interested in obtaining a license to use the set of files on a local network, please contact: Director, Copyrights and Contracts, American Bar Association, 321 N. Clark Street, Chicago, IL 60610, (312) 988-6101. **Please read the license and warranty statements on the following page before using this CD.**

Defending Liberty
Pursuing Justice

CD-ROM to accompany
The Lawyer's Guide to Fact Finding on the Internet, Third Edition